The Wealth Effect

The politics of major banking crises have been transformed since the nineteenth century. Analysing extensive historical and contemporary evidence, Chwieroth and Walter demonstrate that the rising wealth of the middle class has generated 'great expectations' among voters that the government is responsible for the protection of this wealth. Crisis policy interventions have become more extensive and costly – and their political aftermaths far more fraught – because of democratic governance, not in spite of it. Using data from numerous democracies over two centuries, and detailed studies of Brazil, the United Kingdom and the United States, this book breaks new ground in exploring the consequences of the emerging mass political demand for financial stabilization. It shows why great expectations have induced rising financial fragility, more financial sector bailouts and rising political instability and discontent in contemporary democracies, providing new insight to anyone concerned with contemporary policy and politics.

Jeffrey M. Chwieroth is Professor of International Political Economy in the Department of International Relations, and a research associate of the Systemic Risk Centre, at the London School of Economics and Political Science. He is the author of *Capital Ideas: The IMF and the Rise of Financial Liberalization* (2010).

Andrew Walter is Professor of International Relations in the School of Social and Political Sciences at the University of Melbourne. His books include *China, the United States, and Global Order* (Cambridge, 2011, with Rosemary Foot), *East Asian Capitalism* (2012, ed. with Xiaoke Zhang) and *Global Financial Governance Confronts the Rising Powers* (2016, ed. with C. R. Henning).

The Wealth Effect

How the Great Expectations of the Middle Class Have Changed the Politics of Banking Crises

Jeffrey M. Chwieroth
London School of Economics and Political Science

Andrew Walter
University of Melbourne

CAMBRIDGE
UNIVERSITY PRESS

CAMBRIDGE
UNIVERSITY PRESS

University Printing House, Cambridge CB2 8BS, United Kingdom

One Liberty Plaza, 20th Floor, New York, NY 10006, USA

477 Williamstown Road, Port Melbourne, VIC 3207, Australia

314–321, 3rd Floor, Plot 3, Splendor Forum, Jasola District Centre, New Delhi – 110025, India

79 Anson Road, #06–04/06, Singapore 079906

Cambridge University Press is part of the University of Cambridge.

It furthers the University's mission by disseminating knowledge in the pursuit of education, learning, and research at the highest international levels of excellence.

www.cambridge.org
Information on this title: www.cambridge.org/9781107153745

DOI: 10.1017/9781316649992

© Jeffrey M. Chwieroth and Andrew Walter 2019

First published 2019

Printed in the United Kingdom by TJ International Ltd. Padstow Cornwall

A catalogue record for this publication is available from the British Library.

Library of Congress Cataloguing-in-Publication Data
NAMES: Chwieroth, Jeffrey M., 1975– author. | Walter, Andrew, 1961– author.
TITLE: The wealth effect : how the great expectations of the middle class
   have changed the politics of banking crises / Jeffrey M. Chwieroth, London
   School of Economics and Political Science, Andrew Walter, University of Melbourne.
DESCRIPTION: Cambridge, United Kingdom; New York, NY : Cambridge University
   Press, 2019. | Includes bibliographical references and index.
IDENTIFIERS: LCCN 2018042531| ISBN 9781107153745 (hardback : alk. paper) |
   ISBN 9781316607787 (pbk. : alk. paper)
SUBJECTS: LCSH: Financial crises–History. | Middle class. | Wealth. | Monetary policy. |
   Economic policy.
CLASSIFICATION: LCC HB3722 .C586 2019 | DDC 338.5/42–DC23
LC record available at https://lccn.loc.gov/2018042531

ISBN 978-1-107-15374-5 Hardback
ISBN 978-1-316-60778-7 Paperback

CONTENTS

FIGURES

TABLES

PREFACE

We began this project in the wake of the most severe financial crisis in advanced democracies since the Great Depression. We took inspiration from the pioneering work of economists and economic historians who had started to delve deeply into the economic consequences of financial crises over a long stretch of history. They demonstrated the benefits of taking a panoramic historical perspective, identifying systematic patterns in the run-ups and aftermaths of crises. Yet this work largely set aside questions about the political aftermaths of such crises and how politics and institutions shaped the nature of the government policy response.

As scholars of international political economy, these questions were naturally of great interest to us. Theoretically, we wanted to gain a deeper understanding of the importance of time and time-dependent processes in shaping policy and political outcomes after banking crises, as it seemed to us that much economic work emphasized continuity rather than change. Why, for instance, had the policy interventions during and after banking crises in democracies apparently undergone a profound transformation over the course of the previous two centuries? In the nineteenth and early twentieth century democratic governments largely either stood aside or adopted minimalist policy responses to systemic banking crises, but after the 2007–8 crisis we saw governments adopting increasingly extensive and costly publicly funded bailouts.

The observation that many governments in crisis-hit countries lost office in the aftermath of the 2007–8 crisis also motivated us to consider the electoral impact of financial instability. Indeed, politics in many democracies hitherto seen as stable and consolidated became noticeably more fractious, polarized and unpredictable. Had these political aftermaths, like the policy aftermaths, also changed over time? If so, why? Perhaps most interestingly and importantly, this prompted us to think about how the policy and political aftermaths might be related and whether this relationship might itself change over time.

We found that existing accounts did not address these questions in a fully satisfying way. Some scholars explored the relationship between economic crises and political outcomes but gave little attention to financial crises. Other work – both qualitative and quantitative – largely ignored questions related to long-run processes and instead focused on financial crises in narrow time periods or particular regions. In short, surprisingly little was known about how polities themselves might be affected by crises over the long run.

The policy interventions that followed the 2007–8 crisis also made us increasingly sceptical about arguments that democratic institutions could constrain the propensity of governments to implement taxpayer-funded rescues of the financial system. On the contrary, we came increasingly to view democratic institutions as potentially linked to recurrent bouts of financial instability followed by bailouts in a modern age where 'financialization' since the 1970s has increasingly connected middle-class households to the financial system as both investors and borrowers. In contrast to an earlier era when financialization was more limited and wealth more highly concentrated, these processes – often encouraged by successive governments – have given middle-class households in modern democracies 'great expectations' that governments will protect their wealth and access to credit. During major crises, the 'wealth effect' has increasingly entailed governments committing sizeable public resources to stabilize financial markets and bailing out the large, complex financial institutions that have become so pivotal in financial networks.

By focusing on the evolving nature of middle-class household interests and policy preferences, thus far largely overlooked, we developed an account of mass pressure 'from below'. This thesis points to quite different and arguably even more deep-seated causes than the popular post-2007 accounts that attributed bailouts mainly to elite pressure and capture from above by large financial institutions and connected corporate interests.

It also gave us new insight into the electoral impact of financial crises. If the effective demand from middle-class voters for financial stability had risen, then so too should have the political costs of failing to meet this demand. With great expectations, we have seen the preferences of middle-class voters becoming more aligned, albeit still imperfectly, with elites who share similar interests. This has considerably enlarged the constituency supportive of bailouts, placing elected governments facing crises under much greater pressure than in the past to respond quickly and forcibly to protect at-risk wealth. Careful consideration of the importance of time and time-dependent processes thus led us to the view that it was the evolution of these mass preferences that was crucial in understanding why modern governments might suffer greater electoral punishment than those in the past.

At the same time, we noticed that conflicts of interest within this much-enlarged 'bailout constituency' can be acute. Most voters want governments to protect their at-risk wealth in crises, but this is not precisely the same as what the managers, major shareholders and creditors of large complex financial institutions want. Distributional struggles over the allocation of costs and benefits in bailouts continue and, as the size and extent of interventions have increased, in some cases have become more intense. As we conducted the research for this book, we witnessed conflict of this kind taking various forms: between older voters in much of Europe and the United States with defined benefit pensions and negligible mortgages on their homes, and younger voters who had neither; between middle- and upper-income investors in countries who benefited from government protection of 'uninsured' money market funds during the crisis and sustained quantitative easing, and those whose highly leveraged housing wealth evaporated after 2007; and between many comfortable middle-class voters in northern Europe and Greek citizens who faced large pension losses. We also noticed how the preferences of voters could be unrealistic, inconsistent and riddled with conflict, making crisis management exceptionally difficult for governments to navigate. At various points over 2007–8, many voters in crisis-hit countries who initially favoured extensive financial stabilization measures soon complained that politicians had 'bailed out the bankers'.

The intensity and potential inconsistency of these middle-class voter preferences also led us to consider how voters might respond to policy failures and delays that are themselves, in part, due to institutional obstacles. We developed an account that differs from a standard one in the literature that stresses how divided political authority might enable incumbents to avoid political responsibility. In our view, the emergence of great expectations among a large bloc of middle-class voters means that governments facing more severe political constraints – mainly in the form of polarized 'veto players' – will tend to find it harder to retain office following a banking crisis. Modern crises generate particularly acute problems for incumbents because they often increase polarization and gridlock that can produce policy delays and wealth-destroying market contagion. Due to the uneven effects these delays can have on different asset markets, this can exacerbate the distributional conflicts mentioned above.

Our analysis reveals that modern governments now face an unprecedented, harsh dilemma. Simply responding to voters' great expectations for wealth protection does not ensure electoral success. Voter dissatisfaction and electoral punishment is still likely if governments respond in a delayed and limited manner, or in ways perceived as highly costly and redistributive. Such outcomes, we suggest, are more likely to be present in circumstances where political constraints are severe. Managing crises is a fraught business for contemporary governments: escaping punishment is difficult, though not impossible. Doing so depends in large part on delivering prompt, effective interventions that protect most middle-class wealth and that are widely perceived as spreading the burden reasonably fairly across different groups. Such interventions, however, tend to be the exception rather than the rule. And even successful interventions are still far more costly than in the past.

In the end, our analysis has led us to be doubtful about the prospects for sustaining democratic politics, rising financialization and financial stability over time. Great expectations increasingly compel democratic governments to intervene to protect voter wealth. But this in turn has fostered greater financialization, leverage and financial fragility, as well as contributing to larger public sector deficits. The risk, as we may now be observing in some advanced and emerging democracies, is growing disenchantment with democratic institutions. We remain hopeful that political parties of the moderate centre will mobilize sufficient political courage and conviction to convince voters of the need to change course in the interest of preserving not just their wealth, but possibly also democracy itself.

After eight years and several trips from London to Melbourne and many places more or less in-between, we completed this book. Along the way, we incurred a number of intellectual debts. We are indebted to many colleagues at institutions around the world who shared data or offered comments on various parts of the manuscript including, at the risk of omitting some, Christopher J. Anderson, David Andrews, Ben Ansell, Leonardo Baccini, Erik Baekkeskov, Ken Benoit, Leslie Bethell, Sarah Binder, Frederick Boehmke, Carles Boix, Janet Box-Steffensmeier, Mark Buntaine, Richard Carney, Jon Danielsson, Keith Dowding, Zachary Elkins, Manfred Elsig, Lawrence Ezrow, Christopher Gandrud, Lucy Goodhart, Julia Gray, Stephen Haber, Mark Hallerberg, Dominik Hangartner, Jakob de Hann, Eric Helleiner, Philip Keefer, Luke Keele, Jouni Kuha, Katie Lavelle, David Leblang, Amanda Licht, Johannes Lindvall, Abe Lowenthal, Christopher Meissner, James Melton, Daniel Mügge, Abe Newman, Stefano Pagliari, Elliot Posner, Paul Preston, Dennis Quinn, Raphael Reinke, Thomas Sattler, Moritz Schularick, Stephen Topik, Stephanie Walter, Cornelia Woll and Geoffrey Wood. Our research assistants – Chirag Agarwal, Rodrigo Alves-Jafet, Erika Arnold, Hortense Badarani, Bruno Baisch, Pedro Barros, Jeremiah Brown, Noemie Chomet, Andrew Gibbons, Shunran Hu, Alexia Leckie, Pei Xuan Lin, Lukas Linsi, Orian Mahlow, Michael O'Keefe, Alexander Parsons, Victor Pons Pilz, Mike Pottenger, Richard Reid, Bill Roosman, Mike Seiferling, Suzanna Sobolewska, Brenda van-Coppenolle, Kohei Watanabe, Sam Wilkins and Jack Winterton – helped us to gather the data and identify references vital to completing the project.

We are fortunate to have received research support from a number of sources. The support of the Economic and Social Research Council (ESRC) in funding the Systemic Risk Centre (SRC) is gratefully acknowledged (grant number ES/K002309/1). We thank Jon Danielsson and Jean-Pierre Zigrand, co-directors of the SRC, for their support of this project and for providing us with the resources to convene two workshops where we were able to present drafts of chapters and to receive valuable feedback. Ann Law, manager of the SRC, provided administrative support of the highest calibre. Our research also received financial support from Chwieroth's Mid-Career Fellowship from the British Academy for the Humanities and the Social Sciences (MD130026), from Chwieroth's AXA Award from the AXA Research Fund, from Chwieroth and Walter's Discovery Project award from the

Australian Research Council (DP140101877), and from seed fund grants from the Suntory and Toyota International Centres for Economics and Related Disciplines (STICERD) and the Department of International Relations at the London School of Economics and from the Melbourne School of Government. We also owe special thanks to John Haslam at Cambridge University Press, whose enthusiasm, constructive comments and, above all, patience did much to strengthen the quality of the manuscript.

Finally, and most importantly, we dedicate this book to our families, whose even greater patience and support was essential to its completion. We hope that they will continue to fulfil their greatest of expectations.

ABBREVIATIONS

AIG	American International Group
AMC	asset management company
AMLF	Asset-Backed Commercial Paper Money Market Mutual Fund Liquidity Facility
APF	Asset Purchase Facility
APS	Asset Protection Scheme
ARM	Adjustable Rate Mortgage
ATM	automated teller machine
BACEN	Central Bank of Brazil
BB	Banco do Brasil
BEUB	Banco dos Estados Unidos do Brasil
BHCs	bank holding companies
BIS	Bank for International Settlements
BNDES	National Bank for Economic Development [Brazil]
BNH	National Housing Bank
BRB	Banco da República do Brasil
BREUB	Banco da República dos Estados Unidos do Brasil
BRRD	Bank Recovery and Resolution Directive
CAP	Comparative Agendas Project
CDOs	Collateralized debt obligations
CDU	Christian Democratic Union
CDS	credit default swap
CEF	Caixa Econômica Federal
CEO	chief executive officer
CPFF	Commercial Paper Funding Facility

CPS	complementary pension system
CRA	Community Reinvestment Act
DB	defined benefit
DC	defined contribution
DSR	debt service ratio
EBA	Emergency Banking Act
ECB	European Central Bank
EESA	Emergency Economic Stabilization Act
EMGEA	Empresa Gestora de Ativos
Fannie Mae	Federal National Mortgage Association
FDIC	Federal Deposit Insurance Corporation
FDICIA	Federal Deposit Insurance Corporation Improvement Act
FGTS	Fundo de Garantia do Tempo e Serviço
FHA	Federal Housing Administration
FHFA	Federal Housing Finance Agency
FHLB	Federal Home Loan Bank
FHLBB	Federal Home Loan Bank Board
FOMC	Federal Open Market Committee
FSA	Financial Services Authority
FSLIC	Federal Savings and Loan Insurance Corporation
FSOC	Financial Stability Oversight Council
GDP	gross domestic product
GSE	government-sponsored enterprise
HAMP	Home Affordable Modification Program
HARP	Home Affordable Refinance Program
HERA	Housing and Economic Recovery Act
HOLC	Home Owners' Loan Corporation
HUD	Department of Housing and Urban Affairs
IMF	International Monetary Fund
IOF	Imposto sobre Operações Financeiras
IOPS	International Organisation of Pension Supervisors
IRA	Individual Retirement Account
L&V	Laeven and Valencia
LBG	Lloyds Banking Group
LOLR	lender of last resort
LTV	loan-to-market value
MBS	mortgage-backed securities
MMIFF	Money Market Investor Funding Facility

MPC	Monetary Policy Committee
NCC	National Credit Corporation
NMC	National Monetary Council
NPL	non-performing loan
NYCH	New York Clearing House
OCC	Office of the Comptroller of the Currency
OECD	Organization for Economic Cooperation and Development
OFHEO	Office of Federal Housing Enterprise Oversight
OLS	ordinary least squares
OTS	Office of Thrift Supervision
P&A	purchase and assumption
PC	Partido Concentração
PDCF	Primary Dealer Credit Facility
PFL	Liberal Front Party
PMDB	Brazilian Democratic Movement Party
PPP	purchasing power parity
PR	Republican Party [Brazil]
PRA	Principal Reduction Alternative
PRF	Federal Republican Party
PRN	Party of National Reconstruction
PROER	Program of Incentives for the Restructuring and Strengthening of the National Financial System
PRP	Republican Party of São Paulo
PSDB	Social Democratic Party of Brazil
PT	Workers' Party
QE	quantitative easing
RAET	Temporary Special Administration Regime
R&R	Reinhart and Rogoff
RBS	Royal Bank of Scotland
RFC	Reconstruction Finance Corporation
S&Ls	small unit banks, or 'savings and loans'
SBCs	systemic banking crises
SCAP	Supervisory Capital Assessment Program
SEC	Securities and Exchange Commission
SIFIs	systemically important financial institutions
SLS	Special Liquidity Scheme
SPV	special purpose vehicle

SUMOC	Superintendency of Money and Credit
SWIID	Standardized World Income Inequality Database
TAF	Term Auction Facility
TALF	Term Asset-Backed Securities Loan Facility
TARP	Troubled Asset Relief Program
TCI	Tennessee Coal and Iron
TR	Reference Rate
TSLF	Term Securities Lending Facility
TUC	Trades Union Congress
VC	variable contribution
WaMu	Washington Mutual
WVS	World Values Survey

Part I

BANKING CRISES AND THE RISE OF GREAT EXPECTATIONS

1 INTRODUCTION

The financial crises that began in the United States and Europe in 2007 have had dramatic political consequences that have almost certainly not yet fully played out. In their aftermath, some affected Western societies have experienced levels of political instability and polarization that may be unprecedented in the post-war period. Many incumbent governments lost office after extensive and costly interventions that continue to shape public finances and expenditure, as well as public perceptions of the responsibilities and limits of government.

Increasingly, commentators point to worrying parallels with events in earlier, less stable times. Mainstream centre-right and centre-left parties are under pressure from 'populist' parties and candidates that have made substantial electoral inroads in some of the most consolidated democracies by selling a message of elite betrayal (Inglehart and Norris, 2016; Roth, 2017). Economic recovery from these crises has been relatively anaemic by historical standards and many voters are said to remain angry, distrustful of elites and, most alarmingly, of democratic political institutions more generally (Diamond, Plattner and Walker, 2016; Foa and Mounk, 2016, 2017).

In this book, we adopt a long historical perspective so as to consider whether some of these possible consequences of major banking crises are typical or unusual – and whether they are likely to be sustained. At present, we lack systematic knowledge of this kind. Economists and economic historians have provided long-run empirical analyses but have often largely ignored the politics of crises (Cassis, 2013; Jordà, Schularick and Taylor, 2016, 2015; Reinhart and Rogoff,

2009; Turner, 2014). Where they have addressed this topic, we show that they have generally overlooked how and why so much has changed over the course of a century and more (Funke, Schularick and Trebesch, 2016; Mian, Sufi and Trebbi, 2013). Political scientists, meanwhile, have mostly tended to focus on understanding the politics of recent banking crises or on the historical experiences of particular countries and regions (Bartels and Bermeo, 2014; Bermeo and Pontusson, 2012; Crespo-Tenorio, Jensen and Rosas, 2014; Haggard, 2000; Hellwig and Coffey, 2011; Kahler and Lake, 2013; MacIntyre, 2003; Pepinsky, 2012). What is lacking is a systematic assessment of how and why the politics of banking crises has evolved over the long run, and what this means for the ability of governments to manage such crises and their political consequences. This book seeks to fill some of this gap.

Our key message is that the policy and political aftermaths of crises have been transformed over the course of the past two centuries. In the last half-century, financial and political instability have become mutually reinforcing in a way they were not previously. Modern democracies, we argue, have generated powerful tendencies towards increasingly extensive and costly policy interventions. This policy trend is driven primarily by what we term 'great expectations': the heightened demand by large segments of contemporary society – roughly, the middle class – for policies that protect their wealth and incomes from the damage that banking crises can inflict. We focus in particular on the consequences of the rising material stake of this group in wealth protection – or what we call 'the wealth effect'. As Atkinson and Brandolini have noted, much contemporary analysis of inequality focuses on the very rich and the very poor rather than 'the forgotten middle' (Atkinson and Brandolini, 2013, 75). This middle class plays a large part in our story because of its overwhelming political importance. As we discuss in Chapter 3, we view the middle class as 'those [households] "comfortably" clear of being at-risk-of-poverty' but not those households who have sufficient wealth not to need to work (Atkinson and Brandolini, 2013, 79). This now constitutes a majority of potential voters in many democracies with full adult enfranchisement.[1] Cross-country evidence also suggests that

---

[1] Atkinson and Brandolini offer various alternative measures of the middle class, including households with income between 75 per cent and 200 per cent of the national median income, which would include over 70 per cent of Nordic households, over half of British and American households, but under half of Mexican households (Atkinson and Brandolini, 2013, 78–81).

individuals in these households are significantly more likely than their poorer counterparts to vote in elections, maintaining pressure on governments to provide policies that broadly reflect their preferences.[2]

To be sure, the political science literature has a long tradition reaching back to Aristotle of arguing that the emergence of a middle class has been an important driver of democratization and of the effective functioning of democracy (Acemoglu and Robinson, 2006; Glassman, 1995; B. J. Moore, 1966; Mounk, 2018; North and Thomas, 1973). We emphasize a different causal mechanism, with less positive consequences. As middle-class demands for wealth stabilization policies have risen over time, they have tended to generate perverse consequences: increasing financial instability, more and deeper crises, and rising political disruption and dissatisfaction. As in Charles Dickens's famous novel of 1861, great expectations have generated great disappointments – with ongoing consequences for the nature and stability of democratic politics.

Our argument has four main novel elements. First, we underline the central importance of changing societal norms regarding government policy responsibilities, identifying a rising and effective societal demand 'from below' for the protection of relatively recently accumulated at-risk wealth. We contrast this with alternative though generally complementary accounts of how financial elites have captured policy 'from above'. Second, we show how mechanisms of democratic accountability have proven ineffective in limiting the propensity of governments to undertake bailouts during banking crises; indeed, they have increasingly done the opposite. Third, we argue that domestic political institutions have acquired increased importance for voters by shaping how governments intervene in crises. And fourth, we show that great expectations have ultimately fed both financial fragility and voter disappointment in government policy. In this way, our argument points to the macro-level consequences of what others have referred to as the 'financialization of everyday life' (e.g., Finlayson, 2009; Langley, 2009; Seabrooke, 2007).

---

[2] Mahler, for example, finds that there is 'class bias' in voter turnout in most developed democracies (i.e., turnout increases as income rises). The average difference in turnout in thirteen countries in the late 1990s between the 1st and the 3rd–4th (averaged) income quintiles is −8.8 and −3.8 per cent respectively, confirming that middle-class voters are a large group between the relatively pro-redistribution poor and anti-redistribution rich (Mahler, 2008, 175–8). See also Franko, Kelly and Witko (2016); Mahler, Jesuit and Paradowski (2014).

Our analysis also points to a new possible 'policy trilemma'. The classical monetary policy trilemma highlighting the incompatibility of monetary policy autonomy, international financial integration, and exchange rate stability is well known. More recently, some have proposed a financial policy trilemma positing the incompatibility of national responsibility for financial policy, international financial integration and financial stability (Schoenmaker, 2013). Others have suggested a political trilemma for the global economy consisting of democracy, global economic integration and national sovereignty (Rodrik, 2012). We believe that our analysis identifies another trilemma by raising serious concerns about the ability of contemporary societies simultaneously to sustain democratic politics, rising financialization and financial stability over time.

This challenge is not primarily, or merely, driven by what many suggest is the central problem: the increasing political influence of the very wealthiest groups, especially in the United States (Bartels, 2008; Gilens, 2012; Hacker and Pierson, 2010; Johnson and Kwak, 2010). While we do not deny the importance of such 'elite capture' in some cases, large variations in its extent among countries and over time mean that it is unlikely to explain the systematic trends we identify. Instead, we argue, the challenge is arguably even more fundamental because the pressures we identify are rooted in the preferences of a much broader segment of contemporary society than the very wealthiest groups. Nevertheless, our argument has important implications for economic policy and for political strategies that might ameliorate both the damage that democracy is doing to financial stability and the damage that financial instability is doing to democracy.

In the rest of this chapter we proceed as follows. In the first section, we outline our claims about the rise of great expectations regarding the protection of middle-class wealth. In the second section, we preview our argument about its consequences for policy and politics during and after severe banking crises. We end by providing an outline of the remainder of this book.

1.1 The Rise of Great Expectations: From the Nineteenth Century to Today

To clarify our argument about the rise of great expectations, here we divide the period since the early nineteenth century in a very stylized manner into three main eras. This periodization links the evolution of societal wealth, and specifically that of the middle class, to changing household and voter expectations of policy and political outcomes. It is in the third of these eras that great expectations intensify.

In the first era, from the early nineteenth century until the Great Depression, there was a low level of effective societal demand for economic protection in general in most democracies. This expectation was reflected, for example, in the very low levels of social welfare provision by most states compared to the post-1945 era (Briggs, 1961). When banking crises struck in this period, a narrow group of elites connected to insolvent financial firms often requested government rescues, but, with little mass pressure to support this elite demand, elected governments for the most part could avoid bailouts of insolvent banks and their creditors without substantial political risk. Instead, as we explain below, during this period governments and central banks (where these existed) for the most part adopted policies that we describe as largely 'market-conforming', allowing many distressed banks and customers to fail. The disastrous consequences of such policies, notably in the United States and parts of Continental Europe, were demonstrated in the Great Depression. In the political aftermath of this economic calamity, political populism and extremism flourished, a number of democracies collapsed and the world descended into a decade-long spasm of extreme violence.

The second era, roughly dated from 1945 to 1970, was very much a response to the economic and political havoc wrought by the Great Depression and the wars that followed it. These events generated a much more widespread demand for economic stabilization and the establishment of welfare safety nets to provide social stability and thereby to underpin democratic politics. This demand is often summarized by the idea of 'embedded liberalism', which was supported by new Keynesian and social democratic ideas that explained the flaws of the economic orthodoxy of the previous era and provided new policy solutions (Blyth, 2002; Ikenberry, 1992; Polanyi, 1957; Ruggie, 1982). The priority given during this era to national economic stabilization, welfare transfers and the Bretton Woods pegged exchange rate system also required a substantial degree of financial repression in the form of regulatory controls on banking and capital flows. This had the important additional effect of avoiding the deep banking crises of the previous era. For many countries now commonly referred to as 'advanced', this system ensured approximately full employment, stable growth and underpinned the consolidation of democracy. For much of today's emerging and developing world, this system permitted the pursuit of industrial development and nation-building, though with much less commitment to democratic norms.

The third and most recent era began around the mid-1970s and has been strongly associated with extensive financial liberalization and sharply rising societal wealth. Like the second era, it too emerged in part in response to the perceived problems generated by the dominant policy mix of the preceding era. New pro-market policy ideas expounded the benefits of moving away from macroeconomic activism and state-led development and towards the liberalization of markets, including for finance (Frieden, 2006; Helleiner, 1994). In part as a consequence of the financial liberalization that followed, banking crises re-emerged as an important policy challenge and as a growing threat to accumulating societal wealth from the mid-1970s.

It is important to recognize that wealth protection only became a clear policy priority in this third era. During the Bretton Woods era, governments were more strongly committed to the protection of employment income and development promotion than to the protection of wealth. Although, as noted above, financial stability was largely assured in practice during the early post-war decades, most democracies engaged to a substantial degree in the suppression and redistribution of wealth in this period. Post-war marginal tax rates on the very wealthiest peaked after the war and remained high until the 1970s (Scheve and Stasavage, 2016). High levels of wealth expropriation and redistribution in some early post-war banking crises in Western Europe by democratic governments also indicated the low priority given to wealth protection in this era (Scheidel, 2017, 126–73; Tribe, 2001). In most democracies, wealth inequality declined markedly until this time, in part because of these redistributive policies (Piketty and Zucman, 2015).

The shift towards more market-oriented financial policies from the 1970s would, it was hoped, restore more rapid growth. It certainly produced a marked and sustained rise in the value of housing and financial assets in many countries, as well as higher volatility of asset prices. Figure 1.1 shows how rapidly net private real wealth per adult increased in many advanced countries after 1970. As we show in more

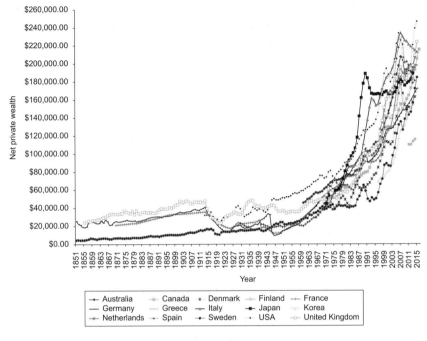

Figure 1.1: Real net private wealth per adult in selected countries, PPP exchange rates and constant 2016 US dollars, 1850–2016.
Source: World Wealth & Income Database (2017).

detail in later chapters, much of this wealth accumulation has been in the form of housing equity and pension assets.

For the middle classes in these countries in particular, this wealth has also been subject to rising market risk. This is because housing assets have become both more important and increasingly leveraged for this large group, and because in a number of countries there has been a shift from defined benefit pensions towards defined contribution schemes (Jordà, Schularick and Taylor, 2017; Piketty and Zucman, 2015). For this reason, and because in some countries this wealth may be needed to purchase increasingly marketized and more expensive services such as education and healthcare, wealth accumulation can be associated with rising anxiety for many households (Langley, 2009). As we show in Chapter 4, this rising anxiety has substantially increased the level of effective demand for government policies that protect this wealth.

We also highlight in later chapters similar trends occurring among households in emerging markets and developing countries, though at lower levels than those observed in more advanced democracies. As economic development and financial inclusion have progressed, a wider segment of the population in emerging markets and developing countries has become linked to the financial system. Bank deposits account for much of this exposure, and thus much household concern in these countries focuses on the limited fiscal capacity of governments to protect this form of wealth. Yet in a number of these countries the wealth portfolios of households of the upper middle class increasingly resemble those of average households in advanced economies. In addition to leveraged housing assets, pension assets held in defined contribution schemes are now prevalent in many parts of the emerging and developing world, most notably in Latin America and Eastern Europe (Brooks, 2005, 2007). Thus, we suggest, the expansion of financial inclusion and the growth in exposure to market-traded assets have also elevated the level of effective demand for wealth protection in emerging market and developing country democracies.

1.2   The Consequences of Great Expectations

This rising demand 'from below' for wealth protection has had crucial policy and political consequences in democracies that largely distinguish the third era from the first two. In policy terms, it has meant that when banking crises occur, governments are now subject to much stronger pressure from a wider political coalition to provide bailouts that prevent extensive wealth destruction. In political terms, it has meant that governments that fail to provide such bailouts, or that do so in a manner that is delayed or perceived as substantially redistributive, experience greater voter dissatisfaction and are thus more prone to lose office than in the past. We discuss both of these below.

1.2.1   The New Bailout Constituency and its Policy Impact

In a low-expectations world, such as that of our first era, the political constituency favouring minimal public intervention in crises generally prevailed over the constituency favouring public sector support of failing banks. This does not mean that governments and central banks never intervened in banking crises that occurred in the pre-1945 period. However, when they did, on average they did so in limited ways that can be described as roughly 'market-conforming'. The key policy recommendation in this tradition is often associated with Walter Bagehot, the famous nineteenth-century author and editor of *The Economist*, who argued that central banks should provide temporary loans at market interest rates in panics only to those banks deemed solvent and that would survive in normal circumstances (Bagehot, 1962 [1873]; Rosas, 2009, 6–7).

In the era of great expectations, more voters will expect governments to go well beyond such a minimalist policy stance during banking crises. As we elaborate in the next chapter, large parts of the middle class now favour intra-crisis policy interventions that minimize potential damage to their employment and their wealth. This is for three main reasons. The first two, following other scholars, we summarize as the financialization of wealth and the democratization of leverage. The third is what we identify as a growing *ex ante* government policy commitment to financial stabilization.

Financialization can be described as 'the increasing role of financial motives, financial markets, financial actors and financial institutions in the operation of the domestic and international economies' (Epstein, 2005, 3). A burgeoning literature has explored its wider social, economic and political implications.[3] The trading of assets in financial markets includes those associated with the pensions and other portfolio financial assets of most middle-class households in modern economies. This process has fostered a highly interdependent, networked financial system in which the level of 'systemic risk' – the risk that failure in one part of the system will propagate failure throughout the system – is substantially elevated. This financialization of wealth not only pertains to pensions and other financial investments; as we note below, financial risk also increasingly shapes housing markets and associated wealth. Although interconnections among banks were also present before the 1970s, their scope and magnitude were of a much smaller scale than in recent decades. Financialization increases the risk that allowing any significant financial firm to fail will generate a system-wide crisis that puts the value of a wide range of assets – and thus the interests of a large number of voters – in jeopardy.

The democratization of leverage, as Jordà, Schularick and Taylor explain, is associated with a long boom in mortgage lending to

---

[3] For one review, see van der Zwan (2014).

households in advanced countries that has generated rising household sector leverage and greater financial fragility (Jordà, Schularick, and Taylor, 2015, 2016, 2017; Jordà, Taylor and Schularick, 2014). This process is at an earlier stage in emerging markets and developing countries, but the level of household borrowing in these countries has reached considerably higher levels than in the past, with concomitant concerns about financial fragility (International Monetary Fund, 2017b). Along with pension and related assets, leveraged housing equity has come to constitute much of the wealth of middle-class households in contemporary societies. It means that they have acquired a much greater interest in the maintenance of the flow of credit – and thus in the protection of the large banks at the heart of the financial system – than before the 1970s.

The growing *ex ante* government policy commitment to financial stabilization stands out as a relatively new political priority in the modern era. Until the second half of the twentieth century, with only a few exceptions most governments refrained from making explicit or implicit commitments to financial stability as a policy priority. Since this time, we have observed a fundamental shift concerning government policy responsibilities in this domain. Although varying in form, these modern policy commitments have tended to reinforce a dominant orientation among voters that governments accept responsibility for preventing financial instability and for mitigating its consequences.

In combination, these three intertwined factors have substantially increased the level of effective demand for bailouts. Since the extent of wealth financialization, household leverage, and voter orientations based on government policy commitments vary across countries, so will the relative intensity of this demand. In country after country, however, these pressures for bailouts have increasingly overwhelmed those forces resisting them. We provide evidence for this in our case study chapters and in Chapter 4, where we show that societal expectations, as captured by our new data based on extensive coding of newspaper editorial commentary, have broadly shifted significantly over time in favour of bailouts.

We are not claiming that governments are mere calculating machines, automatically aggregating and responding in a linear fashion to changing voter preferences. Nor do we deny that other factors, including the partisan configuration of government, can shape policy responses. However, we do suggest that democratically elected

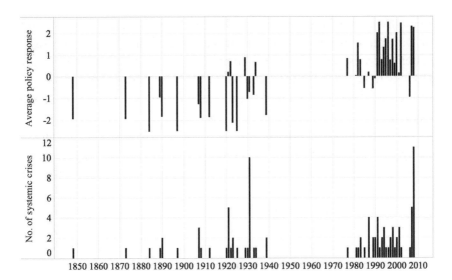

Figure 1.2: From Bagehot to bailout: annual average policy response index for systemic banking crises in democracies (top panel) and annual number of new systemic banking crises (bottom panel), 1848–2010.
Source: Reinhart, 2010 and author calculations. The policy response index captures the character of average policy responses across all countries suffering systemic crises in each year, with negative scores indicating 'Bagehot' policy responses and positive scores indicating bailouts. 'Systemic' or relatively severe banking crises follow Reinhart's coding. For further explanation, see Chapter 5.

governments, by virtue of electoral accountability and legitimacy imperatives, face at least some incentive to implement the dominant policy preferences of voters when they face banking crises. This argument is consistent with scholarship in related fields, including that which demonstrates considerable congruence between changes in public opinion and in policies across a range of issue areas (Barro, 1973; Page and Shapiro, 1983; Seabrooke, 2007).

Moreover, we show that on average, and in our more detailed case studies, elected governments have in practice responded to these great expectations with policies that broadly reflect the growing political dominance of the bailout coalition. Figure 1.2 summarizes this average policy trend over time, indicating, via the prevalence of negative scores on the policy response index we describe in Chapter 4, that Bagehot-style policy responses by democratically elected governments to systemic banking crises (SBCs) dominated in the pre-1945 era. The second era, the Bretton Woods years, saw no SBCs. In the third era, when SBCs re-emerged from the 1970s, there is a strong rising policy trend towards bailouts, as indicated by the prevalence of positive scores on our index. In Figure 1.2 we restrict our analysis to deep and costly systemic crises, so as to indicate that economic consequences alone are unlikely to be responsible for the policy trend we observe. We undertake further analysis in Chapter 5 to rule out this alternative potential explanation.

As late as the 1920s and early 1930s, elected governments in many of today's advanced economies – including Canada, Finland, Belgium, the Netherlands and Switzerland – refrained from extensive interventions as large parts of their banking sector collapsed in the exceptionally deep crises of this period. This was also the case for elected governments in some then-emerging economies, such as Greece, Portugal and Spain. By contrast, governments in these same economies responded over 2007–10 by providing extensive guarantees not only to all banks' depositors, but also of these banks' wholesale creditors. Most significant financial institutions, including many that were potentially insolvent, were rescued by various means or nationalized by the authorities. The bankruptcy of Lehman Brothers was a stark exception to this general trend and is now commonly seen as a catastrophic error of judgement by the George W. Bush administration.

Another alternative possible explanation of this policy trend is simply that policy elites 'learned the lesson' of the Great Depression years. We find this explanation to be unsatisfying. Indeed, prominent economists and policymakers have often interpreted the 1930s crisis rather as reinforcing the Bagehot dictum, that central banks should undertake last-resort lending only to solvent banks in crises in return for adequate collateral (Bernanke, 2015). Furthermore, in the 1980s and 1990s, when SBCs were concentrated in developing and emerging economies, Western policymakers rejected bank bailouts as reflecting 'crony capitalism' and insisted strongly on market-conforming policy responses by crisis-hit governments, often in the context of International Monetary Fund (IMF) conditionality (Van de Walle, 2001; Walter, 2008; Woods, 2006).[4] This evidence suggests that dominant economic ideas by the 1990s favoured market-conforming, Bagehot-style policy responses, not bailouts. When SBCs subsequently struck at home, however, Western leaders ultimately threw their previous advice and

---

[4] This is an important reason why, as Figure 1.2 indicates, Bagehot responses persisted in the 1980s and early 1990s.

ideological inclinations out the window and engaged in extensive and highly costly bailouts. Ignoring these temporal inconsistencies, Ben Bernanke, chairman of the US Federal Reserve, remarked in 2008 that 'there are no atheists in foxholes or ideologues in a financial crisis' (Bernanke, 2015, 164). More accurately, as we suggest in the conclusion, advanced country policy elites revealed their own hypocrisy by going against their own predispositions because of domestic political imperatives, and because their greater fiscal capacity permitted them to do so.

Our position is therefore closer to that of Mervyn King, Bernanke's counterpart at the Bank of England during the crisis. He argues that central banks and governments are now compelled to discard much of Bagehot's dictum because of the fundamental transformation of the financial system in recent decades:

> While banks' balance sheets have exploded, so have the risks associated with them ... Because of its critical role in the infrastructure of the economy, markets correctly believed that no government could let a bank fail, since that would cause immense disruption to everyone's ability to make and receive payments ... If such functions are materially threatened, governments will never be able to sit idly by. Institutions supplying those services are quite simply too important to fail. Everyone knows it. (King, 2016, 94, 95, 96)

Leaving aside the fact that King himself initially advocated a limited Bagehot response in Britain's crisis in 2007, one difference between his analysis and our own is that we locate the ultimate source of this policy shift in the historically unprecedented political pressures placed on elected governments by voters in the middle of the income and wealth distribution. The political path to bailouts, even in modern crises, often remains fraught and is far from linear. As we discuss below, this can have important political consequences.

1.2.2 A Rising Tendency for Political Punishment

Within this average policy trend towards more bailouts there is substantial policy variation. The demand for bailouts has risen in most countries, but elected governments do not provide them in the same ways or to the same degree. Existing scholarship has shown that due to their often severe economic and distributional impact, banking crises can complicate policy responses by fostering greater ideological conflict and political polarization (Blyth, 2002; Funke, Schularick and Trebesch, 2016; Mian, Sufi and Trebbi, 2014). Others have shown how political institutions can provide particular individuals or groups with opportunities to reshape, delay or veto particular policy responses, thereby frustrating voters' policy expectations (Alesina and Drazen, 1991; Crespo-Tenorio, Jensen and Rosas, 2014; Tsebelis, 2002). We build on this literature by showing how political polarization can interact with institutional vetoes to produce policy gridlock during crises, thereby delaying or preventing the kind of intervention preferred by modern voters. The importance of this phenomenon varies greatly across our three eras.

In our first era, a world of low expectations, most voters had a limited stake in financial stabilization and did not see governments as responsible for preventing crises and mitigating their impact. Thus, institutional factors that might delay or block government interventions in financial markets were accordingly less politically consequential during this earlier period. As we show in more detail in Chapter 9, in the very deep crisis of late 1907, the United States government under Theodore Roosevelt undertook very limited policy responses by modern standards. This was in part because there was then little support in Congress for federal Treasury intervention that might have defused the panic. Yet despite this and the very deep recession that followed, the Republicans retained control of the presidency in the 1908 elections.

In the second era, when voter expectations were still moderate, severe banking crises were almost entirely absent. Large distributional shocks emanating from the financial system were also far less common during this period, and political polarization was less important as a policy constraint. We say little more about this tranquil era in the rest of this book.

In the third era, when banking crises returned with a vengeance, policy gridlock had become highly politically consequential because governments now faced voters' great expectations. Any perceived failure to meet these heightened expectations, we argue, is likely to result in much greater electoral punishment. Indeed, we find a systematic trend for voters in the third era to punish incumbent governments after banking crises at much higher rates compared to the pre-1945 era, especially in the presence of veto players with heterogeneous

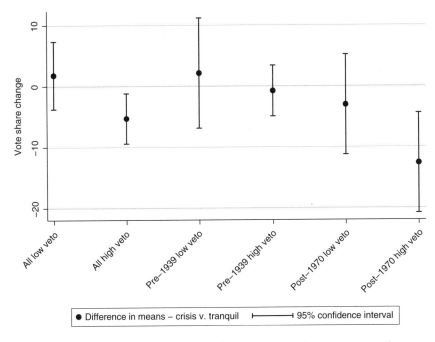

Figure 1.3: Systemic banking crises and changes in incumbent party vote share across veto player environments, 1872–2015.
Source: Reinhart (2010) and Henisz (2017). SBCs follow Reinhart's coding. The Henisz index captures political constraints on the chief executive based on the number of independent actors with veto power over policy decisions and the distribution of political preferences across these actors. For further explanation, see Chapter 6.

preferences. Figures 1.3 and 1.4 summarize this pattern for incumbent ruling parties and coalitions respectively, comparing changes in incumbent vote shares in crisis and crisis-free terms in environments where the government faces 'high' and 'low' political constraints from veto players with heterogeneous preferences (defined respectively as one standard deviation above and below the sample mean).

It is clear from these two figures that incumbent governments only suffer systemically reduced vote shares after crises in the modern era *and* where there are higher levels of veto players with heterogeneous preferences. We argue that this is because such vetoes lead to policy delays or selective interventions that foster voter perceptions of distributional unfairness, disappointing the great expectations now so firmly entrenched among the middle classes. We also point to the way in which rising inequality, often visibly associated with financialization, may have exacerbated political polarization and increased the importance

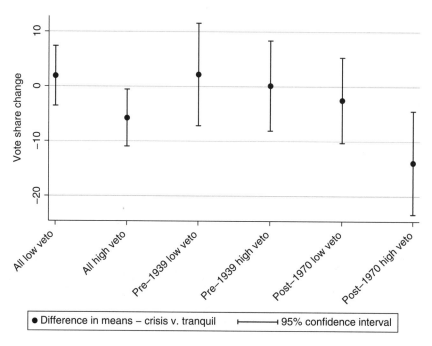

Figure 1.4: Systemic banking crises and changes in incumbent coalition vote share across veto player environments, 1872–2015.
Source: Reinhart (2010) and Henisz (2017).

of institutional vetoes. Inequality can be further increased by costly interventions that require later reductions in welfare spending, emphasizing their negative distributional consequences for many voters (Atkinson and Morelli, 2011; Mian, Sufi and Trebbi, 2014). Bank bailouts can thereby enhance existing perceptions among voters that financial elites have captured politics and policy (Hacker and Pierson, 2010; Johnson and Kwak, 2010).

Government attempts to meet society's great expectations are thus fraught with risk. Political competitors are often provided with multiple opportunities during and after crises to portray policy interventions as delayed, redistributive, misjudged or inadequate. We show in Chapters 8 and 10 how this was the fate of Gordon Brown's UK Labour government and the incumbent Republican Party in the United States, both of which suffered large losses in the elections that followed. Both also suffered from internal contestation over their preferred policy responses, from substantial and visible delays in key policy interventions, and were widely seen as exacerbating existing inequalities.

We also find that the relationship between bank bailouts and voter response is asymmetric. That is, modern voters are more inclined to punish governments for delayed or unfair bailouts, but less inclined to reward them for relatively prompt or less redistributive bailouts. Simply put, avoiding substantial punishment after banking crises is often the best that political incumbents can hope for. High levels of financialization and leverage, along with new orientations about government policy responsibilities, have almost certainly increased the difficulty for any incumbent government of achieving a 'good' outcome. To use a sporting metaphor, the effect of great expectations is equivalent to that of steadily raising the height of the bar in the Olympic high jump: participants find it increasingly difficult to succeed even as they try to learn from past attempts. The onset of a crisis may itself undermine the perceived competence of modern governments, who commit to stabilize finance through an increasingly complex and extensive set of regulations. And even when intra-crisis policy interventions are relatively well executed, banking crises still tend to be followed by unusually severe and sustained recessions, as well as large distributive shocks. Governments that gain good performance bonuses from voters after a crisis are therefore relatively rare.

Our findings thus diverge from the 'clarity of responsibility' thesis that voters will find it difficult to assign blame to incumbent governments for suboptimal policy choices that produce downturns in the presence of veto dispersal, i.e. when voters cannot easily discern who is responsible for policy choices (Duch and Stevenson, 2008; Hellwig and Samuels, 2007; Powell and Whitten, 1993). More generally, in the context of great expectations, crises tend to make voters less forgiving of governments than they might be in non-financial economic downturns, when their wealth is less threatened and distributive effects tend to be less extreme. More worryingly, as financialization and leverage have made crises more frequent and severe, they may also help to explain the growing disenchantment of many contemporary voters with democratic political institutions in general.

1.3   The Organization of This Book

This book is divided into three parts. Part I addresses the relationship between banking crises and the rise of great expectations

(Chapters 1–4). Part II offers a statistical analysis of the evolving policy responses to and political consequences of banking crises in a large sample of democracies (Chapters 5–6). Part III turns to consider how banking crises, policy and politics interrelate in three detailed country case studies since the nineteenth century: the United Kingdom, the United States and Brazil (Chapters 7–12).

Chapter 2 situates our argument more thoroughly in the relevant theoretical literature, explaining why changes in societal expectations of government over the long run can have a powerful impact on policy and on politics. Here, we outline the implications of our theory for the evolution in government policy responses to crises and in the propensity of governments to survive them.

Chapter 3 shows how the financialization of household wealth has evolved over nearly two centuries. It focuses in particular on the experience of the middle classes in Brazil, the United Kingdom and the United States, the three countries that we study in substantial detail in the second half of this book. We explore these cases as countries with a long experience of democratic institutions and banking crises. Political institutions of varying sorts (presidential systems in Brazil and the United States, parliamentary in the United Kingdom) introduced an element of electoral accountability in each country in the nineteenth century. Each country also has a storied history of financial instability. According to one authoritative source, since 1800 there have been nine systemic crises in Brazil, ten in the United Kingdom, and fourteen in the United States (Reinhart, 2010).

In addition, as we show in Chapter 3, financialization has been important in each of these countries, though with variation in its timing and extent. We also observe important differences in the timing of government policy commitments to financial stabilization, with the United States making the earliest observed commitment in the nineteenth century, followed by Brazil in the 1930s, with Britain's commitment coming later. In addition to variation in economic development and fiscal capacity, these countries also display important differences in terms of financial structure and their respective traditions and ideologies regarding state control over banks. The United Kingdom and the United States are liberal market economies with two of the most important financial markets in the world: the City of London and Wall Street. Both are prime examples of an arm's-length approach between the state and the banking sector. Brazil, by contrast, represents a hierarchical market economy with a long tradition of direct intervention in the banking sector (Schneider, 2013). In addition, São Paulo and Rio de Janeiro are two of the largest financial centres in Latin America.[5]

Chapter 4 outlines in more detail the changing nature of voter expectations regarding wealth protection and financial stabilization, drawing on long-run evidence from newspaper editorials in Brazil, the United Kingdom and the United States. It shows that as the wealth of large numbers of voters in the middle class has increased and become subject to rising risk of market disruption, many have come to expect governments to intervene far more extensively during crises than in the past.

Chapter 5 investigates the impact of these changing societal expectations on the policy responses that governments provide during banking crises. We provide evidence from a large number of democracies that the emergence of great expectations has been associated with a rising policy trend towards more extensive bank bailouts during crises.

Chapter 6 considers the impact of great expectations and the policy responses they have engendered for the electoral prospects of incumbent elected governments facing banking crises. We show that post-crisis electoral prospects have deteriorated markedly since the 1970s compared to the pre-1945 era, with polarized vetoes having an important conditioning effect.

Chapters 7 through 12 provide a series of in-depth longitudinal case studies of the policy responses and political consequences of banking crises in individual democracies in different eras. Chapter 7 investigates banking crises in the United Kingdom in a period of low expectations, focusing on crises in 1825 and 1890. Chapter 8 discusses the crisis of 2007–9 in the UK in an era in which great expectations were well entrenched and the policy responses of the government and the political impact of this crisis were very different to those that preceded it. Chapters 9 and 10 turn to consider the United States, which like the UK has a long history of financial instability. Chapter 9 discusses the deep banking crises of 1907 and 1929–33 in an era of low but rising

---

[5] In Chapter 4, we also consider evidence from the Netherlands – a 'coordinated market economy' with a large financial system and, compared with the United Kingdom and United States, a stronger tradition in bank-based finance (Hall and Soskice, 2001; Zysman, 1983). In addition, our statistical analyses in Chapters 5 and 6 include numerous observations from coordinated market economies.

societal expectations. Chapter 10 turns to consider the recent crisis of 2007–9.

Since the focus of the first four case study chapters is on two of the most advanced and financialized countries, Chapters 11 and 12 shift the focus towards an important emerging economy. Brazil has a patchier record of democratic governance than either the UK or the United States, so we consider how it grappled with large crises in the 1890s, a less democratic period, as well as in the 1980s and 1990s during a period of rapid economic and political change. We see Brazil's transition from cronyistic military dictatorship to a vibrant democracy from the mid-1980s as an ideal test of Rosas's argument about the constraining effects of democracy on the propensity for government bailouts (Rosas, 2009).

Chapter 13, the concluding chapter, elaborates the broader implications of our argument, including for policymakers. Our central argument, that many modern governments and central banks have no practical alternative in a crisis but to intervene to rescue the accumulated wealth of large numbers of voters, has a number of implications. The first is that this has fostered continuing increases in financialization, leverage and financial fragility, generating more and deeper crises. Paradoxically, then, the rise of great expectations has helped to reinforce the very threat to financial stability that citizens and governments most fear. As we have suggested, this has generated rising political instability and risks feeding a growing disenchantment with democratic political institutions. We argue that it is essential to escape this financial–political downward spiral.

To do so, we argue that the emphasis of policy must switch firmly towards crisis prevention. Despite concerted attempts in the wake of the most recent crisis to end 'too-big-to-fail', ultimately most such efforts lack political credibility and are of uncertain value. Given this, an important implication of our argument is the need for political parties of the moderate centre to convince voters of the need to accept more radical crisis prevention measures, for the sake both of their wealth and of the stability of democracy.

2 GREAT EXPECTATIONS, BANKING CRISES AND DEMOCRATIC POLITICS

This chapter outlines a theory of how the emergence of great expectations has reshaped the policy and political aftermaths of banking crises. In turn, we suggest, these aftermaths have had important consequences for financial stability, inequality and the political environment in many democratic countries.

After the devastation and social disruption associated with the Great Depression and World War II, societies in many countries wanted greater assurance regarding employment, incomes and economic and social protection generally. Full employment and growth in incomes became perhaps the overriding objective of governments in most democracies, as well as in many non-democracies – as has been emphasized in the literature on post-war 'embedded liberalism' (Blyth, 2002; Ikenberry, 1992; Polanyi, 1957; Ruggie, 1982). Embedded liberalism also had a Southern side, which, in keeping with the commitment to domestic policy autonomy, led much of the developing world to pursue nationalist goals of industrial development and nation-building (Helleiner, 2003).

These goals were eventually replaced in advanced democracies in the 1970s by a new policy priority, the control of inflation, and an inflation-targeting policy framework premised on the pursuit of monetary stability by independent central banks (Blyth and Matthijs, 2017; Helleiner, 1994; Maxfield, 1997). Market deregulation was an important component of this programme, designed to increase price competition and innovation. This included financial deregulation, which unleashed a dramatic increase in the size and complexity of financial markets.

The interests of many middle-class households also became increasingly tied to financial markets through the management of wealth and the provision of financial services, including credit. Aggregate financial wealth grew very rapidly in advanced democracies, including the wealth owned by these households. Since the share of financial assets in the average household's wealth portfolio typically increases with the level of economic development, the degree to which households in emerging and developing democracies have been exposed to similar processes has varied. Yet as these economies have become richer and financial inclusion and deepening progresses, increasing proportions of the population has become linked to the financial system. Many now hold riskier and more sophisticated financial instruments in addition to bank deposits, though at lower levels than those observed in more advanced democracies (Davies, 2008; Honohan, 2008).

We argue that this rising material stake of middle-class households in wealth closely connected to financial markets has increased their effective demand for the protection and promotion of this wealth. We are not claiming that the demand for income, employment and development promotion no longer exists but that these households now assign much greater priority than in the past to wealth protection.[1] This is in keeping with what Ansell describes as a shift from 'Employment Dominance' to 'Asset Dominance' where 'macroeconomic policies (or shocks) have their greatest impact on the price level and volatility of assets like equities and housing – in other words not on citizens' income but on their wealth' (Ansell, 2012, 533).[2]

We refer to this new policy preference as 'great expectations,' with an implied reference to the transformation of the central character of Dickens's novel due to his new-found wealth. However, in sharp contrast to Pip's quest for personal salvation, the modern great expectations of the middle class lead them to seek salvation in *government* policy. As such, they are in deep tension with the (somewhat Victorian) contemporary narrative of individual self-responsibility for managing the increasing risk associated with the 'financialization of everyday life'

---

[1] This demand can conflict with other demands for prioritizing economic growth and employment. For example, mild deflation can favour creditors over debtors and the holders of wealth over citizens that rely on current income and employment.
[2] See also Gourevitch and Shinn (2006, 221).

(Erturk et al., 2007; Langley, 2009; Martin, 2002).[3] We argue that during crises, individuals have strong incentives to set self-responsibility narratives aside, with two important consequences.

First, given the trend toward greater asset accumulation by the middle class, governments have come under greater electoral pressure to preserve such wealth by preventing crises that threaten it. When governments fail to prevent crises, as has been increasingly common since the 1970s, great expectations have heightened imperatives for democratic governments to respond by providing increasingly extensive financial sector and creditor bailouts.

Second, great expectations and the associated government policy responses have had powerful political consequences. One is that democratic governments experiencing banking crises have found it increasingly difficult to retain office in the short to medium term. The rise of great expectations has 'lifted and tilted' the bar regarding citizen assessments of government performance: voters have become increasingly likely to punish governments heavily for failing to protect their wealth, but they are less strongly inclined to reward political incumbents for acting in accordance with these expectations. This asymmetric tendency towards punishment is due to the way in which political institutions condition the policy response to crises and to the powerful distributional effects that often ensue.

The rest of this chapter is organized as follows. The first section considers why the rise of great expectations will raise the demand for relatively extensive policy responses that protect incomes *and* wealth, and how politics and institutions will shape the supply of these policies. The second section provides a theory of why the electoral prospects of incumbent governments will be increasingly conditional on great expectations and more tenuous in an era of high financial fragility. The conclusion briefly considers the longer-run implications of great expectations and related policy responses.

2.1 Crises, Policy Responses and Institutions in Democracies

Public interventions in banking crises are likely to be limited in a world in which most voters have low expectations regarding

---

[3] See Chapter 1, and Carruthers (2015); Gai, Haldane and Kapadia (2011); Haldane (2013); Haldane and May (2011); Kay (2015); Krippner (2005); van der Zwan (2014).

government responsibility for wealth protection. In such a world, the political constituency favouring minimal public intervention is likely to prevail over the constituency that prefers public sector support of failing banks. Voices taking a principled stance in favour of non-intervention may also be present. Yet, as Rosas points out, pure non-intervention by government in crises is rare in practice, since potentially powerful constituencies facing large losses will have a strong incentive to lobby the authorities to intervene to prevent or to absorb such losses. Accordingly, limited and relatively 'market-conforming' lender of last resort (LOLR) interventions as advocated by classical authors such as Henry Thornton and Walter Bagehot constitute the practical end of the minimal intervention spectrum (Rosas, 2009, 6–7).

Such policies are relatively market-conforming in that they provide temporary, emergency public support only to banks that would be solvent in normal market circumstances. As we elaborate more fully in Chapter 5, 'Bagehot' policies include the provision of emergency financial assistance at market or above-market rates of interest to banks that provide good collateral.[4] We also elaborate there how we extend this Bagehot model of crisis resolution to encompass other policies that aim to prevent the failure of institutions that would be solvent in normal times while minimizing potential taxpayer losses.

What we term the 'core' Bagehot constituency includes current taxpayers with a strong interest in avoiding bailouts of insolvent banks that would incur future liabilities for the public sector, while accepting collateralized lending to solvent banks to support, with minimized risk, the overall level of tax receipts. In the era before World War I, direct taxpayers consisted mostly of the relatively wealthy, often a powerful and well-organized group. Those subject to indirect taxes such as import duties were larger if often less influential. This constituency also in principle includes solvent banks – as well as their customers, investors and creditors – who were not threatened by (and might even benefit from) the failure of weak competitor banks. Finally, it also includes public sector beneficiaries, such as public sector workers and welfare recipients, who wish to preserve their share of and access to public

---

[4] In the textbook case, the central bank acts as the LOLR in such circumstances, but the Treasury may also do so. Bagehot also advocated lending at market rather than 'penalty' rates of interest, noting that market rates would typically be elevated during crises (Bagehot, 1962, chap. 7; Turner, 2014, 140–7).

expenditure. In the nineteenth century this group was also relatively small in most countries.[5]

The core bailout constituency, by contrast, includes insolvent banks as well as their customers, creditors and investors who have no easy exit option. These groups should favour the socialization of their losses by the public sector and/or by their stronger bank competitors. Such bailouts work against market forces when the government acts to prevent or to absorb losses by banks that would likely be insolvent in normal circumstances (Rosas, 2009, 6).

It is not immediately obvious which of these two constituencies would secure their policy preferences during earlier banking crises. The Bagehot constituency was probably larger as it included taxpayers and public sector beneficiaries, though both groups were much smaller than today. Important actors on both sides would have strong incentives to mobilize to influence policymakers. In our view, democracy, by virtue of electoral accountability and legitimacy imperatives facing incumbent governments, generally limits the degree to which they can pander to the interests of well-connected elites, and instead incentivizes and orients them to select policies that broadly reflect the dominant policy preferences of their voters. Our emphasis on the importance on mass pressure from below fits with rational choice arguments emphasizing the responsiveness of politicians to 'removal pressures' (Barro, 1973; Ferejohn, 1986) and with constructivist arguments highlighting the responsiveness of elites to mass public understandings (Seabrooke, 2007).

In this regard we see the preferences of voters in the middle of the income and wealth distribution as therefore likely to be decisive in shaping government policy choices. Our key argument is that this middle voter bloc has moved from a soft Bagehot stance towards a strong bailout stance over the course of a century or more. In the earlier era, the interests of this bloc were likely more conflicted, with taxpayers and public sector beneficiaries opposed to bailouts and savers with deposits in distressed banks supporting them. Although the number of taxpayers and public sector beneficiaries was limited, so too was the size of the financial wealth of the middle class.

---

[5] In the UK, for example, public sector employment after the Napoleonic wars fell back to about 3 per cent of total employment, increasing slowly to 7 per cent of the total by 1913 (Thomas and Dimsdale, 2017, sec. A51).

As its wealth rose over time and became increasingly bound up in bank deposits and market-traded assets, this group should have moved to support policies aimed at protecting this wealth. In contrast to the earlier era, bank failures now pose a much more significant threat to a wide segment of this middle bloc of voters. We emphasize two effects: a size effect due to rising average household wealth, and a composition effect due to rising exposure to market-traded assets and growing financial inclusion. The size effect tends to exert greater influence in emerging and developing democracies, while the composition effect tends to feature more prominently in advanced democracies, though neither is unique to either category.

Our argument is therefore different to that of Guillermo Rosas, who argues that electoral competition forces governments to prioritize the interests of taxpayers, who are the largest group of potential losers from costly bailout policies with the capacity to unseat governments that act against their interests. Market actors, understanding this, will view *ex ante* commitments by incumbent governments in democracies as relatively credible and will therefore act more prudently than their counterparts in political systems that lack effective electoral competition. This, Rosas argues, reduces the probability both of deep banking crises and of costly bailouts in democracies (Rosas, 2009, 11).[6] We think this argument underplays important dynamic processes in democracies and effectively assumes that household and voter interests are narrowly defined by their status as taxpayers. Below, we outline three main interconnected developments that have pushed the middle class into the bailout constituency over the past century, especially since the 1970s. These are summarized under headings of the financialization of wealth, the democratization of leverage, and the growing policy commitment to financialization.

2.1.1 The Financialization of Wealth

Banks have become steadily more important in modern complex economies as facilitators of the payments system, as brokers who match lenders with borrowers, and as managers of other actors' savings and financial risk. As large banks have come to take on many or all of

---

[6] Behn et al. offer a weaker version of this argument, arguing that governments will prefer to delay bailouts until after elections (Behn et al., 2015).

these functions, the traditional distinction between commercial and investment banks has been eroded, as has that between banking in 'coordinated' and 'liberal' market economies (Hardie et al., 2013).

As long as the failure of individual banks did not threaten the maintenance of the payments system, actors in the Bagehot coalition could favour market-conforming policies that allowed insolvent banks to fail. However, as financial complexity, interconnectedness and deepening have risen over time, more households and firms have become dependent on the many services provided by banks, especially those that are most interconnected in the financial network. This increasing network complexity raises the level of systemic risk in the financial system, defined as 'the risk that the inability of one or more participants to perform as expected will cause other participants to be unable to meet their obligations when due' (Basel Committee on Banking Supervision, 2015).

Over the past century and more, the biggest shift in this regard has been in the wealth and financial interconnectedness of the rising middle class, especially in advanced countries (Muellbauer, 2008, 293–4). This includes bank deposits and other assets such as stocks, bonds and houses – all now strongly associated with middle-class status. Financialization also means these households have more to lose in financial crashes. Importantly, even as the middle classes have attained levels of wealth that far exceed the aspirations of their grandparents, this has not meant that they have acquired a more relaxed attitude to financial risk. The literature on the democratization of finance documents the profound transformation in 'everyday saving' habits in many democracies in recent decades (Crouch, 2009; Finlayson, 2009; Langley, 2009; Nesvetailova and Palan, 2013; Watson, 2007). A shift toward 'asset based welfare' and what Crouch (2009) describes as 'privatized Keynesianism' in many advanced democracies has meant that households became 'financial subjects' out of necessity to provide for their retirement, to send their children to university, to pay for healthcare, to supplement income, and to access decent housing. These may be seen as relative necessities and basics of modern life, but the demand for them is income-elastic because they also possess substantial 'positional' attributes that shape perceptions of social status. Middle-class wealth, concentrated in owner-occupied housing and domestically managed pension assets, has a stronger home bias and is less diversified than the portfolios of the very wealthy (Hoffman et al., 2009). An important strand of economic sociology has emphasized how these characteristics have fed declining social mobility and rising anxiety (Frank, 2013; Littrell et al., 2010). Rising economic inequality, by increasing competition for key positional goods such as education and housing, can also feed the demand for credit (Ahlquist and Ansell, 2017; Frank, 2013; Rajan, 2010).[7]

There is some evidence of the emergence of 'defensive' wealth acquisition among lower-middle-income households, and more risk-embracing investment approaches to wealth acquisition among upper-middle-income households (Fligstein and Goldstein, 2015). Especially in the former category but possibly more generally, as household wealth portfolios have shifted away from savings deposits with fixed value towards more volatile, market-traded assets such as leveraged housing equity and defined contribution (DC) pensions, the anxiety of house-holders about the value of their total wealth may have increased over time (Watson, 2007). These citizens are more likely to feel that these processes are beyond their control and to reject any suggestion that they should bear personal responsibility for the rising risk to their wealth. Their financial anxiety may have been exacerbated by other factors that have coincided with financialization, including rapid technological change, management, labour market and family structure changes that raised risks for households dependent on labour income (Fligstein and Goldstein, 2015; Kalleberg, 2009; McCloud and Dwyer, 2011; Western et al., 2012). Even those households that actively embrace greater risk during asset price booms will likely adopt more defensive orientations during busts and try to shift blame to others, including governments, if large losses materialize.

Households in other parts of the world have not been insulated from these trends. Rising financial inclusion in emerging and developing countries has brought closer links to the financial system for a wider segment of the population (Demirgüç-Kunt and Klapper, 2012; World Bank, 2014). In recent years, leveraged housing, DC pensions and other market-traded assets have come to form an important component of wealth portfolios for some households in emerging and developing countries. However, the anxieties of many middle-class households in these countries are likely to focus more on the limited fiscal capacity of their governments to protect their wealth only recently stored in less

---

[7] Access to higher-quality government-funded goods and services, such as education, transport, crime prevention and low pollution, also tends to be reflected in house and land values (Muellbauer, 2008, 304).

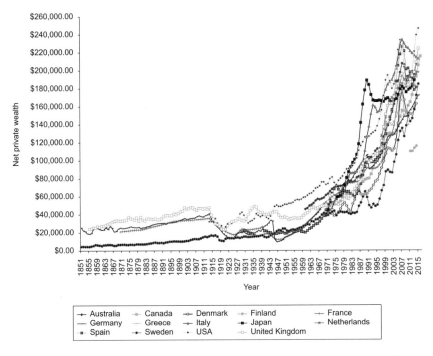

Figure 2.1.a: Net private real wealth per adult in advanced countries, PPP exchange rates and constant 2016 US dollars, 1850–2016.

volatile financial assets. This can create strong incentives for such households to hold savings in banks they deem to be politically protected, including state-owned financial institutions. The very wealthiest households in these countries may hold much of their financial wealth in offshore accounts, thereby benefiting from the protection provided by states with greater fiscal capacity (Zucman, 2015).

Figures 2.1.a and 2.1.b, which use available data to plot net private real wealth per adult in a number of advanced and some emerging market economies, show just how dramatically it has increased since 1970 in most.[8] The contrast between the position of what became the middle class in the second half of the twentieth century and the earlier position of that group is stark. Currently available long-run estimates of

---

[8] South Africa appears as something of an outlier in Figure 2.1.b, due to increased domestic political difficulties from the mid- to late 1970s and international trade and financial sanctions under apartheid (Aron, Muellbauer and Prinsloo, 2008). Since the end of apartheid in 1994, net private wealth has followed the upward pattern of many other advanced and emerging market economies.

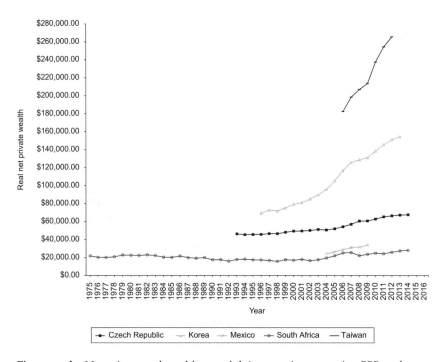

Figure 2.1.b: Net private real wealth per adult in emerging countries, PPP exchange rates and constant 2016 US dollars, 1975–2016.
Source: World Wealth & Income Database (2017).

wealth shares in a few countries reveal that wealth was highly concentrated in the pre-1945 era. In the absence of wealth distribution data, it would seem reasonable to infer based on income inequality estimates that similar patterns of wealth distribution were likely present in most other countries (Bourguignon and Morrisson, 2002). In the years 1870–1939, the share of total societal wealth in the hands of the top 10 per cent of wealth-holders stood in the 70–90 per cent range in Europe and the United States (with Europe then being more unequal). As Piketty and Saez note:

> Wealth concentration was so extreme in pre-WWI Europe that there was basically no 'wealth middle class'. That is . . . the middle 40 percent wealth holders were almost as poor as the bottom 50 percent wealth holders (the wealth share of both groups was close to or less than 5 percent). (Piketty and Saez, 2014, 839)[9]

[9] See also Ohlsson, Roine and Waldenström (2008).

Extreme wealth concentration in this earlier era meant that the richest decile was far more vulnerable than other groups to asset price collapses during banking crises. It is estimated that only one family in twenty was directly affected by the stock market crash during the 1929 banking crisis in the United States (Galbraith, 1955, 78). Financial collapses of an earlier era thus mainly affected a small minority, and what would later become the middle class had no strong interest in bailouts during this period.

In the period since 1970, the wealth share of the top decile in countries for which we have data has ranged from below 60 per cent to above 70 per cent (with the USA now more unequal than Europe).[10] But it is crucial to note that in both France and the USA, for which more detailed data is available, the *level* of real net wealth of the 'middle 40 per cent' of households (from the 50th to 90th percentiles) has risen considerably since 1970, even though the wealth *share* of this group has declined, especially in the United States.[11]

India is the only non-advanced democracy that has had repeated household wealth surveys over a significant portion of time, conducted at roughly decennial intervals since 1961-2. This gives us an important window into trends in a large segment of the emerging and developing world – one comprising roughly 17 per cent of the world's population in 2010. More detailed data from the 1991-2 and 2002-3 surveys indicates that assets per household among the middle 40 per cent more than doubled during this period, even though, like the United States, their wealth share declined somewhat (Subramanian and Jayaraj, 2008).[12] Wealth inequality in India has remained fairly stable since the first survey; in 2000 it was only slightly below the average for other emerging market and developing countries for which data is available (Davies et al., 2008).

Since the United States is now a relatively extreme case of recent wealth inequality, it is reasonable to presume that the level of real net wealth of the middle classes also increased substantially in most other

---

[10] The income share of the middle classes (defined as the middle three quintiles) has fallen further than that of the poor or the very rich in many countries since the 1980s, especially in the United States and the United Kingdom (Atkinson and Brandolini, 2013, 76).

[11] See www.WDI.world, accessed 29 March 2017. The middle 40 per cent still own about 25–35 per cent of total societal wealth in Europe and the USA.

[12] Data from the 2002–3 survey indicates that the middle 40 per cent held roughly 42 per cent of total assets in India.

advanced democracies. With similar wealth inequality to that in other emerging and developing countries, the same might be said of India relative to this group. Thus, although wealth inequality has generally increased since the 1970s, the level of real middle-class wealth today is far greater than in earlier periods. Such levels of wealth accumulation substantiate our 'size effect' claim.

As for the composition effect, the data shows that middle-class wealth in advanced countries has gradually come to be concentrated in houses, pensions, life insurance policies and (now often less so) bank deposits (European Central Bank, 2013, 2016; Guiso et al., 2003; Piketty and Zucman, 2014, 1280–1). The wealth of the middle class in emerging and developing countries, a narrower, but widening group in comparison to advanced countries, has also become more concentrated in housing, bank deposits and in some cases riskier market-traded assets (Aron, Muellbauer and Prinsloo, 2008; European Central Bank, 2013, 2016; Honohan, 2008; Subramanian and Jayaraj, 2008; Torche and Spilerman, 2008).

House ownership rates outside of the wealthiest households have increased remarkably. For example, in the UK in 1918, 77 per cent of all households rented their accommodation, mainly from wealthy private landlords. Ownership rates grew rapidly from the 1950s and by 1971, 50 per cent of households were owner-occupiers (Office for National Statistics, 2013). By 2013, the home ownership rate had reached 64 per cent. Ownership rates before World War II in the United States were higher than in the UK, around 45 per cent from the 1890s, but also rose significantly after World War I (Mazur and Wilson, 2011, 8). By 2013, roughly two-thirds of American households owned their homes. Essentially the same pattern can be found in Canada, Germany, France, Italy and Switzerland (Jordà, Schularick and Taylor, 2016). Nearly three-quarters of Europeans owned their own home in 2008 (Eurostat, 2017). A 2005 United Nations report reveals a similar average home ownership rate among a sample of emerging market and developing countries, as does data from the Housing Finance Information Network (United Nations Human Settlements Program, 2006).[13]

In recent decades, the acquisition of housing assets in a number of countries has reflected more than rising owner-occupation. Housing

---

[13] See also De Ferranti et al. (2004); Guriev and Rachinsky (2008); Torche and Spilerman (2008).

became seen as an investment, an entrepreneurial activity; it reflected a broader trend in some countries – notably in the United States, Britain and Australia – towards the emergence of a 'finance culture', especially among upper-middle-class groups who came to emulate the very wealthy in this regard (Fligstein and Goldstein, 2015). The acquisition of additional housing assets has often been encouraged by taxation policies and by the growing availability of mortgage finance for investment properties.

Long-run data on the portfolio composition of household wealth is limited, even in highly advanced economies. The best available recent data from the United States and the Eurozone household surveys reveals that property assets are far less important in the asset portfolios of the wealthiest households (European Central Bank, 2013, 2016; Guiso et al., 2003; Kuhn, Schularick and Steins, 2017). The same applies in the emerging and developing countries where data is available (European Central Bank, 2013, 2016; Subramanian and Jayaraj, 2008; Torche and Spilerman, 2008). However, in many parts of the emerging and developing world, a large proportion of the poor may not hold formal titles on their home and land (Soto, 2000), which is consistent with the low proportion reporting a mortgage (see below).

These differences mean that during financial crises, interest conflicts can emerge between the wealthiest households and others. The former group has a stronger interest in the protection of their financial market assets than in the protection of the housing wealth of lower- and middle-class households during crises. Yet, as we argue below, the financialization of wealth has led to greater preference alignment as regards the protection of portfolio financial assets.

Financial assets represent a sizeable proportion of household wealth. Household survey data suggests that such assets now make up over 50 per cent of wealth in Norway, over 40 per cent in the United States, about 30 per cent in Australia, Canada, Germany, Italy, the Netherlands and Sweden, 17 per cent in Korea and about 4 per cent in India (Honohan, 2008). The distribution of financial wealth within advanced countries tends to be more concentrated than housing wealth. The same has been found to be the case in emerging Europe (European Central Bank, 2013, 2016), Latin America (Torche and Spilerman, 2008) and Ghana (Honohan, 2008). This may be less true for other emerging markets and developing countries, as suggested by survey data from India, where household portfolios have roughly equal exposure to

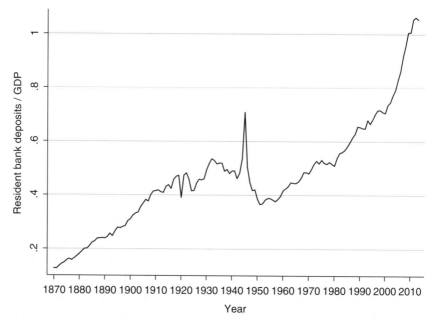

Figure 2.2: Total domestic deposits by non-financial residents / GDP in advanced economies, 1870–2010.
Source: Jordà et al. (2017).

financial assets along the wealth distribution (Subramanian and Jayaraj, 2008). Yet in all countries, the bulk of financial assets is held by relatively wealthy households.

A sizeable fraction of wealth in all economies is held in bank deposits, which have grown significantly in absolute terms in advanced economies since the 1970s (see Figure 2.2). Emerging markets have also experienced considerable growth in bank deposits, though they have only recently attained levels reached in advanced countries in the early 1960s (see Figure 2.3). Bank deposits have also grown in developing countries, though they remain far behind those reached elsewhere, with levels resembling those last seen in advanced countries in the early twentieth century.

A downward trend in the relative weight of deposits in household portfolios is evident in countries where data is available for a longer period of time. In the United States, for instance, the proportion of household financial wealth held in currency and deposits fell from 23 per cent in 1977 to 12 per cent in 2006 (Federal Reserve Board (US) 2017a). In Britain, the proportion fell from 34 per cent in 1980 to 22 per

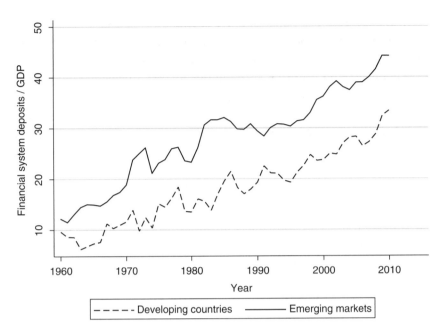

Figure 2.3: Total financial system deposits / GDP in emerging market and developing country democracies, 1960–2010.
Source: World Bank (2017).

cent in 1995 (Banks and Tanner, 2002, 223). Similar declines over this period were observed in Italy and Germany (Eymann and Börsch-Supan, 2002, 294; Guiso and Jappelli, 2002, 254). As we discuss below, such portfolio shifts are part of a wider trend toward greater exposure to market-traded assets in advanced countries in recent decades.

Deposit accounts are very widely held among households in advanced countries, exceeding 95 per cent of households across the wealth and income distribution in recent household wealth surveys (European Central Bank, 2013, 2016; Guiso, Haliassos and Jappelli, 2002; World Bank, 2017). These surveys also reveal that financial asset holdings among households at the lower end of the distribution are highly concentrated in deposits.

The dearth of household wealth surveys elsewhere creates challenges for tracking the extent of exposure to different asset classes across and within emerging and developing countries over time. World Bank household surveys in 2011 and 2014 found that 56 per cent of households in emerging market democracies and 27 per cent of households in developing country democracies had accounts with a formal financial institution (World Bank, 2014, 2015). Access to an account was considerably higher among the richest 60 per cent of households by income, exceeding 62 per cent in emerging markets and nearing 32 per cent in developing countries. Among the poorest 40 per cent, access fell to 46 per cent and 16 per cent in these respective groups.

Household surveys from India – where in 2002–3 bank deposits constituted over 92 per cent of financial assets – indicate asset holdings at banks over a longer time period (1981–2, 1991–2 and 2002–3) than the World Bank surveys. Even at the lowest decile of the income distribution, financial assets represented between roughly 3 and 7 per cent of household wealth (Subramanian and Jayaraj, 2008). Household surveys from sixteen Latin American countries between 1990 and 2000 also indicate that household wealth is stored in bank deposits across the income distribution, though much of it is concentrated in the top quintile (De Ferranti et al., 2004, 429).

Private credit as a proportion of GDP, for which data is available over a longer time period for most emerging markets and developing countries, is closely correlated with account access. Private credit has expanded in both emerging markets and developing countries since the 1970s, though considerably more in the former than the latter (see Figures 2.6 and 2.7 below). The expansion of private credit would suggest a corresponding increase in the share of households with accounts at financial institutions during this time, implying growing exposure to banks as vehicles for storing wealth and facilitating payments.

Data on the supply side of access to financial institutions is consistent with this conclusion. Figure 2.4 plots an index from the IMF that captures the degree of access to financial institutions based on the number of bank branches and automated teller machines (ATMs) per 100,000 adults. The index ranges from 0 to 1, with higher values indicating greater access. Not surprisingly, advanced countries have considerably greater supply-side access to financial institutions. Yet significant improvements have also occurred in emerging markets, particularly since 1990, with marginal improvements in developing countries over the entire time period. In the absence of survey data, these supply-side improvements also suggest greater exposure to financial institutions among households in emerging markets and developing countries.

Alongside bank deposits, households, particularly in advanced countries, have become increasingly exposed to riskier market-traded

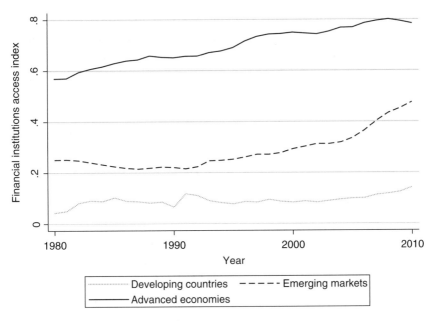

Figure 2.4: Financial institutions access, 1980–2010.
Source: Svirydzenka (2016).

assets. By the early 2000s, the proportion of households in advanced countries with direct or indirect ownership of stocks had grown significantly, reaching nearly 50 per cent in the United States, roughly one-third in Britain and the Netherlands, and nearly one-fifth in France, Germany and Italy (Guiso et al., 2003, 9). Ownership of riskier financial assets among households in advanced economies increases significantly from the fifth decile of wealth distribution upward, as does the share of such assets in the overall wealth portfolio (European Central Bank, 2016, 28).

As with deposits, the limits of available data make tracking household exposure to market-traded assets over time in emerging markets and developing countries difficult. Households surveys from India estimate that eight per cent of households had invested in shares or debentures in 1998.[14] Household survey data from Korea indicates a slightly higher ownership rate, with roughly 10 per cent of households

---

[14] Additional evidence from India suggests that the number of investor households had increased rapidly between 1985–6 and 1998–9, growing at a compound rate of 22 per cent (Subramanian and Jayaraj, 2008, 118).

owning risky financial assets (Honohan, 2008). In Latin America, available data from seven countries indicates that less than 1 per cent of households report income from share ownership, though this figure likely represents, at best, a lower bound estimate due to limited representation of wealthier households taking part in the surveys, and tax evasion (Torche and Spilerman, 2008, 166). Similar to advanced economies, ownership of riskier financial assets shows a strong upward trend along the wealth distribution in emerging markets and developing countries. Based on the limited data available on household financial assets in emerging and developing countries, holdings of risky financial assets below the top 5 per cent of wealth-holders were probably negligible a decade ago (Honohan, 2008).

The pension assets of the middle classes have also grown sharply in many countries since 1945. Since the 1970s, a growing policy trend to constrain the growth in public social insurance and public pension provisions placed a greater onus on individual savings, with tax concessions often used to promote private pensions. There has also been a generalized move since the 1990s away from defined benefit (DB) pensions towards DC schemes, which shifts financial risk onto households and individuals and – as many readers will know from personal experience – increases their incentive to monitor the market value of their pension assets.[15]

Pension privatization diffused around the world in the 1980s and 1990s (Brooks, 2005, 2007). Beginning in Chile in 1981, a growing number of countries across all income categories shifted from publicly funded, pay-as-you-go DB systems to market-based pension provision that includes a DC, funded, privately managed pillar. During the 1980s and 1990s, the number of countries with mandatory privately managed DC schemes increased from one to more than thirty. By 2012, the World Bank indicates that 15 per cent of all mandatory pension schemes worldwide were DC systems (Pallares-Miralles, Whitehouse and Romero, 2012).These schemes are observed most widely in Eastern Europe and Latin America, but are also present in Australia and Nigeria as well as in Ghana, Norway and Sweden on an optional basis. In

---

[15] Under DB schemes, employers are effectively responsible for making up for shortfalls in the value of pension fund assets, reducing the incentive of employees to monitor underlying asset values and portfolio composition.

addition, a number of developing countries have created or maintained publicly managed DC pensions ('provident funds').

Voluntary privately managed DC schemes form an increasingly important part of retirement income in a number of advanced and emerging market democracies. These schemes are particularly widespread in Belgium, Britain, Canada, Ireland, New Zealand and the United States (OECD, 2015a). Voluntary DC schemes also feature prominently in other advanced democracies as well as in South Africa and Brazil.

According to the OECD, private sources provided more than 50 per cent of projected retirement income to an average full career single worker in nine of its thirty-five members in 2010 (in rank order, Iceland, Mexico, Latvia, Denmark, Netherlands, Slovakia, Britain, Australia and Poland). In fourteen other OECD members in 2010, private sources provided more than a quarter of projected retirement income (in rank order, Estonia, United States, Sweden, Ireland, Lithuania, Canada, Hungary, Romania, Bulgaria, Switzerland, Belgium, Germany, New Zealand and Norway). Among countries in Latin America that have mandatory DC schemes, James and Brooks estimate that private sources provided more than 40 per cent of projected income in eight countries (in rank order, Chile, Colombia, El Salvador, Peru (joint-first), Bolivia, Mexico, Argentina and Uruguay) (James and Brooks, 2001).[16]

Thus, in countries in which DC pension schemes play a vital role in retirement income provision, middle-class demand for financial asset price protection should be higher than in countries in which DB systems dominate. Indeed, we expect a growing convergence in this regard between the interest of the middle class and that of the wealthiest households, who as already noted hold the bulk of their wealth in financial assets.

In short, the increased level and changing form of middle-class wealth portfolios over the past century and more has given households in this group a growing interest in financial stability and thus in the protection of systemic banks and other financial institutions, or 'SIFIs' as they have become known. Although SIFIs are not always easy to identify *ex ante,* they are commonly defined as institutions whose

---

[16] Comparable data for other emerging market and developing country democracies are currently unavailable.

'failure or malfunction causes widespread distress, either as a direct impact or as a trigger for broader contagion' (International Monetary Fund, Basel Committee on Banking Supervision, and Financial Stability Board, 2009, 5). They have increasingly become seen by many stakeholders as 'too big to fail' because any such failure would impose unacceptably large costs on them and on the wider financial network and economy (Acharya et al., 2017; Malik and Xu, 2017; Stern and Feldman, 2004). Lower- and middle-income households, whose income, employment and wealth are also increasingly dependent on the stability of the financial system, will share this interest even if public bailouts of large financial institutions are costly. So too do the wealthiest households, who hold the bulk of financial assets, the value of which is increasingly linked to the health and activities of these banks.

Systemic banks are often also market makers in key markets, with responsibilities to provide liquidity during episodes of volatility. They issue debt and equity instruments to non-financial firms and link household savings with securitized lending to such firms through shadow banking markets (e.g. wholesale money markets). Furthermore, such banks have also become among the most important issuers of equity[17] and debt[18] instruments in their own right. SIFIs today dominate corporate bond issuance: at end-2015, outstanding debt issuance by US-based financial firms was $14.97 trillion, compared to $5.52 trillion of issuance by non-financial firms.[19] Financial firms also account for an increasing share of global bond issuance. Vanguard's Global Bond Index Fund, designed to track the global bond market, comprised 56.8 per cent in issuance by governments and supranational agencies, 11.4 per cent in asset-backed securities (issued primarily by banks),

---

[17] In June 2016, the financial sector comprised over 16 per cent of the market capitalization of the Standard and Poor's (S&P) 500 index of the 500 largest listed US firms, second only to the IT sector. Large financial firms comprise the largest sectoral component (20 per cent) of the Morgan Stanley World Index, which covers 85 per cent of the free float-adjusted market capitalization in each of twenty-three advanced countries. All thirty FSB-designated global systemically important banks ('G-SIBs') are listed, often on multiple stock exchanges, and figure prominently in many equity funds. (Data obtained by authors from S&P, Morgan Stanley and the Financial Stability Board as of 8 June 2016.)

[18] Major banks are also deeply involved in the bond markets. As of end-2015, the largest private sector component (22 per cent) of the $40 trillion outstanding US bond market debt was mortgage-related securities, followed by corporate debt (20 per cent). Federal government debt was 38 per cent of total outstanding debt (SIFMA, 2016).

[19] TDSAMRIAOFCUS and TDSAMRIAONCUS series, Federal Reserve Bank of St Louis, FRED database, https://fred.stlouisfed.org/, accessed 8 June 2016.

11 per cent in corporate bonds and 7.6 per cent in other financial firm issuance at end November 2016 (Vanguard Group, Inc., 2017). For all these reasons, middle-class pension and insurance assets increasingly depend directly and indirectly on the health of SIFIs. Thus, since middle-class and wealthy households' financial assets are increasingly concentrated in securitized assets (including bank stock and debt), they have acquired a stronger interest in measures that support these banks and boost their profitability – or at least do not oppose them.

Since financialization is associated with increasing connectedness among financial firms, it also erodes the traditional preference of strong banks for allowing insolvent competitor banks to fail. Because systemic banks increasingly rise and fall together, even relatively strong banks may come to support the rescue of insolvent systemic banks – though they will prefer such rescues to be publicly funded rather than from their own resources. For similar reasons, financialization will intensify the (national) corporate sector interest in bailouts of systemically important banks under all varieties of capitalism.

But the most important shift, we argue, has been in the way that the financialization of middle-class wealth has brought this group into the bailout constituency. As Watson puts it, 'the process of financial socialization has deepened the impression that *more is now at stake than ever before* when the pricing structure of financial markets looks likely to break down' (Watson, 2007, 3).[20] As the size of the financial sector has grown over time, the ability of private sector actors to provide such guarantees has also diminished. This has left the state, with its greater taxation and borrowing capacity, as the preferred residual guarantor in a systemic crisis.

2.1.2   The Democratization of Leverage

A crucially related factor reinforcing this middle-class voter interest in financial stabilization has been rising leverage. Increasingly, lower- and middle-class households borrowed from banks to finance purchases of costly durable goods such as houses and cars. Mortgage lending grew especially rapidly over the course of the twentieth century in advanced countries (see Figure 2.5). According to Jordà, Schularick and Taylor, banking increasingly became the business of household real

---

[20] Emphasis added.

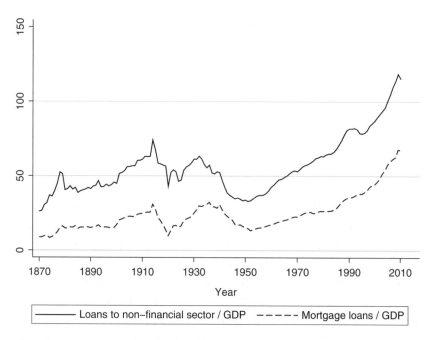

Figure 2.5: Total bank lending and mortgage lending in advanced democracies, 1870–2010.
Source: Jordà, Schularick and Taylor (2014).

estate financing: 'Nearly all of the increase in the size of the financial sectors in Western economies since 1913 stems from a boom in mortgage lending to households and has little to do with the financing of the business sector' (Jordà, Schularick and Taylor, 2014).

The purchase of a house is the largest lifetime transaction for most individuals and families, and mortgage loans constitute the main funding tool. As mortgage lending has risen, so too has the importance of mortgage loans in household debt across countries. By 2011, the median share of mortgages in household debt for a broad set of countries was about 70 per cent (Cerutti, Dagher and Dell'Ariccia, 2015). Moreover, countries with a larger share of mortgage to household debt also have a high share in household debt to total private credit.

Historically, financial repression in much of the developing world meant that the central bank took on a large role in the allocation of domestic credit (Demirgüç-Kunt and Levine, 2001). Yet financial liberalization and deepening, particularly in emerging market democracies, has led banks to take on a greater role in the credit allocation process and has fostered an associated expansion of private sector credit

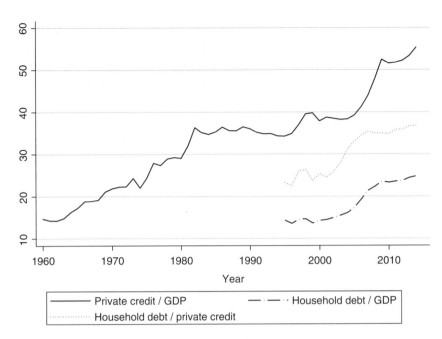

Figure 2.6: Private sector credit and household debt in emerging markets, 1960–2015.
Source: Bank for International Settlements (2017b); Léon (2017a); World Bank (2017).

since the 1970s (see Figure 2.6). Certainly, private sector leverage remains, on average, considerably lower than in advanced democracies. By 2010, leverage in emerging market countries only reached levels last seen in the advanced countries in the early 1970s, while leverage in developing countries retreated in the 1990s and today approximates levels last seen in advanced democracies in the latter part of the nineteenth century.

Long-run data on household borrowing in emerging and developing countries is not available. However, based on data available since 2000 we can gain a reasonable sense of the depth and breadth of recent housing finance and household borrowing in most emerging and developing countries. In general, emerging market and developing countries have far smaller housing finance systems than advanced economies. Warnock and Warnock report that the average mortgage debt-to-GDP ratio for twenty-four advanced economies was 55 per cent of GDP for the 2001–5 period, compared to an average of 10 per cent for thirty-eight emerging economies (Warnock and Warnock, 2008). Based on a larger sample of 118 countries over the 2006–10 period, another study reports slightly lower ratios, roughly 35 per cent in high income countries, 5 per cent in upper-middle-income countries, 3 per cent in lower-middle-income and less than 1 per cent in low-income countries (Badev et al., 2014). Housing finance systems are most developed in East Asia and Eastern Europe and least developed in South Asia and sub-Saharan Africa. In both studies, those upper-middle-income democracies with the largest housing finance systems, ranging between roughly 20 and 40 per cent of GDP (Taiwan, Estonia, Korea, Latvia, South Africa, Latvia, Panama, Thailand and Lithuania), were roughly equivalent to, and in some cases exceeded, levels found in some advanced democracies, including Austria, Belgium, France, Greece and Italy.

Cross-national data on mortgage loan penetration – the share of the adult population with a mortgage from a financial institution – is only available from a 2014 World Bank household survey. Mortgage loan penetration is considerably higher in advanced democracies than elsewhere, reaching nearly 30 per cent as compared to 13 per cent in emerging market democracies and roughly 8 per cent in developing country democracies. Within countries, mortgages tend to be held by the richest 60 per cent of adults, reaching nearly 33 per cent of such adults in advanced countries, 15 per cent in emerging markets and 10 per cent in developing countries. Among the poorest 40 per cent of adults, mortgage loan penetration was 27 per cent, 11 per cent and 6 per cent in these respective groups. While there is considerable cross-country variation, ranging from 1.4 per cent of adults in Burundi to almost 50 per cent of adults in Norway, this data suggests some degree of exposure to mortgage lending even among the poorest groups in less advanced economies.

The size of the housing finance system and mortgage loan penetration are closely correlated with private credit as a proportion of GDP (Badev et al., 2014). More importantly, mortgage lending as a share of overall lending increases with higher levels of private credit to GDP, as does household credit as a share of overall lending (Beck et al., 2012). Figures 2.6 and 2.7 show that household debt in emerging markets and developing countries largely follows this pattern in the post-1995 period. Assuming this pattern held in earlier years, in the 1980s and early 1990s similar levels of household borrowing in emerging markets and developing countries to those observed from the

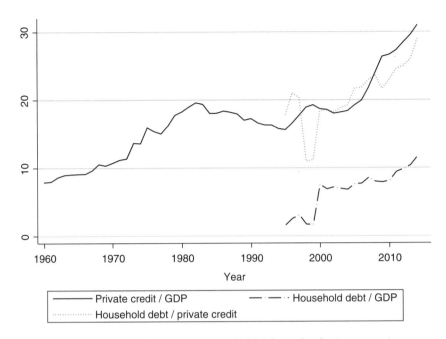

Figure 2.7: Private sector credit and household debt in developing countries, 1960–2015.
Source: Bank for International Settlements (2017b); Léon (2017a); World Bank (2017).

mid-1990s to early 2000s probably prevailed. Household borrowing was almost certainly lower in these countries prior to the 1980s.

Notwithstanding the data limitations, we can conclude with confidence that household borrowing in emerging markets and developing countries in recent decades is considerably higher than in the past, most notably in emerging markets, and that the upward trend likely began in the early to mid-1990s.[21] Household leverage in emerging markets and developing countries recently reached levels last observed in advanced countries in the early 1970s and after the First World War respectively.[22] Taken together, this evidence suggests that rising household leverage accounts for a significant proportion of the credit growth

---

[21] See also International Monetary Fund (2017c, chap. 2).
[22] Badev et al. (2014) also find that the size of the housing finance system, as well as the share of the adult population with a housing loan, tends to increase with countries' income level in a convex manner; that is, it increases slowly with income across developing countries and rapidly with income in emerging and advanced countries.

we observe in emerging and developing democracies over the five decades shown in Figures 2.6 and 2.7, and in some cases in recent years it likely represents the predominant share. Jordà, Schularick and Taylor refer to the trend toward greater household borrowing in advanced countries as the 'democratization of leverage', underlining the deepening connection between the interests of the financial and household sectors. The data we have examined suggests this 'democratization' process is also under way in emerging and developing country democracies, though at a much less advanced stage.

Increasing access to credit for households has, however, come at a significant cost because rising household leverage has produced greater financial fragility, with a risk of substantial wealth losses if asset prices fall (Admati and Hellwig, 2013; Goodhart and Erfurth, 2014; International Monetary Fund, 2017b; Jordà, Schularick and Taylor, 2014, 2015, 2016). We also know that rising household dependence on credit in advanced countries has often been concentrated among lower- and middle-income households, who are relatively dependent on mortgage credit to acquire housing assets and to maintain consumption (Frank, 2013, chap. 5; Kuhn, Schularick and Steins, 2017; Offer, 2014; Rajan, 2010).

Relatively leveraged households have a stronger interest in the continued flow of credit and in policies that prevent house price declines (Admati and Hellwig, 2013).[23] They can also have a general interest in the maintenance of the flow of credit to other leveraged households, as 'fire sales' during crises would depress house prices generally. Thus, rising leverage gives the lower- and middle-income households in advanced countries a further interest in bank bailouts in financial crises.[24] This shift occurred simultaneously with a rise in the political

---

[23] Households facing falling asset prices are also likely to support policies that require banks to offer debt relief to borrowers rather than forced asset sales. However, such policies directly threaten the narrow interests of savers, banks and the relatively wealthy. Protecting the value of housing assets can also conflict with the interests of the young who lack wealth-owning relatives (Muellbauer, 2008, 294).

[24] They also retain an interest in traditional monetary and fiscal stimulus policies. Since many leveraged households depend on labour income to maintain debt payments and avoid default and foreclosure, they have a strong interest in expansionary policies that maintain employment in economic downturns, including those associated with crises. Expansionary monetary policies can also reduce payments on floating rate debt. Thus, expansionary macroeconomic policies may have become important for both income and wealth protection for these households.

importance of these groups due to the expansion of electoral franchises in many countries over the course of the twentieth century (Przeworski, 2009). The 'democratization of leverage' is therefore doubly apt in suggesting how the interest of the household sector has become increasingly aligned with the bailout constituency.

2.1.3   The Growing *Ex Ante* Policy Commitment to Financial Stabilization

Before the mid-twentieth century, most governments made very limited if any commitments to financial stability as a policy priority.[25] This was consistent with a low level of societal demand for financial stabilization. Importantly, this low policy commitment in turn reinforced such societal expectations. As societal demand for financial stabilization policies became more intense in many societies in the later twentieth century, citizen assessments of government competence became more closely associated with their provision.

The experiences of the Great Depression and World War II were crucial in this regard. The associated accumulation of economic knowledge raised policymakers' understandings of the potential for economic stabilization, and new policy ideas fed voter expectations concerning government policy responsibilities (Berman, 2006; Eichengreen, 1992). Accumulated experience with previous crisis responses either at home or abroad may have served to reinforce voter expectations, generating a feedback loop in which financialization and leverage generate rising demand for stabilization policies, including regulation and government promises to prevent financial instability. Such policy commitments foster and reinforce societal expectations that government stabilization measures during financial crises will be forthcoming.[26]

The interwar years were a transitional period in which Bagehot responses remained dominant, whereas voter expectations began to

---

[25] The most basic form of banking regulation operated through company registration mechanisms that first emerged in the eighteenth and nineteenth centuries. Special regulation of banks in addition to rules applied to other firms were gradually introduced in many countries over the course of the nineteenth century, but effective banking supervision emerged later in most countries (Grossman, 2010; Schenk, 2016).

[26] Voters in modern democracies might rely not only on direct experience with crises in their own country but also those in other countries, benchmarking domestic against foreign economic performance when assessing policies and relying heavily on media reporting to make sense of such information (Kayser and Peress, 2012).

increase as governments gradually, if often reluctantly and haphazardly, abandoned market-oriented policy norms of the pre-World War I era. A number of advanced economies experienced widespread banking failures in the 1920s after implementing deflationary policies aimed at returning to the gold standard. At the beginning of these crises, the governments and central banks of some countries, such as Norway, Denmark and Sweden, sought to avoid intervening. As in the United States at the start of the Great Depression (see Chapter 9), this reluctance is evidenced in the continued application of deflationary policy with high interest rates in all three countries in order to return to the gold standard at pre-war exchange rate parities (Larsson, 1991, 96; Olsson, 1991, 32; Knutsen, 1994, 80). In Denmark, a bill introduced in 1921 to guarantee the deposits of seven failed banks was soundly rejected, with a central bank official dismissing it as 'a present to the depositors' (as cited in Hansen, 1994, 70).

Nonetheless, policymakers in some countries increasingly realized that changing political considerations required deviations from pre-World War I policy norms. In outlining its crisis intervention principles at the time, one official of the Danish central bank insisted that it sought to follow Bagehot principles, but noted that it had to bend to the changing political environment by providing public funds to undercapitalized banks. 'It is possible that at other times you would have done things differently and chosen bank failures and deflation,' the central bank official wrote, 'but it was a period of unstable production and banking, and major bank failures would have caused even more interruptions in production, and consequently an enormous unemployment, which would lead to communism and the spread of panic to other banks' (as cited in Hansen, 1994, 70). Fearing the consequences of sustained mass unemployment, the Danish government deferred adherence to the gold standard in favour of protecting the financial system and the broader economy.[27]

Yet the transition to new public policy commitments was not seamless. Even where governments had reluctantly intervened to support banks during crises in the 1920s, political attitudes were slow to change, particularly in countries where there was a strong desire both to return to the gold standard at pre-war exchange parities and to restore

---

[27] Similar concerns existed in Austria in 1931 as well: see Weber (1991, 23).

conditions of limited government involvement in the economy.[28] For instance, in 1924, as economic and political conditions in Denmark stabilized, the central bank returned to a deflationary policy aimed at strengthening the currency and returning to gold, which the country did in 1927. It also shifted back to a harsher policy towards distressed banks (Hansen, 1994, 73). In Norway, a guarantee for new deposits put in place in 1923 for banks taken into public administration for restructuring or liquidation was removed in 1928 when conditions stabilized (Knutsen, 1994, 80).

Some governments were also slow to take on greater responsibility to prevent financial instability via banking supervision and prudential regulation. 'Discussions about bank legislation and control got started,' Olsson notes, 'but the political will to enforce new rules was ... not strong enough' (Olsson, 1991, 32). Attitudes changed in many countries after the start of the Great Depression, but legally effective bank supervision regimes were not put in place in all countries until later, most notably, in addition to the United Kingdom (see Chapter 7), in Austria and the Netherlands (Enderle-Burcel, 1994; Vanthemsche, 1991). Even in the depths of the Great Depression, the Dutch central bank distanced itself from formal oversight, stressing that 'any control over the private banking system is out of the question' (as cited in Vanthemsche, 1991, 116).[29]

Despite differences in form and timing, the 1920s and 1930s did mark the start of a fundamental shift in policy commitment and societal expectations. At this point, as James (1991, 9) observes, 'the position of banks became a highly political issue' in most countries. Politicians in countries worst affected by the devastating banking crises of the 1920s and 1930s often responded by promising to prevent future crises. Parliamentary committees and special commissions were created in numerous countries, often calling for new banking legislation and greater state control over the financial system. Such proposals received increasing support from political parties, particularly, but not exclusively, from those on the left of the political spectrum. Parties began to use policy promises to stabilize banking to compete for voter support. For

---

[28] On adherence to these views in Denmark and Norway, see Larsson (1991, 96), Hansen (1994, 70); Knutsen (1994, 80); in the Netherlands, see Vanthemsche (1991, 116); and in Austria, see Enderle-Burcel (1994, 119–20).

[29] At the time the Netherlands, like Britain, relied on a close and voluntary form of cooperation between banks and the central bank.

instance, after a banking crisis in Sweden in 1922–3 a Banking Committee was appointed that called for tougher regulation; at the same time, the ruling Social Democrats unsuccessfully proposed the creation of a public commercial bank (Larsson, 1991, 89). Later, following the banking crisis in 1932 related to the collapse of Ivar Kreuger's financial empire, groups to the left of the social democratic majority called for bank nationalizations or the creation of public alternatives (Olsson, 1991, 33).

The severe banking crises of the 1920s also brought similar calls for greater state involvement in Denmark and Norway. In Denmark, politicians demanded a tightening of the existing supervisory and regulatory framework that had been put in place in 1919 (Hansen, 1994, 74). The Labour Party opposition in Norway several times demanded that the central bank and the banking system be brought under the supervision of a 'bank council' composed of 'peasants and smallholders, fishermen, workers and white-collar workers' and appointed by Parliament (Knutsen, 1994, 85). Although the Norwegian Labour Party would implement a less radical agenda once in office starting in the 1930s, central figures in the party insisted before and after the war that in the long term, control of the financial system was a key element to achieve its objectives of growth, industrialization and redistribution. Instead, when in office, the essence of the party's proposals was that 'The influence of society on the banking system must be strengthened by developing the state banks, and by a more efficient control with the bank and credit institutions [sic]' (Knutsen, 1994, 90).

Similar patterns can be seen elsewhere in Europe. A call for 'banking control' first appeared in the Belgian Labour Party's 1931 programme; then its famous 1933 *Plan du Travail* called for outright 'nationalization' of the credit sector (Vanthemsche, 1991, 113). It later joined the centre-right Catholic and Liberal parties in a government of national unity that put in place a 'renovation' of economic policy via the establishment of a Banking Commission and new measures of banking control. As discussed earlier, banking control did not come about in the Netherlands until after World War II, but it was publicly discussed and supported before then by some political parties, most notably the Catholic and Socialist ones, and new public banks were created to support industrial growth (Olsson, 1991, 33; Vanthemsche, 1991, 115). An official commission studying greater state control over the banking system was set up in 1937, but its proceedings were still under way when the war broke out. The Social Democratic Party in Switzerland led demands for more state control of the banking sector during the 1930s, though it avoided proposals for outright nationalization (Busch, 2009, 173). In France in 1936, the Banque de France was brought under state control and new plans for the nationalization of other private banks were prepared, though implemented only after World War II (James, 1991, 9).

In many countries, the roots of the government policy commitment were laid in a less democratic era. Substantial extensions of state control and surveillance over banking occurred in a number of non-democratic countries, including Nazi Germany, fascist Italy and Japan (Busch, 2009, 81; Fletcher, 1991, 260; Forsyth, 1991, 200). Elsewhere in Western Europe and in much of the emerging and developing world in Asia, Eastern Europe and the former Soviet Union, Latin America, and sub-Saharan Africa, promises to prevent future banking crises often took a more implicit form, based on extensive state control of the banking system in which major banks were state-owned and/or public sector institutions held a large share of bank assets (Barth, Caprio and Levine, 2006; Quennouëlle-Corre, 2016; Verdier, 2000).[30]

In developing countries, state ownership of the banking system was heavily favoured in the 1960s and 1970s as part of a broader sentiment in development economics that advocated government ownership of firms in strategic sectors. Government ownership of banks was seen as helping to mitigate capital market failures and mobilize savings for strategic projects and sectors (Gerschenkron, 1962; Lewis, 1950; Myrdal, 1968). Government ownership of banks was also a key component of planned socialist economies. 'Without big banks,' Lenin stated, 'socialism would be impossible. The big banks are the "state apparatus" which we need to bring about socialism, and which we take ready-made from capitalism ...' (quoted in Garvy, 1977, 21). These arguments were widely put into practice particularly in the 1960s and

---

[30] As public deposit institutions, postal and national savings banks were established in many countries and may be considered one form of this implicit promise of financial protection. These banks may fall under state control or be subject to special regulatory requirements that limit their allowable activities outside of deposit-taking and investing in government bonds. Due to their origin in most countries as charitable institutions to aid poorer households and community development and to promote saving habits in general, as well as their importance as a source of funds for government expenditure, the regulatory regime for these institutions in some economies, such as England and the Nordic countries, often developed prior to that for commercial banks.

the 1970s, with governments nationalizing existing commercial banks and starting new ones in Africa, Asia and Latin America (La Porta, Lopez-De-Silanes and Shleifer, 2002; Barth, Caprio and Levine, 2006).

Extensive state control of the banking system may have played a particularly important part in heightening voter expectations in developing country democracies where financialization and the democ-ratization of leverage have advanced much less than in more developed democracies. Such control provides a direct link between perceived government competence and financial stability and offers an implicit guarantee of insurance in times of distress.

The commitment to financial stability based on extensive state control also manifested itself via informal forms of influence over lending that operated alongside formal legal frameworks. Such was the case in post-war Japan, where the Ministry of Finance exerted influence on banks via 'administrative guidance'. Explicit and implicit influence and support created a 'convoy' approach to regulation that ensured no financial institution was left behind and no institution moved too fast so as to endanger financial instability. This system encouraged depositors to believe that their savings were safe and polit-icians that banking stability was assured (Amyx, 2013, 107–8).

Thus, while taking different but related forms, the modern era steadily became marked by widespread implicit or explicit commitment to financial stability by the world's democratic governments. Figure 2.8 summarizes the evolution of this trend over time via a measure we develop in Chapter 5 that captures government policy commitments to financial stability. As late as the early 1930s, according to our measure, most democratic governments refrained from making either *de jure* or de facto commitments to financial stability as a policy goal. However, from the mid-1930s onwards, we see a sharp increase in the number of countries making this commitment, such that by the second decade of the post-war era it had become near-universal among the world's democracies. After this time, the demand for financial stability became more firmly rooted in democratic politics as voters increasingly came to expect governments to deliver on their implicitly or explicitly promised policy responsibilities.

Since voters face strong incentives not to invest in the acquisi-tion of knowledge of policy detail unless absolutely necessary, they are unlikely to internalize deeply policy commitments to stabilize the finan-cial system in the absence of real observable improvement in financial

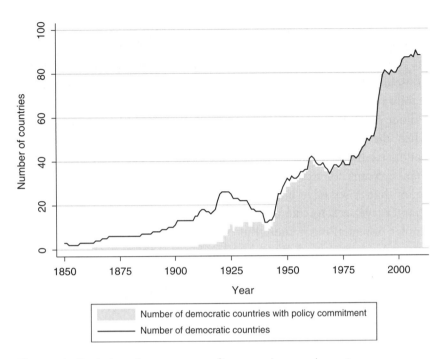

Figure 2.8: Evolution of government policy commitments since 1850.

stability. Voters are likely to be most reassured when effective policy commitments based on past performance follow policy promises. Thus, in economies where such promises were made, the virtual absence of banking crises in the three decades after 1945 likely reinforced voter expectations that crisis prevention was a politically achievable condition.

The re-emergence of banking crises after the 1970s may have damaged the credibility of the commitment to crisis prevention, but has done little to diminish voter expectations of crisis mitigation. As we explore more fully in Chapter 4, recent cross-national household surveys indicate a dominant expectation on the part of respondents that governments would opt for bailouts and other policies aimed at wealth protection during a crisis. The reason for this, we argue, is that the expectations of modern voters have been continually reinforced by a growing material stake in financial stability. Many governments have also greatly extended the scope and depth of financial regulation since the 1970s, signalling to voters that they are attentive to this rising stake. This has reinforced – or at least not undermined – the impact of the financialization of wealth and the democratization of leverage in shifting the middle class toward the bailout constituency.

To summarize, the overall impact of financialization, rising household leverage and a growing government commitment to financial stabilization has been to increase the interest of the rising middle class in bailout policies during banking crises. In the nineteenth century, a time when the middle class was very small, the political strength of the bailout coalition in crises can be assumed to have been much lower than in recent decades. Our argument does not depend on the empirical claim that crises have become deeper over time, and in our empirical chapters we seek to rule out this possibility by focusing on crises of a similar potential magnitude. But by increasing systemic risk, financialization and increasing leverage have blurred the distinction between solvent and insolvent banks and increased the risk to middle-class wealth portfolios. This is likely to have caused the middle class increasingly to support financial sector bailouts aimed at preventing systemic collapse and mitigating the impact of crises.

The main constituencies with a residual interest in Bagehot policies are taxpayers and public sector beneficiaries. Both groups grew in relative size over the course of the twentieth century with the expansion of the national tax base and the welfare state. However, we expect taxpayers and public beneficiaries to be relatively weak sources of support for Bagehot policies for a variety of reasons.

First, the costs of bailouts are widely distributed among both groups (Rosas, 2009, 8). By contrast, the benefits reaped by the beneficiaries of bailouts are highly concentrated, as are the costs of Bagehot policies that might be imposed on them. Second, because the full costs of bailouts may be obscure and only materialize after considerable delay, potential opponents will often lack strong incentives to mobilize against them at the time they are undertaken. Third, as we have already emphasized, taxpayers and public sector beneficiaries are also employees, consumers, investors and (sometimes) firms: real-world actors have composite interests, diluting their incentives to act collectively to limit their tax liabilities or to maximize their share of public spending. Fourth, as the banking sector has itself become increasingly leveraged over time, the possibility of private-sector-led rescues of failing banks is likely to have substantially diminished, with the result that central banks and governments are the only viable source of stabilization. Certainly, governments can face fiscal constraints, especially in emerging and developing democracies, but how much individual voters worry about them is unclear. Creditworthy governments can borrow to cover the additional expenditure for bailouts and they may try to obscure the current costs by allowing central banks to bear the burden or by providing contingent guarantees. This means that it can be extremely difficult for individuals to assess the net costs of bailouts.

Our argument is broadly consistent with the predictions of the general literature on the emergence of a 'risk society' in advanced industrial democracies, but it differs in important respects (Beck, 1992). This literature claims that a general condition of modernity is that 'the costs associated with risks and with risk avoidance are increasingly perceived by the public as the responsibility of the government ... [which] has the dual role of bearing the costs of prevention and compensating the public should the risk materialize' (Alemanno et al., 2013, 4). Societal expectations regarding public risk insurance vary, ranging from more limited risk mitigation in liberal market systems to more extensive mitigation in social democracies (Esping-Andersen, 1990). Our argument suggests, however, that the pressure on governments to provide financial stabilization will be at least as extensive in liberal market economies as elsewhere, because financialization and leverage have reached especially high levels there (Jordà, Schularick and Taylor, 2016; Knoll, Schularick and Steger, 2017). As such, we do not expect that the trend in middle-class voter expectations regarding wealth protection to follow fully trends in their attitudes concerning government responsibility for other aspects of social and economic life. We assess these arguments in Chapter 3.

2.2   Electoral Accountability and Banking Crises

As we have already noted, we expect governments to respond to the changing preferences of the large group of voters in the middle for reasons of electoral accountability and legitimacy. Most scholars have placed less emphasis on the evolving social and historical context at the centre of our argument (Duch and Stevenson, 2008, 1–2). A general political economy literature on the relationship between economic crises and politics finds that modern recessions are usually bad news for political incumbents, though it often focuses on the post-war era and assumes that governments have effective policy tools to mitigate downturns (Alesina et al., 1996; Alesina and Rosenthal, 1989, 1995; Clark, Golder and Poast, 2013; Edwards and Tabellini, 1991). Since banking crises are associated with comparatively deep and long recessions, this literature implies that voters may punish political incumbents presiding over banking crises because they serve as 'recessionary accelerators' (Jordà, Schularick and Taylor, 2013; Reinhart and Rogoff, 2009). This recessionary accelerator mechanism is consistent with some claims made in the literature on economic voting, which finds empirical support for the relationship between economic and electoral performance in democracies.[31]

There has been less scrutiny in this literature of how voters respond to the role of institutions in shaping policy responses to banking crises, compared to how institutions serve as mechanisms for generating political accountability (Crespo-Tenorio, Jensen and Rosas, 2014; Pepinsky, 2012). We build on this literature by emphasizing the need to take account of evolving societal expectations regarding government financial stabilization policy.

In a world of low voter expectations, the question of government responsibility for preventing and managing banking crises may not even emerge and governments may not need to try to deflect blame or take action (Boin, t'Hart and McConnell, 2009, 84). In contrast, we suggest, in a world in which voters have high expectations that governments will act to promote financial stability, they will also be more inclined to assign blame and to punish incumbent governments presiding over banking crises. This might seem at odds with the argument we have already made that governments will respond to modern voter demand for financial stabilization by both acting to prevent banking crises and intervening to mitigate their effects when they occur. If governments do what these voters want, why would they punish them? Our response is that governments find it very challenging in practice to meet the great expectations that many voters have come to hold regarding wealth protection. There are at least three aspects of this tendency for modern governments to disappoint.

First, the very onset of banking crises may be interpreted as an 'incompetency signal' by modern voters who are now primed – by their rising material stakes, by the media, and by the promises that modern politicians make – to evaluate governments on the basis of their

---

[31] For a review of this large literature, see Anderson (2007).

performance in maintaining economic growth and financial stability (Barnes and Hicks, 2012). Prudential regulation is a response to rising voter demand for income and wealth protection, and a political commitment that governments will take measures to protect individuals, businesses and the wider economy from the damaging consequences of financial crises. If crises nevertheless occur, they will disappoint the voter expectations reflected in and reinforced by these policy commitments. In short, great expectations have 'endogenized' political accountability (Boin, t'Hart and McConnell, 2009, 86–8; Bovens and t'Hart, 1996). This is especially likely to be the case with *systemic* banking crises, which are sufficiently disastrous and vivid in their consequences to make it difficult for modern governments to avoid blame for their onset. This aspect of modern banking crises may take on greater importance in developing country democracies where access to formal financial services remains relatively low and state control of the banking system is relatively high.

Second, once crises occur, they constitute a direct threat to voters' incomes and wealth. Improvements in economic knowledge have enabled post-war governments to manage banking crises to avoid deep depressions of the kind that occurred in the early 1930s. As a large literature suggests, crises generally can provide opportunities for politicians, including incumbent governments, to gain or retain power through deft handling of a crisis and its aftermath (Boin, t'Hart and McConnell, 2009; Keeler, 1993). However, even in the best-managed banking crises substantial absolute income and wealth losses remain typical (Bordo et al., 2001; Reinhart and Rogoff, 2009). Furthermore, the increasing size and the changing composition of total household wealth, and the increasing importance of market-traded assets, has almost certainly made it more difficult for governments to protect this wealth during crises. The practical cost of providing guarantees of households' housing and pension wealth could far exceed governments' fiscal capacity, especially in developing and emerging democracies (Reinhart, Rogoff and Savastano, 2003).

It matters in this regard that banking crises are relatively rare events for most voters compared to standard economic recessions. Excluding countries that have never had a systemic banking crisis, the average number of years between systemic crises among independent democracies in our dataset is 29.8 over the 1800–2010 period, making crises a more or less once-in-a-lifetime experience for an average adult. (By comparison, for example, the US economy experienced a recession about every 4.8 years over this same period.) Thus, most voters will have little personal experience with the limits of government crisis interventions and can be expected to be surprised at the size of post-crisis income and wealth losses. Innate loss aversion could amplify this disappointment (Kahneman and Tversky, 1984). Attempts by the incumbent government to deflect blame with counterfactual arguments ('you would be much worse off had we not intervened') may also fail to impress voters, as will many attempts to shift blame to others ('your losses are the fault of greedy speculators or reckless bankers'). Research suggests that counterfactual rhetoric can favour the political opposition, perhaps because it focuses voter attention on the government's mistakes (Catellani, Milesi and Alberici, 2014, 60–1).

Third, the nature and consequences of crisis-related policy interventions are often controversial. The expectations and demands of modern voters may be unrealistic, inconsistent and riddled with conflict, making life very difficult for governments in a crisis. The wealth losses inevitably suffered by at least some households provide the media and political rivals with tactical opportunities and strong incentives to portray a government's policy interventions as delayed, misjudged, inadequate or unfair compared to the 'ideal' intervention that voters would prefer; that is, one that decisively and equitably alleviates financial distress and minimizes income and wealth losses at least cost. That great expectations often embody unrealistic preferences can provide a gift to opposition parties.

By comparison with the rapidity with which financial market actors can move in crises, governments will often move – and be perceived as moving – very slowly indeed. Multiple and polarized veto players can frustrate modern voters' expectations by limiting the ability of governments to respond promptly and effectively to economic shocks (Alesina and Drazen, 1991; Haggard, 2000; Haggard and Kaufman, 1995; Oatley, 2004; Tsebelis, 2002). The 'clarity of responsibility' thesis claims that 'the greater the perceived unified control of policymaking by the incumbent government, the more likely is the citizen to assign responsibility for economic and political outcomes to the incumbents' (Powell and Whitten, 1993, 398). That is, voters may be more forgiving of delay if low political and institutional unity makes it difficult for them to assign responsibility to policymakers (Anderson, 2000; Duch and

Stevenson, 2008; Hellwig, 2008; Hellwig and Samuels, 2007; Powell and Whitten, 1993).

Institutional constraints feature in an earlier general literature that finds that multiple and polarized veto players can limit the ability of governments to respond effectively to economic shocks (Haggard, 2000; Haggard and Kaufman, 1995).[32] Similarly, Oatley finds stabilization after inflationary crises is more often delayed in democracies with highly polarized veto players (Oatley, 2004). In addition, MacIntyre argues that countries with a low dispersal of veto authority can suffer from the different problem of excessive policy volatility during crises, positing a U-shaped relationship between the number of veto players and the costs of financial crises (MacIntyre, 2003).[33]

We build on this literature in arguing that in an era of great expectations, the intensity of voter demand for the protection of wealth – driven in part by growing anxiety about the potential for losses – means that banking crises and crisis resolution delays will be less 'excusable' than the clarity of responsibility thesis suggests. Blurred institutional responsibility may help insulate modern governments from voter disapproval during a comparatively slow-moving non-financial economic downturn, but not when households and voters are exposed to the prospect of a sudden evaporation of their wealth in a fast-moving crisis. Fast-moving banking crises put a premium on a government's ability to act efficiently. Institutional obstacles to efficient interventions should thus have become much more politically salient than in the past.

Another reason why many voters will be less forgiving of incumbent governments facing institutional constraints is because of their informational disadvantage. Most voters will find it difficult to distinguish how much bad policy outcomes in crises are the result of institutional constraints or sheer incompetence.[34] Visible disarray and dissension between different branches of government during a crisis may be perceived by voters as generating costly policy delays *and* reinforce the incompetence signal that the onset of the crisis has already

---

[32] Veto players may also weaken the quality of financial regulation, particularly in developing country democracies, by limiting executive control over who is appointed to regulate the financial system (Satyanath, 2006).

[33] Our results in Chapter 5 are inconsistent with empirical expectations derived from MacIntyre's U-shaped hypothesis.

[34] For a similar argument, see Healy and Malhotra (2013, 296). The same logic could be applied to 'external constraints' on crisis policy responses, such as IMF conditionality or Eurozone membership (Crespo-Tenorio, Jensen and Rosas, 2014; Hellwig, 2008).

sent. By compounding the tendency of market actors to panic in a crisis, the interaction of visible political conflict and institutional constraints could thereby increase risk premia and the depth of the stabilization challenge facing governments. Thus, a vicious cycle could emerge that increases the tendency of voters to interpret intra-crisis constraints negatively.

Banking crises can also generate forces that turn potential institutional constraints into actual policy gridlock. Political polarization tends to increase in the aftermath of modern banking crises because of rising creditor–debtor conflict, a tendency for economic inequality to increase, and because crises can destabilize voter beliefs about appropriate policy and increase ideological fragmentation (Atkinson and Morelli, 2011; Blyth, 2002; Bordo and Meissner, 2012; Funke, Schularick and Trebesch, 2016; McCarty, Poole and Rosenthal, 2015; Mian, Sufi and Trebbi, 2014). Policy gridlock is most likely when polarized actors have access to institutional vetoes (Tsebelis, 2002). If gridlock delays or prevents adequate intervention, it may generate severe spikes in risk premia in debt markets, which can trigger sovereign debt crises, delay recoveries and amplify voter discontent and polarization. Such delays can have uneven effects on different asset markets, exacerbating distributional conflicts. Governments facing greater institutional constraints may also favour selective intervention on terms more favourable to concentrated special interests than to diffuse unorganized groups, compounding perceptions of unfairness, which we discuss below (Johnson and Kwak, 2010; Mian, Sufi and Trebbi, 2014).

Government policy inaction due to polarized veto players will also place more pressure on the central bank to take action, complicating the position of the latter (El-Erian, 2016). As Alan Blinder observes, 'when it comes to deciding which financial institutions shall live on with taxpayer support (e.g. Bank of America, Citigroup, AIG, …) and which shall die (e.g. Lehman Brothers violently, Bear Stearns peacefully), political legitimacy is critically important. The central bank needs an important place at the table, but it should not be making such decisions on its own' (Blinder, 2012, 5). Indeed, as our case study chapters make clear, central banks typically lack the capacity or authority to undertake unilateral guarantees, recapitalizations and other fiscal-related measures essential for stabilization in highly financialized economies. Their interventions are thus, at best, an imperfect substitute for government action.

Our main expectation is that substantial numbers of voters will respond most negatively to readily observable policy gridlock in an age of great expectations. Modern governments will be especially vulnerable to voter punishment if institutional obstacles are perceived to prevent timely and effective crisis resolution. In an age of low expectations, by contrast, policy inaction by governments will have much less serious political consequences. In this way, we suggest, changing societal expectations of government policy have altered the way in which institutional variations across democratic countries matter for the electoral prospects of incumbent governments.

Our argument does not imply that voters will consistently *reward* governments who do respond to crises with bailouts. On the contrary, we doubt that this kind of symmetry will operate. First, the occurrence of a crisis is a reasonable indicator for informationally constrained voters of policy incompetence, a failure to prevent a substantive threat to something about which many voters now care deeply. Second, even when banking crises are accompanied by extensive bailouts and macroeconomic stimuli, they generally result in unusually deep and long recessions and sharp falls in asset prices (Bordo et al., 2001; Jordà, Schularick and Taylor, 2015; Reinhart and Rogoff, 2009). In democracies, such losses give political oppositions and the media opportunities to portray policy interventions as delayed, partisan, misjudged or simply inadequate.

A third reason why informationally constrained modern voters will be inclined to punish governments even when bailouts are forthcoming is that these often have powerful distributional consequences to which media and voter attention will be directed because of societal attachment to norms of fairness and concerns about relative as well as absolute losses (Fong, Bowles and Gintis, 2006; Rosas, 2006, 9; Thaler, 2015, chap. 15). Before World War II, when extensive policy interventions were much less common and wealth was much more highly concentrated, the asset price collapses that typically followed banking crises disproportionately harmed the rich.

Today, in a world of greater financial inclusion, often much higher leverage and more widespread exposure to market-traded assets, financial crises can provoke sharper distributional conflicts. In developing and emerging countries, while a growing segment of households is now exposed to the formal financial system and market-traded assets, costly public interventions by the state could be perceived as especially burdensome for public sector workers, since central government wage bills are relatively high in these countries (World Bank, 2016). Distributional conflict may thus be particularly intense in those developing country democracies where exposure to the formal financial system and market-traded assets remains confined at considerably lower levels than elsewhere.

In more advanced economies, the rapid growth of household leverage means that those households with large mortgages face potentially large housing equity losses during crises. They will have strong incentives to favour policies that support employment and provide relief to household debtors. On the other side, less leveraged taxpayers are likely to see such policies as 'debtor bailouts', or transfers to undeserving borrowers who have taken excessive risks. They are likely to prefer policy interventions that stabilize the financial markets in which most of their wealth is concentrated (Atkinson and Morelli, 2011; Mian and Sufi, 2014a). Such interventions are likely to be perceived in turn by debtors as 'creditor bailouts'.

Policy interventions can also affect age cohorts differently. In most advanced democracies, wealth accumulation has been greatest for the post-war baby boom generation (Blyth and Matthijs, 2017). These baby boomers have accumulated DB pensions whose value is protected compared to the DC schemes that are much more common among younger workers. Older generations' housing assets are also relatively protected from the impact of banking crises because they tend to be less leveraged than those of younger house-owners. And if governments deploy the state's fiscal capacity to rescue the banking sector and its creditors, resulting in higher levels of public indebtedness, this can shift the burden from older savers to younger current and future workers. These differences can produce rising conflicts of interest between generations.

More generally, if increasing inequality is seen as a product of discretionary government policy, many voters may perceive it as unfair. Experiments and surveys have found that people's tolerance of inequality is higher when they judge it is due to diligence and hard work than when it is perceived as a product of 'unfair' factors such as gender, race or connections (Fong, Bowles and Gintis, 2006). High levels of financial sector compensation are often viewed as unfair by voters and this may feed voter perceptions that bank bailouts disproportionately benefit the relatively wealthy (Alessandri and Haldane, 2009; Johnson and Kwak,

2010; Philippon and Reshef, 2012). They may also have reinforced the perception that financial institutions have 'captured' politics and policy (Culpepper and Reinke, 2014; Hacker and Pierson, 2010; Johnson and Kwak, 2010; Zingales, 2015). Thus, modern voters are often conflicted, supporting government intervention to protect their own incomes and wealth while being inclined to see 'bailouts' as unfairly favouring different groups (Gallup, 2009).

We do not expect a simple linear relationship between the length of the period between the onset of a banking crisis and the next election on the one hand, and the extent of voter punishment of the incumbent government on the other (Boin, t'Hart and McConnell, 2009, 99). This is because, as we have suggested, there are multiple reasons why modern voters can react negatively to crises. Some of this voter reaction will be immediate, such as the view that the very onset of a banking crisis signals policy incompetence and the immediate interpretation of bank bailouts as redistributive transfers to the financial sector and the wealthy. These effects on voter sentiment may fade over time and to the advantage of incumbents if the next election is sufficiently distant and the government has been able to demonstrate competence in managing the crisis in the interim. Other effects, however, are likely only to become apparent over time. This includes the income and wealth losses that generally occur despite crisis interventions, as well as the perceived redistributive effects of these interventions. Thus, we expect that the propensity of modern voters to punish incumbent governments will be detectable in most cases whether or not the length of time to the next election is short or relatively long.[35]

In summary, our argument regarding the political consequences of banking crises is that, in contrast to an earlier era, since modern voters expect governments to safeguard their wealth, they have a strong propensity to punish incumbents that preside over banking crises and then respond in a delayed and redistributive manner. Modern governments are effectively caught on the horns of an acute dilemma. Having failed to prevent crises, they find it difficult to avoid extensive interventions to protect household wealth, but in doing so they are increasingly perceived as delivering highly costly and redistributive outcomes. In

---

[35] In order to consider the full range of these effects, our analysis in Chapter 5 takes into account the average election cycle in democracies. Our country case study chapters permit a fine-grained and detailed investigation of the short- and long-run effects of crises.

combination with the rising effective demand for wealth protection, financialization, by raising the extent and cost of bailouts, increases the likelihood that they will be widely perceived as unfair. Many voters will therefore be increasingly inclined to listen to opposition and media critics who frame any delay or blockage as indicators of incompetence, bias and misjudgement. Unfortunately for governments, modern voters' great expectations are also often unrealistic.

Governments thus face a challenging political asymmetry: modern voters tend to punish them when crises occur but offer little reward for crisis interventions. It is not quite a case of 'damned if they do, damned if they don't', since the negative political consequences for political incumbents of a failure to stabilize the financial system are almost certainly greater than intervening, especially in circumstances of extensive financialization. Nevertheless, it is precisely in such circumstances that the electoral rewards for intervention are likely to be most elusive because of the high cost of stabilizing large financial firms. Since incumbents' fear of complete financial collapse will generally trump concerns about generating unwanted distributional consequences, this is a cost that most will ultimately choose to bear. This argument generates three main time-dependent empirical expectations.

Firstly, given the increasing effective demand for financial stability since the 1970s, the propensity of modern voters to punish governments presiding over crises should have increased relative to the pre-1945 period. In addition, we do *not* expect voters to behave similarly in the case of what Funke, Schularick and Trebesch (2016) term 'non-financial macroeconomic disasters', that is, severe recessions not involving a crisis but in which output declines exceed those that follow banking crises. As we show in Chapter 6, these events are less threatening to middle-class wealth and have less powerful effects on inequality and polarization (Atkinson and Morelli, 2011).

Second, rising societal demand for stabilization measures during and after crises means that institutional obstacles to policy responses should have become more politically salient than in the past, conditioning how voters evaluate political incumbents. Modern governments should be more vulnerable to punishment if institutional obstacles prevent timely and effective crisis resolution. Voters, due to their informational disadvantages and the intensity of their demand for wealth protection, are unlikely to forgive incumbents whose hands are 'tied' by institutional constraints.

Third, modern voters are also likely to react negatively to policy responses that are substantively redistributive and perceived as unfair. Greater exposure to the vagaries of asset prices and the vulnerabilities associated with banking crises heightens voter anxiety and their demand for intervention. But if these interventions are interpreted as asymmetrically benefiting large financial institutions and wealthier households rather than those living the 'everyday life of global finance' (Langley, 2009), voters will punish incumbent governments.

2.3   Conclusion

We have provided a theory outlining why the evolution of societal expectations concerning government economic policy responsibilities should have redefined the policy and political aftermaths that follow systemic banking crises in democracies. Before World War II, the absence of a large middle class with substantial wealth and a major stake in financial stability should be associated with low expectations of government responsibility for crisis prevention and mitigation among this group. The rapid accumulation of wealth in middle-class households and their heightened exposure to the financial system since then should have served to reorient societal demands toward the protection of their wealth. Politicians have responded to and thereby reinforced these changing mass impulses via more extensive political commitments to prevent banking crises and to protect household wealth. Commitments of this kind were far less prevalent before the Great Depression but multiplied in various forms thereafter. The absence of systemic crises for decades after 1945 further embedded mass expectations of financial stability.

Our argument puts these trends at the centre of our understanding of the changing policy and political aftermaths of crises, which have thus far been overlooked in most accounts. These emergent middle-class expectations should have prompted modern democratic governments, by virtue of electoral accountability and legitimacy imperatives, to opt for increasingly extensive bailouts and other policies aimed at wealth protection during crises. Put differently, we argue that modern governments implement bailouts because their electoral prospects depend heavily on doing so. Governments in an earlier era, in which voter expectations were radically different, could opt for more market-conforming policies with less far-reaching political consequences.

Having broken their promise to prevent financial instability, incumbents are now expected by many voters to intervene decisively to limit prolonged and acute financial stress and to mitigate its consequences. The intensity of modern societal demands, and the fast-moving nature of modern financial crises, means that voters are less likely to be forgiving of institutional constraints that lead to policy gridlock. Yet governments facing institutional constraints will often struggle to accommodate these demands because modern banking crises tend to unleash heightened political polarization and rising inequality that can produce gridlock.

Indeed, it gets worse for modern governments because modern voters' great expectations are often unrealistic. Our argument suggests that modern governments face an acute political dilemma, in that voters expect timely and effective bailouts but then bridle at their perceived distributional consequences, offering incumbents little benefit for stabilizing the financial system. Voters tend to interpret interventions as asymmetrically benefiting the financial sector and other undeserving groups. Perceptions of unfairness, easily amplified by political oppositions and the media, thus orient modern voters to punish governments even when interventions are forthcoming.

We turn in the chapters that follow to an empirical assessment of our arguments. The evidence strongly confirms that great expectations are a crucial but thus far missing part of the story when it comes to understanding the changing policy responses and political events that follow banking crises. That these expectations are at least partially unrealistic and conflicting, as well as potentially destabilizing, is an important issue to which we return in the concluding chapter.

3

HOUSEHOLD WEALTH AND FINANCIALIZATION IN THE UNITED KINGDOM, THE UNITED STATES AND BRAZIL SINCE THE NINETEENTH CENTURY

> So now, as an infallible way of making little ease great ease,
> I began to contract a quantity of debt.
> Charles Dickens, *Great Expectations* (1861)

We have argued that the emergence of great expectations among the middle class regarding wealth protection was driven by a number of related developments over the past century, including wealth accumulation and its financialization, the democratization of leverage, and new public policy commitments. All of these factors continue to be important in sustaining – and reinforcing – great expectations over time. In the previous chapter, we surveyed dynamic trends across each of these developments in a broad range of advanced, emerging and developing countries and outlined how these should reshape crisis policy responses and political aftermaths over the long run. In this chapter, we dig deeper into the evolution of wealth accumulation, financialization and the democratization of leverage over nearly two centuries in each of three country cases on which we focus in the third part of this book. We show how middle-class households in the United Kingdom, the United States, and Brazil have generally experienced a substantial increase in their wealth portfolios alongside heightened exposure to financial markets in recent decades. This exposure has become especially pronounced in housing and market-traded financial assets, and is enhanced by rising leverage.

As noted in Chapter 1, for the purpose of achieving greater comparability we follow the economic rather than the sociological tradition (Goldthorpe, 2010) in defining the 'middle class' throughout as consisting of 'those [households] "comfortably" clear of being at-risk-of-poverty', but excluding those who are so wealthy as not to need to work (Atkinson and Brandolini, 2013, 79). Over the course of two centuries, the size of this group grew dramatically as the growth of wages in manufacturing and service sector jobs pulled many households significantly above subsistence incomes – pointing to an obvious drawback of 'fixed proportion' definitions of the middle class (Atkinson and Brandolini, 2013).[1] More recently, this process spread to emerging market countries, where the size of the middle class can be significantly smaller than in advanced countries. As Atkinson and Brandolini also note and as we emphasize, wealth (and income from wealth) as well as access to credit have mattered increasingly for middle-class status.

Average levels of household wealth and leverage are considerably higher in the United Kingdom and the United States than in Brazil, and the composition of British and American wealth is weighted much more heavily toward market-traded assets. Inequality *within* Brazil's middle class – as in other highly unequal Latin American countries – is also higher than such intra-class inequality in the United States and Britain (Atkinson and Brandolini, 2013, 77). State-owned financial institutions have also served historically as important financial intermediaries and stores of household wealth in Brazil, in contrast to the United Kingdom and the United States. Yet, as we show below, these differences have lessened in recent years, particularly since the early 1990s. As we outline below, the changing size and composition of the stake of middle-class households in all three countries has important implications for the nature and intensity of their preferences for wealth protection.

We provide evidence on the evolution of household wealth and financialization in all three countries. We do so with the caveat that longitudinal data on wealth and its distribution is patchy and varies substantially across countries. However, we draw on the efforts of

---

[1] At times we refer to different proportions depending on the data available.

various scholars and organizations that have made substantial empirical advances in recent years.

3.1 Household Wealth and Financialization in the United Kingdom since the Nineteenth Century

Over the course of two centuries, wealth in Britain has become less concentrated and its composition has shifted away from landholdings toward housing and financial assets, especially pensions. While wealth inequality remains an important feature of modern Britain and, as elsewhere, is higher than income inequality, the level of wealth accumulated by middle-class households, and their exposure to asset markets, has grown substantially in the twentieth century and particularly rapidly since the 1980s. As a result, the stake that this large group of voters has in financial stability has grown enormously.

Data on the degree to which British households were exposed to housing and financial asset markets is very limited for the early nineteenth century. What data is available suggests that the overwhelming majority of these households lacked significant exposure at the beginning of this period. The 'wealth middle class' then was very small by late twentieth-century standards. Wealth in early nineteenth-century Britain was highly concentrated in the hands of the property-owning aristocracy and 'merchants', who included financiers and industrialists by this time. Over the course of the first half of the nineteenth century, these latter two groups 'soared above the rest of society' (Lindert, 1986, 1136). In 1810, the top 10 per cent of households held more than 60 per cent of total wealth and the top 1 per cent held almost one-quarter (Lindert, 1986, 1141).

Lindert's estimates for the value of average personal occupational estates over the course of the nineteenth century are reproduced in Table 3.1. These suggest that the accumulation of aggregate wealth was rapid as the industrial revolution took hold, but that the major beneficiaries were the merchant classes and secondarily the aristocracy. The average wealth of middle-class professions approximately doubled between 1810 and 1875, but their share of the total diminished. In 1810, the wealth shares of the top 1 per cent and 10 per cent were 55 per cent and 82 per cent respectively and rose steadily over the rest of the century; by 1890, these shares were 61 per cent and 87 per cent

Table 3.1. Estimated average personal estates, selected occupations, England and Wales 1810–1875 (1875 prices)

Occupation	1810	1858	1875
Titled	2,032	3,036	9,855
Merchants	608	5,917	11,804
Professionals	607	1,063	1,201
Farmers, yeomen, husbandmen	220	411	581
Shopkeepers	304	641	606
Industrial trades	345	687	523
Labourers	101	81	143

Source: Lindert (1986, 1137).

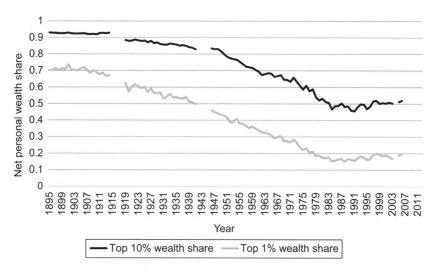

Figure 3.1: Net personal wealth shares, top 1 per cent and 10 per cent of UK adults, 1895–2012.
Source: http://wid.world/country/united-kingdom/.

(Lindert, 1986, 1141; Piketty, and Zucman, 2015, fig. 15.13). Thereafter, wealth concentration fell until the 1980s (Fig. 3.1). As we show below, the middle class was the main beneficiary of this levelling process.

In the early phases of the growing 'democratization' of wealth that occurred from this time, household wealth was being destroyed. As

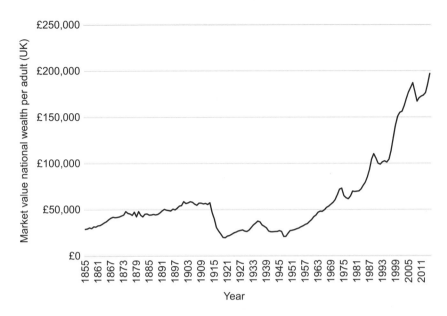

Figure 3.2: Market value of national wealth per adult, 1855–2015 (real 2016 £).
Source: http://wid.world/country/united-kingdom/.

Figure 3.2 shows, real wealth fell sharply in the period of the two world wars and the Great Depression. Recovery began after 1945, and by the 1970s real per capita wealth had reached the levels achieved in 1913. After the 1970s, real wealth per adult rose sharply so that on the eve of the 2007–9 crisis it was two and a half times higher than in 1913. Since the 1980s, Britain, including its middle and upper income groups, has been in a new world of wealth.

What have been the main components of domestic wealth since the early nineteenth century? Around 1826, over 80 per cent consisted of agricultural land or domestic capital, mostly associated with business; less than 20 per cent was in the form of housing. By 1890, over 50 per cent of wealth was business capital, and about a quarter each was held in the form of agricultural land and housing wealth. By 2008, about 55 per cent of domestic wealth consisted of housing assets (Piketty and Zucman, 2015, fig. 15.1). In 1873, more than 90 per cent of property is estimated to have been owned by the top 10 per cent, with the top 1 per cent of households owning more than 60 per cent of property wealth. This was certainly true of agricultural land, where large landowners dominated (and continue to do so today): between 80 per cent and 90 per cent of farmers in the nineteenth century were

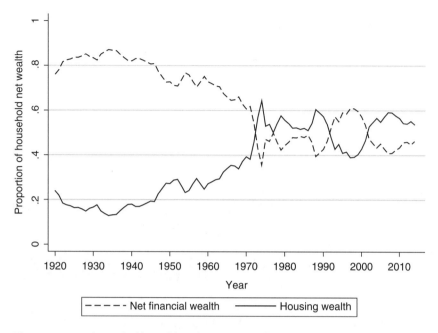

Figure 3.3: UK household wealth in housing and financial assets, 1920–2014.
Source: Office for National Statistics (2016b).

tenants, leasing land from landowners; this proportion fell to 50 per cent by 1960 (Offer, 1991).

Similar levels of inequality in property ownership applied to housing in the nineteenth century. In 1873, less than a sixth of all households owned their own home (Lindert, 1986, 1142). By 1918, only 23 per cent of households were owner-occupiers. This increased sharply after the 1950s, peaking at 69 per cent in 2001 (Office for National Statistics, 2013).

Historical estimates from the Office for National Statistics shown in Figure 3.3 reveal the growing importance of housing wealth in household portfolios. From a low of roughly 14 per cent in 1935, housing has risen to comprise nearly 60 per cent of the wealth in household portfolios (see also Ynesta, 2008). In 1995, non-financial assets – of which housing (land and dwellings) comprised the over-whelming share – constituted 49.3 per cent of household wealth.[2] By

---

[2] Non-financial assets include land, dwellings, other building and structures, machinery and equipment, and inventory. Since 1995, the value of dwellings had comprised over 90 per cent of the value of non-financial assets.

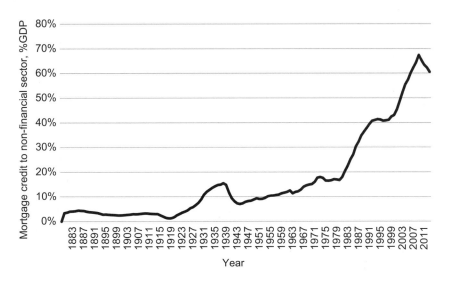

Figure 3.4: Mortgage credit to the UK non-financial sector, per cent of GDP, 1880–2013.
Source: Jordà, Schularick and Taylor (2017).

2006, following a rapid acceleration of house prices, the share of non-financial assets in household sector wealth had reached 64.8 per cent. This was also associated with a rapid growth of mortgage credit to the household sector after 1945, a trend that accelerated sharply after 1980 (Figure 3.4).

Turning to financial assets, bank deposits subject to withdrawal had been in use since the middle of the seventeenth century but did not develop on a large scale or become an important part of the English banking system until well into the nineteenth century (Cameron, 1967; Collins, 1988). Estimates for 1821 put the size of banking system deposits (excluding, wherever possible, interbank deposits and deposits by foreigners) at £56 million, or roughly 16 per cent of GDP.[3] By 1855, the English deposit base had gradually expanded to 25 per cent of GDP, thereafter increasing sharply to 1913, reaching more than 50 per cent of GDP. Across the UK as a whole (including Wales, Scotland and all of Ireland), deposits rose from 27.1 per cent of GDP in 1850 to 43.6 per cent of GDP in 1913.

---

[3] Pre-1870 data on English deposits is from Cameron (1967, 35) and on UK deposits from Collins (1988, 45). We use GDP estimates from the Bank of England's *Millennium of Data* dataset.

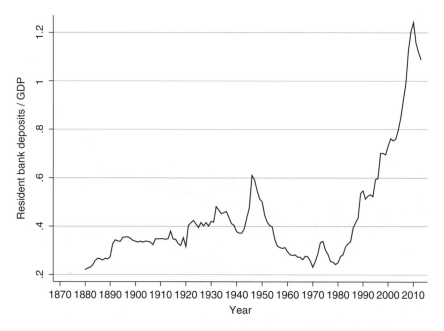

Figure 3.5: Total UK domestic deposits by non-financial residents / GDP.
Source: Jordà, Richter, Schularick and Taylor (2017). Deposits include checking, savings and term deposits of residents. Interbank deposits and deposits owned by foreigners are excluded.

Yet, in comparison to the post-1970 period, banking system deposits still remained at a relatively low level. As Figure 3.4 shows, deposits grew significantly in the three decades leading to the 2007 financial crisis, reaching more than 1.2 times GDP. The data on wealth inequality discussed below also suggests that the middle-class share of deposits is likely to have grown rapidly after World War I from low levels.

Balance sheet data available since 1920, shown in Figure 3.5, indicates that bank deposits represented less than one-sixth of household financial assets in the two decades prior to World War II. After the war, bank deposits grew in importance in household portfolios, reaching roughly one-quarter of financial assets. Changes in the system of national accounts make it difficult to construct a continuous time series for deposits.[4] Yet data available since 1987 suggests the proportion of household financial wealth held in bank deposits has remained

---

[4] Data available from 1957 to 1986 reports combined holdings of currency and bank deposits.

relatively steady, ranging between roughly 20 and 25 per cent, while property and pension assets have risen in importance (see also OECD, (2018)). Other data on the composition of household portfolios indicates that the share of financial assets held in bank deposits increases at the middle and lower end of the wealth distribution (Banks and Tanner, 2002).

Before 1945, household pension scheme assets comprised less than 0.03 per cent of all financial assets in the UK and were insignificant compared to other assets, including bank deposits and shares (Revell, Moyle, and Hockley, 1967).[5] Occupational pension schemes took off after World War II. Membership of such schemes rose from 6.2 million to 12.2 million adults between 1953 and 1967. At the same time, pension fund assets rose to more than 7 per cent of household financial assets (see Figure 3.6) (Roe, 1971).[6]

After this, membership in occupational schemes fell due to a shift towards personal pensions.[7] From the 1950s to the 1980s, most occupational pensions were DB schemes. The Social Security Act of 1986 made membership of occupational schemes voluntary and promoted DC occupational pension schemes and personal pensions. This was also facilitated by the expansion of financial markets in related products (Office for National Statistics, 2014).

As with deposits, changes in the system of national accounts make it difficult to construct a continuous time series for pension assets. Data available from 1966 to 1986 reports combined holdings for pensions and life insurance policies, which show considerable growth over this period. Post-1987 data, which disaggregates this combined series, suggests most of the growth during this period came from pension assets. Pensions grew from less than 8 per cent of financial assets in 1966 to over 40 per cent of financial assets by 1987. Life policies, on the other hand, fell from roughly 13 per cent of financial assets in 1966 to less than 10 per cent of financial assets in 1987.

Thus, the share of pension assets in household financial wealth has grown enormously. Since 1987, pension assets have made up more than 40 per cent of financial assets, and, in some years, more than half.

---

[5] Data from Revell includes household and corporate financial assets.
[6] Data from Roe includes 'persons and unincorporated businesses'.
[7] www.ons.gov.uk/economy/investmentspensionsandtrusts/compendium/pensiontrends/2014-11-28/chapter7pensionschememembership2014edition#trends-in-active-membership.

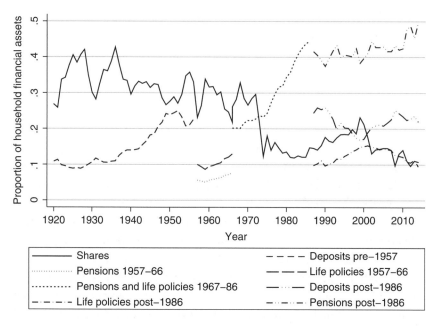

Figure 3.6: Household financial asset portfolios, 1920–2014.
Sources: Roe (1971); Solomou and Weale (1997); Office for National Statistics (2016a, 2016c).

The shift to DC pensions since the 1980s has also increased the exposure of many households to financial market risk. By 2006, it is estimated that only 56 per cent of DB plans remained open or partially open (OECD, 2009, 294). In 2013, private pension assets in the UK stood at $2.8 trillion, an 11.3 per cent share of the OECD pension fund market and the second-largest in the world behind only the United States (OECD, 2015a). Britain is one of only six OECD countries – also including Australia, Iceland, the Netherlands, Switzerland and the United States – where the pension asset-to-GDP ratio (99.6 per cent in 2013) exceeds the OECD weighted average ratio of 82.8 per cent. Britain and the United States are unique among this group of countries in that they are the only two without mandatory or quasi-mandatory private schemes.

In addition to pension assets, it is worth adding that, while the aggregate weight of shares in household wealth portfolios has declined since 1920, a growing *proportion* of British households is exposed to the risk of asset price movements via rising share ownership (Banks and Tanner, 2002). The proportion of households with direct ownership of

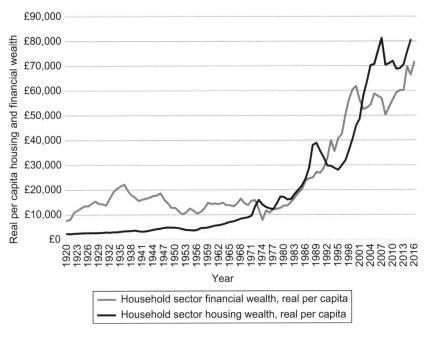

Figure 3.7: Real per capita housing and financial wealth, UK household sector, 1920–2016.
Source: Thomas and Dimsdale (2017).

shares has grown from less than 9 per cent in 1983 (the first year for which this information is available) to 22 per cent in 1998 (Guiso et al., 2003). This suggests that some upper-middle-class households have become more exposed to financial market risk through this channel. While exposure to shares is greater among wealthier households, across all households, such holdings have averaged roughly 15 per cent of financial wealth since 1987 (Office for National Statistics, 2016c).

In summary, both real housing and financial wealth of British households grew rapidly after 1980 (Figure 3.7). The position of most households has thereby been transformed over the past century. During the nineteenth century the overwhelming majority of British households were dependent on labour income as opposed to income from wealth. They therefore faced limited exposure to financial distress associated with bank failures. While potentially exposed to some loss of non-property assets in insolvent banks, the landed gentry – whose living standards depended largely on rental income from land-ownership – would likely have been less at risk than those of financial and industrial interests who were threatened with severe losses or bankruptcy. The landed gentry were strongly associated politically with the Tory Party and, as we discuss in Chapter 7, generally opposed government bailouts of 'speculators' among the rising merchant classes. As we elaborate in the next chapter, the bailout constituency in Britain during the nineteenth century was limited in size and influence, and low expectations generally prevailed regarding government intervention. Incumbent governments accordingly faced less political risk when pursuing Bagehot-style policies.

After the 1970s, the rapid rise in housing and pension wealth substantially increased the stake of middle-class households in financial markets, especially in mortgage credit and markets related to the management of pension assets. As our analysis in Chapter 4 reveals, this greatly heightened societal demand for bailout policies following crises. Moreover, we show in Chapter 8 that as the composition of household wealth shifted more toward housing and market-trade financial assets, responding to societal demand for wealth protection meant providing costlier and more extensive crisis interventions that went well beyond insurance of bank deposits.

3.2   Household Wealth and Financialization in the United States since the Nineteenth Century

As in Britain and most other advanced countries, the importance of housing and financial assets for middle-class American households has risen substantially over the past two centuries. The United States economy generated extraordinary amounts of wealth in the late nineteenth century and especially after 1945. As Figure 3.8 shows, this is also true for average real wealth per capita. Real average individual wealth increased more than threefold between 1970 and 2007.[8]

What have been the main components of this wealth? The relative importance of agricultural land in the geographically large United States was always less than that in Europe, constituting less than 50 per cent of total national wealth at the beginning of the nineteenth

---

[8] For a detailed analysis of the measurement and trajectory of wealth in the United States since 1900, see Wolff (2017a).

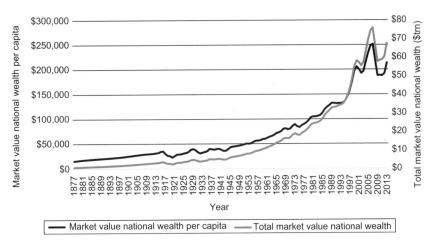

Figure 3.8: Average real wealth per capita ($, left axis) and total real market value of national wealth ($trn, right axis), United States 1877–2013 (2015 dollars). *Source:* www.wid.world dataset, last accessed 13 September 2017.

century (Piketty and Zucman, 2015, fig. 15.3). It has been in continual decline ever since and today is insignificant. Housing wealth grew from the middle of the nineteenth century and continued to rise in importance over the twentieth, reaching about 40 per cent of total wealth by 2007. The more detailed data available from the Federal Reserve for the period since 1945 indicates that in inflation-adjusted terms, real estate, retirement funds and corporate equities have dominated the increase in household sector wealth since the 1970s (Figure 3.9). In 1946, currency and bank deposits were the second largest component of household wealth after real estate assets; although they remain important today, their relative significance has declined substantially, especially since the late 1980s. The overall importance of liquid assets, pension assets and other corporate stockholdings has increased considerably since 1900; by 2007 these represented nearly 23 per cent of total gross household assets.[9]

These trends are strongly consistent with the claim that household wealth has become increasingly connected to financial markets over the course of the twentieth century and especially since the

---

[9] Wolff defines liquid assets as those held in 'checking accounts, savings accounts, time deposits, money market funds, certificates of deposits, and the cash surrender value of life insurance' (Wolff, 2017b, 48). Since the 1980s there has been a shift away from insured to uninsured cash instruments.

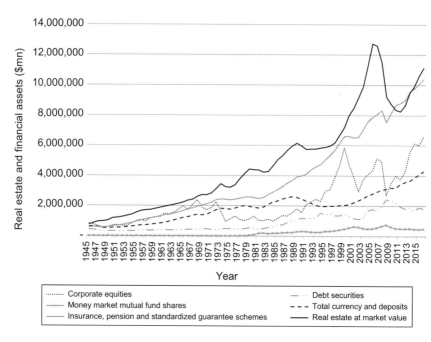

Figure 3.9: Real estate and financial assets by main components, US household and non-profit sector 1945–2015 (real 1982–4 dollars, millions).
Source: Board of Governors of the Federal Reserve System (US), Flow of Funds, Z1: Households and non-profit organizations. Asset values are deflated using the Consumer Price Index for all Urban Consumers (all items, 1982–4=100), US Bureau of Labor Statistics.

1970s. This is especially true for the middle class, for which there are more long-run data available than in the UK and Brazilian cases. For the middle three quintiles in 2007, housing, pensions and liquid assets represented about 86 per cent of total gross assets (Wolff, 2017b, 51). As for Britain, this also means that demand for the protection of household wealth goes well beyond traditional deposit insurance, which poses substantial new challenges to government.

Despite the fragility of America's banking system in the nineteenth century, domestic deposits expanded rapidly in the period after the Civil War, even by comparison with the rapidly expanding economy. In 1870, deposits by households and non-financial firms were about 10 per cent of GDP; by the time of the 1907 crisis we discuss in Chapter 9, they reached 40 per cent of GDP, rising to more than 60 per cent of GDP in the early years of the Great Depression (Figure 3.10). In comparison to other advanced countries at the time, these levels of

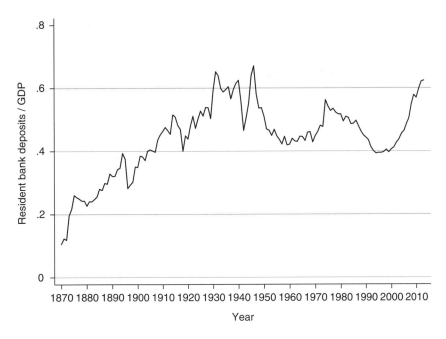

Figure 3.10: Total USA domestic deposits by non-financial residents, ratio to GDP, 1870–2013.
Source: Jordà et al. (2017). Deposits include checking, savings and term deposits of residents. Interbank deposits and deposits owned by foreigners are excluded.

deposit wealth placed the United States in the upper end of the distribution.[10] The relative importance of deposits in the United States peaked in the middle of the twentieth century before declining in the second half, though there has been a substantial increase since 2000. Only in Italy and Switzerland has there been a similar fall in the ratio of total deposits to GDP; on average, this ratio approximately doubled between 1980 and 2008 across all developed countries (Jordà et al., 2017).

Housing assets and secondarily assets connected closely to financial markets ('liquid assets and bonds', including deposits, and 'other financial assets', mostly in retirement accounts) are especially important for the American middle class. Figure 3.11 shows that for households in the 25th to 75th percentiles of the wealth distribution, among whom home ownership rates peaked at nearly 80 per cent in 2004, housing constituted between two-thirds and three-quarters of

[10] At the time of the Great Depression only Switzerland, Japan and Norway had higher levels of deposit wealth as proportion of GDP.

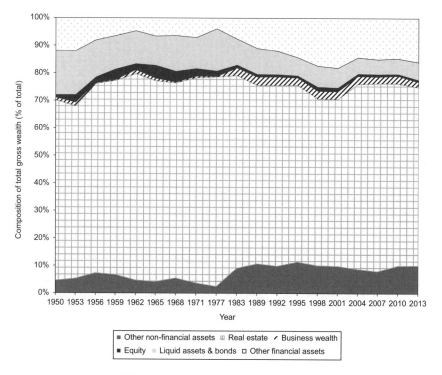

Figure 3.11: Composition of gross wealth, middle-class households, USA, 1950–2013 (per cent of total).
Source: Kuhn, Schularick and Steins (2017, appendix, table I). Middle-class households are defined here as those from the 25th to 75th percentiles of the wealth distribution.

gross household wealth throughout the post-war period (Wolff, 2017b, 51). By 2007, on average 65 per cent of the gross wealth of households in the middle three quintiles was constituted by their principal residence (Wolff, 2016, 44). Rising house prices over the post-war period in America thus play a crucial role in building up the wealth portfolios of the middle class.

Middle-class American households have also become increasingly leveraged since the early twentieth century, especially since the 1980s, as they have taken on more mortgage debt to facilitate the purchase of housing assets.[11] For this group (25th to 75th percentiles), leverage approximately tripled from 22 per cent of household net

---

[11] Housing debt has constituted over 80 per cent of total household debt for this group throughout the post-war period (Kuhn, Schularick and Steins, 2017, appendix, table I).

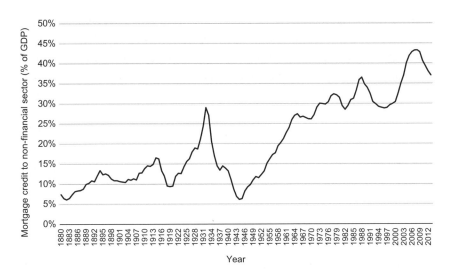

Figure 3.12: Mortgage credit to the non-financial sector, USA, per cent of GDP, 1880–2013.
Source: Jordà, Schularick and Taylor (2017).

wealth in 1950 to 63 per cent by 2007. Since the poor and the relatively rich rely far less on mortgage borrowing, it is middle-class households that are primarily responsible for the sharp increase in aggregate mortgage borrowing in recent decades (Kuhn, Schularick and Steins, 2017) (Figure 3.12). This data reveals that mortgage debt also rose substantially in the 1920s, to be followed by a decade of sharp deleveraging from the time of the Great Depression. A series of policy initiatives from this time aimed to promote home ownership, including the promotion of a secondary market for mortgage debt through the establishment of Fannie Mae and of the Federal Housing Administration (FHA) to insure mortgages. Interest expenses had always been deductible from income taxes when these were permanently introduced in 1913, but as consumer debt rose in the post-1945 period their importance steadily increased. By the 1980s, the large loss of tax revenue this entailed led the Treasury to propose its abolition, but the Reagan administration and the Democrat-controlled Congress agreed to continue to allow mortgage interest deductibility for first and second homes in the Tax Reform Act of 1986 (Klott, 1988).

Today, household debt in America is especially concentrated among the relatively young and the relatively educated. With the Netherlands and Norway, the United States is now among those countries with both the highest level of indebted households (over 75 per cent) and high debt-to-income ratios (OECD, 2015b, 270–1). This has been associated with the rising importance of housing assets in total wealth and a declining share of home equity (Wolff, 2017a, 568). By contrast, the housing wealth of the top 10 per cent in the USA constituted only 31 per cent of their total gross wealth in 2007, with business equity, bonds and other financial assets accounting for 67 per cent; their debt was only 6 per cent of total assets (Kuhn et al., 2017, Appendix, table K). The use of consumer credit, including automobile loans, also increased as a proportion of disposable income from the 1990s.[12]

Housing assets completely dominate the *net* wealth of middle-class American households (Figure 3.13). Assets in retirement accounts are a distant second, though these have grown considerably since the early 1980s. Deposits are even less important, with a sharp decline since the early 1980s. Generally, there has been a long-term shift from liquid to pension assets for middle- and upper-middle-income households (Wolff, 2017b, 16).

The declining liquidity of middle-class asset portfolios has had significant consequences. By 2013, Federal Reserve surveys revealed that about half of all adults either could not cover a small emergency expense costing $400 or would need to do so by selling assets or borrowing money (presumably on a credit card). By 2016, 44 per cent of adults were still unable to cover an unexpected $400 expense from savings (Board of Governors of the Federal Reserve System, 2017a, 26–7). This accords with the findings of other researchers that a significant proportion of people whom we might normally think of as middle-class in income terms are 'asset poor'; in the United States, up to half of middle-class households may fall into this category (Atkinson and Brandolini, 2013, 91). However, as noted above, such households may also be able to access credit to maintain consumption. In the same year (2016), 70 per cent of adults surveyed reported that they could cover expenses over a longer period of extended financial disruption of three months, but 22 per cent of these would need to do so by borrowing or running down assets (Board of Governors of the Federal Reserve System, 2017a, 26–7). US financial institutions have responded by expanding the availability of various credit facilities, including credit

---

[12] Board of Governors of the Federal Reserve System (US), Flow of Funds, Z1: Households and non-profit organizations.

Figure 3.13: Housing wealth and net debt ratios, 1950–2013, middle 50 per cent and top 10 per cent, USA (per cent).

Source: Kuhn, Schularick and Steins (2017, tables M and O, appendix). Middle- and upper-class households are defined as those in the 25th–75th and 90th–100th percentiles of the wealth distribution respectively.

cards, unsecured loans and housing equity withdrawal schemes. Many households may be reducing their liquid savings precisely because of this growing availability of credit; others may have little choice and for them, rising leverage may be the only means by which middle-class status can be retained. There is evidence that this is associated with increased levels of anxiety among many households despite the long-term growth in total household wealth (Board of Governors of the Federal Reserve System, 2017a, 10–14).

Once again, the position of the wealthiest households is starkly different: for the top 10 per cent, business equity is the dominant component of wealth and leverage is low (Kuhn, Schularick and Steins, 2017). As these authors show, without the strong rises in real house prices between 1970 and 2007, which substantially boosted middle-class wealth, the latter group's share of total wealth would have been much lower. When house prices fell after 2006, the leveraged middle classes lost relative to the very wealthy, who benefited from their low leverage and the relatively rapid recovery of stock prices (Kuhn, Schularick and Steins, 2017, 22–7).[13]

Government-provided military pensions were awarded to war veterans and widows from colonial times, though they expanded rapidly after the Civil War (on both sides) and particularly after the 1890 Pension Act, which provided generous pensions to most veterans. According to one source, 'about 20 per cent of all white men age 55 and over received a Union Army pension ... [and by] 1902, the program consumed about 30 per cent of the federal budget' (Short, 2002). Confederate state pensions were much less generous. In the early twentieth century state and municipal governments also began providing pensions to their employees.

Private pensions emerged first as employee benefits provided by some large companies in the United States in the final quarter of the nineteenth century. By 1940, 4.1 million private sector workers received pension coverage, and rapid growth occurred after the war, with nearly

---

[13] These authors use household survey data to construct these estimates of income and wealth inequality. They largely confirm the findings of authors who rely more heavily on income tax data (including Piketty, Saez and Zucman and the World Wealth and Income Database (WID) project) and who show that income and wealth inequality has increased since World War II. However, because survey data picks up untaxed sources of wealth the Kuhn et al. data suggests that the increase in wealth inequality before 2007 was somewhat smaller than WID estimates but larger since 2007.

30 million private workers covered by an employer retirement plan in 1970 (Employee Benefit Research Institute, 1998; US Bureau of the Census, 1975a, 1:343). The relative importance of private pension fund reserves in household wealth portfolios more than quadrupled in the first twenty-five years after World War II, rising from less than 3 per cent of all household financial assets in 1945 to more than 12 per cent in 1970 (US Bureau of the Census, 1975b, 2:977).

Although pension payments were made tax-deductible for companies in 1914, it was not until 1935 with the Social Security Act that the federal government provided DB payments for retirees. The accumulation of savings held as Social Security until the mid-1970s had a powerful effect in reducing wealth inequality, though it also contributed to the declining propensity of Americans to save (Wolff, 2017a, 575). From 1962, self-employed individuals could establish tax-deferred individual retirement savings plans; these were made universally available in 1981. DB pension schemes dominated in the period before the 1980s in both the corporate and public sectors. DC schemes have grown rapidly since then, both as employer-based schemes and personal schemes, especially individual retirement accounts (Figure 3.14).

Thus, as in the British case, the value of pensions to middle-class recipients has become increasingly linked to financial markets since the 1980s. For the middle three quintiles of the wealth distribution, pension accounts became the second largest component of gross household wealth (after housing), at 12.9 per cent of gross assets by 2007 – a substantial increase from only 1.2 per cent in 1983. Equally important, the rate of ownership of pension assets among this group grew from 12.2 per cent in 1983 to 53.4 per cent in 2007 (Wolff, 2016, 44). As Table 3.2 shows, a 2013 consumer survey by the Federal Reserve suggests that only about 18 per cent of Americans had employer-provided DB pensions and substantially more had DC pensions. Younger working-age households are relatively dependent on the latter. About half of prime working-age households had DC schemes, and a quarter had IRAs, with their value dependent on asset prices set in financial markets.

The growing exposure of middle-class American households to market-traded financial assets has been driven in large part by rising stock ownership inside and outside pension schemes. The proportion of middle-class households invested in corporate equities, either directly or indirectly via a mutual fund, retirement account or other managed asset,

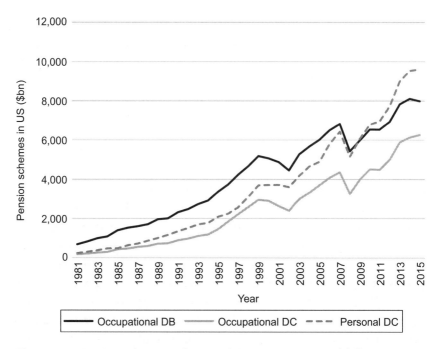

Figure 3.14: Pension schemes in the United States, 1981–2015, $ billions. *Source*: OECD (2016, fig. 1.3).

rose quickly from 16.5 per cent in 1983 to roughly 50 per cent in 2007 (Wolff, 2014, 55). These investments grew from 2.4 per cent of total gross assets in 1983 to 12.6 per cent in 2001 at the height of the dot. com boom, falling somewhat by 2007 as prices fell and middle-class households divested their holdings.

Before World War I, wealth was much more evenly distributed in the United States than in the advanced countries of Europe, not least because of the more even distribution of agricultural land (Jordà et al., 2017). A much higher proportion of Americans also owned their houses than in Britain in the nineteenth century. By 1890, nearly 48 per cent of homes were owner-occupied, a rate that remained fairly stable through to World War II (then, about two-thirds of farmers were owner-occupiers versus 37 per cent for non-farmers). After 1945, home ownership rates rose, especially in urban and suburban areas, until they reached 64 per cent in 1970. This level was sustained until the 1990s, when it began to rise somewhat to peak at 69 per cent in the mid-2000s, before falling back to about 64 per cent since the 2007–9 crisis (US Bureau of the Census, 1975b, 2:646, 2017).

Table 3.2. Federal Reserve Household Wellbeing Survey 2013: retirement savings by respondent age, percentage of respondents*

	18–29	30–44	45–59	60+	Overall
No retirement savings or pension	50.5	27.8	23.0	15.4	30.9
Social Security Old-Age benefits	17.5	31.5	46.4	67.6	36.3
401(k), 403(b), thrift or other DC pension plan through an employer	30.3	52.8	47.9	37.1	43.7
DB pension through an employer (i.e. pension based on a formula, your earnings, and years of service)	7.0	16.0	27.0	25.9	18.2
Individual Retirement Account (IRA)	11.2	23.5	29.2	31.9	23.0
Savings outside a retirement account (e.g. a brokerage account, savings account)	15.4	19.3	28.6	33.3	22.7
Real estate or land	4.4	8.9	16.2	20.5	11.3
Other	1.7	3.4	4.1	4.1	3.2

Source: Board of Governors of the Federal Reserve System (2014, 27). Note: *Among those who are not currently retired. Total respondents: 3,163.

As in Europe, the wealth distribution in the United States became more equal after World War I. This process of rising equality continued until about the mid-1970s, when it began to reverse. According to the World Income and Wealth Database, American households in the 'middle 40 per cent' (those in the 50th to 90th percentiles) steadily improved their position in the wealth distribution in the post-1945 period until the 1980s, when it began to deteriorate (Figure 3.15).[14] Using somewhat different measures, Wolff dates the low point of inequality to the mid-1970s and notes that the post-1929 reduction in wealth inequality is less sharp for individuals than households (Wolff, 2017a, 591–609).[15] The top 10 per cent, 1 per cent and

[14] These results are corroborated by other studies that define the middle class more broadly (Kuhn, Schularick and Steins, 2017; Wolff, 2017a, 2017b). The share of the middle 40 per cent also shows a downward trend since the 1980s for those other countries for which WID data exist (France and China) but the deterioration is less sharp than in the United States.

[15] Average household size fell over the course of the century, and married women became wealthier.

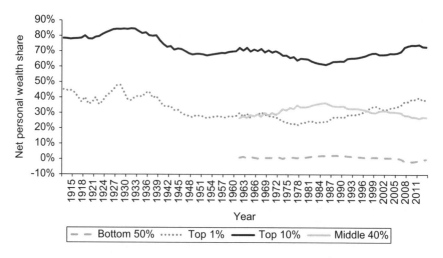

Figure 3.15: Net personal wealth shares, United States, 1913–2014.
Source: http://wid.world/country/usa/.

especially the top 0.1 per cent have been the major winners since then, and on various measures wealth inequality in the United States is now much higher than in almost all other advanced democracies (OECD, 2015b, chap. 6; Scheidel, 2017, 405–10). As Figure 3.15 shows, the share of the middle class has fallen steadily since the mid-1980s. Even so, Figure 3.16 shows that the level of middle-class household real wealth has continued to rise since the 1960s, driven primarily by rising housing wealth (Wolff, 2017a, 2017b). Between 1970 and 2007, aggregate real wealth for the middle 40 per cent increased almost fourfold, before falling sharply after 2007. Thus, the stake of these households in the financial system has continued to rise, as in other advanced countries.

As we discuss in the following chapter, much attention has been given to the rise of 'sub-prime' lending by banks to households with lower incomes and lower credit scores in the years leading up to 2007 compared to the past. However, as we have seen, it would be misleading to suggest that the growing reliance on credit was primarily a lower-income phenomenon. As we argued in Chapter 2, financialization has also become increasingly associated with more aggressive attitudes towards financial risk among higher-income voters, including a tendency to view leveraged housing as an attractive investment option (Fligstein and Goldstein, 2015). Recent research suggests that the growth of mortgage credit over 2001–7 was in fact strongest among

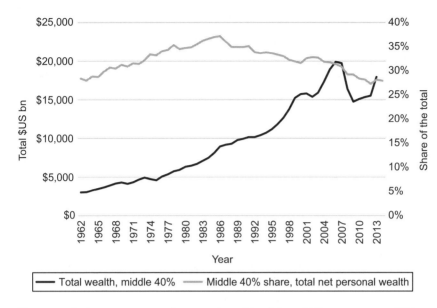

Figure 3.16: Aggregate net real personal wealth of the middle 40 per cent, USA, 1962–2014, total US$ billion (left axis) and share of the total (right axis). *Source*: http://wid.world/country/usa/. Total personal wealth is calculated in 2015 US dollars (billions). The middle 40 per cent is defined here as adults in the 50th to 90th percentiles.

prime borrowers, who were using the growing availability of mortgage credit to invest aggressively in property assets (Albanesi, Giorgi and Nosal, 2017). These authors also find that most mortgage defaults after 2006 were concentrated among real estate investors in the middle of the credit score distribution.

Our expectation is that all of these developments – defensive reliance on credit by lower income households, more aggressive use of credit by higher income households, and a general increase in middle and upper income exposure to traded assets – will have substantially boosted the demand by a wide swathe of lower-middle- to upper-middle-class voters for the protection of wealth and the maintenance of the flow of credit. As we show in Chapter 10, this made it difficult even for 'small government' Republican politicians to avoid bailing out the financial sector after 2007.

The changing composition of household wealth also has important implications for the kinds of wealth protection policies the middle classes are likely to prefer. For the great majority of households, it is clear that historic deposit insurance limits since 1935 have

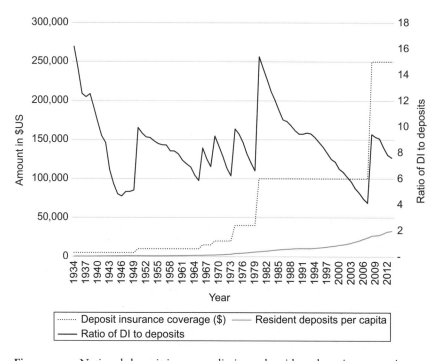

Figure 3.17: National deposit insurance limits and resident deposits per capita, USA, 1934–2013 (US$, left axis) and ratio (right axis).
Source: Jordà et al. (2017); Jordà, Schularick and Taylor (2017), author calculations. The FDIC was established in 1934 and deposit insurance limits were first set at $5,000. Insurance coverage is provided per individual per institution. Given the skewness of the distribution of deposits, median per capita deposits are substantially lower than the average per capita deposits shown above.

consistently far exceeded the value of per capita bank deposits (Figure 3.17). Given this substantial effective over-insurance of deposits and the fact that the wealth of most households has become increasingly concentrated in leveraged housing assets and in portfolio assets connected to financial markets, deposit insurance has become less relevant as a form of wealth protection. It remains important to the extent that it deters bank runs, but as we note in Chapter 10, this became increasingly less true by 2007. More directly relevant by then were policies that could protect non-deposit forms of wealth. The challenge this presents both for governments and citizens, however, is considerable because the value of portfolio financial assets and housing is far greater and very difficult for policymakers to control. Modern governments possess a large range of tools that affect asset prices, including tax, regulatory,

Table 3.3. Estimated real estate and financial assets at risk, US households and non-profits, 2007 (US$ billions)

	Flow of funds estimates	Hypothetical 30% fall	Fall as % of federal government revenue
Real estate	20,707	6,212	242%
Checking & time deposits	7,555	2,267	88%
Money market funds	1,346	404	16%
Debt securities	3,955	1,187	46%
Corporate equities	10,018	3,005	117%
Mutual fund shares	4,319	1,296	50%
Life insurance reserves	1,077	323	13%
Pension entitlements	15,077		
of which estimated DC proportion	9,235	2,770	108%
Estimated non-housing, non-deposit financial assets at risk	24,285	8,985	350%

Source: Author calculations from Board of Governors of the Federal Reserve System (US), Flow of Funds, Z1: Households and non-profit organizations. The estimated proportion of assets in DC pensions is taken from the OECD estimate for that year of 61.2 per cent (OECD, 2016).

fiscal and monetary policies, but these prices are also substantially determined by market behaviour, including expectations (Shiller, 2005).

The real estate and financial assets now at risk would be extraordinarily costly for governments to guarantee in the same way as they do bank deposits, for the simple reason that their aggregate value far exceeds government tax revenues. As Table 3.3 shows, by 2007, American households and non-profits owned aggregate financial and real estate assets of about $64 trillion, nearly four and a half times annual GDP of $14.5 trillion. In contrast to bank deposits, the insurance of which has been funded (in principle) over time via Federal Deposit Insurance Corporation (FDIC) member bank contributions, guarantees of other assets would constitute extremely large contingent liabilities for the government. Assuming a plausible hypothetical fall of 30 per cent in at-risk real estate and non-deposit financial assets, the final column in

Table 3.3 estimates the size of this liability relative to federal government revenue. If real estate and non-guaranteed financial assets fell by 30 per cent, the cost to taxpayers would be nearly six times total current government revenue. As we discuss in Chapter 10, this represents an upper bound on the potential cost of such interventions since less costly measures to limit such wealth losses are possible. Nevertheless, it is suggestive of why the government in 2008 chose only to guarantee money market funds in addition to insured bank deposits. Many households accordingly suffered no deposit or near-deposit losses after 2007 but, as we discuss in Chapter 10, they experienced falls in housing and financial wealth greater than the aggregate size of bank deposits and near-deposits.

To summarize, although household wealth in America has continued to rise over the long run and especially since the 1970s, it has also become more unequally distributed in recent decades, to the point where the United States has emerged as one of the most unequal developed democracies – a stark contrast with its position in the nineteenth century. The middle class, broadly defined, emerged relatively early in the United States, with significant real estate and financial assets. This added substantially to existing pressure from the very wealthy to protect their financial and business assets. In contrast to Britain and much of the rest of developed Europe, the bailout constituency in the United States is therefore likely to have been stronger at an earlier stage. The presumption of laissez-faire in economic policy was also less strong in the nineteenth-century United States than in Britain, as US policies were influenced by Listian and Hamiltonian ideas favouring government-supported development. Thus, we expect incumbent governments in the United States to face greater political risk from pursuing Bagehot policies at an earlier stage than in most other countries.

We also expect the size and influence of the bailout constituency to have grown substantially from the mid-twentieth century as the incomes, wealth and leverage of middle-class households expanded rapidly. The rapid rise in housing and pension wealth since the 1970s in particular increased the stake of middle-class households in financial markets, especially in mortgage credit and in markets related to the management of retirement assets. This further increased the political risk for governments of pursuing Bagehot policies, as we explore later in the case of the 2007–9 crisis. As we also suggest, however, sharply rising income and wealth inequality in recent decades, and the growing importance of non-deposit wealth, has made the risks of intervention almost as fraught.

3.3 Household Wealth and Financialization in Brazil since the Nineteenth Century

The limited availability of data on household balance sheets makes estimation of wealth levels and household portfolio composition more difficult in the case of Brazil, particularly over a long time frame and especially prior to the late 1990s. Available data indicates that few Brazilian households owned housing and financial assets in the nineteenth century; for as much as 50 per cent of households in parts of Brazil, or 70 per cent of the population, the value of their possessions was close to zero (Frank, 2004, 180–1; Silveira, 1985, 106, 110).[16] Wealth was highly concentrated in the hands of the traditional landed elite and the emergent mercantile families from the start of the Empire in 1822. It has remained highly concentrated in Brazil ever since, and a sizeable middle class in wealth terms took far longer to emerge than in Britain and the United States.

Frank (2004, 2005) and Silveira (1985) provide the best available estimates over a long time frame. This data is derived from estate inventory samples largely drawn from the city of Rio de Janeiro, with more limited data from the counties of São João del Rei and São José in Minas Gerais and the city of São Paulo. We must allow for some margin of error in these estimates, since poorer households were less likely to have their estates inventoried. Much higher estimates of wealth concentration would result if we assume a larger proportion of households held zero wealth. In addition, these estimates apply only to selected areas of Brazil, and the wealth distribution could be different in areas where we lack data. In the period since 2000 we use regression-based estimates for the whole of Brazil provided by Credit Suisse.

In 1820, the top 10 per cent of wealth-holders in Rio de Janeiro held nearly 60 per cent of total wealth; in São João–São José they held

---

[16] Frank (2005, 252) suggests an estimate of 50 per cent is credible for highly urbanized and expensive Rio de Janeiro, but that an estimate of 33 per cent is more likely for other areas, such as São João–São José.

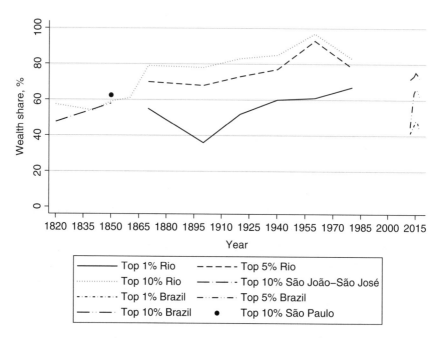

Figure 3.18: Wealth shares, top 1 per cent, 5 per cent and 10 per cent of Brazilian wealth-holders and households.
Sources: Credit Suisse (2017a, 156; 2016, 148; 2015, 149; 2014, 147; 2012, 150); Frank (2005, 251; 2004, 84); Silveira (1985, 77).

roughly half of total wealth. The wealth shares of the top decile thereafter rose steadily for more than a century, peaking at 97 per cent in 1960. By implication, the 'wealth middle class' during this long period was close to non-existent (Figure 3.19). The top 1 per cent and 5 per cent of wealth-holders enjoyed similar rates of wealth accumulation over this period, though the former appear to have fared worse than the latter during the financial instability of the 1890s and 1900s. Estimates of the wealth Gini coefficient among Rio de Janeiro wealth-holders also increase over the period from 1870 to 1960, rising from 0.855 to 0.90 (Silveira, 1985, 78).

The peak of wealth concentration likely occurred sometime during the period between the 1960s and the end of the 1980s (Silveira, 1985, 108). Unfortunately, wealth data covering the period from 1980 to 2000 is not available. The wealth share of middle-class households had shown some improvement since the 1940s, rising from 0.75 per cent to 1.2 per cent by the early 1980s. But the period of high and accelerating inflation in the late 1980s likely eroded these limited

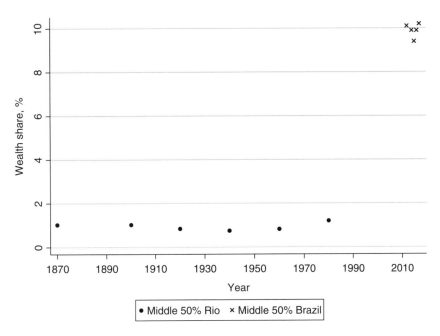

Figure 3.19: Wealth shares, middle 50 per cent of Brazilian wealth-holders and households.
Sources: Credit Suisse (2017a, 156; 2016, 148; 2015, 149; 2014, 147; 2012, 150); Frank (2005, 251; 2004, 84); Silveira (1985, 77).

gains. Inflation tends to be a highly regressive wealth tax, since the ability to protect wealth via portfolio adjustments is generally held to be increasing in income, at least over an initial period (Easterly and Fischer, 2001; Romer and Romer, 1999). Barriers to enter asset markets – including those denominated in foreign currencies – aimed at protection from inflation were widespread in Brazil, restricting access to wealthy households (Neri, 1995). Thus, it is likely that the period of accelerating inflation served to concentrate wealth in Brazil in the same manner it did for income (see Figure 3.20). The income distribution tends to be highly correlated with the wealth distribution, though the latter tends to be more unequal than the former (Davies et al., 2008).

The evolution of the income Gini coefficient shows that income inequality rose from 1981 to 1989 at the height of hyperinflation in Brazil, before falling to significantly lower levels when monetary conditions stabilized, particularly after the *Real* Plan in 1994. If income became more evenly distributed after 1989 then we can conclude with

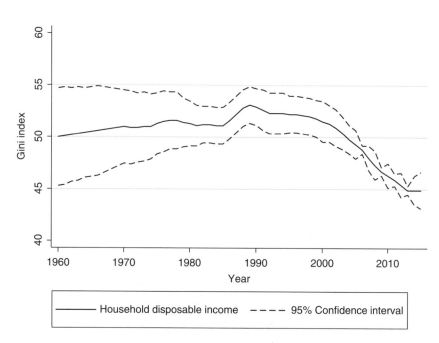

Figure 3.20: Evolution of the income Gini coefficient in Brazil, 1960–2015. *Source*: Solt (2016).[17]

some confidence that wealth likely did as well. In fact, decomposition of the evolution of the Gini coefficient suggests that some of the decline since 1989 was due, in part, to rising asset ownership among households outside the top end of the income distribution (Ferreira, Leite and Litchfield, 2008, 212). This finding would be consistent with estimates of the wealth Gini coefficient, which indicate it fell from 0.86 in 1980 to 0.78 in 2000 (Davies et al., 2008, 404). Thus, we can be reasonably confident that the early 1990s saw the start of an accelerating trend toward greater middle-class wealth in Brazil.

Indeed, like middle-class households elsewhere, those in Brazil now find themselves in a new world of wealth, albeit at levels considerably lower than those observed in advanced countries (see Figure 3.21). To put it in perspective, at constant prices, total wealth in Brazil in 2017 is comparable to that of the United States in 1901 (Credit Suisse

[17] Data is from the Standardized World Income Inequality Database, which utilizes a multiple imputation algorithm to provide estimates. We thus include confidence intervals around these estimates. Data from household surveys depicts a similar evolution (Ferreira, Leite and Litchfield, 2008).

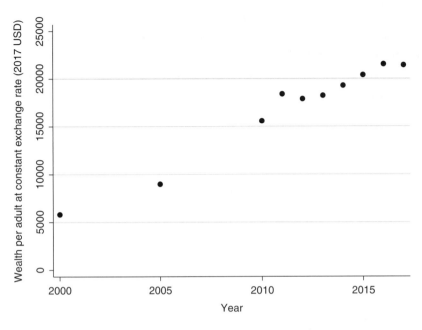

Figure 3.21: Net wealth per adult in Brazil at constant exchange rate, 2000–15. *Source*: Credit Suisse (2017a, 151).

Research Institute, 2017b, 43).[18] Yet the middle class of Brazil has grown substantially in recent decades. Using the 'clear of being at-risk-of-poverty' definition, World Bank estimates of the size of Brazil's middle class by the mid-1990s range from 20 to 40 per cent of the total population, with the upper range today at about 50 per cent (Ferreira et al., 2013, 140). Like much of the rest of Latin America, although Brazil is not yet a 'middle-class society', it may be in the process of becoming one.

This middle class now holds a much greater level of wealth than it did more than a century or even a generation ago, and as we discuss below, the composition of its wealth portfolio has become increasingly weighted to assets of considerably greater market risk. As we discuss in Chapter 12, average Brazilian households are also relatively dependent on current income, fungible wealth and increasingly credit to provide for large necessary expenditures such as emergency medical payments.

---

[18] The US population in 1901 was 77.6 million; Brazil's was 207.7 million in 2016, nearly 2.7 times larger.

This greater vulnerability compared to households in many upper-middle- and high-income countries is likely to intensify demand for the protection of wealth.

By 2012, Credit Suisse estimates that the middle 50 per cent of the wealth distribution in Brazil held somewhere in the range of 10–17 per cent of the country's wealth, a level that has remained fairly constant in subsequent years (Credit Suisse Research Institute, 2012, 150; 2017a, 156).[19] When compared to the earlier estimate of the share of middle-class wealth-holders in Rio de Janeiro, this would suggest a remarkable tenfold increase since 1980 and a sizeable growth in the middle-class wealth share over the crisis period we analyse in Chapter 12. Over the same period, the wealth shares of the top one per cent, five per cent, and 10 per cent had all fallen considerably (see Figure 3.18).

What have been the principal components of household wealth since the nineteenth century? Brazil was a slave society until 1888, when it became the last country in the so-called New World to outlaw slavery. Slaves, as a form of property, constituted an important component of household wealth for most of the years of the Empire. So central were slaves to the Brazilian economy that at one point they represented nearly half of the population of Rio de Janeiro (Barman, 1988, 49).

Frank's analysis of estate inventories in Rio de Janeiro over the course of the nineteenth century reveals that middle-class wealth-holders – as noted above, then a fairly small group – invested more heavily in slaves than their wealthier counterparts and owned few financial and housing assets: the portfolio share of slave wealth in middle-class households was more than double that found in wealthy households (Frank, 2004, 60).[20] Even the poorest 20 per cent of wealth-holders in Brazil invested heavily in slaves, as it was the only affordable asset within their reach. Until slavery was outlawed, slaves accounted for roughly 10 per cent of wealth among the wealth-holders of Rio de Janeiro, with considerably higher shares in São João–São José (33 per cent) and São Paulo (39 per cent) (Frank, 2004, 40, 73, 88; 2005, 244).

[19] The Credit Suisse data is provided according to wealth deciles. We thus compute the lower bound as that held by households in the 2nd to 7th deciles of the wealth distribution, and the upper bound as that held by households in the 3rd to 8th deciles of the wealth distribution.
[20] The ratio of slave prices to house prices was about 5 to 1 in the 1820s (Frank, 2004, 43).

Land has historically been an important form of wealth in Brazil, serving as a hedge against inflation and macroeconomic instability. Available data from the nineteenth century suggests that Brazil, like Britain, was characterized by a high concentration of land-ownership. In the state of Minas Gerais, one study estimates the Gini coefficient for landholding to have ranged from 0.71 to 0.77 (Bergad, 1999, 69, 207–8). In the century and a half since then, the pattern of land ownership has become even more concentrated. Decadal estimates since the Second World War consistently place the Gini coefficient for land-ownership for the country as a whole at around 0.85 (Silveira, 1985, 145; Torche and Spilerman, 2008, 162–3). However, as urbanization rapidly increased after the Second World War, rising from 31 per cent in 1940 to over 80 per cent by 2000 (World Bank, 2002, 11), other forms of wealth have become more important. This tendency was observable much earlier in major cities. In Rio de Janeiro, urbanization in the nineteenth century led to higher house prices, which, as discussed below, boosted the weight of housing assets in wealth portfolios and diminished the value of rural property holdings, even among rural landowners with only minimal property connections to the city (Frank, 2004, 40, 73, 88; 2005, 247–8).[21]

For any given level of land-ownership, higher levels of rural population density should heighten the weight of land as an asset in household wealth portfolios (Ansell and Samuels, 2010). Ansell and Samuels provide data that weight the proportion of all cultivable land worked by families of four individuals or fewer by the proportion of the population living outside urban areas.[22] Lower values would be suggestive of less weight given to land in wealth portfolios, which is precisely what is to be expected in Brazil as urbanization progressed in the twentieth century (see Figure 3.22). Notwithstanding this trend, periods of macroeconomic instability, such as the late 1980s, have led to periodic increases in land prices, as households sought to hedge against

[21] Among all wealth-holders in Rio de Janeiro, Frank (2004, 40, 88) indicates the weight of rural property holdings in wealth portfolios fell from 12.2 per cent in 1815–25 to 2 per cent in 1885–9. In São João–São José, where rural property holdings were more extensive and urbanization more limited, and the area largely isolated from the effects of the coffee boom, the weight of property holdings also fell, from 40.4 per cent in 1815–25 to 33.7 per cent in 1850–60 (Frank, 2005, 244).

[22] Formally, this is calculated as (1 − Proportion of Family Farms)*(1 − Urbanization). The first term provides a sense of land-ownership concentration; the second term provides the rural population density weight.

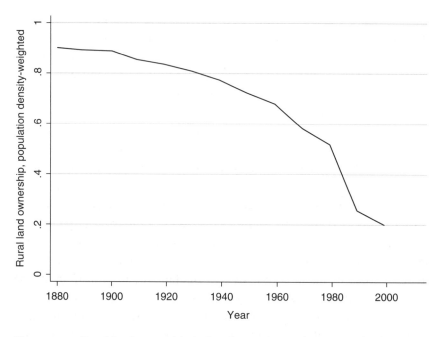

Figure 3.22: Rural land ownership in Brazil, population density-weighted, 1880–2000.
Source: Ansell and Samuels (2010).

uncertainty (Assunção, 2008). But, as we discuss below, the general trend has been for other forms of wealth to have taken on greater importance.

Owner-occupied housing has long been of paramount importance in Brazilian household wealth portfolios. For most of the nineteenth century, Frank's estimates indicate that residential property made up the single largest category of wealth – averaging 38 per cent of holdings – for the wealth-holders of Rio de Janeiro, São João–São José and São Paulo (Frank, 2004, 40, 73, 88; 2005, 244). During this time, home ownership was widespread, at least among wealth-holders, of whom nearly 60 per cent owned at least one property. Housing wealth, however, was highly concentrated: estimates from 1815–1825 indicate that the richest 20 per cent owned 78 per cent of housing wealth, with the remainder held by the middle 60 per cent (Frank, 2004, 42). The Gini coefficient for urban residential property wealth in Rio de Janeiro was 0.83 in 1820 and 0.82 in 1855; wealthy residents typically owned multiple houses from which they derived significant rental income (Frank, 2004, 60).

Home ownership was increasingly democratized after the Second World War, becoming widespread even among lower socio-economic strata (De Ferranti et al., 2003, 431; Torche and Spilerman, 2008, 159). This pattern is due to the prevalence of squatting settlements in urban areas (*favelas*) and government housing policies. By 1988, the home ownership rate had reached nearly 59 per cent, climbing to over 70 per cent since the early 1990s – above levels in Britain and the United States (Fay and Wellenstein, 2005, 93; Torche and Spilerman, 2008, 157; World Bank, 2002, 12). Among middle-class households (defined either as the middle three quintiles or the third to eighth decile), ownership rates have averaged more than 67 per cent since 1990, not far below levels in these advanced countries.

Housing has become the most widespread asset in Brazil; indeed, for a large proportion of the population, particularly at the lower end of the wealth distribution, owner-occupied housing is the only asset in their portfolio (De Ferranti et al., 2003, 194). Since 2000, non-financial assets – principally housing (land and dwellings) – have, on average, comprised more than 58 per cent of household wealth (Credit Suisse Research Institute, 2017a). However, due to the prevalence of squatting, a large proportion of the poor do not hold formal title. Many self-declared home owners may in fact be squatters, which is consistent with the low proportion reporting a mortgage (see below). The absence of legal title for these households – estimated to be as high as one-third of the population – has clear negative implications for a household's ability to collateralize its home equity. Yet for the middle class, residential property likely provides a more accessible store of value. By the 1990s, these households (defined here as the middle three quintiles) held 42 per cent of total housing wealth, while the top quintile held 50 per cent (Torche and Spilerman, 2008, 161).

The historically high level of ownership has not been accompanied by elevated levels of household debt. The housing finance system in Brazil is considerably smaller than that found in advanced countries. Whereas mortgage debt to GDP averaged 55 per cent in advanced countries from 2001 to 2005, it averaged just 2.6 per cent over the same period in Brazil (Warnock and Warnock, 2008). Yet mortgage borrowing has increased substantially in recent years, rising from 4.6 per cent of GDP in 2007 to 9.4 per cent of GDP in 2015 (Housing Finance Information Network, 2018). Data on mortgage loan penetration in Brazil indicates that 10.5 per cent reported having a mortgage from a financial institution in 2014, a much smaller proportion than the 33 per cent reported in advanced countries. Within Brazil, the richest 60 per cent of households report higher rates of mortgage borrowing (13.2 per cent) than the poorest 40 per cent (6.4 per cent), suggesting that housing finance is making inroads among the middle and upper classes.

Banks provided limited credit to households during the years of high inflation, but the success of the *Real* Plan in stabilizing prices led Brazilians in 1994 to take out consumer credit in what Baer and Nazmi describe as 'unprecedented amounts' (Baer and Nazmi, 2000, 9). Private bank credit to households soared by more than 180 per cent in one year. Household debt, most notably consumer loan products and mortgages, has registered a substantial increase since the early 2000s but remains at a level roughly equivalent to that last observed in advanced countries in the 1960s (Ferreira et al., 2013, 141; International Monetary Fund, 2013).

The lack of available data makes it difficult to describe with high certainty the pattern of household borrowing before 1995. As discussed in Chapter 2, the size of the housing finance system and mortgage loan penetration are closely correlated with private credit as a proportion of GDP. In addition, mortgage lending as a share of overall lending increases with higher levels of private credit to GDP, as does household borrowing as a share of overall borrowing. The household debt data in Figure 3.23 seems to follow this pattern in the post-1995 period. As such, the 1970s might have seen household borrowing levels similar to that observed from 1995 to 2003, with less elevated levels likely present during the 1960s and 1980s. Notwithstanding the data limitations, we can conclude with certainty that household borrowing has grown rapidly over the past decade and presume with some confidence that by 1980 it reached a level similar to that observed in 1995, then fell sharply in the 1980s and again in the early 1990s, before rising to the level observed in 1995.

Only a small number of banks operated in Brazil for much of the nineteenth century, and for much of the twentieth century the banking system was regionally concentrated. In 1888, Brazil had twenty-six banks, located in only seven of the twenty states, with half of the deposits stored in Rio de Janeiro (Topik, 1987, 28). Banks did not play an active role in providing household credit in the nineteenth century, specializing instead in discounting short-term paper and

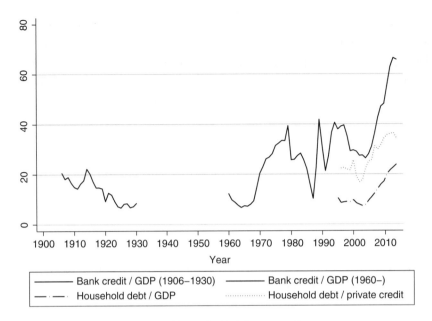

Figure 3.23: Private credit and household debt in Brazil, 1906–2014.
Source: Bank for International Settlements (2017b); Musacchio (2009, 64)
(per cent).

providing short-term credit to finance agricultural exports and working
capital for firms (Hanley, 2005; Musacchio, 2009, 60–6; Triner, 2000).
Households instead obtained credit through personal connections
(Triner, 2000, 24–5). Such informal credits were an important form of
wealth, particularly for wealthier households, comprising until the
1890s more than 10 per cent of household portfolios (Frank, 2004,
40, 73, 88; 2005, 244).

Even as the banking system expanded after the creation of the
republic in 1889 (see Chapter 11), bank credit continued to focus
mostly on short-term commercial transactions, such as discounted
paper, short-term loans, advances on commercial paper, and mortgage
loans largely to the agricultural sector (Hanley, 2005, 138–9, 168;
Triner, 2000, 70). Moreover, the stock of loans remained small compared to those recorded in advanced countries.

By the 1920s, the banking system was dominated by the Banco
do Brasil (BB). The government had effectively nationalized BB
following a series of severe banking crises in the late nineteenth and
early twentieth centuries (see Chapter 11), though it did not take a
controlling share in the bank until 1923 (Deos, Ruocco and Rosa,

2017, 69). As the government's agent in international debt markets, the bank received government surpluses as deposits, extended loans to the Treasury based on expected revenues, and enjoyed a monopoly on note issuance. BB accounted for about one-third of domestic banking activities, with the remaining share controlled by a small number of domestic banks. Foreign banks also held a commanding position in Brazil, providing about 56 per cent of total loans, most of which were concentrated in financing foreign trade (Goldsmith, 1986, 99–101).

Brazil experienced substantial growth in the number of banks between the two world wars, but banking remained regionally concentrated. In 1936, the cities of Rio de Janeiro and São Paulo accounted for two-thirds of the country's bank deposits and mortgages; many parts of the country lacked banking services. At the end of the Second World War, two-fifths of banks had their head offices in Rio de Janeiro and one-quarter in São Paulo. Branches were somewhat more diversified: the state of São Paulo had one-third, Minas Gerais one-fourth and Rio Grande do Sul one-tenth (Goldsmith, 1986, 166).

The failure of BB and private banks to adequately satisfy the credit demands of the agricultural sector led many state governments to create commercial banks in the 1920s and 1930s.[23] By the 1970s, there were twenty-four state commercial banks operating in Brazil. As in other countries in the developing world, the objective behind these banks, as well as state development and savings banks that were also later created, was to help overcome capital market failures by allocating credit to productive sectors not served by private banks, especially agriculture and small and medium-sized firms. At the federal level, in the 1950s the government established the National Bank for Economic Development (BNDES) to promote financing for infrastructure and industrial investments as well as some regional development banks (Ferreira and Rosa, 2017). In the 1960s it also created a Housing Bank (BNH) to finance housing and related infrastructure construction, which was merged with the state-owned Caxia Econômica Federal (CEF) in 1986 (Deos, Ruocco and Rosa, 2017, 70). By the early 1970s, government banks had come to dominate Brazilian domestic banking activities, holding 55 per cent of deposits and accounting for 60 per cent of loans to the private sector (Baer and Nazmi, 2000, 6).

---

[23] Prior to that time only two state governments – Minas Gerais (in 1889) and Paraiba (in 1912) – had created banks.

Government-owned financial institutions maintained these shares of the banking system deposit and loans until the late 1990s (Nakane and Weintraub, 2005, 2265). Private domestic banks held roughly 40 per cent of deposits and 33 per cent of loans, with foreign banks accounting for the remainder.

As in advanced countries, the holdings of financial assets in Brazil are considerably more concentrated than those for housing assets (Frank, 2004, 82). The principal source of data on the distribution of financial asset ownership comes from household surveys, though under-reporting by and under-representation of wealthier households often make them even more problematic than usual in the case of Brazil (De Ferranti et al., 2003, 64; Torche and Spilerman, 2008, 166). Estimates of asset ownership distribution based on these surveys thus likely provide, at best, a lower bound.

Household surveys asking about 'capital income, land rents, and profits' provide an approximation of the distribution of financial asset ownership in more recent years. Given the high concentration of income in Brazil, it is expected that capital assets will be clustered at the top end of the distribution. Surveys since 1990 reveal that, although income from 'capital, rents, and profits' is concentrated in the top income quintile – on average more than 80 per cent of asset income – the middle three quintiles also derive a modest share – on average more than 17 per cent (De Ferranti et al., 2003, 429). Thus, the stake of modern Brazilian middle-class households in financial assets is far from insignificant.

Turning to different types of financial assets, available data indicates rapid growth in deposits since the early 1990s (see Figure 3.24). The volume of deposits remained fairly constant until a brief sharp rise and rapid fall in the late 1980s and early 1990s as the economy experienced hyperinflation. Growth in bank deposits has since then carried on largely uninterrupted, recently reaching levels last observed in advanced countries during the early 1990s.

Data on the size of deposit holdings before 1960 is limited but it was almost certainly smaller, especially in the nineteenth century. Per capita bank deposits stood at US$17.50 in 1921 and US $20.00 in 1928, compared to $152.10 and $235.80 respectively in these years in the United States (Topik, 1987, 52). By 1930, the banking system was about thirteen times the size it had been in 1906, measured in terms of real price-adjusted deposits. Yet despite

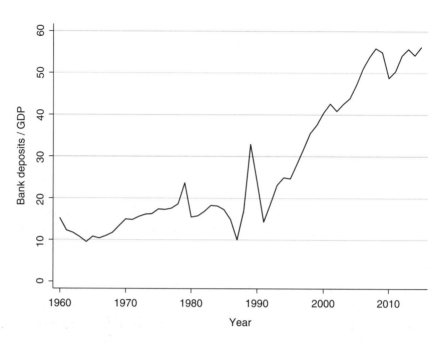

Figure 3.24: Bank deposits / GDP in Brazil, 1960–2015 (per cent).
Source: World Bank (2017).

this rapid growth, Brazil in 1930 continued to exhibit a level of financial depth that was considerably lower than that observed in advanced countries in the nineteenth century (Triner, 2000, 81, 101). In 1930, Brazil had 0.15 financial establishments (bank headquarters and branches) per 10,000 people, a very low level of bank density. By contrast, the United Kingdom had a density rating of 0.77 when it began its industrialization more than a century earlier, and the United States in 1920 had a density rating of 2.94 (Cameron, 1967, 20–4; Topik, 1987, 52). As noted already, banking was also highly concentrated in Rio de Janeiro and São Paulo.

Until the 1890s, cash and bank deposits made up less than 10 per cent of total wealth among wealth-holders in Rio de Janeiro (Frank, 2004, 40, 73, 88). Cash and bank deposits were far more important in the capital than elsewhere where informal personal credit instruments dominated (Frank, 2005, 244). Following the outlawing of slavery and a period of exceptional monetary easing (see Chapter 11), bank deposits and cash grew in importance, at least among wealth-holders of Rio de Janeiro, reaching nearly 20 per cent of household wealth over the period from 1890 to 1895.

Unfortunately, it is difficult to make claims about the weight of deposit holdings in wealth portfolios until more than a century later, by which time households had become increasingly exposed to market-based financial assets. Data from the OECD indicates that deposit holdings have constituted more than 20 per cent of financial assets since 2009 (OECD, 2018). In addition, World Bank household surveys found that 56 per cent of households in 2011 and 68 per cent in 2014 had an account at a formal financial institution. As with mortgages, access was higher among the richest 60 per cent of households, exceeding 67 per cent in both surveys. Among the poorest 40 per cent of households, account access was nearly 40 per cent in 2011 and roughly 58 per cent in 2014. The growth of private credit since the late 1980s – which is closely correlated with account access – would also suggest growing exposure to banks as stores of deposit wealth. This is also consistent with data from the IMF showing rapidly expanding supply-side access to financial institutions, particularly since the early 1990s when the index approaches, and later exceeds, the average level found in advanced countries (see Figure 3.25). It suggests financial institutions are responding to growing demand from Brazilian households for financial services.

As Brazilian households have become wealthier, their portfolios have shifted toward riskier market-traded assets connected to financial markets in a manner not observed in the nineteenth century. Between 1815 and 1825, stocks and bonds comprised less than 2 per cent of the holdings of Rio de Janeiro wealth-holders and just 0.2 per cent of the holdings of those in São João–São José (Frank, 2004, 40; 2005, 244). After 1850, following changes to the commercial code, the number and size of joint-stock companies grew rapidly, though not as fast as in the 1880s and 1890s following additional reforms discussed in Chapter 11. In addition to these developments, the availability of government bonds and the introduction of railroads and state-subsidized railroad bonds increased the avenues for investment, especially for residents of Rio de Janeiro. In the six decades after 1885, stocks and bonds averaged roughly 8 per cent of portfolios of Rio de Janeiro wealth-holders (Frank, 2004, 73, 88). By contrast, in the period between 1850 and 1860, their weight was 5.6 per cent in the portfolios of wealth-holders in São João– São José and 1.6 per cent for those in São Paulo (Frank, 2005, 244).

By the late 1880s, owing to institutional reforms that facilitated an equity market boom (see Chapter 11), public and private securities

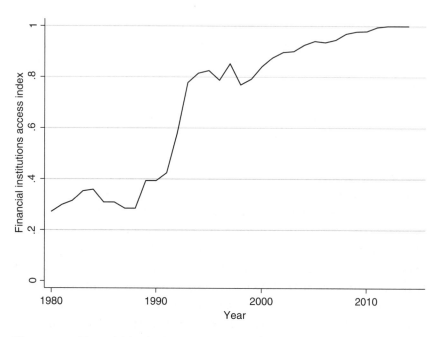

Figure 3.25: Financial institutions access in Brazil, 1980–2015.
Source: Svirydzenka (2016).

traded in the stock exchanges of Brazil increased their importance as a share of household wealth. The share of household wealth invested in stocks and bonds grew from 11.5 per cent of estate valuations in Rio de Janeiro in 1868–73 to over 32 per cent between 1885 and 1889. In Rio, these assets were largely concentrated in the hands of the wealthy, with the top quintile of wealth-holders accounting for more than 90 per cent of the holdings (Frank, 2004, 89, see also 41). In São Paulo, holdings of company stocks were more equally distributed across income strata between 1881 and 1895, but more heavily concentrated in the hands of wealthier households in earlier periods (Hanley, 2005, 78).

Aggregate financial wealth grew rapidly after the macroeconomic stabilization achieved by the *Real* Plan in the mid-1990s. According to Brazil's central bank, 'mutual funds' as a proportion of GDP increased from 11.6 per cent in 1995 to 30.2 per cent by 2001 (Goldfajn, Hennings and Mori, 2003, 22). This wealth was clustered in the top end of the income distribution. In 2001, the top quintile accounted for more than 88 per cent of income from stock dividends, with the top decile receiving nearly 77 per cent of the income (Torche and Spilerman, 2008, 167). As the middle-class share of wealth increased from the early 1990s, it is likely that so too did its exposure to this asset class. In 2001, the middle three quintiles accounted for nearly 12 per cent of the income from stock dividends. Across Brazil as a whole, ownership of stocks and securities outside pension funds has comprised more than 40 per cent of financial assets since 2009, which is considerably more than observed in Britain (16 per cent) and only somewhat less than that found in the United States (52 per cent) (OECD, 2018).

Pension assets have made up more than 12 per cent of household financial assets since 2009, roughly the level observed in Germany and Denmark over the same period (OECD, 2018). The Brazilian private pension scheme is the oldest in Latin America. The first regulations, which established the Complementary Pension System (CPS), were issued in 1977, though there are some private pension funds that are more than 100 years old. The CPS is composed of both a closed system managed by corporate pension funds instituted in 1977 and covering employees of a specific firm or group of firms, and the open system, a product of the *Real* Plan in 1994, managed by banks and insurance firms open to any individual worker.

The basic social security system, which first emerged in 1923, covers private sector workers and is a conventional pay-as-you-go system providing defined benefits.[24] The system combines low qualifying conditions for a full pension with large benefit payments as a percentage of average earnings, making it one of the most generous in the world and one of the costliest among emerging and developing countries (OECD, 2015a). The replacement ratio is relatively high for the 92 per cent of the working population earning less than the benefit salary ceiling. The average earner entering the workforce in 2014 could expect a net replacement rate of 80 per cent of her earnings upon retirement (OECD, 2015a, 28). Compared to the private sector social security scheme, public sector employees receive even higher pensions for lower contribution rates and qualifying conditions. These pension privileges were entrenched in the 1988 Constitution (Cardoso and Graeff, 2012, 20). Until pension reforms in 2002, civil servants retired

---

[24] The Brazilian social security system is notable for the existence of unequal access and benefits. Until the 1988 Constitution, access to retirement pensions was generally restricted to workers formally employed in urban areas, which excluded the vast majority of the population in rural or informal employment. Moreover, some occupational categories, such as civil servants and military staff, enjoy privileged benefits vis-à-vis other workers.

on 100 per cent of their final salary and were not able (or did not need) to join private schemes. As a result, the overall coverage rate of the private pension system has been somewhat limited.

Membership (active participants and retirees) in the closed system was 1.18 million in the 1970s and 1.84 million in the 1980s. It later grew to 1.98 million in the 1990s, 2.91 million in the 2000s and now stands at 3.24 million (Associação Brasileira das Entidades Fechadas de Previdência Complementar, n.d.). The coverage rate has remained fairly constant at 2.2 per cent of the active labour force, or 3.7 per cent of the population when non-active beneficiaries are included (Pugh and Pinheiro, 2009, 9; Reis and Paixão, 2004, 3). While low, it is important to recall that the proportion of the working population earning above the monthly social security salary ceiling stands at just 8 per cent. If we assume these workers are the principal participants in the private pension market, then the coverage extends to more than a quarter of this segment of the population.

Closed entities manage the largest proportion of pension assets, but open entities grew in importance from roughly 2 per cent of the private pension market in 1994 to 15 per cent in 2003. Before 1990, private pension assets were limited in size, averaging 1.4 per cent of GDP in the 1970s and 2.3 per cent of GDP in the 1980s. Pension assets then increased steadily between 1990 and 2003, reaching nearly 16 per cent of GDP, a level that has been more or less maintained in subsequent years. By 2003, Brazil had accumulated the seventh largest private pension assets and the twelfth largest pension assets to GDP ratio in the world (Reis and Paixão, 2004, 3).

Initially, the closed entity market grew based on employment ties in large state-owned firms, but later large private firms began to offer benefit plans to employees, and since 2003, coverage has been extended to small and medium-sized private firms, labour unions, professional associations and civil servants. But state-owned company pension funds remain the largest players in the market, holding nearly two-thirds of closed-entity assets, with the three largest pension funds accounting for more than 40 per cent of the assets (Reis and Paixão, 2004, 5).

Pension law in Brazil recognizes three distinct plan designs: defined benefit (DB), defined contribution (DC) and variable contribution (VC). VC plans are 'mixed plans' that are pure DC during the accumulation phase but retain a life annuity obligation after retirement. The individual is thus subject to market risk during the accumulation phase but then transfers that risk upon retirement.

The shift toward DC private pensions began in the 1980s and accelerated in the 1990s. DB schemes are still dominant in the market but most are closed to new entrants (Pugh, 2009, 2). By law, new funds sponsored by unions, professional associations and the government must be DC. Available data since 2003 shows the steady exposure of Brazilian pension wealth in closed entities toward DC schemes in terms of the proportion of operating plans, membership and assets (see Table 3.4).

In summary, the wealth of Brazilian households has grown significantly in recent decades from a considerably lower base than that observed in Britain, the United States and other advanced economies. During the nineteenth century the overwhelming majority of Brazilians

Table 3.4. Brazilian closed pension market by scheme type, percentage of total

	2003	2008	2009	2016
Plans				
DB	37	36	35	30
DC	16	33	35	37
VC	47	31	30	33
Membership				
DB			38	33
DC			20	26
VC			42	41
Assets				
DB			81	67
DC			6	11
VC			13	22

Sources: Associação Brasileira das Entidades Fechadas de Previdência Complementar (n.d.); Pugh (2009, 3); Pugh and Pinheiro (2009, 9); Reis and Paixão (2004, 5).

held little, if any, wealth and instead were largely dependent on income from labour, much of it outside the formal sector. This remained the case for much of the twentieth century. Although housing assets became increasingly democratized after the Second World War, a great many Brazilians, especially the poor, lacked legal title for the property. Nonetheless, by the 1990s, middle-class households laid legal claim to a substantial proportion of housing assets.

The success of the *Real* Plan and growing financial inclusion induced a rapid rise in financial assets held by the middle class. Rising household wealth – what in Chapter 2 we called the size effect – led to a sharp increase in the stake that middle-class households had in financial markets. In recent decades a growing number of Brazilian households, like those in advanced countries, have become exposed to DC pension assets and rising leverage. As market-traded assets and credit markets have become increasingly important for Brazilian households, this has undoubtedly heightened their stake in financial stability. Yet when compared to households in advanced economies, the average Brazilian middle-class household has seen less change in the composition of its wealth portfolio; instead, traditional bank deposits continue to dominate.

Much of this less volatile deposit wealth remains held in state-owned financial institutions. Both the composition of household wealth and the market share of state-owned banks should have important implications for the kinds of wealth protection policies that households are likely to prefer. Deposit insurance will likely feature as a crucially important form of wealth protection. Moreover, given the substantial share of deposit wealth held in private domestic banks (roughly 40 per cent in the mid-1990s), this should heighten preferences for formal deposit insurance – a measure that Brazil did not put into place until 1995 during a systemic crisis (see Chapter 12). By contrast, societal demand for a larger range of policy measures to stabilize asset prices and credit markets should be considerably more muted than observed in advanced countries.

3.4   Conclusion

The evidence provided in this chapter reveals an unmistakable trend: households in the United Kingdom, the United States and even

Brazil have experienced a rapid accumulation of wealth and a heightened exposure to the financial system. Wealth accumulation, financialization and the democratization of leverage are common features across each of these countries. Financial markets now hold great sway over modern household fortunes and livelihoods in each of these countries in a manner that differs sharply from earlier times.

The wealth portfolios of modern households in each of these countries mean that middle-class voters now have a much greater stake in financial stability. We would expect the size and composition effects to be associated with this rising middle-class wealth and exposure to leverage and market-traded assets, and growing financial inclusion in these countries. Empirically, the changing material stake of middle-class households in financial stability should be associated with the rise of great expectations in each of these countries, as household demand for financial stability grows in intensity and the middle class joins the bailout constituency during crises. We now turn to evidence in the next chapter to assess this claim.

4 THE EMERGENCE OF GREAT EXPECTATIONS IN THE UNITED KINGDOM, THE UNITED STATES AND BRAZIL

> What sound reason is there why the Government should undertake to protect depositors in banks, any more than it should endeavour to protect those depositors in dealings with each other?
> *New York Times*, Congress and Finance, 10 February 1873

> Continental Illinois Bank is being nationalized. Much as it must pain the Administration to find that free market remedies aren't always best, Government is taking over. Thanks be for Government.
> *New York Times*, A Bank Held Up by Government,
> 29 July 1984

A critical component of our argument is that great expectations held by citizens about government responsibilities for preventing and mitigating the impact of financial crises emerged in the first half of the twentieth century and evolved and intensified after the 1970s. In this chapter, we provide more substantive empirical justification for this central claim.

We noted in Chapter 1 that the experience of the Great Depression led many governments after 1945 to protect society against the effects of financial crises on incomes and employment. More generally, the perceived need for governments to manage financial markets in the broader public interest prompted a variety of new policies and regulations during and after the war (Allen et al., 1938; Busch, 2009; Helleiner, 1994, 25–50; Hall, 1993).

We also noted that there was a strong component of wealth suppression and redistribution in this early post-war policy consensus. Over time, the emphasis on employment protection and wealth suppression shifted to one of wealth protection and accumulation and we seek to show in this chapter how this reflected the changing expectations of an increasingly wealthy middle class. We present the results of our analysis of the evolution of newspaper opinion in the United Kingdom, the United States and Brazil concerning responsibility for and appropriate policy responses to banking crises from the nineteenth century to the present. Our argument leads us to expect that the evolution of newspaper opinion, as a proxy for changing mass expectations, should reveal that, when compared to the earlier era, extensive government interventions to stabilize the financial system for purposes of wealth protection now command stronger support and public officials now are held more responsible for financial instability. The evidence is strongly consistent with this expectation.

In addition, we show that changing newspaper opinion was paralleled by evidence from longitudinal household surveys examining public attitudes regarding public responsibility for and appropriate policy responses to banking crises. This evidence also suggests that the broader trend in voter expectations regarding financial stability and wealth protection diverged somewhat from changing voter attitudes concerning government responsibility for other aspects of social and economic life. That we observe each of these broader trends in all of our country cases strongly supports our argument that great expectations took hold during an era of wealth accumulation, financialization, democratizing leverage, and new financial policy commitments.

4.1 Utilizing Newspaper Opinion: Justification and Method

Ideally, we would use longitudinal household surveys to measure voter responses to these developments. Yet extensive data of this kind is not available. Public opinion surveys began in the mid-1930s in only a few countries and even in these cases contain little information pertinent to our study.[1]

---

[1] George Gallup founded the American Institute of Public Opinion in 1936 and established a British subsidiary; other pioneers such as Elmo Roper and Louis Harris helped to launch scientific polling in the 1930s and 1940s.

Accordingly, we follow others in making use of newspaper coverage in our three country cases as an alternative indicator of public opinion. Epstein and Segal (2000), for instance, find that front page newspaper coverage by major national newspapers provides a 'reproducible, valid, and transportable measure' of citizen attention to political issues. Drawing on this important finding, Culpepper (2010) makes use of cross-national data on front-page press coverage to study the political salience of issues of corporate control in Europe and Japan.[2] Lodge and Wegrich make use of patterns of national discourse on financial regulation following the 2007–8 financial crisis to investigate 'the extent and direction of public attention' (2011, 727).

We are also interested in the content of argumentation in newspaper editorials following banking crises and accordingly we go well beyond merely measuring article counts. Editorials are of value for our purpose because they can provide indirect evidence of changing voter expectations of government financial stabilization over the long run. Editorials may primarily reflect elite opinion and suffer from political bias, but over long periods of time they are likely to bear a general relationship to broader societal opinion, particularly if the mass public take their cues from these opinion leaders (Lupia, 1998; Popkin, 1994) and newspapers have strong incentives to tailor their opinions to the beliefs of their consumers (Gentzkow and Shapiro, 2010, 64).[3] To counter concerns about political bias, we use editorials from leading newspapers with long publication histories and large circulations that represent a diverse range of partisan leanings, as well as financial centre and regional opinion.

We use content analysis of the argumentation patterns in these editorials, employing comparable search terms and queries for each of our country cases. However, the availability of digitized newspapers

---

[2] Other studies include Jones and Baumgartner (2005) and Smith (2000).

[3] We assume opinion diffuses in social groups from individuals who read newspapers, despite lower literacy rates (roughly 50 per cent in England in 1825, 80 per cent in the United States in 1857, and 15 per cent in Brazil in 1890) during some of the earlier crises in our analysis (Love, 1970, 8; Mitch, 2004, 344; United Nations Educational, Scientific and Cultural Organization, 2005, chap. 8). For example, there is evidence of a vigorous print media influencing political debate in the United Kingdom well before the nineteenth century (Stasavage, 2011, 161). Importantly, the literate population comprised all eligible voters in Brazil until the removal of the literacy requirement in 1985, and, in all likelihood, a large segment of eligible British voters until male suffrage was gradually expanded over the course of the nineteenth century. The spread of formal schooling and other learning opportunities contributed to a transition to widespread literacy in each of these countries by the second half of the twentieth century.

with sophisticated Boolean search capabilities was uneven within and across our three country cases. We thus adapted the search protocol to best approximate a Boolean search in cases where it was not available. We provide a full specification of our search protocol and methods in the online appendix for this chapter.[4]

The writing of editorials as a practice, distinguishing between the opinion of the editors and 'factual' reporting, emerged in the nineteenth century in Europe and the United States and diffused later to other countries. All of the British and American newspapers in our sample contained for the full search period separate opinion editorials that represented the views of the respective publication's editorial board. However, opinion editorials did not appear in most Brazilian newspapers until the post-1945 period. Staff from the Brazilian newspapers that remain in print were unable to provide information that would enable us to identify the precise year when opinion editorials were introduced. As a result, when clearly identifiable opinion editorials were unavailable, we coded relevant articles that expressed an editorial-like opinion (asking: 'Does the article make statements that express judgments about the attribution of blame or the appropriateness of policy responses to banking crises?') and that did not include an author byline. This procedure provides us with a reasonable depiction of the content of newspaper opinion at given moments. However, since articles with editorial-like opinion appear with much greater frequency than distinct opinion editorials, the sample generated from Brazilian newspapers is typically considerably larger than that for American and British newspapers.

Our analysis involved two manual coding tasks: first, the identification of claims of blame apportionment for public and private actors; and second, identifying support for or opposition to measures related to the Bagehot and bailout models of crisis intervention that we outline in greater detail in Chapter 5. In each case, we began at a far more granular level, first specifying various different private and public actors (see below), and various different policies that we associate with either Bagehot or bailout responses. We then asked coders to characterize blame and support/opposition expressed in each newspaper document. Finally, we aggregated these codings into private/public blame, and support/opposition to Bagehot/bailout responses. We employed a scale ranging from 1 to 5, with higher values indicating greater blame of

---

[4] www.cambridge.org/TheWealthEffect

public (private) actors, and lower values indicating greater exoneration of public (private) actors. We use the same scale for policy responses, with higher values indicating greater support of (opposition to) bailout (Bagehot) measures, and lower values indicating greater opposition to (support of) bailout (Bagehot) measures. As in our analysis throughout this book, we focus only on banking crises designated as systemic in major datasets (Laeven and Valencia, 2013; Reinhart, 2010; Reinhart and Rogoff, 2009). This reduces the likelihood that editorial opinion might vary simply due to the relative severity of crises. As in Chapter 5, we considered all newspaper documents published within a window that extends from the onset of a crisis to three years after the end-date specified in major datasets.[5]

Ten coders carried out the content analysis after extensive training and reliability testing. A reliability pre-test using eight editorials across four crisis windows in the United Kingdom and the United States confirmed that the coders were applying the protocol with the acceptable levels of agreement and inter-coder reliability. Each country team of coders received a detailed summary of each crisis window to provide them with background knowledge for the coding. Coders were then randomly assigned newspapers and crisis windows to ensure that any remaining coding error would distribute randomly. We used a double-blind sampling method to check for intercoder reliability (giving a kappa intercoder score of 0.83). Every fifth editorial within each crisis window was assigned to more than one coder. For each crisis window we set a threshold of 10 per cent as the minimum number of editorials that would be cross-checked.

4.2   The Evolution of Editorial Opinion on Crisis Policy Responses

We begin with newspaper opinion in the United Kingdom, the United States and Brazil concerning appropriate policy responses to banking crises from the nineteenth century to the present. Economic knowledge about policy responses to banking crises improved considerably over the course of the nineteenth century (Grossman, 2010,

---

[5] In cases of follow-up crises, where the new crisis start-date and post-crisis horizon overlap, we truncate the post-crisis horizon.

chap. 4). As we detail in Chapter 5, the intellectual foundations for market-conformist crisis resolution policies and the conceptual framework for LOLR operations were laid in the early nineteenth century. As the nineteenth century progressed, experience accumulated with measures associated with bailouts, such as creditor guarantees and indiscriminate, uncollateralized, open-ended or subsidized liquidity support that ran against Bagehot's famous dictum. It was thus not the case that newspaper editorialists resembled Sidney Webb in the 1920s in being unable to imagine policy measures outside the confines of free-market orthodoxy (Cairncross and Eichengreen, 1983, 5). On the contrary, observers had already become aware that government rescues of failing financial institutions were within the realm of possibility.

4.2.1 United Kingdom

The United Kingdom has a long history of financial crises, national newspaper publishing, and iconic status in the history of central banking policy. Figure 4.1 provides an overview of the

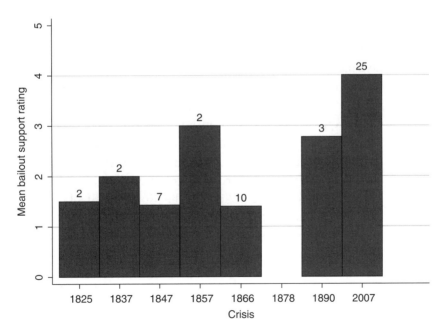

Figure 4.1: Government policy responses and newspaper opinion in the United Kingdom across eight systemic crises.
Note: Newspaper document counts above bars. None were found in 1878.

argumentation patterns of five British newspapers (the *Daily Telegraph*, *The Economist*,[6] *The Times*, the *Financial Times* and *The Guardian*) for eight systemic banking crises (1825, 1837, 1847, 1857, 1866, 1878, 1890, 2007). There is an unambiguous trend towards rising support over this period in British newspaper editorials for public assistance to banks during financial crises. During the nineteenth century the mean level of support for bailouts across all editorials was 1.74 on our five-point scale. This places average opinion at the time in strong to moderate opposition to public assistance to ailing banks. Yet by the time of the 2007 crisis editorial opinion had shifted sharply to moderately strong support for bailouts (4.01 on our five-point scale). This difference in means across these two sample time periods is highly significant ($t = 8.81$, $p < 0.001$).

Throughout the nineteenth century British newspaper editorialists usually articulated a firm market-conformist conviction that ailing financial firms should be permitted to fail without assistance. In the course of widespread banking failures during the deep 1825 crisis (see Chapter 7), *The Times* worried that ailing banks might gamble for resurrection and insisted that public assistance should be withheld:

> ... it would be for the good of society that an insolvent firm [bank] should sink. Difficulty leads to desperation – the partners plunge, and try experiments and speculate – their demands, often successful, upon the credit of great capitalists, are more serious – their mode of living manifests an increase of ostentatious expense and as their means diminish, and their debts accumulate, the destruction they inflict is more extensive the longer they can manage to retard it. Therefore, we assert, and we do so, as well on the strongest grounds of deliberate conviction as with an earnest anxiety for the protection of all innocent and honest men, that to inspire confidence in houses which can at last only repay it by insolvency, is to perpetrate direct wrong, and dreadfully enhance a great commercial evil. If a house fails ... a foolish cry is often raised, that a little reasonable help would have saved it. Saved what? A house that was in relation to its debts, one quarter worse than nothing. Ought such a

---

[6] Walter Bagehot edited *The Economist* from 1861 to 1877, thus covering only the 1866 crisis.

house to be left standing – we again put it to any reasonable man – in a condition where it was every hour made the depositary of other people's money? … He is not a legitimate banker.[7]

The Guardian articulated a similar view during the 1866 crisis:

One great advantage, however, has been obtained from the crisis. It has extinguished the finance companies, which, ever since their origins, have proved themselves perfect nuisances in the Money Market, by diverting the loanable capital from its legitimate employment – from that of discounting against goods, or real transactions, to that of discounting for speculation.[8]

Over the course of the nineteenth century British editorialists often expressed support for the proposal that the then privately owned Bank of England should provide limited collateralized lending consistent with Bagehot's rule. In 1847, *The Guardian* praised efforts by the Bank of England to lend to solvent but illiquid firms ('men engaged in the more quiet and routine business of life [that] cannot long afford to pay discounts rated according to the perils or the temptations of a crisis') on terms that were 'safe to themselves' (i.e. by requiring sound collateral).[9] As commentators came to accept and support the Bank's role as a lender of last resort, they rejected fiscal intervention by the government. In the 1847 crisis, *The Guardian* explicitly disavowed any government responsibility:

We are in no degree driven from this position by the loud cries for what they call 'assistance' that are daily heard from the masses of losing speculators, whose numbers and whose importunity are on the increase, and who seem desirous to bully the Government – that is to say, the public – into an interference in their favour at the expense of every other class.[10]

---

[7] *The Times*, The Perplexities in the City, 15 December 1825.
[8] *The Guardian*, The Government Has Authorized the Directors of the Bank of England, 13 May 1866. Note that before 1959 *The Guardian* was known as the *Manchester Guardian*, but we use the abbreviated form throughout.
[9] *The Guardian*, It is impossible to commit, 4 October 1847.
[10] *The Guardian*, There is no feature more remarkable, 24 October 1847.

In later crises, such as 1866, editorialists endorsed the government's willingness to suspend the 1844 Bank Charter Act, which permitted the Bank of England to issue notes freely (see Chapter 7). *The Times* suggested:

> It may, therefore, be plausibly urged that the discount business of the Bank of England should be enlarged so as to satisfy the pressing wants of the hour, and that the capital necessary for such enlargement should be raised, under the sanction of the Executive Government, by such means as may appear best fitted for a purpose purely temporary.[11]

The Guardian praised the Bank of England's support as '[i]t prevented the failure of every really solvent company and house.'[12] Similarly, *The Times* wrote, '[H]ad it not been for the large assistance and aid afforded by the Bank of England there is great probability that the failure of banking companies would have resembled that in the year 1825, when, with the exception of the Bank of England, nearly the whole of the London banks stopped payment.'[13]

We found no evidence that editorialists supported interventions involving a direct fiscal contribution from the government, with one exception. As mentioned in Chapter 2, national savings banks were present in several countries during the nineteenth century and fell under state control or were subject to special regulatory requirements that limited their allowable activities outside of deposit-taking and investing in government bonds. These quasi-charitable institutions emerged in the United Kingdom in the late eighteenth century with the aim of encouraging the poor to save to protect themselves against old age and illness. An 1817 Act required that funds deposited in savings banks were invested in government bonds or deposited at the Bank of England. Depositors were provided with an explicit government guarantee of the nominal value of their savings so long as their funds were invested in bonds or deposited at the Bank of England. The government sought to discourage the use of savings banks by the upper and middle classes by setting a maximum deposit threshold.

---

[11] *The Times*, The shock which agitated the City of London, 11 May 1866.
[12] *The Guardian*, The question put last week in the House of Commons, 12 August 1866.
[13] *The Times*, If anything can justify a suspension of the Bank, 12 May 1866.

Importantly, the 1817 Act extended the deposit guarantee only once the funds had reached the safe custody of the National Debt Commissioners or the Bank of England. This opened up the possibility of depositor losses due to fraud and embezzlement (Roberts, 2013b; Ross, 2013). Such was the case during the 1857 crisis. As a result, the government introduced legislation that would extend protection to all savings bank depositors, even those whose savings had yet to reach safe hands. At the same time the government cut the maximum deposit protection in half, explicitly to limit its responsibility and to ensure that it would not aid the middle class.[14]

The initial deposit guarantee had provided a very low level of wealth protection for a specific and limited category of households as part of paternalistic state efforts to promote frugality. The 1857 legislation extended its scope but reduced the amount of this guarantee. The episode thus reflects how government guarantees are like a ratchet: they often expand in crises because in circumstances of asymmetric information there are always some households who believe they are deserving of protection and pressure governments to extend existing commitments. At the same time, it also indicates how the relative weakness of this pressure compared to a century later allowed the government to disavow extensive responsibility for wealth protection by reducing the level of coverage present in the guarantee.

Contemporary newspaper opinion, as offered in *The Times*, supported this effort while calling for greater oversight of these institutions:

> It is evident that, with deposits to the amount of nearly £35,000,000, belonging to thirteen hundred thousand depositors, the Savings-Banks require cautious legislation, and stricter control than has yet been exercised over them. In fact, the Government has always been, and still is, in a false position respecting them. The Banks have in the eyes of the depositors, and of the greater part of the public, a national character; and this belief, though unfounded, has been sufficient to induce Government to make, in more than one case, compensation to

---

[14] An 1824 revision of the 1817 Act put a limit of £50 on deposits in the first year, and £30 in subsequent years, with a maximum total of £200. The 1857 revision lowered the threshold to £100. See http://hansard.millbanksystems.com/commons/1857/may/11/savings-banks-considered-in-committee#S3V0145P0_18570511_HOC_29.

those who have suffered by mismanagement or fraud ... A national guarantee is desired by the depositors, and is offered by the Government. Such a guarantee would restore the whole system to efficiency, and effect a great and lasting improvement in the habits of the people. It is for sensible men to consider whether they will reject this offer, offered so freely, and on terms so little burdensome.[15]

More than three decades later, the Bank of England's intervention in the 1890 crisis – which involved organization of a guarantee of Barings' liabilities by private London banks and finance houses – departed sharply from previous policy precedents in the United Kingdom. Although Barings was to be liquidated, unbeknownst to the public at the time, the government had given verbal assurances that it would accept half of the potential losses that might have fallen on the Bank of England. *The Economist* supported the decision to allow Barings to go into liquidation, arguing that:

It would, no doubt, be very gratifying to big loan and finance houses to have it laid down that if they only over-commit themselves to the extent of a sufficient number of millions, the combined resources of the Bank of England and the leading joint stock banks throughout the country will be used to tide them over their difficulties with as little loss as possible, whereas people with smaller commitments would be left to shift for themselves ... But it certainly would not be to the public advantage if any countenance were given to such principles.[16]

A number of editorials strongly endorsed the actions of the Bank of England in defusing the crisis, but there is no evidence to suggest that any of them were aware of the hidden contingent liability to which the government had exposed itself, and no suggestion of any government responsibility for crisis resolution. Writing three years after the crisis, the *Financial Times* reiterated its endorsement of the value and magnitude of the response of the Bank of England:

The formation of the Baring Guarantee Fund by Mr. Lauderdale [the Bank's governor] was a magnificent example of a

---

[15] *The Times*, No one will, we think, be disposed to deny, 13 May 1857.
[16] *The Economist*, 22 November 1890.

strong man's capacity for prompt action in a crisis. That action
THE FINANCIAL TIMES has always unhesitatingly endorsed,
and we still do so. It is very easy to be wise after the event, and
Mr. Lauderdale himself, in view of three years' subsequent
experience, cannot fail to see that the results of his policy are
not entirely satisfactory. ... [H]ad the Bank of England not
acted as it did, the most vivid imagination cannot paint what
would have occurred. If the crisis of November, 1890, had been
allowed to work itself out to its own conclusion, we should not
have had, in its present form, the crisis of November, 1893.
What lay before Mr. Lauderdale in 1890 was the choice
between such a financial collapse as has never occurred before
in the financial history of London, and a prolonged agony such
as the City has gone through during the past three years.[17]

By the time of the 2007 crisis British newspaper editorialists,
including those philosophically attached to market principles, had abandoned their earlier support for market-conformist responses, articulating
instead a very different consensus. 'The lesson of history', *The Economist*
said, 'is that early, decisive government action can stem the pain and cost
of banking crises,'[18] and: 'Banks have a special status in the economy:
that is why they receive bail-outs when other companies should not.'[19]
Principled stances in favour of market-conforming policy solutions, such
as those initially adopted by the Bank of England (see Chapter 8), found
little support in the face of financial collapse. As *The Guardian* observed:

Mr. King [governor of the Bank of England] ... held out on
financiers last summer when they demanded he pump more
money into the system. After all, ran the reasoning, why should
the Bank bail out financiers from their own mess? A bit of pain
might encourage reflection and reform. That was a good policy,
but eventually the banking turmoil got so bad – threatening to
turn a slowdown in the wider economy into something much
worse – that the Bank of England relented ... Faced with that
kind of turbulence, Mr King and his colleagues have no alternative but to lend money to banks.[20]

[17] *Financial Times*, November, 1890 and 1893, 11 November 1893.
[18] *The Economist*, Saving the System, 9 October 2008.
[19] *The Economist*, Banking Bail-outs: Leaving Las Vegas, 20 November 2008.
[20] *The Guardian*, Banks: in trouble again, 21 March 2008.

Editorialists repeatedly stressed that government intervention was justified to avoid generating a system-wide crisis that would put the economy and the value of a wide range of assets at risk. *The Guardian* worried that the 'the collapse of a major mortgage lender [Northern Rock] would have had much bigger consequences for our economy' than intervention.[21] *The Times* emphasized the strong societal interest in the continued flow of credit, and, like *The Economist* editorial above, the consequences of policy inaction: '[I]t is far better to expose the taxpayer to limited risk now than to risk systemic failure in a panic-stricken banking system, which could turn the current shortage of loans into a prolonged drought and land the taxpayer with a bigger long-term headache.'[22]

By this time, the interest in preventing systemic collapse appears in many editorials as overriding the concerns about limiting immediate taxpayer exposure. *The Guardian* described the rescue of British banks as 'eye-wateringly expensive. But by throwing a lifeline he [the Prime Minster Gordon Brown] has done the right thing.'[23] Later, *The Guardian* wrote, 'This [rescue] will be a messy, costly, business, but fixing the plumbing often is'[24] and it will have 'prevented a wide banking collapse'.[25] *The Times* expressed concern about 'taxpayer exposure to the banking sector', but stressed 'the Government was right to recapitalise the banks'.[26]

Such support for government intervention was not uncondi-tional. 'Not all banks are equally worth preserving,' wrote *The Guardian*.[27] Those 'which are no longer viable ... should be wound up'.[28] Highlighting voter perceptions of distributional unfairness, it called for 'A Bail-Out for Savers, too', urging that 'London should follow Dublin's example and ... extend a total guarantee ... [to] stop this anxiety turning into a panic.'[29] Yet blanket guarantees, while protecting small savers, generate large contingent liabilities of uncertain value for the taxpayer and can have regressive implications for the wealth

[21] *The Guardian*, Banks and Markets: Northern Exposure, 15 September 2007.
[22] *The Times*, Saving Banks from Themselves, 22 April 2008.
[23] *The Guardian*, Financial Crisis, Launching the Lifeboats, 9 October 2008.
[24] *The Guardian*, Banking crisis: Unblocking the Pipes, 15 January 2009.
[25] *The Guardian*, Financial crisis: Our money, our banks, 17 February 2009.
[26] *The Times*, The Risks of Currency Weakness, 21 November 2008.
[27] *The Guardian*, Banks: in trouble again, 21 March 2008.
[28] *The Guardian*, Banking Crisis: Time for Action, 7 October 2008.
[29] *The Guardian*, Bank Accounts: A Bail-Out for Savers, too, 4 October 2008.

distribution as taxpayers' money is used to insulate large depositors and bank creditors from losses. This episode illustrates how the expectations and demands of modern voters are often inconsistent and conflictual.

4.2.2 The United States

As in the British case, Figure 4.2 shows a rising trend of support for bank rescues in editorials of six major US newspapers (the *New York Times*, the *Chicago Tribune*, the *Boston Globe*, the *Washington Post*, the *Los Angeles Times* and the *Wall Street Journal*) for ten systemic banking crises (1857, 1873, 1884, 1890, 1893, 1907, 1914, 1929, 1984, 2007). It indicates that average editorial opinion prior to the Great Depression was in strong opposition to public assistance to ailing banks (1.16 on our five-point scale, even lower than in the United Kingdom). The Great Depression then marked a transitional era where editorial opinion became increasingly open to the possibility of government intervention (2.98 on our five-point scale, or slightly less than the 'neutral position'). Thereafter, editorial opinion became significantly

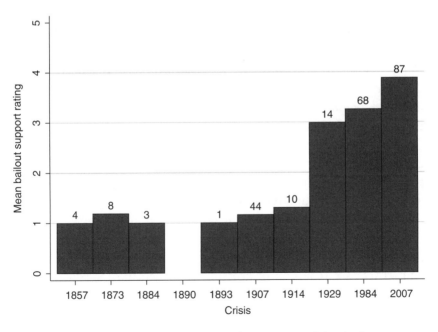

Figure 4.2: Government policy responses and newspaper opinion in the United States.
Newspaper document counts above bars.

stronger in its support for government intervention, averaging 3.61 on our five-point scale in the post-1970 era, with support peaking during the 2007 crisis period. As for the United Kingdom, the difference in means between pre-1939 and post-1970 crises is highly significant $(t = 11.79, p < 0.001)$.

Like their counterparts in the United Kingdom, American editorialists in the nineteenth century generally praised decisions to permit insolvent banks to fail, even if it imposed losses on households. Writing during the Panic of 1873, the *Boston Globe* asserted:

> The great house of Jay Cooke and Company was known in almost every household in the land, and its downfall will set not only those who may have suffered by investing their money in its railroad bonds, but the people generally thinking of financial subjects ... [Yet,] they must pay the penalty like any other unwise investor.[30]

At the same time, the *New York Times* editorialized that 'the business of a bank of deposit and discount has nothing in it that requires Government supervision' (15 October 1873) and advocated private sector solutions to financial distress (19 September 1873). The newspaper also opposed insulating savers from losses due to bank failures, as indicated in the quote at the top of this chapter.

Editorial opposition to deposit insurance remained strong through the early twentieth century. In the aftermath of the 1907 crisis, the *Washington Post* disparaged proposals from Democratic presidential candidate William Jennings Bryan for a national deposit insurance scheme as 'socialistic'.[31] Similarly, the *Wall Street Journal* opined that government insurance of bank deposits 'is distinctly socialist in its character. It is another of those schemes which are intended to destroy individual initiative and responsibility.'[32]

However, unlike other newspapers in our sample, the *Los Angeles Times* was an early supporter of public deposit insurance, partly for the reason that it would reduce the incentive for bank runs, and partly as a reflection of growing voter demand for protection of household wealth: 'If assured by Uncle Sam that he could not lose a

---

[30] *Boston Globe*, The Financial Catastrophe, 24 September 1873.
[31] *Washington Post*, A Vicious Proposition, 1 October 1908.
[32] *Wall Street Journal*, Unloading Responsibility Upon the Government, 27 November 1907.

dollar, a depositor would not rush to withdraw his funds from a bank in time of panic ... [and] ... we would have an additional and even more important insurance against loss through bank failures.'[33] Recall from Chapter 3 that the level of deposit wealth held by American households at the time was high by contemporary global standards. As we detail in Chapter 9, the growth of deposit wealth since the Civil War and pressure from poor Southern and Western farmers for financial protection induced several states to adopt deposit insurance for state-chartered banks after the 1907 crisis. It is thus not surprising that the *Los Angeles Times* reflected these growing demands from voters, as did some Western and Southern members of Congress who authored virtually all of the failed federal legislative proposals for deposit insurance between 1907 and 1931 (Calomiris and White, 1994, 155).[34]

In the absence of a central bank, editorial opinion, with the exception of the *Boston Globe*, generally supported the Treasury's provision of limited emergency liquidity consistent with Bagehot's principles.[35] A *New York Times* editorial during the Panic of 1893 is representative: 'Free loaning on reasonable collateral will avert the worst feature of the possible panic – money stringency.'[36] Editorials in this period also made clear that more extensive government intervention should be neither expected nor demanded, as the *New York Times* stated after liquidity provision during the Panic of 1857: 'Mr. Cobb [Secretary of the Treasury] has done his whole duty, and more, to avert the trouble to the banking movement ... [This] relieves the Government of all responsibility [for further measures].'[37] Later, during the Panic of 1873, the *New York Times* warned against 'drifting into a position of dependence on the Government in all sudden and great emergencies'.[38] Editorials in the *New York Times* during the 1884 crisis also raised

---

[33] *Los Angeles Times*, To Insure Bank Depositors, 23 January 1907.
[34] Many local newspapers also supported proposals for public deposit insurance at this time. For example, in Oklahoma, the first American state to adopt such a scheme (in 1908), the *Orlando Clipper* from Logan County editorialized that 'No bank can fail in any town in the United States without injury to every other bank in the town. The ... loss of business and loss of confidence amounts to far more than the amount of tax the bank would have to pay into the proposed guaranty fund.' *Orlando Clipper*, Regarding a Guaranty Law, 24 January 1908.
[35] *Boston Globe*, The Dangers of Expansion, 24 November, 1873; *Boston Globe*, New Schemes of Inflation, 29 December 1873.
[36] *New York Times*, The Wiser Heads in Wall Street, 22 December 1895.
[37] *New York Times*, The Panic and the General Government, 19 October 1857.
[38] *New York Times*, 4 March 1874.

concerns that even limited liquidity provision would weaken market discipline by 'offer[ing] money to those who do not need it and who could get it without difficulty on the bonds which it is offered to pay'.[39]

By the time of the 1907 crisis, contemporary policymakers and opinion leaders were aware that bouts of monetary stringency and panic were likely to be recurrent without a central bank with note issuing and rediscounting privileges that could provide greater elasticity to the money supply (see Chapter 9). In its wake, editorial opinion, while supportive of the Treasury's limited liquidity provision and the private rescue led by J. P. Morgan, strongly endorsed the creation of a central bank.

Importantly, contemporary opinion saw a would-be central bank as responsible for addressing liquidity shocks rather than problems of insolvency. As such, we code editorials advocating the creation of a central bank as supporting Bagehot measures. 'What we want', wrote the *Wall Street Journal*, 'is elastic circulation to prevent panics.'[40] 'A central bank, organized under a proper system, would afford elasticity of the circulation. It would meet the demands for an increased issue of notes in the crop-moving season, without imposing undue strain upon the New York money market. It would prevent those violent fluctuations ... It would afford support for country banks ... It would put an end to the pressure of the country banks upon the central reserve cities for legal tender money.'[41] The *Journal* emphasized 'the utility of the central bank in saving the money market from disaster'.[42]

At the start of the Great Depression, editorialists still preferred limited central bank liquidity provision and a private-sector-led response to the crisis. The *New York Times*, for instance, praised Hoover's plans to create the National Credit Corporation – a government-encouraged private sector initiative that would rescue solvent but ailing banks – as 'convincing and reassuring' without calling for more extensive government involvement.[43] Exclaiming that 'economic recovery will begin. President Hoover has clearly marked

---

[39] *New York Times*, The Wall Street excitement, 15 May 1884.
[40] *Wall Street Journal*, Working Together, 19 November 1907.
[41] *Wall Street Journal*, A Central Bank of Issue, XIV, Summary of the Argument, 6 November 1909.
[42] *Wall Street Journal* 12 October 1909. See also *New York Times* 27 October 1907; *Los Angeles Times*, Two Democrats and Finance, 29 October 1907.
[43] *New York Times*, To mobilize banking resources, 8 October 1931.

the path to its door,' the *Wall Street Journal* endorsed the creation of the Reconstruction Finance Corporation (RFC) – an institution to provide collateralized lending to local and state governments, banks and business – as 'amply justified'.[44] The *New York Times* called the RFC 'a great piece of work'.[45] It also opposed the idea of abandoning the gold standard – which some claimed constrained the Federal Reserve from lending freely to stem the panic – as one found 'only in inexperienced minds'.[46] The *Boston Globe*, however, remained sceptical of even limited efforts like the RFC, calling on members of Congress to 'resist this amazing effort to put the Government Treasury into the business of financing of private undertaking that are plainly extravagant for industry and Nation alike'.[47]

As the banking crisis intensified in the early 1930s, there are clear signs of a shift of editorial opinion towards supporting more extensive interventions, though not yet as wholeheartedly as would be the case by the 1980s. Many editorialists shifted to support Roosevelt's early actions to restore financial stability and protect the remaining wealth of lower- and middle-class Americans. Editorial opinion reflected the growing demands of many of these voters to stabilize the banking system and protect their (often diminishing) access to mortgage credit. But support did not yet extend, as it would in later crises, to protecting a wider range of financial assets and services. The *Washington Post* supported 'a high degree of liquidity'[48] provision from the Federal Reserve 'to bolster up the credit system'.[49] The *Boston Globe* praised Roosevelt's declaration of a bank holiday and measures taken while the banks remained closed – which included de facto 100 per cent deposit insurance (see Chapter 9) – as 'actions which only a powerful Government could have taken ... The net result of all this was to establish a center of order and power in the midst of panic and confusion.'[50] And the *Washington Post* supported the deposit guarantee as

[44] *Wall Street Journal*, The Path to Recovery, 5 February 1932.
[45] *New York Times*, As Europe Sees Us, 26 June 1932.
[46] *New York Times*, The Gold Standard, 10 January 1932.
[47] *Boston Globe*, A dubious scheme, 13 June 1932.
[48] *Washington Post*, Banking outlook improves, 2 March 1933.
[49] *Washington Post*, Banking Difficulties, 4 March 1933.
[50] *Boston Globe*, The First Roosevelt Year, 27 February 1934. See also *Wall Street Journal*, Do the New Dealers Understand the New Deal?, 8 June 1933.

having 'served a useful purpose ... to induce people to restore hoarded funds to the banks'.[51]

Like British editorialists, those in the United States articulated a very different set of views during more recent crises, going far beyond the comparatively modest expectations articulated during the Great Depression. In both the 1980s Saving and Loans crisis and the 2007–8 crisis, editorialists repeatedly stressed the enormous costs of policy inaction and supported policies to protect household wealth and the flow of credit put at risk from bank failures. In 1984, following the costly and extensive intervention to rescue Continental Illinois, which at the time was likely insolvent and became the largest bank failure in US history, the *Washington Post* wrote:

> Rapid and massive federal intervention only barely averted a banking panic last week on a scale that this country has not seen in half a century. The federal government is totally justified in organizing this huge rescue. If this panic had not been caught in time, the damage would not have been limited to one Chicago bank. Much of the cost would have fallen, as usual, on depositors and borrowers who deserve none of the blame for it.[52]

In a reversal of the earlier 'liquidationist' orthodoxy (see Chapter 9), the *Post* claimed, 'Everybody agrees that assuring the stability of the financial system is more important than consistently letting badly run businesses fail.'[53] The *New York Times* was also enthusiastic in its praise for what it described as the government's nationalization of Continental Illinois, as indicated in the quote at the top of this chapter. Three years later, even as costs of the savings and loan crisis accumulated, the *Post* emphasized the greater consequences of systemic collapse: 'Congress is setting an important precedent here. It is acknowledging the federal government's responsibility as the lender of last resort. Averting the collapse of financial institutions is usually expensive. But it is far less expensive than the alternative.'[54]

---

[51] *Washington Post*, A banking reform program, 28 July 1936.
[52] *Washington Post*, Editorial, 20 May 1984.
[53] *Washington Post*, Protecting the System, Not Depositors, 22 May 1984.
[54] *Washington Post*, Bailing Them Out Is Better, 11 September 1987. See also *Washington Post*, S and L Indecision, 10 March 1991.

The *New York Times*, writing in the early stages of the 2007 crisis, called not only for assistance to Wall Street but also for a 'government bailout' to provide 'aid to people or industries in financial distress ... [and] shield them from the full losses they would incur if left entirely to the vagaries of the market'.[55] After the government rescue of Fannie Mae and Freddie Mac in July 2008 (see Chapter 10), the *Chicago Tribune* commented: 'No one likes to see privately owned companies bailed out for bad decisions. But letting these two fail would punish untold millions of innocent people as well as the guilty.'[56] Emphasizing the consequences of the failure of two pillars of the American housing finance system, the *Tribune* later wrote: 'The Treasury intervention over the weekend was deemed essential to avoid a collapse that would have done to the economy what Hurricane Katrina did to New Orleans.'[57] Although reflecting voter concern about the costs, the *New York Times* emphasized that 'dangers to our jobs, our credit transactions and or savings'[58] made the expensive rescue necessary to 'stop the stock market from failing ... and to save us all from economic Armageddon'.[59]

As in the United Kingdom, there were voices that cautioned against unconditional taxpayer support of ailing banks. 'Perhaps our ears are deceiving us,' wrote the *Wall Street Journal* during the savings and loan crisis, 'but we seem to be hearing speculation that ultimately the nation's taxpayers will have to bail out sick banks and thrift institutions. That might be one idea of solution. It is not ours.'[60] Calling for more safeguards in rescuing banks during the 2007–8 crisis, the *Boston Globe* urged members of Congress not to 'abdicate their responsibility to protect taxpayers' interests. Maybe, just maybe, companies that allocated their money recklessly shouldn't be rewarded by simply having the government take soured investments off their hands.'[61] However, the overall trend in US editorials towards supporting bailouts in the interest of broader financial stabilization is clear.

---

[55] *New York Times*, B Is for Bailout, C Is for ... , 10 September 2007.
[56] *Chicago Tribune*, Fannie and Freddie mess, 17 July 2008.
[57] *Chicago Tribune*, Bail out of future bailouts, 9 September 2008.
[58] *New York Times*, Rescue the rescue, 30 September 2008.
[59] *New York Times*, The Final Debate, 16 November 2008.
[60] *Wall Street Journal*, Bad Banking Deserves Penalties, 30 May 1988.
[61] *Boston Globe*, The blank check buyout, 23 September 2008.

In supporting financial rescues, editorials called for early and decisive measures, capturing concerns about the costly consequences of delayed intervention. The *Washington Post*, for instance, channelled voter frustration with the legislative stalemate that had led to the escalation of the costs of the savings and loan crisis:

> BEFORE CONGRESS adjourns, it is going to have to come up with more billions for the S and L cleanup. Otherwise the operation will run out of money sometime around the end of the year and come to a full stop for several months until the next Congress can pass legislation. That would mean more delays in the process of putting the failed savings and loan associations out of business, with still higher costs to the public.[62]

In a similar vein, during the 2007–8 crisis, the *Boston Globe* admonished that 'Congress shouldn't drag its feet in formulating a systematic response to the financial crisis.'[63]

Lastly, as in the United Kingdom, US editorials reflected the tension in voter expectations: a demand for financial stabilization but dissatisfaction with perceived distributional unfairness. The *Boston Globe* aptly summarized this view: 'Many US taxpayers were understandably outraged at the thought of bailing out bankers who have made unwise bets, but that was the only way to prevent the global financial system from locking up.'[64] Concerns about distributional unfairness featured on both sides of the political spectrum. On the centre-left, the *New York Times* expressed concern that the interventions 'would in effect shift most of the risk of the banks' bad debts onto taxpayers'.[65] It later criticized the government for doing 'more to shield the banks from losses than to help homeowners and stabilize the market'.[66] On the centre-right, the *Chicago Tribune* warned the interventions would 'create a nation of bailout junkies'.[67] Similarly, the

---

[62] *Washington Post*, More Money for the S and Ls, 20 October 1990. See also *Washington Post*, Costs of the S and L Cleanup, 6 August 1989 and *Washington Post*, Last Installment for the S and Ls, 28 June 1993.

[63] *Boston Globe*, Bailout temptations, 23 September 2008.

[64] *Boston Globe*, Mass. should join mortgage deal, giving economy a way forward, 2 February 2012.

[65] *New York Times*, Bank Bailout, Redux, 8 February 2009.

[66] *New York Times*, The Mortgage Challenge, 2 December 2012.

[67] *Chicago Tribune*, Bailout Nation, 16 November 2008.

Boston Globe argued against 'new programs designed to make life better for selected groups holding more debt than they can manage'.[68]

4.2.3 Brazil

We find a similar trend in newspaper opinion in Brazil to that in the United Kingdom and the United States. Figure 4.3 indicates a sharp rise in support for government intervention, in newspaper documents of six major Brazilian newspapers (*Jornal do Brasil, O Paiz, O Estado de São Paulo, O Globo, Folha de São Paulo, Jornal do Commercio*) for seven systemic banking crises (1890, 1897, 1900, 1914, 1920s, 1985, 1990, 1994). Prior to the 1990s, average newspaper opinion remained in fairly strong opposition to intervention to rescue failing banks (1.5 on our five-point scale). Support for intervention was significantly higher in the 1990s (3.4 on our five-point scale, $t = 7.09$, $p < 0.001$), though – as we would expect – it remained somewhat lower than that observed in the more highly financialized United Kingdom and the United States. What is particularly striking is that we detect the strongest support for bailouts to be during the 1990 crisis when the government implemented a decidedly Bagehot response that imposed losses on depositors (see Chapter 12). As we detail later in the book, the government suffered politically when it disappointed voter expectations. Newspaper opinion remained, on average, supportive of bailouts in the following crisis, but the intensity of the support was somewhat tempered by the distributional implications. This suggests that in 1990s Brazil the support of newspaper opinion (and, by implication, modern voters) for bailouts was most intense precisely when the government was failing to provide them.

The earliest crisis in Figure 4.3 followed an expansionary credit programme in which the government authorized a number of banks to issue inconvertible paper currency (see Chapter 11). The resulting inflation and asset boom and bust triggered a systemic crisis in 1890, with subsequent crises in later years, as banks fell under the weight of unrecoverable loans made during the boom years. Newspaper opinion, like that in the United Kingdom and the United States, favoured permitting distressed institutions to fail. *O Paiz* editorialized: 'Continuing to liquidate the banks is the only feasible solution after the horrendous

---

[68] *Boston Globe*, Helping the economy?, 31 October 2011.

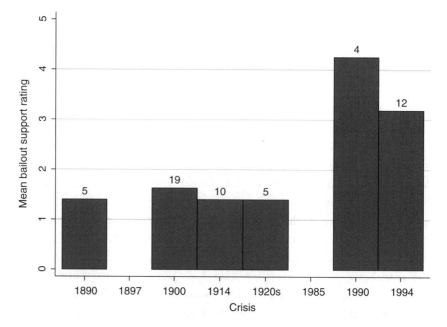

Figure 4.3: Government policy responses and newspaper opinion in Brazil. Newspaper document counts above bars.

actions of the institute of credit [note-issuing banks].'[69] It praised the government's efforts to close and restructure insolvent banks: 'We must applaud the minister of finance. His ideas are driving a sensible and beneficial change.'[70] 'The government of Dr Campos Sales [president from 1898 to 1902] has, with honourable and undeniable sincerity, tried to finish its difficult mission to reconstruct the national financial organism.'[71]

In the absence of a central bank, opinion in the earliest crisis supported limited emergency liquidity provision by the Treasury so long as it was consistent with Bagehot's principles and did not the entail the issuance of inconvertible paper currency. Adherence to the latter principle became even more pressing after the government signed a

[69] O Paiz, Factores de desconfiança [Factors of distrust], 4 March 1901. These and the following translations were provided by specialist coders with native Brazilian Portuguese language skills.

[70] O Paiz, Circulaçao Ouro [Gold Circulation], 7 March 1901.

[71] O Paiz, Os Fundos Publicos [The Public Funds], 14 January 1900. See also Jornal do Commercio, A Crise da Praça. O Thesouro e o Banco da República [A Crisis in the Square. The Treasury and the Banco da República], 23 February 1900.

funding loan in 1898 with the Rothschilds that prohibited paper currency issuance. The *Jornal do Commercio* supported collateralized lending to distressed firms as part of the 'aid to industry' campaign in 1892 (see Chapter 11): 'We beg, once again, the government, that it meets the requirements of our national firms.'[72] However, amidst widespread banking failures in 1900, *O Paiz* rejected the idea of issuing paper currency to provide liquidity support: 'The solution that appeals to all is the issuing of more paper currency; however, this solution is absolutely impossible.'[73] It applauded when 'The government quickly rejected the ruinous idea of issuing more paper currency.'[74]

There was no consensus on this issue after the disruption of World War I, when the government's decision to issue paper currency for the first time since 1891 to provide liquidity support to banks that could provide the necessary collateral aroused significant controversy. *O Estado de São Paulo* claimed 'the banks need physical cash to boost the cash cycle within the economy'.[75] Three months later, it asserted: 'Given our country economic and financial facts of the present, I dare to affirm, gentlemen, that there is no financier who is against the inconvertible paper currency that does not recognize the necessity of the emissions as an essential contingency of the moment.'[76] *O Paiz* disagreed: 'Unfortunately, the governing plans of any politician are always equal to that of the most ignorant bar-clerk: taxes, loans, and paper money.'[77] Thus, the tension in Brazil at the time was largely between those who advocated non-intervention and those who favoured intervention consistent with Bagehot's principles.

Support for the latter position grew over time, particularly as contemporary opinion increasingly came to favour the creation of a central bank. The nation's largest commercial bank and the Treasury's financial agent – the Banco do Brasil (BB) – gained a monopoly on note issuance in 1923 and gradually developed some functions of a central

[72] *Jornal do Commercio*, Commercio e lavoura [Trade and farming], 30 January 1892.
[73] *O Paiz*, A praça [The square], 16 September 1900.
[74] *O Paiz*, A Crise da Praça [The Crisis in the Square], 19 September 1900.
[75] *O Estado de São Paulo*, Importância do aspect econômico [Importance of the economic aspect], 22 September 1915.
[76] *O Estado de São Paulo*, Marcha depressiva de nossa economia [The depressive march of our economy], 22 December 1915. See also *Jornal do Brasil*, Banco do Brasil, 30 April 1917.
[77] *O Paiz*, A carestia da vida. Inércia Criminosa do Governo [The high price of life. The criminal inertia of the government], 24 December 1915.

bank, including rediscounting the notes of other banks, but it was not a central bank and its role as a lender of last resort remained informal. As in the United States, when newspaper opinion advocated the creation of a central bank, it did so in part based on the need to strengthen policy-maker capacity to respond to liquidity shocks, not solvency concerns. Therefore, we consider such arguments to be in favour of Bagehot measures. 'The universal solution [to a series of liquidity shocks facing banks in the 1920s]', wrote *Folha da Manha*, 'is given by the almost one hundred years in the mobilization of the reserve banks through a central reserve bank.'[78] Creation of a central bank, observed *O Estado de São Paulo*, would provide 'help in case of a truly exceptional crisis'.[79]

The response of newspaper opinion to the government's intervention in the Banco da República do Brasil (BRB) in 1900 represents a partial exception to opinions opposing any government responsibility for crisis resolution. The BRB, like its successor the BB, had a semi-public status as the nation's largest commercial bank and the Treasury's financial agent; the government selected some of its senior management (see Chapter 11). Since the government also relied on the BRB to acquire and liquidate the assets of failed banks, the BRB itself became steadily illiquid as the quality of its loan portfolio deteriorated. The government provided the ailing bank with collateralized liquidity support, but was ultimately forced to nationalize it, imposing a tough settlement on its shareholders and creditors (this eventually led to the creation of the 'new' BB).

Newspaper opinion largely endorsed this intervention, which combined elements of both Bagehot and bailout. *O Paiz*'s defence invoked a peculiar combination of both nationalism and a need to maintain Brazil's credibility to foreign investors: 'To deny the bank the patriotic assistance it asked for would be to sacrifice the credit of the nation, to condemn the most intelligent forces of the country to a state of dismay.'[80] It supported the government's nationalization: 'It is evident that the direct intervention of the government in the management of the business of Banco da República do Brazil guarantees to all

---

[78] *Folha da Manha*, Problema bancario e creditorio [The banking and credit problem], 5 September 1928. See also *Folha da Manha*, O Banco do Brasil e a crise financeira [Banco do Brasil and the financial crises], 28 June 1926.

[79] *O Estado de São Paulo*, Situaçao Bancaria [Banking situation], 27 July 1915.

[80] *O Paiz*, A Crise da Praça. A soluçao da crise [The crisis in the square. The solution to the crisis], 15 September 1900.

the best of the possible solutions.'[81] O *Estado de São Paulo* called the government's response 'commendable'.[82]

It worth noting the reasons *not* articulated in support of the intervention, namely that the BRB's collapse would put household wealth and access to credit at risk. In fact, the loss of shareholder and creditor wealth posed little concern in newspaper documents at the time.

Such was not the case when crises struck Brazil in the 1990s.[83] Then, Brazilian editorialists articulated a new consensus that underscored the importance of protecting growing household wealth and dependence on credit. Brazil was without formal deposit insurance until 1995 (see Chapter 12), but when in 1990 the government froze financial assets and imposed losses on depositors as part of its strategy to combat rising inflation, newspapers such as the *Jornal do Brasil* opposed it as a 'savings confiscation ... in flagrant violation of the constitutional text'.[84] It later argued that 'the investor must be protected by a creditor's insurance, such as the American FDIC [Federal Deposit Insurance Corporation], in order not to discourage savings'.[85] In addition to wealth protection, the *Folha de São Paulo* raised the need to maintain the flow of credit: 'Those who cry 'let them fail' forget that it is not only the interests of bankers that are at stake. So are those of the depositors and borrowers, who have not caused the difficulties of the banks.'[86]

Like those in the United Kingdom and the United States, Brazilian newspapers by this time supported financial rescues to avoid the greater consequences that would result from systemic collapse. As newspapers did in earlier crises, the *Jornal do Brasil* highlighted the 'interest of preserving Brazil's creditworthiness in the international financial market, preventing the illiquidity of paper from troubled state banks from hurting other issuers, starting with the National

[81] O *Paiz*, A Crise da Praça [The crisis in the square], 19 September 1900. See also O *Paiz*, A Crise da Praça. A soluçao da crise [The crisis in the square. The solution to the crisis], 15 September 1900, and O *Paiz*, O Governo e a Praça [The government and the square], 17 September 1900.

[82] O *Estado de São Paulo*, A soluçao da crise [The solution to the crisis], 16 September 1900.

[83] There were no recorded editorials relating to the 1985 banking crisis. We suspect this is because, in this year of political transition and an ongoing debt crisis, editorialists focused their attention on other issues, including debt and macroeconomic policy.

[84] *Jornal do Brasil*, O enigma da inflaçao [The enigma of inflation], 22 November 1991.

[85] *Jornal do Brasil*, Dividas e Duvidas [Doubts and Debts], 19 May 1994.

[86] *Folha de São Paulo*, Precisamos de bancos que nao precisem se salvos [We need banks that do not need to be saved], 2 December 1995.

Treasury'.[87] The *Jornal do Commercio* opined: 'In the cost–benefit evaluation, the Central Bank technicians have no doubt that the government needs to intervene and inject resources. Failure to do so will result in a greater loss.'[88] The *Folha de São Paulo* articulated this rationale at length:

> What should be emphasized is preservation of integrity of the financial system and not the rescue of individual banks ... Who pays the bill? In this case, the credibility of the system would fall to zero and a localized problem would detonate in a domino effect that would drag down the entire system, with unforeseeable consequences for the economy. The government correctly described the lesser evil as a restructuring of the banking sector in order to strengthen the system as a whole. In this episode the interest of depositors was preserved and not that of the majority and minority owners of the banks. The cost to the Treasury, reflected in the low increase in the financing granted, was certainly much lower than that which would result from a financial crisis at the national level.[89]

Later, the *Folha da São Paulo* praised the 1990s intervention as critical in avoiding future negative economic and financial consequences: 'The resilience of the Brazilian financial system to the Asian crisis highlighted PROER's [Program of Incentives to the Restructuring and Strengthening of the National Financial System] effectiveness as a private bank rescue programme undertaken two years ago by the Brazilian government. If it were not for that state initiative, Brazil, like so many other countries, would be facing the bankruptcy of its banking system, irreversibly jeopardizing the national development process and its hard-won economic stability.'[90]

Yet newspapers also vented concerns about the interventions. While supporting government interventions in ailing state-owned banks

---

[87] *Jornal do Brasil*, Dividas e Duvidas [Doubts and Debts], 19 May 1994.
[88] *Jornal do Commercio*, Saneamento total [Total sanitation], 22 January 1998. See also *Jornal do Commercio*, Quatro anos em oito [Four years in eight], 22 February 1998.
[89] *Folha de São Paulo*, É papel do governo preserver a integridade do sistema [It is government's role to preserve the system integrity], 2 December 1995. See also O *Estado de São Paulo*, Diferenças e semelhanças com a Asia [Differences and similarities with Asia], 21 January 1998.
[90] *Folha de São Paulo*, Editorial, Atração por bancos [Editorial, Attraction for banks], 7 April 2000.

in the 1990s, the *Jornal do Commercio* argued: 'it is not enough to promote financial relief alone. Either the state banks play the role of regional development agencies, and play an invaluable role, especially in the more backward regions, acting under strict technical criteria, or they must be extinguished or privatized.'[91] The *Jornal do Brasil*, also a supporter of intervention, wrote: 'Nothing justifies, however, the return of paternalism to the financial market. Banks – official or private – must face the brunt of falling inflation through tough domestic sanitation [i.e. cleaning up] measures.'[92] Similarly, the *Folha da São Paulo* called for 'transparent incentives to accelerate the processes of merger and extinction of fragile banks'.[93] As we discuss in Chapter 12, these criticisms derived in part from the widespread perception that state banks had been used by successive governments for narrow political purposes.

Moreover, as in the United Kingdom and the United States, newspapers focused on perceptions of distributional unfairness. While backing the case for intervention, the *Jornal do Brasil* suggested, 'It is a grave mistake, however, to channel public resources, which are lacking in hospitals and schools, to maintain in operation instruments of political support (public banks) and the employment of bankers.'[94] The *Jornal do Commercio* expressed a similar view on PROER, which, as we discuss in Chapter 12, provided assistance to private banks:

> Proer was another scandal! Proer was a bailout program for [private] banks that were in financial difficulty. In order not to prevent collapse, the Government came in to help and the bankers were saved. It's a shame that the Government has got the rotten part of the story! But who swallowed it? The rotten thing remained for the people, who certainly did not see the advantage of this help. But, why is this not done with micro and small business owners?? Why did the Government let these 'small entrepreneurs' close their doors and increase the number of unemployed?? For sheer political convenience![95]

---

[91] *Jornal do Commercio*, Saneamento total [Total sanitation], 22 January 1998.
[92] *Jornal do Brasil*, Dividas e Duvidas [Doubts and Debts], 19 May 1994.
[93] *Folha de São Paulo*, Bancos e saltimbancos [Banks and acrobats], 28 November 1995.
[94] *Jornal do Brasil*, Dividas e Duvidas [Doubts and Debts], 19 May 1994.
[95] *Jornal do Commercio*, A mao do governo [The hand of the government], 1 November 2001.

Lingering perceptions of distributional unfairness undoubtedly contributed to the *Folha da São Paulo*'s conclusion that 'operations to rescue banks are still far from having convinced public opinion'.[96]

Lastly, it is worth highlighting that Brazilian newspapers were also critical of policy delays. *O Estado de São Paulo* opined: 'Politicians do not seem to realize the gravity of their omission when they postpone indefinitely the reforms for which the country asks.' Veto players, it effectively argued, were creating gridlock: 'The state banking sector has not yet been shrunk because of economic reasons, but due to political impositions by the resistance of governors and the incomprehension of parliamentarians.'[97]

4.3 The Evolution of Editorial Opinion on Crisis Blame

We now turn to evidence about changing newspaper opinion toward public responsibility for banking crises. The emergence of great expectations implies that newspaper opinion should reveal that, when compared to the earlier era, public sector officials are now blamed more intensely when crises occur. The growing material stake of voters in financial stability and effective policy commitments based on past performance should heighten expectations about government responsibilities for preventing crises.

We do not expect governments to escape blame in the earlier era, but rather that they should be blamed less intensely because voters expect less of them. Moreover, with the exception of the United States – for reasons we outline below – the relative weight of blame on private sector actors should be greater in the earlier period. Since the intensity of blame on public actors should rise over time, our argument does not imply that there should be any significant difference in the relative weight of blame on public and private actors in the modern era.

Banking crises are, of course, the result of a complex set of causes that can vary from one case to another. Our focus here is on blame apportioned to public sector and private sector actors. Public

---

[96] *Folha de São Paulo*, Editorial, Atração por bancos [Editorial, Attraction for banks], 7 April 2000.

[97] *O Estado de São Paulo*, Diferenças e semelhanças com a Asia [Differences and similarities with Asia], 21 January 1998.

sector actors could include any regulator with responsibility for oversight and/or supervision of the financial system, any agency responsible for monetary policy, members of the executive, legislative or judicial branches of government, any political parties, and any other public sector actor not listed above. Private sector actors could include any private universal, commercial, or investment bank, any other financial institutions (securities firms, brokers, insurers, hedge funds, etc.), any individual investor, any non-financial corporation, households and consumers, and any other private sector not listed above.

For most crises the distinction between public and private sector actors is relatively clear cut. However, our treatment of the Bank of England – which remained a private institution, albeit with public responsibilities, until its nationalization in 1946 (see Chapters 7 and 8) – requires clarification. Here we follow both contemporary opinion and that of economic historians in considering the Bank of England as a de facto public lender of last resort by 1873 (Bignon, Flandreau and Ugolini, 2012; Fetter, 1965; Sayers, 1936).[98] After this date we treat the Bank of England as a public sector actor. We consider the Banco do Brasil (and its predecessors) in a similar manner, coding it as a public sector institution after its nationalization in 1900.

Table 4.1 shows the average blame rating apportioned to public actors across the time periods. Irrespective of the time period, the evidence in Table 4.1 casts doubt on the possibility that voters generally view financial crises as 'acts of God' (cf. Achen and Bartels, 2012, abstract). In fact, the evidence below reveals that writers of newspaper opinion, at the very least, were always sufficiently sophisticated to assess relevant economic factors and causal relationships (even if inexpertly) and to assign blame.

Public sector actors do not escape blame in the earlier era, but as expected, in each country they were blamed with significantly greater intensity in the modern era (column 6). In addition, with the exception of the United States, the relative weight of blame assigned to private sector actors is greater in the earlier period (column 7).

---

[98] As late as 1866 *The Guardian* stated, 'the Bank of England is nothing more than a great joint-stock bank'. *The Guardian*, A meeting of the Manchester Chamber of Commerce, 9 December 1866.

Table 4.1. Average public and private sector blame apportionment in United Kingdom, United States and Brazil

	Pre-1939 public	Pre-1939 private	Post-1970 public	Post-1970 private	Public: post-1970 v. pre-1939 Mean difference	Public v. private: pre-1939 Mean difference
United Kingdom	2.72 (25)	4.38 (78)	4.16 (24)	4.47 (21)	1.44*** (t = 4.41)	−1.66*** (t = 8.15)
United States	3.98 (55)	3.93 (68)	4.62 (83)	4.64 (67)	0.64*** (t = 3.73)	0.06 (t = 0.19)
Brazil	3.69 (111)	4.19 (58)	4.8 (69)	3.2 (5)	1.11*** (t = 5.41)	−0.5** (t = 2.17)

Newspaper document counts in parentheses.
*** $p < 0.01$, ** $p < 0.05$

Given the United Kingdom's and Brazil's much more recent formal policy commitments to financial stability (see Chapters 8 and 12), the difference in public sector blame intensity across the time periods is largest in these countries, and it is where private sector actors receive greater blame in the earlier era. The United States, which made its first formal policy commitment considerably earlier (1863), registers the smallest difference in public sector blame intensity across the time periods, though one which still reveals greater blame in the modern era. The presence of this formal commitment in the earlier era, unique among country cases, helps account for no observed difference in the relative weight of blame for private sector actors in the earlier period. As we also argued in Chapter 2, the absence of crises serves a critical role in ratcheting up expectations that financial stability is a normal and politically achievable condition. Thus, as the United States' experience with recurrent financial instability moved further into the past, expectations of government responsibility to prevent crises likely intensified in the modern era, helping to account for the observed difference across the time periods. We provide more detail on our three country cases in what follows.

4.3.1   United Kingdom

British newspaper opinion assigned comparatively little blame to public sector actors in the nineteenth century. In fact, the results in Table 4.1 reveal that, on average, newspaper opinion exonerated them from responsibility for financial instability. This result is in line with what we would expect in an era of low financialization when the government had made no prior public policy commitment to prevent financial instability, and monetary policy was in the hands of the then private Bank of England.

Before the Bank became a de facto public institution, newspapers often saw its lending policies as contributing to crises. In 1837, *The Guardian* wrote: 'This recklessness assuredly could not have been carried so far had it not been for the unbounded confidence of the bill brokers, who must have discounted their paper to an extent perfectly unparalleled, and whose means of doing so were doubtless at one period greatly aided by those loans from the Bank of England.'[99] Later, in 1847, *The Times* took the Bank to task for abusing its position as a private institution enjoying special public privileges: 'It is very true that the Directors of the Bank of England have sins enough to answer for. With a vast, and, so to speak, a preponderating amount of public money in their hands, they have used the deposit without public principle and spirit. They have conducted their business just as the most private and irresponsible traders would have done.'[100]

There was much discussion in the mid- to late nineteenth century as to whether the government could be blamed for financial instability following the passage of the 1844 Bank Charter Act. *The Economist* wrote: 'We do not attribute any very important share of the present crisis [to it].'[101] Similarly, *The Guardian* concluded, 'the cry against the bill of 1844 is based upon an evident misunderstanding of what is really the present want in the country'.[102] In 1847, *The Times* argued, in contrast, that 'The Bank Charter, with its Ministerial and city

---

[99] *The Guardian*, The State of the Money Market, 12 April 1837.
[100] *The Times*, 1 November 1847. See also *The Guardian*, It is impossible to commit, 4 October 1847, and *The Guardian*, The Bank of England and the Act of 1844, 8 December 1847.
[101] *The Economist*, The Crisis, 1 May 1847.
[102] *The Guardian*, The Bank Regulation Act, 12 May 1847. See also *The Guardian*, Among the many deplorable features, 14 May 1866, and *The Guardian*, The currency discussion in the House of Commons, 5 August 1866.

promoters, is to blame for fettering the discretion of the Directors.'[103] Later, during the 1866 crisis, it reversed this opinion, asserting that 'the existence of the Bank Charter Act is not the cause of a Panic'.[104]

When blame was apportioned to public sector actors, it was typically for the ineffectiveness of government warnings about speculation. In 1847, *The Economist* editorialized, 'We had no faith even in the attempt of the Legislature to stop or check the folly, except by such means as would have been contrary to the spirit of our institutions and the free disposal of capital; and we saw, without any surprise, the entire failure of the attempt made by the Legislature last year to bring the community to a just sense of their danger.'[105]

The failure of Overend Gurney in 1866 also led to questions about the principle of limited liability, which Parliament had extended to banks in 1857. Overend Gurney, though insolvent at the time, had converted itself into a limited liability company in 1865 to salvage its position. New shareholders, whose uncalled capital was called, suffered losses as a result of the bank's failure under the new legal structure. *The Times* articulated dissatisfaction:

> The worst effect of the panic is due to an unforeseen operation of the new principle of Limited Liability. Practically, as too many victims have found to their cost, liability remained as unlimited as ever. Worse could not have happened in the OVEREND and GURNEY case if the partnership had been on the old conditions. The liability of an investor was indeed limited to the amount of his shares, but not to the amount of his investment.[106]

Yet newspaper opinion at this time largely failed to blame public actors for financial instability. In fact, some editorials emphasized the limits of government responsibility for the economy. 'The Legislature cannot always regulate the movements of commerce,' wrote *The Guardian* in 1857.[107]

By the time of the 2008 crisis societal expectations were rather different. Newspaper opinion reveals a strong expectation that public actors should prevent crises and deserved intense blame when they

---

[103] *The Times*, 26 May 1847.
[104] *The Times*, The Panic may be said to have passed away, 15 May 1866.
[105] *The Economist*, The Railway Struggle for Capital, 18 September 1847.
[106] *The Times*, The stagnation of commerce, 30 September 1867.
[107] *The Guardian*, The 'financial crisis', 29 November 1857.

failed do so. 'The regulator, whose job it is to spot trouble, ... failed. It must get its act together,' argued *The Guardian*.[108] *The Times* added, 'Regulators failed to perceive the risks inherent in the financial system ... The tripartite system of regulation introduced by new Labour has proved wholly inadequate for the task of scrutinising the banks and protecting consumers.'[109]

The Bank of England also received its share of criticism. *The Times* subjected the Bank's governor to intense and withering criticism:

> Having failed to see the risk building up in the banking system, Sir Mervyn seemed like a rabbit caught in headlights when the crisis hit. He did too little too late to prevent the implosion at Northern Rock and the first run on a British bank in more than a century. An academic economist, suspicious of the money makers in the City, he was determined that bankers should not be saved from the consequences of their own mistakes. He refused for months to provide struggling banks with the funding they needed. But it was not the bankers who suffered, it was the broader economy and London's reputation as a financial centre.[110]

Newspaper opinion was also unconvinced by government attempts to shift blame from itself to foreigners (usually the United States). A typical case comes from *The Guardian*:

> Though the current crisis may have had its trigger in the US, over the past decade the gun has been loaded at home. Now the government's biggest critics will probably include other savers who feel cheated. As chancellor, Mr Brown was proud of his light-touch financial regulation. That is what allowed Northern Rock to grow so quickly. Now it has ended up in a mess, and the markets are in turmoil. That may cast a shadow over Labour's popularity, and it certainly means the economy will be squeezed.[111]

---

[108] *The Guardian*, Banks and markets: Northern exposure, 15 September 2007.

[109] *The Times*, A Crisis of Confidence, 24 November 2008. See also *The Times*, Bank Balance; Banks must be made safe without doing unnecessary damage to the economy, 28 March 2013.

[110] *The Times*, Bank Record; Sir Mervyn King's reign as Governor was better in theory than in practice, 29 June 2013. See also *Financial Times*, UK Regulation, 22 June 2011, and *The Guardian*, World economy: Banking on disaster, 9 July 2012.

[111] *The Guardian*, Banks: A government rocked, 18 September 2007.

4.3.2 The United States

In the United States, newspaper opinion in the earlier era attributed recurrent crises, in part, to the nation's insufficiently inelastic money supply and system of unit banking. Both were artefacts of public policy. 'The stubborn fact is', wrote the *Chicago Tribune* in 1857, 'that no sufficiency of money is in the land, and that the condition of things is owing to a panic.'[112] Writing in 1907, the *Los Angeles Times* similarly argued, 'Clearly the business of the country has outgrown its financial system. There is not money enough to carry on our commerce, and this is true not only of us, but of the entire commercial world. Money is tight everywhere because of insufficient supply.'[113] Crises were also linked to debates about monetary policy, which centred on the commitment to the gold standard, silver coinage and bimetallism. 'In 1893 there was a financial panic,' wrote the *New York Times*, 'the cause of which, as the great body of public opinion recognized, was the silver legislation of 1890.'[114]

The National Banking Act of 1863 marked the first clear commitment by the federal government to financial stabilization, though one that was narrowly confined to an initially small number of nationally charted banks (see Chapter 9). In addition to creating a new supervisory authority for national banks, it provided for the first time specific minimum reserve and collateral requirements for these banks. This early policy commitment made the regulatory authorities an early target for blame in a manner not observed in the United Kingdom or Brazil. In fact, the *New York Times* attributed the 1873 panic in part to these two new regulatory requirements:

> The experience of the last six days has brought out very clearly two grave defects in our national banking system. One of these is the requirement that a fixed percentage of the liabilities of the banks in greenbacks shall be held as a reserve; the other is the arbitrary limit placed on the issue of banknotes secured by United States bonds.[115]

[112] *Chicago Tribune*, The Real Cause of our Financial Distress, 7 August 1857.
[113] *Los Angeles Times*, Two Democrats and Finance, 29 October 1907.
[114] *New York Times*, The Gold Standard or Run, 25 February 1896.
[115] *New York Times*, A Lesson of the Hour, 24 September 1873. See also *New York Times*, The Financial Crisis, 21 September 1873, and *Washington Post*, Administrative Reform, 19 June 1884.

In the Great Depression, American editorialists continued to call into question the effectiveness of policymakers' commitment to financial stability. The *Washington Post* raised concerns about the competitive chartering of banks by the federal and state governments: 'The system of divided authority, permitting thousands of small unit banks to operate under the laws of 48 States and Federal Government, was largely responsible for the scandalous record of bank failures during the postwar period. The safeguards established under national banking laws were steadily weakened and standards lowered to enable the national banks to compete more effectively with State banks. As a result of this competition and laxity the banking system became more and more vulnerable and failures mounted steadily in years prior to the collapse of 1933.'[116] Similarly, the *New York Times* opined, 'The public may be inclined to regard the banking crisis as just another phase of the depression, but its origin lies in the weaknesses of the American banking system.'[117]

By the time of the savings and loan crisis, the expectation that government had a responsibility to prevent financial crises had become firmly entrenched. 'The regulator's job is to defend the stability of the banking system as a whole and to prevent one bank's troubles from spreading. Those are the standards that count,' wrote the *Washington Post*.[118] Editorialists showed little tolerance, in the words of the *Wall Street Journal*, for 'Congress ... bending all its efforts in the wrong direction, toward perpetuating a badly flawed banking and regulatory framework'.[119] In some cases, editorialists argued public policy had been captured: 'The failures are the product of a weak and degraded regulatory system that has historically been dominated by S and L owners, their trade associations and their friends in Congress and in successive administrations.'[120]

Similar arguments were voiced during the 2007–8 crisis. The *New York Times* wrote: 'The White House is complicit in the current

[116] *Washington Post*, A banking reform program, 28 July 1936. See also *Washington Post*, Unified banking, 7 December 1933.
[117] *New York Times*, Chance for bank reform, 7 March 1933.
[118] *Washington Post*, Rescuing Banks, 5 October 1984.
[119] *Wall Street Journal*, Bailout Time Again, 5 May 1987.
[120] *Washington Post*, The End of the S and Ls, 11 October 1988. See also *New York Times*, S and Ls, The Price of Prevarication, 20 October 1988; *New York Times*, Facing the S and Ls, Not So Squarely, 7 February 1989; *Washington Post*, S and L Failure, 5 February 1990.

mess for advancing an absolutist notion that self policed markets self-correct, and therefore require little or no regulation. The Federal Reserve and other regulators are complicit because they failed to rein in clearly reckless lending. The Congress of the bubble years is complicit for failing to oversee the derelict regulators.'[121] As we detail in Chapter 10, debate about the causes of the latest crisis in the United States has proven highly contentious. Yet what unites most commentators is a view that places intense blame on public sector actors.

4.3.3 Brazil

In Brazil, newspaper opinion in both time periods drew a close link between high inflation, financial instability and the government's monetary and financial policy decisions. For instance, in 1891, the *Jornal do Brasil* pointed to the 'abuse of money printing and its pernicious influence ... as leading to this financial situation'.[122] During the same crisis, it later suggested, 'How bad it is that politicians' actions aren't only horrible and cruel, but also corrupt and unaware, of how they ruin us.'[123] Writing in the 1920s, *O Paiz* highlighted 'repetition' in 'our financial policy to emit paper'.[124] In the 1980s, *Folha da São Paulo* called the government the 'main cause of inflation'.[125]

It is only at the end of the 1920s that we observe claims that the government should take greater responsibility for financial stability. At the time, banks were only required to submit audited financial reports to the Treasury similar those all corporations were required to publish for their shareholders. It is unclear how the Treasury enforced this regulation and how it verified the reported data. No regulatory oversight to establish minimal standards of bank safety, such as capital or reserve requirements, was present (Triner, 2000, 145–6). *O Paiz* editorialized, 'The conclusion to be drawn is: the banks' balance sheets

---

[121] *New York Times*, B Is for Bailout, C Is for ..., 10 September 2007. See also *New York Times*, Wall Street Casualties, 16 September 2008; *Boston Globe*, Eight wishes for 08, 1 January 2008; *Boston Globe*, A parachute for the markets, 23 January 2008; *Chicago Tribune*, Tough love from taxpayers, 16 September 2008.

[122] *Jornal do Brasil*, A Baixa do Cambio [The Exchange Rate Dip], 26 August 1891.

[123] *Jornal do Brasil*, A reforma finançeira [The Financial reform], 26 June 1893.

[124] *O Paiz*, A Actualidade Politica no Senado [The actual politics of the Senate], 29 December 1929.

[125] *Folha de São Paulo*, O inconstitucional ajuste fiscal [The unconstitutional fiscal adjustment], 24 November 1988.

cannot faithfully express the truth, and from this can be deduced the insufficiency of our banking supervision apparatus ... [and] ... facts would not be necessary to prove the inefficacy of banking supervision in its current form.'[126]

In the modern era, extensive state control of the banking system enhanced government responsibility for crises, attracting greater blame. The *Jornal do Brasil* asserted that 'The continued deterioration of the state banks is today the "Achilles heel" of the national financial system.'[127] It later added: "The state-owned bank is considered by many a magical institution. It is imagined that it can create money for everything ... The result has been an endless succession of insolvency situations, interventions, scandals, which so far have always ended up debited in the accounts of the Treasury, that is, in the personal accounts of each one of us, citizens and taxpayers.'[128]

Finally, it is also worth noting that, as in the British case, Brazilian governments could not easily shift the blame to external actors, including the International Monetary Fund. As *Folha São Paulo* remarked, 'The government ... tries to transfer the source of all evils in Brazilians to the easily hateful IMF, causing them to forget the problems of the recession, unemployment, and hunger increasingly present in the country. Not because of impositions of the IMF but because of the negligence and incompetence of economic ministers.'[129]

4.4 Great Expectations Elsewhere and Everywhere?

In addition to the evidence from newspaper editorials, our comprehensive search for cross-national longitudinal survey data on voter attitudes toward wealth protection and financial stabilization came up with two available national household surveys, one in the Netherlands in 2010 and multiple waves in the United Kingdom from

---

[126] *O Paiz*, Os Bancos e a Fiscalizaçao Bancaria [The Banks and Banking Supervision], 14 May 1929. See also *Folha da Manha*, O banco do Brasil e a crise financeira [Banco do Brasil and the financial crises], 28 June 1926.

[127] *Jornal do Brasil*, O Absurdo Problema dos Bancos Estaduais [The Absurd Problem of the State Banks], 13 October 1986.

[128] *Jornal do Brasil*, Em busca da realidade [Searching for reality], 9 October 1995.

[129] *Folha de São Paulo*, FMI e armadilhas para os democratas [IMF and the traps for Democrats], 13 April 1983.

2003 to 2012.[130] Both provide striking evidence of the emergence of great expectations among voters in these financialized economies. Respondents in both countries held high expectations for regulators and supervisors to meet and expected that governments would opt for bailouts and other policies aimed at wealth protection during crises.

Roughly two-thirds (63 per cent) of Dutch respondents agreed with the view that supervisors must ensure that banks never go bankrupt. Three-quarters of the respondents also incorrectly assumed that supervisors will refund *any* deposits when a bank goes bankrupt.[131] A substantial majority (59 per cent) also believed that supervisors have to ensure swift reimbursement of guaranteed savings when a bank fails. Whereas the survey reveals that Dutch households (80 per cent) expected repayment in three days, the average repayment period in the Netherlands is three months (Van der Cruijsen et al., 2013).

Similar expectations are found among British households. Since the question was first posed in 2003, less than a third of British respondents believed that financial firms are ever allowed to go bankrupt. When asked in 2012 why they held this belief, over a third responded that the government or regulator would always bail them out and another fifth thought that some firms are too important to be allowed to fail. The remainder responded that otherwise people would lose confidence in the financial system (14 per cent), too many consumers would be affected (12 per cent) or the government would never allow consumers to lose money (8 per cent) (Financial Services Authority (UK), 2012). These expectations are quite different from nineteenth-century understandings and from the employment protection focus of the Bretton Woods era.

Furthermore, as we detail throughout this book, these survey respondents have plausible grounds for believing in the inevitability of government bailouts, which have become increasingly common in crisis-hit democracies since the 1980s (Chwieroth and Walter, 2017; Goodhart, 1999, 356–7). Faced with the prospect of engendering moral hazard, governments have often pushed in vain against these new expectations. In the British case, for example, respondents' expectations about bailouts persisted despite repeated efforts by British regulators to

---

[130] These are the 2010 De Nederlandsche Bank Household Survey in the Netherlands and the 2003–2012 Financial Services Authority Consumer Awareness Survey in the UK. Both are surveys of approximately 2,000 households in each country.

[131] In practice, repayment depends on the type of account and is capped at €100,000 per person per bank.

articulate a 'non-zero-failure' regime (Financial Services Authority (UK), 2012, 33–4).

These two cases have particular characteristics of relevance to our argument. First, both have experienced rising middle-class wealth and financialization, growing household leverage and an accumulating policy commitment to financial stabilization, which, as we suggest, should diminish the size and influence of the Bagehot coalition. That we find evidence that our argument holds in these cases increases our confidence that similar voter expectations are likely to be present in other cases with similar characteristics.

Second, the two countries represent different varieties of capitalism, but societal demands for wealth protection apply just as strongly in the liberal market United Kingdom as in coordinated market Netherlands. The same can be said when we consider the content of newspaper opinion in the liberal market United Kingdom and the United States as when we consider hierarchical market Brazil (Schneider, 2013; Schneider and Soskice, 2009). Thus, as argued in Chapter 1, the weight of this evidence suggests that the mass demand for bailouts has become high in a wide variety of political economies with varying levels of financialization and leverage.

Finally, it is worth noting that at the time of the surveys, the Netherlands and the UK utilized different models of supervision, the former relying on the 'twin-peaks' model where market conduct and prudential supervision are housed in separate agencies, and the latter using a single integrated supervisor model. As such, we can plausibly rule out variation in the model of supervision as one potential influence on voter expectations.

What about the possible confounding effect of voter understandings of the changing role of the state? Could great expectations simply reflect the emergence of a 'risk society' in which voters expect public risk insurance in many facets of modern life? (Beck, 1992). If the role of the state has changed greatly since the nineteenth century, then the expectations we emphasize might have been associated with a general normative shift in recent decades towards greater individual reliance on government. While this could explain some of the long-run change in voter expectations, we remain sceptical of this possibility. Ansell (2014), for instance, draws a crucial link between surging housing wealth in democratic countries and individual social policy preferences. Using microdata on social preferences from panel surveys in a cross-national sample of democratic countries, he demonstrates that home owners experiencing house price appreciation and thus growing wealth portfolios become *less* supportive of general redistribution and social insurance policies.[132] To be sure, support for some social welfare institutions remains broad and deep in countries such as the United Kingdom and the United States, including the National Health Service and Social Security respectively. In the latter case, this seems to be in part because Social Security is viewed by many Americans – including conservatives – as a form of personal saving (Jacobs, 2010; Skocpol and Williamson, 2016, 80–1).

We use data from the World Values Survey (WVS) to further investigate general voter attitudes to government responsibility. The WVS provides cross-national data for various years from 1981 to 2014, covering voter survey responses about government responsibility on a scale ranging from 1 to 10, with higher values indicating government should take more responsibility for aspects of life, and lower values indicating people should take more responsibility. We calculate country-specific averages for each year this survey question was posed to voters in democratic countries. This provides us with 134 observations.

Figure 4.4 plots the country-specific averages from each survey and the best-fitting line. We use ISO3C country labels to identify any observations that may appear as outliers. If voters expect more from government in many aspects of life, then we should observe an upward trend in this data over time. Yet such a trend does not appear in this data. On average, voters have expressed views on government responsibility that fall in the intermediate range of the survey scale, and these views have shown little variation over time. Over the same period, Bagehot policies have become much less common. This suggests that the shift in voter expectations regarding wealth protection may be issue-specific; and, in this case, likely due more to the rising material stake of middle-class voters in financial stabilization than to rising generic support for public risk insurance.

4.5 Conclusion

Great expectations have become a fundamental component of the changing politics of banking crises, but they were not always so.

---

[132] See also Powdthavee and Oswald (2016).

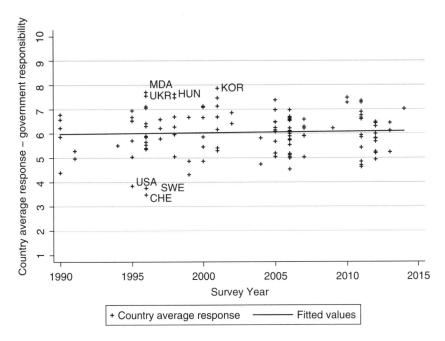

Figure 4.4: Voter attitudes toward government responsibility.
Source: World Values Survey (2017).

Before the mid-twentieth century, our newspaper evidence suggests that understandings of government responsibilities generally coalesced around a Bagehot model of financial stabilization. After this point, far more extensive expectations about government policy responsibilities have become entrenched, even in less financialized emerging economies. Evidence from changing newspaper opinion in our three country cases, as a proxy for voter expectations, reveals significantly stronger support for extensive government interventions following crises in recent decades compared to those in an earlier era. Importantly, in each of our country cases newspaper opinion invokes the very long-term dynamic trends – wealth accumulation, financialization and the democratization of leverage – that we have argued are so critical in reshaping societal expectations and which were shown in Chapter 3 to have accelerated in recent decades.

In addition, evidence from newspaper opinion is also consistent with our argument that people's expectations and demands of government can be inconsistent and conflicting. Newspaper opinion in recent decades reveals support for intervention to stabilize the financial system and protect household wealth and the flow of credit, but also deep dissatisfaction with the costs and distributional consequences. Such opinion provides evidence of the very political dilemma for incumbent governments that we highlighted in Chapter 2: modern governments are expected to protect wealth, but, when they attempt to do so, they face heightened criticism that makes reaping political reward difficult. This is particularly the case when, as newspaper opinion evidence suggests, such interventions are delayed or perceived to be substantively redistributive.

Lastly, evidence in this chapter revealed the changing nature of blame apportionment for financial instability. Consistent with our argument that modern voters are more demanding about government responsibilities to prevent financial instability, we found that public sector actors received significantly greater blame for crises in recent decades than in the earlier period. In addition, we found that, with the exception of the United States, newspaper opinion placed greater relative blame on private actors in the earlier period. Importantly, evidence from newspaper opinion suggests that the United States was an exception for reasons consistent with our argument, namely its considerably earlier public policy commitment to financial stability.

Finally, the changing opinion we identify does not appear to have followed fully from changes in voter attitudes concerning government responsibility for other aspects of social and economic life. But these great expectations in the world of finance have nonetheless had far-reaching policy and political consequences. It is to these consequences that we now turn.

Part II

EVOLVING POLICY RESPONSES TO AND POLITICAL CONSEQUENCES OF BANKING CRISES SINCE THE NINETEENTH CENTURY

5 CHANGING EXPECTATIONS AND POLICY RESPONSES TO BANKING CRISES

A central plank of our argument is that the emergence of great expectations regarding financial stabilization has been a primary factor driving changes in the nature of government policy responses to crises over the long run. This evolution in the policy expectations of households and voters has been driven by three key interrelated developments: financialization, the democratization of leverage, and an accumulating policy commitment on the part of governments to financial stabilization. Great expectations have reconfigured the relative size and influence of the Bagehot and bailout constituencies. As the interests of households in modern democracies have become increasingly linked to financial markets, and governments have accumulated a policy commitment to financial stabilization via regulation, this has broadened and intensified the effective demand by households and voters for wealth protection during crises. Thus, in many modern democracies, the once dominant Bagehot constituency now faces a bailout constituency of greater strength and breadth and one whose great expectations favour far more extensive policy interventions following crises than those observed in the past.

To investigate this claim, this chapter explores evidence related to the changing nature of government policy responses to banking crises over nearly two centuries. Specifically, we expect that rising financialization, growing household leverage and an accumulating policy commitment to financial stabilization should heighten powerful tendencies in modern democracies toward bailouts.

We assess these empirical expectations against competing explanations using a considerably longer time frame and larger sample of systemic crises than found in earlier studies.[1] Our findings are inconsistent with the claim that democratic governments generally seek to minimize the public burden of bank insolvency to avoid electoral sanction. Such imperatives, to the extent they are present, are conditional on the expectations of voters which earlier studies have overlooked or conceived too narrowly (i.e. modern voters are more than taxpayers seeking to minimize state exposure to bank insolvency). Before the Second World War, democratic governments did often respond to crises in ways that approximated the Bagehot idea. However, our findings are strongly consistent with our argument that these policy choices were not due to the threat of electoral sanction alone but instead depended on voters having 'low expectations' of government intervention that fit with the interests and policy beliefs of a more politically dominant elite Bagehot coalition.

Modern governments appear responsive to a very different standard of democratic accountability. In recent decades, we find that dynamic developments in financialization, household leverage and policy commitments omitted in previous studies have increased the propensity for elected governments to respond to systemic banking crises with more extensive bailouts. Arguments that democratic institutions provide for an effective representation of narrow taxpayer interests in the modern era thus seem misplaced. Middle-class voters, as we argued in Chapter 2, have more complex and sometimes conflicting preferences; recently, they have come to expect extensive public intervention in crises to protect their wealth.

The rest of this chapter proceeds as follows. We start by outlining our data and methods. We then present the results of our analysis linking the three crucial developments driving the emergence of great expectations to the changing nature of government policy responses to crises. We conclude by considering the implications of these dynamic tendencies for democratic accountability.

---

[1] As detailed below, our sample consists of 112 systemic crises from 1848 to 2010. Rosas (2006, 2009), on the other hand, considers a sample of 40 crises – including several borderline or non-systemic crises – over a much shorter time frame, 1976 to 1998.

5.1   Government Policy Responses: Conceptualization and Measurement

Popular accounts often lump together all policies that support banks and related entities as essentially providing a bailout to the financial sector. Yet government policy responses to banking crises are not discrete binary events. Analytically, it is more useful to conceptualize these responses as mapping on a policy continuum that ranges in the abstract from the absence of any government assistance to banks to complete government socialization of all banking sector losses.

The first pole of the continuum, which we label the *Market* pole, would correspond to a government refraining from any intervention to stabilize the financial system and simply allowing distressed institutions to fail. At this Market pole, banks generally perceived to be solvent but which suffer liquidity problems may receive loans or other forms of support from other *private sector* banks and investors. The other pole, which we call the *Socialization* pole, would represent policy responses in which government support permits institutions to continue operating whether or not they remain commercially viable and the taxpayer fully subsidizes any losses. Both poles are ideal types and in practice, policy responses often fall short of these extremes. More precisely, as Figure 5.1 shows, most responses fall between the two poles that approximate models that Guillermo Rosas summarized as 'Bagehot' and 'Bailout' (Rosas, 2006).

Bagehot and bailout responses are thus best conceptualized as occupying ranges rather than points on this policy continuum. A 'Bagehot' model is meant to conform to Walter Bagehot's doctrine of crisis resolution, which called for central banks to establish LOLR facilities to provide unlimited assistance to banks by 'freely advancing on what in ordinary times is reckoned a good security' (Bagehot, 1962

Pure			*Pure*
market	Bagehot	Bailout	*socialization*
responses	responses	responses	*responses*

Figure 5.1: Conceptualizing policy responses to banking crises.

[1873], 97). Such lending should also take place at 'penalty' interest rates to ensure that the government was not subsidizing banks in need. This doctrine has often been summarized as saying that the authorities should lend only to solvent but illiquid banks. However, in a crisis, bank solvency is often by definition in doubt and Bagehot was careful to stress that solvency could only be defined in reference to 'normal times' (DeLong, 2012, 21–2). Since markets can be expected to provide clearly solvent but illiquid banks with loans, the LOLR is generally only needed when there is some uncertainty about solvency: the 'LOLR is, almost always, only sought, or needed, when there is some potentiality for loss ... [which in turn] raises the possibility [of] taxpayer [loss]' (Goodhart, 1999, 352). Thus, illiquidity and solvency concerns are related.

As Bagehot was well aware, even under the gold standard this policy commitment necessarily included the government, since the value of the central bank in providing liabilities to distressed banks ultimately depended on the fiscal capacity of the state that stood behind it (Goodhart, 1999, 347–8). This response diverges from the strict non-intervention of the Market pole in that it involves policy intervention to prevent *ordinarily solvent but illiquid* banks from failing. It places the burden of *permanent insolvency* on banks and related creditors rather than on taxpayers and thus can also entail enforcing the closure of insolvent banks, forcing write-downs of banks' non-performing loans (NPLs) and other distressed assets, permitting their recapitalization by private investors and protecting few if any depositors. However, as Goodhart points out, a Bagehot policy response does entail an implicit taxpayer liability.

A 'bailout' response falls closer to the Socialization pole in that it involves government-sponsored measures to delay the closure of banks that are almost certainly insolvent even in 'normal' times via the more extensive use of taxpayer resources. That is, in contrast to the Bagehot model, a bailout response provides LOLR facilities (or some equivalent) to banks comparatively indiscriminately and at length. Essentially, it buys time in the hope that banks will work their way out of insolvency or on the assumption that taxpayer losses will only materialize in the future. Even so, since delay may not prevent some bank closures or private sector losses, even extensive bailouts differ from the Socialization pole. In addition, this strategy often in practice includes the transfer of distressed assets from banks at public expense, the recapitalization of banks with public funds, regulatory forbearance, the provision of blanket protection to depositors, and allowing insolvent banks to continue operating indefinitely. Each of these options, which may be used independently or in combination with other measures, involves an additional burden to taxpayers, who ultimately will be called upon in some manner, either implicitly or explicitly, to absorb financial losses.

Thus, the main conceptual differences between a Bagehot and a bailout policy response lie in the intention of the government in providing support to banks, in the targets of support, and ultimately in the willingness to impose (in the latter case) a much higher burden on taxpayers. Analytically, like Rosas, we view government policy responses as generally falling in a continuum between the Bagehot and bailout models. We identify five policy areas crucial to classifying the response to banking crises: *Liquidity Support, Liability Resolution, Asset Resolution, Bank Capitalization* and *Bank Exit*. We now describe the response that a government pursuing a coherent Bagehot or bailout strategy would implement in each of these five areas.

In terms of *Liquidity Support*, the hallmark of a Bagehot response would be LOLR advances to solvent[2] institutions based on good collateral and lent at a premium to normal market rates. As noted above, liquidity support may be extended to institutions that ultimately fail, but governments and central banks should avoid assisting banks that are clearly insolvent on a continuing basis. Very quick decisions often need to be made in crises, and insolvent institutions are strongly incentivized to hide the true nature of their accounts (Brunnermeier, James and Landau, 2016, 116–19; Swagel, 2015). This problem led Bagehot and others to emphasize the importance of collateralized lending and premium rates to limit the likelihood, with considerable probability, of the central bank making a loss and to dissuade those borrowers who have little prospect of restoring solvency or who are not in genuine distress. When such advances become indiscriminate, uncollateralized, open-ended or carry an interest-rate subsidy, we view it as characterizing a bailout response in this area.

In the area of *Liability Resolution*, bailout responses would include cases where governments offer explicit full protection of liabilities or extend guarantees to non-deposit liability holders of banks,

---

[2] In what follows, we define solvency in terms of 'normal' market conditions.

ensuring that all or a specified set of creditor claims will be honoured with taxpayer resources. Such guarantees, as we examine more fully below, have become increasingly necessary in highly financialized economies to stop market contagion during a crisis. Explicit guarantees also could be targeted specifically at depositors via the introduction of new deposit insurance schemes or the extension of existing schemes. Implicit guarantees may also be present in some financial systems such as those where the government already exerts extensive control over the banking system but does not explicitly pre-commit to a guarantee of controlled banks. Alternatively, governments may institute deposit freezes, bank holidays, or payment suspensions that revise the payment schedules to claimants. Creditors incur different distributional consequences from these respective policies, but none of them entails imposition of losses. Whereas guarantees and deposit insurance permit creditors access to their claims and shift the cost of compensation to taxpayers, deposit freezes and payment suspensions restrict creditor rights and in principle require no taxpayer resources. Yet both fit with the bailout response in that they serve to lengthen the life of insolvent banks after the immediate crisis has abated.

Implicit or explicit guarantees may already be present when a crisis strikes. An example of an existing implicit guarantee is state ownership of the banking system, a policy intervention that extends well beyond those considered by Bagehot in his day. We treat such commitments as fitting with the bailout response because they provide depositors and counterparties with some assurance that forbearance on normal solvency requirements for state-controlled banks will be applied, or if not, public support will follow given sufficient fiscal resources, as occurred in Brazil in the 1980s and 1990s (see Chapter 12). Should insolvent state-owned banks be permitted to fail in a crisis, this would represent a shift from the socialization pole towards the market pole (as in Indonesia in 1998 when the state faced severe fiscal difficulty). A now-common explicit guarantee is deposit insurance – a less radical intervention than state ownership of banking but still potentially transformative. Retracting it in a crisis would also represent a shift towards the market pole, whereas extending its size or scope would be a shift towards the socialization pole. Therefore, we view sustaining existing deposit insurance as consistent with a Bagehot response, withdrawals as a shift toward a pure market response, and extensions as a shift towards the socialization pole.[3] In addition, rather than socializing liabilities, a Bagehot response in the area of Liability Resolution would include 'bail-in' provisions whereby creditor claims are written down or converted into equity to stabilize a distressed institution (Sommer, 2014).

Governments confront the issue of NPLs or other distressed assets when dealing with *Asset Resolution*. The Bagehot response to distressed assets is to require banks to identify them and then to write them down to their real value on their books. Consistent with this approach, bank closures would result should such write-downs reveal insolvency. Under the bailout ideal type, by contrast, the government may tackle distressed assets through three basic mechanisms. One mechanism allows banks to hide them to defer their recognition, via lax valuation and accounting regimes or regulatory forbearance (Walter, 2008, 45). A second provides support or relief for distressed bank borrowers, enabling these borrowers, at taxpayer expense, to continue to service their debt. A third mechanism removes distressed assets from the balance sheet of the banks at taxpayer expense, acquiring assets of uncertain but generally low value in exchange for support. If the government pays market value, it could force banks into immediate insolvency, and recapitalization (see below) would have to be part of the same transaction. If the government pays current book value (the accounting value on a bank's balance sheet), this overpayment would constitute a subsidy to the bank's shareholders and creditors. In acquiring these assets, governments may utilize an asset management company (AMC or 'bad bank') to recover collateral and dispose of distressed assets. Alternatively, banks may be required to participate actively in this process as a condition of support.

Bank Capitalization captures the loss absorbency of an institution. Well-capitalized institutions have more resources to absorb losses arising from distressed assets. Bank solvency can be defined as when the estimated market value of a bank's assets exceeds its debt liabilities. Although private sector analysts now deploy a range of indicators to assess bank solvency, regulators have often defined it as the ability of a bank to meet one or more minimum ratios, usually including a specified equity to assets ratio (Mishkin and Eakins, 2014,

---

[3] Rosas (2006, 2009) implements a similar coding strategy regarding implicit and explicit guarantees.

chap. 17; Moody's Investor Services, 2016). If a bank does not meet these regulatory minima, it would, under a Bagehot policy, be forced to raise additional capital from private sources and asset sales, or face a process of restructuring or closure.

Bailout policies will seek to prevent or delay the closure of a bank that would probably be insolvent in normal times without public support. They may achieve this by regulatory forbearance or by revising the regulatory framework (loan classification, loan loss provisioning, valuation mechanisms, or the regulatory definition of insolvency), by fund-matching arrangements to subsidize private recapitalization efforts or by nationalizing the bank. As with Liability Resolution, the distributional consequences of these policies vary. In some cases (regulatory forbearance), shareholders do not face dilution or losses; in others, they face dilution and either lose partial control (fund-matching) or complete control (nationalization) of the bank. In all cases, as with those for Liability Resolution, the bank remains in operation after insolvency, with taxpayers carrying the immediate cost.

Exit Policy refers to restructuring treatment applied to financial institutions after insolvency is detected. Bank exit is a process rather than an event and usually ends with the institution's absorption by another solvent institution or its liquidation (Lindgren, 2005). Closure means the end of a financial institution as a legal entity. It may occur upfront followed by a resolution and liquidation process, or be part of or the end result of an intervention and resolution process. Intervention occurs when the supervisor takes over management and ownership control of a failing institution, possibly resulting in restructuring or closure and liquidation. Resolution follows intervention. It entails a number of options aimed at reorganizing an institution's operations, including closure but also potentially involving mergers, partial sales, purchase and assumption (P&A) operations, liquidation, bridge banks or reorganizations. Mergers and sales involve the transfer and absorption of all the assets and liabilities of the failing institution by another institution. In a P&A operation, another institution purchases a portion of the failing institution's assets and part or all of its liabilities.[4]

---

[4] Partial sales or P&A operations may or may not entail government support. In a government-supported merger or P&A operation, a government agency or deposit insurer will guarantee or pay the purchasing institution for the difference between the value of the assets and liabilities.

Liquidation is the process through which the assets of an institution are sold and the proceeds used to settle its liabilities. A failing bank may also be closed and some or all of its assets and liabilities transferred to a temporary bridge bank until permanent resolution is determined.[5]

In a sense, all other policy areas are linked to government decisions regarding exit policy. Under the bailout ideal type, banks known to be insolvent on an ongoing basis are permitted to continue operations. By contrast, under the Bagehot ideal type, the bank exit process would follow immediately from the detection of regulatory insolvency.

With the above in mind, how should we measure the general character of crisis policy responses? Previous studies of the determinants of bank bailouts largely rely either on fiscal cost measurements (Gandrud and Hallerberg, 2015a; Grossman and Woll, 2014; Honohan and Klingebiel, 2000; Keefer, 2007) or on a limited number of policy response indicators (Culpepper and Reinke, 2014; Weber and Schmitz, 2011). These modelling decisions may not always be appropriate. Fiscal costs can take many years to be settled and are not wholly determined by the same factors that shape government policy responses. Some policy responses, such as guarantees, liquidity assistance and AMCs, generate contingent liabilities that are realized in the future only if some event (e.g. a bank is unable to pay its publicly guaranteed liabilities) occurs (Gandrud and Hallerberg, 2015a). More broadly, eventual economic outcomes that follow from any set of policy choices may also influence fiscal costs. Moreover, the drawback of limiting focus to a narrow set of policy indicators is that government responses to systemic banking crises are typically multifaceted, often encompassing a wide range of policies that can be substitutes or complements.

For these reasons, we follow a similar procedure to Rosas in devising a broader description of policy response (Rosas, 2006). Rosas classifies different microeconomic policy measures according to whether they fit with either the 'Bailout' or 'Bagehot' ideal type – measures that taken together either serve to prevent clearly insolvent banks from failing, or alternatively that ensure that losses by such banks are crystallized and borne by their owners, employees and investors. Our aim is to measure the overall tendency for governments to conform to one of these ideal types in their response to banking crises.

---

[5] The bridge bank would require separate capitalization, normally via government support.

Table 5.1. Policy responses to banking crises, Bagehot v. bailout

Policy Issue	Bagehot	Bailout	Indicator
Liquidity support	Authorities lend on good collateral at penalty rate, for a limited duration to screened applicants	Authorities provide indiscriminate, uncollateralized, open-ended or subsidized support, as requested by banks	Indiscriminate, uncollateralized, open-ended or subsidized liquidity support (+1)
Asset resolution	Banks forced to write down distressed assets on their balance sheets	Public sector assumes distressed assets Debt relief programme for distressed borrowers	Public asset management company or debt relief programme for borrowers (+1)
Bank capitalization	Private sector recapitalization	Public sector recapitalization	Recapitalization or nationalization (+1)
Liability resolution	No additional implicit or explicit protection extended to liability holders	Implicit or explicit protection of major categories of liability holders	High state bank presence or explicit guarantee (+1) New or extended deposit insurance (+1) Deposit freeze, bank holiday, or payment suspension (+1) Losses imposed on depositors (−1)
Exit policy	Banks closed or restructured after insolvency detected	Insolvent banks permitted to continue operations	Bank restructuring (−1)

Building on Rosas's earlier depiction, Table 5.1 extends our earlier discussion of the crucial elements of policies one would expect from a coherent Bagehot or bailout response. The first column of Table 5.1 identifies the five crucial policy areas discussed earlier: Liquidity Support, Liability Resolution, Asset Resolution, Bank Capitalization and Bank Exit Policy. Entries in the two subsequent columns refer to the policy decisions that characterize a Bagehot or a bailout response.

Honohan and Klingebiel – who are the principal data source for Rosas – compile and code government policy responses to crises observed during 1970–2000 (Honohan and Klingebiel, 2000). We extend their coding scheme to develop eight binary indicators – Bank Liquidity, Public Asset Management, Recapitalization, Guarantees, Deposit Insurance, Deposit Freeze, Deposit Loss and Bank Restructuring – that we relate in the fourth column to the five policy issue areas detailed in the Bagehot–bailout classification.[6]

We provide detailed explanations of our coding scheme in the Appendix to this chapter. We code policies consistent with the bailout ideal type as '+1' and code those policies consistent with the Bagehot ideal type as '−1.' Liquidity Support, for instance, is coded as +1 where we observe indiscriminate, uncollateralized, open-ended or subsidized liquidity support consistent with a bailout response. As another example, Liability Resolution is coded as −1 where we observe losses imposed on depositors consistent with a Bagehot response.

Table 5.1 shows how the other six indicators relate to the various policy issue areas. In coding government policy responses, we draw on a wide range of sources detailed in the supplementary online materials. We consider all policy responses that occur within three years after the crisis window ends.[7] Clearly, this produces a score that aggregates crisis responses over the full time window after the outbreak of the crisis and does not take into account that government policy responses may vary over the time window. We explore such intra-crisis policy response variations in our qualitative case studies.

Our primary banking crisis measure is from Reinhart and Rogoff (R&R), who provide the most comprehensive data on crises since the early nineteenth century (Reinhart, 2010; Reinhart and Rogoff, 2009). The R&R measure is an expansive definition that identifies banking crises as occurring whenever there is any distress in the banking system. We focus on episodes of *systemic* banking crises (such as the Global Financial Crisis of 2008) rather than isolated banking failures

---

[6] Honohan and Klingbiel (2000) and Rosas (2006) also consider regulatory forbearance as a potential indicator. Yet Rosas (2006, 185–6) finds that it performs poorly in identifying underlying government proclivity towards bailouts. Since most governments experiencing crises are likely to choose forbearance but it is often difficult to detect, we exclude it in our analysis.

[7] So, for example, for a country experiencing a crisis over 1907–8, policy responses occurring in the period 1907–11 would be included.

(such as the solvency problems at Crédit Lyonnaise in France in 1994–5) so as to investigate policy responses only in those crises that threaten the stability of the whole banking system.[8] We also consider a measure from Laeven and Valencia (L&V) (2008, 2013), which extends from 1970 to 2011 and covers nearly twice as many countries as the R&R dataset and records only systemic crises. We use these measures to produce two sets of responses: both sets use the R&R crisis dating for the pre-1945 era, then separately for the post-1970 era one set includes the R&R dating and the other relies on the L&V dating.

We identify democracies using data from Boix, Miller and Rosato (2014). Importantly, in addition to free and fair contestation, this dichotomous measure of democracy requires countries to meet a minimal suffrage requirement, defined as a majority of the male adult population – a criterion omitted from the Polity dataset and many other alternative measures. This suffrage requirement, as Boix, Miller and Rosato show, has important implications for historical work prior to World War II, when there was substantial variation in the extent of the franchise. By emphasizing results using this measure, we aim to rule out possible objections that the changing politics of banking crises may be due to suffrage expansion and democratization alone.

In addition, as we discuss below, our results are robust to the consideration of an alternative sample of democracies using the Polity dataset (Marshall, Gurr and Jaggers, 2017). The Polity index aggregates several components that help to differentiate the institutional features of democratic and non-democratic countries: competitiveness and openness of the selection process for the chief executive, the degree of institutional constraint on the decision-making authority of the chief executive, and the regulation and competitiveness of political participation. The Polity project uses these components to create an eleven-point index of each country's democratic features and an eleven-point index of its autocratic features. The difference between these two indices creates a summary regime type score that ranges from −10 to 10, with lower values indicating a highly autocratic country and higher values capturing a highly democratic country. We follow convention by defining a country as democratic if its summary regime type score is above 6 during the crisis spell (Marshall, Gurr and Jaggers, 2017).

---

[8] Systemic and non-systemic crises are distinguished in Reinhart (2010).

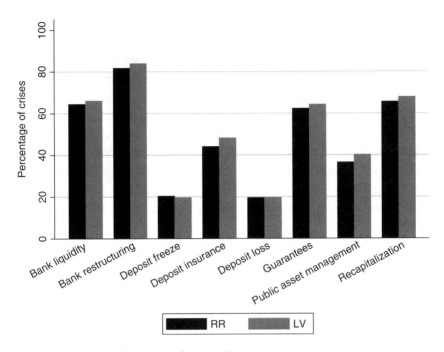

Figure 5.2: Relative frequency of crisis policy responses, 1848–2008.

Our analysis of policy responses begins with the raw data. Both the R&R and L&V data include government policy responses in democratic countries with start dates from 1848 to 2008. We record responses to 38 crises in 17 democracies in the pre-war era.[9] In the post-1970 era, we record responses to 55 crises in 41 democracies using the R&R measure, and 74 crises in 58 democracies using the L&V measure.

We plot the relative frequency of each of the policy response indicators in Figure 5.2. We observe similar values across all the policy responses for both the R&R and L&V crises. Figure 5.2 shows that Liquidity Support and Bank Restructuring are two of the most commonly used policy responses to crises since 1848. Indiscriminate, uncollateralized, open-ended or subsidized liquidity support was extended in roughly two-thirds of all crisis episodes, and restructuring was implemented in more than 80 per cent. It is little surprise that liquidity support features as one of the most popular policy responses. Laeven and Valencia (2008, 21) refer to it as 'the most common first line

[9] Unless otherwise stated, we rely on the Boix, Miller and Rosato classification scheme.

of response in systemic crisis episodes', observing it in all the post-2007 crisis episodes and even in Argentina in 1995 when a currency board was in place. Indeed, its historical ubiquity is remarkable: the strictures of the gold standard did not prevent governments in the pre-1914 era from extending liquidity support,[10] and nor did the absence of a central bank or legal frameworks prohibiting intervention by fiscal authorities. As we detail in Chapter 9, before the creation of the Federal Reserve in 1913, the US Treasury was often called upon to provide liquidity in times of crisis and stringency.[11] Lacking a formal central bank until 1964, the Treasury in Brazil, as discussed in Chapter 11, was called on to take similar actions during crises in the nineteenth and early twentieth century.

Bank restructuring also commonly follows a crisis. Returning to the example of the 1995 crisis episode in Argentina, 15 institutions encountered problems, of which 5 were liquidated, 6 were resolved under a P&A operation, and 4 were absorbed by stronger institutions. There were 13 additional mergers involving 47 banks. Closures also may extend to non-bank financial institutions, such as Thailand following the 1997 crisis in which 56 finance companies were closed (Laeven and Valencia, 2008, 22). The developments in Norway after the 1921 crisis provide a notable pre-1939 example: a total of 47 commercial banks, including several of the country's biggest banks, were restructured, with only six avoiding liquidation. Similarly, following a contemporary crisis in Denmark, a total of 32 commercial banks were liquidated during the 1920s, while 16 banks on the brink of liquidation were taken over by healthier banks (Larsson, 1991, 97). In the United States, significant waves of restructuring occurred during the 1907 crisis, the Great Depression era of the 1930s, the savings and loan crisis of the 1980s, and the recent crisis starting in 2007.

Guarantees and recapitalizations are also common policy responses following a crisis. Guarantees featured in about three-fifths of all crisis episodes. Underscoring their virtually essential nature in

---

[10] Governments could do this, for example, by temporarily suspending gold standard rules to facilitate LOLR provision, as in Britain after 1844.

[11] The US Treasury would pay interest and/or principal on its debt in advance, place deposits in banks despite prohibitions against it doing so, offer to accept securities other than government bonds as collateral for deposits of government funds, or buy and sell silver (Conant, 1915, 714).

highly financialized economies, significant guarantees on non-deposit liabilities featured in nearly every crisis episode that began over the 2007–8 period. In the case of Ireland, for instance, the government introduced unlimited guarantees of most liabilities of ten banks. Other measures during the 2007–8 crisis were much narrower in scope, such as the guarantees extended to interbank loans in Belgium, Germany and the Netherlands. Implicit protection to creditors was also present following crises in countries with high levels of state ownership of the banking system, such as Bolivia, Ecuador, Colombia and Peru in the 1980s, and India and Italy in the 1990s.

The Bank of England's response to the 1890 Barings crisis provides what Kindleberger and Aliber describe as 'the most famous guarantee of liabilities' from the pre-1939 era (Kindleberger and Aliber, 2011, 217). As we discuss more fully in Chapter 7, the Bank's governor extended a guarantee of Barings' liabilities and organized a rescue fund with assistance from other banks that would offset any losses it might incur. Denmark's response following the 1907 crisis provides a less well-known example. Here the Ministry of Finance and the Treasury orchestrated a consortium of five leading banks to assist and extend an unlimited guarantee of the liabilities of weaker banks (Bordo and Eichengreen, 1999, 46; Conant, 1915, 300–1).

Governments relied on recapitalizations in roughly two-thirds of all crisis episodes. In all of the 2007–8 crises, for instance, public capital support was extended, with governments taking a stake in at least one bank. In some countries, as well as earlier crisis episodes, such as Colombia in the early 1980s, Finland, Norway and Sweden in the late 1980s and early 1990s, and Thailand and South Korea following the Asian financial crisis, governments nationalized failing institutions. Recapitalizations were also used, on occasion, in the pre-1939 era. The Dutch government, for instance, provided public funds in 1924 to stabilize the share price of a large commercial bank (Colvin, 2014). During the 1934 crisis in Belgium, the banking system was in such a weak position that none of the banks, with the exception of the unusually large Société Générale, could publish accounts. The government lent support to two bankrupt middle-sized banks and later extended a special credit line to save the country's second largest bank from collapse (Vanthemsche, 1991).

Protection for depositors – either via the creation of new insurance arrangements or the extension of existing schemes – follows as the next most frequently observed response, featuring in nearly half of all crisis episodes. Following the 2007–8 crisis, for instance, all governments in our database enhanced protection for depositors. In some countries, such as Austria, Germany, Iceland and Ireland, the government extended unlimited coverage to depositors. New depositor protection was also put in place following a number of crises in the 1980s and 1990s, including the aforementioned crises in Colombia, Scandinavia, Argentina and East Asia. With the exception of the United States during the Great Depression, the creation or extension of formal deposit insurance was absent in all other crises in the pre-1939 era.[12]

Public Asset Management features in about 40 per cent of the crisis episodes. We observe only two instances where a democratic government assumed direct responsibility for distressed bank assets in the pre-1939 era. In Germany in the final years of the Weimar Republic, the Reichsbank created a 'bad bank' to purchase distressed assets from ailing financial institutions (James, 2009, 86–8). Similarly, as we detail in Chapter 9, the Home Owners' Loan Corporation (HOLC) in the United States served as a 'bad bank' during the Great Depression. Such public asset management companies are now much more common and were used, for instance, in Finland and Sweden in the early 1990s and in a number of countries during the Asian financial crises and again after 2007 (Gandrud and Hallerberg, 2013). We see debt relief as a form of public asset management much less frequently – both recorded instances in democracies occurred during crises in the 1980s and 1990s in Ecuador (Caprio and Klingebiel, 2003; Honohan and Klingebiel, 2003).

Deposit freezes, bank holidays and payment suspensions are less frequently used than other measures aimed at delaying the exit of insolvent banks, occurring in 20 per cent of crisis episodes. Deposit freezes are most prevalent in crises affecting Latin America: in Argentina in 1989 and 2001, Brazil in 1990, Ecuador in 1999 and Uruguay in 2002. The United States features as the most frequent user of these instruments in the pre-1939 era. Bank holidays were implemented during the 1907 crisis and the Great Depression in the 1930s, while a number of important banks suspended payments during the 1873 and 1884 banking panics (Bordo and Eichengreen, 1999).

---

[12] In Norway, a guarantee fund for savings banks with voluntary membership was put in place in 1921. A separate guarantee fund for commercial banks was introduced in 1939. Yet neither fund was a pure deposit insurance scheme (Gerdrup, 2003).

Deposit losses are the most seldom-used measure, appearing in roughly one-fifth of crisis episodes. Argentina is one example where losses have been imposed on depositors more than once since 1970. Under the Bonex plan in 1989, domestic currency time deposits were converted into long-term dollar denominated bonds. After the conversion, depositors suffered large losses as they retained only the secondary market value of Bonex holdings, which traded at a discount that reached as high as two-thirds before recovering to about 50 per cent, in lieu of their deposits. Then, in 2001, severe losses were again imposed when dollar deposits were 'pesofied' via conversion into the domestic currency at an exchange rate below the prevailing market rate.

In Chapters 9 and 12, we explore multiple crises in the United States and Brazil in which depositors incurred losses. Canada provides another example where losses were imposed on depositors more than once following systemic crises in the pre-1939 era. Following a crisis in 1908, depositors recovered less than a third of the value of their savings when the small Banque de St Jean failed. Later, when the somewhat larger Farmers' Bank of Canada failed, depositors, whose assets exceeded $1.31 million, were fully wiped out. It is notable that when shareholders and depositors campaigned for compensation from the government, their request was denied. According to Carr, Mathewson and Quigley, 'to reimburse the depositors without an explicit mandate from the royal commission would implicitly introduce deposit insurance in Canada, a concept for which there appears to have been little general support' (Carr, Mathewson and Quigley, 1995, 1141). Indeed, members of both major political parties opposed a proposed bill to provide full compensation for depositors in the Farmers' Bank. A similar approach was taken when the small-sized Bank of Vancouver failed in the aftermath of a crisis in 1912. Losses to depositors reached 88 per cent of their claims. It appears that depositor losses in American banks in this era were usually smaller, though it could take years for depositors in failed banks to be (partially) repaid (Federal Deposit Insurance Corporation (US), 2014, 24–5). Canada's line appears to have been unusually harsh. Carr, Mathewson and Quigley indicate that the central bank and the finance ministry failed to consider 'any course other than liquidation in which depositors would bear the full brunt of their assigned losses' (Carr, Mathewson and Quigley, 1995, 1142).

Our argument leads us to expect that democratic governments responded to systemic crises with more far-reaching interventions

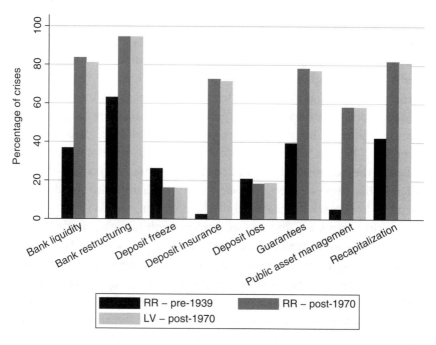

Figure 5.3: Relative frequency of crisis policy responses, pre-1939 v. post-1970.

aiming to delay the exit of clearly insolvent banks in the post-1970 period than in the past. Some evidence supporting this claim can be seen in Figure 5.3, which compares the relative frequency across both time periods for each of the policy response indicators. We then test the difference in proportions. As can be seen, post-1970 governments provided extensive liquidity support, guarantees and recapitalizations roughly twice as often as those governments in the pre-1939 era. As suggested earlier, the most striking difference can be found with respect to deposit insurance and public asset management, where such measures were on average used much more frequently in the post-1970 period. Post-1970 governments on average also opted more frequently for bank restructuring. We find no significant differences for the remaining policy response indicators across the two time periods.

Our data suggests that governments typically employ a range of responses when responding to crises. For instance, even a very pro-market government may provide extensive liquidity support as it restructures the banking system and closes clearly insolvent banks. Likewise, extensive bailouts involving recapitalizations and guarantees often involve closing and merging some failing banks. Since the raw binary data does not reveal which indicators are correlated and potentially exaggerate the dimensionality of the data, we use the *first principal component* of the eight indicators as our preferred measure of government policy responses to banking crises.

This index constructed from the R&R crisis data ranges from −2.56 to 2.52, with higher values indicating a more coherent set of bailout policy responses and lower values indicating a more coherent set of Bagehot policy responses. The index generated from the L&V data ranges from −2.81 to 2.36. In a world where governments implement a range of policy responses, principal component analysis informs us how these responses co-vary along the Market–Socialization continuum, enabling us to assess the extent to which particular governments approximate the Bagehot or bailout ideal types.

Our analysis of the R&R data reveals, in order of importance, that the first principal component is strongly correlated with Recapitalization, Liquidity, Deposit Insurance and Public Asset Management, with Guarantees having moderately high correlations. This suggests that these five policy indicators vary together. Deposit Freezes have almost no correlation with the first principal component. Not surprisingly, Bank Restructuring has a moderately high negative correlation and Deposit Loss a weakly negative correlation. The direction and magnitude for all the policy indicator correlations are generally similar for the L&V data, although the magnitude varies somewhat.

This suggests that the first principal component can be viewed as a measure of the coherence of the bailout response. The principal component scores that comprise our policy response index show that cases with positive scores will tend to have greater values on indicators associated with delaying the exit of insolvent banks (Recapitalization, Liquidity, Deposit Insurance, Public Asset Management and Guarantees) and lower values for the remaining indicators related to the aim of minimizing the burden to the taxpayer (Bank Restructuring and Deposit Losses). The opposite is the case for negative policy response index scores.

Using the R&R data, Figure 5.4 plots the annual number of systemic banking crises and the annual average crisis policy response in democracies since 1848. We find that bailout interventions before 1945 were exceptional, whereas by the 1990s they had become the rule. The policy responses using the L&V data, plotted in Figure 5.5, reveal a

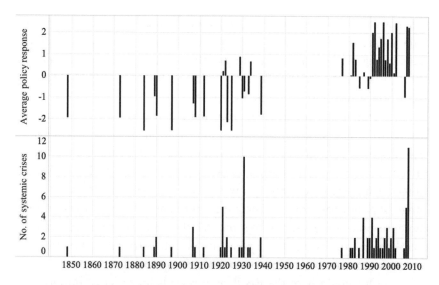

Figure 5.4: Banking crisis policy responses, 1848–2008 – R&R sample.
Note: Democracies identified via Boix, Miller and Rosato classification scheme.

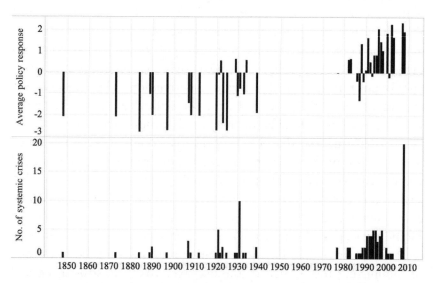

Figure 5.5: Banking crisis policy responses, 1848–2008 – L&V sample.
Note: Democracies identified via Boix, Miller and Rosato classification scheme.

similar tendency in the post-1970 period. For both the R&R and L&V data, the average crisis policy response in the pre-war period (−1.05 on the R&R index, −1.21 on the L&V index) stands in stark contrast to that in the post-1970 period (1.33 and 1.15, respectively). This difference in means attains a high level of statistical significance for both indexes (t = 9.09 and t = 9.59, p < 0.001).[13]

Indeed, democratic governments in the low expectations pre-war period generally implemented policy responses that adhered more closely to the Bagehot ideal type. The average response remains below zero for nearly all of the pre-1945 period. In years with a relatively large number of new crises, as in the early 1920s and the 1930s, policy responses tend toward the Bagehot end of our index. Of the three policies our analysis suggests to be most identifiable with a coherent bailout response, we observe only one pre-war case of deposit insurance (the United States in the Great Depression), two instances where the government assumed responsibility for distressed bank assets (the United States in the Great Depression and Germany in the final years of the Weimar Republic) and roughly a third of the cases where guarantees were employed. Only nine of the thirty-six pre-war cases (23.6 per cent) record a response index score leaning in the bailout direction: Denmark (1907), Italy (1921), Netherlands (1921), Norway (1921), Sweden (1922), United States (1929), Denmark (1931), Germany (1931) and Belgium (1934) (Hansen, 1994). Most of this small number of bailout cases are found in the interwar period, supporting our view that it was a transitional era, but one in which Bagehot responses were still dominant, representing roughly 70 per cent of the twenty-six crisis episodes. Indeed, we discussed the transitional nature of many of the above cases in Chapters 2 and 3, and we explore in greater detail in Chapter 9 how the United States made this transition between 1929 and 1933–5.

The rising tendency for bailout interventions from the mid-1970s, especially since the 1990s, is consistent with our argument that the protection of household wealth became an increasingly important objective of governments. We observe a striking departure from pre-war policy norms after the 1970s, most notably, as discussed earlier, with respect to government protection of deposits and use of the public sector's balance sheet to recapitalize banks and to assume responsibility for bad assets and debts. As Figure 5.3 showed, these defining features

[13] In R&R systemic crises after the 1990s the average response rises to 1.63 and the difference with the pre-war period increases in statistical significance (t =10.14, p < 0.001). For L&V systemic crises, the average response rises to 1.33 in the post-1990 period (t = 10.35, p < 0.001).

of bailout interventions were used prominently in the vast majority of post-1970 systemic crises in democracies.

5.2   Empirical Tests of the Argument

To test the causal claims in our theory more rigorously, we use our policy response measures to investigate the role of our main independent variables: the financialization of wealth, the democratization of leverage, and the accumulating policy commitment on the part of governments to financial stabilization. We expect to see more extensive interventions in democracies where we observe higher levels of these three variables.

We begin with the financialization of wealth. Our focus here concerns the extent to which households have acquired greater stakes in the stabilization of the market value of housing and financial assets. Ideally, we would employ data on the changing nature of household asset ownership and wealth portfolio composition to assess the importance of this mechanism. Yet, as discussed in Chapter 2, such data is not consistently available over a long-run period even for highly advanced economies. We explore more disaggregated data, when available, in Chapter 3 and the case study chapters.

The best available data over a long-run period is aggregate in form. Although households vary greatly in their asset ownership and wealth holdings, the data examined in Chapter 2 indicates rising average household wealth, rising exposure to market-traded assets and growing financial inclusion. As economies have grown richer and financial deepening has progressed, home ownership rates have increased and more voters have become linked to the financial system via deposits and riskier market-traded assets. Aggregate measures of such trends almost certainly capture the growing stake of many households in the stabilization of the value of these housing and financial assets.

Housing assets constitute the largest share of wealth holdings for middle-class households (see Chapters 2 and 3). Typical middle-class households, particularly in advanced democracies, have also become more highly leveraged. Their wealth portfolios are thus highly sensitive to changes in residential property prices: rising property prices create substantial wealth gains for these households, whereas the threat of large losses can loom when financial crashes portend falling housing values. This is the essence of the composition effect we outlined in Chapter 2.

Measuring national-level residential property prices in a cross-national comparative manner presents challenges (Scatigna, Szemere and Tsatsaronis, 2014). We make use of two different national series (Bank for International Settlements, 2017a; Knoll, Schularick and Steger, 2017). Knoll, Schularick and Steger provide an annual nominal house price index for 14 advanced economies since 1870 with the base equal to 100 in 1990. The Bank for International Settlements data offers an annual nominal house price index for fifty-nine advanced and emerging market economies since 1966 with the base equal to 100 in 2010. We use the Knoll, Schularick and Steger data as our primary source and then supplement it with data from the Bank for International Settlements. We link the two series of index numbers, setting the base of the new consolidated series to 100 in 2010. We focus on the property price level as it helps to capture the extent of housing equity wealth within a country.[14]

As we have seen, financial assets also represent a sizeable proportion of middle-class household wealth (Chapters 2 and 3). The failure of a financial institution would have clear negative implications for the wealth of those households whose savings were potentially at stake. This is the essence of the size effect we outlined in Chapter 2. As households' deposits in the financial system have grown over time, we would expect the size and intensity of the preference for government protection of this wealth to have strengthened, prompting more extensive interventions. Indeed, strict implementation of Bagehot policies would constitute a serious threat to this wealth, including in circumstances where the government reneged on pre-existing guarantees or such guarantees proved insufficient to insure this wealth in practice.

We measure the importance of household deposits using two different national series (Jordà et al., 2017; World Bank, 2017). Jordà et al. provide data on total domestic deposits by non-residents for seventeen advanced countries since 1870. The World Bank provides

---

[14] We use nominal rather than real indices on grounds of practicality and because theory and empirical evidence suggests that most people (as opposed to economists) think of asset prices in nominal rather than real terms (Brunnermeier and Julliard, 2008; Shafir, Diamond and Tversky, 1997; Shiller, 2005, 55–6).

data on deposits in banks and other financial institutions since 1960. We normalize both measures by GDP. Then, we use the Jordà et al. data as our primary source and supplement it with data from the World Bank.

Financialization also entails greater household exposure to market-traded financial assets, such as stocks and bonds. Defined contribution (DC) pensions constitute the primary vehicle in which many of these market-traded financial assets are held. As with property assets, the composition effect we outlined in Chapter 2 suggests that households have much more to lose when financial crashes threaten sudden collapses in the value of their pension assets. The prospect of such losses should prompt intense effective societal demand for intervention where middle-class households are exposed to this risk, most notably where private sources provide a substantial projected share of retirement income.

As with housing and deposit assets, long-run data on the size and composition of DC pension assets is not available. Nonetheless, using a range of sources, we are able to identify countries where households were exposed to DC pension assets via one or more of the following arrangements: (1) a mandatory privately or publicly managed DC scheme for all workers; (2) widespread participation in voluntary private DC schemes; (3) a mandatory privately or publicly managed DC scheme for workers in some sectors; and (4) limited participation in voluntary private DC schemes (Brooks, 2005, 2007; International Organisation of Pension Supervisors, 2017; International Social Security Association, 2017; Organisation for Economic Cooperation and Development, International Social Security Association and International Organisation of Pension Supervisors, 2008). Following OECD (2015a), we identify countries with widespread participation in voluntary schemes as those where coverage of private pension schemes exceeds 40 per cent of the working-age population (15–64 years). Limited participation designates countries where regulations permit voluntary DC schemes but coverage is short of this threshold.

Table 5.2 identifies the country and L&V crisis-years where we identify exposure to DC pension assets based on one or more of these four arrangements. As discussed in Chapter 2, DC pension schemes exist in various forms in countries of all income categories. We use this data to create four different measures to test our empirical

Table 5.2. DC pension scheme arrangements

Mandatory DC scheme – all workers[15]	Widespread voluntary DC participation	Mandatory DC scheme – sectoral	Limited voluntary DC participation
Argentina 1989	Belgium 2008	India 1993	Austria 2008
Argentina 1995	Germany 2008	Thailand 1997	Brazil 1990
Argentina 2001	Iceland 2008		Brazil 1994
Bolivia 1994	Ireland 2008		Bulgaria 1994
Colombia 1998	United Kingdom 2007		Costa Rica 1994
Denmark 2008	United States 1988		Czech Republic 1996
Hungary 2008	United States 2007		France 2008
Sweden 2008			Hungary 1991
Switzerland 2008			Hungary 2008
Uruguay 2002			Italy 2008
			Luxembourg 2008
			Netherlands 2008
			Norway 1991
			Portugal 2008
			Slovenia 2008
			South Korea 1997
			Spain 2008
			Thailand 1997
			Ukraine 2008

expectations. The first measure is an additive index that seeks to capture the degree of exposure to DC pension assets based on the four arrangements discussed above. We assign a value of 1 to those arrangements (3) and (4) where DC schemes are mandatory for only some sectors of the economy or voluntary participation is limited. We assign a value of 2 to those arrangements (1) and (2) where DC schemes are mandatory for all workers or voluntary participation is widespread. In principle, this measure can range from 0 to 4, with higher values indicating greater exposure to DC assets (i.e. a mandatory DC scheme and widespread voluntary participation). However, in practice, we observe variation ranging from 0 to 3.

---

[15] Argentina (in 2008) and Bolivia and Hungary (in 2010) have since reversed their implementation of mandatory DC pension schemes.

We also explore three alternative binary measures that aim to capture the different configurations of the above arrangements. One measure captures the presence of arrangements (1) and (2) where DC asset holdings are likely to be more wide-ranging based on mandatory or widespread voluntary participation. Another measure captures the presence of any mandatory DC arrangement either for all workers (1) or specific sectors (3). A final measure captures the presence of any of the above DC arrangements.

We now turn to the democratization of leverage. Here we focus on the extent to which households have developed a stronger stake in financial stabilization based on rising leverage from mortgage and consumer borrowing. We measure the importance of household leverage using three different national series (Bank for International Settlements, 2017b; Jordà, Schularick and Taylor, 2016; Léon, 2017a). Jordà, Schularick, and Taylor provide data on bank credit extended to households in seventeen advanced countries since 1870. In addition to commercial banks' balance sheets, these data also include credit from savings banks, credit unions and building societies. This series includes data for both mortgage and consumer borrowing, but the latter for a shorter period. Since mortgage borrowing constitutes the bulk of household leverage, we use this data for years in which data on consumer borrowing is unavailable. The Bank for International Settlements (BIS) data is available for 44 advanced and emerging market countries since 1944. This data offers the broadest coverage of financial intermediaries, including all credit from domestic and foreign sources. The Léon data extends from 1995 to 2014, covering 143 countries but is limited to commercial banks as the source of credit. All measures are normalized by GDP. We use Jordà, Schularick and Taylor as our primary source, then supplement it with the BIS data, before turning to the Léon data to fill any remaining gaps.

Lastly, we turn to measuring the evolving commitment on the part of governments to financial stabilization. Here we wish to capture the extent to which governments have exhibited an accumulating commitment to financial stability as a policy priority. Our measure of these promises focuses on the most concrete forms of pre-commitment: prudential regulation, the creation of financial regulatory agencies, and extensive state control of the banking system. We use the creation date of the first regulatory agency at the national level charged with responsibility for financial supervision or, alternatively, when the government took extensive control of the banking system. We view these institutional innovations as clear and vivid manifestations of an explicit or implicit promise by governments to voters to prioritize financial stability as part of their responsibility to the public. For creation dates we draw largely on the regulatory agencies data from Jacint, Levi-Faur and Fernández-i-Marín (2011). We supplement this, where necessary, with information from the websites of national central banks and financial regulatory agencies. We use available data on government ownership of the banking system to identify extensive state control (Abiad, Detragiache and Tressel, 2008; Honohan and Klingebiel, 2000).

Figure 5.6 shows the evolution of government policy commitments to financial stability since 1850, first previewed in Chapter 2, based on the introduction of legislation or the creation of regulatory authorities providing for banking supervision as well as the establishment of extensive state control of the banking system. We understand regulatory authorities here in a broad sense. Some countries commit to

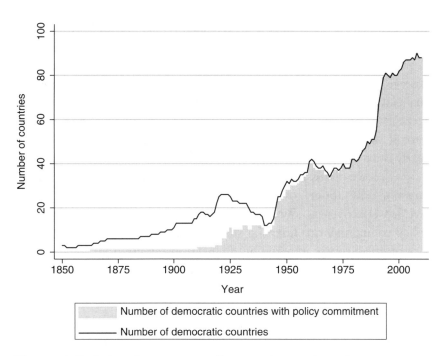

Figure 5.6: Evolution of government policy commitments since 1850.

regulation by central banks, some by having the finance ministry take on this responsibility, and some by establishing stand-alone regulatory agencies (Gandrud, 2013). Others reveal this commitment through extensive state ownership of the banking system, defined here as when state-owned institutions hold more than 50 per cent of assets or 75 per cent of deposits (Abiad, Detragiache and Tressel, 2008; Honohan and Klingebiel, 2003). Our interest here is to identify when governments first make this commitment, which, we assume, once made, is not retracted by institutional change that relocates regulatory authority.

We identify the creation of the Office of the Comptroller of the Currency in the United States in 1863 as the first instance when a democratic government made an explicit commitment to financial stability via the creation of supervisory authority based on statutory law. This agency, part of the US Treasury, was created to charter, regulate and supervise all national banks and thrift institutions. Other early creators of regulatory authorities included Sweden (1907) and Denmark (1919).[16] Effective bank regulation and oversight developed in Brazil in 1933 when the Treasury imposed reserve requirements on banks along with other measures (see Chapter 12). But as late as the early 1930s most democratic governments lacked such regulatory authorities. Britain, for instance, did not create this authority until the nationalization of the Bank of England in 1946. From the mid-1930s onwards, we observe a sharp increase toward more democracies committing to financial stability as a policy goal either via the creation of regulatory agencies or by imposing state control over the banking system. By the start of the post-war era, promoting financial stability had become a nearly universal de facto policy commitment among democracies.

As we discussed in Chapter 2, our argument implies that voters care not only about government promises but, more crucially, their revealed effectiveness. We thus develop a proxy measure of stronger policy commitment to financial stabilization based on a country's history of effectiveness in avoiding financial instability. Our logic is that voters in countries with longer experiences of policy effectiveness will have higher expectations of financial stability than voters in countries

---

[16] An inspectorate for savings banks was established earlier via statutory legislation in Austria (1844), Denmark (1880), Finland (1895) and Norway (1900). Yet these acts omitted supervision of commercial banks. Our results are unchanged if we use this alternative dating.

with shorter experiences. Formal government commitments to financial stabilization such as the establishment of a financial regulatory authority, the introduction of statutory banking regulation or extensive state control of banking will be devalued in voters' eyes if crises subsequently occur. Our measure thus uses the date of financial regulatory authority creation, statutory banking regulation implementation and/or extensive state control of the banking system (whichever occurs first) as the baseline for counting the number of years since a country last experienced a systemic crisis, with higher values indicating an accumulating policy commitment. An accumulating policy commitment should orient more voters toward expecting continued financial stabilization, prompting more intense effective societal demand for public intervention when it is threatened.

Figure 5.7 plots the years of accumulated policy commitment for a sample of L&V crisis-years. At the upper end of the distribution, we find crisis-years after a prolonged period of financial stability following the creation of a regulatory authority or statutory banking regulation (Austria 2008, Germany 2008, Denmark 2008, Japan 1997, Sweden 1991) or an extended period of state control of the banking system (Lithuania 1995, Albania 1994, Poland 1992, Estonia 1992). At the lower end of the distribution, we observe crisis-years where either the country lacked a regulatory authority, statutory banking regulation, or extensive state control (Belgium 1934, France 1930, Canada 1923, Netherlands 1921) or it had experienced recent financial distress (Denmark, for instance, experienced a crisis in 1931 and 1921 following creation of a regulatory authority in 1919).

We also include control variables for degree of democracy, GDP per capita, public debt burden, exchange rate regime and partisanship. We control for degree of democracy because the representation of taxpayer interests may be stronger in regimes with stronger democratic institutions (Rosas, 2006). We consider the level of economic development – the natural log of per capita GDP – and public debt burdens to account for the fiscal constraints on governments to afford the expense associated with bank bailouts. We use GDP per capita data from the Maddison Project and Penn World Tables 9.0 (Feenstra, Inklaar and Timmer, 2015; Maddison Project, 2013), and data on gross government debt as proportion of GDP (Abbas et al., 2011; Mauro et al., 2013). In some model specifications GDP per capita is highly correlated with the measures testing our argument. To avoid

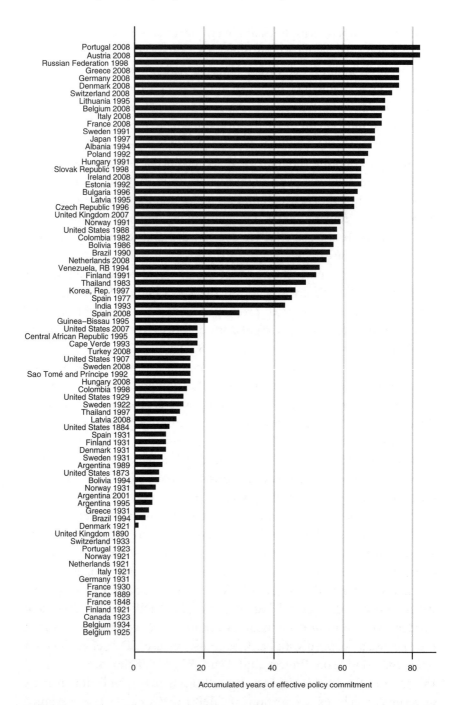

Figure 5.7: Accumulated years of effective policy commitment.

complications with multicollinearity, in these specifications we substitute a binary variable for 'advanced economies' based on the IMF income classification scheme. Following Flandreau and Zumer, we supplement this scheme by classifying Greece, Portugal and Spain as emerging economies during the pre-1945 era (Flandreau and Zumer, 2004).

Exchange rate commitments may also constrain the capacity of governments to undertake the fiscal and monetary measures associated with bank bailouts. We might expect governments to move closer to a more coherent Bagehot response under a fixed exchange rate regime. We obtain data on exchange rate commitments from three sources (Bordo and Meissner, 2006; Ilzetzki, Reinhart and Rogoff, 2017; Reinhart, 2010) and create a binary variable indicating the presence of a fixed exchange regime, including a commitment to the gold standard.

It is also essential to control for political partisanship, which we argued in Chapter 2 should be unrelated to the propensity of governments to provide bailouts due to the rise of great expectations. We use data from Brambor and Lindvall and the Database of Political Institutions to create a measure of government partisanship, coded as 1 = 'Right,' 2 = 'Centre,' and 3 = 'Left' (Brambor and Lindvall, 2017; Cruz, Keefer and Scartascini, 2016).

We provide our sample, summary statistics and correlation matrix in the online appendix. We estimate a series of ordinary least squares regressions that model government policy responses to banking crises. Missing values pose some concern in this analysis. Banking crises are relatively rare events. The summary statistics show that partisanship exhibits a somewhat higher level of missingness. Inclusion of all the covariates above further depletes the already small number of crisis windows. We thus estimate both a reduced-form specification where partisanship is excluded and a more comprehensive specification where this variable is included. Results are similar across both specifications.

The results provide strong confirmation of our argument. Table 5.3 reports the results from the larger sample of L&V crises, and we provide the results from the R&R sample in the online appendix. Turning first to financialization, we find that more extensive bailouts follow crises in countries where residential property prices have reached elevated levels. The magnitude of the effect is substantively large. Based on the results from Model 1 in Table 5.3, we can say for an increase in property prices on the level experienced in the United

Table 5.3. Great expectations and banking crises policy responses, 1873–2008 – L&V

Variables	(1)	(2)	(3)	(4)	(5)	(6)	(7)	(8)
Property prices (ln)	0.398*** (0.103)	0.401*** (0.108)						
Deposits/ GDP (ln)			0.216*** (0.0639)	0.220*** (0.0629)				
DC scale					0.737*** (0.157)	0.753*** (0.168)		
DC mandatory or widespread							1.099*** (0.276)	1.120*** (0.297)
DC mandatory								
DC any								
Household debt/GDP (ln)								
Years effective commitment	0.0128 (0.00835)	0.0123 (0.00898)	0.0224*** (0.00555)	0.0233*** (0.00588)	0.0256*** (0.00544)	0.0254*** (0.00583)	0.0283*** (0.00567)	0.0285*** (0.00592)
Degree of democracy	0.0125 (0.117)	0.00952 (0.120)	0.0769 (0.0661)	0.0400 (0.0682)	0.0440 (0.0622)	0.0289 (0.0671)	0.0730 (0.0619)	0.0551 (0.0675)
GDP per capita (ln)			0.000560* (0.000319)	0.000621* (0.000317)				
Advanced market	0.0538 (0.645)	0.0644 (0.658)			−0.202 (0.239)	−0.188 (0.240)	−0.255 (0.246)	−0.248 (0.250)
Public debt/ GDP (ln)	0.0555 (0.304)	0.0667 (0.315)	0.137 (0.221)	0.123 (0.218)	0.0121 (0.157)	−0.0111 (0.155)	0.00351 (0.170)	−0.0183 (0.167)
Fixed exchange rate	0.258 (0.288)	0.262 (0.288)	0.377 (0.272)	0.429 (0.284)	0.0938 (0.202)	0.132 (0.210)	0.137 (0.235)	0.172 (0.246)
Partisanship		0.0706 (0.128)		0.0927 (0.131)		0.189 (0.127)		0.154 (0.131)
Constant	−1.054 (1.083)	−1.197 (1.255)	−1.761* (0.932)	−1.601 (0.994)	−1.074 (0.744)	−1.224 (0.810)	−1.176 (0.813)	−1.243 (0.895)
Observations	48	48	95	93	104	102	104	102
R-squared	0.726	0.727	0.354	0.366	0.424	0.433	0.373	0.381

Robust standard errors in parentheses. *** $p < 0.01$, ** $p < 0.05$, * $p < 0.1$

Policy Index

(9)	(10)	(11)	(12)	(13)	(14)	(15)	(16)
1.066*** (0.312)	1.059*** (0.324)						
		1.299*** (0.271)	1.328*** (0.284)				
				0.805*** (0.151)	0.793*** (0.169)		
0.0309*** (0.00557)	0.0312*** (0.00583)	0.0236*** (0.00519)	0.0232*** (0.00562)	0.0255*** (0.00432)	0.0259*** (0.00515)	0.0300*** (0.00571)	0.0305*** (0.00598)
0.0743 (0.0573)	0.0570 (0.0644)	0.0394 (0.0614)	0.0277 (0.0653)	−0.0730 (0.0768)	−0.0759 (0.0763)	0.103* (0.0610)	0.0836 (0.0663)
0.000982** (0.000432)	0.000981** (0.000433)						
		−0.151 (0.251)	−0.133 (0.252)	−1.480*** (0.319)	−1.478*** (0.317)	−0.253 (0.274)	−0.254 (0.282)
−0.0334 (0.219)	−0.0481 (0.218)	0.0347 (0.155)	0.0134 (0.154)	0.424** (0.186)	0.421** (0.189)	0.0476 (0.187)	0.0298 (0.187)
0.118 (0.269)	0.150 (0.277)	0.0258 (0.211)	0.0594 (0.221)	0.153 (0.243)	0.159 (0.238)	0.196 (0.274)	0.226 (0.286)
	0.129 (0.126)		0.193 (0.125)		0.0409 (0.112)		0.104 (0.124)
−1.206 (0.916)	−1.251 (0.990)	−1.112 (0.717)	−1.302 (0.791)	−2.522*** (0.822)	−2.536** (0.940)	−1.469* (0.871)	−1.445 (0.964)
103	101	104	102	67	66	104	102
0.358	0.364	0.428	0.436	0.657	0.658	0.309	0.314

States between the 1929 and 2008 crises (from 3.5 to 129.8 on the index), we would expect the policy response index to increase by 1.43 [0.74, 2.18].[17] Even a smaller increase in property prices, such as that experienced between the 1988 and 2008 crises in the United States (from 47.6 to 129.8 on the index), generates a 0.40 [0.21, 0.60] increase in the policy response index, an effect of reasonably large size given the sample mean of 0.35. Higher property prices undoubtedly tap into the build-up of concentrated wealth in housing assets among middle-class households, capturing aspects of the composition effect we outlined in Chapter 2. Sharp falls in asset prices during crises can also quickly threaten highly exposed banks with insolvency, intensifying financial distress and creating additional wealth losses (especially for leveraged households, which we consider below). Financial crashes therefore place the value of these more volatile housing assets at serious risk, thus prompting governments to respond to the more intense effective societal demand for intervention that follows from the growing stake that households have in financial stabilization.

We also find that democratic governments have tended to move sharply away from the strict implementation of Bagehot policies when households have acquired a sizeable share of wealth stored in financial system deposits. This result, demonstrative of the size effect we outlined in Chapter 2, dovetails with the earlier analysis of the raw data, which revealed the introduction and extension of deposit insurance to be a core feature of post-1970 policy responses and the imposition of losses on depositors from this time to be a rare occurrence. As deposit wealth has grown in size and, more critically, broadened across the wealth distribution, it has generated stronger propensities among democratic governments to intervene. We can say, based on the results from Model 3 in Table 5.3, that for an increase in deposit wealth experienced in emerging economies, such as Ecuador between its crises in 1982 and 1998 (13.4 per cent to 23.3 per cent of GDP), we would expect the policy response index to increase by 0.08 [0.03, 0.13]. Alternatively, using the example of an increase in deposit wealth of a developing country, such as Bolivia between its crises in 1986 and 1994 (4.6 per cent to 33 per cent), we would expect the policy response index to

---

[17] 95 per cent confidence intervals are in brackets, binary covariates are set to zero, and all other covariates are held constant at their means.

increase by 0.31 [0.12, 0.48]. These are both fairly sizeable effects given the sample mean.

We also find that household exposure to market-traded financial assets held in DC pension schemes heightens the likelihood that governments will intervene with more expensive bailouts. Table 5.3 reports substantively large coefficients across all four measures of household exposure to DC pension schemes, suggesting that the composition effect associated with housing assets also extends to pension assets. To provide a sense of this propensity in our sample, we use Figure 5.8 to compare the simulated expected policy response index of countries in terms of household exposure to any of the four DC arrangements analysed. Figure 5.8 shows that the expected policy response index score in countries where DC arrangements are present is significantly more oriented toward bailouts than in countries where such arrangements are not found.[18] The results suggest that governments are exceptionally responsive to growing household anxiety about the value of market-exposed pension assets following a crisis.

We also find that governments appear responsive to the stronger stake that households have in financial stabilization in democracies with elevated leverage from mortgage and consumer borrowing. Using the results from Model 13 in Table 5.3, we can say that for an increase in household leverage equivalent to that experienced in the Netherlands between its 1921 and 2008 crises (14.5 per cent to 109.7 per cent of GDP), we would expect the policy response index to increase by 1.63 [1.02, 2.22]. Even for a smaller increase in a less highly leveraged economy, such as that experienced in Germany between its 1931 and 2008 crises (26.2 per cent to 59.7 per cent), we would expect this index to increase by 0.66 [0.42, 0.91].

The democratization of leverage has been associated with more extensive bailouts, in all likelihood, due to government efforts to support aggregate demand and to prevent 'fire sales' of assets that would threaten household wealth and harm the wider economy via the 'wealth effect'. Weaker demand and weaker investment depresses output, particularly in highly financialized economies where growing leverage drives higher asset market valuations (Brunnermeier and Schnabel, 2015; Jordà, Schularick and Taylor, 2015). To avoid losing political support from

---

[18] For R&R systemic crises the difference is 2.05 ($t = 6.15$, $p < 0.001$) and for L&V crises the difference is 1.86 ($t = 6.47$, $p < 0.001$).

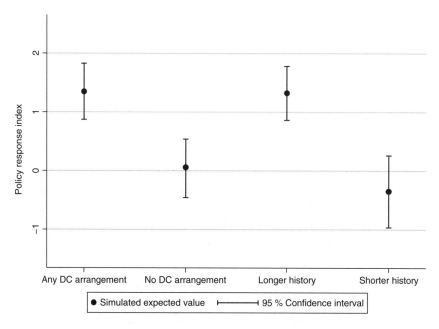

Figure 5.8: Simulated expected policy responses.

households, the results suggest governments have become increasingly prone to public intervention to stabilize the financial system.

Lastly, we also find that bailouts are more likely in democracies where voters have observed a longer accumulated policy commitment to financial stabilization. Once governments pre-commit to financial stability via concrete institutional arrangements, voters come to expect them to deliver on this promise as experience demonstrates that it is an achievable condition. The results in Table 5.3 support this conclusion, with democratic governments opting to intervene more extensively in countries with a longer track record of accumulated policy commitment.

Figure 5.8 provides a sense of this effect by comparing the simulated expected policy response index of countries with 'longer' and 'shorter' accumulated histories as defined by those observations one standard deviation above and below the sample mean. The expected policy response index score in countries with longer histories is significantly more oriented toward bailouts than in countries with shorter histories.[19] The results suggest governments are responsive to

---

[19] For R&R systemic crises the difference is 1.92 ($t = 6.56$, $p < 0.001$) and for L&V crises the difference is 1.65 ($t = 6.02$, $p < 0.001$).

the emergence of heightened voter expectations of financial stability that are grounded in an accumulating history of policy commitment.

As for our control variables, several models indicate that richer economies are more likely to choose bailout policies. This result may reflect their greater fiscal capacity to engage in taxpayer-funded financial rescues. We find little evidence that exchange rate commitments or public debt burdens constrain (or enable) particular policy responses. Lastly, we find no evidence to suggest that degree of democracy or partisanship drives government policy responses to crises. This is consistent with the doubts our argument raises as to the importance of either feature in the modern period. Indeed, the evidence confirms that the great expectations of voters, brought on by financialization, the democratization of leverage and an accumulating policy commitment to financial stability, overwhelm any effects that partisanship and democratic institutions might have in shaping bailouts.

5.3   Conclusion

Some claim that democratic politicians, as electorally accountable representatives of taxpayer interests, seek to avoid extensive interventions following banking crises compared to their counterparts in non-democratic settings. The evidence in this chapter fails to support that contention. On the contrary, consistent with our argument, it indicates that democratically elected politicians in the modern era have become increasingly prone to respond to the demands of a broader and more influential pro-bailout coalition. The emergence of great expectations and the growing political influence of this coalition have come from the three interrelated developments – the financialization of wealth, the democratization of leverage and an accumulating policy commitment to financial stability – that have been the focus of the empirical analysis in this chapter. We find clear and robust evidence that these three developments have encouraged powerful tendencies toward bailouts in modern democracies.

We show in the following chapter that democratic governments that are unable to prevent crises and that fail to respond effectively to mitigate their consequences for household wealth are now far more likely to suffer political punishment from voters than in the past. As these great expectations have diffused and become entrenched, modern democratic politicians may now see no alternative but to intervene to stabilize the financial system, not least of all to avoid electoral sanction. Yet such tendencies, and the great expectations driving them, may themselves be destabilizing. If voters have come to expect crisis prevention and mitigation policies, and governments intervene at growing cost, this may produce rising moral hazard and continuing increases in financialization, leverage and financial fragility. This can generate more, deeper crises and interventions down the line. The paradox to which we return in the concluding chapter then is that great expectations may ultimately reinforce the very threat to financial stability from which voters demand protection.

6 BANKING CRISES AND VOTERS OVER THE LONG RUN

In this chapter we test the theoretical propositions about voter punishment following banking crises that we developed in Chapter 2. Using a new dataset, we aim to identify how variations over time and variations within democratic countries affect the electoral success of incumbent political parties in the aftermath of banking crises. We expect that rising modern voter demand for wealth protection and stabilization during and after crises should heighten the political salience of institutional obstacles to policy responses compared to the past, conditioning how voters evaluate incumbents. In contrast to the 'clarity of responsibility' literature, we expect that the intensity of modern voter demand for wealth protection has become so high that crises are less excusable, even for those governments in which institutional constraints have seemingly blurred electoral accountability. Modern governments should find it more difficult to escape voter punishment when institutional constraints limit their capacity to act decisively and fairly to protect wealth during such crises.

Assessing different forms of electoral accountability, we test our argument after accounting for the effects of other economic and political variables. The results provide strong support for our claims. Political punishment in the aftermath of a banking crisis is mainly a modern phenomenon and most evident in systems where political incumbents face institutional obstacles to policy interventions. We also provide supplemental evidence that links the aftermath of modern crises and institutional constraints to increased inequality, rising voter polarization, greater policy gridlock, and declining voter satisfaction with incumbents.

A potential concern with these findings is that recessions that follow modern crises could be more severe than non-financial downturns and so the observed effect could be due to the depth of the output loss and not to the crisis itself. We address this issue by comparing banking crises to what Funke, Schularick and Trebesch term 'non-financial macro disasters'; that is, severe recessions not involving a crisis but in which output declines exceed those that follow banking crises (Barro and Ursua, 2008; Funke, Schularick and Trebesch, 2016). We find that the political aftermaths of banking crises stand out even from these more severe downturns as particularly disruptive for incumbent party electoral prospects. One reason, our supplemental evidence suggests, is that in contrast to non-financial disasters, modern banking crises appear particularly threatening to the housing and financial wealth we have shown to be of such importance to the contemporary middle class.

The rest of the chapter proceeds by first outlining our data and methods. We then present the results of our primary analysis of voter punishment before turning to our supplemental evidence on polarization, inequality and policy gridlock. We conclude by emphasizing the new insights that a long-run perspective provides.

6.1 Data and Method

A core implication of our argument is that, among crisis-hit democratic governments since the 1970s, those incumbent parties that hold political power in systems with polarized veto players are likely to incur greater voter punishment than those that do not. Resting on a minimalist Schumpeterian conception of democracy, most of the literature on economic voting offers a thin notion of accountability, insisting that incumbent parties need not lose elections for political accountability to be present (Samuels and Hellwig, 2010). Instead, voters need only *reward* or *punish* incumbents, as measured by changes in incumbent party vote shares. A decline in incumbent party votes represents accountability via punishment, incentivizing the government to change policy direction or risk not being re-elected in the future (Barro, 1973; Ferejohn, 1986).

Removing incumbent parties from office, as opposed to giving them fewer votes, offers a thicker, more demanding requirement for accountability (Samuels and Hellwig, 2010). We would expect to observe less evidence of accountability when using this requirement, for the obvious reason that even substantial voter punishment need not automatically translate into changes in the partisan control of the executive. In their analysis of post-World War II elections, Samuels and Hellwig (2010) find that even when incumbent parties suffer large declines in their vote share (greater than 5 per cent), they are removed from office only about half the time. In addition, changes in partisan control should be expected only when voters perceive viable alternatives to the incumbents (Sanders and Carey, 2002). For example, in Germany, the Christian Democratic Union (CDU) has won four successive elections since 2005 despite a rise in voter dissatisfaction after the 2008 banking crisis and the 2015 migrant crisis, partly because the opposition Social Democrats have not been perceived as offering a viable alternative government.

Yet it would be misleading in these cases to interpret the absence of partisan turnover as indicative of an absence of voter dissatisfaction. In these cases, a decline in incumbent party vote share signals voter preferences for a change in policy direction, to which incumbent politicians can feel a need to respond – even if it falls short of a wholesale change of government.

Given our emphasis on voter punishment, at a minimum, our argument requires that we uncover evidence of declining vote shares for incumbent parties that preside over banking crises in political systems with polarized veto players. We should expect weaker results as we move from 'thin' to 'thick' notions of accountability. Voters should punish incumbents in the circumstances we specify, but the political and institutional context, including the absence of viable alternative government, may preclude removing them from office.

Our primary interest is to assess how institutional constraints associated with the veto player environment condition the impact of crises on the incumbent political party's or coalition's electoral success. To achieve this goal, we begin by considering the vote share of incumbent political parties. We compile a new dataset of 484 elections from 1872 to 2013 for 33 countries in our sample.[1] We use the last election in a given year in cases where there are two or more elections in one year.

---

[1] All sample and summary statistics are provided in the online appendix.

We consider only elections for the chief executive.[2] Thus, we focus on the incumbent vote share of the president's party in presidential systems and that of the governing party – or of the dominant party in the governing coalition – in parliamentary systems.

We then extend the analysis by making use of a second new dataset on political survival, following others by constructing an annual indicator of 'incumbent spells' based on the partisan affiliation of the chief executive (Crespo-Tenorio, Jensen and Rosas, 2014). This *Partisan spells* indicator, which encompasses the years 1822–2013, measures when incumbent political parties, not individual leaders, lose office – a higher bar for electoral accountability than loss of votes. It allows us to take into account institutional features, such as term limits and fixed v. endogenous electoral cycles, which would otherwise make comparison between parliamentary and presidential regimes difficult.[3]

The key mechanism driving our argument is how modern voters respond to governments facing political constraints in the context of a banking crisis. We thus limit our focus to democratic countries. As in Chapter 5, we rely on the Boix, Miller and Rosato data as our primary means for classifying democracies and show our results to be robust to the consideration of an alternative sample of democracies using the Polity dataset.

The exact timing of a *Banking crisis* is difficult to ascertain, so we follow convention in measuring the incidence of crises by country-year. We code a country-year as '1' when an incumbent spell includes a systemic banking crisis, and '0' otherwise, with some spells experiencing multiple crises. As in Chapter 5, our primary banking crisis measure is from Reinhart and Rogoff (R&R) (Reinhart, 2010; Reinhart and Rogoff, 2009). In the sample analysed here, the R&R measure yields 113 systemic crises spread across 59 democratic countries from 1822 to 2010. We observe 45 crises in 17 countries in the pre-war period and 68 crises in the full sample in the post-war period. Crises were rare in the post-war period until the mid-1970s (only three crises spread over four years in three countries), after which they occurred more frequently and with longer duration. As a robustness check, we also use the measure from Laeven and Valencia (L&V) (Laeven and Valencia, 2008, 2013). This measure yields 49 systemic crises across 60 countries in our dataset.

---

[2] E.g. presidential elections in the United States and parliamentary elections in Japan.
[3] The online appendix provides coding rules and data sources.

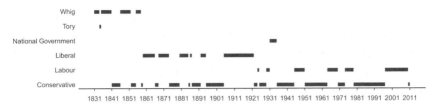

Figure 6.1: Visual representation of partisan spell indicator in Britain, 1831–2011.

In analysing the vote share data, we code the *Banking crisis* measure as '1' when a banking crisis occurred during the incumbent party's term preceding the election, and '0' otherwise. For the survival data, following other authors, we focus on the full five-year period after a systemic crisis (Funke, Schularick and Trebesch, 2016; Mian, Sufi and Trebbi, 2014).[4] In the case of a new systemic crisis in this five-year post-crisis period, we restart the five-year horizon from the most recent crisis. We analyse 592 partisan spells when we use the R&R sample, of which 173 overlapped with a post-crisis window (29.2 per cent), and 313 spells when we use the L&V sample, of which 64 (20.5 per cent) experienced a post-crisis window. We observe similar results when we use the vote share data.

Figure 6.1 shows the basic structure of our survival data for the case of Britain over 1831–2011. The horizontal bars capture the duration of unique partisan spells. We see multiple partisan spell terminations in Britain across six different partisan configurations.

Our argument emphasizes the importance of ideological differences among veto players as a core element shaping government policy responses. From the standpoint of testing our conditional theory, the major independent variable is Veto Players. This variable captures the degree of political constraint on policy change in a particular country in a given year, based on the number of independent actors with veto power over policy decisions and the distribution of political preferences across these actors. The lack of available data on veto player preferences prevents us from directly capturing polarization for our broad sample. Instead, we use Witold Henisz's Political Constraints Index Dataset,

---

[4] We use this time window to take into account the average election cycle in democracies (3.41 years), with more than 95 per cent of democracies having election cycles of three years or more. Data is from Gandrud (2015).

which considers the number of independent branches of government, the extent of alignment across these branches, and the heterogeneity of preferences within these branches (Henisz, 2017).[5] Given the absence of data on veto player preferences, Henisz utilizes partisan fractionalization in the legislature to calculate preference heterogeneity for a broad sample of countries over two centuries. In addition to its international comparability and availability since 1800, like Mansfield and Milner (2012), we view the strength of this measure as based on the connection between the theory underlying it and our own argument. The Henisz measure is based on a simple single-dimensional spatial model of political interaction that permits the status quo and the preferences of all actors to vary across the entire space.

We see a single policy dimension as useful for our analysis. As discussed in Chapter 5, we follow Rosas in suggesting that government responses to banking crises, and thus political preferences with respect to these responses, range on a continuum from 'Bagehot' to 'bailout' (Rosas, 2009). The single policy dimension underlying Henisz's model thus provides a simple means to assess our argument about the influence of domestic institutional arrangements and political preferences. Finally, Henisz's measure fits with our argument that additional political constraints on policy change in the form of homogeneity (heterogeneity) of party preferences within the opposition (governing) coalition have a positive but diminishing constraining effect on policy change (Henisz, 2002, 363).

The Henisz measure is a continuous variable that ranges from 0 to 1, with higher values indicating a greater number of veto players with distinct political preferences. When Veto Players equals 0, no veto players exist in a particular country. When Veto Players equals 1, party control across institutional arrangements diverges from the executive's party with sufficient intensity to balance its power.

The Henisz measure of political constraints differs substantially from the Checks measure developed by Thorsten Beck, George Clarke, Alberto Groff, Philip Keefer and Patrick Walsh (Beck et al., 2001). The Checks measure is based on the degree of electoral competition in

---

[5] Henisz develops two measures of political constraints, one that includes the judiciary and one that does not. We use the latter measure since we have little reason to suspect that the judiciary would influence decisions about crisis resolution policy. Nonetheless, our results are similar when we use the former measure.

a country, the type of institutions that permit actors to check the executive (i.e. presidential versus parliamentary systems, open versus closed list voting systems), and the partisan differences across these actors. Countries score very high on the Checks measure where electoral competition is high and strong partisan differences exist across institutions that can check the executive.

While this measure is simpler than Henisz's measure, it has some drawbacks that lead us to prefer the latter. The two most notable drawbacks are its weak connection to our theoretical argument and its availability. The Checks measure, which does not capture preference heterogeneity, fits poorly with our argument that the number of veto players has a positive but diminishing constraining effect on policy change. Unlike the Henisz measure, the Checks measure assumes a simple linear relationship between additional independent vetoes and executive constraints, treating the effect of one additional veto player as constant regardless of whether it is the first veto point or the fourteenth. In addition, Checks is only available from 1975 and thus does not permit a panoramic analysis.[6] We thus primarily use the Henisz measure in our empirical analysis.

For reasons similar to those outlined in Mansfield and Milner (Mansfield and Milner, 2012, 99), we rely on Henisz's more general measure of veto players rather than constructing a measure specific to banking crisis resolution policy. First, the detailed information required to produce a more specific measure is unavailable for most countries across the long time span of our analysis. The selective availability of information would also provide a potential source of bias. Second, like Mansfield and Milner, we see it as reasonable to presume that a more specific veto player measure would appear similar to the more general one we are using because crisis resolution policies face the same institutional obstacles and constraints as other policies. In the United States, for instance, the Bush administration had to overcome congressional opposition to secure approval of the Troubled Asset Relief Program (TARP), which constituted one of the president's main initiatives to rescue the financial system in 2008 (see Chapter 10). Crisis resolution policies typically require some policy change and thus tend to face the same institutional veto players shaping other policy areas.

---

[6] The Checks measure is also available for a smaller number of countries than the Henisz measure.

Alternative measures of institutional constraints on policymaking are also available (see Jahn, 2011). Yet these measures cover only a limited number of advanced economies over a narrow range of post-war years. While these limitations rule out their use in the statistical analysis provided here, where possible we make use of these measures in our country case studies. This enables us to consider alternative institutional constraints and preference configurations not captured in the Henisz measure.

The statistical analysis includes control variables for age and degree of democracy, economic growth, GDP per capita and prior history of financial instability using a cumulative number of systemic crises. We control for age and degree of the democracy because incumbents in more consolidated democracies may be more likely to survive crises. We use the cumulative democracy score from Polity IV to measure the degree of democracy, with higher values indicating greater democracy (Marshall, Gurr and Jaggers, 2017). The Maddison project and the Penn World Tables provide data on growth and GDP per capita.

Growth is a crucial control variable since we seek to account for its confounding effect on banking crisis onset and incumbent party electoral prospects. However, since banking crises usually create or amplify economic downturns, we later take steps to identify more clearly the effects of the crisis itself as opposed to the recession that follows it. In the spirit of Barro and Ursua (2008), we address this issue by comparing banking crises to severe recessions not involving a crisis but in which output declines *exceed* those that follow systemic banking crises. Specifically, we follow Funke, Schularick and Trebesch (2016) by identifying an event as a 'non-financial macro-disaster' when the annual output decline is higher than the average output decline that follows banking crises and occurs outside a five-year crisis window. We apply this cut-off separately for the pre-1945 sample (with a threshold of 4.5 per cent) and for the post-1970 sample (with a threshold of 3.8 per cent). On average, these disasters see an annual GDP contraction of 9.8 per cent in the pre-1945 sample and 6.9 per cent in the post-1970 sample.

We control for prior history of financial instability as voter expectations of governments may vary depending on their past experiences. Expectations of incumbent governments may be highest in countries where crises have been less frequent, so voters in such countries may always punish incumbent governments severely, irrespective of the time period or institutional environment. All variables enter the model as annual data lagged by one year.

Our conditional theory leads us to employ an interaction term to test our argument. We create an interaction term that combines the effect of a banking crisis with the Henisz measure of veto players. This interaction term permits us to assess the conditional effect of banking crises across various levels of Veto Players on the expected electoral prospects for incumbent parties.

We use ordinary least squares (OLS) for the vote share data. Using the survival data, we estimate a series of Cox proportional hazard models that model the expected length of a partisan spell for an incumbent party.[7]

6.2   Results: Accountability Models

Given our emphasis on voter punishment, we begin with the vote share data. We first estimate models that use the full sample from 1872 to 2011 but exclude the 1946–69 period because the virtual absence of systemic banking crises in these years risks biasing the result.[8] Table 6.1 provides the results. The preferred method to interpret the effect of interaction terms is graphical presentation of the relationship between changes in the variables constituting the interaction term and the outcome of interest (Brambor, Clark and Golder, 2006, 74). We therefore plot the simulated marginal effect of a banking crisis as the veto player variable varies from its observed minimum to its maximum values, and include a histogram of the distribution of the veto player variable.

[7] Since we emphasize how changes over calendar time (i.e. years elapsed since 1800) shape the occurrence of partisan spell termination within a country – an event that occurs more than once – we use a conditional elapsed time model with stratification (Box-Steffensmeier and Jones, 2004). This model is capable of addressing the possibilities that partisan spells develop sequentially and that their timing is different across occurrences (or strata). Hausman tests indicate the baseline hazard varies across each stratum, which supports our model specification. When we account for unobserved heterogeneity by adding a country-specific frailty term to the model, we find the estimated frailty parameter to be insignificant, with plots of the frailty estimates showing no significant variation across countries. Diagnostic tests do not reveal any violation of the proportional hazards assumption.

[8] Our results are quantitatively similar when we include this period, but the standard errors are expectedly smaller.

Table 6.1. *Banking crises and incumbent party vote share, 1872–2013*

Variable	R&R 1872–1938 / 1970–2013	R&R 1872–1938	R&R 1970–2013	L&V 1970–2013
	(1)	(2)	(3)	(4)
Crisis	13.29	−6.244	18.22**	9.403
	(10.47)	(19.16)	(8.039)	(7.001)
Veto players	−27.84***	−80.03***	−13.45**	−17.87***
	(6.436	(11.41)	(6.160)	(5.812)
Crisis × veto players	−38.73*	6.846	−50.85***	−28.47*
	(22.24)	(40.86)	(17.40)	(15.68)
Boix age	−0.0255	0.112***	−0.0149	−0.00657
	(0.0172)	(0.0400)	(0.0165)	(0.0175)
Degree of democracy – polity	−0.0165	0.109	−1.160***	−0.799**
	(0.306)	(0.337)	(0.376)	(0.354)
GDP per capita (ln)	−0.301	0.487	−1.456	−0.965
	(0.965)	(3.070)	(1.558)	(1.554)
Growth	0.520***	0.418***	1.027***	0.935***
	(0.124)	(0.134)	(0.222)	(0.242)
Cumulative crises	0.446**	−0.765**	0.462**	1.899*
	(0.214)	(0.357)	(0.212)	(0.982)
Constant	50.22***	67.23***	64.59***	59.42***
	(8.29)	(22.90)	(15.16)	(15.16)
R-squared	0.183	0.332	0.199	0.188
Observations	477	190	321	320

Figure 6.2, which uses the results from Model 1, shows that banking crises lead to a significant decline in incumbent party vote share in high veto player environments in the full sample using the R&R data. Yet Figure 6.2 obscures as much as it reveals. If one focused solely on variations in the veto player environment across the complete sample, one might reject the possibility of a time-dependent conditional relationship between crises and the institutional environment. Our theory

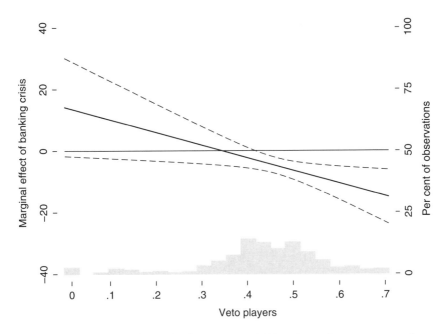

Figure 6.2: Marginal effect of banking crisis (R&R) on incumbent party vote share conditional on veto players, 1872–2011.

leads us to suspect otherwise. To test our argument, we subset the data into two time periods that capture the long-term shift in voter expectations: 1872–1938 and 1970–2011. We then re-estimate Model 1 across these different subsets using the R&R data, and re-estimate the same models using the L&V data for 1970 to 2010. We then plot the marginal effect by using the results from Models 2, 3 and 4.

Figures 6.3–6.5 support our argument that, in combination, societal expectations and institutional contexts shape the propensity for voters to punish incumbent parties in the aftermath of a banking crisis, showing clearly that observations in the modern period underpin the earlier result in Figure 6.2. Figure 6.3 shows that in the pre-war era the marginal effect of banking crises on incumbent party vote share is statistically insignificant and of trivial magnitude for all observed values of veto players.[9] Crises appear less disruptive to the wealth and orientations of voters during this time, consistent with the lower

---

[9] Separately, we removed the interaction and found no unconditional relationship between crises and incumbent party vote share.

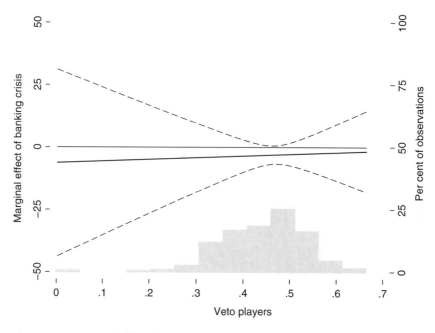

Figure 6.3: Marginal effect of banking crisis (R&R) on incumbent party vote share conditional on veto players, 1872–1938.

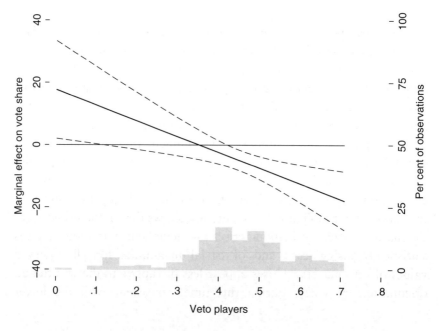

Figure 6.4: Marginal effect of banking crisis (R&R) on incumbent party vote share conditional on veto players, 1970–2013.

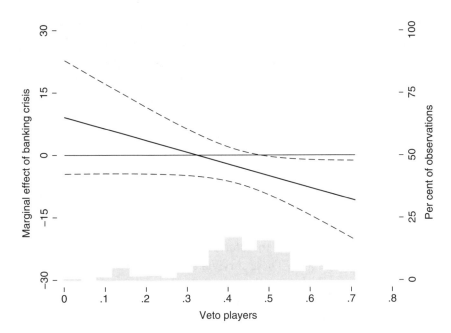

Figure 6.5: Marginal effect of banking crisis (L&V) on incumbent party vote share conditional on veto players, 1970–2013.

expectations regarding government policy responsibility that then prevailed. Since we limit our sample of democracies to countries where the electoral franchise was extended to a majority of the adult male population, these results are unlikely to be due to restrictions on suffrage.

Figures 6.4 and 6.5 show the conditional relationship between crises and veto players in the post-1970 era to be *negative* and significant when we use both the R&R and L&V data. The histogram in both figures shows that a sizeable number of observations fall within the range of statistical significance. After 1970, incumbent governments suffered a much harsher verdict from voters in high veto player environments following a crisis, especially when compared to the pre-war era. These electoral losses were particularly pronounced following the crises of the 1980s in Latin America, in Scandinavia in the early 1990s, in emerging markets in East Asia and Latin America in the late 1990s and early 2000s, and in Western democracies after 2008.

The post-1970 era results suggest that following a crisis the vote share of governments in 'high' veto player environments drops by 14.44 [−21.67, −7.21] percentage points using the R&R measure and 8.87 [−16.57, −1.18] percentage points using the L&V measure

(95 per cent confidence intervals in brackets).[10] This effect compares to a mean value of 36 per cent for the incumbent vote share. These are large effects that we would expect to negatively impact government survival, which we discuss below. We find no significant effect when post-1970 crises occur in 'low' veto player environments. These results are consistent with our argument about the very different expectations of post-1970s voters. The results from a Chow test provide additional evidence in support of our argument, indicating that our findings are not stable across the two time periods in our sample and suggestive of the time-dependent relationship we posit.[11]

Turning to a thicker notion of accountability, Table 6.2 reports the results for the survival data. As with the vote share data, marginal effects plots are necessary to interpret interaction effects (Brambor, Clark and Golder, 2006). These survival results confirm the conditional relationship uncovered using the vote share data.

The use of the full sample once again reveals the pitfalls of overlooking the time-dependent relationship that our theory suggests. Figure 6.6, which uses the results from Model 1, indicates that banking crises have no significant effect on partisan spell termination for any values of Veto Players across the full sample. Yet when we subset the data we find otherwise. Figure 6.7 indicates for the pre-war era a similar result to that uncovered using the vote share data: crises have an insignificant conditional effect on partisan spell termination in this period. The same cannot be said for the post-1970 era. Consistent with the vote share data results, Figures 6.8 and 6.9 reveal a positive and significant conditional relationship between crises and veto players when we use either the R&R or L&V data. The histograms in both figures show that a sizeable number of observations fall in the range of statistical significance – nearly 50 per cent for the R&R measure and over 60 per cent for the L&V measure.

Risk ratios, which compare the estimated hazard rate of governments experiencing a crisis against the hazard rate of governments that do not experience a crisis ('tranquil' spells), also provide a sense of the magnitude of the effect plotted in Figures 6.8 and 6.9. When

---

[10] 'High' and 'low' values of the veto players variable correspond to one standard deviation above and below the mean in the sample (all other covariates are held constant at their mean).

[11] The test statistic $F(6, 505) = 8.21$ ($p < 0.01$).

Table 6.2. Banking crises and partisan spell termination, 1822–2010

Variables	R&R 1822–1938 / 1970–2010	R&R 1822–1938	R&R 1970–2010	L&V 1970–2010
	(1)	(2)	(3)	(4)
Crisis	0.093	1.949	−0.519	−0.588
	(0.370	(1.575)	(0.513)	(0.642)
Veto players	−0.348	1.660*	−0.563	−0.274
	(0.493)	(0.885)	(0.649)	(0.544)
Crisis × veto players	0.922	−4.759	2.423**	2.381**
	(0.801)	(3.461)	(1.124)	(1.159)
Boix age	−0.00147	−0.0301***	−0.000407	−0.00160
	(0.00297)	(0.0111)	(0.00293)	(0.00294)
Degree of democracy – polity	−0.0886***	−0.00698	−0.102**	−0.0979**
	(0.0251)	(0.0415)	(0.0416)	(0.0411)
GDP per capita (Ln)	−0.245**	−0.804**	0.0322	0.0163
	(0.113)	(0.405)	(0.144)	(0.154)
Growth	−0.0151	−0.0663**	−0.00974	−0.0215
	(0.0131)	(0.0295)	(0.0237)	(0.0224)
Cumulative crises	−0.00954	−0.0574	−0.0196	−0.252*
	(0.0289)	(0.0872)	(0.0269)	(0.151)
Observations	2382	727	1743	1743

Robust standard errors in parentheses
*** $p < 0.01$, ** $p < 0.05$, * $p < 0.1$

comparing two post-1970 governments in a 'high' veto player environment, the one experiencing a banking crisis (according to the R&R measure) is 2.21 [1.38, 3.41] times more likely to suffer a partisan spell termination than a government in a tranquil environment, and 1.66 [1.03, 2.82] times more likely using the L&V measure (95 per cent confidence intervals in brackets). In addition, when comparing two post-1970 governments following a crisis, the one in the high veto player environment is 1.66 [1.03, 2.82] times more likely to suffer a partisan spell termination for R&R crises, and 1.78 [1.02, 3.15] times more likely for L&V crises, compared to the government in a low veto

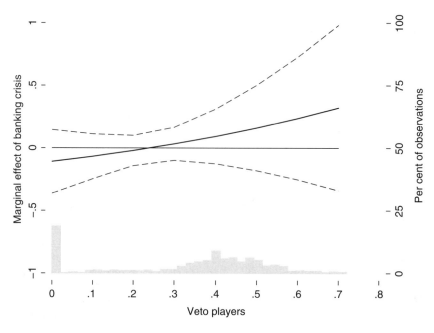

Figure 6.6: Marginal effect of banking crisis (R&R) on partisan spell termination conditional on veto players, 1822–2010.

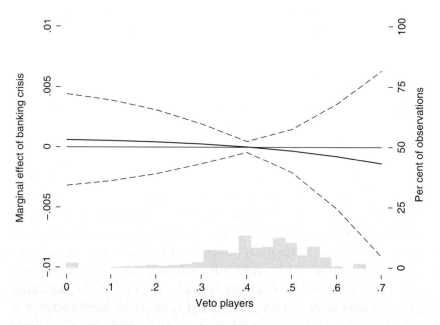

Figure 6.7: Marginal effect of banking crisis (R&R) on partisan spell termination conditional on veto players, 1822–1938.

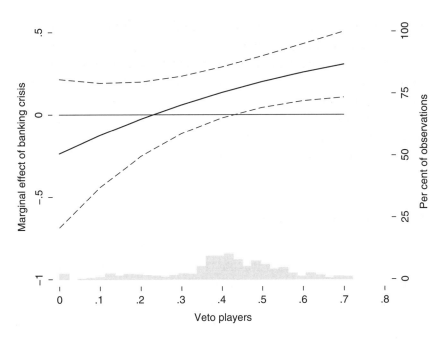

Figure 6.8: Marginal effect of banking crisis (R&R) on partisan spell termination conditional on veto players, 1970–2010.

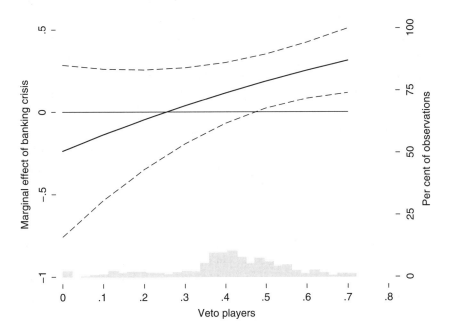

Figure 6.9: Marginal effect of banking crisis (L&V) on partisan spell termination conditional on veto players, 1970–2010.

player environment. We also find no significantly elevated termination risk when a crisis hits governments in 'low' veto player environments. As with the vote share data, the Chow test statistic is again significant.[12] Overall, these results strengthen our conclusion that modern voters punished governments more severely in political systems more prone to policy gridlock and selective interventions in the aftermath of crises. Modern voters act in ways consistent with both thin and thick notions of electoral accountability after banking crises.

6.3   Supplemental Tests

We perform a number of robustness checks, reported in the online appendix. Whether we use a somewhat different sample of democracies based on the Polity IV measure, consider the role of austerity policies in the wake of banking crises, include IMF conditionality and Eurozone membership as additional institutional constraint control variables, or address collinearity between veto players and democracy using residualization, our results still hold. We also consider alternative indicators of the domestic structure of political competition, including a measure of whether the executive's party enjoys majority status in the law-making house(s) of the legislature, and another that captures the effective number of parties in the legislature. That we fail to uncover significant results for either suggests that our results are not merely a function of the presence of divided government or a consequence of turnover being more likely in more fractionalized party systems. Our results are also robust when we take into account the possibility that some governments are more prone to banking crises (endogenous selection) as well as imbalances in the data (covariate balance and covariate overlap).

When we compare the political aftermath of systemic banking crises with severe non-financial macro-disasters, the results, reported in Table 6.3, indicate that voter responses to modern banking crises are different and particularly disruptive for incumbency survival. In contrast to modern banking crises, in macro-disasters voter punishment tends, if anything, to weaken in higher veto player environments. This result – consistent with an extensive literature – suggests that the institutional environment may indeed blur the clarity of responsibility

---

[12] The test statistic is χ^2 (6) = 20.92 ($p < 0.01$).

in macro-disasters, at least in the modern era. In the pre-war era, like systemic banking crises, macro-disasters do not significantly affect incumbency electoral prospects.

What might explain this difference? Macro-disasters may be more readily perceived by voters as forgivable because they are often driven by factors beyond the apparent control of governments, such as commodity price collapses, natural catastrophes or geopolitical tensions (Funke, Schularick and Trebesch, 2016). Our argument suggests that modern voters will instead see systemic banking crises as both preventable and highly damaging to their wealth. Another possibility is that macro-disasters have less severe negative wealth effects than modern banking crises and thus less impact on inequality and polarization.

We carry out a simple empirical test of the second possibility by examining available data on real house price changes and real stock market returns since 1970 (Bank for International Settlements, 2017a; Dimson, Marsh and Staunton, 2016). We estimate a simple fixed effects OLS model where each of the variables is regressed on our post-crisis and post-macro-disaster indicators, controlling for GDP per capita. The results, presented in Tables 6.4a and 6.4b, are supportive of our argument: housing and stock market wealth tends to contract sharply in the aftermath of modern banking crises, but not after macro-disasters. The former clashes with the great expectations of modern voters, but the latter may seem less threatening.

Having identified the impact of modern systemic banking crises on incumbency survival and differentiated it from more severe downturns, we now turn to further supplemental tests of our argument to assess the causal mechanisms at work. Our argument suggests that modern crises tend to induce rising inequality and increasing voter polarization, generating policy gridlock when polarized actors gain access to veto players and eroding incumbency survival prospects in – and only in – the era of great expectations.

To assess the first implication, we employ data on Gini coefficients of income distributions from Bourguignon and Morrisson and the Standardized World Income Inequality Database (SWIID), and data on voter attitudes from the World Values Survey (WVS) (Bourguignon and Morrisson, 2002; Solt, 2008, 2016; World Values Survey, 2017). Long-run data on wealth inequality is unavailable for most countries in our analysis. We thus investigate income inequality, which tends to be highly correlated with wealth inequality. Higher Gini

Table 6.3. Macro-disasters and incumbency survival

Variable	Survival 1822–1938 Boix	Survival 1822–1938 Polity	Survival 1970–2010 Boix	Survival 1970–2013 Polity	Vote 1872–1938 Boix	Vote 1872–1938 Polity	Vote 1970–2013 Boix	Vote 1970–2013 Polity
	(1)	(2)	(3)	(4)	(5)	(6)	(7)	(8)
Macro-disasters	-3.678* (2.141)	-8.736*** (1.895)	1.829* (0.952)	0.745 (0.735)	-17.6 (13.110)	-40.12*** (10.070)	-19.15 (14.000)	-16.81 (13.400)
Veto players	0.356 (0.857)	-3.989** (1.647)	0.0661 (0.547)	0.00402 (0.512)	-80.44*** (22.110)	-107.3*** (12.620)	-21.54*** (5.868)	-18.86*** (5.858)
Macro-disasters × veto players	8.556 (5.805)	20.56*** (4.987)	-5.074** (2.562)	-1.441 (1.881)	29.67 (27.590)	76.35*** (21.380)	34.86 (33.790)	25.8 (30.780)
Democracy age	-0.0704*** (0.017)	-0.0360*** (0.012)	-0.00273 (0.003)	-0.00517* (0.003)	0.0541 (0.033)	0.0613** (0.030)	-0.00668 (0.018)	0.0487*** (0.015)
Degree of democracy – polity	-0.0418 (0.058)	0.174** (0.072)	-0.0910** (0.041)	-0.114*** (0.041)	0.233 (0.337)	-1.269 (0.854)	-0.924** (0.377)	-2.170* (1.242)

GDP per capita (ln)	-1.075**	-0.823*	0.00677	0.0127**	-0.549	-0.893	-1.435	-2.659*
	(0.542)	(0.487)	(0.007)	(0.005)	(3.074)	(2.804)	(1.610)	(1.446)
Growth	-0.114***	-0.142***	-0.0235	-0.0435*	0.391***	0.435***	0.969***	0.958***
	(0.028)	(0.043)	(0.023)	(0.026)	(0.129)	(0.136)	(0.242)	(0.215)
Cumulative macro-disasters	0.402**	0.255*	-0.248*	-0.147*	0.233	0.707**	-0.533	-1.082
	(0.158)	(0.152)	(0.131)	(0.080)	(0.314)	(0.304)	(1.500)	(1.536)
Constant					72.48***	100.2***	67.39***	87.36***
					(21.10)	(22.62)	(16.02)	(15.08)
Observations	727	614	1743	1695	191	155	321	318
R-squared					0.315	0.451	0.16	0.169

Robust standard errors in parentheses
*** $p < 0.01$, ** $p < 0.05$, * $p < 0.1$

Table 6.4a. House prices, banking crises and macro-disasters

Variables	R&R Boix (1)	L&V Boix (2)	R&R Polity (3)	L&V Polity (4)	R&R Boix (5)	L&V Polity (6)	R&R Boix (7)	L&V Polity (8)
Crisis	-7.258*** (1.015)	-7.563*** (0.996)	-7.556*** (0.898)	-7.393*** (0.872)				
Macro-disaster					2.287 (2.251)	2.275 (2.373)	0.791 (1.755)	1.490 (2.005)
GDP per capita (ln)	2.290 (2.008)	3.539* (2.015)	3.615* (2.019)	4.280** (2.028)	1.678 (2.098)	1.709 (2.105)	2.632 (2.018)	2.783 (2.033)
Constant	-19.77 (20.47)	-32.47 (20.53)	-33.53 (20.60)	-40.27* (20.68)	-14.77 (21.40)	-15.08 (21.47)	-24.96 (20.59)	-26.54 (20.75)
Observations	462	462	534	534	452	452	553	553
R-squared	0.108	0.120	0.126	0.128	0.004	0.003	0.004	0.004
Number of countries	36	36	38	38	35	35	37	37

Standard errors in parentheses
*** $p < 0.01$, ** $p < 0.05$, * $p < 0.1$
Fixed effects included.
Boix: 1970–2010; Polity 1970–2013.

Table 6.4b. Stock market valuations, banking crises and macro-disasters

Variables	R&R Boix (1)	L&V Boix (2)	R&R Polity (3)	L&V Polity (4)	R&R Boix (5)	L&V Polity (6)	R&R Boix (7)	L&V Polity (8)
Crisis	−11.92*** (3.796)	−9.794** (3.801)	−11.55*** (3.358)	−9.441*** (3.325)				
Macro-disaster					0.690 (7.366)	−0.0106 (7.612)	0.460 (5.830)	0.338 (6.330)
GDP per capita (ln)	3.559 (4.187)	2.929 (4.198)	2.234 (3.958)	1.740 (3.996)	−0.0631 (4.063)	−0.0972 (4.068)	−0.804 (3.705)	−0.796 (3.707)
Constant	−26.32 (42.86)	−20.04 (42.97)	−12.83 (40.55)	−7.935 (40.93)	9.749 (41.69)	10.11 (41.75)	17.43 (38.09)	17.35 (38.11)
Observations	824	824	871	871	824	824	886	886
R-squared	0.012	0.008	0.014	0.010	0.000	0.000	0.000	0.000
Number of countries	21	21	21	21	21	21	21	21

Standard errors in parentheses
*** $p < 0.01$, ** $p < 0.05$, * $p < 0.1$
Fixed effects included.
Boix: 1970–2010; Polity 1970–2013.

values indicate greater inequality. The WVS provides cross-national data for various years from 1981 to 2014, covering voter survey responses about ideological self-positioning on a political scale ranging from 1 to 10, with higher values being more conservative. We use the standard deviation of these responses to capture the dispersion of voter beliefs within countries. We are not aware of similar data available for the pre-1945 era.

In exploring inequality and voter polarization we follow other scholars in restricting our analysis to observations that fall within five years before or after a crisis.[13] We estimate a simple fixed effects OLS model where the Gini coefficient is regressed on our post-crisis indicator, controlling for GDP per capita. Since the SWIID uses a multiple imputation algorithm to standardize missing observations, we take this uncertainty into account in our estimates. The results, presented in Table 6.5, are supportive of our argument: inequality rises strongly in the aftermath of modern banking crises, but falls sharply in the aftermath of pre-war crises. In the modern era, the estimates suggest the Gini coefficient increases 10 per cent over the full five-year post-crisis window relative to the sample mean; in the pre-war era, the Gini coefficient *falls* over six per cent. Effects of this size are plausibly perceived by voters.

We posit that a post-crisis *rise* in inequality should be associated with growing voter polarization in the modern era. We assess this mechanism by estimating a simple fixed effects OLS model where the standard deviation of voter responses is regressed on our post-crisis indicator, controlling for GDP per capita. Our results, reported in Table 6.6, point to countries becoming more polarized after crises, with voter beliefs showing greater dispersion compared to the pre-crisis period. In our limited sample we observe sizeable increases in voter belief dispersion following the 2007–8 crises in the United States, the Netherlands and Sweden as well as after crises in the 1990s in India, Japan, South Korea and the Philippines. We do not observe similar effects on inequality and polarization following macro-disasters.[14]

---

[13] Funke, Schularick and Trebesch (2016); Mian, Sufi and Trebbi (2014). Pre-crisis and post-crisis years are non-crisis years before or after the start of a crisis. In cases of follow-up crises, where the pre-crisis horizon and post-crisis horizon overlap, we truncate the pre-crisis horizon.

[14] Atkinson and Morelli also provide evidence that inequality rises more strongly in the aftermath of banking crises, but less so in macro-disasters (Atkinson and Morelli, 2011).

Table 6.5. Inequality and banking crises

Variables	R&R Boix 1859–1938 (1)	R&R Boix 1859–1938 (2)	R&R Boix 1970–2010 (3)	L&V Boix 1970–2010 (4)	R&R Polity 1970–2013 (5)	L&V Polity 1970–2013 (6)
Crises	-0.00529*** (0.00185)	-0.00585*** (0.00205)	.6565771*** (0.1993527)	.5574107*** (0.203397)	.5566123*** (0.1883383)	.5649112*** (0.1834944)
GDP per capita (ln)	-0.0311*** (0.00354)	-0.0298*** (0.00384)	-2.124608** (0.9433994)	1.063804 (0.9402988)	-1.659934 (1.090939)	2.848775*** (0.9666899)
Constant	0.713*** (0.0289)	0.702*** (0.0314)	57.21954*** (57.21954)	25.86994*** (9.070214)	52.9247*** (10.65229)	7.83517 (9.499201)
Observations	426	345	410	385	416	390
R-squared	0.176	0.178				
Number of countries	20	17	47	45	43	41

Robust standard errors in parentheses

*** $p < 0.01$, ** $p < 0.05$, * $p < 0.1$

Fixed effects included.

Since the SWIID uses a multiple imputation algorithm to standardize missing observations, we take this uncertainty into account in our estimates. Models 3–6 are multiple imputation estimates based on 100 imputations.

Models 1–2 use the Bourguignon and Morrison post-tax, post-transfer net income Gini index (0–1). Models 3–6 use the SWIID Gini index (0–100).

Table 6.6. Voter polarization and banking crises

Variables	R&R Boix 1970–2010 (1)	L&V Boix 1970–2010 (2)	R&R Polity 1970–2013 (3)	L&V Polity 1970–2013 (4)
Crisis	0.0903* (0.0443)	0.0960* (0.0429)	0.0880* (0.0399)	0.0931** (0.0390)
GDP per capita (ln)	0.591 (0.759)	0.546 (0.763)	1.738*** (0.313)	1.722*** (0.293)
Constant	−3.570 (7.301)	−3.204 (7.466)	−14.60*** (2.995)	−14.73*** (2.855)
Observations	17	18	16	17
R-squared	0.531	0.520	0.830	0.784
Number of countries	9	9	9	9

Robust standard errors in parentheses
*** $p < 0.01$, ** $p < 0.05$, * $p < 0.1$
Includes only country and year observations within five years before or after a crisis.

Rising social conflict after modern banking crises should increase the gap between the initial build-up of financial stress and the government policy intervention to contain it. We expect that polarized veto player environments will be associated with a larger gap ('delay') and place pressure on the central bank to take action.

Gandrud's and Hallerberg's Financial Market Stress (FinStress) index, available at monthly intervals since 2003, provides the most comprehensive granular data available on perceived banking sector stress. For each crisis we identify the initial build-up of financial stress as the date when a smoothed line of this index first begins its upward trajectory prior to the onset of the crisis. Figure 6.10 provides an illustration for the United States and Hungary; the former is a case of a gradual build-up of stress, the latter of a more sudden onset of stress from a higher initial level.

As we argued in Chapter 2, central bank interventions will likely prove insufficient for financial stabilization in highly financialized

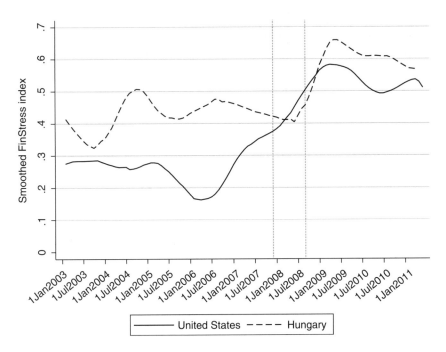

Figure 6.10: Financial stress and crises in United States and Hungary, 2003–2011. *Note:* Lines represent a loess smoother of the FinStress series. Vertical dotted lines indicate L&V crisis onset dating (1 December 2007 for United States; 1 September 2008 for Hungary).

systems. The same can be said for deposit guarantees. In highly financialized systems, governments will likely need to guarantee bank liabilities well beyond traditional insured deposit accounts. When credible, blanket guarantees can prove essential in restoring confidence and thus provide a reasonable indicator of the type of government response necessary to stabilize the financial system.[15] Yet guarantees are rarely implemented as soon as financial stress is felt because of political conflict over their fiscal implications and potential side effects; in most cases, guarantees are made only when a full-blown systemic crisis is already unfolding. Our argument suggests that veto players are one leading cause of this delay.

We calculate as our measure of delay the time elapsed between the initial financial stress onset date and the guarantee announcement

[15] In addition, with the exception of Laeven and Valencia's dating of the announcement of blanket bank liability guarantees, available sources provided limited information on the timing of particular interventions.

Table 6.7. Sample of crisis intervention delays

Country	Initial build-up	Guarantee announcement	Delay (months)
Austria	June 2008	December 2008	6
Belgium	August 2008	October 2008	14
Denmark	November 2007	February 2009	15
France	March 2007	October 2008	19
Germany	December 2007	October 2008	10
Greece	February 2008	October 2008	8
Hungary	August 2008	October 2008	2
Iceland	June 2008	October 2008	4
Ireland	May 2007	September 2008	16
Italy	December 2007	November 2008	11
Latvia	June 2007	December 2008	18
Luxembourg	September 2007	October 2008	13
Netherlands	February 2007	October 2008	20
Portugal	January 2008	October 2008	9
Slovenia	November 2008	December 2008	1
Spain	August 2007	October 2008	14
Sweden	April 2008	October 2008	6
United Kingdom	February 2008	October 2008	8
United States	June 2006	October 2008	28

date. This provides us with nineteen observations (see Table 6.7). The small sample size limits us to carrying out simple empirical tests of our argument. We estimate a Cox proportional hazards model where we regress our measure of delay on the average veto player score over the delay period, controlling for the change in FinStress over the delay period.[16] The results in Table 6.8 support our argument: higher veto

---

[16] Diagnostic tests do not reveal any violation of the proportional hazards assumption.

Table 6.8. Crisis intervention delays, financial stress, and incumbent party vote share

Variables	Delay	FinStress over electoral cycle	FinStress over electoral cycle	Incumbent party vote share
	(1)	(2)	(3)	(4)
Veto players	−0.569** (0.242)	0.609** (0.271)		
FinStress change	−0.507** (0.256)			
Growth		0.209 (0.232)	0.224 (0.202)	3.99* (2.05)
Delay			0.101** (0.045)	
FinStress over electoral cycle				−2.34** (1.07)
Constant		−0.297 (1.62)	1.440* (0.719)	33.38*** (2.76)
Observations	19	16	16	16
R-squared		0.215	0.227	0.256

Robust standard errors in parentheses: *** $p < 0.01$, ** $p < 0.05$, * $p < 0.1$

player environments are associated with longer crisis intervention delays. In line with our argument, we also find in additional tests that veto players and longer crisis intervention delays are associated with larger increases in financial stress over the electoral cycle, which in turn are linked to lower vote shares for the incumbent party following a crisis.[17]

To further assess the claim that polarized veto player environments are prone to post-crisis policy gridlock, we searched for

---

[17] Financial stress may reach more elevated levels in higher veto environments because pre-crisis regulation is more lax (Satyanath, 2006), although this is less likely in our European Union-dominated sample because of harmonized bank regulation.

cross-national measures of legislative performance. Excepting Binder's data on legislative deadlock in the post-war United States, we were unable to identify data related to post-crisis stabilization during the time frame of this analysis (Binder, 2003, 2015). The United States is recorded with an intermediate value in the Henisz index, and it is commonly claimed that its policymakers had a relatively 'good' crisis in 2007–9 (Culpepper and Reinke, 2014; Drezner, 2014, 177; Geithner, 2015). If we find substantive policy delay with negative consequences for wealth and voter perceptions of unfairness in this case, then cases with higher values in the Henisz index are likely prone to larger effects. Importantly, this case also permits us to exploit the DW-NOMINATE ideological scores for members of Congress to assess more directly the effect of actual veto player preferences on post-crisis gridlock (Carroll et al., 2015).

Binder captures legislative gridlock by identifying the set of salient legislative measures on the agenda and determining a ratio of failed measures to all measures for each Congress. Binder also identifies the policy topic of each legislative measure using the codes from the Comparative Agendas Project (CAP). We use these codes to create a gridlock ratio of legislative measures related to post-crisis stabilization, specifically those for the CAP policy topics identified as 'Macroeconomics' and 'Domestic Commerce'. These CAP policy topics include many areas relevant to post-crisis policy interventions, including interest rates, unemployment, monetary policy, national budget (Macroeconomics), banking, securities and commodities, and financial regulation (Domestic Commerce).

Following Binder, we estimate a grouped logit model to account for the variation in the size of the legislative agenda. Positive coefficient values suggest an *increase* in gridlock (i.e. fewer legislative measures are passed). Our model includes the post-crisis variable, the DW-NOMINATE measure of congressional polarization (defined as the difference between party means on the liberal–conservative dimension) and their interaction, while controlling for the presence of divided government (Mayhew, 2005). Table 6.9 presents the results, which are supportive of our hypothesized mechanism. We find polarization induced greater economic policy gridlock in years following crises. When comparing two crisis-hit Congresses, whereas the one in the more polarized environment is predicted to experience 3.45 [1.81, 5.09] legislative failures, the one in the less polarized environment is predicted

Table 6.9. Banking crises and policy grid-lock in the United States, 1947–2014

Variables	(1)
Crisis	−2.238
	(1.842)
Polarization	2.098**
	(0.883)
Crisis × polarization	1.99
	(2.21)
Divided government	0.487*
	(0.269)
Constant	−1.945**
	(0.559)
Observations	25
F (4,20)	3.17**

Coefficients are weighted least squares logit estimates for group data. Standard errors in parentheses.
*** $p < 0.01$, ** $p < 0.05$, * $p < 0.1$

to experience 2.03 [0.46, 3.61] legislative failures (95 per cent confidence intervals in brackets).[18] This statistically significant difference of nearly 70 per cent across the two environments represents a sharp increase relative to the sample mean of only 2.04 legislative failures per Congress. We explore some of these episodes of gridlock in the United States in Chapter 10.

6.4 Conclusion

In this chapter, we have examined one of the core empirical implications of the argument we developed in Chapter 2, namely that incumbency electoral success is linked to variations in societal

---

[18] 'More' and 'less' polarization correspond to one standard deviation above and below the sample mean respectively (in the presence of divided government).

expectations over time and institutional variations among democratic countries. In combination, the post-war entrenchment of great expectations and the presence of veto players constraining policy change greatly influence the propensity of voters to punish incumbent political parties in the aftermath of banking crises. We tested this implication by accounting for a number of economic and political conditions, exploring a range of demanding robustness checks, and addressing thin and thick concepts of electoral accountability. Based on analysis using our panoramic dataset stretching back to the early nineteenth century, we found strong support for our argument.

We provided much evidence supportive of our claim that there has been a structural break in the relationship between banking crises and the electoral prospects of incumbent governments. Our panoramic analysis revealed the importance of great expectations as a vital precondition shaping the effect of institutional configurations on voter responses. Our analysis suggests the sharp rise in societal expectations and household wealth after the experiences of the Great Depression and the long era of stability associated with Bretton Woods redefined how modern voters react to institutional factors that impact the ability of governments to respond to crises. In contrast to severe non-financial macro-disasters, the sudden evaporation of wealth that often follows modern banking crises appears particularly threatening to voters whose fortunes have become increasingly linked to housing and financial markets. Moreover, modern crises seem to be associated with the unleashing of powerful political and economic forces, namely heightened voter polarization and rising inequality. Such forces can foster a tendency toward policy gridlock and arouse voter perceptions of distributional unfairness. As we explore in more detail in Chapters 8 and 10, modern voters also appear to be relatively impervious to counterfactual claims by policymakers that their absolute and relative losses would have been far greater had the interventions not been undertaken.

Our results show that this matters less in the low expectations world that prevailed in an earlier era. Then, most voters had considerably less wealth stored in housing and financial assets and did not see governments as responsible for preventing crises and mitigating their impact; as we saw in the previous chapter, financial institutions and their creditors also bore more of the costs of financial distress at this time. By contrast, in a great expectations world, inequality and political polarization matter far more. Our results suggest that in these circum-stances, institutional constraints and distributional fairness have become highly consequential because a failure to meet the heightened expectations of voters is likely to result in severe electoral punishment.

In conjunction with evolving societal expectations, crises and the institutional constraints that shape policy interventions have come to carry much greater political significance. This is only apparent from a long-run historical perspective. In the next part of this book, we provide detailed evidence in support of our claims from systemic crises in Britain, the United States and Brazil across two centuries.

Part III

BANKING CRISES, POLICY AND POLITICS IN THE UNITED KINGDOM, THE UNITED STATES AND BRAZIL SINCE THE NINETEENTH CENTURY

7 BANKING CRISES IN THE UNITED KINGDOM IN AN ERA OF LOW EXPECTATIONS

The next two chapters explore the policy and political consequences of major banking crises in the United Kingdom, beginning with the crises in the early nineteenth century through the most recent crises in 2007–9. As the country[1] with the most advanced industrial and financial system of the nineteenth century it is an important case. We show in these two chapters that the policy and political consequences of a series of intense systemic banking crises across this period of nearly two centuries changed substantially over time.

The focus of this chapter is on the nineteenth century, when financialization in the United Kingdom was embryonic, wealth was highly concentrated in a narrow group of elites, and the government had made no prior commitment to prevent financial crises via regulation. These circumstances, as shown in Chapter 4, contributed to low expectations among voters as to government responsibility to protect them from financial shocks. We find that the bailout constituency during nineteenth-century banking crises remained confined largely to merchant and financial elites linked to insolvent banks. With limited pressure from below, the government and the Bank of England, then a private institution with public privileges and responsibilities, responded to crises with measures that aligned largely with the Bagehot model

---

[1] We generally refer throughout to 'the United Kingdom', formed as a union of Great Britain and Ireland in 1801 (later modified to a union of Great Britain and Northern Ireland in 1922), though we follow common usage in using 'British' and 'English' throughout as identifying adjectives (e.g. 'British banks', 'British economy', 'English banking system', etc.).

outlined in Chapter 5. Furthermore, despite the severe economic down-turns that often followed such crises, voters largely overlooked them when evaluating incumbent governments in elections that followed.

We begin by elaborating our logic for selecting the systemic banking crises – 1825–6, 1890 and 2007–9 – that feature in our analysis in this chapter and the next. We then survey the political-institutional landscape of the United Kingdom since the Napoleonic Wars. We high-light the presence of mechanisms that offered voters, albeit in limited ways in earlier crises, the possibility to sanction governments, thereby exposing them to electoral accountability and legitimacy imperatives when responding to crises. The two sections that follow describe the policy responses and political impacts of the crises of 1825–6 and 1890 respectively. A final section concludes by discussing how, given limited financialization of middle-class wealth and no prior government commit-ment to prevent financial instability, the expansion of British democracy over the course of the nineteenth century was consistent with crisis policy interventions that by today's standards were very market-conforming.

7.1   Which Crises?

According to Reinhart and Rogoff, there were numerous sys-temic banking crises in the United Kingdom in the nineteenth century and only one in the twentieth (2007–9). Figure 7.1 shows that systemic crises were highly concentrated in the first half of the nineteenth century and thereafter became increasingly less frequent. However, there are in practice few to investigate during the period of full democracy, which according to Boix, Miller and Rosato begins in 1884, though Polity

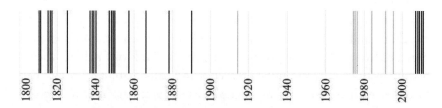

Figure 7.1: Timeline of banking crises in the United Kingdom, 1800–2015.
Sources: inclusive of all banking crises indicated in Laeven and Valencia (2013), Reinhart (2010), and Reinhart and Rogoff (2009). Lighter bars indicate non-systemic banking crisis codings by Reinhart and Rogoff. Laeven and Valencia only code crises from 1970.

provides the earlier dating of 1880 (Boix, Miller and Rosato, 2014; Marshall, Gurr and Jaggers, 2017). As we discuss below, for most historians the electoral reforms of the first half of the 1880s were crucial, expanding the franchise significantly. This leaves the 1890 Barings crisis as the main comparator with the 2007–9 systemic crisis during the period of full democracy.

However, in this chapter we also examine the 1825–6 crisis because the systemic status of the 1890 crisis is contested among economic historians, and because the 1825–6 crisis was an unambiguously deep and virulent one. J. D. Turner argues that it was the only systemic crisis of the nineteenth century and the most serious before that of 2007–9 (Turner, 2014, 57–61). Furthermore, the policy and political aftermath of this crisis, during a period of less democratic government in the United Kingdom, also provides an interesting vantage point from which to consider the two later crises in the era of fuller democracy.

How deep were British banking crises in the nineteenth century? Figure 7.2 indicates annual real GDP growth outcomes in the UK for the banking crises indicated in Figure 7.1. It suggests that the crises of

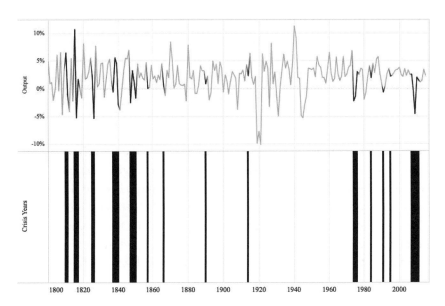

Figure 7.2: United Kingdom: real GDP growth (per cent) with banking crisis years highlighted.
Sources: Bank of England, three centuries of data; Laeven and Valencia (2013); Reinhart and Rogoff (2009). The GDP measure is the chained composite measure of UK GDP at factor cost, annual percentage change.

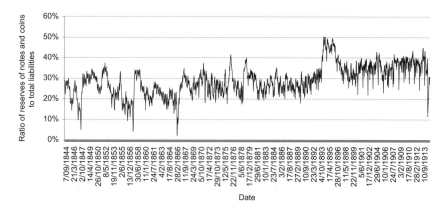

Figure 7.3: Bank of England: ratio of reserves of notes and coins to total liabilities, 1844–1913.
Source: Huang and Thomas (2016a).Weekly data.

1815–17, 1825–6 and 2007–9 were associated with unusually deep recessions. Interestingly, for the 1890 crisis there was no recession, though one did occur in 1892.

Using the depth of associated recessions to measure the severity of a banking crisis is problematic. It reflects a general problem in crisis coding, which is that it is difficult to define this severity independently of the policy responses – potential and actual – that can accompany them and thereby influence the trajectory of the economy. The fact that these policy responses – as we argue in this book – have become significantly more extensive over time increases the difficulty of making cross-time comparisons using output data.

The only systemic crises during the classical era of the pre-1914 gold standard in which the Bank's reserves of notes and coin were seriously depleted – a measure of a possible scramble by market actors for liquidity – were those in 1847, 1857 and 1866 (see Figure 7.3).[2] These instances necessitated the suspension of the 1844 Bank Act to permit the Bank to issue unbacked notes so as to allow it to meet its liabilities. By this measure, the outbreak of world war in July–August

---

[2] Note that after the 1844 Bank Act, the reserve of notes in the Bank's 'Banking Department' became the first line of defence in a crisis, because there would be a sharp increase in the demand by other financial firms for such notes in a crisis even if there were sufficient gold reserves to back its note issue (unbacked note issuance was disallowed under the Act). As the note reserve shrank, this could induce a scramble for liquidity. See Huang and Thomas (2016b).

1914 was the next closest episode, though Reinhart and Rogoff do not identify it as a systemic crisis.[3] The 1890 crisis does not count by this measure, but this may have been because policy interventions in this episode successfully deterred a market panic.

Taken together, this would suggest that the dislocation accompanying the 1825–6 banking crisis was much deeper than that surrounding the Barings crisis of 1890. Financial historians, past and contemporary, also generally agree that the crisis of 1825–6 was exceptionally deep (Bagehot, 1962 [1873], 98; Conant, 1902, 477; Kindleberger and Aliber, 2011, 111).

Whether the 1890 crisis was 'systemic' is, unsurprisingly in light of this data, contested among historians. Some dispute the designation by Reinhart and Rogoff, among others, of the Barings failure in 1890 as a systemic banking crisis (Reinhart, 2010, 114). Capie, who defines a banking crisis proper as one that threatens the viability of the payments system that is typically centred on deposit-taking institutions, is one example (Capie, 2014, 9–11). J. D. Turner agrees and argues that this position is supported by the fact that bank stocks generally did not decline sharply in the month before the Bank's intervention to rescue Barings (Turner, 2014, 61). However, Turner's preferred crisis indicator, the change in bank stocks relative to overall stock market indices, could be substantially influenced by market expectations of lender of last resort interventions, which he says had become expected in the United Kingdom by the 1890s.

On the other side, Flandreau and Ugolini argue that Barings was a merchant bank of systemic importance, whose failure would have undermined the stability of London's money market and international position (Flandreau and Ugolini, 2014, 93).[4] White agrees that Barings was of systemic importance and argues that the prompt intervention by the Bank of England in the 1890 case – in contrast, for example, to its initial hesitation in 1825 – successfully averted a major crisis: 'What frightened the Bank here was the imminent failure of a SIFI, which had

---

[3] According to Roberts, a systemic banking crisis began a week before the outbreak of war in August 1914 that resulted in a massive intervention in which Bagehot's principles were set aside; all large banks were saved and in the 'Cold Storage Scheme' the Bank of England purchased up to a third of outstanding bills of exchange (Roberts, 2013a). Since this intervention was associated with a national security emergency rather than a peacetime crisis, we set it aside here.

[4] See also Cain and Hopkins (2016, 159).

not been encountered before. Overend Gurney's failure in 1866 was smaller and yet it had occasioned a panic, magnifying a recession; since that time financial institutions had grown considerably and global financial networks had expanded' (White, 2016a, 5). Some knowledgeable contemporaries agreed that this was *potentially* a major crisis that was only averted by skilful and decisive intervention. Nathan Rothschild feared Barings' collapse would threaten London's position as a global financial centre; George Goschen, Chancellor of the Exchequer, said it would have made the 1866 crisis look like 'child's play'; and William Lidderdale, Governor of the Bank of England, thought '[a]ll houses would tumble one after the other' if Barings failed (Elliot, 1911, 170).

Ultimately, this disagreement is difficult to resolve because no one can be certain whether the banking system would have been seriously destabilized had Barings not been rescued. The positive impact of the announcement of the guarantee fund, discussed below, appears to have been immediate: 'The news of the guarantee allowed knowledge of Barings' troubles to spread beyond the inner circles [of City and government] without causing panic; indeed, anxiety lifted' (Pressnell, 1968, 207).

In summary, we can say that the financial and economic turmoil that accompanied the 1825–6 banking crisis was comparable with that of 2007–9 and for this reason it is a valuable case. The 1890 crisis was a *potential* systemic crisis since it is possible that the Bank of England's timely intervention prevented it from developing – in contrast to the experience of 2007–9 (see Chapter 8). Since one of our crucial concerns is to investigate the nature and consequences of such policy interventions, we also investigate the 1890 crisis in this chapter as the best available case during the period of democracy in this earlier era.

7.2   The Changing Institutional-Political Environment

The Glorious Revolution of 1688 entrenched the influence of an aristocratic parliament that nevertheless constrained the sovereign, with powerful consequences for financial and economic development (North and Weingast, 1989). Democracy took at least a further two centuries to achieve, but as Stasavage points out, the 1688 revolution was accompanied by other developments that improved the ability of British electors to acquire information about their parliamentary representatives, and thus to hold them to account: 'First, the invention of modern political party organizations gave constituents a new technology for monitoring their representatives[.] Second, the development of a very active print news culture also certainly lowered costs of information acquisition' (Stasavage, 2011, 161).

Effective control over governance in the United Kingdom passed from the sovereign to his or her first minister and cabinet during the eighteenth century. In this period, the label of 'prime minister' became attached to this first minister. Although the convention that the sovereign must choose the prime minister from the party that effectively controls Parliament was not firmly entrenched until after the Great Reform Bill of 1832, in practice these ministers had already become more dependent on the confidence of the parliament than the crown to remain in power (Blick and Jones, 2010). The monarchy was weak in the final decade of the reign of George III after 1810 and during that of George IV in the 1820s; effectively, the prime minister was in control of government. Thus, by the beginning of the nineteenth century, although the United Kingdom was far from a full democracy, the executive branch of government was to a substantial extent responsible to Parliament, to parties and to the electorate, which had a growing if indirect role in their selection and replacement.

During the eighteenth century and until the mid-nineteenth century, the main groupings in British politics were the Whigs and Tories. Both drew their support from the aristocracy, but the Whigs had somewhat more progressive tendencies in that they favoured a more constitutional (constrained) monarchy. They also opposed the restoration of the Catholic Stuart monarchy ('Jacobitism'), which some Tories favoured. The Tories were strongly associated with the landed gentry and royal family, whereas over time the Whigs gained increasing support from wealthy merchants in London, including those associated with the Bank of England and the financial sector generally. They were a broad coalition that allied this 'monied interest' with other groups, and its coherence contributed substantially to the United Kingdom's financial development and credibility. So did Robert Walpole's strategy of adopting moderate policies on land taxation so as to minimize the incentive for radical Tories to ally with land-owning Whigs (Stasavage, 2003, 99–123). Increasingly, Whigs came to support more 'liberal' causes including Catholic emancipation, free trade, the abolition of slavery and the expansion of the franchise, all of which conservative Tories opposed.

After a long period of Whig supremacy, the Tories dominated government between 1783 and 1830 and thus during the first of our major banking crises. The Tories controlled the British prime ministership from 1807 through 1830, when Wellington lost power due to a vote of no confidence in Parliament on 15 November 1830. However, party boundaries were sometimes fluid. Some members of the government of Lord Liverpool (Robert Jenkinson, prime minister from 1812 to 1827) called themselves Whigs (Christie, 1982, 283). The Tories were increasingly split in the 1820s between anti-Catholic 'ultra-Tories' and a more moderate wing. However, most commentators accept that these were years of Tory rule.

On the eve of the 1826 election, although political participation in the United Kingdom was greater than in most other countries at the time, the property-based electoral franchise was still very narrow. Prior to the 1832 Reform Act, estimates put the size of the British electorate at roughly 516,000, or about 3 per cent of the total population of 16.4 million (House of Commons Library, United Kingdom, 2013, 3–4). In rural constituencies, elections were often uncontested, so that many voters had only a hypothetical voice. In the 1831 elections, for example, one-third of 380 seats were contested.

The result of this system was that the aristocracy retained a powerful hold on Parliament, including on the (lower) House of Commons. Over 1820–32, membership of the Commons included '150 heirs of peers[,] ... 141 younger sons of peers ... and 11 peers' bastards' (Fisher, 2009, 1:243). This was 22 per cent of the total membership of the House over this period, but this underestimates the political dominance of the aristocracy as other MPs were linked to it via their mothers and by marriage ties, and because of the deference accorded by many to the higher ranks of society.

Thus, although Britain had moved some distance after 1688 away from a monarchical regime, its parliamentary system of government by 1825 was far from fully democratic, and thus not coded as such in the Boix–Miller–Rosato (2013) dataset. The Polity IV score for the United Kingdom in 1825–6 is −2. It codes the recruitment of the chief executive as regulated and institutionalized, but as selected by the monarch (Marshall, Gurr and Jaggers, 2017). Polity also codes the prime minister as substantially constrained by other accountability groups, notably the cabinet, the party and the Parliament itself.

However, as we have noted, by the 1820s the monarchy was weak and the dominant party chose the prime minister. Political parties and their senior leadership were also playing a much more important role in policymaking than the sovereign, and competition between the two major parties was considerable. They competed for the votes of a narrow electorate, but according to 'selectorate theory' measures, at this time the size of the selectorate was large and the 'winning coalition' required to gain office was of intermediate proportion (Bueno de Mesquita et al., 2003). Narrow economic interests were well represented and influential. The landed gentry defended their interests vigorously, including the protection of agriculture and limited taxation of land. The rising mercantile and financial elite was also directly represented. Over the 1820–32 period, about 140 elected members (10 per cent) of the House of Commons were bankers, financiers, merchants and industrialists. Of the approximately sixty-five bankers, about a third were also involved in commerce or industry; about half were Whigs; twenty-eight were London-based partners and the rest were in the provinces (Fisher, 2009, 1:270).

For these reasons, elections by this period provided a mechanism of accountability through which a limited group could shape incumbent survival. Even public opinion had a growing influence on the behaviour of political representatives. Occasional bouts of rioting and other forms of public violence were one means by which the disenfranchised periodically exercised some influence (Holmes, 2002, 283; O'Gorman, 1997, 360).

After the Whigs returned to power in the elections of 1830, they introduced the 1832 Reform Act, which widened the franchise to all male householders in borough constituencies living in properties worth at least £10 a year. This increased the size of the electorate by about 50 per cent (House of Commons Library, United Kingdom, 2013, 4). The reform indicated the Tories' increasing unpopularity and the growing influence of extra-parliamentary pressure groups, such as the Birmingham Political Union. But the low degree of electoral competition limited the damage to aristocratic control of Parliament. In the election that took place over December 1832 to January 1833, only a third of the seats were contested and, as Bagehot later noted, the 'ten pound householders' granted the vote in 1832 on the whole remained deferential towards the upper classes and continued to vote for them (Bagehot, 1882, xii–xiii).

Over the longer term, the widening of the franchise led to significant change in the House of Commons, which increasingly became the house of the (upper) middle classes (Bagehot, 1882, xxv–xxvi). New middle-class members were joined by some radicals, and by mid-century the Whigs were succeeded by the Liberal Party, which rose to prominence in the governments of Gladstone from 1868. However, as we saw in Chapter 3, this rising political importance of the middle class was not matched by their share of societal wealth, which remained very low by mid-twentieth-century standards – with important consequences for the politics of banking crises in this period. After the 1832 Act, the rise of 'conservative associations' among the Tories also led to the emergence of the modern Conservative Party, the principles of which were elaborated in the Tamworth Manifesto of 1834 and first associated with the governments of Sir Robert Peel in the 1830s and 1840s.

The 1867 Reform Act further extended the franchise by granting the vote to relatively skilled working-class males residing in towns. This increased voting rights from about one in seven males to one in three (Boix, Miller and Rosato, 2014, 13). The middle and upper middle classes dominated the electoral system numerically after this reform, extending their influence in the House of Commons – and thus the gap between it and the aristocratic House of Lords.

The momentum for the further extension of the franchise built over the course of the following decade. In the 1884 Reform Act, Parliament accepted that the vote should also be extended to most men in counties, increasing the franchise to nearly two-thirds of adult males (House of Commons Library, United Kingdom, 2013, 4). In the following year, the Redistribution of Seats Act substantially reduced inequalities across electoral districts and most were to be represented by single members. As reflected in the Boix–Miller–Rosato (2013) and Polity datasets, in the five years leading up to the 1890 crisis, then, it can be said that the United Kingdom was a highly imperfect but functioning parliamentary democracy.[5]

---

[5] Boix et al. code the UK as democratic from 1884, noting that the House of Lords never successfully exercised its pre-1911 authority to veto legislation (Boix, Miller and Rosato, 2014, 13). Universal male suffrage and the extension of the vote to some women were granted in 1918; equal suffrage was granted in 1928.

7.3   The 1825–6 Banking Crisis

A number of contemporaries blamed this crisis on the previous actions of the government and the Bank to promote easier credit conditions after the Napoleonic wars so as to refinance the heavy burden of war debt. An overissue of notes, critics claimed, allowed a speculative mania to develop that peaked in 1825 (Kindleberger and Aliber, 2011, 88; Thomas, 1934, 1:61–4; Turner, 2014, 67). A number of Tory members had historically taken the position that the Bank's dominance of note issuance was unacceptable and the source of financial instability, but the criticism also came from some Whig members and leading newspaper editorialists (see Chapter 4). As the Marquis of Lansdowne, a Whig, argued in the House of Lords in February 1826:

> [T]he Bank directors deserved great credit for the promptitude with which they endeavoured to arrest the effects of the late panic by a great issue of small notes. But, having said thus much, it would be uncandid in him not to add, that the Bank, in the first instance, so far from having arrested the progress of the late evils, had increased them by the extent of its issues of paper.[6]

Country banks were the first to be affected by the developing panic in 1825, but by December it had spread to London and had become systemic. Kindleberger records nearly 10 per cent (73 of 770) of country banks failing during this crisis and cites informed contemporaries to support the claim that the United Kingdom came near to complete financial collapse (Kindleberger and Aliber, 2011, 111; Thomas, 1934, 1:55–6). As the remarks of Lord Lansdowne indicate, the Bank of England provided extensive assistance to banks during the crisis and came under pressure to do more from financial and mercantile interests, as well as from key figures in the government. The government itself resisted calls for it to provide additional assistance, preferring to rely on the Bank to do so.

The Bank came under considerable fire for worsening the crisis. Conant notes that it created 'financial paralysis' by raising its discount rate from 4 per cent to 5 per cent on 13 December (Conant, 1915, 621).

---

[6] House of Lords debate, 'State of the Currency', *Hansard*, 9 February 1826, vol. 14, cc132–45.

Contemporary critics also blamed the London-based structure of the Bank for the chronic lack of liquidity outside of London during the crisis (Calomiris and Haber, 2014, 114). Bagehot (in *Lombard Street*) argues the Bank also erred by allowing its gold reserve to deplete precipitously and then trying to protect it by lending as little as possible, inducing a 'tremendous panic' (Bagehot, 1962 [1873], 178–9).

However, the Bank's actions eventually stemmed the financial crisis in late December 1825. The subsequent effects on the real economy were substantial, with a 'massive' wave of bankruptcies that peaked in April 1826. Over 2,500 bankruptcies were recorded in 1826 – more than two and a half times the annual number observed in the two years preceding the crisis (Gayer, Rostow and Schwartz, 1975, 1:205). Real GDP also fell in 1826 by over 5 per cent (Thomas and Dimsdale, 2017).

7.3.1 The Politics of Policy Responses

The years before this crisis were a period of growing ascendance of liberal philosophical aversion to government interference in the economy. Thus, the intellectual foundations for market-conformist liquidity provision policies had already been laid. Leading figures – including Sir Francis Baring and Henry Thornton – had clearly elaborated much of the conceptual framework for lender of last resort operations now associated with the later writings of Bagehot (Grossman, 2010, 99–101). Both Baring and Thornton concurred that the Bank of England should serve as what Thornton called the *dernier resort*, the court of last appeal, temporarily expanding its loans when there was a heightened demand for liquidity. In speeches in Parliament, evidence given to a parliamentary committee, and in a published volume, Thornton strongly opposed the idea of bailouts of mismanaged banks but supported judicious lending to avert a generalized collapse. Explicitly recognizing the need for a balanced policy, Thornton wrote in 1802:

> It is by no means intended to imply, that it would become the Bank of England to relieve every distress which the rashness of country banks may bring upon them: the bank, by doing this, might encourage their improvidence. There seems to be a medium at which a public bank should aim in granting aid to inferior establishments, and which it must often find very difficult

to be observed. The relief should be neither so prompt and liberal as to exempt those who misconduct their business from all natural causes of their own fault, nor so scanty and slow as deeply to involve the general interests. (Thornton, 1802, 188)

In spring 1825, Lord Liverpool had publicly warned about the excesses of speculation and he seemed attentive to concerns about moral hazard. He stated that assistance would not be forthcoming in the event of a crisis. When the crisis came later that year, Liverpool held fast to his commitment and refused escalating demands for government assistance, saying that he would rather resign – and indeed he seems to have come close to doing so (Brock, 1967, 209–10). Intellectually, he adhered strongly to the principles of laissez-faire, favouring the principle that market discipline should be preserved. Echoing Thornton's concerns about moral hazard, Liverpool stated, 'I have always thought that the precedent of 1793 ... was not a favourable one and therefore ought not to be followed ... What would be the effects of such a measure [the issuance of Exchequer bills]? Not to leave the people to rely upon themselves. What is that but the very evil I have deprecated; namely looking to government for aid, to relieve them from the consequence of their own extravagance' (Brock, 1967, 210).

Liverpool's reference to the precedent of 1793 is revealing. The United Kingdom had joined its continental allies in waging war against the French revolutionary regime, leading to a sharp escalation in public debt and the Bank seeking to conserve its gold reserves. When facing a financial crisis later that year, the government had intervened to stabilize markets by issuing Exchequer bills to lend against collateral to some distressed banks and merchants (Brock, 1967, 189–91, 201–2, 209; Thomas, 1934, 1:25–30). Some insolvent borrowers were promised funds because of the 'mischief that might result from ... bankruptcy' (as cited in Grossman, 2010, 191, fn.13). As it would in a later national security emergency in 1914, the government in 1793 seems to have gone further than it did during crises that occurred during the long period of peace after the end of the Napoleonic Wars. The restoration of peace in 1815 also coincided with a gradual move from mercantilism towards economic liberalism, and in this new context Liverpool was determined not to repeat the interventions of 1793.

As noted above, the Bank of England initially responded to the crisis in mid-December 1825 by acting to protect its own position.

Of course, the Bank was then a privately owned institution, albeit one with special privileges granted by government, including its monopoly on joint-stock banking and on note issuance within London – in return for its fulfilling certain public policy objectives (notably regarding the efficient issue of public debt). Thus, while caution needs to be exercised when speaking of 'policy responses' by the Bank, its governors were keenly aware that their position, and decisions about its next charter renewal in 1833, would depend in part on how well it served the public good.[7] The Bank was also faced with its responsibility to maintain the gold convertibility of the pound, which limited its ability to expand liquidity during a crisis.

The Bank stood by as the first bank runs occurred in December. According to Bagehot, the Bank 'at first acted as unwisely as it was possible to act … The reserve being very small, it endeavoured to protect that reserve by lending as little as possible' (Bagehot, 1962 [1873], 98).[8] This stance did it few political favours. There were always those – including Members of Parliament (MPs) connected with other banks – willing to use a crisis to curtail the Bank's privileges. The main constituency pushing for more extensive intervention was the financial and connected merchant community in London and in the country, where financial and commercial distress was acute. It should be noted in this regard that it was common practice in the early nineteenth century (one sustained through at least mid-century) for the Bank to accept bills of exchange for discount not only from merchant banks but also from a variety of non-bank firms including 'cabinet makers, flax spinners, publishers, and umbrella manufacturers' – and in at least one case in 1857, slave merchants (Anson et al., 2017, 46).

Four MPs' own banks failed in the 1825 crisis (Fisher, 2009, 1:270). As 'fear of general disaster' spread, the Bank and other bankers pressured the government to suspend the requirement for the Bank to convert its notes into gold, as it had done from 1797 to 1821. But the government rejected this request (Thomas, 1934, 1:56). Nor did the

---

[7] The Bank was subject to nine charter renewals between its founding in 1694 and the Bank Act of 1844 that provided it with exclusive note-issuance authority (Broz and Grossman, 2004).

[8] It also maintained bank rate at 5 per cent through the crisis. This was the maximum interest rate the Bank could charge until the repeal of usury laws in 1833 (Anson et al., 2017, 36). Bank rate changes did not become an important part of the Bank's crisis management strategy until the 1847 crisis.

government wish itself to accept responsibility to act as a lender of last resort.

Instead, the prime minister (Liverpool) convened a meeting with the Bank's governor on 14 December and encouraged him to print money and lend extensively against sound collateral (Brock, 1967, 205). The Bank's reluctant acceptance of this task, according to Kindleberger and Aliber, was 'the sulky answer of driven men' (Kindleberger and Aliber, 2011, 217). The Bank, according to another source, 'had taken a firm and deliberate resolution to make common cause with the country as far as their humble efforts would go' (cited in Thomas, 1934, 1:56). As the accelerating run on country banks spread to London, the Bank lent extensively to other firms by discounting bills and issuing £5 million in new notes, accepting any and every form of acceptable security and refusing advances to none of the more than 2,500 applicants for assistance (Thomas, 1934, 1:56).

By 17 December, this initial intervention had the effect of easing the panic in London, but it persisted for another week in the countryside. The Bank issued a further £1 million in old notes found in its basement (Brock, 1967, 206). The Bank's provision of collateralized lending and the prompt closure of dozens of insolvent financial institutions largely aligned with what we described in Chapter 5 as the Bagehot policy model – excepting in that, as noted above, the Bank also provided assistance to non-bank firms. Since the UK fell short of the democratic thresholds in the Boix and Polity databases, the 1826 crisis does not appear in our analysis in Chapter 5. Nonetheless, the data we collected for this crisis generates a highly negative score that falls toward the upper range of the market-conforming response pole (see Figure 7.4).

Pressure to do more than this built quickly. Parliamentary representatives associated with the merchant class, led by the Whig George Tierney, also called for government intervention in the form of an emergency issuance of Exchequer bills to distressed merchants in exchange for collateral in the form of goods.[9]

The rising prominence of liberal economic ideas may in part have shaped the government's approach and in turn informed public expectations about government responsibility for financial and economic

---

[9] See particularly House of Commons debate, 'Commercial Distress – Petition of Merchants of London for Relief', *Hansard*, 23 February 1826, vol. 14, cc698–733 (Brock, 1967, 209).

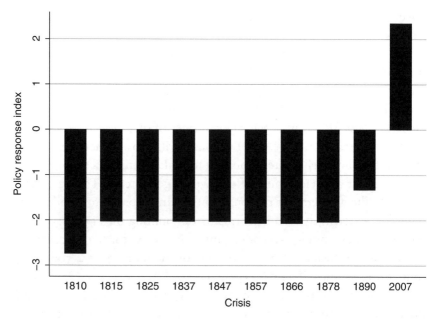

Figure 7.4: Policy responses to banking crises in the United Kingdom, 1810–2007.

stabilization. However, many in Liverpool's Tory Party were not converts to laissez-faire, and the government felt it necessary to deflect this pressure for intervention by asking the Bank to take further action. There is direct evidence of this in a letter that Bagehot later cited from the home secretary, Sir Robert Peel, to the Duke of Wellington, and which is worth citing at length. Peel stated:

> We have been placed in a very unpleasant predicament on the other question – the issue of Exchequer Bills by Government. The feeling of the City, of many of our friends, of some of the Opposition, was decidedly in favour of the issue of Exchequer Bills to relieve the merchants and manufacturers. It was said in favour of the issue, that the same measure had been tried and succeeded in 1793 and 1811. Our friends whispered about that we were acting quite in a different manner from that in which Mr. Pitt did act, and would have acted had he been alive. We felt satisfied that, however plausible were the reasons urged in favour of the issue of Exchequer Bills, yet that the measure was a dangerous one, and ought to be resisted by the Government ... We found that the Bank had the power to lend

money on deposit of goods. As our issue of Exchequer Bills would have been useless unless the Bank cashed them, as therefore the intervention of the Bank was in any event absolutely necessary, and as its intervention would be chiefly useful by the effect which it would have in increasing the circulating medium, we advised the Bank to take the whole affair into their own hands at once, to issue their notes on the security of goods, instead of issuing them on Exchequer Bills, such bills being themselves issued on that security. They reluctantly consented, and rescued us from a very embarrassing predicament. (Cited in Bagehot, 1962 [1873], 98–9)

Although the Bank expanded the scope of its normal emergency lending in response to this government pressure, it seems to have done so on terms largely consistent with the Bagehot approach, including collateralized lending and screening of borrowers.[10] Notably, Bagehot himself applauded the Bank's actions. He also cites Jeremiah Harman, a prominent London banker and a director of the Bank of England:

We lent it by every possible means and in modes we had never adopted before; we took in stock on security, we purchased Exchequer bills, we made advances on Exchequer bills, we not only discounted outright, but we made advances on the deposit of bills of exchange to an immense amount, in short, by every possible means consistent with the safety of the Bank, and we were not on some occasions over-nice. Seeing the dreadful state in which the public were, we rendered every assistance in our power. (Bagehot, 1962 [1873], 25)

Thus, the policy response to the 1825 crisis can be said to have stemmed directly from the pressure that financial and business elites were able to bring to bear on both the government and the Bank, with the government insisting that the costs be borne largely by the Bank. Both the government and the Bank also strongly preferred that the measures were broadly market-conforming, though the Bank lent extensively to banks and non-banks in exchange for a wide range of

---

[10] As noted above, existing usury laws prevented it from lending at penalty rates above 5 per cent.

collateral. That it did so reflected the heavy dependence of contemporary merchants on bills of exchange.

In the parliamentary post-mortem in February 1826, when commercial distress remained high, MPs connected with the mercantile elite supported the Bank's actions, including its direct lending to merchants, although some made it known that they believed the government could have done more. Matthias Attwood, member for Callington (in Cornwall) and a banker himself, was one:

> If it were contrary to any principles of political economy for the government to give extraordinary assistance to the merchants, in a state of commercial difficulty such as the present, it was at least a legitimate proceeding for the Bank to give such assistance. That was opposed to no principle of political economy. The Bank was a commercial establishment. It was precisely such an establishment as the commercial body was entitled to look to, for extraordinary assistance in a crisis of extraordinary emergency.[11]

Unsurprisingly, prominent members of the government maintained that only the Bank could so act. This included William Huskisson, President of the Board of Trade, and Frederick Robinson, Chancellor of the Exchequer.[12] Direct government intervention would have been a step too far and would only have fostered the moral hazard that Liverpool was insistent on avoiding. The government indicated a willingness to repay the Bank any advances it made on the limited quantity of Exchequer Bills outstanding, but this was upon a different principle than direct government relief. Liverpool stated in the Lords that:

> If the Bank would administer that species of relief, he, as a member of the government, would have no hesitation, at a future period of the session, to apply to parliament for a grant to repay it any advances which it might eventually have occasion to make. In what other way the government could interfere, with propriety, he confessed he could not see. If the

---

[11] House of Commons debate, 'Bank Charter and Promissory Notes Acts', *Hansard*, 14 February 1826, vol. 14, cc368–407.

[12] House of Commons debate, 'Bank Charter and Promissory Notes Acts', *Hansard*, 14 February 1826, vol. 14, cc368–407.

effect of this declaration should be to deprive the government of the confidence of those who had hitherto supported it, he should regret the circumstance; but he could not consent to purchase the confidence of any class of individuals, by acquiescing in a request which he was, in his conscience, convinced would be more dangerous than beneficial to the interests of the country.[13]

Liverpool also supported other temporary liberalizing measures to reduce the tariff on corn to provide relief to the distressed manufacturing districts and committed to further trade liberalization – though his own colleagues later sabotaged this plan (Brock, 1967, 222–7). The crisis also induced some regulatory changes. In response to the concern that the Bank's structure had not permitted it to provide adequate assistance to country banks, the Country Bankers' Act of 1826 allowed and encouraged the Bank to open branches outside of London, which it did in the following years (Calomiris and Haber, 2014, 115). The Act also diluted the Bank's monopoly on joint-stock banking by permitting the establishment of other joint-stock banks on the condition that they operated beyond a sixty-five-mile radius of London. This did little in practice to erode the Bank's effective monopoly on note issuance.[14]

7.3.2 Political Impact

Lord Liverpool had led a stable Tory government since the elections of 1820 that followed the death of George III. It had a comfortable majority in the House of Commons although the Whig opposition was able to organize an occasional government defeat on controversial issues. The 1825 banking crisis was a matter of considerable interest for the political economists in the House. The Bank's response to the crisis received widespread praise, though as noted earlier some blamed the crisis in part on its policy during the boom period and its monopoly on joint-stock banking. Notably, they did not generally direct criticism at Liverpool's market-conforming policy response

---

[13] House of Commons debate, 'Bank Charter and Promissory Notes Acts', *Hansard*, 14 February 1826, vol. 14, cc368–407.

[14] Other banks could in principle issue notes, but the Bank's refusal to deal with those that chose to do so prevented such competitive issuance in practice (Calomiris and Haber, 2014, 115).

(Grossman, 2010). Those who actually lost money in failing country banks seem to have lacked the political influence needed to receive assistance or compensation.

There is also little indication that Liverpool's government was seriously destabilized by its principled policy stance. The dissolution of the Parliament, which had run from January 1820 for most of the seven-year maximum duration permitted under the 1716 Septennial Act, took place on 2 June 1826.[15] Liverpool had initially favoured a dissolution in September 1825, but pro-emancipation colleagues convinced him to delay elections until the following year when they hoped that the then intense anti-Catholic sentiment might have dissipated (Fisher, 2009, 1:221–2).

In the election that followed over June–July 1826, only 112 of 380 constituencies were contested (29 per cent), a slight increase on 1820 but a standard proportion for that era (some constituencies had multiple members, making up a total of 658 members). The main issue of the election was Catholic emancipation, and about a dozen new anti-Catholic MPs were elected. Overall, the election resulted in the Liverpool Tory government being comfortably returned, albeit under a very constrained electoral system. It is not clear that there was any substantial swing against the Tory Party, which was itself split on the question of Catholic emancipation (Fisher, 2009, 1:329–30).

One possibility is that the shortage of elections in a less democratic environment short-circuited the potential for a crisis-induced political backlash against the incumbent Tory government. Of the many areas of England that experienced bank failures in this crisis, only a minority had contested elections in 1826. Of the twenty-eight individual bank failures that we have identified from one key historical source, only eleven were located in counties or boroughs that had elections in 1826 (Fisher, 2009; Orbell and Turton, 2001). However, it is also possible that the presence of a contesting candidate was endogenous to voter sentiment. That is, the absence of a contested election could indicate the limited potential impact that localized bank failures had on the incumbent candidate's prospects for defeat.

Furthermore, when we consider contested elections where bank failures were observed, we find that even in these cases the political impact was limited. Indeed, in almost all cases where sitting Tories ran

---

[15] www.historyofparliamentonline.org/volume/1820-1832/survey/v-general-elections-1820-1831.

in these constituencies, they enjoyed an *increase* in their vote share.[16] In Hereford, the two sitting members were returned, with the incumbent Tory, a strong supporter of Liverpool's government, topping the poll.[17] In Bristol as well, the sitting Tory came first in 1826 after a second place result in 1820.[18] In the City of London, of the four MPs returned, two were Tories and two were Whigs. Since there were three Tories and one Whig elected in 1820, this meant a loss of one seat for the Tories. However, only two Tories ran in the election, William Thompson and William Ward, and both were elected; both also saw their vote shares increase by 24.7 per cent and 19.0 per cent respectively, with William Thompson leading the whole field, unlike in 1820 (Smith, 1844, 1:211). In Surrey, the only sitting Tory lost his seat to a Whig, though it appears that the main animus against him was from mercantile interests angered at his opposition to Corn Law reform.[19] In short, even in contested constituencies that had suffered local banking failures, there is little evidence of a systematic negative impact for political incumbents from the banking crisis that immediately preceded it.

At the time of the 1826 elections, suffrage restrictions based on property ownership mean that, as discussed earlier, the limited group of voters likely derived an important part of their wealth and income from landholdings. Estimates suggest that the value of and rental income from land were relatively stable following the 1825 crisis.[20] As Offer points out, landowners could renegotiate yearly rents with tenant farmers and shifted much of the economic risk of fluctuating farm incomes to them (Offer, 1991). In fact, Gayer, Rostow and Schwartz report that rent per acre increased in the years following the crisis (Gayer, Rostow and Schwartz, 1975, 1:269). This limited group of

---

[16] Authors' analysis. Surrey was the exception, where a Tory lost his seat, but as he was elected unopposed in 1820 it is not possible to calculate the change in his vote share.

[17] The Tory, John Somers Cocks, had previously been elected unopposed in 1820.

[18] www.historyofparliamentonline.org/volume/1820-1832/constituencies/bristol.

[19] www.historyofparliamentonline.org/volume/1820-1832/member/holme-sumner-george-1760-1838.

[20] The only available data series on land prices during this period reveals 'wide fluctuations' that Gayer, Rostow and Schwartz describe as 'random in some years' due to low transaction numbers: '[T]he accident of a fine estate being sold in one year, and poor one in the next, or of forced sale, elevate or depressed the price' (Gayer, Rostow and Schwartz, 1975, 1:929). An 'abnormally low price in 1827 in conjunction with the relatively large acreage disposed of' leads them to describe a sharp decline in land values in that year as 'random' and 'without doubt, spurious'. We thus conclude that land values remained largely stable in the post-crisis period, which is the general trend until 1970 (Jaevicius, Huston and Baum, 2015, 18).

voters also minimized their vulnerability to the failures of country banks by maintaining their primary accounts with London-based private bankers, including the Bank of England (Pressnell, 1956, 246–7).

Taken together, then, the majority of voters at the time likely experienced limited negative exposure to bank failures. The policy response from the Bank of England meant most voters were much less at risk than exposed financial and mercantile interests, and these groups were were largely satisfied by the extensive assistance eventually provided by the Bank. Hence, the bailout constituency favouring *government* action was very vocal but not sufficiently influential to secure more extensive policy measures, allowing the government to deflect pressure for limited intervention onto the Bank. Liverpool's government thus also faced a low level of political risk in supporting the Bank's provision of Bagehot-style emergency lending.

One reason for low expectations at this time may be that the government had made no prior commitment to prevent crises via financial regulation. Banks were not subject to minimum capital or reserve requirements, nor were they required to file with the government or to publish any financial data. England's first comprehensive banking code – which required publication of basic elements of firm governance and specified minimal thresholds for nominal and paid-in capital – was not enacted until 1844. This was also a period in which bank directors faced full liability for losses, which provided a further signal to banks that government protection would not be forthcoming in the event of failure.[21] One indication of this expectation is that banks engaged in self-protection by holding very large (by modern standards) reserves and pools of 'uncalled capital' to protect against losses (Haldane, 2011).

There does appear to have been some agitation related to the financial crisis and its aftermath in some urban constituencies, perhaps related to the frustrations of those groups lacking the right to vote. 'In some of the larger industrializing towns, there were calls for further reductions in corn import duties and other imposts and demands for relief from distress caused by unemployment' (Fisher, 2009, 1:222). There was also extensive rioting and violence in a number of areas in England and Ireland during the elections, though much was due to

---

[21] Banks were not granted limited liability until 1857, when the banking code was repealed and replaced by corporation law. Even then, limited liability joint-stock banking did not take off until after the failure of Glasgow City Bank in 1878 (Haldane, 2011).

contestation between anti-Catholic and pro-emancipation groups. At the height of the panic in December 1825, Pressnell suggests that police were called in to disperse surging crowds in the City [of London] (Pressnell, 1956, 488). But, interestingly, Pressnell's authoritative study of country banks provides no evidence of social unrest in areas where these banks failed. The primary holders of country bank deposit accounts and notes were drawn from the lower middle classes and upwards. Pressnell suggests that attempts to address the anxieties of these individuals were often made 'in the traditional form of public meetings to express confidence in local banks, of guarantees by local worthies, and of declarations by tradesmen that they would accept the threatened local notes' (Pressnell, 1956, 489). Those who lost money in failing country banks seem simply to have lacked the political influence needed to receive assistance or compensation.

The period of government over 1826 to 1830 was one of considerable instability, particularly compared to the period that preceded it, and pressure for reform built steadily. However, it is unlikely this was due to any longer-term impact of the 1825–6 crisis. Lord Liverpool's retirement in 1827 was due to his having suffered a severe stroke (he died the following year). Wellington and William Pitt then refused to serve under the relatively moderate Tory, George Canning, in 1827, who was asked by the King to form a government. Canning then invited several Whigs into his cabinet. However, Canning died after only four months in office. He was succeeded by Viscount Goderich, who lasted no longer than Canning and who could not hold his coalition together. Goderich in turn was succeeded by the Duke of Wellington, who restored a 'high' Tory cabinet in 1828.

From this time, the fortunes of the Whigs revived. In the election of August 1830 the government returned to power, but it lost about fifteen members ('1830 | History of Parliament Online' n.d.). The Whigs gained in this election under Lord Grey, and after Wellington's resignation they were asked by the new king to form a government. This government introduced the 1832 Reform Act, which widened the franchise.

7.4   The Barings Crisis of 1890

As its name implies, this crisis was focused on one of the City's major finance houses, though its repercussions were felt much more widely. Many sources point to Barings' increasingly heavy exposure to South America from 1885, particularly Argentina, which enjoyed a large inflow of lending in the five years preceding the crisis. Barings played an important role in the issuance of Argentine bonds used to finance substantial investments in banking, utilities, infrastructure and services. The bank was by this stage the country's largest single creditor, holding £8.3 million by 1890 (White, 2016b).

By this time there were many signs of financial excesses in the recipient countries, as well as growing political instability. Rising concern about the Argentinian situation was increased by growing civil unrest and a failed coup in July 1890, which prompted the resignation of the president, who was widely seen as incompetent and corrupt (Ferns, 1992, 258–9). Although governance improved in Argentina, it came too late for Barings. London banks experienced a flight to quality; Barings and other banks closely connected with Argentine interests were now in serious difficulty and fear was spreading throughout the British banking system. Over November 1890, private deposits at the Bank of England increased sharply as depositors moved money from private banks thought to be exposed to Barings, such as Martin's. Lloyds Bank, which had expanded rapidly through acquisition to become one of the largest joint-stock banks, was unable to sell £500,000 of gilts to improve its cash position (Conant, 1915, 662–4; White, 2016b).

The Bank of England and the government were increasingly concerned about the wider impact of a failure of Barings. In mid-November they agreed that Barings should be rescued initially by a combination of Bank and Treasury financial support, allowing the Bank of England to assemble a predominantly private sector guarantee fund to make good on any losses that it might incur. This action stabilized the markets and may have prevented a deeper banking and economic crisis from developing. As we explore further below, it was also a crisis in which the potential electoral ramifications of a serious financial and economic downturn were far different to those in 1825–6.

7.4.1 The Politics of Policy Responses

The first policy measures were taken by the Bank of England. In the week before the rescue was launched, the Bank injected liquidity into the market by sharply increasing its discounts over 7–14 November (White, 2016b). This action was consistent with the Bank's evolving understanding of its role as a lender of last resort and the accumulation of more than a century of experience – though the Bank continued to resist an explicit acceptance of this role out of a fear of fostering moral hazard (Calomiris and Haber, 2014, 121–2; Fetter, 1965, 282).[22] As had also happened in the three major banking crises that followed the 1844 Bank Charter Act,[23] the chancellor (Goschen) offered to suspend the Act to allow the Bank to issue notes freely. At this stage, the government refused to lend its own funds to rescue Barings or any other bank in difficulty.

This much was effectively standard practice during panics since at least mid century. But the authorities soon went further. Lidderdale declined the government's offer of suspension of the Bank Act, but insisted in a meeting with the chancellor on 10 November that the government support its intention to rescue Barings with the Bank's own funds and those it could raise from the City. Specifically, he wanted the government to provide a short-term guarantee of half of the Bank's exposure while he organized the rescue fund in the City. White argues that the Bank had learnt from the recent example of the Banque de France-led rescue in 1889 of the Comptoir d'Escompte, which was well known to London bankers including the Rothschilds, who were heavily involved in both crises. Barings' large exposure to Argentine securities meant that it would be difficult for the Bank to lend to it on good collateral – though this raised the question of whether Barings was in fact insolvent, as a Bank report on its position denied (White, 2016a, 5). Goschen refused this request, though he agreed to ask for assistance from the Banque de France via the Rothschilds and to form a committee to negotiate with the Argentine government (White, 2016a, 4).

On 14 November, Lidderdale once again requested direct government assistance and threatened to allow Barings to collapse. Under this increased pressure, Goschen and the Prime Minister (the Marquess of Salisbury) agreed verbally to meet half of the loss until the afternoon of 16 November to allow the Bank to organize a guarantee fund in the

---

[22] From the 1866 crisis, commercial banks increasingly dominated the lists of acceptors from which the Bank would discount bills (Anson et al., 2017, 46–8). These authors analyse micro-level data to show that the Bank had 'evolved towards' a consistent application of the Bagehot rule in its discounting behaviour during crises by mid century. They find that even in previous crises, the Bank took sufficient collateral from borrowers for its last resort lending to have been profitable.

[23] The 1844 Act required that the Bank issue notes only up to the value of £14 million in excess of its gold reserves.

City (White, 2016a, 6). Although Lidderdale asked Goschen to confirm this in writing some days later, he did so only in very general terms (Pressnell, 1968, 203–4). This calculated vagueness enabled Goschen later to deny in Parliament that any guarantee had been given by the government. His biographer records Goschen as worrying that the Bank could lose as much as 50 per cent of a £1 million commitment and was thus 'entirely convinced … that we could not carry direct aid in Parliament if we had wished' (Elliot, 1911, 172).[24]

The final point underscores that there was insufficient political support for a government bailout. There was little of the clamour among parliamentarians for emergency assistance to private firms that had been present in the 1825 crisis. This may be because the 1890 crisis was not, or more likely, was not allowed to become, as systemic as that of 1825.

Was it also due to the greater dominance of laissez-faire ideas by the end of the nineteenth century? As most participants in the long and heated debate over whether the nineteenth century was an 'age of laissez faire' in the United Kingdom agree, the final three decades of the century in fact saw a marked increase in state interventionism in a range of areas, including legislation to provide for compulsory state-supported education, slum clearance, factory regulation, arbitration of labour disputes, employer liability and workplace insurance. Nevertheless, the drift towards interventionism should be kept in perspective: by 1900 there was still no housing policy, old-age pensions or national health insurance (Evans, 2011). And '[f]or each proposed act of governmental regulation a case had to be made – the general presumption against the meddlesome state was at least that strong' (Paul, 1980, 24). This lingering general presumption of Conservatives and Liberals against intervention, particularly in the area of crisis resolution in which the arguments of Baring, Thornton and Bagehot emphasized the need for market-conformity, also played out in the Barings case. Publicly at least, the government left crisis management mainly to the Bank of England.

The rescue fund that Lidderdale assembled consisted of an initial Bank of England loan of £7.5 million to Barings to permit it to discharge its existing obligations. Barings was split into a privately recapitalized, limited liability 'good' bank, Baring Brothers & Co. Ltd,

---

[24] See also Turner (2014, 155).

which would continue to provide financial services to its clients in the usual manner from a solvent position, and a 'bad' bank retaining the old name and the distressed assets. The bad bank would be managed by the Bank of England, but Barings brothers retained unlimited liability for any losses. The new Barings firm was responsible for repaying the initial loan from the Bank. The Bank intended to liquidate the distressed assets in the bad bank in a phased manner to recover maximum value. The Bank also insisted that the family's assets, including their properties and contents, were auctioned with the cash proceeds going to the bad bank.

The Bank of England also secured participation from leading merchant banks in a Guarantee Fund, where contributors would share, pro rata to their participation, any residual loss after three years (later extended to five) from the disposal of bad assets. The Bank reduced its commitment to £1 million, but the Guarantee Fund, amounting to £17.1 million, ensured that the private banks – including some of Barings' creditors – would bear most of any loss from the rescue.[25] Indeed, major shares were assigned to banks who had lent heavily to Barings, as in the French example the year before (White, 2016a, 8). The old Barings bad bank was eventually sold by the Bank of England to investors for £1.5 million in 1894. The final result was that the British guarantee syndicate, as in the French case of 1889, did not in practice have to cover any losses.

Thus, although the rescue of Barings did not require any immediate outlay of public funds, it did involve the acceptance of a contingent government liability, albeit one where the private sector would bear the lion's share of any losses. This loss-sharing arrangement, the liquidation of the old Barings bad bank, and the provision of collateralized lending to the new Barings entity mostly aligns with the Bagehot policy model outlined in Chapter 5. However, the government's acceptance of some of the potential losses that might have fallen on the Bank, and the lingering uncertainty about the solvency of Barings, positions this policy response further away from the market-conforming pole than that observed in 1826. As such, our data generates a negative score that falls within the middle range of the Bagehot continuum (see Figure 7.4).

---

[25] The Bank also provided nearly half a million pounds of assistance to Murrieta's, an Anglo-South American finance house, over four months from the time of the Barings rescue, before reversing this decision.

This unusual intervention by the Bank and (less transparently) the government was controversial at the time. *The Economist* thought that the rescue, despite the punitive measures applied to the Barings family, went considerably beyond standard Bank practice. The main objection was the familiar refrain that it supported special interests and risked encouraging bad behaviour:

> From the fact that it [the guarantee] is to extend over a period of three years, it would appear as if there were some intention of nursing the assets of Messrs Baring, incurring obligations in regard not only to their mercantile operations, which are stated to be perfectly sound, but also to their financial transactions with the Argentine and other South American Governments, which are of a doubtful character. And if anything of this kind is intended, the banks are going beyond their province.[26]

J. D. Turner goes further to argue that although the public justification for the rescue was Barings' economic importance, the more likely explanation is that British political and financial elites wished to rescue 'one of their own' engaged in the project of empire-building (Turner, 2014, 154–7). In a similar vein, Grossman (2010, 94) points to the fact that members of the Barings firm had been directors of the Bank of England since 1840 and that seventeen members of the extended Baring family sat in Parliament between 1812 and 1918.

Barings' political connections likely did matter, particularly when one contrasts the Bank's rescue of Barings with its notorious refusal to provide assistance to Overend Gurney in the crisis of 1866, the largest bank at the time.[27] These connections may also have influenced the Bank's perceptions about the solvency of Barings, about which White (2016b) expresses scepticism.

Yet it is difficult to find further support for the claim that the rescue was driven by imperial objectives. Cain and Hopkins, who pay particular attention to the relationship between the City and British imperialism, agree that relations between the Bank, government and the City elite, including Barings, were as cosy as 'a gentleman's club'. They cite evidence that other houses, including that of the Rothschilds,

---

[26] *The Economist*, 22 November 1890, 1466.
[27] The Bank also refused to provide assistance to the relatively distant City of Glasgow Bank in 1878, on grounds of insolvency.

felt a collapse of Barings would threaten their own position. The Roths-childs' important role in the Barings crisis does support the view that special interests mobilized to support the rescue, but this is common in crises. These authors argue instead that 'what was at stake [in this crisis] was the position of London as an international financial centre', rather than any 'conspiratorial' attempt to shore up the United Kingdom's specific position in Latin America (Cain and Hopkins, 2016, 157–9). Intervention that went somewhat beyond Bagehot's rule, in short, could have been a product of a coincidence of elite political and economic interests in the maintenance of the City's pre-eminent position. The Bank, Grossman (2010, 71, 97) adds, may also have acted to avoid a potential twin crisis. The collapse of Barings – an internationally oriented firm – might have led to foreign withdrawals, threatening the Bank's gold reserves. In contrast to the fallout from the failure of domestically oriented Overend – which could be addressed via note issuance – the potential fallout from Barings would have been more difficult to address with the toolkit available to the Bank.

There was no substantial opposition in Parliament to the Bank's role in the Barings rescue. Sir William Harcourt, Chancellor of the Exchequer in Gladstone's Liberal governments in the 1880s and 1890s, supported the Bank's intervention in November 1890, but asked Goschen in May 1891 to reassure the House of Commons that the government had played no part in 'propping up' Barings via a guarantee: 'it is a most pernicious and dangerous precedent, and I hope we shall learn from the Chancellor of the Exchequer that he has taken no such course'.[28] Whether Harcourt had heard about the government's verbal agreement with Lidderdale is unknown, but Goschen denied that any such thing had been done:

> I am glad to be able to state that the guarantee for Barings' house was undertaken by the great banking institutions of this country without any undertaking or guarantee by the Government directly or indirectly. I do not deny that great pressure has been put upon the Chancellor of the Exchequer and upon the Government with regard to it; and there was a time, in that memorable week, when it was believed that without the

---

[28] House of Commons debate, 'Customs and Inland Revenue Bill', *Hansard*, 26 May 1891, vol. 353, cc1096–132.

assistance of the Government it would be impossible to carry through the saving of that great house and all those other houses which might be imperilled by its fall.[29]

The Chancellor of the Exchequer was, of course, being economical with the truth on this occasion, but it seems that the verbal understanding of the previous November with Lidderdale had not become public knowledge. The Prime Minister, Salisbury, similarly chose not to divulge any indication of the government's role in his answer to a question in the House of Lords a week after the rescue.[30]

The secrecy concerning the government's role supports the conclusion that there was very little mass political support for such an intervention, even of a limited and temporary nature. In such a context, the government faced strong incentives to shift uncertain costs to the future and keep Parliament and voters in the dark via the creation of a substantial contingent liability (Gandrud and Hallerberg, 2015a).

Another indicator of the very low level of politicization surrounding economic policy at the time is that there is literally no discussion to be found in Parliament concerning the setting of the bank rate over the whole of 1890–1.[31] The expansion of the franchise to include most adult males, and the emergence of a Parliament in which the middle classes were now well represented, was not an important driver of the Barings rescue or of other policies relevant to the resolution of the crisis. There was, in short, no 'pressure from below'. Rather, policy responses seem to have been the result of an elite consensus view among key players in the City, notably the Bank of England, leading merchant banks and the government, especially Goschen, that Barings needed to be saved to preserve the stability and pre-eminence of the City of London as the leading global financial centre.

7.4.2   Political Impact

The Conservatives had been in power since the election of August 1886, with the Marquess of Salisbury as prime minister. The

[29] House of Commons debate, 'Customs and Inland Revenue Bill', *Hansard*, 26 May 1891, vol. 353, cc1096–132.
[30] House of Lords debate, 'Address in Answer to Her Majesty's Most Gracious Speech', *Hansard*, 25 November 1890, vol. 349, cc5–31.
[31] Author search for 'Bank' and 'rate', 1890 and 1891 (UK Parliament 2018).

Liberal Party had split before the election over the question of Irish Home Rule, with the Liberal Unionists aligning with the pro-Union Conservatives. This compact allowed Salisbury to form a Conservative government and to prevent Gladstone from pursuing his home rule agenda (Pearce and Stewart, 2002, 49–53). Generally, the Conservatives enjoyed a resurgence in the final two decades of the nineteenth century under Salisbury's strategy of adjusting to further democratization and the United Kingdom's relative international decline by appealing to non-aristocratic voters in the burgeoning suburbs who were attracted by values of property, empire and nationalism (Green, 1995; Shannon, 1996).

By the next election of July 1892, the home rule debate had subsided. This posed a great challenge to the Liberal Unionists and to Salisbury's ability to remain in government (Cawood, 2010, 332). In this election, the Conservatives lost 47 of their 317 seats, though they remained the largest party. Together, the Conservatives and their Liberal Unionist allies suffered a swing in the popular vote of −4.4 per cent compared to 1886. The Liberal Unionists lost nearly a third of their MPs, compared to 19 per cent for the Conservatives (Cawood, 2010, 349). The Liberals gained eighty seats, though the vote swing in their favour was only 0.3 per cent.[32] Gladstone was able to form a minority government with the support of the Irish Nationalists, though Salisbury's position, especially in the Lords, was still sufficiently powerful to block his ambitions on home rule (Pearce and Stewart, 2002, 95).

There is no indication from our extensive search of contemporary newspapers and other documents that the Barings crisis and rescue played any significant role in the 1892 elections. There was little controversy in Parliament on the matter, and the costs of the rescue were largely concentrated on the owners of Barings and its creditors. Salisbury had decided to call the election because the Parliament was nearing the end of its term and he believed that the divisions within the Liberal Party over Home Rule would allow the Conservatives to retain power. The management and aftermath of the Barings crisis was not a matter of discussion. The Irish question continued to dominate the

---

[32] For the vote share figures, we use those in Boothroyd rather than Craig, as the former adjusts for vote shares in two-member seats and other discrepancies (Boothroyd, n.d.; Craig, 1976).

election, though other issues raised during the campaign included tariffs, land reform, temperance, factory and electoral reform (Cook and Stevenson, 2014, 80–3).

The economy continued to grow during 1890 and 1891 and taxpayers suffered no losses from the rescue; nor was there any deterioration in the overall fiscal balance or public debt burden (Mauro et al., 2013; Thomas and Dimsdale, 2017). Unemployment initially declined slightly from a level of 4.3 per cent in 1890, but it increased to 6.1 per cent following a recession in 1892. However, during this period those dependent on labour income experienced a 6 per cent increase in average weekly earnings. In addition, as far as we can tell from available data, wealth and income inequality did not increase following the crisis; in fact, income inequality may have fallen slightly (Bourguignon and Morrisson, 2002). This and the apparently successful strategy of shifting the burden to the Bank of England and hiding the risk to taxpayers helped to shield the Conservative government from criticism. In the whole of 1892, there were only two references to the Barings crisis made in Parliament, neither of them in the context of the July election.[33]

In summary, we can say fairly confidently that the Bank of England-led rescue of Barings was not a factor in the Salisbury government's eventual loss of office. The government saw it as politically essential to avoid any perception that it would or should provide assistance to distressed financial or non-financial firms in this crisis. In 1825, by contrast, another Tory government had to resist stronger calls in Parliament to intervene. It is difficult to know whether, had Barings been allowed to fail, significant numbers of voters and opposition parliamentarians would have called on the government to shift from its official laissez-faire stance. However, it is likely that the government would have been able to mount a robust defence by pointing to Barings' probable insolvency and by appealing to lingering norms of limited government.

7.5   Conclusion

This chapter explored banking crises spanning nearly a century during which a vigorous, industrializing and globalizing British

---

[33] Author search (UK Parliament, 2018).

economy generated an extraordinary amount of wealth compared to previous experience and by the standards of most other countries at the time. Although this wealth was threatened periodically by severe banking crises that shook its rapidly expanding financial sector, by today's standards British governments by and large resisted crisis interventions that placed substantial taxpayer funds at risk. By the end of the period, the Barings crisis showed that this was becoming more difficult, but also that it was politically essential for these governments to stick closely to the Bagehot script. In doing so, despite the considerable expansion of democracy and the growth of mass political parties over this period, successive crises did not jeopardize incumbents' hold on political office.

We have argued that this can be explained by the high concentration and composition of societal wealth during this period. Following the further extension of franchise in the 1880s, the overwhelming majority of British voters now depended upon income from labour as opposed to income from wealth. Banking crises posed less of a risk to the living standards of this large group of voters and to the landed gentry, than to those financial and industrial interests that were threatened with severe losses. The bailout constituency was thus of limited size and influence; moreover, it could largely be satisfied through the provision of collateralized lending by the Bank of England. The absence of any explicit government commitment to provide financial stability via banking regulation further served to dampen the clamour for government bailouts. Low expectations continued to prevail among the majority of society despite the rapid accumulation of wealth and the expansion of finance.

Accordingly, despite the pressure on policymakers from financial and industrial elites, policy responses in both the 1825–6 and 1890 crises were relatively market-conforming. In neither crisis did we observe systematic and widespread protection of insolvent banks and their creditors. Depositors and note holders of failed banks incurred losses during the 1825–6 crisis. Even in the 1890 crisis, where a liability guarantee was extended, the family and other shareholders of Barings incurred severe costs, as did Barings's creditors, who were compelled to accept the largest share of the potential burden in the guarantee. If Barings had been a deposit-taking institution, it is likely that depositors would also have been forced to take losses.

Our theory suggests that the political fallout from these responses should be muted, if even present at all. The evidence confirms this expectation. In neither post-crisis election did we observe a significant swing away from the incumbent party due to the crisis itself. In fact, in the 1826 election, we found evidence that support increased for the incumbent party in a number of constituencies where bank failures occurred. The 1890 crisis played little part in the election that followed two years later. Our argument also suggests that in an era of low expectations, the political importance of institutional obstacles to policy interventions will be muted. In both 1825 and 1890, incumbent governments understood that securing parliamentary agreement for intervention by the Exchequer would be difficult. In 1825, the Liverpool government successfully pressured the Bank of England, presumably because of the ongoing threat of non-renewal of its monopoly charter, to intervene more extensively after its initial delay worsened the crisis. Despite this delay and the extensive economic disruption that ensued, it was the privately owned Bank that attracted criticism, not the government. In 1890, the government and the Bank both agreed that a rescue of Barings was needed and the Bank was able to move quickly with this political support. The government avoided a potential veto by Parliament through a gentlemen's agreement with the Bank.

Nor do we observe in either of these two crises intense voter dissatisfaction with the policy responses due to perceptions of distributional unfairness – in contrast to the crisis we discuss in the next chapter. A narrow set of failed financial institutions, their wealthy creditors and business interests bore most of the cost of the financial distress. Much would change in the era that followed. Financialization would accelerate rapidly, boosting the wealth of the middle class to an unprecedented level and exposing their living standards to greater risk of financial disruption. Alongside these developments, the British government committed in various ways to prevent major banking crises. As we argue in the following chapter, the emergence of great expectations among British voters led to markedly different policy and political consequences following the crisis in 2007–9.

8 A BANKING CRISIS IN THE UNITED KINGDOM IN AN ERA OF GREAT EXPECTATIONS

By the time that the most recent major banking crisis began in the United Kingdom in 2007, great expectations were well entrenched. In this chapter, we show that in this environment, the policy and political aftermaths of this crisis differed considerably from those in the nineteenth century. This difference, we argue, is a consequence of the dramatic changes since the 1970s in the level and composition of British household wealth and the democratization of leverage that we surveyed in Chapter 3.

We begin by highlighting some associated post-1945 developments, notably a growing British policy commitment to financial stabilization. The introduction of formal banking regulation and deposit insurance in 1979 came later in the United Kingdom than in some other countries, but it reinforced earlier promises by political incumbents to prevent banking crises. We argue that these stronger policy commitments enhanced voter expectations of wealth protection and inclined them to view the outbreak of the crisis in 2007 as a 'broken promise'. The first British bank run since Victorian times provided a vivid demonstration to many voters that pre-crisis financial regulation – with which the incumbent Labour government was closely linked – had failed to meet their expectations. We show that public perceptions of the government's policy competence fell sharply, an effect that was difficult to detect in the crises examined in the previous chapter.

In an effort to respond to voters' heightened expectations, the government adopted a range of policies that went well beyond those in past crises in offering widespread protection of banks and their creditors. Although this response eventually stabilized the financial system, we show that it was accompanied by serious delays and redistributive effects. Rather than electoral reward, these characteristics of the government's response generated rising voter resentment and eventual defeat in the 2010 election.

8.1   A Growing Policy Commitment to Financial Stabilization

Unlike some other developed countries, including France and the United States, the United Kingdom did not adopt a formal framework of bank regulation in the aftermath of the Great Depression; indeed, it did not do so until the 1979 Banking Act. This was linked to the fact that the United Kingdom did not suffer a banking crisis in the 1930s and the presumption that the Bank of England would be able to guide the banking system through its informal 'nods and winks'.

The experience of relative stability in the banking sector reinforced this tendency towards informality until the 1970s. The British banking system had become an increasingly important source of public borrowing from the outbreak of World War I, increasing the government's interest in ensuring sectoral stability. By the 1920s, with the dramatic sectoral consolidation and the rise of the 'Big Five' clearing banks, which now controlled over 80 per cent of deposits and lending, the Bank and Treasury recognized that they would be forced to rescue any of these banks if they were threatened with failure. Indeed, so cautious had the authorities become that they rescued or assisted in the rescue of a number of small banks in the interwar period (Turner, 2014, 13–14, 160–72). These rescues, though unrecorded in other sources, may have been seen by some voters as indicating that the government was taking greater responsibility for financial stability. The state interest in the banking system expanded during World War II, when the government worked closely with the Big Five to manage the war effort (Calomiris and Haber, 2014, 136).

However, the full flowering of great expectations would occur after 1945. After the war, the collapse of the United Kingdom's creditor position engendered a reliance on trade and capital controls that curtailed the City's international position for three decades, with the important exception of the 'offshore' dollar-based Euromarkets (Cassis, 2010, 209–25; Schenk, 2005). The priority of sterling monetary and financial policy from 1945 to about 1970 was to manage and reduce the heavy public debt burden that had built up over the course of the two wars. This was achieved by a policy of extensive financial repression that kept real interest rates low and which required close cooperation with the major banks.

The emergence of a stable banking system was also associated with the rise of a degree of self-regulation (Goodhart, 2000, 9). British banking had long been highly compartmentalized, with self-restrictions on competition persisting until the 1980s. Self-regulation was backed by the implicit threat of nationalization that hung over the heads of bankers in the post-war decades (Turner, 2014, 181–6). The Labour Party had threatened radical measures against the financial sector, but like many of their counterparts in other European countries at this time they backed off from such threats on taking power after the war. In the first two post-war elections in 1945 and 1950, both of which Labour won, the party's manifestos maintained that 'the operations of the ... banks [must be] harmonised with industrial needs' (1945) and promised to 'take whatever measures may be required to control financial forces, so as to maintain full employment and promote the welfare of the nation' (1950) (Kimber, 2017). Labour's most radical policy measure was the Bank of England Act of 1946, which nationalized the Bank and marked the start of the government's effective regulatory commitment to financial stabilization. The Act delegated general regulatory authority to the Bank, giving it the power to 'request information from and make recommendations to bankers'. If authorized by the Treasury, it could issue directions to make these recommendations effective. Although no such directions were ever made, the threat was there (Robb, 1997, 29). Until the 1970s, supervision was undertaken by a small unit in the Bank's discount office, an indication of the strength of self-regulation and the importance of informal guidance by the Bank's leadership.

Post-war British Conservative Party manifestos opposed radical measures and tended to focus more on the need for government policy to promote saving and growth. However, they also accepted large parts of the post-war consensus concerning the need for more national economic management (Kimber, 2017). Virtually all post-war Conservative prime ministers continued to promote the longstanding party nostrum of fostering 'a property-owning democracy' in which wealth and prosperity were shared more equally. Churchill, for example, asserted in the 1945 election campaign that the Conservatives would promote wealth and protect it – mainly by ensuring that inflation, then seen as a greater threat to the value of savings than banking crises, was kept under control:

> We will not permit any monkeying with the people's savings. Our desire is to see property widely spread, and we rejoice that the savings movement, which must go on, has now made almost everyone a property-owner. An object of our financial policy is to keep prices from rising, and make sure that savers do not see the purchasing-power of their savings dwindle. (Kimber, 2017)

In short, both major political parties had made public commitments to the need to prevent financial instability and for more widely shared prosperity. During the era of the wars, financial stability had already become a strategic priority of the state. As post-war recovery took hold and wealth accumulated, both parties would make further promises to protect it, especially by controlling inflation and by increasing the real value of pensions.

The stable banking system that had prevailed since the 1920s began to unravel in the 1970s. After two terms of Labour government under Harold Wilson, the Conservative government of Edward Heath (1970–4) launched the trend towards financial deregulation. The new policy of 'Competition and Credit Control' begun in 1971 sought to increase the scope for competition and innovation in the banking sector (Goodhart, 2014). This shift in the emphasis of policy led to growing competition for the Big Five from international banks based in London and from non-bank financial firms. The Big Five in turn lobbied for the removal of the straightjacket of credit control (Turner, 2014, 188). They were supported in this by small firms and savers, who increasingly sought to evade the government-controlled banking cartel by shifting into the 'secondary' banking sector (Calomiris and Haber, 2014, 141–2).

Following the economic turmoil of 1973–4, a number of secondary banks that had invested heavily in real estate began to fail as interest rates rose rapidly. The Bank organized a 'lifeboat' scheme that supported this sector with loans from major banks and the Bank of England (Bank of England, 1978). After these non-systemic bank failures, the Bank accepted the need for more formalized regulation and supervision and for greater protection of deposits (Robb, 1997, 30). Banks and other deposit-takers were 'invited' to accept voluntarily prudential supervision by the Bank, which they duly did by 1975. The rapid growth of foreign banks operating in the City and the entry of the

United Kingdom into the European Economic Community in 1973 provided further encouragement in the form of a growing need for international regulatory harmonization. The Wilson government stated in 1975 that it would provide the Bank of England's new prudential regulatory framework with formal statutory backing. This eventually materialized four years later in the final weeks of the government.

The April 1979 Banking Act gave formal legal powers and sanctions to the Bank to provide it with more authority to undertake its evolving supervisory role. It also created a two-tier system of authorizing 'recognized' banks and 'licensed' institutions, with the former receiving greater regulatory and supervisory relief; until that point, there was no statutory restriction on deposit-taking. It also introduced the first formal depositor protection scheme, against the wishes of the major banks.[1]

Financial deregulation resumed after the election of the Thatcher government in May 1979, which removed capital controls in October of that year and the remaining constraints on bank lending in 1980. The Latin American debt crisis that broke in 1982 revealed the increasing riskiness of the activities of some major British banks. Their subsequent move into mortgage lending would add to systemic risk. As Offer explains, the secondary banks facilitated the first phase of the housing boom that followed the deregulation after 1971, but the major banks entered the mortgage lending market only from 1985 (Offer, 2014). The Thatcher government continued to advocate further deregulation, culminating in the 'Big Bang' reforms of 1986 that deregulated financial trading (Dimsdale and Hotson, 2014). In its aftermath, many building societies converted from mutual ownership structures to publicly listed banks.

The Thatcher government also strengthened the formal statutory framework for bank supervision after another mini-crisis. In 1984, a small though 'recognized' bank, Johnson Matthey, failed under the prudential watch of the Bank of England and was ultimately nationalized by the Bank to prevent a loss of confidence in the banking system. This prompted a White Paper on Banking Supervision in 1985, which specified that the Bank of England as banking sector supervisor should

---

[1] The Act provided for the insurance of the first 75 per cent of deposits up to £10,000 in authorized institutions. The major banks opposed it because they would become the largest contributors to the guarantee fund and the least likely to use it (Turner, 2014, 193).

'ensure that [each] bank is managed in such a way as not to put at undue risk the interest of depositors, with that institution or more generally' (cited in Robb, 1997, 31).

The subsequent Banking Act of 1987 strengthened the Bank's supervisory powers, eliminating the two-tier system of supervision, and bolstered deposit insurance. Not long after this, the Bank also reached a bilateral agreement with American regulators to set minimum regulatory capital standards for all banks, including foreign subsidiaries, operating in British and US markets. This agreement in turn facilitated the 'Basel I' agreement on bank capital adequacy in July 1988, which promoted the adoption of minimum capital regulatory standards for internationally active banks in the G10 countries (Basel Committee on Banking Supervision, 1988; Kapstein, 1996).

The 'New Labour' government led by Tony Blair and Gordon Brown that won office from the Conservatives in the 1997 election inherited much of the legacy of Margaret Thatcher's strong emphasis on market deregulation combined with more formalized statutory regulation for key sectors such as banking. On gaining office, Gordon Brown's first major act as Chancellor of the Exchequer was to give the Bank of England formal independence in the setting of monetary policy and to announce the intention to establish a new Financial Services Authority (FSA) that would be responsible for the implementation of financial regulatory policy.

In practice, the FSA focused more on 'conduct of business' regulation than on prudential regulation (Banking Supervision and Regulation – Economic Affairs Committee, House of Lords (UK), 2009, pt 117). As a number of post-crisis reports pointed out, including some by the FSA itself, its 'light touch' approach to prudential regulation was a product of an intellectual consensus supporting the existing Basel capital adequacy approach; deference to contemporary private sector risk management practices; insufficient capacity; and a 'sustained political emphasis [by the government] on the need for the FSA to be "light touch" in its approach and mindful of London's competitive position' (Financial Services Authority Board, 2011, 260–1; see also House of Commons Treasury Committee, 2012, 47).

The City of London boomed in the years that followed; the direct and indirect tax revenues it generated were crucial for the government's objectives of modest redistribution and increased spending on public services. As we discussed in Chapter 3, house prices and household leverage also began once again to rise rapidly, but the capital-based regulatory framework was seen as providing reassurance that banking crises were unlikely to occur in advanced markets like the United Kingdom's (Davies and Green, 2010, chap. 3). However, the political risks of failing to protect housing wealth had already been underlined by the sustained downturn in house prices after 1990, triggered by the doomed attempt by the Conservative government to remain in the European Exchange Rate Mechanism. These were important factors in the removal of Thatcher as prime minister and in the improving election prospects of Labour under Blair (Pattie, Dorling and Johnston, 1995). The growing interconnection between the interests of households with leveraged housing equity, the banking sector, and the commitment of successive governments to financial deregulation and stabilization would have powerful consequences for the government's policy responses in and the political aftermath of the much bigger crisis to come.

8.2   The Crisis of 2007–9

The dating of this crisis is still disputed. In February 2007, one of the world's largest banks, HSBC, headquartered in London, announced that some of its US sub-prime mortgage assets were experiencing delinquency rates significantly higher than had been expected. Then, on 9 August 2007, the large French bank BNP Paribas revealed that investors would not be able to take money out of two of its funds. This led to a sharp rise in interbank lending rates. Liquidity in the wholesale interbank market evaporated as banks with surplus funds became unwilling to lend. The panic soon spread to London and exposed banks that were highly dependent on access to this market. Mortgage lender Northern Rock, which had borrowed large sums from wholesale markets to finance mortgages for customers, soon faced a severe funding crisis. As the panic spread, many depositors also sought to withdraw funds, producing the first depositor run on a British bank for 150 years (House of Commons Treasury Committee, United Kingdom, 2008).

The Bank of England announced that, with Treasury authorization, it had provided a specific temporary liquidity support facility to Northern Rock on 14 September 2007; three days later the government provided a guarantee for all its deposits, and for any other bank that found itself in a similar position (National Audit Office (UK), 2009a, 5). Over the next few months, the Treasury extended these guarantees to cover up to £51 billion of the bank's liabilities, including indemnifying the Bank of England for providing additional emergency support to Northern Rock (something only announced by the chancellor to Parliament on 25 November 2009).[2] This crossed another line that had successfully been resisted in the 1890 Barings crisis. Until 2009, the UK lacked a special resolution regime for banks that would permit British officials to wrest control of Northern Rock from its shareholders and senior management while the bank remained solvent. With no early resolution, the bank continued to lose franchise value, making a private sector sale more difficult. Eventually, the government was forced to relent, announcing the nationalization of the bank on 17 February 2008 in what the chancellor claimed would be a temporary measure (Bank of England, 2008, 17–19; Brown, 2010, 29). As we detail below, in delaying nationalization, the government effectively permitted Northern Rock to continue to write high-risk loans that would heighten taxpayer exposure. Moreover, as noted in Chapter 6, we can see that perceptions of financial stress increased significantly from this time (Table 6.7).

Deteriorating conditions in the US securities markets backed by sub-prime mortgages continued to weigh heavily on foreign markets, particularly London's given the high level of financial integration between these two major centres. Prospects for a gradual approach to the resolution of accumulating financial sector losses were dashed when the US investment bank Lehman Brothers filed for bankruptcy on 15 September 2008, prompting a 'system-wide loss of confidence in financial institutions' (Bank of England, 2008, 10). This was the deepest financial shock to hit US markets since the 1930s and it reverberated globally, rapidly affecting London, which now lacked the resilience its banking system had shown in the Great Depression years. Interbank markets froze up completely, as did most senior unsecured, covered bond and securitization markets. As we discuss below, this led the British government and central bank to follow many other developed democracies in taking a series of unprecedented measures to prevent complete collapse (International Monetary Fund, 2009, 32–48).

---

[2] https://publications.parliament.uk/pa/cm200910/cmhansrd/cm091125/debtext/91125-0004.htm, accessed 28 April, 2018.

8.2.1 Policy Responses

The institutional setting in the United Kingdom, with its majoritarian political institutions, is often said to confer considerable authority on the prime minister and cabinet, thus reducing potential vetoes and the need for political compromise in introducing new policies. But it would be an overstatement to suggest that the government faced few institutional obstacles that could delay its response. The Labour government enjoyed a dominant position in Parliament, but three potential veto players shaped its response over the course of the crisis: (1) the Labour Party on which the prime minister and chancellor depended for legislative support; (2) the Bank of England, which wielded operational independence over monetary policy and retained residual responsibility for financial stability, and (3) the European Union, which oversaw policy harmonization and single market rules.[3]

All three of these veto players had a role in delaying the government's response to the deepening crisis. By October 2007, the government had already put in place plans and draft legislation to enable it to nationalize Northern Rock, but it took a further four months for this to occur (Darling, 2011, 54). The government faced serious difficulties crafting a consensus that would gain support across the Labour Party, which was divided between a left wing of 'Old Labour' members – who pushed for nationalization early on – and a more market-oriented 'New Labour' wing that had led the party to three consecutive election victories for the first time in its history and which feared the reputational consequences of nationalization (Darling, 2011, 68, 174).[4] 'I was against nationalization, especially of a failed bank,' then prime minister Gordon Brown later wrote:

> [A]t that stage I would not let it be considered ... [E]ver since the 1970s, the Labour Party had been losing elections on the question of economic competence. Tony Blair and I had spent twenty years building New Labour on the foundation of market competition, private enterprise, and economic stability as the

---

[3] On the role of independent central banks and the European Union as potential veto players, see Jahn (2011). We do not consider the FSA to have operated as an important veto player, partly because its authority had been undermined by its strong association with the light-touch regulation that characterized the pre-crisis period and partly because crisis management focused on the Bank and the Treasury.

[4] See also Wachman (2007).

path to growth and I was not prepared to undermine that painstaking work with one instant decision. (Brown, 2010, 23)

Darling, Brown's successor as chancellor, also feared that nationalization 'would hark back to the wilderness years when Labour appeared unelectable' (Darling, 2011, 65). Touching on the tensions within the Labour Party, he further added:

[I]t was a highly controversial proposition. The Labour Party had in the past held the belief that the state should own the key sectors of the economy ... New Labour was very much built on the proposition that in a modern economy there is a limit to what the state needs to own ... Owning the banks, however, once the battle-cry of the left, was anathema to New Labour. Put simply, I did not want to nationalize a bank if it could be avoided. Nationalization had to be an option for us, but, as I told the House of Commons throughout autumn, only one of last resort. (Darling, 2011, 54)

Vince Cable, Treasury spokesperson for the opposition Liberal Democrats, exploited the Labour split by demanding the government nationalize the stricken bank, calling the prime minister 'petrified by indecision' (Griffiths, 2007). Hewing to New Labour ideology, however, the government continued to delay resolution by insisting on a private sector solution. Darling later conceded that the decision to nationalize should have been made earlier, but adds:

I was in no doubt about just how difficult the politics of nationalization would be; it would be only too easy for the Tories to say that this was evidence of the fact that we hadn't changed from the days of Clause 4 of the Labour Party constitution which committed us to public ownership of key sectors of the economy ... If we had done it in the autumn of 2007, it would have been hugely controversial with the public in general and in the City. (Darling, 2011, 66–8)

The Bank of England was a second source of policy delay. As Northern Rock's difficulties reverberated through the markets, the Bank announced on 19 September 2007 that it would provide liquidity in the money markets via a series of three-month auctions against a range of collateral that included mortgage obligations. The Treasury and the

FSA argued that the Bank's auctions were insufficient and pushed it to inject system-wide liquidity into the banking system, as had been done in the United States and the Eurozone. Yet Mervyn King, the Bank's governor, reportedly opposed such measures, fearing that it would foster moral hazard in a banking system he saw as undercapitalized.[5] Much to the dismay of the Treasury and British bankers who insisted – or hoped – the problem was one of market illiquidity, King sought to enforce a narrower view of Bagehot's dictum (Darling, 2011, 21–3, 57, 61).

The government was unable to force the Bank to shift its position. As Darling later put it:

> My frustration was that I could not in practice order the Bank to do what I wanted. Only the Bank of England can put the necessary funds into the banking system ... The Bank was independent and the Governor knew it. We did not agree on what to do ... The fact that we had given the Bank independence had a downside as well as an upside. (Darling, 2011, 22–3)

The Bank withheld the generalized systemic support that the Treasury wanted until December, during which time financial stress continued to build. In Darling's view, the government's sometimes strained relationship with the Bank 'contributed to the fact that our response to the crisis was not as sharp and decisive as it might have been' (Darling, 2011, 20). It was not until 12 December, as stresses in the interbank market continued, that the Bank joined other major central banks in announcing a further series of measures to improve money market liquidity.

The third factor shaping the timing of the government's policy response was that the European Union rules on state aid required the notification of the emergency support of Northern Rock that began in September 2007 to the European Commission, which approved the aid on condition that it would be temporary and that the Treasury submit a restructuring or liquidation plan by March 2008 (National Audit Office (UK), 2009a, 7). These conditions further constrained the government and consumed valuable time.

Meanwhile, even larger problems loomed. On 21 April 2008, the Bank launched its Special Liquidity Scheme (SLS), which provided

---

[5] King defended auctions as less destabilizing due to their anonymity, and noted that the Bank soon reached its statutory limits in providing LOLR assistance to Northern Rock (King, 2016, 205).

extensive liquidity to the British banking system. Banks and building societies could swap their illiquid assets for UK Treasury Bills for a period of up to three years. The Bank acquired £287 billion in nominal value of mostly mortgage-related securities by early February 2009 (Bank of England, 2009a).[6] This scheme was later extended, closing only in January 2012. These liquidity operations produced a rapid expansion in the size of the Bank's balance sheet. Yet even these measures the Bank appeared to undertake only with reluctance, requiring the Treasury to engage in extensive persuasion. In the government's view, the delay this caused proved costly: 'Had we had it in place during the autumn of 2007, it would have been of huge benefit to the banks' (Darling, 2011, 94).

The Bank's SLS failed to stem the gathering panic, eventually forcing the government to intervene in ways that vastly exceeded its rescue and nationalization of Northern Rock. As noted earlier, on 17 September 2007 the Treasury had announced that it would guarantee the deposits of any banks that experienced difficulties. This open promise went well beyond the existing formal deposit insurance scheme, which guaranteed only the first £35,000 of individual savings (Eaglesham et al., 2007). Then, on 30 September 2008, the Irish government, responding to the growing turmoil in its banking sector, provided a blanket guarantee of Irish bank deposits that prompted a series of other governments to follow. The FSA responded with an announcement on 3 October that the new limit of the deposit guarantee was £50,000, effective on 7 October 2008 (Financial Services Authority (UK), 2008).

In the wake of the Lehman Brothers failure, the UK's largest mortgage lender, HBOS, saw its share price collapse. The British authorities encouraged Lloyds TSB to take over HBOS, but the merger announced on 18 September cast doubt on the viability of the merged bank. On the same day, the Bank of England agreed a reciprocal swap agreement with the US Federal Reserve to relieve pressures in short-term dollar funding markets and the FSA issued new rules prohibiting the short selling of financial shares. Bradford & Bingley, another distressed specialist mortgage provider, was the next to be nationalized on 29 September. One year later, in October 2010, the government would

---

[6] British banks also obtained some additional liquidity support via the European Central Bank, which had begun injecting additional liquidity into the Euro interbank market in August 2007 after the BNP Paribas announcement.

establish UK Asset Resolution Limited – a public asset management company ('bad bank') to facilitate the orderly management of the closed mortgage books of both Northern Rock and Bradford & Bingley.

On 8 October 2008, the British government was among the first European countries to announce a bank support scheme, less than two days after the FTSE 100 stock index had suffered its largest ever one-day fall. The £500 billion support package contained a series of measures designed to stabilize the financial system (Swaine, 2008), including £200 billion to be made available for short terms loans through the Bank of England's Special Liquidity Scheme, and a new Bank Recapitalisation Fund to provide up to £50 billion for the government to invest as equity in banks (initial investments were made in Royal Bank of Scotland (RBS) and Lloyds Banking Group in December 2008 and January 2009 respectively). A further £250 billion Credit Guarantee Scheme would be available to underwrite short- and medium-term unsecured debt until April 2009. Although the chancellor announced that the assistance package was available to all major British banks, only RBS and Lloyds together with HBOS sought government assistance.[7] Darling noted that the senior management and board at RBS would be restructured as part of the deal with this bank. On the same day, the Bank of England announced a further interest rate cut of 0.5 per cent, coordinated with other major central banks. Larger interest rate cuts were announced in the following months that by March 2009 brought bank rate to an historic low of 0.5 per cent.

The October 2008 bank support package was undoubtedly embarrassing for the government. Putting aside the fact that his government's reluctance to depart from New Labour's pro-market stance had delayed the adoption of stabilizing measures, Prime Minister Gordon Brown defended it by arguing that the government's actions had 'led the way' for other nations to follow:

> This is not a time for conventional thinking or outdated dogma but for fresh and innovative intervention that gets to the heart of the problem . . . These decisions on stability and restructuring are the necessary building blocks to allow banks to return to their basic function of providing cash and investment for families and businesses. (Swaine, 2008)

---

[7] Other banks such as Barclays were able to obtain additional capital from investors.

The opposition parties provided qualified support for the package while criticizing the government relentlessly for having reached the point where it had become necessary. Shadow Chancellor George Osborne (Conservative) stated that 'This is the final chapter of the age of irresponsibility and it's absolutely extraordinary that a government has been driven by events to today's announcement' (Barker, 2008).

Arguments that the Labour government was seeking to shift blame from itself to foreigners (especially the United States) and to banks while bailing out the City and wealthy bankers resonated strongly among traditional Conservative voters and even among relatively sophisticated Labour partisans (Hellwig and Coffey, 2011; see also Table 4.1). To compensate, the government announced loan guarantees of more than £20 billion to assist small and medium-size businesses on 14 January 2009 ('House of Commons Debate, 14 January 2009,' n.d.). On 19 January the government announced a second bank rescue package, designed to increase the amount of money that banks could lend to businesses and private individuals, composed of the Asset Purchase Facility (APF) and the Asset Protection Scheme (APS). The APF authorized the Bank of England to purchase up to £50 billion more bank collateral; the APS provided further guarantees against exceptional future credit losses, with the government's liability under this scheme fixed at £200 billion. The government also extended the window of the Credit Guarantee Scheme from April to December 2009, and launched a new Asset-Backed Securities Guarantee Scheme to stabilize the housing market by guaranteeing newly issued AAA-rated mortgage backed securities.

In March 2009, the Bank of England's Monetary Policy Committee (MPC) decided that the stimulative effect of successive interest rate reductions was insufficient, and that the APF should be used to purchase assets financed by the creation of central bank money. This became known as 'quantitative easing', focusing primarily on the purchase of UK government bonds and a smaller amount of high-quality commercial paper and corporate bonds. Over March 2009 to January 2010, £200 billion of assets, mostly government bonds, were purchased. Combined with the Bank's liquidity support measures, this tripled the size of its balance sheet in proportion to GDP compared to the pre-crisis period (Bank of England, 2011, 200–12).

On 21 February 2009, the UK Banking Act 2009 came into effect, replacing the temporary powers provided by an emergency

2008 act with a new Special Resolution Regime. This gave the authorities a series of options to deal with failing banks individually.[8] Very soon after this, the scale of government support needed by the most troubled banks increased sharply. On 26 February, RBS announced an annual loss of £24.1 billion and the government revealed that RBS would participate in the APS in return for increased lending commitments. The next day, Lloyds Banking Group (LBG) announced a pre-tax loss of £10.8 billion for HBOS; the government reached an agreement on its participation in APS on 7 March.

In April 2009, the government added £5 billion to its initial £15 billion stake in RBS. It added a further £25 billion in December, taking its stake to 62 per cent of the voting share capital at a cost of £45.5 billion (including non-voting shares, the government's stake in RBS peaked at 84.4 per cent). In the case of LBG, investments in January, June and December 2009 totalled £20.3 billion, with a peak voting share capital stake of 43.4 per cent (UK Financial Investments Limited, 2015, 17, 23). By the time of the 2010 election, the taxpayer would suffer a paper loss of £12.5 billion on its holdings of RBS and LBG due to depreciation of the value of the stocks (National Audit Office (UK), 2010, 13).[9] In April 2009, the government also launched its Asset-backed Securities Guarantee Scheme, which provided guarantees on banks' residential mortgage-backed securities.[10]

The Bank of England summarized the fiscal impact of these bank rescues and guarantees at the end of 2009:

> Since the start of the crisis, [the government] has injected £66 billion of capital, around a half of the total raised, nearly all of which has been provided to the Royal Bank of Scotland (RBS) and Lloyds Banking Group (LBG). Around £31 billion of that has been provided since June in the context of the Asset Protection Scheme (APS) and LBG's recent rights issue. The APS protects RBS against losses on £282 billion of assets,

---

[8] These included a transfer of assets of the failing bank to a private sector purchaser, the creation of a bridge bank or asset management vehicle, temporary public ownership, and a bail-in of existing investors and creditors.

[9] In 2017, the government sold its remaining stake in LBG, generating an overall profit of more than £500 million. However, at the time of writing, the government retains a 72 per cent ownership stake in RBS, with the government expecting an eventual loss of £29.2 billion from the rescue (Dunkley, 2017a, 2017b).

[10] This scheme was never used.

particularly loans, consumer finance and commercial real estate. The £40 billion of commercial real estate assets protected represent 20% of the major UK banks' exposures to this sector. Overall, RBS's participation in the APS accounts for £141 billion of the sector-wide reduction in risk-weighted assets of £316 billion since end-2008. (Bank of England, 2009b, 31–4)

Overall, at the end of 2009, the National Audit Office estimated the maximum taxpayer exposure had reached £955 billion, with net cost to the taxpayer to lie between £20 billion and £50 billion (National Audit Office (UK), 2010, 6). The effect of these measures and of the deep recession on public finances was dramatic. The general government fiscal deficit increased sharply, from an average of 3.0 per cent of GDP in the five years ending in 2007 to an 8.1 per cent average over the following five years. General government debt doubled from 51 per cent of GDP in 2007 to 103 per cent by 2011 and continued to grow thereafter (OECD, 2017).

It is clear, then, that the British government's rescue package after September 2008 went far beyond the policy interventions during other systemic banking crises in the previous two centuries. Taken together the UK policy response, consisting of extensive liquidity support to undercapitalized institutions, the extension of new guarantees for deposits and bank debt, the creation of a new public asset management company, and the injection of capital, strongly aligns with the bailout policy model outlined in Chapter 5. These measures vastly outweighed the bank restructuring that occurred following the crisis. As such, in contrast to the government's response in the earlier era, our data for this crisis generates a highly positive score that falls near the top end of the bailout continuum (see Figure 7.5).

It is also evident that the bank rescue measures and the stimulative effects of expansionary macroeconomic policy provided substantial direct benefits to the weaker intervened banks, though they came with considerable costs for these banks. Within the banking industry there was significant opposition to parts of the government's rescue package, particularly its plans to provide capital injections (Woll, 2014, 104–5). According to Darling, one bank chairman labelled government recapitalization as 'expropriation, nothing less than a return to the 1970s – or worse, the 1940s' (Darling, 2011, 134–5). Instead of making the recapitalization mandatory, as King at the Bank wanted and as the US administration did (Chapter 10), the government offered banks a choice: banks would have to raise capital to the level individually assessed by the financial regulator, but they could do so via private sources or public money. Culpepper and Reinke argue that British authorities failed to achieve their preferred method of mandatory government recapitalization because stronger banks whose future income came largely from outside the UK, namely HSBC and Standard Chartered, could threaten to exit (Culpepper and Reinke, 2014, 439–43). As a voluntary recapitalization scheme that lacked contributions from healthier institutions, the British plan thus served both to stigmatize participating institutions and to drive up costs for the taxpayer.[11]

Weaker banks strongly opposed the scheme and insisted that what was needed was additional liquidity (Brown, 2010, 58). But their survival depended on government support. In exchange for this support, the senior management teams of the intervened banks, as noted earlier, were generally replaced. There was also a substantial reduction in employment in these banks, and their shareholders lost most of their money despite the government interventions. The harsh treatment provided to participating weaker banks supposedly led Fred Goodwin, RBS's resigning CEO, to say of the government talks, 'This is not a negotiation; it is a drive-by shooting' (Rawnsley, 2010).

The main beneficiaries of the bailouts lay elsewhere. The political coalition that supported the rescues, explicitly and perhaps more often implicitly, extended far more widely than these intervened banks, their senior management, their employees and their investors. Depositors in all the intervened institutions were protected, even when their deposits exceeded the pre-crisis insurance commitments. Given the potential for a wider run on British bank deposits, this guarantee also safeguarded the interests of all depositors and thus relatively healthy banks. More generally, the creditors of all the intervened banks were protected, consistent with the authorities' policy of stabilizing the

---

[11] The design of the recapitalization plan included high upfront fees without warrants for future stock purchases. The pricing of the recapitalization – set initially at a dividend of 12 per cent – was aimed at deterring excessive use of the scheme, but had the effect of leaving the taxpayer worse off. Charging high fees to weak banks in which the government has taken a large stake means the government ends up charging itself. The same could be said for the government's use of risk-adjusted fees in charging for its guarantee, which imposed higher fees on these weaker banks. If share prices recovered in the ten years following the capital injection, the absence of warrants meant the government could not in the future buy more shares at the price they had paid in October 2008.

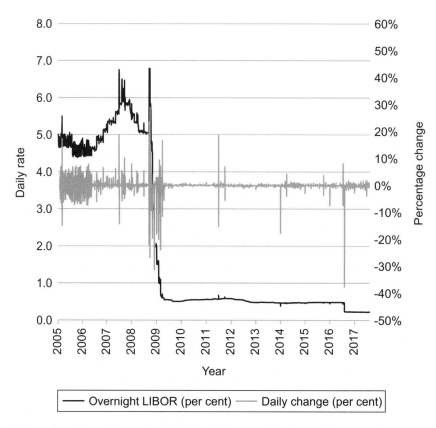

Figure 8.1: Overnight sterling LIBOR, daily rate (left axis) and per cent change (right axis), 2005–17.
Source: FRED Database (2016b).

wholesale capital markets associated with financial sector funding (National Audit Office (UK), 2009b, 15).

This also meant that stronger UK-based banks benefited from the bailouts of weaker banks and especially from the general protection of bank creditors.[12] The sterling interbank market lending rate spiked suddenly after the failure of Lehman Brothers in mid-September 2008 and remained volatile through March 2009 (Figure 8.1). By the end of 2008, this interbank rate was falling sharply and it has remained at historically low levels ever since. This supports the view that the stabilization measures undertaken by the authorities benefited the whole financial sector

---

[12] Weaker banks also, in principle, benefited from the Credit Guarantee Scheme, but participation was conditional on recapitalization, which, as discussed, involved considerable costs.

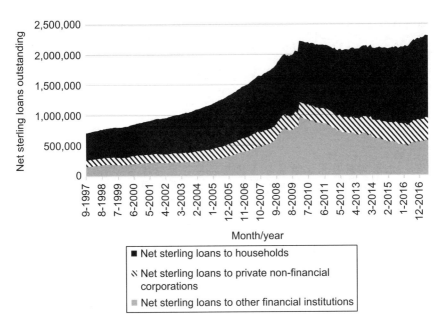

Figure 8.2: UK banks, net sterling loans by sector, £ millions, 1997–2017.
Source: Bank of England (n.d.).

and especially the large, most creditworthy banks. Banks such as HSBC, Barclays and Standard Chartered were also able to issue new equity to investors in the months following September 2008.

Nevertheless, it would be wrong to see the government and central bank as responding simply to pressure from these beneficiary banks. The government's primary concern was to ensure that the banks continued to lend to business and especially to household customers, which by 2008 was the dominant source of credit demand in the economy (Figure 8.2). Government officials were deeply concerned about the impact that failure of a systemically important institution would have on British households and firms. As Brown wrote later in explaining his motivation for intervention:

> It was clear that if there was no resumption of lending in the economy there would be a crash. Worse, if we had a run on the Royal Bank of Scotland, there would be people and shops and schools and hospitals trying to function with no money ... I knew doing nothing was not an option. We were days away from a complete banking collapse: companies not being able to

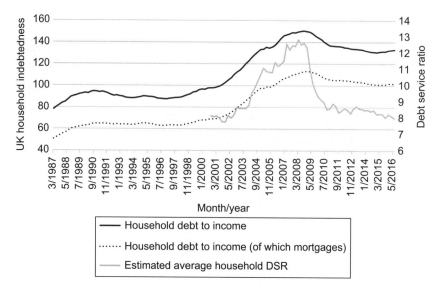

Figure 8.3: UK household indebtedness (left axis) and debt service ratio (right axis), 1987–2016.

Source: Bank of England (2016, A27, A29).

Notes: Debt ratios are calculated as total debt/total mortgage debt as a percentage of a four-quarter moving sum of disposable income. The debt service ratio (DSR) is calculated as household interest and mortgage principal repayments as a percentage of household disposable income.

> pay their creditors, workers not being able to draw their wages and families finding the ATM had no cash to give them.
> (Brown, 2010, xix, xvii)[13]

Mortgage holders were major beneficiaries of the financial stabilization and of the rapid reduction in interest rates. Most of these had taken out mortgages at floating interest rates or at short-term fixed rates, which posed significant financial risk to the household sector given the sharp increase in debt burdens since 2000. The large falls in interest rates that occurred in the first eighteen months of the crisis and the persistent low interest rates that prevailed thereafter led to a substantial reduction in mortgage interest payments (Figure 8.3).

---

[13] The independent National Audit Office reached a similarly bleak conclusion in December 2009: 'If the support measures had not been put in place, the scale of the economic and social costs if one or more major UK banks had collapsed would be so large as to be difficult to envision. The support provided to the banks was therefore justified' (National Audit Office (UK), 2010, 10).

As a group, the household sector was the largest beneficiary of the financial stabilization once the protection it afforded to employment income and to pension assets is taken into account (on which we elaborate below). Nevertheless, as we argue in the following section, justifying the cost of these bailouts to voters as taxpayers, even when they were net beneficiaries of the government's actions, proved exceptionally challenging.

8.2.2 Political Effects

Part of the reason for this was that despite the government's attempt to gain political advantage from the intervention measures, the opposition parties were able to neutralize this advantage by openly supporting the need for financial stabilization. As the crisis reached a climax in late September 2008, the Conservative leader, David Cameron, stated that it was crucial that Parliament avoid the 'political deadlock' that had characterized the response in the United States and that the stabilization of the financial sector be the immediate priority. To this end, the Conservatives pledged to drop their objections to the government's emergency legislation to ensure a quick passage through Parliament: 'Today is a day for safety, security and for protection' [Cameron said] … '[though] that doesn't mean excusing inexcusable behaviour' (Summers, 2008).[14] Nick Clegg, leader of the Liberal Democrats, had only weeks earlier opposed 'bailouts' for bank shareholders, but now also pledged support for the stabilization measures and specifically called for a 'cast iron guarantee' of all deposits (Summers, 2008). These pledges also focused attention on internal Labour Party conflict, which as we have seen had helped to produce the series of policy delays that had occurred in the year from August 2007.

This tactic also permitted the opposition the opportunity to take some credit for the country's eventual stabilization. At the same time, and damagingly for the government, it allowed the opposition to frame specific aspects of the package as overly costly, distributionally unfair and, as the economic costs of the crisis accumulated, ineffective in preventing

---

[14] The Conservative Party adopted a similar position with respect to legislation to nationalize Northern Rock (see Darling, 2011, 67–8).

substantial harm to many voters. This political opportunity expanded as the government was forced to take additional measures over the following months. In January 2009, Shadow Chancellor Osborne stated that:

> This is not some long-planned, carefully thought-through second phase of Government policy; it is instead the clearest possible admission that the first bail-out of the banks has failed ... a bail-out whose size we still do not know, whose details remain a mystery and whose ultimate cost to the people of Britain will be known only when this Government have long gone. Of course we cannot allow the banking system to fail – but for two months now, the Opposition have warned the Government that bank recapitalisation was not working, that the cost of the preference shares was too high, that the liquidity operations had to be extended, that the promised lending to businesses was not taking place, and that Government guarantees to get lending flowing to the real economy were needed ... The Prime Minister has finally been forced to confront the truth: he has not saved the world, he certainly has not saved the economy, and he has not even saved the British banks yet ('House of Commons Debate 19 January 2009,' n.d., column 486).

The Liberal Democrats were temperamentally more inclined than the Conservatives to criticize the banks and by January 2009 were arguing for the nationalization of RBS and Lloyds (Parker and Pickard, 2009). Although the natural supporters of the Labour government accepted the need for the measures, they too were highly critical of the banks. Brendan Barber, general secretary of the Trades Union Congress (TUC), said:

> The government is absolutely right to take further action to bail out the banks. The alternative would not just be a prolonged recession, but a slump. But ministers must also realise that there will be public anger that even more taxpayers' money has had to be put into the banking system, particularly among those who face losing their jobs or homes because of the irresponsible policies pursued by the banks. There needs to be a public inquiry into the behaviour of the banks, their advisers and their auditors. (Sparrow, 2009)

These arguments appealed to a basic tension in the position of many voters: emphatic in their belief that the government should protect their jobs, incomes and wealth, but uncomfortable and often angry about the means by which this was done and their fairness. At best, many voters gave only grudging support to the government's actions. Unfortunately for the government, its electoral position had already been eroding well before the policy interventions of September–October 2008.

As our theory predicts, the initial stage of the crisis, dominated by the failure of Northern Rock, appears to have sent a strong signal to voters that Gordon Brown's own much-vaunted economic policy competence was in serious doubt (BBC News, 2007; Croft, 2007). Brown and Darling were keenly aware of these reputational consequences and, as we noted, delayed nationalizing Northern Rock as a result. While the taxpayer continued to fund and bear the commercial risks of Northern Rock, the Treasury failed to take effective action to limit the origination of new high-risk loans by the bank. Under the terms of the emergency support, Northern Rock was required to significantly reduce the volume of new mortgage loans. However, prior to nationalization, the Treasury permitted Northern Rock to continue to write high-risk loans up to 125 per cent of a property's value, exposing the taxpayer to additional risk (House of Commons Public Accounts Committee, 2009, 8–9; National Audit Office (UK), 2009a, 7, 32). These high-risk loans represented around 30 per cent of Northern Rock's mortgage book, but accounted for about 50 per cent of overall arrears and 75 per cent of repossessions.

Brown also sought to deflect responsibility for the crisis by arguing that it was 'global' rather than national in nature, pointing to the problems experienced by banks in the United States and Europe that were significantly larger than Northern Rock. However, this lacked credibility because Brown had based his own leadership qualifications largely on his unrivalled economic and financial expertise and had visibly embraced a booming financial sector via a loudly trumpeted 'light touch' regulatory regime for the City in the years before 2007–8 (Coates, 2009, 424–5; Foley, 2009).

Labour's support in opinion polls fell from about 40 per cent of those polled in September 2007 to about 25 per cent by June 2008, by which time the Conservative opposition had a commanding lead (Figure 8.4). Support for the government recovered somewhat in the second half of 2008, including during the peak of the crisis in

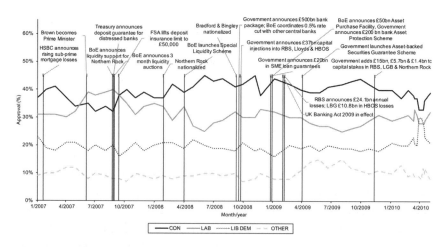

Figure 8.4: Guardian/ICM monthly polling: voter intentions by preferred party, January 2007–May 2010.
Source: ICM Research (n.d.).
Note: CON=Conservative Party; LAB=Labour Party; LIB DEM=Liberal Democrats.

September–October 2008 and the large interventions that followed this, before deteriorating again in 2009.

Data shown in Figure 8.5 from the Continuous Monitoring Survey as part of the British Election Study reveals a similar pattern. When Brown first became prime minister in June 2007, the electorate rated his competence highly, consistent with his generally successful decade-long tenure as chancellor, with a mean competence rating of 5.8 on a 0–10 scale (higher values indicating greater competence). His competence rating then collapsed in late autumn of 2007 following the run on Northern Rock, bottoming out at about 3.5. It then briefly revived in the wake of the October 2008 rescue package, reaching nearly 5.0, before collapsing again after the second phase of policies was announced in January 2009. By mid-2009 it was back at levels reached at the nadir the previous autumn. Voters' perceptions of Brown's competence would change little in the subsequent months leading to the election.

Consistent with our argument, voters responded positively when the government acted with speed and purpose during the peak of the crisis in late 2008. Gordon Brown's claims of Britain 'leading the world' in its bank rescue plans may not have been seen as entirely hollow by voters. The United Kingdom was said to be a 'pace-setter'

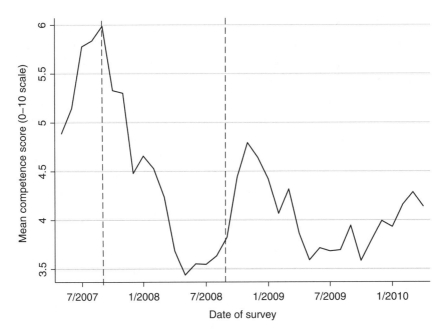

Figure 8.5: Mean competence score for Gordon Brown, May 2007–April 2010. *Source*: British Electoral Study (2010). Dotted lines indicate the run on Northern Rock and the announcement of the October 2008 package.

due to its quick and decisive intervention (Quaglia, 2009). But, as Darling notes, 'global success' came with 'domestic failure' (Darling, 2011). Indeed, in addition to the competence shock delivered by the crisis, the policy delays in dealing with Northern Rock, the onset of income and wealth destruction in 2009 and its perceived distributive unfairness combined to undermine the government.

While the government may have gained some credit from voters for its policy interventions in late 2008, this was also effectively limited by the opposition parties' tactic of supporting the need for financial stabilization. As was the case in the United States (see Chapter 10), the British public was not opposed to government intervention during the crisis. On the contrary, consistent with our theory, voters initially appear to have supported public assistance to financial firms and households. This support, however, declined considerably as concerns about the distributional consequences of the bailouts increased. Voter support for Labour from the onset of the Northern Rock crisis through the period to the next election in May 2010 never attained levels sufficient for the government to retain office.

This initial competence shock thesis is supported by the fact that in the immediate aftermath of the Labour government's nationalization of Northern Rock, the wider economic consequences of the crisis seemed modest. Unemployment in particular remained low (Figure 8.6). By the middle of 2008 it was clear that the economy was slowing sharply: for the first time since the early 1990s, growth in the second quarter was negative; it continued to worsen thereafter (Office for National Statistics, n.d., b). Wage growth was also falling quickly and unemployment was rising (Figure 8.6). Yet it was from about this time that electoral support for the government improved somewhat through the end of 2008, albeit only modestly and briefly.

In launching the bank rescue package in September–October 2008, the government understood that it faced a severe challenge in justifying to voters the need to commit so much public money to the banking sector with its high-flying senior bankers and traders. For many voters outside of the capital, it was made worse by the fact that many of the perceived recipients of this largesse were located in London.

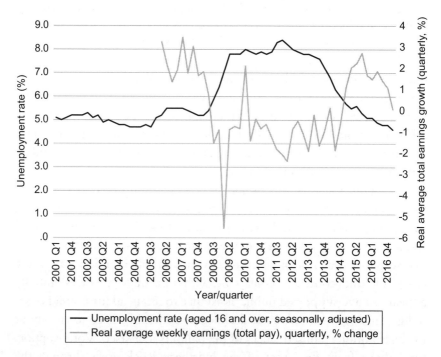

Figure 8.6: Unemployment rate (left axis) and real average total earnings growth (right axis), 2001–16 (quarterly, per cent).
Source: Office for National Statistics (n.d., a).

In October 2008, Gordon Brown and other ministers embarked on a regional tour of Britain to explain the rescue package to a public that was shocked by both the enormity of the crisis and the proposed remedy. Brown also released a podcast on 9 October to sell the bailout. In it, he sought to frame the bailout package as 'investments . . . with strings attached' that would earn a return and ensure that the banks would 'continue to lend to homeowners and small businesses'. His government, Brown claimed, was 'leading the world' in this policy response. He told voters: 'I want you to know that we are doing this for you . . . , not to help banks as an end in itself':

> The bottom line is that if we don't take this action to help stabilise the banking system, the cost to savers, homeowners and small businesses would be far higher . . . Businesses would go to the wall and families would really suffer. (*PM Special Podcast on the Financial Stability Programme*, n.d.)

This framing may have had a modest positive effect in rallying voter sentiment around the government – from mid-2008, support for the government improved from a low of about 25 per cent to about 33 per cent of likely voters by the end of 2008. But most voters seemed unconvinced by Brown's counterfactual reasoning and thus unwilling to provide much electoral reward for the government's response. Asked in an October 2008 Guardian/ICM poll whether the government's response had made them more or less likely to vote Labour, only 13 per cent said more, against 27 per cent who said less (Glover, 2008). Most voters, 60 per cent, said the response made no difference, at a time when Labour's support among the electorate stood at just 30 per cent. By early 2009, the costs of the policy interventions and the deep recession that followed the crisis were becoming ever more apparent to the public. These costs were multiple.

First, even had Brown's counterfactual reasoning been valid, the vivid size of the support package underlined the costs that would be borne by taxpayers and public sector beneficiaries. Over the course of the next few months, the size of the public commitments and the associated deterioration of public finances continued to escalate, suggesting that government expenditure would need to be diverted away from voter priorities such as schools, hospitals and welfare payments. The fiscal deficit rose from 2.6 per cent of GDP in April 2007 to 10 per cent by April 2010. Public sector net debt (excluding nationalized banks) also increased sharply from 36 per cent of GDP at the end of 2007 to 55 per cent by mid-2009; by the time of the election in May 2010 it was 66 per cent, about double the pre-crisis figure (Office for National Statistics, 2017a). The prime minister tried to reassure voters that the bailout would 'not be at the expense of better public services', but this claim seemed increasingly to lack credibility among voters. This allowed the opposition parties to blame the deterioration of public finances on the government.

Second, by early 2009 and in the period leading up to the election of May 2010, the real economy deteriorated sharply and many voters now faced substantial, growing costs. Voters who may initially have accepted the need for the extraordinary policy measures and who may even have been inclined to reward the government for the relative efficiency of the rescue increasingly deserted it. Data from public opinion polls conducted during this period provide supportive evidence. In a June–August 2009 poll, while a slim majority of respondents (55 per cent) favoured 'financial support to banks in trouble', nearly two-thirds (62 per cent) expressed dissatisfaction with the government's action to address the financial crisis (BBC World Service, 2009). Strikingly, by the time of a June–September 2010 follow-up survey, the level of public support for aiding troubled banks had declined significantly. The 2010 poll revealed that an overwhelming majority of respondents (61 per cent) now opposed financial support to banks in trouble (BBC World Service, 2010).[15]

Having observed the government implement extraordinary policy measures, voters had not seen much in the way of economic improvement. Bank lending to firms, which had grown at over 15 per cent per annum in 2007, continued to shrink in 2009 (this would continue through mid-2015). Lending to households (mostly mortgages) was more resilient but still barely grew from late 2009 through 2013 – a period of unprecedented stagnation in the period since the 1960s (Figure 8.7).

Unemployment rose to nearly 8 per cent by mid-2009; it did not return to pre-crisis levels until 2015 (Figure 8.6). Real wages fell sharply for many employees, who would have felt a considerable reduction in

[15] Respondents were not asked in the 2010 survey to indicate their satisfaction with government action to address the crisis.

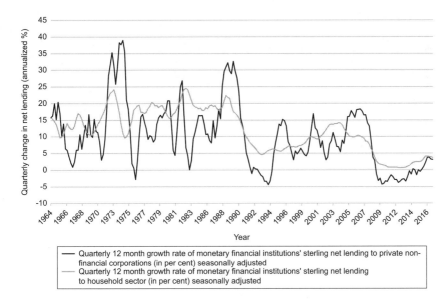

Figure 8.7: UK banks: quarterly change in net lending to private firms and households (annualized percentage rates), 1964–2016.
Source: Bank of England (n.d.).

their purchasing power. Household real incomes had grown rapidly in the period leading up to 2007, with lower income households doing slightly better than upper income households.[16] With the exception of the bottom two quartiles, most households saw their real incomes fall or stagnate in the period before the 2010 election – a pattern that was sustained for some years after this (Figure 8.8).

Third, and perhaps most importantly, the emerging costs associated with the aftermath of the crisis were distributed unevenly, further undermining the government's ability to sell the interventions as a success story. The government was successful in limiting the costs of the crisis for low-income households, who were the only group to see real increases in income in the two years before the May 2010 election. However, the wealth share of the top 1 per cent of households increased over the period 2007–10 (Atkinson et al., 2017; Office for National Statistics, 2017b, 5). Moreover, most voters seem to have perceived that

---

[16] Average real household disposable income grew at 2.9 per cent from 2000 to 2007. The average annual growth rate for the top 20 per cent was 2.4 per cent, while that for the bottom two quintiles was 3.4 per cent (Office for National Statistics, 2017b).

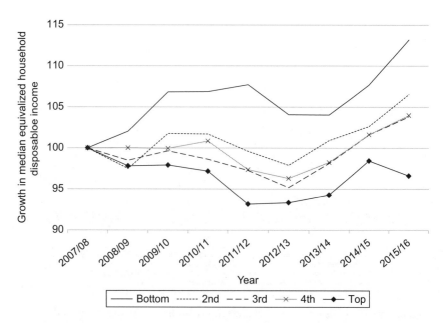

Figure 8.8: Growth in median equivalized household disposable income by quintile, financial year ending 2008 to financial year ending 2016 (2007–8 = 100).
Source: Office for National Statistics (2017b).
Notes: Income figures have been deflated to 2015/16 prices using the consumer prices index including owner-occupiers' housing costs (CPIH). Households are grouped by their equivalized disposable incomes, using the modified OECD scale.

inequality worsened in this period.[17] Middle income households in particular fared relatively poorly and these voters were the most likely to desert the incumbent Labour Party for the Conservatives or the Liberal Democrats.

This was especially true of younger voters, who bore a greater share of the costs and who have historically been more inclined to vote Labour. Whereas the median real income of households composed of individuals aged 60 years or over continued to rise after 2007 and was about 7 per cent higher by mid-2010, the incomes of the middle-aged (31–59 years) stagnated and those of the relatively

---

[17] A Pew Research Center survey in 2013 found that 72 per cent of those surveyed thought that 'the gap between rich and poor has increased in recent years'; 22 per cent thought it had stayed the same and only 3 per cent thought it had decreased. 65 per cent of respondents also thought that the economic system 'favors the wealthy', compared to 30 per cent who thought it was 'fair to most' (Pew Research Center, 2013, 21–2).

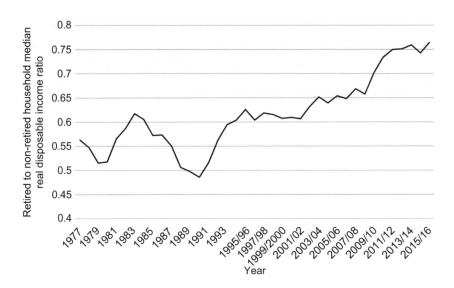

Figure 8.9: Retired to non-retired household median real disposable income ratio, 1977–2016.
Source: Office for National Statistics (2017b, 11). The ratio compares median equivalized disposable income of retired and non-retired households using ONS public data. Financial years from 1994.

young (22–30 years) fell by nearly 5 per cent.[18] A study by the Institute for Fiscal Studies explained this as the result of policies that produced 'sizeable increases in private pension incomes … [alongside] relatively poor income growth observed for working-age individuals' (Cribb et al., 2017, 19).[19] Figure 8.9 shows that the ratio of median retired household income to that of median non-retired households had remained fairly stable since 1992, but then rose considerably following the crisis.

[18] This divergent pattern continued after 2010. By the 2015/16 financial year, real median household incomes for the oldest cohort were 10 per cent higher, whereas for the youngest cohort they were 7 per cent lower than the pre-crisis peak, and even 4 per cent lower than in 2002/03 (Cribb et al., 2017, 18–21).

[19] The main driver of the rising incomes of retirees has been the growth in income received from private pensions: the percentage of such households with private pensions rose from 44.5 per cent in 1977 to 78.8 per cent in 2015/16, and the percentage of gross income received by retirees from private pensions rose from 18 per cent to 43.8 per cent over the same period (Office for National Statistics, 2017b, 11). One reason for this relative resilience of retired household income is that retirees and other older workers are more likely to be enrolled in defined benefit pensions than younger workers.

In fact, the post-crisis deterioration in the position of the relatively poor and the relatively young is even greater than this suggests, because the cost of housing for these groups increased sharply while that for richer and older Britons fell. Older households, which are much more likely to own their own home, benefited substantially from falling mortgage interest rates, while younger households became increasingly dependent on rented housing, the cost of which has continued to increase since the crisis. The ratio of housing costs to disposable income for renters reached a post-war peak at 37 per cent in 2010, whereas the ratio for mortgagors fell by 5 percentage points over 2007–10 to 14 per cent and that for outright home owners remained at a constant 5 per cent (Corlett and Judge, 2017, 30). This disparity is especially stark in the high-cost South-East.

Widespread perceptions of distributional unfairness were exacerbated because the largest post-crisis gains were also experienced in regions where income was already high (London and the South-East), whereas those experiencing the largest losses were in regions where income was already low (Northern Ireland and Yorkshire and Humberside) (Haldane, 2016, 8; Rodríguez-Pose, 2018). London was among those global cities that from 2009 experienced rapid rises in prime real estate prices, as investors from many countries shifted their portfolios from emerging markets and commodities towards high-end property investments in major cities (Brooker, 2018). This supported the widespread view that the capital and the financial sector so closely associated with it were the main beneficiaries of the post-crisis interventions – although this is not true on average for London's relatively young and those in middle-class and poorer households lacking housing investments.

Meanwhile, average real per capita wealth fell by 9 per cent from 2007 to 2009 (World Wealth & Income Database, 2017). The main stock market index fell 44 per cent in nominal terms from a peak in October 2007 to its trough in February 2009 (Figure 8.10), negatively affecting households with defined contribution pensions and others holding portfolio financial assets. Of the 47 per cent of the employed population covered by private occupational pension schemes, more than a quarter were in defined contribution schemes over 2008/9 (Office for National Statistics, 2016d).

Average house prices also fell by about 15 per cent in real terms from 2008 to 2010, after having risen sharply from the mid-1990s to

Figure 8.10: UK FTSE All-Share Index, monthly closings, 2000–16.
Source: Global Financial Data (n.d.).

the eve of the crisis (Knoll, Schularick and Steger, 2017, 344).[20] These initial absolute falls in wealth for many households occurred despite the large government interventions. This almost certainly contributed to the erosion of political support for the government among households experiencing losses.

Wealth inequality also increased significantly after the crisis. Across age cohorts, '[a]ll of the £2.7 trillion rise in wealth since 2007 has been harvested by those over the age of 45, two thirds by those over the age of 65. By contrast, those aged 16–34 have seen their wealth decline by around 10%' (Haldane, 2016, 11). The wealthiest households, who hold most of their assets in the form of financial assets, suffered large initial losses in the few months after September 2008. However, financial asset prices recovered quickly, in part because of the stimulative effects of fiscal policy and unconventional monetary policy

---

[20] Average real house prices in the United Kingdom approximately trebled between 1995 and 2007–8, rising much faster than real incomes over the same period (Belfield, Chandler and Joyce, 2015). At their pre-crisis peak, average house prices were 7.6 times average net household incomes, compared to 6.4 times at the peak of the previous housing boom in 1989.

on financial markets.[21] By April 2010, the FTSE All-Share index was back at 83 per cent of its October 2007 peak. Average house price indices began rising again in 2010 (Bank of England, 2014, 13, 15).

By comparison with countries such as Ireland, Spain and the United States, the destruction of British housing wealth was much lower. Large pre-crisis increases in real house prices compounded the relative disadvantage of the young by increasing the cost of attaining home ownership. Millennials are now about half as likely as their baby-boomer parents to own their own home; indeed, their home ownership rates are now lower than those of their great-grandparents' generation (Corlett and Judge, 2017, 13). Post-crisis, falling house prices in some areas did not fully reverse this shift but had a disproportionally negative impact on the housing equity owned by more leveraged households that had purchased houses relatively recently. Most owners of housing over sixty years old have relatively little mortgage debt, so they retained large windfall gains in housing equity even when prices fell.[22] Housing gains and losses were also unevenly geographically distributed, with London and the South-East seeing increases and other regions often experiencing falls (Haldane, 2016, 9).

The pension assets of older households were also largely protected, in contrast to the employment incomes of younger workers. By the time of the crisis, household wealth consisted primarily of pension, property and savings assets, with pensions and property the dominant components. Most such wealth is held by older households, with those whose highest income-earner is 55–74 years old owning most pension wealth (more often in protected defined benefit schemes), and those aged 55 and older owning most net housing wealth (Figure 8.11). The shift in recent decades from relatively generous DB to DC pensions has also disfavoured younger people, who are more likely to hold assets in the latter (Cribb, Hood and Joyce, 2016).

---

[21] This effect has accelerated in the period since 2010. By 2015, individuals in the bottom two-fifths of the income distribution had experienced no wealth gains, whereas the wealth of those in the top quintile increased by nearly 20 per cent (Haldane, 2016, 10).

[22] This also means that because most mortgage debt is concentrated among working age households, these households have a stronger interest than the retired in the continued flow of mortgage credit (Crawford, Innes and O'Dea, 2015, 20). Since 2010, however, the renewed rise in house prices relative to incomes and a reduction in mortgage availability for the young has further reduced the proportion of younger people buying rather than renting accommodation (Haldane, 2016, 11).

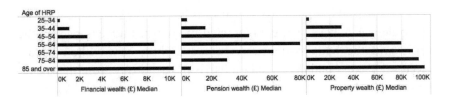

Figure 8.11: Median financial, pension and property wealth by age cohorts, UK 2010–12.

Source: Crawford, Innes and O'Dea (2016, table 2). HRP = household reference person, or the age of the individual with the highest salary in the household. The estimate is derived from a weighted sample of all households interviewed in the ONS Wealth and Assets Survey Wave 3 (2010–12).

In summary, the main losers in the two years leading up to the elections of May 2010 were high- and middle-income households in income terms, those households who were net asset-poor, renters, the highly leveraged who experienced falling house prices, and the relatively young in general. New Labour, whose electoral strategy depended on the support of relatively prosperous centrist voters, was hesitant to alienate these voters by proposing substantial redistributive measures to compensate the losers. Among the negatively affected group were many young to middle-aged voters who had voted for Labour in successive elections from 1997. Results from the October 2008 Guardian/ICM poll indicate that even among those voters who backed Labour in the 2005 election only 25 per cent said the government's response made them more supportive of Labour. The main winners were those at the top of the wealth distribution, the asset-rich, and the relatively old – none of them key Labour constituencies. Indeed, results from the October 2008 Guardian/ICM poll reveal that among Conservative voters, only 3 per cent stated they were now more likely to vote Labour after the announcement of the bank rescue package. The policy interventions that favoured relatively older voters, an increasingly important electoral constituency, were a potential source of support for Labour, but the Conservative Party effectively neutralized this with policy proposals that were at least as attractive to older voters (Conservative Party (UK), 2010, 42).[23]

---

[23] By the time of the crisis, the percentage of the total population that was aged sixty-five or older was over 16 per cent. These voters exercise disproportionate influence in elections because their turnout rates are significantly higher than average, especially compared to young voters. One polling organization estimated that turnout by voters aged 18–24 and

Internal Labour Party constraints limited the government's ability to deliver policies that counteracted the redistributive impact of the crisis and the bank bailouts. As noted earlier, New Labour's past electoral success had depended on its visible departure from the socialism of 'Old' Labour. 'In order to win an election,' Hopkin and Viarengo (2012, 119) observe, 'Labour needed to convince the aspirant middle-income groups that the party was on their side, while at the same time offering something to its supporters at the bottom of the income scale. The acuteness of the political dilemma resided in the hostility of many middle income voters towards the kinds of redistributive policies that would imply higher taxes in order to help the poor' (Hopkin and Viarengo, 2012, 119).[24]

This problem was compounded by the fact that the government needed to raise taxes to limit borrowing after the crisis. Tax increases on high-income and wealthier households offered one such mechanism that would have potentially limited perceptions among the middle classes of distributional unfairness. But in each election since 1997, New Labour had made (and thus far kept) a specific promise not to increase either the basic marginal rate (20 per cent) or the top rate of income tax (40 per cent). Raising the latter would break a party manifesto commitment and potentially further damage its electoral chances. 'To raise it', Darling later wrote, 'would be to cross the political Rubicon for New Labour' (Darling, 2011, 185).

These electoral considerations boxed in the government because it was difficult to raise sufficient revenue from other sources. After much internal debate, it had already committed to an increase in National Insurance contributions, paid by employees and employers, which the Conservatives would later deride as a 'tax on jobs'. In addition, in Brown's last budget as chancellor in 2007 he had sought to portray Labour as the tax-cutting party by reducing the basic rate of income tax to its lowest level in seventy-five years. To pay for this reduction, he planned to abolish the 10 per cent starting rate for income tax, which would produce losses for many low-income families, even after an internal Labour Party revolt forced the government to change course by providing compensation to some families (Kavanagh and Cowley,

25–34 was 52 per cent and 57 per cent respectively in the 2010 election, compared to 70 per cent and 75 per cent for voters aged 55–64 and 65+ respectively (Burn-Murdoch, 2017).
[24] See also Smith (2010, 237).

2010, 51). 'Those [families who lost out from this reform]', according to Darling, 'were the voters who deserted us, alienated by the idea that we're doing nothing for them, in 2010' (Darling, 2011, 186). Other households also lost out from Labour's tax and benefit reforms during its final term of office. This included a net loss of £8.1 billion (£316.57 per household per year) concentrated among middle- and high-income households, with most of the losses suffered after the crisis (Browne and Phillips, 2010, 16).

Breaking its manifesto commitment, the government did make some efforts to raise additional revenue from those at the top. It raised the top marginal tax rate (applied to earnings above £150,000) to 50 per cent, restricted the tax-free allowance available to individuals earning over £100,000, and began to remove the tax relief that top-rate earners could claim for pension contributions. It also introduced a 50 per cent tax on banker bonuses above £25,000 in 2009. While the bonus tax proved popular, Darling later conceded that it was largely drowned out by the 'negative message we were sending out on aspiration [which] contradicted everything we had argued for over the past fifteen years' (Darling, 2011, 230). Even so, these measures brought in little additional revenue. As Hopkin and Viarengo observe, 'Labour's redistributive strategy was therefore inherently limited in its ambition, due to self-imposed constraints the party leadership considered essential to electoral success' (Hopkin and Viarengo, 2012, 121).

This fed a widespread perception, even among groups that were relative beneficiaries in the crisis aftermath, that the very richest groups in society had continued to prosper. The crisis prompted a sharp increase in media reporting of the very high incomes and bonuses of the most successful City financiers, reflecting their increased political salience. These had further negative political effects at a time when banks were seen as being rescued by taxpayers. As Figure 8.12 shows, even in a Conservative centre-right newspaper such as *The Times*, hardly a standard vehicle of 'banker bashing', City remuneration practices suddenly became much more politically salient and newsworthy after 2008, with a peak in February 2009.[25] Perhaps the most prominent example followed revelations of the substantial retirement payments

---

[25] Article titles indicative of the changing public mood included 'No one pays back a bonus' (7 February 2009), 'Barclays' £600m pushes banker bonuses past £2bn' (9 February 2009) and 'What's fairness got to do with anything, Gordon?' (1 October 2009).

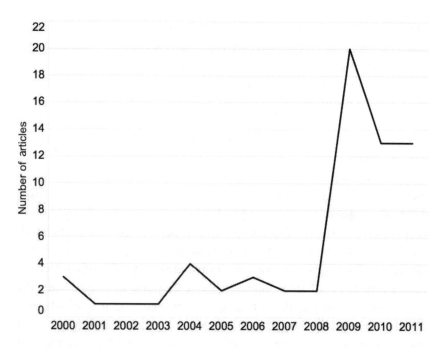

Figure 8.12: Articles mentioning banker pay or bank bonuses in *The Times* (London), 2000–11.
Source: The Times Digital Archive. Article counts containing keywords 'banker pay' or 'bank bonuses'.

that were to be made to Fred Goodwin, the CEO of RBS. A searing public debate followed over whether the government, which now controlled the bank, should honour the contract. Goodwin ended up losing his knighthood but retained most of his retirement package. The intensity of the bonus and retirement debate drowned out discussions of new policy measures introduced in January 2009, and limited the credit the government could earn from them (Woll, 2014, 106).

Public trust in banks had collapsed.[26] In late 2009, there were reports that 5,000 City bankers would receive bonus payments of over £1 million in early 2010 and that some individuals would receive as much as £15 million. Responding to reports that a substantial proportion of these payments would be made to bankers at RBS, the largest of

[26] In 1987, 91 per cent of respondents in the British Social Attitudes Survey agreed with the statement that 'banks were well run'. By 1994, this figure had fallen to 63 per cent and in 2009 it reached only 19 per cent. In the latter year, banks were by far the least trusted major institutions in British society among those mentioned in opinion surveys (trade unions were next at 35 per cent) (British Social Attitudes, n.d.).

those banks rescued by the government, Lord Myners, the City minister, said: 'I think they [City leaders] have got to come back into the real world and to understand that the banking industry has needed huge support from the taxpayer and the taxpayer simply finds these expectations unacceptable.'[27] Unhelpfully for the Labour government, it had presided over this outcome.

The accumulating costs of the crisis, related changes in the distribution of income and wealth, and voter perceptions that government policies had unfairly favoured already advantaged groups eventually overwhelmed any gains that accrued from the Brown government's relatively efficient management of the crisis in late 2008 (Gamble, 2009, 459–60). Opinion polls suggested that the government trailed the opposition Conservative Party by nearly 20 percentage points over much of 2008 and 2009, and the Guardian/ICM poll in June 2009 even put Labour in third place behind the much smaller Liberal Democrats (Glover, 2009). Although the very large Conservative lead was not sustained into 2010, in the months before the May election in that year, swing voters shifted to the Liberal Democrats rather than back to the Labour government.

Labour was decisively defeated in the election, gaining 29 per cent of the vote compared to 36 per cent for the Conservatives and 23 per cent for the Liberal Democrats. Labour suffered a swing in the popular vote of −6.2 per cent compared to 2005. The seat distribution was 258, 306 and 57 respectively. In a Parliament of 650 seats, the Conservatives formed a coalition government with the Liberal Democrats. This was the second worst post-war electoral result for the Labour Party, only marginally better than the disastrous 1983 election. This outcome was striking for a government that had done its best to prevent a disastrous collapse of the financial system and to protect the incomes and wealth of large parts of the middle class.

8.3   Conclusion

Labour's electoral demise in 2010 is consistent with our argument that in spite of the now high level of effective voter demand for financial stabilization, governments who respond to this demand when

---

[27] Grice (2009).

crises occur often achieve little electoral benefit. The Conservatives and Liberal Democrats were clear beneficiaries of the crisis, having supported the need for intervention while effectively focusing the blame for its substantial costs and associated perceived inequities on the Labour government. The crisis had already significantly damaged the perceived competence of the incumbent government in the eyes of British voters, but given the serious risk it posed to the living standards of many of these voters, it had felt compelled to intervene extensively. Darling, later posing the question, 'So why not let the banks fail?', answered:

> The risk of one bank collapsing and taking all the others with it was acute. I suppose it could have been tried, but I would not have wanted to be responsible for the economic and social catastrophe that might follow ... What was vital now was to prevent a complete collapse of the financial system ... On any view, these were eye-watering sums of money, but if we were to stop the panic and loss of confidence, to avert what even the least excitable commentators were calling economic Armageddon, we had to do whatever it took. The alternative would have been a financial and economic meltdown, not just in the UK but right across the world ... If we got this wrong, the livelihoods of millions of people would be at stake.
>
> (Darling, 2011, 141, 142, 157)

The government's response prevented the economic and social catastrophe that Darling and other policymakers feared, but it could not save the Labour government from electoral defeat. Delays and substantial costs, including absolute wealth losses, were still incurred by substantial numbers of voters. Furthermore, the distributive impact of the crisis and the associated interventions was widely perceived as unfair. Voters rewarded the government for financial stabilization only fleetingly in late 2008, but as the perceived costs accumulated over the following year, they increasingly deserted the government. This outcome could not have been more different to the nineteenth-century systemic banking crises in the United Kingdom considered in the previous chapter. This evolving pattern of crisis intervention and political consequences can also be seen in the United States, to which we turn in the following chapter.

9 BANKING CRISES IN THE UNITED STATES BEFORE THE ERA OF GREAT EXPECTATIONS

In this and the following chapter we consider the changing policy and political consequences of major banking crises in the United States since the early twentieth century. The United States experienced much earlier than any other country a combination of relatively high levels of both democratization and banking instability – there were nine major banking crises in the period 1818–1907 alone.[1] The degree of democracy in the United States at the beginning of this period, despite its limitations, was substantially higher than in almost every other country. For much of the nineteenth century, this provided American voters with a greater ability than elsewhere to sanction incumbent governments, with the consequence that government was more responsive to voter preferences.

The distribution of income and wealth was also less unequal in the United States during this period than in Britain and much of the rest of Europe. This and the rapid development of the American economy in the nineteenth century meant that a sizeable middle class emerged earlier there than in Europe and the stake of this group in the stability of the financial system was also greater at an earlier period. The US administration, in 1863, also became one of the first governments to make a formal commitment to financial stabilization via regulation. Banking crises thus displayed somewhat different dynamics than in the United Kingdom in this era.

[1] For an excellent historical survey, see Calomiris and Haber (2014, chap. 6).

We begin this chapter by investigating the very deep crisis of 1907, which broke in the 'progressive' era of US politics when popular pressure was building for reform and a greater role for the federal government in the economy. This was also a time when the United States lacked a central bank, so that unlike in the British case the political pressure for government intervention during the crisis was focused on the Treasury. Despite this, we show that the government did not provide a large financial sector bailout and relied heavily on private sector actions that were in themselves insufficient to prevent a deep downturn. Even so, the political repercussions were minor.

This gradually changed by the early 1930s, when the United States experienced the intense and extended banking crisis of the Great Depression era. Although a standard understanding of the policy response to this crisis is that laissez-faire ideology inhibited a government-led stabilization role until Franklin Delano Roosevelt took office, we show that interventions took place before this that were more extensive than those in 1907. Despite this changing policy stance, the wealth destruction that occurred during this crisis was far greater and the political repercussions more powerful than any that preceded it. The post-crisis policy reforms were also more extensive, with the US government adopting a more extensive financial regulatory framework and a system of deposit insurance well ahead of other advanced democracies. We can see in this crisis, and the policy response, the impact of emerging great expectations regarding financial stabilization among large numbers of American voters, which became even more extensive and consequential after the 1970s. In this sense, the transitional nature of the interwar period is particularly apparent in the case of the United States.

The organization of this chapter is as follows. We first set the evolving political and financial context for the three systemic banking crises – 1907, 1929–33 and 2007–9 – that we address in this chapter and the next. The remainder of the chapter is devoted to assessing the relationship between policy responses and politics in the first two of these crises. Although American voters expected less from government with respect to financial stabilization during the nineteenth century than they did by the middle of the twentieth, there were increasingly widespread calls for monetary and financial reform by its end. Although the middle-class stake in financial stability was rising and was stronger than in the United Kingdom at this time, American politics was deeply divided as to how the federal government should respond. This left the United States without a central bank until 1913 and hampered the government's ability to respond during crises. These political divisions continued after World War I and limited the ability of the newly established Federal Reserve to act decisively to stabilize a still volatile financial system. These flaws were seriously exposed in the late 1920s and early 1930s, with lasting political consequences.

9.1 Banking Crises and the Evolution of Banking Regulation in the United States

In contrast to most of Europe, the level of democracy in the United States was relatively high from the beginning of the nineteenth century. At the outset of the nineteenth century the United States is scored at 9 in degree of democracy in the Polity IV dataset; it suffered only a modest temporary regression in the 1850s and 1860s to a score of 8 (Marshall, Gurr and Jaggers, 2017). It receives the highest score of 10 in the period of the three crises on which we focus in this and the following chapter. Boix, Miller and Rosato also code the United States as a democracy for the full period (Boix, Miller and Rosato, 2014). US political institutions have been remarkably stable over the whole period, with institutional checks and balances providing multiple potential veto points to different actors.

According to Reinhart and Rogoff, there was more than one systemic banking crisis per decade in the century between the end of the Napoleonic wars and World War I alone (Figure 9.1). The deepest of these crises occurred over 1929–33, when thousands of banks failed and ultimately the financial system faced complete collapse. A long period of tranquillity during the Bretton Woods era was followed by a return to the historical norm of financial instability from the mid-1980s.

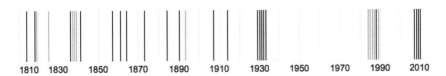

| 1810 1830 | 1850 | 1870 | 1890 | 1910 | 1930 | 1950 | 1970 | 1990 | 2010 |

Figure 9.1: United States: systemic and non-systemic banking crises, 1810–2015. *Sources*: Laeven and Valencia (2013), Reinhart (2010), Reinhart and Rogoff (2009). Crisis years indicate any years in which crises are mentioned in these sources. Darker bars indicate crises designated as systemic by any of these sources.

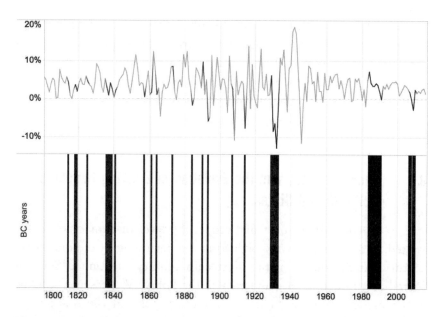

Figure 9.2: United States: real GDP growth (annual percentage change) with banking crisis years, 1800–2016.
Sources: Johnson and Williamson (2017); Laeven and Valencia (2013); Reinhart (2010); Reinhart and Rogoff (2009). GDP is deflated by the CPI data provided in Johnson and Williamson (2017). Banking crisis years (BC years) indicate any crises coded by L&V and the different R&R sources.

This wealth of cases of systemic crises in a large democracy over a long period provides an important laboratory to test our argument further. The crisis of 1907 is of particular interest because of its virulence – Kindleberger refers to it as a 'full-scale panic' (Kindleberger and Aliber, 2011, 88) – and its impact. As Figure 9.2 shows, it was followed by a sharp recession in 1908 that was deeper than any in the nineteenth century. Usefully for our study, this crisis also occurred in the period before the establishment of the US Federal Reserve in 1913. It provides an interesting contrast with the 1825 and 1890 crises in the United Kingdom, where the government was able to deflect much of the pressure for intervention to the Bank of England.

The iconic 1929–33 crisis was so consequential for politics and policy in the following half-century that it would be remiss to omit it from our study. As shown in Figure 9.2, it was associated with the deepest and most extended contraction of the American economy in its history, providing a major test of its political institutions. This crisis is also a valuable case because it is an early indicator of the growing pressure for government intervention in the modern era, which we discuss below.

The crisis that began in 2007 was another of the deepest over the past two centuries and prompted unprecedented policy interventions. In part for this reason, the 'Great Recession' that followed it was less deep than those after previous major crises. As we discuss in the next chapter, however, the recovery phase was anaemic by historical standards and fed rising voter dissatisfaction. This crisis also permits us to explore our argument about the policy and political consequences of rising societal wealth and inequality.

The distinctive volatility of the American financial system has been of considerable interest to many scholars. Calomiris and Haber argue that from the 1810s through to 1980 the dominant political coalition shaping American finance was between small unit bankers, chartered by states and enjoying local monopolies, and agrarian populists opposed to metropolitan elites and large banks (Calomiris and Haber, 2014, 153, 160–5). Most states consistently opposed interstate bank branching – a position supported by the Supreme Court in 1839 – as well as attempts by 'Hamiltonian' federalists to establish nationally chartered banks with monopoly privileges.

Despite continuing bouts of financial instability, the federal government did not take explicit responsibility for stabilization until the Civil War. Even then, this responsibility was a narrow one, limited to supervising 'national banks' that were much less numerous than state-chartered banks and trust companies.[2] The First Bank of the United States (1791–1811) played a modest role in lending to state-chartered banks such as during the 1810 panic, but Congress allowed its charter to expire the following year (Timberlake, 1978, 10). The Second Bank of the United States (1816–36) exacerbated the panic of 1819 with

---

[2] Starting in 1837, some states began to enact free banking codes that broke from the previous practice of requiring an application for charter to the state legislature. State legislation typically specified minimum capital requirement and shareholder liability and usually required note issuances to be secured by state bonds rather than deposits. State-level deposit insurance schemes existed at various times in six states between 1829 and 1866 and again at various times in eight other states after 1907. Yet none of these schemes implied *federal* responsibility for financial stability. In fact, after the passage of the National Bank Act, national banks that would be supervised at the federal level were prohibited from taking part in state deposit insurance schemes. As a result, many healthier state banks switched to federal charters to opt out of the schemes (Grossman, 2010, 241).

its policy of credit contraction and did not survive Andrew Jackson's campaign against it in the 1830s. Beginning in 1833, Jackson ordered that federal government deposits from the Second Bank of the United States be placed in state-chartered banks, which his political opponents called his 'pet banks'.

A consensus emerged that these selected state 'deposit banks' had to be regulated, partly due to the general antipathy of Congress toward discretionary executive powers and partly as a result of hard-money advocates seeking to stabilize bank credit and contain inflation (Timberlake, 1978, 46–7, 65). In 1836, Congress passed the Deposit Bank Act, which gave the Treasury the authority to set discretionary minimum specie reserve requirements for all custodial deposit banks to render these banks 'a safe depository of the public moneys' (Timberlake, 1978, 54). But the Treasury did not act on this authority: banks were left 'practically unregulated ... [and] did not even face state restrictions' (Timberlake, 1978, 48).

The fiscal demands of the Civil War led to the establishment of nationally chartered banks issuing national banknotes backed by government bonds in the National Banking Act of 1863. Importantly, this Act represented the first clear commitment by the federal government to financial stabilization, even if narrow in scope and uncertain in its broader implications. It required nationally chartered banks to adopt minimum reserve requirements on notes and deposits that were, in contrast to the 1836 Act, specified and set at 25 per cent for banks in reserve cities and 15 per cent for country banks. The reserves were to be held as cash or in the form of deposits in reserve centre cities, of which New York as a central reserve city was by far the most important. The number of reserve cities was expanded over time and in 1887 Chicago and St Louis joined New York as central reserve cities. National banks were also required to hold government bonds as collateral for their note issues, set at a minimum of one-third of their capital (Timberlake, 1978, 87).[3] The Act protected local banks by requiring national banks to operate out of a single building and effectively preventing them from

---

[3] The relationship between bank capital, bond holdings and note issuance was revised over time in laws enacted in 1874, 1882 and 1900 (Grossman, 2010, 230). Regulatory practice regarding reserve requirements in states varied widely; in some states there were none, though the crises of 1893 and 1907 led a number to emulate national requirements (White, 1983, 29–31).

branching, even while a few states permitted their own banks to establish branches. Importantly, it also established the Office of Comptroller of the Currency (OCC, part of the Treasury) with supervisory authority for national banks.

The credibility of this new policy commitment was uncertain, not least because state banks were outside the federal supervisory remit. Many states also lacked supervisory capacity and where it existed it was often weak (White, 1983, 33–5). Other regulatory requirements were very modest. Under the original National Banking Acts, minimum capital requirements for national banks were set at $50,000–$200,000, depending on the size of the town or city in which they were located. Capital requirements set by state banking regulation varied for state banks and were often lower than for national banks, in some cases as low as $10,000, providing them with a regulatory advantage. State banks, unlike national banks, also faced relatively few regulatory restrictions on real estate lending, which allowed them to dominate this market (White, 1983, 16–23). These competitive pressures led the federal government to reduce the minimum capital requirements for national banks in 1900 (Grossman, 2010, 231).

The federal government and most states imposed 'double liability' on bank shareholders during this period (Grossman, 2001, 2007). In the event that a bank failed, double liability meant that shareholders, in addition to losing their initial investment, could be called upon to pay an additional amount roughly equal to this investment. Some states went further, mandating triple and even unlimited liability. Although multiple liability for shareholders signalled a low political commitment to creditor protection, the National Bank Act made it difficult for the government to avoid blame for the outbreak of financial instability (see Table 4.1).

The policy contradiction that emerged was that this federal government commitment to financial stabilization was not matched by adequate means to prevent and manage the periodic crises that a fragile banking system generated. The competitive chartering of banks by state and federal governments fostered an increasingly interdependent but still very fragmented system. Private banks also thrived in the nineteenth century, though they were in decline in the years before the First World War, a time when state-chartered trusts were flourishing and moving into commercial banking and deposit-taking. The almost complete prohibition of branch banking, and limited regulation, promoted rapid growth in the number of banks and trusts. The number of banks in the United States grew from roughly 1,500 in 1860 to nearly 20,000 in 1905; most had no branches (Calomiris and Haber, 2014, 181).

New York was emerging as the nation's dominant financial centre, itself a matter of considerable resentment in states in the West and South, in part because federal policy was seen as having assisted New York's rise via its privileged status as a central reserve city. In the second half of the nineteenth century, private 'clearing houses' had been established by consortia of banks to facilitate payments and account settlement. The most important of these was the New York Clearing House (NYCH), established in 1853; more were set up in other cities in the following decades. During panics, when bank runs could threaten even relatively healthy banks, the clearing houses could also assist banks suffering from liquidity problems – effectively, acting as a private lender of last resort in the absence of a central bank (Gorton, 1984, 4–6). This liquidity support usually took the form of loan certificates jointly backed by the assets of all member banks and was provided to applicant banks on the provision of adequate collateral – thereby approximating Bagehot's rule for central banks (Cannon, 1910, chap. 10).[4] Although the Treasury had provided some liquidity support to banks in the earliest days of the Republic (Sylla, Wright and Cowen, 2009; Taus, 1943), in the crises of 1884 and 1893 it largely stood by and allowed the NYCH to take the lead in stemming the panic, including by issuing certificates and other forms of emergency credit to its member banks (Timberlake, 1978, 138, 171). Clearing houses also established supervisory functions and regulation for member banks to minimize risky practices. After the National Bank Act of 1863, they did this by drawing on statutory regulation for nationally chartered banks and sometimes on state rules for state-chartered banks (Gorton, 1984, 9–10). Banks that failed to meet regulatory standards could be expelled.

Despite these innovations, by the beginning of the twentieth century the US banking system was multifaceted and lacked competitive and regulatory coherence. One of the principal motivations for the

---

[4] In the crisis of 1873, the New York City Clearinghouse Association innovated by guaranteeing checks to individual depositors, creating a form of quasi-money. In 1893 and 1907, clearing houses went further by effectively printing their own money (Gorton, 1984, 7).

National Banking Act was to develop a uniform national currency, which was accomplished by introducing differential tax treatment for notes issued by state and national banks, imposing a 10 per cent tax on those issued by the former but only a 1 per cent tax on those of the latter. In the short run, the number of state banks declined sharply while national banks expanded rapidly. However, many state banks responded by increasing deposit-financed lending, aided in some cases by state-legislated reductions in minimum capital requirements. In the decades that followed, state-chartered banks vastly outgrew national banks, both in terms of their number and total assets. By 1890, state banks outnumbered national banks (over 8,300 compared to less than 5,000 of the latter) and controlled about 55 per cent of total bank assets (Calomiris and Haber, 2014, 181).

Meanwhile, large industrial and oil firms had become increasingly connected with major New York banks. The reserve city system established by the National Banking Acts had given rise to a system of pyramided reserves in which national banks held a portion of their reserves in larger reserve city banks, which in turn held a portion of their reserves in the central reserve city banks. In practice, this led to a build-up of reserve balances in New York. Demand for money in the interior of the country intensified during the autumn harvest and spring planting seasons, creating substantial outflows from New York and periodic tightening of money market conditions (Grossman, 2010, 232–5). Recurrent bouts of monetary stringency due to the nation's insufficiently elastic money supply and system of pyramided reserves were well known to policymakers by the time of the 1907 crisis (Taus, 1943, 112). Without a central bank with note-issuing and rediscounting privileges it fell to the Treasury to provide greater elasticity to the money supply.

During the tenure of Leslie Shaw as Treasury Secretary (1902–6), it acquired a more extensive liquidity management role. While the government had deposited funds in the banking system for decades, under Shaw the Treasury managed its banking sector deposits more strategically to mitigate seasonal fluctuations in the demand for money (Timberlake, 1978, 176–80). It also removed reserve requirements on these deposits. This left the government increasingly exposed to criticism in Congress and among academics that it was fostering moral hazard and increasingly beholden to powerful interests on Wall Street. Shaw's defence was straightforward:

It has been the fixed policy of the Treasury Department for more than half a century to anticipate monetary stringencies, and so far as possible prevent panics. It should not be necessary to defend such a policy. Extraordinary measures to prevent the spread of epidemics are always commended, though this country has never witnessed a pestilence which has left in its wake so great an aggregate of suffering and sorrow as mark the presence of epidemics of financial disorder and industrial stagnature. (Shaw, 1905)

This robust defence of a government role in financial stabilization, albeit one aligned with Bagehot's dictum, seemed consistent with Roosevelt's Progressive Era 'Square Deal', which asserted a general need for federal responsibility for conservation, business regulation and consumer protection. But Shaw's plan did not envisage stricter banking supervision to counterbalance Treasury support for banks and it proved very unpopular. According to Taus it was 'well in advance of prevailing opinions of his day and certainly well beyond the banking laws of his time' (Taus, 1943, 118). Although Shaw's proposals received Roosevelt's support, he was replaced by the less adept George Cortelyou in March 1907. His system faltered in the crisis of 1907, which we discuss below.

In the wake of this crisis, many New York bankers favoured the creation of a central bank, albeit one they would control, to allow more flexible liquidity provision. Many bankers in the rest of the country remained opposed and were able to shape the Federal Reserve System, established in 1913. The Federal Reserve Act gave the United States the central bank that it had long lacked, but in a very particular form (Timberlake, 1978, 186–206; Wood, 2014, 64–7). In 1914, an organizing committee of the new bank decided to establish twelve Federal Reserve Districts with associated Federal Reserve Banks. The Federal Reserve Act established a new national currency with the Federal Reserve ('Fed') able to issue its own notes, and it allowed member banks to obtain liquidity in the form of additional reserves or Fed notes by providing their local Federal Reserve Bank with high-quality collateral (short-term commercial paper and agricultural loans). This institutionalized Bagehot's rule. The Act also created a new layer of banking regulation. Banks that joined the Federal Reserve System would be subject to more stringent capital and reserve requirements than non-member banks, as well as restrictions on invest-ments deemed by Federal Reserve regulators as too risky, insufficiently liquid or against the public interest. Member banks were required to hold their reserve balances with their local Federal Reserve Bank. State-chartered banks were eligible to join the Federal Reserve System on condition that they accept the Fed's regulations and supervisory authority. Since many local banks viewed the new regulations as excessively onerous, few initially opted to join the System. This subse-quently emerged as a major weakness in the crisis of 1929–33.

This system of regulation for Fed member banks created serious regulatory imbalances, engendering growing pressure from this quarter for reform. The McFadden Act of 1927 levelled the playing field for national banks by providing equal treatment for branching as permitted by state law. Some states had liberalized restrictions on branching due to failures of unit banks in the 1920s, though it was still banned in others. The McFadden Act also harmonized regulation for banks that were members of the Federal Reserve System and those that were not – the latter constituting about two-thirds of all commercial banks in the 1920s.

The deep banking crisis associated with the Great Depression from 1929 produced a further decisive shift in the regulatory frame-work for banking. The failure of thousands of small banks prompted a further liberalization of state-level branching regulations, but the Hoover administration proved unable to deliver extensive financial reform despite congressional initiatives over 1931 and 1932. In October 1932, the retiring president of the state bank division of the American Bankers' Association declared that state banks were 'unalterably opposed to the so-called unification of all banking under federal control in place of the present dual system of state and national banks' (cited in Hammond, 1933, 622).

After Franklin Delano Roosevelt took office in March 1933, the new administration hoped to ensure that finance was sufficiently regu-lated such that it could no longer disrupt economic and social life. Roosevelt promised in his inaugural address the 'strict supervision of all banking and credits and investments'.[5] The key legislation that followed was the Banking Act of June 1933, more commonly known

---

[5] Franklin D. Roosevelt, 'Inaugural Address', 4 March 1933. Gerhard Peters and John T. Woolley, *The American Presidency Project*, www.presidency.ucsb.edu/ws/?pid=14473.

as Glass–Steagall after its two main legislative proponents. Consistent with the New Deal philosophy, one early commentator argued that 'the new law makes banking more of a social enterprise and increases the responsibility of the federal government for banking stability' (Preston, 1933, 585). The Act tightened regulation by requiring bank holding companies (BHCs) and other affiliates of state member banks to report triannually to both their regional Federal Reserve Bank and the Federal Reserve Board in Washington.

However, the populist coalition wishing to preserve local unit banking was still able to shape banking legislation in this period. Glass–Steagall established a federal system of deposit insurance (funded by levies on bank members of the Federal Deposit Insurance Corporation), which proved highly popular with the public (Maues, 2013). It also provided for the separation of commercial and investment banking, and the control of interest rates on deposit and savings accounts via what became known as Regulation Q. Although these new regulations were justified on the grounds of financial stabilization, they also protected local banks from competition (Calomiris and Haber, 2014, 154, 189). Roosevelt himself, the Treasury Secretary, the Comptroller of the Currency, Senator Glass and the Senate Banking Committee had all opposed federal deposit insurance, and so did large banks who perceived inefficient small banks as its main beneficiaries – as Steagall, the populist chair of the House Banking Committee, had intended. Indeed, following its introduction, nearly 2,000 banks opened in 1934 (Figure 9.3).

Small unit banks, or 'savings and loans' (S&Ls), that focused on taking deposits and financing house purchases had already been provided with a secure source of liquidity and cheap finance via the Federal Home Loan Bank, established in the FHLB Act of 1932. The FHLB itself comprised twelve regional home loan banks that were federally sponsored but owned by their member banks; each of the regional HLBs was under the supervision of the Federal Home Loan Bank Board (Federal Deposit Insurance Corporation (US) 1997, 170). The Home Owners' Loan Act of 1933 also gave the FHLBB the right to charter and regulate federal S&Ls. The National Housing Act of 1934 further established the Federal Savings and Loan Insurance Corporation (FSLIC) – also subject to FHLBB supervision – to provide federal deposit insurance for S&Ls. These initiatives reflected the growing government emphasis on promoting home ownership in urban centres.

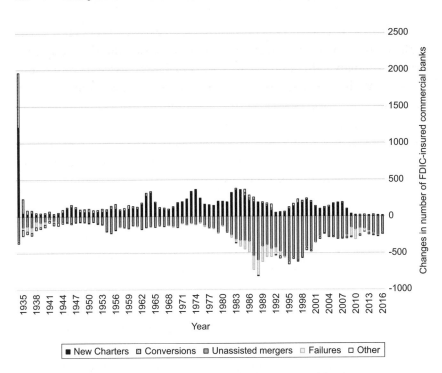

Figure 9.3: Changes in number of FDIC-insured commercial banks, 1934–2016. *Source*: Federal Deposit Insurance Corporation, www5.fdic.gov/hsob/HSOBRpt .asp, last accessed 25 September 2017.

Under this regulatory regime, the banking system would experience decades of stability after the Great Depression. The number of bank insolvencies declined sharply and until the 1980s S&L crisis remained at a comparatively lower level than that observed in the past. As in other countries, the emphasis on tighter financial regulation became a cornerstone of post-war economic policy.

9.2 The 1907 Banking Crisis

Although speculative pressure and banking sector fragility had been building for some time before late 1907, a failed scheme to corner the copper market unleashed a sudden panic in mid-October (Bruner and Carr, 2007, 7–55). Problems developed first with some smaller banks connected with the copper speculation. These banks applied to the NYCH for financial assistance, which we discuss in more detail below (Conant, 1915, 711–16). On 21 October, the third largest trust[6] in the country, with nearly $60 million in deposits, the Knickerbocker Trust Company, also applied to the NYCH for assistance, without success. With the suspension of payments by Knickerbocker the following day, panic spread to other significant trust companies and to the stock exchange. Banks that had lent to Knickerbocker and others were affected, and within days the panic had spread across the country. Some states, including Oklahoma, Nevada, Washington, Oregon, and California, declared bank holidays (Conant, 1915, 715; Kindleberger and Aliber, 2011, 212).

The impact of the crisis was severe. About seventy banks and trusts (the latter sector being especially distressed) collapsed over the final months of 1907 despite interventions by the clearing houses in major cities and by the US Treasury (see below) (Conant, 1915, 714–18; Moen and Tallman, 1992). Total commercial failures in 1908 increased by nearly 40 per cent over the average levels of 1905–7, especially in the Middle, Southern and Western states (US Department of Commerce and Labor, 1910, 547–9). After average annual real growth of 6 per cent over 1905–7, the economy shrank by nearly 11 per cent in 1908. Estimated unemployment in the manufacturing, transportation, building trades and mining sectors rose from 7 per cent in 1907 to 16.4 per cent in 1908 (Douglas and Director, 1931, 28).

The impact of the crisis on wealth was more mixed. Total US deposits fell by about 6 per cent from September to December 1907 (Jaremski and Rousseau, 2018). Depositor losses occurred primarily in state banks, whereas losses were minimal in the generally better-capitalized national banks (Gorton, 1988).[7] Stock prices fell sharply in the lead-up to the October 1907 crisis, with real stock prices down about 40 per cent from their peak in September 1906. After a further modest decline in November, they began a rapid recovery that saw the real stock price index rise by nearly as much by the time of the November 1908 elections.[8] Real average house prices, however, were

[6] American financial trusts had evolved to take on most of the characteristics of banks, though they were generally more lightly regulated.

[7] It was common for depositors in failed banks to wait years to receive funds, which generally occurred only after bank assets were liquidated. Between 1865 and 1933, on average it took six years at the federal level to pay depositors and other creditors and to close the bank (Federal Deposit Insurance Corporation (US), 2014, 24–5),

[8] Data from this point from Shiller (n.d.), unless otherwise indicated.

less resilient and steadily fell by about 15 per cent from their peak in 1907 to their trough in 1910, though this affected only a minority of households. Hence, the impact of the crisis was felt more heavily in the real sector of the economy.

9.2.1 Policy Responses

As in previous crises since the 1860s, distressed banks turned to the clearing houses for assistance. As a leading financier and key figure in the NYCH, John Pierpont Morgan took the lead in 1907.[9] Morgan's deputy, Benjamin Strong, had determined that Knickerbocker was insolvent. The NYCH therefore refused to assist it, but announced that all its members were solvent and would if necessary be protected. It then moved, at Morgan's behest, to stem the panic by supporting the Trust Company of America and brokers at the New York Stock Exchange (Bruner and Carr, 2007, 83–102). However, the inner circle of New York bankers centred on Morgan found it difficult to convince the many trusts to cooperate in similar ways.

Morgan had also summoned the US Treasury Secretary, George Cortelyou, to New York on 22 October to explain the gravity of the situation and to request assistance.[10] Cortelyou accepted the invitation and announced on 24 October that the Treasury would deposit more government cash in approved banks, a practice that had become, as indicated earlier, the main means by which the Treasury managed previous financial disruptions (McCulley, 1992, 100–47). According to Conant, these deposits amounted to about $80 million in the period from late August through 3 December (Conant, 1915, 714). In a further effort to relieve monetary stringency, the Treasury also announced that it would broaden the acceptable range of instruments that national banks could use as backing for note issuance (Taus, 1943, 123–5). However, by early November the Treasury was itself running out of cash and was unable or unwilling to do more to stabilize what remained a dangerous situation (Bruner and Carr, 2007, 22, 34, 86–7, 136).

---

[9] Earlier, following the 1893 crisis, during which government's gold holdings declined sharply, Morgan had engineered a rescue of the US Treasury by arranging to sell gold to it directly in exchange for a bond issue.

[10] Roosevelt had appointed Cortelyou to replace Leslie Shaw as Treasury Secretary in March 1907.

The combination of private sector and Treasury action was insufficient to stem the panic. By 25 October, money market interest rates reached 150 per cent (Bruner and Carr, 2007, 102). Although Morgan had initially resisted the emergency issue of NYCH loan certificates, in the absence of a central bank and with the Treasury unable to release more cash the escalation of the liquidity shortage forced the New York banks to accept this measure. Over $100 million of NYCH loan certificates were issued and cash payments were suspended (McCulley, 1992, 146–7). As mentioned earlier, further suspensions of bank payments spread across the country. The panic eventually subsided in early November with the provision of further substantial private sector assistance to major New York trusts, the news that nearly $100 million in gold had arrived from Europe, and the announcement that US Steel would acquire the financially distressed Tennessee Coal and Iron (TCI) company, the collapse of which would have triggered further market panic (Bruner and Carr, 2007, 108, 124–39).

The US president, Theodore Roosevelt, had been on an extended holiday in the build-up to the crisis, but in a speech on 22 October in Nashville, Tennessee, he blamed the crisis on speculators rather than government policies. On Cortelyou's advice, two days later he praised the joint work of leading bankers and the US Treasury. More crucially, Roosevelt agreed to the proposed takeover of TCI by US Steel, setting aside anti-trust (competition) concerns (Bruner and Carr, 2007, 109, 129–33). In mid-November, he announced that the crisis was over and that no further policy measures were required. After 19 November the Treasury issued $150 million in government bonds, in part related to the construction of the Panama Canal, apparently aimed at absorbing hoarded cash and relieving the shortage of collateral carrying the note-issuance privilege (Bruner and Carr, 2007, 139; Conant, 1915, 719). The proceeds were deposited in national banks, which were also temporarily relieved of OCC reporting obligations (Taus, 1943, 124). However, by this stage the crisis had subsided and new flows of gold from Europe may have played a more important role in stabilizing America's financial system (Kindleberger and Aliber, 2011, 232).

Overall, the federal government response to the 1907 crisis was slightly greater than in the two prior crises but was still very limited. It allowed the major private banks to do most to resolve the crisis. This

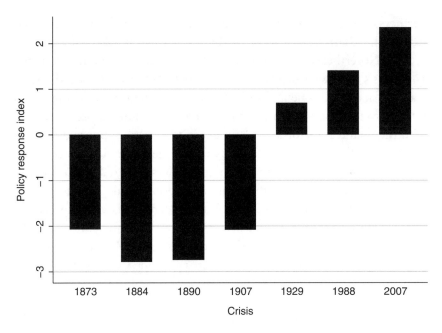

Figure 9.4: Policy responses to banking crises in the United States, 1873–2007.
Note: Crisis dating from those crises designated as systemic by Laeven and Valencia since 1970 and by Reinhart and Rogoff before 1945.

assessment is consistent with our policy response index for the 1907 crisis, which indicates that it tended strongly towards the market-conforming end of the policy spectrum, even if somewhat less so than the policy response to the 1884 and 1890 crises (Figure 9.4). It is also consistent with the limited pressure for federal government intervention from most voters, whose stake in the crisis was limited. As we discuss in more detail below, the response to the deep crisis that began in 1929 was (eventually) more interventionist but still much less so than in the 2007–10 crisis (discussed in the following chapter).

The onus placed on clearing houses to organize private sector coordination in crises probably reduced the political pressure on the government to intervene. However, there was no strong clamour from the opposition Democrats or their constituents for more extensive government assistance – with the partial exception of deposit protection, discussed below. Indeed, there was much suspicion that by having deposited Treasury cash in banks, the administration was beholden to Wall Street interests. 'The panic of 1907 belongs to and should be borne by the Republican party without any partners except their silent partners, the corporation magnates and trust beneficiaries,' charged Adolph J. Sabath in the House of Representatives in May 1908.[11]

Nevertheless, the very limited intervention undertaken in the 1907 crisis and its virulence fed concern that America's financial system was unusually unstable and isolated those who had until then opposed reform (McCulley, 1992, 143). Many voices, including those associated with the financial sector and a number in Congress, supported reforms that would allow the authorities to issue emergency liquidity in crises, as European central banks were commonly understood to do (*Washington Post*, 1907). In May 1908, the Republican-dominated Congress passed the compromise Aldrich–Vreeland Act; no Democrats voted in favour. The Act allowed the emergency provision of currency by national banks based on their reserves and established a National Monetary Commission to undertake an official enquiry. In 1911, the Commission recommended the establishment of a national central bank, to which Congress eventually agreed in December 1913 in the Federal Reserve Act.

The Democratic opposition portrayed these proposals as designed to favour the Republicans' major bank allies. Led by William Jennings Bryan, they pushed instead for a system of national deposit insurance (funded by a levy on bank deposits) to prevent bank runs, a proposal which they claimed supported the interests of average citizens.[12] Bryan's refrain that the Republicans had used the Treasury to assist Wall Street rather than depositors had considerable appeal in the South and West where the radical agrarian Populist Party had made inroads in the 1890s before merging with the Democrats to support Bryan in the 1896 presidential election. In the decade after 1907, eight states adopted deposit insurance systems (Federal Deposit Insurance Corporation (US), 1998, 12–17). This movement reflected the pressure from poor farmers in the South and West for financial protection and the rapid growth of bank deposits since the Civil War. As we saw in Chapter 4, proposals for deposit insurance received mixed reviews in newspaper opinion elsewhere.

The proposal for national deposit insurance was supported by many small regional banks but opposed by the Republicans, including

[11] Adolph J. Sabath (Democrat, House, Illinois), on 29 May 1908, *Congressional Record*, vol. 42, appendix, p. 468.
[12] See, for example, the speech of John G. McHenry (Democrat, House, Pennsylvania) on 14 May 1908, *Congressional Record*, vol. 42, appendix, pp. 141–9, and *New York Times* (1907).

by Roosevelt's chosen successor William Taft, on the standard moral hazard grounds that it would foster reckless lending. It was opposed by major banks, the American Bankers Association and orthodox economists (McCulley, 1992, 155–8). Republicans did, however, feel the need to respond to this popular pressure and Taft promoted the idea of a postal savings system, culminating in the Postal Savings Bank Act of 1910. Political agitation for deposit insurance nevertheless continued, though all of the state deposit insurance schemes had ceased operation prior to the Great Depression.[13]

9.2.2 Political Consequences

The Republicans roundly rejected the argument that the crisis was a product of their government. 'All these assertions show the disposition to ascribe undue importance to the effects of legislation and political action upon business conditions,' argued Theodore Burton of Ohio (Republican, House).[14] Indeed, there is little indication that the Democratic charges of collusion between the ruling Republicans and Wall Street in the crisis had a substantial effect in the elections held the following year.

Theodore Roosevelt, who had acceded to the presidency in 1901 on the death in office of McKinley, had won a landslide election victory in 1904 with 56.4 per cent of the vote. Yet he had promised in this campaign not to run for re-election and had groomed his friend Taft as his Republican successor in 1908. The recent crisis, its powerful negative impact on the economy,[15] and Taft's less charismatic personality might have been a deadly combination in a more contemporary presidential contest. But Taft easily beat his Democratic opponent, Bryan, by 51.1 per cent of the popular vote to 43 per cent in the presidential elections of November 1908. To be sure, Taft garnered fewer votes in many districts than Roosevelt in 1904, but states that had more bank failures were not more likely to inflict greater

[13] The schemes suffered from several flaws that led to the closure. First, all the schemes contained provisions that enabled healthier banks to opt out of the system by becoming national banks. Second, since the economies of these states were not well diversified, they were vulnerable to failures concentrated in the states' main economic sectors (Grossman, 2010, 241).

[14] 42 Congressional Record, House of Representatives, 17 April 1908.

[15] Although the economy began recovering from mid-1908, industrial output did not return to pre-crisis levels until 1910.

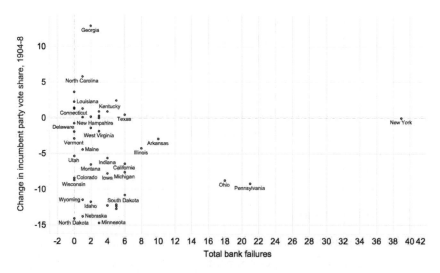

Figure 9.5: Bank failures by US state, 1907–8, and per cent change in Republican presidential candidate vote share, 1904–8.
Source: Comptroller of the Currency (US) (1909); Moore (1985). The bivariate relationship is insignificant including (-0.072, $p = 0.6364$) and excluding (-0.2450, $p = 0.1132$) potential outliers.

punishment on the Republican candidate in November 1908 (Figure 9.5). Nor was the vote swing against the Republicans greater in those states in which national banks failed (these represented 16 per cent of all bank failures over 1907–8) – where it might be expected that voters would hold the *federal* government more responsible for such failures.

    Despite the government's limited role in supervising national banks, it seems that many voters retained low expectations as to the federal government's responsibility to prevent and respond to crises. In part, this may be due to the government's revealed inability to fulfil this commitment effectively, as indicated by the three systemic crises (1873, 1884, 1890) that occurred after the creation of the OCC. As discussed above, the greater prevalence of state banks, which were outside the regulatory framework of the OCC, and the prevalence of double liability rules for bank shareholders also likely contributed to lowering voter expectations.

    The crisis also had little substantive impact on the 1908 congressional elections. As with the presidential vote, we do not find a significant relationship between state-level bank failures between 1907 and

1908 and the percentage of state congressional seats lost by the incumbent Republicans in 1908.[16] Although they lost five seats in the House and two in the Senate in these elections, the Republicans retained a dominant position in both houses (Moore, 1985, 863–7).[17] Republican seat losses in the House elections in 1908 occurred in Indiana (7), Colorado (3), Ohio (3), Nebraska (2), Illinois (1) and Kentucky (1); gains occurred in North Carolina (3), Missouri (2), New Jersey (1), Oklahoma (2), Pennsylvania (2), Rhode Island (1) and Wisconsin (1). In the states in which a bank holiday was declared, presumably those in which the crisis reached serious proportions, only one (Oklahoma) saw a net change in the party seat tally – and in this case, the incumbent Republicans actually *gained* two seats from the Democrats. The party seat tallies were notably unchanged in New York, where the crisis was centred and at its most virulent (20 per cent of all failed banks over 1907–8 were located in this state). Here, twenty-six of thirty-seven seats continued to be held by Republicans, and a majority of these Republican incumbents were returned with increased vote shares (and in the presidential election, Taft's vote share in New York was unchanged from Roosevelt's). In the state most affected by the banking crisis after New York, Pennsylvania, the Republicans also *gained* two seats in the House.

Although the crisis therefore had very limited impact on Republican political dominance in the short term, its reverberations continued in the years thereafter as it had exposed the inadequacies of the status quo and, in the eyes of many progressives and populists, the excessive power of Wall Street. The ongoing debate over financial reform divided Republicans with closer links to Wall Street from those on the progressive wing of the party who saw the major banks as excessively powerful. The latter included Theodore Roosevelt, who became disillusioned with Taft's presidency and eventually ran on an independent progressive ticket in the 1912 presidential elections, as well as 'Main Street' Republicans such as Charles Lindbergh, Sr (McCulley, 1992, chap. 8).

With Taft unable to unify the Republicans, the Democrats took control of the House of Representatives in the 1910 elections.

---

[16] The bivariate relationship is insignificant including (0.0047, p = 0.795) and excluding (−0.005, p = 0.709) potential outliers.

[17] Senate elections were held in the first few months of 1908, House elections in November. Republicans held 219 seats in the House compared to 172 for the Democrats; in the Senate, they held 59 seats to the Democrats' 31.

They would use this position to launch the Money Trust Investigations of the House Committee on Banking and Currency in 1912 to investigate the role and influence of Wall Street (United States Congress, House Committee on Banking and Currency, 1912). In 1912, Woodrow Wilson's successful bid for the Democratic presidential nomination promised tariff reduction and other progressive causes such as ending monopolies. He opposed the 'vast confederacies of banks and railways' as well as the Republican proposal for a central bank that he argued placed too much power in the hands of private banks. Instead, Wilson's platform proposed 'such a systematic revision of our banking laws as will render temporary relief in localities where such relief is needed, with protection from control of dominion by what is known as the money trust'. In short, it appeared to promise a more stable banking system less influenced by major banks but without much detail on how to achieve this. The platform condemned 'present methods of depositing government funds in a few favored banks, largely situated in or controlled by Wall Street, in return for political favors' (Democratic Party, United States, 1912).

Wilson won the presidency in November 1912 in an unusual four-way contest, with the Republican vote split between Taft and Theodore Roosevelt's independent progressive candidacy. The Democrats also won four Senate seats, thereby gaining control of both houses and ending a long period of Republican ascendancy (they won sixty-one seats to control two-thirds of all seats in the House). In his speech to Congress on banking in June 1913, President Wilson asserted that 'the control of the system of banking and of issue which our new laws are to set up must be public, not private, must be vested in the Government itself, so that the banks may be the instruments, not the masters, of business and of individual enterprise and initiative' (Wilson, 1913). By this time, his proposals for banking reform had become more solid. He switched tack to support the need for a central bank, albeit one that he believed would provide for a strong measure of public control.

Congress finally passed the Federal Reserve Act in December 1913. Section 9 of this Act provided for the Federal Reserve Board, to be based in Washington DC, to require non-national bank members of the federal reserve system to meet the reserve and capital requirements required under the National Banking Act. Nevertheless, the regional structure of this system would subsequently allow Wall Street banks to retain considerable influence through the Federal Reserve Bank of New York.

In summary, the Republicans suffered little short-term political damage from the 1907 crisis, consistent with our argument that prevailing low societal expectations regarding financial stabilization generated low levels of political punishment for the incumbent party. Nevertheless, the crisis did underline the need for currency and banking reform and the aftermath showed the Republican Party unable to provide it. This provided the Democrats with an opportunity to capitalize on a current of popular opinion that saw Wall Street as wielding excessive economic and political power, though without fostering a national consensus on banking sector reform and regulation. This was demonstrated, for example, by the move among a number of states, rather than the federal government, to adopt deposit insurance schemes after 1907. These schemes seem to have fostered increased risk-taking by insured banks and many such schemes collapsed in the 1920s, reducing political support for deposit insurance (Calomiris and Haber, 2014, 188). No national scheme would be forthcoming until 1933.

In this respect, the greater degree of democracy and of middle-class wealth in the United States compared with the United Kingdom over the course of much of the nineteenth century produced modest steps, notably at the state level, towards greater government involvement in financial protection and stabilization that built on the earlier creation of the OCC. In the context of federalism, government at the state and federal levels responded to these nascent pressures unevenly over time. This movement would be accelerated sharply at the federal level by the experience of the Great Depression, to which we now turn.

9.3   The 1929–33 Crisis

The Great Depression and associated US banking crisis is generally thought to have begun with the Wall Street Crash of late October 1929, which followed an exuberant bull market run in the 1920s (Kindleberger and Aliber, 2011, 31). The stock market crash directly worsened the position of banks that had provided brokers' loans in the booming market. On 7 November 1930, the Bank of Tennessee in Nashville – a subsidiary of Caldwell & Co., the largest financial holding

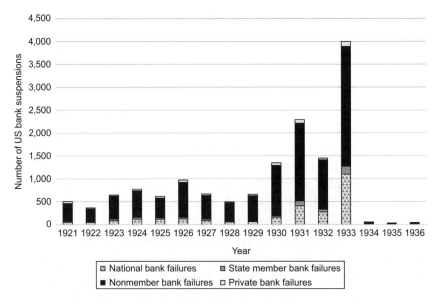

Figure 9.6: Number of US bank suspensions, 1921–36: national, state, non-member and private banks.
Source: US Federal Reserve (1937). Bank 'suspensions' refer to temporary or permanent closures of individual banks. Closures during bank holidays are not included. 'Non-member' banks refer to non-membership of the Federal Reserve System.

company in the South – failed and within a week other Caldwell affiliates closed. Bank failures mushroomed rapidly in the South. On 11 December, the fourth largest bank in New York City, the Bank of the United States, was forced to close after an attempted New York Fed-sponsored merger fell through. These high-profile failures received considerable media attention and panic spread rapidly (Richardson, 2013). Although the waves of bank failures ebbed and flowed over the next few years, the authorities failed to stem the collapse, which peaked in 1933 (Figure 9.6). From 1929 to the end of the crisis in 1933, nearly 10,000 banks failed, over 40 per cent of all the banks that existed at the beginning of the period. Over the period 1930–3, this represented 26.3 per cent of all national banks, 32.4 per cent of state member banks, and 43 per cent of non-member banks (excluding private and mutual savings banks) (US Federal Reserve, 1937). Losses incurred by depositors during this crisis were also far higher than in the nineteenth-century crises, estimated by Calomiris and Gorton at over 3 per cent of GDP (Calomiris and Gorton, 1991). As noted earlier, at this time it also took years for depositors in closed banks to be repaid (Federal Deposit Insurance Corporation (US), 2014, 24–5).

Prominent authors have blamed the Federal Reserve System for failing to act to prevent the stock market crisis from turning into a systemic banking crisis (Bernanke, 1983; Friedman and Schwartz, 1963). Key members of the Fed during the early 1930s blamed the earlier policy of Benjamin Strong of the New York Fed for ignoring the 'real bills doctrine', thereby fostering excessive credit growth and fuelling speculation (Meltzer, 2010, 1:274–5).

At the beginning of the crisis, over 8,000 banks were members of the Fed system, whereas nearly 16,000 were non-members. These two separate banking systems were nevertheless highly interdependent. Sectoral fragility was increased by banks' reserve practices and inadequate regulation in a national system that banks could not be compelled to join. Double-counting of 'floating' cheques as cash reserves was common practice, and non-member banks held most of their deposit reserves in Fed member banks in reserve cities. When deposit runs began, this uncovered a shortage of useable cash reserves and concentrated pressure on reserve city banks (Richardson, 2013).

The collapse of the banking system and the hoarding of cash by banks and the public raised the cost of credit for most non-bank firms; some firms could not obtain any credit and many collapsed (Bernanke, 1983). As Figure 9.7 shows, the collapse in lending after 1929 was the most severe in the past 150 years and applied to mortgage lending to households as well as to total lending.[18] In 1939, total lending was still 52 per cent lower than in 1929; mortgage lending was still 33 per cent lower. The lending collapse was concentrated most heavily in regions in which local Federal Reserve banks refused to provide LOLR facilities to banks, such as the Eighth District headquartered in St Louis (Jalil, 2014; Richardson and Troost, 2009). This also points to the failure of New Deal policies focused on the rehabilitation of banks and other financial institutions to reinvigorate aggregate demand (Olson, 1988, 177–82). We discuss both of these last points below.

---

[18] In 1920, mortgage lending constituted about a quarter of total bank lending. Although mortgage lending fell in aggregate by 20 per cent from 1929 to 1933, its relative importance, which had risen steadily throughout the 1920s, continued to rise through the Great Depression, reaching 55 per cent of all lending by 1933. However, as shown in Figure 3.12, even mortgage lending also fell sharply as a percentage of GDP in the 1930s.

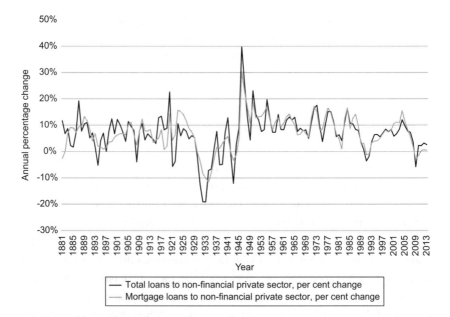

Figure 9.7: Annual percentage change in total banking sector loans to the non-financial private sector and mortgage loans to households, 1881–2013.
Source: Jordà, Schularick and Taylor (2017).

The economic impact of this banking sector collapse and associated financial disintermediation was catastrophic. Nominal GDP fell by 45 per cent between 1929 and 1933. Over the same period, consumer prices fell 24 per cent and real GDP per capita fell by 29 per cent (Jordà, Schularick and Taylor, 2017). Unemployment rose from negligible levels in 1929 to over 20 per cent by 1932 and peaked at over 25 per cent in 1933 (National Bureau of Economic Research, n.d.). This produced substantial social hardship at a time when public welfare provision was still very low by post-1945 standards.[19] Defaults by businesses, including farmers, were extensive. Commercial bankruptcy rates were already high in the late 1920s but rose 40 per cent from 1929 to 1932.[20]

The impact of the Depression on aggregate wealth, including household sector wealth, was even more dramatic and far greater than in the 1907 crisis. Average real wealth per adult fell by a third between

[19] In 1930, social transfers as a percentage of GDP were still negligible at 0.6 per cent, though they began to increase thereafter (Lindert, 2017, 40, 45).

[20] U.S. Number of Business Failures, All Commercial FIRST, m09029a, www.nber.org/databases/macrohistory/contents/chapter09.html.

1929 and 1932 (World Wealth & Income Database, 2017). Total deposits in commercial banks fell by 45 per cent from their peak in October 1929 to their trough in March 1933; the ratio of cash held by the public to deposits more than doubled over the same period.[21] As noted earlier, depositor losses were also historically large. The net savings of life insurance policyholders fell 83 per cent from a peak in 1928 to the trough in 1932. The Dow Jones Industrial Stock Price Index fell 84 per cent between September 1929 and March 1933; Shiller calculates that real (S&P Composite) stock prices fell by 73 per cent over the same period (Shiller, n.d.).

Shiller also calculates that average house prices fell by 24 per cent in nominal terms and 6 per cent in real terms (note that by 1929 real house prices were still 29 per cent below their pre-1914 peak). Mortgage lending had grown very rapidly during the 1920s with the emergence of high-leverage lending for house purposes, and the non-farm home ownership rate reached 46 per cent. After 1929, delinquency rates on home mortgages were high; mortgage foreclosures reached 1,000 per day by 1933, and 20–25 per cent of the total mortgage market was estimated to be in default (Federal Housing Finance Agency, 2011, 1).[22] Eighty per cent of all real estate bonds (securitized mortgages) were in default by 1935 (Snowden, 2010, 19).

The available data also suggests that economic inequality peaked in the 1920s. The pre-tax income share of the top 10 per cent of adults peaked in 1928 and had fallen 3 percentage points by 1931; the share of the top 1 per cent fell by over 6 percentage points. The income shares of these wealthiest segments then improved by the mid-1930s, before falling after the outbreak of World War II (World Wealth & Income Database, 2017). Wealth inequality rose very quickly over the period 1922–9 and then fell sharply from 1929 to 1933 (Wolff, 2017a, 607–9). This pattern is strongly related to the stock market boom and subsequent crash, and the high concentration of stock market wealth among the wealthiest households. The net personal wealth share of the top 10 per cent of adults remained relatively stable during the Great Depression years but began a long-term decline after 1933 (Figure 3.15).

---

[21] All remaining data in this paragraph, unless otherwise indicated, is from the NBER Macrohistory Database (NBER, n.d.), part X.

[22] Other sources suggest that more than 40 per cent of home mortgages (and about half in urban areas) were in default (Olson, 1988, 94–5; Wheelock, 2008, 138–9).

However, the share of the top 1 per cent fell by nearly 8 percentage points over 1929–33 and, after an increase in the mid-1930s, resumed a long-run decline thereafter (see also Wolff, 2017a, 591–609). The high and rising levels of wealth inequality before the Depression and the very negative and sustained impact of the crisis on asset prices, including business assets, also meant that the very wealthiest households experienced a sharp decline in net wealth (Piketty and Zucman, 2015, 1313). As we discuss in the following chapter, this experience was not replicated after 2007.

9.3.1 Policy Responses

Although the Federal Reserve System broadly failed to provide adequate liquidity to banks during the crisis, there was considerable variation in the policy of different Federal Reserve District banks. The 1930 crisis began in Nashville, located in the Fed's Sixth District, headquartered in Atlanta. The Federal Reserve Bank of Atlanta was much more activist than other Federal Reserve Banks during the crisis, providing emergency discounted liquidity to its member banks, encouraging these banks to extend loans to non-member banks, and delivering cash to communities affected by bank runs.

Recent research has shown that this activist policy substantially reduced the failure rate of banks in the Sixth District compared with those in adjoining districts overseen by 'liquidationists' who believed that the panic should be permitted to purge the system of unhealthy practices (Jalil, 2014; Richardson and Troost, 2009). Although the New York Fed also preferred a Bagehot policy response and undertook substantial government bond purchases in the early phase of the crisis, the belief that enough had been done became the dominant view by early 1930. Even after the situation deteriorated with the beginning of a wave of bank failures in late 1930, the majority of Federal Reserve Banks and the Board of Governors in Washington remained opposed to consistent liquidity expansion (Chandler, 1971, 142; Kindleberger and Aliber, 2011, 236, 240–1; Meltzer, 2010, vol. 1, chap. 5; Mishkin and White, 2016, 21). There was no provision in the Federal Reserve Act to ensure policy coordination between the twelve semi-autonomous reserve banks, whose boards were dominated by private bankers (Meltzer, 2010, 1:3). Boston and Chicago were mostly against the New York policy throughout the crisis. This replicated the conflicts that occurred under the previous system, in which clearing houses had dominated crisis responses.

Perhaps even more important than these coordination problems were the dominant policy norms that constrained the willingness of many within the Fed system to take more vigorous action. This even applied in the New York Fed. In summer 1931 as bank failures continued, against the advice of his own advisors its hesitant governor, George Harrison, did not accept the need to provide rediscounting facilities and saw the failures as a product of poor management and enhanced supervision by regulators (Meltzer, 2010, 1:336–7). Many in the Fed system adopted a principled opposition to extensive liquidity provision – based on the 'real bills' doctrine – in an economy in which nominal interest rates and the demand for credit by business were very low. They notably failed to distinguish between low nominal and high real interest rates (Meltzer, 2010, 1:322).

As the deflationary spiral accelerated over 1931, bankers and businesses set aside their qualms about government intervention and began to demand government action. Hoover himself still preferred a private-sector-led response and sought to encourage this (Olson, 1972, 1988, 9–10). In his address to Congress in December 1930, he stressed the need for self-reliance:

> Economic depression cannot be cured by legislative action or executive pronouncement. Economic wounds must be healed by the action of the cells of the economic body—the producers and consumers themselves. Recovery can be expedited and its effects mitigated by cooperative action ... The best contribution of government lies in encouragement of this voluntary cooperation in the community. (Hoover, 1930)

In a meeting at Andrew Mellon's New York apartment in October 1931, Hoover encouraged banks to establish the National Credit Corporation (NCC), effectively a bank-led fund that would provide assistance to solvent but distressed banks. The NCC was to be authorized to use subscribed capital and borrowed funds to rediscount assets ineligible for discount in the Federal Reserve System and to purchase the assets of insolvent banks. However, the Fed itself was unwilling to commit to the NCC, and the latter's directors were unwilling to risk their money on loans to weak banks. The 1930 congressional elections had led to Democratic control of the House of Representatives and an improved position in the Senate, so the shortcomings of the Republican policy agenda received growing attention. More initiatives were forthcoming from the House, in particular from the House Banking and Currency Committee under its Democratic chairman, Henry Steagall (Burns, 1974, 15–16).

The NCC's failure represented the end of the road for Hoover's search for a private-sector-led solution and he now looked to the wartime-era War Finance Corporation as a source of inspiration (Olson, 1972). With the cooperation of congressional Democrats, the administration established the Reconstruction Finance Corporation (RFC) in January 1932, to provide collateralized loans to local and state governments, banks and businesses. Hoover announced at its launch that its main objective was to provide collateralized loans to non-member solvent banks unable to access Federal Reserve funding. The Treasury committed $500 million of capital to the RFC, which could borrow a further $1.5 billion from the Treasury or the private sector.

In June, Congress authorized a doubling of its borrowing capacity to $3 billion. The RFC was also authorized to lend to railroads, to which banks had lent heavily, and to self-liquidating public works projects and agricultural credit corporations. But it did not provide a solution to the deepening depression and very little of this money found its way into new loans to firms and into job creation. Critics charged that it lent too conservatively in its first year, requiring high-quality collateral that may have worsened the liquidity position of some banks. Others charged that the RFC made politically connected loans to large banks. This was a political and policy disaster for the administration, generating a perception that at best it supported big banks and businesses (Olson, 1988, 19–21). A controversial $90 million loan was made in July 1932 to the Central Republic Bank of Chicago, of which the former US vice president and recently departed first president of the RFC, Charles Dawes, had just become chairman. This garnered media attention and angered many in Congress, prompting new legislation in July 1932 that required the RFC to publish the identities of the recipients of its loans. It probably reduced RFC lending to banks by increasing their fear of stigmatization (Butkiewicz, 1995; Patch, 1935). It also worsened prospects for cooperation between the parties and different branches of government (Burns, 1974, 22).

Over 1931, Steagall had been pushing with his Democratic Senate colleague, Carter Glass, for legislative reform in banking policy – an initiative supported by Hoover (Burns, 1974, 16). In February 1932, Congress passed the first Glass–Steagall Act that extended the Fed's ability to discount – a step towards greater state intervention that was seen at the time as radical by its proponents (Meltzer, 2010, 1:347, fn.83). This, and growing concerns within the Fed that further inaction would encourage more radical measures in Congress, prompted the Fed to undertake further sizeable government bond purchases (Meltzer, 2010, 1:360–1). In July 1932, Congress passed the Federal Home Loan Bank Act, to promote lending for housebuilding and to reduce foreclosures, and the Emergency Relief and Construction Act, which amended the RFC to provide funds for public works programmes. The momentum for greater policy action appeared to be growing.

By the middle of the year, however, the Fed's purchase programme swung back towards caution. Although the RFC had lent $951 million to banks and trusts and $325 million to railroads in the Hoover era, the financial system continued to deteriorate (US Department of the Treasury 1959, sec. Appendix).[23] Bank failures accelerated in late 1932 before a final collapse in March 1933, but the Federal Reserve system failed to renew its expansionary policy before it was too late (US Federal Reserve, 1937, 909).

The long political transition from Hoover to Roosevelt after the election of November 1932 encouraged inaction by the Fed, Congress and the Hoover administration in these final months (Meltzer, 2010, 1:379–80). The lack of clarity in FDR's own views on financial reform and differences of opinion among the Democrats also contributed. FDR had proposed 'vastly more rigid supervision of banks' to reduce speculation and supported the separation of commercial and investment banking, but like Carter Glass he did not support deposit insurance (Burns, 1974, 22–3). By Roosevelt's inauguration day on 4 March 1933, 70 per cent of all states had declared bank holidays and withdrawals were restricted in the rest. Neither the Fed nor the RFC was able to stop the systemic collapse. A week before he left office, Hoover asked the Fed's Board of Governors its opinion of a proposed federal government guarantee of bank deposits and the issuance of clearing

---

[23] Business loans, like loans made to banks, were made on the condition 'that, in the opinion of RFC's Board of Directors, the borrower be solvent and the loan "adequately secured"'. This security condition was somewhat loosened in January 1935 to 'so secured as reasonably to assure repayment' to encourage more lending (US Department of the Treasury, 1959, 65).

house certificates. The Board responded that it could recommend neither, though it supported the proposal for a national bank holiday
(Kindleberger and Aliber, 2011, 221; Meltzer, 2010, 1:384–5).

Eichengreen argues that the Hoover administration constrained
the Fed by failing to suspend the gold standard, thereby preventing the
central bank from lending currency freely to stem the panic (Eichengreen, 1992, 297–8). Meltzer, however, argues that gold reserves were
not a serious constraint on Federal Reserve action and shows in an
extensive analysis of Fed documents that the most important policy
determinant was that key figures inside and outside the central bank
were convinced by prevailing monetary doctrine that expansion was not
the appropriate response (Meltzer, 2010, vol. 1, chap. 5).

At his inauguration, Roosevelt argued that a New Deal was
needed that would involve more government activism, including more
spending for public works, relief for the poor and unemployed, and a
raft of financial reforms. Although he cast Hoover as the archetype of
bankrupt conservatism, FDR in fact borrowed heavily from proposals
that had originated in the Hoover administration but which had foun-
dered due to the hesitancy of his predecessor and disagreements among
policymakers (Olson, 1988, 35–41). One of FDR's first acts as president
was to declare a four-day bank holiday, subsequently extended by two
days. Roosevelt was willing to experiment with a range of policies
previously seen as unthinkable, such as suspending the gold standard
and cancelling the gold clause in debt contracts, which effectively bailed
in private creditors and reduced the burden of corporate debt by almost
one third (Kroszner, 1998). Even so, he remained committed to balanced budget ideas until the downturn of 1937–8 shifted political
power from fiscal conservatives such as Henry Morgenthau to Keynes-
ians such as Alvin Hansen and Marriner Eccles (Olson, 1988, 179–85).
Before then, new spending initiatives, such as the advent of Social
Security in 1935, which provided social insurance programmes such
as pensions, unemployment and disability insurance, and the Works
Progress Administration, which employed workers to build public projects, were to be paid out of current taxes.

More important in stabilizing the banking system were the
measures that accompanied the initial national bank holiday. The Federal Reserve and Treasury developed an emergency plan to protect
depositors, reopen sound banks and reorganize others, and empower
the Fed to lend more decisively (Burns, 1974, 46–7). Congress passed

the Emergency Banking Act (EBA) on 9 March, sanctioning the bank closures as well as providing the president with powers to restructure and reopen closed banks and the RFC to take equity stakes in national and state banks (Hoover had belatedly come to accept the need for such recapitalizations in 1932 but his proposal stalled in Congress (Olson, 1988, 39)). The support this provided to state banks who were not members of the Federal Reserve System reflected FDR's persistent inclination to support the continuation of the dual banking system – something Glass viewed as an abomination (Burns, 1974, 183).

Under the EBA, the RFC purchased $1 billion in preferred stock in more than 6,000 banks that were audited by teams of examiners from the RFC, the Federal Reserve System and the Treasury. By September 1934, it owned stock in half the banks in the country (Olson, 1988, 64–5, 81). Major banks in New York and elsewhere were convinced by FDR and Jesse Jones, RFC President, to accept government equity stakes so as to reduce the stigma of recapitalization for others (Burns, 1974, 123–4). This recapitalization programme enabled the gradual reopening of banks that were designated by the OCC in the Treasury as solvent. Bad assets were charged off against capital and, if recapitalization was required, the RFC and investors would inject new capital, with the RFC providing no more than private investors. As a rule, the RFC avoided intervening in bank management but it often took action to limit executive salaries, helping to deflect criticism that it was enriching the wealthy (Olson, 1988, 126).

The Act also authorized the RFC to provide collateralized loans to closed banks to unfreeze deposits. FDR understood the need to respond to the political pressure from closed banks, their depositors and Congressmen in the South and Midwest to support these banks, going against the preferences of Jesse Jones, who favoured the liquidation of many weak banks. There was also pressure on the RFC to enable banks to join the new deposit insurance system by January 1934 (see below). Jones therefore had to accept that the RFC should evaluate assets at less exacting standards than he wished, employing assumptions that their value would improve under a three- to five-year recovery scenario (Olson, 1988, 74–5). Those banks deemed to be truly insolvent were placed in the hands of conservators. Between March 1933 and June 1935, the RFC lent $823 million to closed banks to release depositors' funds (US Department of the Treasury, 1959, Appendix). Under Jones's vigorous leadership, the RFC became the primary instrument of what Olson describes as the 'state capitalism' of the New Deal and a politically useful instrument for both the administration and members of Congress for distributing funds without the need for appropriations: 'To one degree or another, every member of Congress ended up in Jones's debt' (Olson, 1988, 44).

The EBA also allowed the Federal Reserve to make advances in 'exceptional and exigent circumstances' to member banks on any acceptable assets – a provision that was later made permanent in the 1935 Banking Act as section 13(3) of the Federal Reserve Act.[24] The OCC was given powers to monitor national banks with impaired assets. The Treasury, rather than the Fed, was now firmly in charge; the Fed would largely follow administration policy for the remainder of the decade. FDR's first Treasury Secretary, William Woodin, informed New York Fed Governor George Harrison on 11 March that 'there is definitely an obligation on the federal government to reimburse the 12 regional Federal Reserve Banks for losses which they may make on loans made under these emergency powers' (Greene, 2013).[25]

According to Silber, the commitment to lend Fed money as needed to Treasury-vetted banks created 'de facto 100 per cent deposit insurance' well before the establishment of the formal deposit insurance regime associated with the FDIC, and was largely responsible for the programme's success in restoring public confidence in the banking system (Silber, 2009, 20). We can also interpret the use of the RFC to unfreeze the deposits in closed banks as de facto deposit insurance. This priority was also reflected in the willingness of auditors to err on the side of official lending to reopen banks that fell into a grey area between clear solvency and insolvency (Burns, 1974, 118).

The Banking Act of 1933 that succeeded the EBA was driven more by Congress than the president and had its origins in Hoover-era

---

[24] Section 13(3) of the latter act refers to the Fed's discounting powers in 'unusual and exigent circumstances' (Federal Reserve Board (US), 2017b).

[25] In June 1934, the Industrial Advances Act added section 13(b) to the Federal Reserve Act, allowing the Fed to provide secured lending to non-financial firms for working capital purposes for up to five-year maturities. The RFC was similarly authorized at this point. However, this industrial lending was much less important than lending to banks and railroads. To the end of 1935, the Fed system lent $125 million for this purpose and the RFC lent $23 million (Fettig, 2002; Hackley, 1973, 134). Patch argues that Republicans on the House Banking and Currency Committee did not oppose this industrial lending, but rather thought too little had been done (Patch, 1935). However, bankers were generally opposed, as were key figures in the Federal Reserve (Olson, 1988, 158–9). Section 13(b) was only repealed in 1958.

legislative proposals and investigations (Moley, 1966, 317). Public indignation over the role of bankers in producing the financial collapse – a perception that the Fed and other policymakers had an interest in fostering – was amplified by the often lurid hearings led by Ferdinand Pecora, Chief Counsel to the United States Senate Committee on Banking and Currency, that had begun in April 1932 (Kennedy, 1973, 103–28). This reduced the ability of bankers to resist key proposals, though small banks and their political allies were able to block Glass's proposal to extend branch banking substantially and thus to promote consolidation in the sector.

The Banking Act accordingly tightened banking regulation and intensified supervision. Notably, building on the view that the crisis was a product of excessive speculation in securities markets driven by bank credit, it separated commercial and investment banking by preventing affiliations between banks and securities firms.[26] The Federal Reserve Banks were now also required to ensure that member banks did not provide credit that facilitated speculation in securities, commodities or real estate. They were also prohibited from paying interest on checking accounts and limited interest payable on other forms of deposit, so as to prevent excessive competition for deposits between banks ('Regulation Q', promulgated on 29 August 1933). Branching was liberalized somewhat for national banks, but remained relatively restrictive, protecting small unit banking and ensuring that banking competition would remain limited for decades.

Large banks had generally opposed both the separation of commercial and investment banking and deposit insurance, which they viewed variously as socialism and as favouring small banks, but public pressure for deposit insurance eventually overwhelmed this opposition (Burns, 1974, 53–61, 89ff.; Maues, 2013). Henry Steagall agreed to support the legislation on the condition that it included deposit insurance. The Act established the Federal Deposit Insurance Corporation (FDIC) and a system of deposit insurance that protected each account holder up to $2,500 from January 1934.

We can interpret the earlier measure to provide a de facto guarantee of bank deposits and the later decision to adopt a formal

---

[26] The Banking Act was followed by the Securities Act of 1933, which provided for new regulation of the securities industry, and the Securities Exchange Act of 1934, which established the Securities and Exchange Commission to oversee securities markets.

national system for deposit insurance as a reflection both of the widespread view that it would reduce depositor runs and of the growing voter pressure for wealth protection in this form. Deposits in the Postal Savings system – which already enjoyed a de facto guarantee – had increased rapidly as private bank failures accelerated, increasing fears among some bankers that this could encourage what they perceived as a radical government in Washington to nationalize and control the banking system (Burns, 1974, 72–3, 182). Although FDR never seriously considered full banking nationalization and appointed orthodox figures to key financial policy positions to assuage such concerns, public distrust of bankers was running high, as the Pecora hearings demonstrated.

Multiple liability had been meant to serve as a stability-enhancing mechanism that would dampen the incentives for bank runs, but the widespread bank failures had revealed its inadequacy and by 1941 virtually every state had repealed it. The bankruptcies of many shareholders who had taken no part in the management of failed banks also generated political pressure for the repeal of double liability laws (Macey and Miller, 1992, 38). In its place, deposit insurance represented an alternative means to stabilize the banking system before it encountered distress. According to Friedman and Schwartz (1963, 434), 'Federal insurance of bank deposits was the most important structural change in the banking system to result from the 1933 panic ... and ... the structural change most conducive to monetary stability.'

Growing voter demand for protection of household wealth, particularly small depositors, also drove adoption of deposit insurance. As Grossman (2010, 130) observes, the initial level of deposit protection, even after adjusting for inflation, was far below the level of protection offered in the United States today, and 'underscores the aim of protecting small savers'. As Figures 3.5 and 3.10 show, by 1929 deposits reached 60 per cent of GDP in the United States compared to 40 per cent in the UK, and levels of middle-class wealth were higher in the former. By the 1920s, the experience with state-level deposit insurance funds had been disappointing, with many having been exhausted by the stream of bank failures during that decade. Although this experience increased the concerns of many policymakers regarding the risks of public deposit insurance, it boosted the constituency favouring federal government protection of deposit wealth, as reflected in growing calls within Congress for federal action to protect the 'average family'. This objective of protecting middle-class savings came to be shared by Roosevelt. When Steagall in 1934 proposed increasing the level of deposit insurance to $10,000, Roosevelt opposed this on the grounds that it:

> ... would aid only the three percent of rich depositors who have more than twenty-five hundred in any one bank. The bill as passed by the Senate takes care of the other ninety-seven percent who are people like you [Henry Rainey, Speaker of the House] and me. (cited in Burns, 1974, 128)

They compromised by raising the limit to $5,000 from July 1934, when all FDIC-insured banks were required to become members of the FDIC.[27]

Although the level of financialization achieved in the United States by the late 1920s was substantially lower than that reached after the 1970s, it was high by contemporary standards. This can also be seen in the housing market, where a boom in mortgage financing in the 1920s and relatively high rates of owner-occupation compared to Europe created a substantial constituency for protecting wealth in the form of housing assets. This included distressed urban home owners and farmers, the construction industry and employees, banks, buildings and loan associations, mutual savings banks and insurance companies (Olson, 1988, 94). The post-crisis policy response included a series of initiatives to promote home ownership and associated building via intervention in the distressed mortgage market (Fishback, 2017). The Home Owners' Loan Corporation (HOLC) was established as a government-sponsored corporation in June 1933 with RFC capital to borrow so as to refinance mortgages in default to prevent foreclosure and to buy bad loans from banks (Wheelock, 2008). In the three years after the creation of the HOLC, '[it] received applications from 40 percent of all residential mortgagors and wrote new loans on ten percent of the owner-occupied homes in the U.S.' (Snowden, 2010, 21).[28] It appears to have had a substantial positive effect on house prices and enabled many of these families to retain their homes (Fishback, 2017, 1476–9). The FHA was also established in 1934 as a government agency to, among other things, insure and thereby subsidize mortgage

---

[27] The Federal Savings and Loan Insurance Corporation (FSLIC) was also established in 1934 to administer deposit insurance for savings and loans institutions.
[28] See also Fishback, Rose and Snowden (2013).

lending. By 1935, real average house prices had risen 14 per cent from their nadir in 1932 (Shiller, n.d.). In 1938, another government-sponsored corporation, the Federal National Mortgage Association (Fannie Mae), was established to purchase mortgages, mostly those insured by the FHA, and thereby create a large secondary market in securitized mortgage debt.

The 1935 Banking Act also resolved the coordination problems in the Federal Reserve by permanently shifting power to the Board of Governors in Washington and establishing the governance structure that persists today (Meltzer, 2010, 1:5). The measure was strongly supported by the new Fed governor Marriner Eccles, but opposed by Jeffersonian Democrats such as Carter Glass (Burns, 1974, 139–77). This Act also authorized the Board of Governors to set reserve requirements for member banks. It designated the FDIC as liquidator of failed banks and eliminated double liability for bank shareholders.[29]

To summarize, the policy responses adopted by the US authorities after the 1929 stock market crash did not begin with a Bagehot policy response. Instead, both the Federal Reserve and the government opted for an even more market-conforming response in which LOLR facilities were withheld in the early phases of the crisis. By 1932, the Hoover administration moved towards greater fiscal intervention to halt the spread of the banking crisis. The Fed also shifted towards a Bagehot-style policy stance in 1932 but then retreated from it. Then, with the final collapse of the financial system in the weeks before FDR took office, the new administration moved well beyond Hoover's modest measures and the provision of LOLR facilities to a much more thoroughgoing intervention that first provided de facto full liability guarantees to much of the banking system, government recapitalizations and bank restructuring, followed by other measures that included an explicit deposit insurance regime. In this way, the authorities lurched from what some have called a 'liquidationist' policy stance, to an inconsistent Bagehot policy with some support from the Treasury, and finally to a bailout.

This suggests that US policymakers groped their way slowly and haphazardly towards a more interventionist policy stance as the crisis that began to accelerate in 1930 failed to resolve itself as they had

---

[29] Over the long run, this is likely to have increased the propensity of banks to take more risk (Mitchener and Richardson, 2013).

hoped. By early 1933 the system faced complete collapse. The dominant economic ideas and policy norms in both the Federal Reserve and the Hoover administration – which initially favoured a policy stance that accepted large numbers of bank failures as inevitable and as not even requiring liquidity provision – proved completely inadequate. These elite ideas were also at odds with the rising financialization of the US economy and the growing stake of many American households not only in the stabilization of working incomes, but also in the financial system itself. Many urban householders and farmers had deposits and had borrowed to acquire property. Various government policy initiatives had aimed to protect and promote the private ownership of housing at a much earlier time than most other countries.

However, the size and influence of the bailout constituency was still of modest influence by comparison to the post-1970s era. It was weakest regarding demand for intervention in securities markets, where relatively wealthy interests had more at stake and where more puritanical views prevailed. There was a consensus in Congress that 'speculation' was an evil to be avoided, producing a series of policy initiatives to prevent assistance from the Fed from finding its way into speculative activities. This can also be seen in the 1933 Banking Act's separation of commercial and investment banking.

9.3.2 Political Consequences

The spiralling financial and economic crisis that began in late 1929 worsened considerably in late 1932 and the electoral outcome was in sharp contrast to that which followed the crisis of 1907. The indecision of Hoover's administration was a political gift to Roosevelt and the Democrats. The failure of the Federal Reserve to take decisive action to stabilize the banking sector made matters worse for the incumbents. FDR highlighted the inaction and fatalism of the Republicans and promised action to address the social and economic consequences of the crisis. He was able to contrast his own record of providing public employment programmes as governor of New York with Hoover's philosophical reliance on voluntarism. In accepting the Democratic nomination as presidential candidate in July 1932, he stated:

> Our Republican leaders tell us economic laws – sacred, inviolable, unchangeable – cause panics which no one could prevent.

But while they prate of economic laws, men and women are starving. We must lay hold of the fact that economic laws are not made by nature. They are made by human beings. Yes, when – not if – when we get the chance, the Federal Government will assume bold leadership in distress relief. For years Washington has alternated between putting its head in the sand and saying there is no large number of destitute people in our midst who need food and clothing, and then saying the States should take care of them, if there are. Instead of planning two and a half years ago to do what they are now trying to do, they kept putting it off from day to day, week to week, and month to month, until the conscience of America demanded action (Roosevelt, 1932).

Roosevelt won by a landslide with 89 per cent of the electoral college vote and 57.4 per cent of the popular vote (compared to Hoover's 39.6 per cent). The seeming inability of the lame duck Hoover administration to provide the necessary leadership in the midst of a deepening crisis also gave FDR the opportunity to portray himself as a 'man of action' immediately on gaining office. Although the economy did not fully recover until the 1940s, the success of the EBA and associated banking stabilization measures and the popularity of Social Security and unemployment protection allowed FDR to achieve an even larger landslide victory in the 1936 elections with 60.8 per cent of the popular vote. He went on to win comfortably a record two further elections in 1940 and 1944.

To what extent was Hoover's loss and FDR's emphatic victory in 1932 a product of the banking crisis? This is difficult to determine with certainty. Hoover had won by a landslide in 1928 against his opponent, Al Smith, representing a Democratic Party divided over prohibition. By 1932, his administration's indecisiveness in handling the crisis after 1929 and the evident failure of Hoover's exhortations to business and consumers to remain confident undermined his general reputation for policy competence. So too did his failure to prevent a growing federal fiscal deficit (which increased to 4.6 per cent of GDP in 1932 as tax receipts collapsed and spending pressures rose), whilst continuing to emphasize his belief in balanced budgets. In May 1932, he told Congress that 'the course of unbalanced budgets is the road to ruin' and proposed a tax hike to reduce it (Leuchtenburg, 2009, 135).

As this episode and others suggest, Hoover's failure was not a product of inactivism so much as of the appearance of being forced by events into action. Even then, his achievements disappointed: his RFC was intended to tackle the unemployment crisis but it was implemented in such a way that it had minimal impact. In other important areas, Hoover simply made poor choices – though it should be emphasized that much of the policy elite at the time – including many of those surrounding FDR – agreed with his fiscal orthodoxy. He was also visibly unable to convince Congress to accept major new policy proposals as the economic crisis worsened. With unemployment at nearly a quarter of the adult male workforce and in some cities far higher (in Cleveland it was 50 per cent, in Toledo 80 per cent), Hoover fatally became personally associated with the human cost of the Depression: the homeless and destitute were living in urban slums called 'Hoovervilles'; turned-out pockets of men standing in bread lines were referred to as 'Hoover Flags'.[30] He also appeared to be insensitive to and even to deny the very reality of this hardship. His authorization of the Army, led by the headstrong General Douglas MacArthur, to clear the remainder of a core of Great War veterans and their families demonstrating for the early payment of promised bonuses from Anacostia Flats in Washington DC in July 1932 captured for many Americans this insensitivity (Leuchtenburg, 2009, 132–4).

Many voters thus perceived that the government had failed in its responsibility to understand and to prevent the worst consequences of the Depression; many were also clearly willing to assign blame for this failure. Few observers gave the Republicans any chance of retaining the White House in the November election, which Hoover himself seemed to understand. By 1932, he instead largely resorted to a rhetorical but doomed campaign strategy of defending the integrity of his policies, character and political philosophy, while at the same time conjuring the spectre of revolution if the people chose unwisely to elect Roosevelt (Carcasson, 1998). All of this by itself would have been sufficient to doom most candidates.

---

[30] Leuchtenburg relates another telling anecdote of a Republican couple who in 1928 had named their son Herbert Hoover Jones and in 1932 petitioned a court to change his name to Franklin D. Roosevelt Jones, 'desiring to relieve the young man from the chagrin and mortification which he is suffering and will suffer' (Leuchtenburg, 2009, 142).

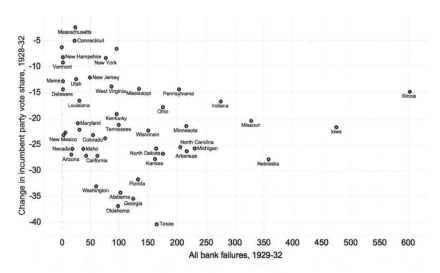

Figure 9.8: Bank failures by US state, 1929–32 inclusive, and per cent change in incumbent presidential candidate vote share, 1928–32.
Source: Moore (1985); US Federal Reserve, (1937). The bivariate relationship is insignificant including potential outliers ($-0.1711, p = 0.245$). Excluding potential outliers, it is significant at $p < 0.10$ ($-0.277, p = 0.059$).

In a single case such as this it is difficult to separate the effects on voting of general economic collapse from those of bank failures. Moreover, the transitional nature of the interwar period implies that voter expectations regarding federal government responsibility for crisis prevention and mitigation were still rapidly evolving in the lead-up to the 1932 election.[31] As such we find, excluding a likely outlier, a weak negative relationship between state-level bank failures between 1929 and 1932 and the electoral swing against the incumbent Republican Party in the 1932 election (see Figure 9.8).[32] The Democrats won a landslide victory in the House of Representatives, capturing ninety-seven seats. The incumbent Republican Party suffered large losses in states in which bank failures were higher than average, including Ohio (nine seats), Michigan (eight), Pennsylvania (eight), Illinois (seven), Iowa (six), Minnesota (six) and Wisconsin (five). While we fail to detect

[31] Bank failures accelerated after the election, but thousands of banks had already failed over the previous two years.
[32] Diagnostic tests suggest that Illinois represents a likely outlier. A leverage-versus-residual-squared plot reveals that it exerts higher-than-average leverage and that it has an above average residual. Additional tests for leverage and influence – including DFBETA and Cook's distance – also suggest that Illinois may be a problematic observation.

a systematic relationship between state-level bank failures between 1931 and 1932 and the percentage of House congressional seats lost by the Republicans in 1932, when we compare these results to the 1908 election, they suggest the political costs of financial instability were increasing.[33] In states in which bank failures were higher than average, the incumbent Republicans suffered significantly greater losses in 1932 than they did in 1908.[34]

The interventions undertaken by the Roosevelt administration proved highly popular and its reforms were sustained for a generation. The administration took pains to ensure that the RFC interventions in banks were not perceived as mere bailouts by extensive auditing of banks and tighter financial regulation. Moreover, as we have noted, it balanced these with interventions that protected ordinary urban and rural households, including mortgage relief, deposit insurance, Social Security and public works programmes. As we explore in the next chapter, the impact of these policies was significantly greater than those adopted after 2007 and, unlike in the later case, they seem to have been perceived by voters as distributing the costs and benefits of government intervention reasonably fairly. The Democratic Party was able to protect this policy legacy of the 1930s for nearly half a century through its control of Congress, although the Republican presidencies of Eisenhower and Nixon did not seek to reverse it.

9.4 Conclusion

The initial policy response of Republican governments to the crises of 1907 and of 1929–33 tended towards the Market pole on our continuum. The Treasury and Federal Reserve respectively failed to provide adequate liquidity to the banking system in 1907 and in the first phase of the later crisis. This resulted in accelerating bank failures. The earlier crisis was halted largely by private sector initiatives rather than state intervention, and despite its severity the incumbent Republicans survived the elections of 1908. This outcome is consistent with our

---

[33] The bivariate relationship is insignificant (-0.0004, $p = 0.424$). Diagnostic tests failed to detect any outliers.

[34] The difference in means for both seat losses (4.9 in 1932 versus 1.4 in 1908, $t = 2.30$, $p < 0.05$) and seat share swing (-42.7 per cent in 1932 versus -5.2 per cent in 1908, $t = 2.76$, $p < 0.05$) is significant.

theory that in this era, prevailing low levels of financialization, leverage and varied but narrow and contested government commitments to financial stabilization generated both low public expectations of government financial stabilization and a politically weak bailout constituency.[35] However, the crisis did prompt the political class to establish the Federal Reserve System to promote greater financial stability, an indicator that they recognized that the political costs of financial stability were increasing.

The bailout constituency was still politically weak when the next major crisis broke in 1929–30. Indeed, prevailing economic doctrine among policy elites did not even favour a Bagehot-style solution and the incumbent Republicans felt sufficiently politically secure to persist with a market-oriented policy response through 1931. But pressure for more extensive policy interventions grew as the crisis deepened. In 1932, under growing political pressure to act, the Fed moved towards providing more extensive liquidity to the banking system, though it did so inconsistently. The Hoover administration also tried belatedly to step into this policy vacuum with a series of measures in 1932, especially in establishing the RFC, although it too was incapable of devising a viable solution to the crisis.

Political support for a more extensive set of government interventions reached new heights in 1933 as the Roosevelt administration took office. The collapse of production and employment over 1929–32 was arguably sufficient in itself to produce this dramatic result, but many perceived that it was closely connected to the crisis of the banking system. Furthermore, the policy priorities of the Roosevelt administration are revealing. The immediate actions of the Roosevelt administration were to restore financial stability and to protect the livelihoods and remaining wealth of the lower and middle classes. The political movement for deposit insurance and credit protection reflected the unusual

---

[35] Some argue that the political impact of the 1893 crisis was very negative for the incumbent Democrats, contributing to their major losses in the mid-term House elections in 1894 (e.g. McCarty, Poole and Rosenthal, 2013, 174). Once again, however, our analysis finds that at the state level, bank failures (total, state or national) over 1893–4 had no significant effect on the seat share swing against Democrats in November 1894 (including and excluding outliers as well as results for states in which no Democrats ran in 1892). Nor is there evidence that these bank failures had a significant effect on the subsequent 1896 presidential elections, in which William Jennings Bryan ran (and lost) for the incumbent Democrats – at the state level, there is no significant relationship between bank failures over 1893–4 and the change in Democratic vote share between 1892 and 1896.

fragility of America's banking system, but also the severity of the threat it posed to the accumulated wealth of its middle classes.

This political impact reflected more a size rather than a composition effect of rising middle-class wealth: these voters wanted to protect the basic components of wealth and their access to mortgage credit. There was little popular support for the protection of more sophisticated financial instruments and investment banking. Only state pensions would be protected. Congress gorged on populist attacks on 'speculators' and passed associated legislation separating commercial and investment banking, leaving the latter much less protected. Greater protection for this political coalition was also reflected in its unevenness. Social Security coverage was low for African Americans, who were often disenfranchised, especially in the South where the Democrats dominated, and for women, who had received the vote in 1920 but who were framed in the legislation as dependants (Katznelson, 2006, 25–52; Kessler-Harris, 2003, 131; Rodems and Shaefer, 2016). In addition, the HOLC appears to have taken into account racial and ethnic composition when assessing the relative riskiness of lending to different neighbourhoods, contributing to institutionalized discrimination in lending practices among financial institutions (Aaronson, Hartley and Mazumder, 2017; Jackson, 1980).

Thus, in its late phase, the 1930s crisis represented a turning point in the standard policy response to banking crises and also in their political consequences. This shifting stance proved popular and reinforced an emergent mass democratic bailout constituency. FDR's landslide re-election in November 1936 suggests that voters approved of the series of new policy measures undertaken by the administration in its first term, including deposit insurance, Social Security, mortgage market interventions, more stringent financial regulation and reform of the Federal Reserve System. By the end of the period under review, then, the government had shifted to offering a large group of voters a set of policies that protected their wealth. Indeed, in some ways it did this more rapidly and effectively than it promoted and protected employment. These policies were a harbinger of financial stabilization policies that became well entrenched in the post-war era and which were embraced by Republican and Democratic administrations alike in banking crises since the 1980s. We explore these later policy responses and the political impact of the crisis of 2007–9 in the following chapter.

10 THE 2007-2009 CRISIS AND ITS AFTERMATH IN THE UNITED STATES

> Old Testament vengeance appeals to the populist fury of the moment, but the truly moral thing to do during a raging financial inferno is to put it out . . . even if some arsonists escape their full measure of justice.
> (Geithner, 2015, 9).

In this chapter we address the policy and political consequences of the most recent major banking crisis in the United States, which came at a time in which processes of financialization, rising leverage and deepening government commitments to financial stabilization had become entrenched. Initially often referred to as the 'sub-prime' crisis, it became seen as the primary source of what became known as the 'Global Financial Crisis' (GFC).[1] As we noted in Chapter 9, it was one of the deepest in US history and its origins, course and aftermath remain highly contested.

One of the reasons for this was the complex and extensive set of policy responses undertaken by both the George W. Bush and Obama administrations – often described by policymakers and academics as an unprecedented financial sector bailout (Barofsky, 2012; Culpepper and Reinke, 2014). Many have attributed this to the capture of US political actors and institutions by Wall Street banks and related firms (Bair, 2012; Barofsky, 2012; Johnson and Kwak, 2010).

---

[1] Like previous multi-country crises, the GFC was in practice largely focused on one region – in this case, the North Atlantic. As we discuss later in this chapter and in Chapter 8, some actors sought political advantage by framing the crisis as 'global' in nature.

Although Figure 9.4 suggests that the policy responses of both administrations inclined strongly towards the bailout end of our policy spectrum, our argument provides a different emphasis. We argue that this policy response was driven as much by the preferences of a large segment of middle-class voters whose stake in financial stability had become ever larger and who now had great expectations regarding government action to protect their wealth. The government sought to respond to these preferences, but it did so in a way that was delayed and seen as ineffective and unfairly redistributive by many voters of different partisan persuasions. As in the British case examined in Chapter 8, government officials were unable to convince these voters that they were much better off relative to a no-intervention scenario.[2] The political consequences were very serious, first for the incumbent Bush administration and subsequently for the Democratic Party's position in Congress in 2010.

The rest of this chapter is structured as follows. The first section discusses the heavily contested origins of the crisis. The second section discusses the policy responses of the George W. Bush and Obama administrations, as well as those of the Fed and other agencies. The third section addresses the political consequences of the crisis and the associated policy interventions, with a focus on their impact on the presidential and congressional elections in 2008 and those that followed over the following four years. A final section concludes by setting these outcomes in a longer historical perspective.

10.1   The Origins of the 2007–9 Crisis

The origins of this crisis have been as hotly contested as any covered in this book. It has been substantially framed by a highly partisan debate over whether private actors and markets or government policies and institutions were most to blame – as reflected, for example, in the Democratic majority and Republican minority dissenting reports of the congressional commission on the subject (Financial Crisis Inquiry Commission, 2011). The basic contours of the build-up in financial vulnerabilities are relatively uncontested: rapid growth in

---

[2] According to one widely cited estimate, the cumulative impact of these responses by 2010 was to boost real GDP by 13.5 per cent and reduce unemployment by 5.4 per cent (Blinder and Zandi, 2015, 3). As we discuss below, the interventions also almost certainly prevented even larger wealth losses from occurring.

mortgage credit to households with lower creditworthiness; rapid growth in the securitization of such mortgage debt; rising financial sector and household sector leverage; a growing dependence of banks on short-term wholesale funding from relatively unregulated markets such as the 'repo' market; a rising current account deficit; and rapidly rising asset prices.

The first category of arguments concerning the origin of these developments accepts that private sector actors and markets were the primary drivers of these developments, though they can differ on the underlying motivation of the actors.[3] Some also argue that market actors subjected policymakers and government agencies to extensive lobbying, who may have been primed to listen due to a dominant deregulatory ideology that underestimated the potential for financial market failure (Stiglitz, 2009). Most authors who focus on the role of market failure point to generalized expectations that increasing house prices reduced credit risk for sub-prime households[4] and related risks for financial firms and investors in securitized mortgage markets (Foote, Gilardi and Willen, 2012). The percentage of households taking out riskier mortgages increased rapidly, including adjustable rate mortgages ('ARMs'), interest-only mortgages and 'low-doc' and 'no-doc' mortgages in which borrowers could provide limited evidence of borrowing capacity. Mortgage brokers with little 'skin in the game' seeking to maximize fees by signing such loans became common by 2004–5. Household sector leverage, already at historic highs, also grew rapidly: by 2006, 46 per cent of first-time homebuyers made no downpayment and the median downpayment was only 2 per cent of the purchase price (Calomiris and Haber, 2014, 19).

Although many large commercial and investment banks played an important part in mortgage and security markets, the 'shadow banking' system played an increasingly central role. This included uninsured money market funds that purchased asset-backed securities composed of mortgage debt (including 'collateralized debt obligations', CDOs), the off-balance sheet special purpose vehicles (SPVs) that major

---

[3] Many emphasize greed and the role of real estate and financial sector compensation systems as the primary driver; others emphasize 'bubble' expectations, especially the pre-crisis view that house prices would continue to rise (Foote, Gilardi and Willen, 2012; Shiller, 2015).

[4] Sub-prime borrowers are those with a below-average credit history, including those with prior records of default, usually defined by an industry 'FICO' consumer credit score of below 640.

banks established to issue CDOs, the government-sponsored corporations Fannie Mae and Freddie Mac that both issued mortgage-backed securities and invested in CDOs, and the market for quasi-insurance contracts (credit default swaps, CDSs) that insurers like AIG Financial Products sold that offered protection to purchasers of CDOs and other securities (Bair, 2012, 54–6; Bernanke, 2015, chap. 5).[5] This shadow banking sector was comparatively unregulated but closely connected to the traditional banking sector in ways that were poorly understood. Crucially, through the use of SPVs and CDSs, many banks were able to take highly leveraged bets on housing-related securities while still meeting minimum regulatory capital ratios. These were highly profitable until housing markets faltered (Acharya and Richardson, 2009).

In the second category are a variety of arguments that assign primary blame to pre-crisis monetary policy, regulatory policy and legislation. Conservative, pro-market commentators mostly emphasize an excess rather than a lack of government intervention. Wallison, for example, emphasizes the importance of actions by the collective political class since the 1970s in a series of 'well-intentioned ... efforts to increase home ownership, especially among minority, low-income, and other underserved groups, through hidden financial subsidies' (Wallison, 2009). In the George H. W. Bush and Clinton years, banks seeking to expand into new markets via acquisition or branching were encouraged to meet expanded 1977 Community Reinvestment Act (CRA) targets for lending to traditionally under-served, lower-income households. Groups representing these household interests knew that they could target banks seeking merger approvals to encourage increased local lending commitments (Calomiris and Haber, 2014, 208–29; McCarty, Poole and Rosenthal, 2013, 126–44; Raghuram Rajan, 2010, 21–45).

The disagreement between those who blame government policy and those who blame market failure is particularly visible in the debate over the role of the CRA and the related Housing and Community Development Act (1992), including in the majority and minority reports of the Financial Crisis Inquiry Commission (Bhutta and Ringo, 2015; Financial Crisis Inquiry Commission, 2011, xxvii). Home ownership

---

[5] Some speculative investors, especially hedge funds, also bought CDS as they (correctly) believed that the insurance premiums charged were cheap relative to the underlying risk of default.

was a political objective on which conservative and progressive politicians could agree: it was a 'marriage of egalitarian ideology and the
"ownership society" offshoot of free market conservatism' (McCarty,
Poole and Rosenthal, 2013, 126). In the context of rising income
inequality, increasing the supply of mortgage credit had the distinct
short-term political advantage that it required no immediate additional
government expenditure, but it generated a large contingent public
financial liability (Raghuram Rajan, 2010; Weir, 1998). Since extending
lending to low- and lower-middle-income households would directly
increase the risks faced by banks, they in turn lobbied politicians to
require the government-sponsored enterprises (GSEs) to purchase the
mortgages they provided to these groups.[6]

Certainly, regulation of the large mortgage finance sector and
the associated real estate sector was lax. The tax deductibility of mortgage interest was also retained, some state governments exempted home
equity in personal bankruptcy and others reduced property taxes in
response to voter pressure. Over the course of the 1990s and early
2000s, the GSEs loosened their own credit underwriting standards as
they met expanded mortgage repurchase targets: by the mid-1990s,
Fannie Mae and Freddie Mac accepted bank mortgages carrying 3 per
cent downpayments (down from 20 per cent in 1990) and mortgages
provided to households with low credit scores. By 2004, they accepted
'no-doc' mortgage loans. The GSEs were compensated with especially
low regulatory capital requirements and by relatively weak regulation
and supervision provided by an agency of the Department of Housing
and Urban Affairs (HUD), the Office of Federal Housing Enterprise
Oversight (Calomiris and Haber, 2014, 209, 236). This appeared to
matter little to most market actors, who assumed that while ostensibly
private, the GSEs enjoyed an effective government guarantee (Acharya
et al., 2011).

Others argue that government policy was less important than
over-optimistic beliefs about the future trajectory of house prices shared
by private and government-connected institutions alike (Foote, Gilardi
and Willen, 2012). 'Private label' mortgage securitizations, which were
concentrated in Alt-A and sub-prime mortgages, grew much more
rapidly than GSE MBS over 2003–6 (Housing Finance Policy Center,

---

[6] The main GSEs included Fannie Mae, Freddie Mac and the twelve Federal Home
Loan Banks.

Urban Institute, 2017b, 6–10). The default risk taken on by private investors substantially exceeded that taken on by the GSEs.[7] The GSEs thus arguably followed rather than led the market trend towards increasingly risky lending to sub-prime borrowers and sharply deteriorating private sector lending standards (Financial Crisis Inquiry Commission, 2011, chap. 5). Market actors may have done so in part because after the 2001 dot.com stock market crash and recession, the US financial system was awash with surplus liquidity due to the influx of savings from abroad and a long period of easy money policy from the Federal Reserve (Taylor, 2009). Others add that the Fed policy of cutting interest rates aggressively in previous crises fostered investor over-confidence by generating expectations of a floor under asset prices – the so-called 'Greenspan put'.

Many also emphasize the contribution of a broad deregulatory trend in the years leading up to the crisis (Jabłecki and Machaj, 2009). Financial deregulation had accelerated in the wake of the savings and loan (S&L) crisis that began in the 1980s, itself a consequence of a political consensus favouring cheap mortgage finance for households and a congressional unwillingness to appropriate funds to resolve insolvent thrifts (Calomiris and Haber, 2014, 154; Federal Deposit Insurance Corporation (US), 1997, 167–88; McCarty, Poole and Rosenthal, 2013, 136, 164). In December 1991, Congress passed the Federal Deposit Insurance Corporation Improvement Act (FDICIA) to tackle the forbearance that was seen as having produced a delayed regulatory response and ultimately much greater costs for taxpayers.[8] The 1994 Riegle–Neal Interstate Banking and Branching Efficiency Act fully deregulated branching within and between states, accelerating a process of consolidation already under way. These policy responses reinforced the government commitment to regulate banking to preserve financial stability while fostering the emergence of large, complex banks with nationwide operations.

In short, there is no shortage of blame that can be assigned to private and public sector actors (see also Table 4.1). All sides shared beliefs about the benefits of a combination of banking sector

---

[7] See Housing Finance Policy Center, Urban Institute (2017a).

[8] The FDICIA required that federal bank regulators henceforth take automatic regulatory actions when a bank's capital ratios fell below specified thresholds and that the FDIC resolve failing banks at least cost to taxpayers (termed 'Prompt Corrective Action').

deregulation and of continued government intervention in housing markets. Private sector actors often appear to have perceived the risks of taking rising and profitable stakes in securitization markets connected with housing and other assets as low. Middle- and lower-middle-class households took decisions that produced rising leverage and linked their housing and portfolio assets with financial markets. Together, these interconnected decisions generated rising financial fragility that few perceived before problems emerged in 2007 (Figure 10.1; see also Figure 6.10 and Table 6.7).

This rising fragility was almost certainly obscured by the fact that most banks easily met minimum regulatory risk-weighted capital and leverage requirements. These provided strong incentives to banks to economize on equity capital issuance and maximize the return on equity

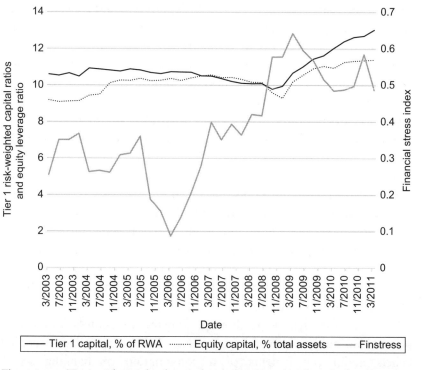

Figure 10.1: Tier 1 risk-weighted capital ratios (per cent) and equity leverage ratio (per cent) (left axis), and Financial Stress Index (right axis), March 2003–11, quarterly average for all FDIC-insured banks.
Source: ('BankRegData,' n.d.), drawing on FDIC Quarterly Call Reports; financial stress indicator from Gandrud and Hallerberg (2015b), on right-hand scale. RWA = risk-weighted assets. FDIC data are quarterly.

via securitization and CDS purchases. The lax regulation of the financial derivatives market, aided by a now-dominant pro-market ideology in Congress and extensive lobbying by major banks and securities firms, was enshrined in the Commodity Futures Modernization Act of 2000 (Bair, 2012; McCarty, Poole and Rosenthal, 2013, 109).

As indicated in Figure 9.3, bank failures accelerated sharply in 2008 and 2009. Figure 10.1 shows that US banks' capital and leverage ratios showed only marginal deterioration in the years preceding the crisis and Tier 1 capital remained above 8 per cent, in spite of the sharp increase in financial stress from its low point in 2006. In contrast to the S&L crisis (though not to the Latin American debt crisis of the 1980s), this time a number of very large US banks were threatened with collapse. This included Washington Mutual, which at the time of its failure in September 2008 was the sixth-largest bank with $307 billion in assets and the largest bank failure in US history (Dash and Sorkin, 2008). As we discuss below, even larger banks would have failed had not the government intervened extensively to support the sector.

FDIC analysis shows that reported regulatory capital ratios were unrelated to the probability that banks failed after 2007. Of 510 banks that failed between 2008 and 2014, 486 (95.4 per cent) had reported risk-weighted Tier 1 capital ratios at the end of 2007 of above 8 per cent, earning a designation by US regulators as 'well-capitalized'; a mere seven (1.4 per cent) of the failed banks had previously reported regulatory capital ratios of less than 6 per cent, earning regulatory designations of either 'undercapitalized' or 'significantly undercapitalized'.[9] Ironically, only these seven 'undercapitalized' banks would have been subject to formal prompt corrective action procedures by regulators under the 1991 FDICIA. The regulatory regime failed to focus regulatory attention on the real danger, which was the increasing levels of systemic risk among the much larger population of supposedly 'well-capitalized' banks. All of the ten largest US banks fell into this latter category.[10]

The structure of financial regulation made matters worse. Some financial firms were able to choose those regulators least likely to restrict

---

[9] Seventeen banks fell into the 'adequately capitalized' range of Tier 1 capital ratios of 6–8 per cent (data obtained from Federal Deposit Insurance Corporation (US), 2007).

[10] The largest banks were also regarded by the regulatory agencies as 'well-capitalized' as measured by their unweighted minimum Tier 1 leverage ratio (Haldane, 2017, 29; Hoenig, 2013).

their activities. AIG's ability to have its London-based Financial Products division regulated by OTS is one example. Countrywide, the leading national mortgage lender, switched to OTS from the Fed as late as March 2007 when OTS promised to be 'less antagonistic'. Many mortgage lenders were regulated by state authorities, while Fannie and Freddie were supervised by the Office of Federal Housing Enterprise Oversight, OFHEO (Bernanke, 2015, 95). The multiplicity of regulators with segmented responsibilities left none effectively responsible for monitoring levels of risk in the system as a whole (US Government Accountability Office, 2010).

Over-confidence in the resilience of the US financial system was rife in key agencies. Ben Bernanke, Federal Reserve Chairman, testified to Congress in March 2007 that the housing market was going through a 'substantial correction', with sub-prime delinquencies rising and house prices falling (Bernanke, 2015, 134). At that point, however, the economy was still very strong, bank profits and capitalization were high, and the Fed expected that the impact on financial markets would be limited. Within months, however, financial stress intensified. In June, Bear Stearns, the fifth-largest US investment bank, announced that it would make a large secured loan to one of its off-balance sheet hedge funds that was suffering losses in its mortgage securities portfolio. Then in late July, it announced that one of these funds had lost 'all of its value' and another had experienced losses of more than 90 per cent (Pruzan, 2008). European banks with significant exposures to the US mortgage market made similar announcements from this time, including one of France's major banks, BNP Paribas (Simensen, 2007; *New York Times*, 2007). Countrywide's woes intensified as its commercial paper funding dried up and its stock price plummeted; it was saved by an equity injection from Bank of America on 22 August, which eventually acquired the mortgage lender.

Stress suddenly built up in the international interbank market as banks became increasingly conservative in lending to peers perceived to be exposed (to an uncertain degree) to these markets, as indicated by the 'TED spread' between interbank and Treasury bill interest rates (Figure 10.2). The interbank market turned out to be especially prone to funding runs because the lending was short-term and uninsured.

The most intense phase of the crisis began a year after the emergence of severe problems in the securitization and interbank markets, with the bankruptcy of Lehman Brothers in September 2008.

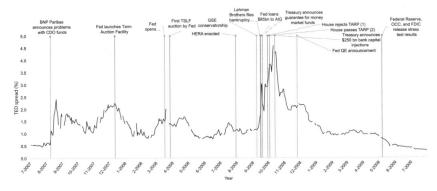

Figure 10.2: TED spread (per cent) and major crisis events, July 2007–July 2009. *Note:* The TED spread is the difference in percentage points between the three-month LIBOR rate based on US dollars (FRED Database, 2017c) and the three-month Treasury Bill rate (FRED Database, 2016a). The series is lagged by one week because the LIBOR series is lagged by one week due to an agreement with the source.

This fuelled an intense panic in the interbank markets (Figure 10.2). Equity markets collapsed and measures of stock market volatility spiked. Other markets related to wholesale finance including senior unsecured debt markets, covered bond and securitization markets froze in this phase of the crisis, when policymakers faced a meltdown of a kind not seen since February–March 1933.

10.2 Policy Responses to the Crisis

Beginning in August 2007, the main policy responses in the first nine months of the crisis were undertaken by monetary authorities and approximated a Bagehot response. In this period, the main demand for intervention came from financial firms and investors. When markets for asset-backed securities failed to recover, it became difficult for the authorities to determine the value of illiquid securities portfolios and thus whether major banks were illiquid or insolvent (Geithner, 2015, 138). House prices began falling in the second half of 2006 but it was not until the second half of 2008 that the decline threatened to turn into a rout. Pressure on the authorities to prevent a systemic financial collapse increased sharply from this time as the wealth of many voters became threatened, pushing the ideologically pro-market Bush administration into a series of unprecedented interventions. However, as we discuss below, as in the British case policy responses to these problems were delayed due to the policy gridlock produced by the link between partisan polarization and political institutions. Nevertheless, as the scope and generosity of support measures increased in fits and starts from mid-2008, this pushed the overall shape of the policy response along the spectrum from Bagehot to bailout. As Figure 10.2 indicates, the most intense phase of policy responses occurred in the last quarter of 2008, in the final months of the Bush administration.

10.2.1   Policy Responses under the Bush Administration

Most of the burden of managing the evolving crisis initially fell upon the Federal Reserve. The New York Fed injected $62 billion into the money markets in the immediate aftermath of the BNP Paribas announcement (the European Central Bank (ECB) had injected more than three times that amount into the Eurozone markets) (Bernanke, 2015, 144). On 17 August 2007, the Fed's Open Market Committee (FOMC) lowered the spread between the discount rate and federal funds target rate by 50 basis points (b.p.) so as to make discount window borrowing more attractive to banks. As bad news about bank losses and funding problems continued to emerge over the following months, a series of Fed rate cuts followed (Figure 10.3). By May 2008, the Fed funds target rate had been reduced by 325 b.p. to reach 2 per cent and the spread of the discount rate over the former had been lowered to 25 b.p. Concerns about the continuing stigma attached to discount window borrowing by banks also led the Fed to establish in December 2007 a new, temporary Term Auction Facility (TAF) to auction Fed funds at a rate lower than the discount rate.

Mishkin and White argue that the TAF was a significant departure from the Bagehot rule of lending at a penalty rate and marked the beginning of a series of other even more extensive departures (Mishkin and White, 2016). These included the Term Securities Lending Facility (TSLF) and the Primary Dealer Credit Facility (PDCF), both designed to lend to primary dealers, including major investment banks, in March 2008 (Geithner, 2015, 145). After the Lehman collapse in September 2008, other new lending facilities were created that allowed the Fed to purchase a variety of asset-backed securities. These included the Asset-Backed Commercial Paper Money Market Mutual Fund Liquidity

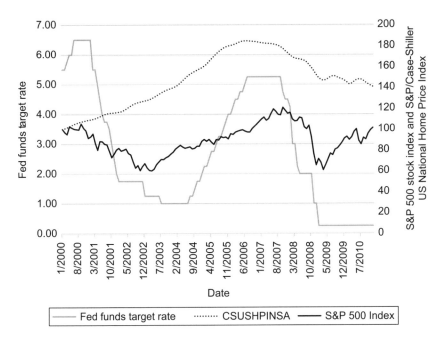

Figure 10.3: Fed Funds Target Rate (left, per cent), S&P 500 Stock Index and S&P/Case-Shiller US National Home Price Index (CSUSHPINSA) (both right, January 2000 = 100).
Source: CBOE (2018); FRED Database (2017a, 2017b, 2017c). The Federal Reserve discontinued a single Fed Funds target on 16 December 2008, replacing it with an upper and lower target. The upper target is used from this date.

Facility (AMLF), the Commercial Paper Funding Facility (CPFF), the Money Market Investor Funding Facility (MMIFF), and the Term Asset-Backed Securities Loan Facility (TALF). This extension of liquidity support beyond the commercial banking sector while accepting 'an unprecedented range of collateral' required the Fed to invoke Section 13 (3), which permitted it 'in unusual and exigent circumstances' to lend to any entity so long as certain requirements were met. The Fed classifies all these facilities as liquidity assistance, which in total reached $1.5 trillion by November 2008 (Figure 10.4).

In addition to these domestic measures, from December 2007 the Federal Reserve established swap facilities with the ECB and Swiss National Bank to allow them to provide further dollar liquidity to their own banks and to reduce demand by these banks for onshore liquidity. These swap lines were subsequently expanded to include Japan, the UK, Canada, Australia, Sweden, Norway, Denmark, New

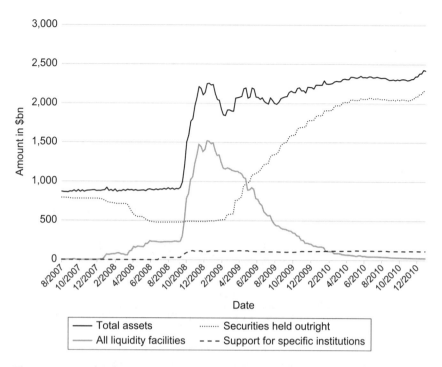

Figure 10.4: Federal Reserve balance sheet, major components, August 2007–December 2010, $billion.
Source: Board of Governors of the Federal Reserve System (2017b). All liquidity facilities includes: Term Auction credit; primary credit; secondary credit; seasonal credit; Primary Dealer Credit Facility; Asset-Backed Commercial Paper Money Market Mutual Fund Liquidity Facility; Term Asset-Backed Securities Loan Facility; Commercial Paper Funding Facility; and central bank liquidity swaps. Support for specific institutions includes: Maiden Lane LLC; Maiden Lane II LLC; Maiden Lane III LLC; and support to AIG.

Zealand, Mexico, Brazil, South Korea and Singapore and peaked at $583 billion in December 2008. Timothy Geithner, then President of the New York Fed, remarked that by then the Fed had become 'the world's lender of last resort' (Geithner, 2015, 141).

The contrast with the Fed's tentative and inconsistent actions in the early 1930s could not have been greater – as Bernanke in Washington and Geithner in New York fully intended. In contrast to Mishkin and White and many other critics, Bernanke argues that the Fed's interventions – including lending to the shadow banking sector at rates barely above the Fed funds rate on a variety of non-traditional collateral – were consistent with Bagehot's philosophy because they met the requirement that such lending be provided in unlimited amounts to solvent institutions (solvent because the collateral was deemed adequate) (Bernanke, 2015, 268, 410). He accepts that the Fed went beyond Bagehot 'in a few instances', particularly in funding the Bear Stearns acquisition, in lending to AIG and in reluctantly providing a temporary line of credit for Fannie and Freddie in July 2008, but defends these as necessary because of their systemic implications (Bernanke, 2015, 410).

Our position, which we elaborate below, is that the Fed's and the government's actions collectively went well beyond Bagehot, reflecting an underlying political imperative to prevent drastic consequences for the economy, the financial system, and ultimately households from Bear's collapse. This political imperative was heightened by the long-term process of rising financialization, which had accelerated since the 1990s. It accords with the view that even 'independent' central banks are necessarily embedded in an evolving political environment and especially dependent on the government during a crisis (De Haan and Eijffinger, 2016). Bernanke was clearly aware of these political constraints. Although the Fed's liquidity provision was far greater than its direct support to specific firms, by late October 2008 the latter reached $117 billion (Figure 10.4). Such direct support would prove particularly controversial, testing the political limits of the Fed's role and of the Treasury's legal authority.

In March 2008, Bear Stearns faced collapse as its market financing dried up. The Treasury was barred from spending money without a specific congressional authorization and thus lacked the authority to inject capital to ensure the solvency of an investment bank. It was also prohibited from indemnifying the Fed against any losses it incurred. The political difficulty of obtaining these congressional authorizations led the Fed, which feared a systemic collapse, to agree with JP Morgan Chase that the latter would purchase Bear. It provided a sweetener: the New York Fed would guarantee Bear's illiquid assets via a non-recourse loan of $30 billion to Morgan, which would be exposed only up to the first $1bn of losses. This left the Fed with a total risk of $29 billion, backed by $30 billion of Bear's investment-grade assets. The Treasury could not formally assist, but Secretary Paulson provided a 'comfort letter' stating that the Fed would be permitted to reduce its annual profits transfer to the Treasury if it suffered losses (Geithner, 2015, 150). Paulson later wrote that the letter was 'an indirect way of getting the Fed the cover it needed for taking an action that should – and would – have been taken by Treasury if we had had the fiscal authority to do so' (Paulson, 2010, 115). However, the Fed's primary role in the Bear rescue was a political liability for the government. Over 60 per cent of voters polled later that month opposed federal government rescues of Wall Street investment firms, whereas a majority then favoured government assistance to financially distressed home owners (Jacobe, 2008). The Fed resisted pressure from 'monoline' insurers of mortgage securities, Lehman Brothers, hedge funds and others for similar assistance (Geithner, 2015, 145, 156). But in crucial instances, the Fed was induced to go well beyond traditional LOLR intervention.

The first major financial intervention by the Treasury occurred in mid-2008. As the housing market crisis intensified, Fannie Mae and Freddie Mac came under increasing pressure as losses eroded their thin capitalization. With their equity capital only about 1 per cent of their total mortgage exposure the Fed judged both firms to be insolvent, but all the key authorities agreed that they must be supported (Frame et al., 2015, 33–4; Geithner, 2015, 170). The GSEs were massive, holding or guaranteeing about $5.2 trillion of home mortgage debt. They were also cornerstones of the mortgage securitization markets. Many investors, including foreign government agencies, saw their debt as effectively government-guaranteed. In contrast to the subsequent battles over TARP, Congress, including a majority of Republican senators, overwhelmingly approved a bailout of unprecedented size via the Housing and Economic Recovery Act (HERA), which became law on 30 July 2008. As we discuss below, this was a year after the bill had been introduced in Congress.

Paulson justified this intervention by emphasizing the dire consequences of not acting for the wealth portfolios of American households:

> Fannie Mae and Freddie Mac are so large and so interwoven in our financial system that a failure of either of them would cause great turmoil in the financial markets here at home and around the globe. This turmoil would directly and negatively impact household wealth from family budgets, to home values, to savings for college and retirement. A failure would affect the

ability of Americans to get home loans, auto loans and other consumer credit and business finance. And a failure would be harmful to economic growth and job creation. That is why we have taken these actions today.[11]

HERA gave the US Treasury unlimited authority to invest in both GSEs on a temporary emergency basis – an indication of the broad political commitment in Washington to the stabilization of the market for housing finance. It also provided for the FHA to guarantee up to $300 billion in new fixed rate thirty-year mortgage loans to sub-prime borrowers on the condition that lenders wrote down principal loan balances to 90 per cent of the current value of the property. The Fed also announced that it could provide finance to the GSEs as needed. In September, the Treasury purchased senior preferred stock in both GSEs, and the new regulator, the Federal Housing Finance Agency, took them into 'conservatorship' – a solution that avoided the politically toxic alternatives of receivership or nationalization. The government would invest $187.5 billion in these firms over 2008–11, though the fair value estimate of total government support to the GSEs is about $290 billion (Lucas, 2017). The government's capital injections also effectively bailed out the creditors of both firms, which receivership would not have done, though shareholders took large losses (Frame et al., 2015).[12]

In sharp contrast to the Bear and GSE interventions, the Fed and other government agencies allowed Lehman Brothers – a much larger bank than Bear – to go into bankruptcy in September 2008 on the grounds that they had no other option once a mooted purchase by the British bank Barclays was vetoed by its regulator (Bernanke, 2015, 268; Paulson, 2010, 209). The Fed claimed that, unlike Bear, Lehman was insolvent and that section 13(3) of the Federal Reserve Act prohibited it from knowingly lending at a loss (Geithner, 2015, 174; Swagel, 2015). Why the previous offer of Fed assistance to the GSEs, which it also judged insolvent, was legal remains unclear – perhaps because simultaneous Treasury assistance plausibly guaranteed that the Fed would take no loss.

Going to Congress as the administration had done for the GSEs in July was evidently a political non-starter in the case of Lehman. As

---

[11] As cited in Davidson and Hansen (2008). See also Paulson (2010, 17).
[12] In 2012, a new law was passed that transfers all profits and losses to the Treasury, narrowing the difference between conservatorship and nationalization.

Paulson recalls, 'All of us were well aware that after Fannie and Freddie, the country, Congress, and both parties were fed up with bailouts' (Paulson, 2010, 181). Barack Obama and John McCain, the Democratic and Republican candidates in the looming presidential elections, were then close in national polls, and each had felt compelled to oppose bailouts on the campaign trail. Prior to Lehman's failure, McCain and his running mate, Sarah Palin, though conceding the need to rescue Fannie and Freddie as 'the only short-term alternative for ensuring that hard-working Americans have access to affordable mortgages,' published a *Wall Street Journal* op-ed, entitled 'We'll Protect Taxpayers from More Bailouts' (McCain and Palin, 2008). Having placed calls to more than twenty members of Congress, Paulson received support on action taken on the GSEs, but also 'an earful about bailouts and ... [warnings] that they didn't want to see taxpayer money put into Lehman' (Paulson, 2010, 183). The media commentary that followed was mixed and sometimes supportive of the decision of the government not to rescue a failing investment bank (Washington Post, 2008; see also Chapter 4).

This temporary deviation from a bailout strategy proved unsustainable as the Lehman bankruptcy greatly exacerbated the financial panic and threatened a systemic collapse. The Bank of America solved one immediate problem by agreeing to purchase another troubled investment bank, Merrill Lynch, but weakened itself in the process. Concerns grew about Citigroup, then the largest US financial conglomerate. Most immediately, the authorities, like the markets, feared that AIG, with over $400 billion of outstanding CDS contracts on mortgage-backed securities, was likely to fail, which would in turn threaten the entire financial system. On 16 September, the New York Fed proposed an $85 billion direct loan to AIG at 11 per cent interest, in return for 79.9 per cent of its stock and the exit of the CEO; the Treasury provided another 'comfort letter' though Paulson realized he would now have to go to Congress to request emergency lending authority for the Treasury (Andrews, Merced and Walsh, 2008; Geithner, 2015, 187).[13] This intervention

---

[13] The NYFRB set up special purpose vehicles 'Maiden Lane' II and III to hold the various AIG assets that were acquired. (The original Maiden Lane SPV held Bear Stearns' assets.) These were sold off gradually and the NYFRB loans repaid in full, completing on 19 June 2012.

punished shareholders but protected bondholders. It also enabled AIG to pay out on CDS contracts to banks, which was widely interpreted as providing a back-door bailout of major banks, including many foreign ones (CBS News, 2009; Pirrong, 2009). The authorities argued that they lacked the legal means to impose haircuts (partial losses) on the banks holding these contracts and that any attempt to do so would only exacerbate the panic in funding markets (Geithner, 2015, 246; Swagel, 2015, 116).

President Bush noted that '[t]here was nothing appealing about the deal [which] was basically a nationalization ... Less than forty-eight hours after Lehman filed for bankruptcy, saving AIG would look like a glaring contraction. But that was a hell of a lot better than a financial collapse' (Bush, 2011, 458). Paulson agreed, again emphasizing the importance for household wealth portfolios of saving AIG: '[I]f this company were to go down, it would hurt many, many Americans ... In addition to providing all kinds of insurance to millions of US citizens, AIG was deeply involved in their retirements, selling annuities and guaranteeing the retirement income of millions of teachers and healthcare workers' (Paulson, 2010, 233). At this time, a majority of voters supported a financial sector rescue, but worried that the costs would fall mainly on taxpayers (Goldman, 2008; Pew Research Center, 2008). Recognizing this ambivalence, Paulson sought to frame his actions as 'rescues or interventions, not bailouts'.

Both the Treasury and the Fed were now intervening extensively to prevent what they feared would be a collapse of even wider proportions than in early 1933. Three days after the AIG bailout, with turmoil spreading to the uninsured deposits market, the Treasury announced that it would guarantee all money market funds, worth over $3.4 trillion, with a mere $50 billion from its emergency Exchange Equalization Fund. The Fed dramatically expanded its liquidity assistance from this point, accepting much lower-quality collateral, including BBB-securities. The MBS (mortgage-backed securities) market was a particular focus because rising default rates on sub-prime mortgages after 2006 had eroded market confidence, making it increasingly difficult for banks to sell them in the repo market. It launched the Government Sponsored Entities Purchase Program in November 2008, under which the Fed purchased $1.25 trillion of MBS guaranteed by Fannie Mae and Freddie Mac. This became known as 'quantitative easing' (QE) because it expanded the Fed's balance sheet and the monetary base (Mishkin and White, 2016).[14] This hybrid policy was a mixture of traditional monetary expansion and extraordinary liquidity provision.

The Fed, in Bernanke's view, had reached the outer limit of its authority and tools to intervene without congressional action. On 17 September, in a conversation with Paulson, Bernanke insisted: 'We can't keep doing this. Both because we at the Fed don't have the necessary resources and for reasons of democratic legitimacy, it's important that Congress come in and take control of the situation' (cited in Cassidy, 2008).

The Treasury then unveiled its plan to intervene to deal with the problem of illiquid assets on major banks' books. Its first Troubled Asset Relief Plan (TARP) proposal of 18 September to Congress provided little detail about how it would achieve this and was met with hostility, including by many Republicans. President Bush sought to build political support for the plan in an address to the nation on 24 September 2008, stating:

> I propose that the federal government reduce the risk posed by [banks'] troubled assets and supply urgently needed money so banks and other financial institutions can avoid collapse and resume lending. This rescue effort is not aimed at preserving any individual company or industry. It is aimed at preserving America's overall economy. It will help American consumers and businesses get credit to meet their daily needs and create jobs ... I also understand the frustration of responsible Americans who pay their mortgages on time, file their tax returns every April 15th, and are reluctant to pay the cost of excesses on Wall Street. But given the situation we are facing, not passing a bill now would cost these Americans much more later. (*New York Times*, 2008)

This plea was ineffective, perhaps because Bush's political standing was then so low (with a net approval rating of less than 30 per cent). But it would not be the only time that voters were

---

[14] The Fed subsequently launched 'QE2' in November 2010 in announcing that it would purchase $600 billion of long-term Treasury bonds (about $75 billion per month) to lower long-term interest rates. It announced 'QE3' in September 2012, committing to the purchase of $40 billion of MBS and $45 billion of long-term Treasuries per month on an open-ended basis until labour markets improved. In December 2013, it announced that this programme would be phased out gradually ('tapering').

unpersuaded by counterfactual policy justifications. In a meeting with Bernanke and Paulson on 24 September, House Republicans rejected the argument that further financial stabilization measures were urgently needed. For these members, Bernanke recalled:

> Bailing out Wall Street fat cats would be a gross injustice, a gift from Main Street to Wall Street. One member told us that he had spoken to small-town bankers, auto-dealers, and others in his district … So far, he said, they had not seen any meaningful effects of the Wall Street troubles. (Bernanke, 2015, 316)

On 26 September, the FDIC placed Washington Mutual ('WaMu') in receivership and facilitated a sale of its assets to JP Morgan Chase (Sidel, Enrich and Fitzpatrick, 2008). The FDIC followed standard procedure in requiring WaMu's senior creditors to take losses, but in the eyes of the Fed and Treasury this worsened the panic in funding markets (Geithner, 2015, 213). Just after this, the country's fourth-largest bank, Wachovia, avoided bankruptcy but was said to be in sale negotiations with Citigroup, a deal brokered by the FDIC, with the government offering to absorb all losses exceeding $42 billion.[15] In both cases, the bankruptcy procedure and private sector solutions appeared to be working. Furthermore, with elections looming in November, many Democrats and Republicans baulked at the perceived political costs of the TARP proposal.

At this point, pressure from constituents was not sufficiently strong to incentivize members of Congress to support the Treasury proposals. Those members of Congress who were retiring in November were more supportive of the bill, but Paulson found that many others believed that the weight of opinion in their constituencies opposed a banking sector bailout (McCarty, Poole and Rosenthal, 2013, 214–23; Paulson, 2010, 286). Opposition was greater on the Republican side, where anti-government ideology also played a role. Only one-third of Republican House members supported the bill compared to 60 per cent of Democrats in spite of pressure from the White House, both parties' presidential nominees and their congressional leaderships (Bush, 2011, 463; Hulse and Herszenhorn, 2008).

---

[15] Wells Fargo subsequently acquired Wachovia with a better offer that required no government assistance.

Paulson had been aware of the potential for gridlock to produce severe wealth-destroying market reactions and it had been one reason he had hesitated to submit the TARP request.[16] The market reaction to Congress's rejection of TARP on 29 September was indeed severe. By the end of the day, the stock market had fallen by about 7 per cent and the Vix (stock market volatility) index and the TED spread (interbank market stress) both hit new peaks and continued to rise over the following days. The market panic in turn threatened a more severe downturn and wealth losses. Bush noted: 'Every constituent with an IRA, a pension, or an E*Trade account would be furious' (Bush, 2011, 463). This reaction may have begun to convince more voters that the rescue package was necessary if distasteful. Geithner reports that members of Congress began receiving calls from constituents concerned about their life savings (Geithner, 2015, 221). Opinion polls conducted in early October, however, produced conflicting results, suggesting the public remained divided.[17] This seems to have left many members of Congress uncertain at this crucial stage of how voters would react, particularly since voters were unlikely to experience any benefits from approving TARP before the November elections. 'So it was easy,' McCarty, Poole and Rosenthal observe, 'given the time frame, to cater to populist rage' (McCarty, Poole and Rosenthal, 2013, 233).

After Senate amendments including business tax breaks and a temporary increase in deposit insurance to $250,000 per account, sufficient numbers in the House switched position to pass the Emergency Economic Stabilization Act (EESA) on 3 October. Those members with tighter upcoming re-election races were less likely to switch to support the bill. Some cited 'a torrent of calls from constituents' and the increase in the deposit insurance limit as a reason why they now voted in favour (Herszenhorn, 2008). In 2009, the temporary increase in deposit insurance was extended and in 2010 it was made permanent.[18]

---

[16] Paulson later wrote: 'If Congress failed to come through, the markets would implode' (Paulson, 2010, 147).

[17] CBS News (2008); McCarty, Poole and Rosenthal (2013), 234–7; Morales (2008). Over the following months, support for TARP seems to have diminished, especially among Republican voters.

[18] On 8 February 2006 the Federal Deposit Insurance Reform Act had raised the limit on deposit insurance for Independent Retirement Accounts (IRAs) from $100,000 to $250,000. EESA then raised the insurance limit on individual checking accounts to $250,000 until 31 December 2009 (the IRA limit was left at $250,000 and the maximum total coverage for an individual was set at $500,000). This decision was pushed by the

The House vote on EESA was 263 for to 171 against; 46 per cent of Republicans voted against the bill compared to 27 per cent of Democrats. At the time, John Boehner, House Republican leader, remarked that 'we know if we do nothing this crisis is likely to worsen and put us in an economic slump the likes of which we have never seen' (Herszenhorn, 2008). After this point, however, Boehner and other Republicans reversed their position, suggesting they were concerned that further support would have risked delivering political benefits to the Democrats. After the November elections, most Republican members distanced themselves from past and future government interventions. This strategy allowed the party to claim some credit for the country's stabilization while also siding with rising voter dissatisfaction with the bailout (including many voters who came to believe that TARP was an Obama administration programme) (Heimlich, 2010).

The bill provided up to $700 billion (with a tranche of $350 billion released initially) to purchase distressed sub-prime-related assets directly from banks. However, agreeing on mechanisms to price illiquid assets proved difficult; credit market stress indicators continued to worsen after the passage of TARP. The Fed introduced the CPFF to purchase uncollateralized commercial paper, in its own estimation stretching its 13(3) authority to the limit (Geithner, 2015, 226).

With pressure growing on the administration to act, it announced on 13 October that it would use TARP funds to buy up to $250 billion in preferred non-voting stock in banks paying 5 per cent dividends rising to 9 per cent after five years, with warrants to purchase common stock (Landler, 2008). Encouraging the participation of all nine major banks in the programme was a top priority, and for this reason the Treasury did not accede to congressional Democratic requests for restrictions on executive compensation, and CEO removal, in recipient banks. The FDIC, under pressure from the Fed and Treasury and following decisions by many European governments to introduce blanket bank liability guarantees, simultaneously issued a guarantee of commercial bank business checking accounts (Bair, 2012, 110–13). The Treasury also used TARP to inject a further $40 billion into AIG (later

---

Treasury and Fed; Bair at the FDIC had thought it unnecessary (Bair, 2012, 109–10). On 20 May 2009, the Helping Families Save Their Homes Act of 2009 extended the coverage period to 31 December 2013. On 21 July 2010, the Dodd–Frank Act made the increase permanent.

increased to $70 billion), which became a 'lightning rod' for critics of the bailout (Geithner, 2015, 248). After the initial round of capital injections, further injections and guarantees would follow for Citigroup and Bank of America. As the financial crisis spread to the real economy, General Motors and Chrysler also faced bankruptcy and with Bush's support the Treasury provided an initial $17.4 billion from TARP to these auto firms (Bush, 2011, 468–9).

That an ideologically pro-market administration had come this far indicates the extreme political pressure it was under. Republicans knew that the electoral stakes were high and that Wall Street was politically toxic. 'In asking for this,' Paulson later wrote, 'we would be bailing out Wall Street. And that would look just plain bad to everyone from free-market devotees to populist demagogues. But not doing this would be disastrous for Main Street and ordinary citizens' (Paulson, 2010, 256). This justification could be seen as disingenuous, though Paulson's former association with Goldman Sachs probably made it more, rather than less, difficult for him to support Wall Street, even if he shared their 'world-view' (Johnson and Kwak, 2010, 185). Certainly, TARP was lenient to many banks' executives and senior creditors, but in some respects – notably the requirement that all major banks accept capital injections and provide the government with warrants – the US bailout was tougher than its British counterpart (Culpepper and Reinke, 2014).

The overriding consideration of the main protagonists was to prevent a second Great Depression – they simply believed that this could not be done without a wholesale rescue of major financial firms (Bernanke, 2015, 145, 416; Bush, 2011, 458; Geithner, 2015, 248; Paulson, 2010). Bush's view was that 'the only way to preserve the free market in the long run was to intervene in the short run ... I had made up my mind: The U.S. government was going all in' (Bush, 2011, 458–9). Paulson was equally pragmatic in setting aside his free market principles: 'Government owning a stake in any private US company is objectionable to most Americans, me included. Yet the alternative of leaving business and consumers without access to financing is totally unacceptable' (cited in Guha, Politi and Mackenzie, 2008). Others like Sheila Bair and Neil Barofsky, whom Bush appointed as TARP Inspector General, were more inclined to the populist view that letting major financial firms fail was appropriate and would be less destabilizing than the Fed and Treasury believed.

The key policy actors also favoured earlier intervention than Congress allowed, particularly in the GSEs (Frame et al., 2015).[19] Bernanke had warned as early as March 2007 that Fannie and Freddie might trigger a crisis and believed that taxpayer money would need to be spent to rescue banks (Bernanke, 2015, chap. 11; Wessel, 2009, chap. 10). As we saw in the US context in Chapter 5, polarized veto players had contributed to policy gridlock and delays in responding to the onset of financial stress. Growing congressional opposition to bailouts after Bear Stearns and differing partisan views on GSE reform made prompt action difficult. Democrats wished to link GSE reform to proposals for mortgage debtor relief and block grants to state and local authorities to purchase distressed mortgages, which Bush threatened to veto. As Wessel notes, 'Bernanke and Paulson agreed that there was no point in offering Congress a plan so far-reaching unless the crisis was so severe that Congress would see no other option' (Wessel, 2009, 177–8). Aware that failure in Congress could trigger a severe market reaction, Barney Frank, the Democratic chair of the House Financial Services Committee, asked Bernanke and Paulson not to request additional powers and resources until they were sure Congress would grant it (Paulson, 2010, 139; Wessel, 2009). Essentially, the crisis had to reach a much more acute phase a year later before Paulson and Bernanke could command sufficient political support. In the meantime, the Treasury opted to push GSEs to raise capital and to encourage lawmakers to compromise in the hope it would be enough.

Paulson also describes continuing problems with Congress blocking GSE reform over the course of a year. The legislation that eventually became HERA in July 2008 had been introduced in Congress by House Democrats in July 2007.[20] The problem for the administration's strategy was that continuing inaction on the bill generated increasing market disruption and further deterioration in the position of Fannie and Freddie. Paulson noted his frustration with members of his own party in Congress:

---

[19] Bush makes the somewhat partisan point in his memoirs that his administration had been concerned about the stability of the GSEs from the beginning but that congressional Democrats blocked new legislation to constrain them in 2003 and 2005. 'All it took was the prospect of a global financial meltdown' for Congress finally to pass new legislation in summer 2008 providing for a stronger GSE regulator (Bush, 2011, 454–5).

[20] Pelosi (2008). See also the timeline and compilation of GSE-related developments leading up to the later interventions in *Wall Street Journal* (n.d.).

Meantime, the housing and GSE reform legislation continued to move much slower than expected. Initially, we'd thought it would be done by the July 4 [2008] recess, but that deadline had slipped away as Republicans dug in against homeowner bailouts, placing much of the burden for passage on the Democrats. While Congress dithered, the markets got jittery ... Fannie had raised some equity, but Freddie had missed the opportunity, and Congress still had not acted on the proposed reforms. Now, we would need much more. For the first time, I seriously considered going to Congress for emergency powers on the GSEs. Before, with Democrats and Republicans at war, it had been impossible to get relatively modest things done without a crisis. (Paulson, 2010, 139, 143)

The same problem applied to bank recapitalization. Treasury officials had prepared a plan for bank recapitalization in April 2008, but the political incentives for Congress to agree were not sufficiently strong before the catastrophic collapse of Lehman Brothers and AIG in September. It was only then, Paulson wrote, that 'for the first time I believed Congress would likely give us what we needed. The extreme severity of the market conditions made it clear that no good alternatives existed' (Paulson, 2010, 244). Even then, Congress only accepted the plan after initially rejecting it and generating a deeper market collapse (McCarty, Poole and Rosenthal, 2013, 184).

10.2.2 Policy Responses under the Obama Administration

The victory of Barack Obama in the November presidential elections and the Democratic gains in both houses of Congress suggested to some that a fundamental shift in policy direction towards a more progressive politics was possible (Bartels, 2013, 47–8). As Bartels notes, this hope was soon disappointed. The new administration was very concerned to reassure financial markets that it would maintain policy continuity as regards financial stabilization. An important signal was the assembly of an economic policy team that many associated with both financial deregulation and Bush-era bailouts, particularly Larry Summers and Tim Geithner (Calmes, 2008). It demonstrated that the administration would not adopt policies pushed by the left of the Democratic Party, including bank nationalization.

Geithner as the incoming Treasury Secretary continued to push hard for additional financial sector support measures and to avoid radical measures (Geithner, 2015, 4). New equity injections using TARP funds in Citigroup and AIG respectively followed in February and March 2009, indelibly associating TARP with the new administration. Even insiders, including Bair at the FDIC, believed that both firms were treated too leniently, alleging that Geithner deferred to his mentor and former Treasury Secretary, Robert Rubin, who had become chairman of Citigroup (Bair, 2012, 121–5, 168). The Obama administration also continued the Bush administration's policy of avoiding costly direct purchases of illiquid assets on banks' balance sheets, with the minor exception of an $18.6 billion programme that used some TARP funds to co-invest with private investors in a Public–Private Investment Fund.

The Treasury also ensured that the first Obama budget included a $750 billion placeholder for a second TARP that would allow the government to provide further recapitalizations, though this was never tapped. Instead, Geithner pushed a 'stress test' strategy, whereby the nineteen largest banks would be placed under the Supervisory Capital Assessment Program (SCAP) in which the Fed and other regulators would estimate the potential erosion of bank capital in different recession scenarios and require them to raise additional capital to meet a minimum 4 per cent Tier I capital ratio (Geithner, 2015, 347). The government committed to provide the additional capital if private markets would not. Although Geithner's initial announcement of this approach was widely seen as botched and many critics doubted that the scenarios were sufficiently stringent, the release of the results in May 2009 when the economy appeared to be stabilizing were better received. The TED spread fell thereafter (Figure 10.2) (Andrews, 2009). In an environment of extremely low interest rates and plentiful Fed liquidity, banks could rebuild capital through retained profits. This allowed the administration to avoid the difficult political choice of further public recapitalizations or 'bad bank' solutions involving the deployment of taxpayer funds. As investor sentiment recovered, banks raised private capital, and by the end of 2009 stronger banks had repaid two-thirds of the total TARP capital investments.

The administration portrayed these as successes, but like its predecessor it struggled to convince the public that it was not siding more with the financial sector than with most voters. Support for intervention began to drop across the political spectrum as the crisis

382 | Banking Crises, Policy and Politics in the UK, US and Brazil

subsided. As early as December 2008, approximately equal numbers of voters supported and opposed the TARP rescue package (Morales, 2008). Support for intervention bottomed out in early 2009, as the public became increasingly disillusioned with TARP. After Obama's inauguration a partisan gap opened up, with Democrats more likely to support bailouts (McCarty, Poole and Rosenthal, 2013, 235–6). In July 2009, Sigtarp Inspector-General Barofsky reported that the total gross government commitment to the financial system was $23.7 trillion (164 per cent of GDP) – a shocking figure that the administration said was misleading because it failed to take government assets into account. It nevertheless played into the increasingly popular narrative among Republicans that spending was out of control and fiscal retrenchment was necessary (Fox News, 2009; Office of the Special Inspector General for the Troubled Asset Relief Program, 2009, 137–58).

Even when the new administration did tilt policy towards supporting 'Main Street' and 'middle America', it obtained little short-term political benefit. It used TARP funds to provide additional loans to GM and Chrysler, bringing government support to the automobile sector to $80 billion. This intervention was important for the depressed Midwest and eventually proved unexpectedly successful in reviving Detroit's prospects, but by placing both firms in bankruptcy it was widely interpreted as another example of the privileged treatment of large banks (Goolsbee and Krueger, 2015).

Most importantly, the administration launched a major fiscal stimulus package, envisaged in part as providing more effective support to struggling home owners by creating jobs and allowing them to maintain mortgage payments (Geithner, 2015, 264). Despite much talk of 'strategic defaults' in cases where home owners had negative equity, the evidence suggests that default was mainly driven by income shocks due to a loss of employment (Farrell et al., 2017, 3–4, 17–19). Delinquency rates on mortgages and the unemployment rate had risen together sharply since 2007 (Figure 10.5). These problems were also heavily concentrated among certain groups, particularly the relatively poor, the less skilled, ethnic minorities and the relatively young – many typically Democrat voters.

The need to obtain some Republican senators' votes to overcome the filibuster hurdle required compromises that may have reduced the impact of the package, including by reducing its size (Herszenhorn and Hulse, 2009; McCarty, Poole and Rosenthal, 2013, 204). But at

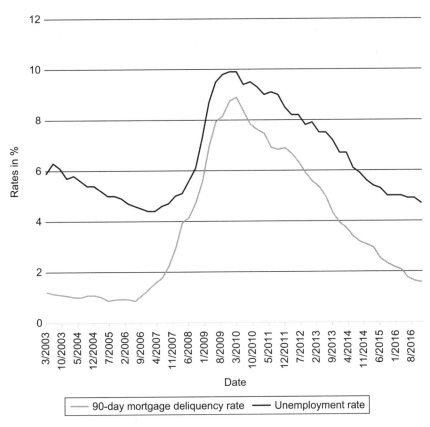

Figure 10.5: Civilian unemployment rate and ninety-day delinquency rate on residential mortgages, 2003–16 (per cent).
Source: Federal Reserve Bank of New York (2017), and US Bureau of Labor Statistics, retrieved from FRED, Federal Reserve Bank of St Louis, 13 December 2017.

$787 billion (later revised to $831 billion), the American Recovery and Reinvestment Act of February 2009 was bigger than TARP. Although it provided for new spending on infrastructure, education, health, energy, unemployment benefits and other welfare programmes, as well as tax cuts focused on families, no House Republican voted for the bill, with many citing concerns about deficits and government waste. Obama was seen as too aloof from the process, and the perception spread that he and Geithner had delegated the details of the bill to liberal congressional Democrats (Galston, 2010, 2). As with much else in this period, the package was interpreted very differently by committed partisan voters: positively by Democrats and negatively by most Republican voters.

Rising unemployment in the year after its passage only reinforced the latter view that the package was ineffective and wasteful (McCarty, Poole and Rosenthal, 2013, 39, 204).

This episode indicates the continuing relevance of institutional political constraints after the 2008 elections, especially in the Senate. In the context of high ideological polarization, this placed the Obama administration in a much more constrained position vis-à-vis Congress than that facing Roosevelt even before 1935 (McCarty, Poole and Rosenthal, 2013, 163). Even the more independent Federal Reserve had seen its unusually large interventions erode its support in Congress, requiring it to keep a wary eye on the political limits of its actions.[21]

These institutional constraints were also important in shaping the administration's mix of indirect (fiscal stimulus) and direct assistance to struggling home owners. The aggregate housing balance sheet of the household sector had already turned negative in late 2006 as the value of housing equity plunged and debt remained relatively constant. By the second half of 2009, about 25 per cent of all households had negative equity on their home.[22] As noted in Chapter 3, it was well beyond the bounds of fiscal and political plausibility to place a hard floor under the housing market. A government guarantee of the value of the household sector's real estate assets alone, given a 30 per cent fall in average values, could have cost more than double the annual federal budget (Geithner, 2015, 273, 300). The collapse of the stock market, given the rising dependence of middle-class Americans on DC retirement plans, compounded the massive loss of wealth produced by the crisis – about 44 per cent for the median household (see below).

Compared to this aggregate wealth loss, the Obama administration's measures were bound to look inadequate. The Bush administration's initiatives to encourage banks to restructure mortgages were generally seen to have been half-hearted and ineffective; a similar judgement would also ultimately be passed on Obama's. The Obama team estimated that at least eight million households were at risk of foreclosure and more were distressed, but given the Senate filibuster they

---

[21] As it was, a number of conservative Republicans and liberal Democrats viewed the Fed's interventions as unacceptable and thirty voted against confirming Ben Bernanke's second term as Fed chairman in February 2010, producing the weakest Senate endorsement ever given to a sitting chairman (Chan, 2010).

[22] In late 2012, over 20 per cent of households still had negative equity (Housing Finance Policy Center, Urban Institute, 2017b, 6, 22).

operated within a very constrained fiscal envelope. They had hoped to deploy about $50 billion of TARP money to subsidize mortgage modifications, but Geithner claimed that all the remaining TARP funds – up to $300 billion – would likely be needed for further banking sector support. They were also acutely aware of the political need to target assistance only to the demonstrably needy so as to avoid the criticism they were providing handouts to the undeserving and to those who would lose their homes in any event (Geithner, 2015, 273, 300). Nevertheless, under pressure to respond to the housing crisis, the administration announced on 18 February 2009 that it would help between seven and nine million families avoid foreclosure (US Department of the Treasury, 2009a).

The Home Affordable Modification Program (HAMP) 'tier 1', launched in March 2009, required applicants to provide evidence of default, foreclosure or imminent default on their principal home mortgage and provided successful recipients with reductions in their monthly payment-to-income ratio to a maximum of 31 per cent. The Home Affordable Refinance Program (HARP) launched at the same time was aimed at assisting home owners to refinance their mortgage at the lower rates that prevailed post-crisis. Initially, the government was reluctant to force banks to write down the value of their assets, which could have increased its bank recapitalization costs. The Principal Reduction Alternative (PRA) programme introduced in 2010 aimed to assist underwater borrowers with loan-to-market value (LTV) ratios greater than 115 per cent with principal reductions to meet an LTV target of 105 per cent. Related GSE programmes, which began in 2010, were aimed at assisting struggling borrowers ineligible for HAMP by reducing monthly payments by at least 20 per cent. HAMP modifications were granted to just over one million borrowers by end-2012, far below initial administration estimates. In its first year, 82 per cent of applicants for HAMP loan modifications were rejected, suggesting that even this limited programme disappointed many of those who hoped to benefit (Office of the Special Inspector General for the Troubled Asset Relief Program, 2009, 148). The administration was unwilling to adopt more radical measures to stem the tide of foreclosures, such as permitting bankruptcy judges to modify mortgage terms (Galston, 2010, 7). This conservatism left it overly dependent on the cooperation of lenders, who in some cases had instructed employees to maximize fee income by automatically denying most mortgage restructurings via 'robo-signings' (Dayen,

2015; Kiel, 2013). By comparison, other programmes, including private sector modifications, eventually provided assistance to another five million (Housing Finance Policy Center, Urban Institute, 2017b, 23).[23]

Not surprisingly in these circumstances, the government struggled to obtain any political benefit from these initiatives. It claimed it had provided over $200 billion in ongoing support to Fannie and Freddie to keep the mortgage market alive (Geithner, 2015, 300), but this only reinforced the perception that it had done more for large financial firms than for home owners. So did the administration's use of TARP money to inject more capital into Citigroup and AIG over February–March 2009, only to be confronted shortly thereafter by lurid headlines detailing how AIG was planning to pay $165 million in bonuses to staff in the Financial Products division that had produced its massive losses. Although the firm was legally committed to make the payments, the administration appeared powerless and complicit (Andrews and Baker, 2009; Dennis and Cho, 2009). The total intervention in the mortgage market remained small compared to the financial sector support measures. As of 30 November 2017, total disbursements under the TARP programme were $438.5 billion. Only 6.1 per cent ($27.1 billion) went to mortgage relief, compared to 55.9 per cent for the banking sector, 18.2 per cent for the automobile sector, 15.5 per cent for AIG and 4.4 per cent for credit market support (US Department of the Treasury, 2017, 5).

According to Mian and Sufi, 'The fact that Secretary Geithner and the Obama administration did not push for debt write-downs more aggressively remains the biggest policy mistake of the Great Recession' (Mian and Sufi, 2014). In the short term, HAMP failed to assist enough households to be of substantial electoral benefit, while also alienating other voters who thought the programme was undiluted socialism (McCarty, Poole and Rosenthal, 2013, 236–7).[24] In the longer term, the housing crisis likely compounded the problem of declining social and geographical mobility.[25] Underwater borrowers would find it even more

---

[23] Only payment reductions were in practice effective: a 10 per cent payment reduction reduced default rates by about 22 per cent (Farrell et al., 2017, 3–7).

[24] Bernanke confessed that he was 'perplexed that helping homeowners was not more politically popular. But Americans apparently were no more disposed to bail out their neighbours than they were to bail out Wall Street' (Bernanke, 2015, 390).

[25] On the decline of social and geographical mobility in the United States, see Chetty et al., 2014a, 2014b; Sharkey, 2013).

difficult to relocate from distressed to more buoyant communities. This likely contributed to the political backlash Obama faced early in his first term, and to subsequent political developments in the 2016 election.

The Republican Party successfully exploited these political divisions and aligned itself firmly against further government spending, citing concerns about fiscal rectitude (a stance party leaders have consistently set aside when in power in recent decades). Due to the progressivity of the US income tax, mortgage interventions would mostly have benefited households in the lower half of the income and wealth distribution, but their cost would have been borne primarily by those in the upper half. As Figure 10.6 shows, the bottom half of earners in the United States pay almost no income tax. The payment of taxes is highly skewed to the wealthy: 5 per cent of earners paid more than half of all income tax in 2008 and the top 1 per cent paid 37.5 per cent. On this issue, the interests of the majority of the middle class and the very wealthy largely aligned (Branham, Soroka and Wlezien, 2017; Enns, 2015).

The argument that government-sponsored mortgage relief was unjustified was the key impetus behind the Tea Party movement, which tapped a deep vein of distrust of government among conservative white, older middle-class voters. It began spontaneously in the immediate

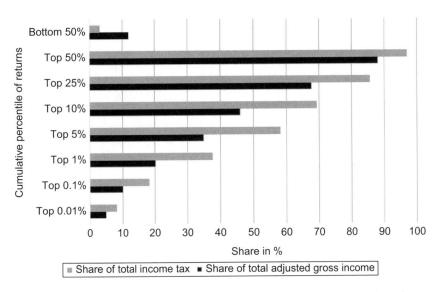

Figure 10.6: Share of adjusted gross income and total income tax by selected expanded descending cumulative percentiles of returns, 2008.
Source: Dungan (2014).

aftermath of Obama's inauguration, as a protest against what they perceived as a potentially catastrophic government bailout of 'irresponsible' and 'undeserving' home owners who had overborrowed before the crisis, though it came to focus on a broader set of concerns about immigration and welfare (Skocpol and Williamson, 2016). Tea Party members often saw the pre-crisis expansion of credit to sub-prime borrowers as an unwarranted, government-promoted transfer to 'unproductive' members of society. Now, after the crisis, 'good' government programmes such as Medicare and Social Security on which 'productive workers' deservedly drew were threatened by such redistributive transfers (Skocpol and Williamson, 2016, 80–1). Obama himself was closely associated with an elitist government that represented the interests of the undeserving, particularly illegal immigrants and the young. This standpoint reflected a strong element of generational and cultural resentment by baby boomers who viewed themselves as having contributed taxes over their working lives, only to see government programmes that benefited them threatened (Skocpol and Williamson, 2016, 66). As Figure 10.7 shows, Obama's approval ratings commenced a steady downward trend from early 2009 through most of 2010 before improving slightly in the first half of 2011. They resumed a downward trend through the end of 2011 before recovering with the economy in 2012.

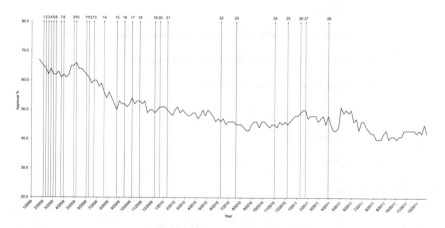

Figure 10.7: Obama's approval ratings and major policy and political events, 2009–11.
Source: Gallup (n.d.). Weekly figures, percentage responding that they approved of the way Barack Obama was handling his job as president.

Timeline:

Event	Week beginning	Event details
1	2 February 2009	Fed announces expansion of TALF up to $1 tn 10 February
2	9 February 2009	Bank stress tests announced 10 February
3	16 February 2009	Stimulus package passes Congress 17 February; Obama says admin. will prevent 7–9 million foreclosures 18 February
4	23 February 2009	Treasury says it may need additional $750 bn to stabilize financial system 26 February; agrees to increase its stake in Citicorp to 36% 27 February
5	2 March 2009	Treasury injects more equity into AIG 2 March; HAMP and HARP announced 4 March
6	9 March 2009	AIG announces bonuses to FP division 15 March; FDIC extends debt guarantee portion of TLGP 17 March
7	23 March 2009	Treasury announces public–private toxic asset programme 23 March
8	30 March 2009	Treasury extends Money Market Funds Guarantee Program 31 March
9	27 April 2009	Chrysler files bankruptcy, Treasury injects equity 30 April
10	4 May 2009	Bank stress tests results announced 7 May
11	1 June 2009	GM files bankruptcy, Treasury injects equity 1 June
12	8 June 2009	Treasury approves TARP capital repayments by 10 banks 9 June
13	22 June 2009	Fed extends all emergency liquidity support programmes 24 June
14	20 July 2009	Barofsky reports $23.7 tn in govt support of financial system 20 July
15	24 August 2009	Obama nominates Ben Bernanke for second term as Fed chairman 25 August
16	14 September 2009	Treasury ends Money Market Funds Guarantee Program 18 September
17	05 October 2009	Unemployment reaches 10 per cent 6 October

(cont'd)

Event	Week beginning	Event details
18	26 October 2009	FDIC Temporary Liquidity Guarantee Program expires 31 October
19	7 December 2009	Bank of America repays $45 bn in TARP capital 9 December
20	21 December 2009	Citicorp repays $20 bn and Wells Fargo $25 bn in TARP capital 23 December; Treasury lifts $400 bn cap on aid to Fannie & Freddie 24 December
21	11 January 2010	Financial Crisis Inquiry Commission holds first hearing 13 January
22	7 June 2010	Treasury announces TARP repayments exceed TARP disbursements for first time 11 June
23	19 July 2010	Dodd–Frank Act passes Congress 21 July
24	1 November 2010	Republicans regain control of House in mid-term elections, 2 November
25	6 December 2010	Treasury disposes of remaining Citicorp shares 7 December
26	10 January 2011	Fed Reserve Bank of NY announces end of AIG support programme & full repayment of its loans to AIG 14 January
27	24 January 2011	Financial Crisis Inquiry Commission releases final report 27 January
28	28 March 2011	Fed releases information regarding borrowers at its discount window & emergency lending facilities under section 13(3) for period 8 August 2007 to 1 March 2010 (31 March)

Do Tea Party voters share the great expectations of most American voters regarding government financial protection? On the one hand, they tend to attribute economic problems to 'big government' and 'public employees' rather than to Wall Street or the private sector in general (Cramer, 2014). On the other, they insist strongly on the protection of their own justly earned property, income and wealth. Although they commonly oppose FDR's New Deal, like most Americans they are typically strongly attached to Social Security, show ambivalence toward financial issues, and do not oppose key federal programmes such as deposit insurance.[26] As one Tea Party respondent offered, he opposed 'government meddling in the market' and 'big government folks ... [who are] taking the struggle out of normal life issues' by providing handouts to the undeserving (cited in (Skocpol and Williamson, 2016, 46). An April 2010 CBS News–*New York Times* poll revealed that Tea Party supporters were distrusting of government intervention and opposed to its expansion and redistribution to the poor, but confident in the Federal Reserve's ability to promote financial stability (*New York Times*, 2010). This older, middle-class white demographic – like that in Britain – is generally much less leveraged and their accumulated wealth is less vulnerable to income shocks than younger and minority groups. Above all, they feared that Obama would raise public spending on others by taxing 'people like themselves' (Skocpol and Williamson, 2016, 30–2).

Thus, it is not clear that a substantial 'rebalancing' of government intervention away from banks towards struggling home owners was politically achievable. This would have been supported most strongly by lower-income households but adamantly opposed by most Republican voters and significant numbers of wealthier Democrats. This was arguably a case in which the dominant preferences of the wealthy and the middle classes jointly helped to block a policy that would have favoured mainly the relatively poor who had been most negatively affected by the crisis (Branham, Soroka and Wlezien, 2017).

The Obama administration had more success on financial regulatory reform – an area in which voters were less polarized and which a majority appeared to support. Mitch McConnell, the Senate Republican leader, indicated to Geithner in January 2010 that financial regulatory reform was the only issue on which they were willing to cooperate with the administration, because voters supported it (Geithner, 2015, 398). The House Financial Services Committee, chaired by Barney Frank, and the Senate Finance Committee, chaired by Christopher Dodd, had begun work in 2009 on providing new regulation, supervision and resolution tools for large financial conglomerates. Treasury also provided a white paper setting out the administration's proposals in these areas and on a new consumer protection agency (US Department of the Treasury,

---

[26] On the entrenched, widespread public support for Social Security in the United States, see Jacobs (2010).

2009b). The proposals included a new Treasury-based national bank regulator and adding the requirement to the Federal Reserve's Section 13 (3) emergency lending authority that the Fed should first obtain the permission of the Treasury Secretary (US Department of the Treasury, 2009b, 78). These proposals, opposed by the FDIC, did not survive subsequent negotiations with Congress (Bair, 2012, 182–99, 213–29).

Once again, the House bill received no Republican votes despite McConnell's earlier signal. In fact, it seems that a majority of Republican voters never strongly supported tighter financial regulation even though most blamed Wall Street for the crisis (Jordan, 2015). In late April 2010, Senate Republicans agreed to allow debate on the proposed bill after having blocked it for three days – seemingly because they calculated that continuing to do so had political costs (Herszenhorn and Wyatt, 2010). As with the stimulus package, each of the three Republican senators who eventually voted for the bill extracted substantial concessions, including the elimination of authority to spend the remaining $225 billion of TARP money (Geithner, 2015, 418–29).

The Dodd–Frank Act, formally the Wall Street Reform and Consumer Protection Act of 21 July 2010, was nevertheless the most extensive set of regulatory reforms since the Great Depression era. Importantly, although the Fed's Section 13(3) authority remains, the Act prohibits lending to specific firms and requires any emergency facilities to have 'broad-based eligibility' (Board of Governors of the Federal Reserve System, 2015). It also prevents the Treasury from using the Exchange Stabilization Fund to guarantee money markets. The FDIC must now obtain congressional approval to make broad debt guarantees (Swagel, 2015, 120). At the same time, it creates other new authorities, including a non-bank resolution authority that can use taxpayer funds to prevent a collapse, with provisions to ensure losses for investors (Title II). In principle, these new rules are intended to signal that 'too big to fail' will no longer be tolerated and that insolvent financial conglomerates will be resolved rather than rescued. In practice, many doubt their credibility (Acharya, Anginer and Warburton, 2016).[27]

---

[27] As the Office of Financial Research stated in 2016, the 'living wills' Dodd–Frank required of large financial conglomerates to demonstrate their ability to be wound up in bankruptcy were 'still weak' and in almost all cases 'not credible' (US Office of Financial Research, 2016, 71). Regulators in 2017 judged that things had improved but significant shortcomings remained for some major banks (Board of Governors of the Federal Reserve System and Federal Deposit Insurance Corporation, 2017).

Nor did the Act achieve much simplification of the complex financial regulatory and supervisory framework. Dodd–Frank established a new inter-agency Financial Stability Oversight Council (FSOC) to oversee the largest financial institutions and systemic risk, an Office of Financial Research to support FSOC, a new Bureau of Consumer Financial Protection within the Federal Reserve, an Office of National Insurance within the Treasury, an Office of Credit Rating Agencies within the SEC, and the Federal Housing Finance Agency (FHFA). The OTS was eliminated and the Fed was given responsibility for supervising thrift holding companies and subsidiaries, the OCC federal thrifts and the FDIC state thrifts. The SEC was required to regulate all investment advisors with funds over $100 billion, including hedge funds.

Dodd–Frank required the agencies to provide higher risk-based capital requirements for banks, particularly equity capital, as well as new liquidity requirements and resolution plans ('living wills') for financial conglomerates. However, it delegated much of the detail of regulatory tightening to the Fed and its negotiations with its international counterparts in the Basel Committee and Financial Stability Board (Bair, 2012, 257–72). Although substantial regulatory tightening in these areas was eventually agreed, it did not satisfy many who called for far higher equity requirements for major banks (Admati and Hellwig, 2013; Hoenig, 2013). The Act contained a swathe of new securities regulation, including credit risk retention for ABS securitizers (at least 5 per cent of issues), more detailed disclosure of securities exposures, regulation and oversight of the derivatives market, mandatory clearing of most swaps on an exchange and capital and margin requirements for swap dealers. Credit rating agencies were subject to new requirements, including separating their rating activities from other businesses and SEC oversight. Shareholders were also given more influence on executive compensation and firms were required to adopt procedures to claw back pay in the event of accounting restatements. The 'Volcker rule', one of the most controversial parts of the bill, was intended to constrain most proprietary trading by banks and restricted them from owning, sponsoring or investing in hedge funds or private equity funds. Summers and Geithner were sceptical of its value but Obama was attracted to its politics (Geithner, 2015, 404). As we discuss below, however, it is difficult to detect any lasting political benefit.

10.3 Political Consequences of the Crisis

In contrast to the British case in the same period, the US case exhibits even greater delay, deeper political polarization and greater contestation over the purposes and impact of the policy interventions. The higher level of institutional vetoes accessible to political opponents in the US helps to explain extended legislative delays in crucial areas. We discuss why this, as well as widely perceived distributive inequities of the interventions, produced a voter backlash first in the George W. Bush era and subsequently in that of Obama.

High political polarization was one important reason why even when interventions had their intended effect (notably, preventing another Great Depression), many voters were still inclined to view them negatively. Political opponents in Congress were consistently able to frame these interventions as ineffective and unfair – something we also see in the British case. Opinion polls reveal that the level of public support for aiding troubled banks and financial institutions declined in the months and years following the height of the crisis (BBC Press Office, 2010; McCarty, Poole and Rosenthal, 2013, 234–6). As Bermeo and Bartels conclude, '[H]aving experienced varying doses of these policies, and seeing no dramatic improvement in tangible economic conditions as a result, most citizens were in no mood for counterfactual arguments that, as one US study [(Blinder and Zandi, 2010, 10)] put it, "the comprehensive policy responses saved the economy from another depression"' (Bartels and Bermeo, 2014, 17). Indeed, by April 2010, a CBS News–New York Times poll found that 51 per cent of respondents – and 74 per cent of Tea Party supporters – believed that the economy would have improved on its own without the bailouts (New York Times, 2010).

The deep unpopularity of the Iraq War and George W. Bush's exceptionally low approval ratings weighed heavily on the Republican Party and the administration.[28] By 2008, the economic downturn associated with the developing financial crisis had become the most salient national problem for voters and the crisis had eliminated what little remained of Bush's reputation for policy competence (Jacobson, 2010, 210). Bush's approval ratings lingered at about 30 per cent and showed no strong overall upward trend in the final months except among

[28] Obama's opposition to the war had helped him gain the Democratic nomination and hurt the Republican presidential candidate, John McCain, who had supported the war.

Republican voters (Gallup, n.d.). Unlike in the British case, there was no substantive temporary 'bump' in political approval for the administration after the interventions over July–October 2008. Efforts by the administration to justify the interventions on the grounds that had it not done so everyone would have been far worse off fell flat, as did half-hearted attempts to shift blame to foreigners via Bernanke's argument that the Asian 'savings glut' was one cause of America's crisis (Bush, 2011, 448). TARP was consistently unpopular with most voters, including when the Obama administration subsequently sought to use it to assist industry and distressed households.

This suggests that voters associated the crisis, which peaked in September–October, with Republican policies from which John McCain was unable to distance himself in the lead-up to the November 2008 elections. Voters were also unwilling to reward the incumbent party for the interventions that it had proposed. The congressional Republicans were also in difficulty, having neither consistently opposed the administration's policy proposals nor ensured their smooth legislative approval. The Democrats had been a crucial source of support for HERA and TARP. Congressional approval ratings continued to deteriorate over 2007–8 and were even lower than those of the president.

Although Obama's 2008 victory over McCain was not unusual in that it followed a very unpopular two-term Republican presidency and a deteriorating economy, most agree that the dramatic worsening of the crisis in September 2008 benefited the Democrats (Bartels, 2013; Hill, Herron and Lewis, 2010; Jacobson, 2010; Saad, Jones and Newport, 2008). In fact, Antoniades and Calomiris suggest the sharp contraction of mortgage credit in the lead-up to the election may have been decisive in swinging voters away from the incumbent party – and much more important than increasing unemployment (Antoniades and Calomiris, 2018). The financial crisis was therefore probably important both in terms of its negative impact on wealth and because the drama of September reinforced voter perception of the incompetence of the incumbent Republicans. Obama opened up a substantial lead over McCain in the final month of the campaign (Jacobson, 2010, 216; RealClearPolitics, n.d.; Saad, Jones and Newport, 2008). As Bartels points out, however, Obama's victory margin of 7.2 per cent was far from a landslide, let alone comparable to FDR's election victories in the 1930s – perhaps because the policy interventions undertaken by the Bush administration and the Fed had prevented another Great

Depression (Bartels, 2013, 53). The Democrats gained 21 seats in the House to reach 257 seats to the Republicans' 178; in the Senate, Democrats won 8 seats to control 57 seats to the Republicans' 41.

Despite the extensive interventions, unemployment was 6.8 per cent by November 2008 – not yet unusually high for a recession and, as noted above, probably not politically decisive. Far more dramatic were the negative wealth effects of the crisis, almost certainly worsened by the delays in the policy responses discussed above. In a Pew survey in early 2009, 36 per cent of respondents aged 30–49 believed their investment losses exceeded 20 per cent; the figure for those aged 50–64 was 43 per cent. Three-quarters of the latter group reported that they believed the crisis had made it difficult for them to afford retirement (Morin and Taylor, 2009). Over the longer period from 2007 to 2010 between Fed household surveys, estimated median real household wealth fell precipitously by 44 per cent to its lowest level since 1969. The percentage of households with zero or negative net worth increased from 18.7 to 21.8 per cent over the same period, a level greater than in 1962. '[T]he Great Recession hit and like a tsunami wiped out 40 years of wealth gains' (Wolff, 2017b, 36).

Wealth losses of this magnitude in a context of great expectations were politically catastrophic. Consistent with the findings of Antoniades and Calomiris cited above, Hill, Herron and Lewis find in their county-level analysis of the 2008 presidential vote that the swing to Obama (compared to John Kerry's vote share in 2004) was not significantly boosted by higher unemployment rates, but that it was higher in counties with higher mortgage delinquency rates and average per capita wages over $15,000 (Hill, Herron and Lewis, 2010, 51–3). They interpret this as suggesting that the housing crisis had the greatest political impact among middle-class households. They also find that the swing to Obama was higher in counties with higher stock dividends per capita, also consistent with our theory that wealth losses would be of particular concern to middle- and upper-income households in the initial aftermath of the crisis.

As in Britain around the same time, voters had complex reactions to the Bush interventions. They expected the government to intervene to protect their wealth and incomes and reacted badly when they experienced losses. At the same time, most disliked the means by which the government intervened. As we discussed in Chapter 3, middle-class wealth had become increasingly concentrated in housing and portfolio financial assets, especially pensions in the years leading up to the crisis. This was particularly true in the US case for sub-prime borrowers who purchased houses on highly leveraged terms and who were most vulnerable to house price falls and falling labour income. In many cases, the net wealth of these households completely evaporated; their access to credit has also been substantially curtailed since 2008 (Housing Finance Policy Center, Urban Institute, 2017b, 17). Democratic voters often perceived these relative losses as evidence that the Obama administration was beholden to Wall Street, while Republican and centrist voters more often blamed the Obama administration for its modest attempts to support lower-income households.

A majority of Americans also believed that the crisis and associated policy interventions had worsened inequality. A 2009 BBC World Service poll found that 54 per cent of Americans believed that the benefits and burdens of recent economic developments had been distributed unfairly; a follow-up poll in 2012 found this figure had increased to 65 per cent (BBC World Service, 2012). Similarly, a Pew Research Center poll in 2013 found that 66 per cent of Americans surveyed agreed that 'the gap between rich and poor had increased in recent years', 25 per cent thought it had stayed the same and only 5 per cent thought it had decreased. Moreover, 61 per cent of respondents thought that the economic system 'favors the wealthy', compared to 35 per cent who thought it was 'fair to most' (Pew Research Center, 2013, 21–2). These perceptions were probably reinforced by the extensive media coverage of the bailouts and of continuing high levels of executive compensation (Figure 10.8). Measured wealth inequality also increased significantly in the post-crisis period (Bricker et al., 2017, 1–2). The wealth Gini coefficient increased from 0.834 to 0.866 over 2007–10 and the share of the top quintile rose by 3.6 percentage points; after 2010, wealth inequality continued to increase, though at a lower rate (Wolff, 2017b, 10). In contrast, income inequality initially fell over 2007–10, with the income Gini falling from 0.574 to 0.549 and the income share of the top 1 per cent fell from 21.3 to 17.2 per cent over the same period. After 2010, income inequality began once again to increase sharply, with the Gini reaching its pre-crisis level by 2012 and the share of the top 1 per cent rising to 19.8 per cent (Wolff, 2017b, 12).

With highly leveraged housing assets dominating the wealth portfolios of the middle class, falling house prices were especially

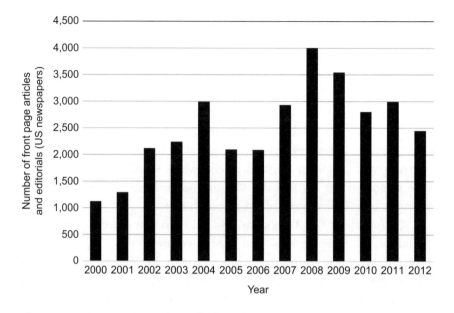

Figure 10.8: Front page articles and editorials on inequality and executive compensation, US newspapers, 2000–12.
Source: US Newspapers, ProQuest. Search term: 'inequality AND bonus* OR executive pay', front page/cover stories and editorials, annual counts.

important drivers of wealth losses for households below the top quintile. The impact of the housing crisis on most households was also indicated by the sharp fall in levels of house ownership. The average home ownership rate fell from 69.1 per cent at its peak in 2004 to 63.7 per cent by 2016. Falling home ownership actually hit the middle classes hardest: for the middle three quintiles it fell by over 10 percentage points, from 78.2 to 67 per cent (Bricker et al., 2017, 1–2; Wolff, 2017b, 51).[29] The impact of the destruction of wealth fell especially hard on younger households, which tend to have purchased houses relatively recently, have lower pension wealth, be highly leveraged and relatively dependent upon labour income. Over 2007–10, the net housing wealth of households with heads under thirty-five fell by 53 per cent and their total real wealth by nearly half (Wolff, 2017b, 30–1).

As these figures indicate, the wealth destruction and rising inequality associated with the Great Recession likely had a political

---

[29] The payments burden of indebted households who retained their home eased somewhat due to the fall in interest rates and as borrowers paid down debt.

impact that extended well beyond the elections of November 2008. As soon as Obama took office, his administration was beset by the growing public distaste for the bailouts and by the partisan framing of his new policy proposals. By mid-2009, public anger about the crisis and associated bailouts had become latent. There were few public protests, but news of the payments of bonuses to AIG financial products division employees focused attention on the misuse of government funds, disappointed Democratic voters and reinforced the beliefs of Republican voters (McCarty, Poole and Rosenthal, 2013, 130–1). As these authors point out, the continued deterioration of the economy in 2009 also led many centrist voters to accept the Republican narrative that the stimulus package had damaged rather than helped the economy, short-circuiting the administration's plan to introduce further fiscal stimulus (McCarty, Poole and Rosenthal, 2013, 204). As noted earlier, the administration's assistance to the automobile industry and to struggling and poorer households was often viewed by these voters in particularly negative terms.

All of the administration's crisis-related interventions, with the exception of financial regulatory reform, tended to be viewed negatively by most voters by 2010. In a September 2010 Gallup poll, 61 per cent of respondents expressed disapproval of government assistance to financial institutions, 56 per cent of the auto assistance programme, and 52 per cent of the stimulus (by contrast, 61 per cent approved of tighter financial regulation) (Saad, 2010). As Mann noted:

> The well-documented successes of the financial stabilization and stimulus initiatives are invisible to a public reacting to the here and now, not to the counterfactual of how much worse it might have been. The painfully slow recovery from the global financial crisis and Great Recession have led most Americans to believe these programs have failed and as a consequence they judge the president and Congress harshly. (Mann, 2010, 21)

Furthermore, most voters believed that the interventions had benefited Wall Street more than middle America: 'TARP may have succeeded as policy, but it certainly failed as politics' (Jacobson, 2011, 43).

At the same time, public deficits and debt levels reached new peaks. Austerity was less extensive than in Europe at the time, including in the UK after May 2010, but social transfers were relatively limited in the United States and the labour market remained depressed.

Unemployment peaked at nearly 10 per cent and the number of long-term unemployed remained higher than at any time since the 1930s.

Even Dodd–Frank provided little political benefit to the Obama administration (Jacobson, 2011, 47–8). Although a majority of voters in 2009 thought 'more regulation' of financial markets was needed, by 2010 such support was eroding, though only 20–25 per cent of voters favoured 'less regulation' (Jordan, 2015). Support for more regulation continued to decline in the years after this. Republican voters seem increasingly to have accepted the view of their representatives that the bill reflected ideological overreach by Democrats. A 2013 Pew poll found that about two-thirds of Republican voters (and about 80 per cent of Tea Party partisans) believed that the government had 'gone too far … in regulating financial institutions and markets'; about the same percentage of Democratic voters thought it had not gone far enough (Drake, 2013). To the extent that Republican voter support for tighter financial regulation had ever been strong it quickly evaporated, and congressional Republicans shifted to a strategy of repealing significant components of Dodd–Frank.

The electoral backlash began with some early election victories by the Tea Party movement (e.g. that of Scott Brown in the special Senate election of January 2010 in Massachusetts). It continued with the Republican victory in the 2010 mid-term congressional elections in the House of Representatives. To the extent that the Bush and Obama administrations' interventions prevented an even worse downturn they may have helped to forestall an even greater Democratic loss (Bartels, 2013, 54–5). Yet the size of the defeat was unusual, with the swing against the Democrats in the House over 8 per cent. Democratic losses were especially high in the South and Midwest, where more conservative voters had reacted badly to what they viewed as two years of ideological overreach by liberal Democratic partisans. Tea Party Republicans showed particular hostility towards Obama and were highly mobilized during the campaign (Jacobson, 2011). Seventeen new Republican members were affiliated with the Tea Party and combined with another forty-three who were returned formed the Tea Party Caucus. Overall, Republicans gained sixty-three House seats to achieve a clear majority; they gained six Senate seats to hold forty-seven in total, to the Democrats' fifty-one. The Republican Party moved significantly further to the right and undercut the Obama administration's legislative agenda. Republican opposition to redistribution to younger and poorer

Americans, whether in the form of mortgage relief to struggling house-holds or in the form of the Affordable Care Act – seen as a real threat to Tea Partiers' existing Medicare benefits – was now even more deeply entrenched. The remainder of Obama's presidency was spent defending the domestic legislative achievements of its first two years; rebalancing the post-crisis bailout was politically unachievable.

Exit polls taken during the election reveal that the result likely arose from both adverse economic conditions and from negative voter perceptions of the policies and priorities of the Obama administration (Bartels, 2014, 213). Analyses of the direct electoral impact of major roll-call votes suggest that the government's response to the crisis was particularly salient for voters, though there is some disagreement about which specific measures exerted the largest impact. Silver finds voters punished Democrat incumbents harshly for supporting TARP, while McGhee emphasizes the political costs for Democrats of supporting the stimulus package (McGhee, 2010; Silver, 2010). Both analyses suggest that Democratic performance in the 2010 election was likely partly attributable to policy measures related to the crisis, even though the bailouts were initiated under the Bush administration. It is also worth noting that Democrats who supported TARP in the first House roll-call vote (29 September 2008) experienced a smaller increase in vote share between 2006 and 2008 than their fellow Democrats who opposed it (Green and Hudak, 2009).

It could be said that the administration was a victim of the simple fact that economic downturns after systemic financial crises tend to be unusually deep and long in duration. But as we saw in the previous chapter, its fate was quite different to that of the Democrats after 1932, when the economy took much longer to recover. The much more extensive financialization of the economy by the 2000s and the different wealth effects of the crisis and associated interventions likely played an important part in the rapid political reversal experienced by the Demo-crats after 2008. Obama and his senior officials also bear part of the blame. Geithner was singularly ineffective in the politics of delivering and selling Treasury policies, although in his defence Obama apparently told him to devise the best policies and to 'leave the politics to me' (Geithner, 2015, 7). Obama himself was far less effective in this task than his own belief in his rhetorical skills had led him to assume. He failed when in office to pursue the post-partisan political agenda he had advocated during his campaign (Galston, 2010). Although by 2012 a recovering economy enabled him to win a second term, Republican opposition in Congress ensured that he could do little to build on the legislative achievements of his first two years (Bartels, 2013, 63–7).

10.4 Conclusion

The policy response to the 2007–9 crisis in the United States, both from government and from independent agencies such as the Federal Reserve, is consistent with our argument that there are growing pressures on modern governments from below to protect people's wealth and living standards. The Bush administration, despite its ideological aversion to government intervention, eventually undertook the most extensive financial sector rescue in American history. Bush himself was 'furious the situation had reached this point [and] would have been happy to let [the banks fail]'. He accepted the advice of Bernanke and Paulson, however, that 'as unfair as it was to use the American people's money to prevent a collapse for which they weren't responsible, it would be even more unfair to do nothing and leave them to suffer the consequences … If we're really looking at another Great Depression [Bush told his staff], you can be damn sure I'm going to be Roosevelt, not Hoover' (Bush, 2011, 440). This homely summary indicates how much had changed in the politics of finance over the course of eight decades.

Even then, the administration's Republican colleagues in Congress were very reluctant to provide it with a blank cheque, with the notable exception of support to the GSEs in July 2008. Opposition within the Republican Party and in Congress more generally produced substantial delays in the policy response, though eventually this opposition was overcome when a 1933-style financial meltdown appeared imminent.

Our analysis therefore supports the conclusion of Bermeo and Pontusson that political polarization and supermajoritarian features of the US political system 'profoundly shaped (and hampered)' the policy response to the crisis (Bermeo and Pontusson, 2012, 15). More generally, rising political polarization since the 1980s in combination with supermajoritarian institutions such as the Senate filibuster had made the US political system unusually resistant to policy innovation (Hetherington and Rudolph, 2015; McCarty, Poole and Rosenthal, 2015). It is impossible to know whether the crisis as it developed in 2008 would have been less severe had policy intervention been timelier, though experience elsewhere suggests that speedy crisis interventions tend to produce stronger macroeconomic performance and lower long-run costs (International Monetary Fund, 2014). In the United States, partisan gridlock in Congress likely increased the fragility of the system and the extent and cost of the eventual interventions of September–October 2008. In this respect, the story of the crisis interventions has parallels with the delayed response to the S&L crisis in the 1980s. As we argued, the policy interventions that were eventually implemented also appeared ineffective, selective and highly redistributive to many voters – though often in different ways, depending upon partisan frames. The Bush administration and the Republican Party more generally were unable to gain much electoral benefit from these interventions in the November 2008 elections, when the Democratic Party was swept to power.

But the political benefit for the Democrats proved short-lived. The interventions did not prevent extensive wealth and income losses among middle-class and poorer households. The value of pension assets fell sharply, as did the leveraged housing assets that dominated the wealth portfolios of families below the top 10 per cent. The Obama administration soon also became tainted like its predecessor by being seen as embracing the bailout of the financial sector. Many of its own voters were disappointed by its apparent failure to adopt more redistributive policies, while Republican voters were repelled by what they often perceived as radical policies aimed at assisting unionized firms and undeserving householders who had overborrowed in the pre-crisis years. Congressional Republicans built on this voter opposition and used the Senate filibuster process to constrain the new administration's macroeconomic, housing and regulatory reform agenda. This strategy proved successful when Republicans, fuelled by a rising anti-government grass-roots movement, regained control of the House in November 2010. Although Obama won re-election in 2012, by comparison with the political dominance achieved by FDR by 1936, his administration's legacy of financial and welfare reforms was far less secure. As we note in the concluding chapter, this would become particularly apparent by 2016.

11 BANKING CRISES IN BRAZIL IN AN ERA OF LOW EXPECTATIONS

In this and the following chapter we explore the political and policy aftermaths of crises in Brazil. In the late nineteenth century Brazil developed a relatively large, advanced and integrated financial system by the standards of emerging market economies. In the span of a little more than a decade, at a time when quasi-democratic institutions were being introduced and consolidated, the country experienced three systemic banking crises of varying intensity. We show that these crises had considerably different policy and political consequences than those of the 1990s that we explore in the following chapter.

Financialization during this earlier period of Brazilian history was rather limited and wealth was highly concentrated in the hands of land-owning agrarian elites (Bértola and Ocampo, 2012, 119–23). As in the United Kingdom at the time, the government had made no prior commitment to prevent crises via regulation. The limited group of voters, as well as the large number of disenfranchised citizens, had low expectations regarding government responsibility to protect them from financial instability. A succession of governments acted in accordance with these expectations in implementing largely market-conforming policies – as did their British and American counterparts around this time. Measured from the height of the boom, over the course of the events surveyed in this chapter the result of these policies led to the closure of roughly 40 per cent of domestic banks and the loss of nearly 85 per cent of their market capitalization.[1]

---

[1] Data is from Calomiris and Haber (2014, 426).

Voters were far from passive during this period. They reacted negatively to inflation, currency depreciation, and instances of fraud and corruption over the course of the preceding credit boom. But we show that, despite the severity of downturns that followed these crises, the policies adopted in their aftermath were largely unchallenged and had little effect on the ruling party's hold on office. Notwithstanding the constrained nature of Brazil's democracy (which we discuss below), the degree of voter support that the ruling party and its policies were able to command during this period stands in contrast to that which we examine in the next chapter.

We begin by identifying the systemic banking crises – 1890–2, 1897–8, 1900–1, 1990–3 and 1994–8 – that feature in this chapter and the next. We then explore Brazil's political-institutional landscape during the early part of the period known as the Old Republic (1889–1930). We stress the constrained nature of Brazil's democracy during this period, but also highlight the mechanisms that offered elites opportunities to compete for political power, thereby exposing governments to accountability and legitimacy imperatives when responding to crises.

Indeed, we discuss how the first president of Brazil was removed from office precisely because of his attempt to implement policies that went against the dominant market-conforming policy preferences of influential agrarian elites. On regaining power, these agrarian elites responded to crises with policies that largely aligned with the Bagehot model. In an era of low expectations, their hold on office was uninterrupted and, equally important, their crisis policy measures were largely unopposed.

11.1   Banking Crises in Brazil since 1890

Brazil was subjected to repeated bouts of financial instability almost from the beginning of the Old Republic (1889–1930). According to Reinhart and Rogoff, there were three systemic banking crises in its first decade (Figure 11.1). The origin of these crises (1890–2, 1897–8 and 1900–1) can be traced to an extraordinary credit and asset boom from 1888 to 1891 called the *Encilhamento*, a term literally meaning 'saddling up' and intended to capture the similarities between last-minute bets placed at the Jockey Club of Rio de Janeiro and the speculative frenzy that pervaded the financial system at the time. This frenzy was so fierce that there was a shortage of names for new companies (Bordo and Eichengreen, 1999, 52). After the bubble burst, banks continued to fail

Figure 11.1: Brazil: systemic and non-systemic banking crises, 1870–2010.
Sources: Laeven and Valencia (2013); Reinhart (2010); Reinhart and Rogoff (2009). Crisis years indicate any years in which crises are mentioned in these sources. Darker bars indicate crises designated as systemic by any of these sources. As noted in the text, there is some inconsistency over the systemic status of the 1990–3 crisis in the sources.

throughout the 1890s under the weight of unrecoverable loans made during the boom years. Ongoing financial fragility culminated in a deep crisis in 1900, which Hanley (2005, 172) describes as a 'great bank panic' and Fritsch (1988, 8) labels 'one of the severest in Brazilian economic history'.

As Figure 11.2 shows, recessions followed the 1890–2 and 1900–1 crises, with the sharpest output decline experienced following the initial collapse of the *Encilhamento*. Banking failures were widespread over this period. In 1891, there were sixty-eight banks listed on the Rio de Janeiro stock exchange. By 1906, there were only ten; their declared capital was only one-ninth of their 1891 value and their cash reserves were only half of the 1891 level (Neuhaus, 1974, 11). Triner's study of banking during the Old Republic describes a 'generalized collapse of banking' and 'generalized failure among banks' (Triner, 2000, 45, 47).

Like earlier crises in the United States (see Chapter 9), those that followed the *Encilhamento* occurred prior to the establishment of a central bank in Brazil (which occurred in 1964). Pressure for policy intervention before this was thus focused on the Treasury and to some extent various commercial banks that acted as Treasury agents. Like the 1907 crisis in the United States, the crises of this period generated some political momentum for creating a central bank, though this step was only taken decades in the future. Taken together, this series of crises, due to both their intensity and impact, stand out as the defining period of financial instability in pre-World War II Brazil and thus form the focus of this chapter.[2]

---

[2] On the centrality of these crises in Brazil's financial history, see Bordo and Eichengreen (1999, 52–4); Calomiris and Haber (2014, 415–27); Hanley (2005, 90–3, 172–8); Musacchio (2009, 42–4); Schulz (2008); Topik (1987, 25–40); Triner (2000, 44–9, 69–74).

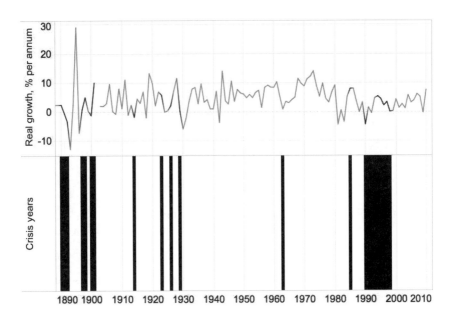

Figure 11.2: Brazil: real GDP growth (annual percentage change) with banking crisis years, 1890–2010.
Source: Growth data are from Mauro et al. (2013). Crisis years indicate any years in which crises are mentioned in Laeven and Valencia (2013); Reinhart (2010); Reinhart and Rogoff (2009).

In the next chapter, we explore two crises – one beginning in 1990, the other in 1994 – that followed the passage of a new democratic constitution in 1988, replacing legislation that had been in place under the military dictatorship that had ruled Brazil from 1964 to 1985. By the time of the onset of these crises, Brazil had regained its democratic status according to Boix, Miller and Rosato (2013), with Polity scoring the regime at 8 in terms of its degree of democracy. The crisis literature offers conflicting views of the severity of these crises. Reinhart and Rogoff identify the 1990 crisis as systemic and the 1994 crisis as borderline (Reinhart, 2010). By contrast, Laeven and Valencia identify both crises as systemic in one study (2008) but then in a later study (2013) code the 1994 crisis as systemic and the 1990 crisis as borderline. Whereas during the 1994 crisis numerous bank restructurings and closures occurred as part of the government's response, during the 1990 crisis continuing high inflation and the government's introduction of a deposit freeze prevented widespread banking failures. Figure 11.2 indicates the economy declined severely following the 1990 crisis but

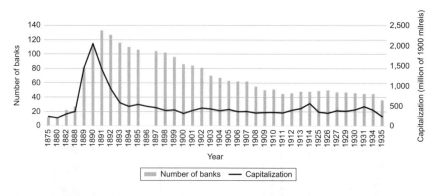

Figure 11.3: Size of the Brazilian banking system, 1875–1935.
Source: Calomiris and Haber (2014, 426). Capitalization is measured here as estimated nominal paid-in capital.

failed to experience a recession after the 1994 crisis, though as we noted in Chapters 7 and 9, this could be due to differences in policy intervention.

Our analysis in the next chapter considers both crises, in part to rule out any uncertainty as to the systemic nature of either. In addition, as the two crises prompted contrasting policy interventions – the former closer to the Bagehot model and the latter closer to the bailout model – they provide an interesting setting to explore our core arguments in an emerging market characterized by both comparatively high inequality and rising societal wealth.

11.2 The Political and Institutional Environment of the Old Republic, 1889–1930

In September 1822, Brazil gained independence from Portugal, keeping the administrative structure established by its colonial power. The country's first constitution, enacted in 1824, created a parliamentary monarchy where the emperor, as head of state, enjoyed considerable prerogatives, which he repeatedly employed, including the right to dissolve parliament and to select the prime minister. Political parties competed in elections decided by a narrow electorate, but the power of the emperor significantly reduced the importance of regularly held parliamentary elections (Love, 1970, 5–7).

A military coup, led by Marshal Deodoro da Fonseca, toppled the monarchy in 1889. Deodoro thereafter ruled by decree as head of an

interim military government until the adoption of a new republican constitution in 1891. The constitution, which ushered in the Old Republic,
democratized the formal political process by increasing the number of
elected offices at all levels of government, broadening suffrage, and decen-
tralizing political authority. Although the republican era thus opened up
the political process to greater contestation and participation, the new
government that emerged was far from fully democratic and is not
designated as such in the Boix–Miller–Rosato (2013) dataset. The Polity
IV score for Brazil during the Old Republic is −3, which makes it
slightly less democratic than Britain prior to the 1832 Reform Act
(see Chapter 7). On some measures, however, such as the openness of
executive recruitment and competitiveness of participation, Polity suggests the Old Republic may have been more democratic than Britain
before 1832 (Marshall, Gurr and Jaggers, 2017).

Many factors constrained Brazil's emergent democracy. Until
the presidential election of 1894, changes in the chief executive occurred
through actual or threatened forceful seizures of power and the president faced few constraints on the exercise of authority. As discussed
below, Deodoro secured victory in the first republican presidential
election in 1891 via the threat of military intervention, then later, when
Congress attempted to constrain his authority, undertook a coup before
himself being ousted from office. Both Deodoro and his successor, also a
military officer, often ruled by decree, with Polity suggesting both
presidents enjoyed unlimited authority.

Beginning with the 1894 presidential elections, Brazil moved to
a system where elections were largely decided by informal competition
among an elite, and where the president faced moderate limits on executive authority. Before elections, the political elite would reach agreement
on their preferred presidential candidate in a process that, though constrained, was at times contentious (Cable, 1976). The governing elite's
designated candidate then typically secured victory either through the
absence of an organized opposition candidate, as in 1894, or via intra-
elite arrangements and patron–client relationships that provided the
designated candidate with sufficient electoral support to defeat the opposition candidate.

The provisions of the 1891 constitution facilitated these
intra-elite arrangements and patron–client relationships. It created a
presidential system alongside a federal structure that gave extensive
fiscal powers to the states, allowed them to raise foreign loans and to

organize armed militias without federal interference, and made state representation in the federal lower house of Congress proportional to population.[3] The nature of the electoral system, and Brazil's regionally uneven demographic and income distribution, had the effect of concentrating political power in a limited group of wealthier and more populous states.

This created a threefold classification among states in terms of political influence: first, the dominant wealthier and populous states, São Paulo and Minas Gerais; second, the intermediary states Bahia, Rio Grande do Sul, Rio de Janeiro and Pernambuco; and third, the remaining fourteen poorer and less populated minor states. Separately, the federal capital, which at the time was the city of Rio de Janeiro, ranked near the upper end of the second group of states. Nearly two-thirds of Brazil's population in 1890 were concentrated in the six major states. The most powerful state delegation in the lower house was from Minas Gerais, consisting of thirty-seven deputies, followed by São Paulo and Bahia, each with twenty-two deputies. At the bottom end of the distribution were nine smaller states with the minimum representation allowed, but which together had fewer deputies than Minas Gerais. It was thus a common complaint that the five most populous states together constituted a majority in Congress.

Within this federal structure the national government came under the control of state-based political parties representing agrarian oligarchies of the most powerful states. After the election of the second civilian president in 1898, a style of rule became institutionalized known as the 'politics of the governors' – an arrangement between state-level political parties and the president in which the former assured the latter that they would win elections in their respective jurisdictions in exchange for support of the president's policies in Congress and electoral support of the president's successor. However, as discussed below, this did not prevent rival parties or factions, often from the intermediate states which nurtured ambitions to have greater influence and representation, from opposing the president and contesting elections.

---

[3] Fiscal decentralization gave a considerable share of tax receipts to state and local governments, with one estimate indicating both levels each received roughly one-fifth of all revenues (Love, 1970, 8).

Below the state governors and their party committees stood the *coronéis* (colonels or local bosses). These local bosses, particularly in the more developed states of São Paulo, Minas Gerais and Rio Grande do Sul, were generally dependent on the influence of the state's oligarchies in government for obtaining favours, including land, loans, public employment and public works projects, that provided the basis of their power over their local region. In some states of the north and north-east, a powerful family would exercise control at all levels, minimizing the distinction between local bosses and the state oligarchy. Yet, in other states in the same region, '*coronéis* of the interior' emerged with considerable autonomy from the state oligarchy and party (Fausto, 1989, 269). The colonels, usually owners of large agricultural estates themselves, largely monopolized political and economic power in their district via patron–client relationships with the rural population.

The rules governing elections under the Republic enabled the colonels to wield significant political power. The president was to be elected by direct popular ballot with the right to vote extended to all literate males above the age of twenty-one. While this represented a significant expansion of the electorate from Empire to Republic, the literacy-based electoral franchise was still very narrow, with less than one-tenth of the population qualified to vote under the 1891 Constitution. This was never more than 6 per cent of all Brazilians, roughly the same size as observed in Britain prior to the 1832 Reform Act (Love, 1970, 8; see also Chapter 7).

However, unlike in Britain, in Brazil an open vote compromised the freedom of the electorate. Under the Empire, the most common voting method was a publicly taken voice vote. The *Rosa e Silva* Law, enacted in 1904, gave voters the possibility of casting a secret ballot, but the secret ballot was not fully established until 1932 and was included in the 1934 Constitution. Balloting, particularly in rural areas, often took place in small groups, which enabled the local bosses to monitor and sanction or reward voters for their behaviour.

Under these arrangements, a patriarchal system of domination, known as the *coronelismo*, concentrated power in the hands of the rural oligarchy. The colonel would instruct his dependants on how to vote, and the term *voto de cabresto* (the 'herd vote') was used to describe this abuse of expanded suffrage. In exchange, the colonel would offer protection in the form of land, financial assistance or employment. In addition, the colonels often controlled private militias to intimidate voters and rival candidates. Rural oligarchs could thus stack elections, which were subject to fraud and inefficient voter registration systems, in their favour. While the urban middle class of professionals and commercial employees was relatively independent of the coronel regime, the system strengthened the position of the landed oligarchy, as the country remained 90 per cent rural in the early years of the Republic (Love, 1970, 10).[4] Not surprisingly, the middle class was often in conflict with the rural oligarchy in its struggle to introduce the secret ballot and to create an electoral commission to curb fraud (Fausto, 1989, 285).

Brazil lacked a true national party after the end of the Empire, and thus regional contestation between the two economically leading states – São Paulo and Minas Gerais – came to define Brazilian politics from the start of the second decade of the Republic. The landed gentries of São Paulo's coffee industry and Minas Gerais's dairy interests dominated their respective state structures to their advantage. The leader of the federal delegation was the governor of the state, with congressmen following his leadership. Leaders of the Paulista and Mineiro Republican parties (and other states) focused more on the interests of their state than on national concerns. Starting with the 1906 election, a system of alternating the presidency that became known as *café com leite* (coffee with milk) is often said to have emerged from their competition, signifying a pact to alternate control of the national government. Yet the process of electing the president was often much more chaotic and contentious, with each state party seeking to maintain its hold on the presidency rather than share it. Four of the five Paulista presidents during the era of the Old Republic were not succeeded by Mineiros.

In fact, Paulistas won all three elections held during the period examined in this chapter, and these early years of the Republic are often said to be an era of Paulista hegemony. Nonetheless, there existed considerable contestation among several factions of republicans. The 'historic' or pre-1889 republicans – those who identified themselves as republicans before the fall of the monarchy – were divided into radicals and moderates. Both groups were committed republicans and, as discussed below, shared many of the same economic policy preferences,

---

[4] According to the 1920 census, nationwide 84 per cent of the population lived in rural areas. The country's middle class – made up of public and private administrators, professionals, and military and public safety officers – represented under 4 per cent of the country's total employed population (Topik, 1987, 8).

but they differed after the 1889 coup over the treatment of *adesistas* or former monarchists who later became republicans. While the radicals sought to exclude them from power, the moderates, with whom the Paulista presidents generally aligned, preferred reconciliation.

In addition to these factions, a Jacobinist movement emerged in the late nineteenth century. Jacobinism, which prevailed widely among the urban middle and working classes, emerged as a radical nationalist republican movement rooted in discontent surrounding corruption and inflation during and following the *Encilhamento*. The Jacobins focused their discontent less on government policies and more on Portuguese merchants whom they perceived as causing inflation via their control and manipulation of commerce (Cable, 1976, 92–3; Fausto, 1989, 286).[5] The Jacobin movement was centred in the federal capital, but there were also organizations in Minas Gerais, Bahia, São Paulo, Rio Grande do Sul and several minor states.

Thus, despite restrictions on political participation and competition, factions competed for the votes of a narrow electorate. During the period of Paulista hegemony, governing state elites needed to forge agreements with other influential state leaders and make sufficient concessions to secure their support in elections. Indeed, according to 'selectorate theory' measures, starting with the 1894 election, the size of the selectorate in Brazil was as large as that in Britain and the United States at this time, and the 'winning coalition' required to maintain office was as large as that in Britain following the 1890 crisis and larger than that observed before the 1832 Reform Act.[6] Rival factions to the Paulista-led governments did gain representation in the Congress and control of some state governments. Indeed, at times support for the opposition party in Congress was nearly equal to that of those committed to the incumbent party (Cable, 1976, 108). At one point, the Jacobins, as rivals to Paulista hegemony, had become so significant that Brazil's first ambassador to the United States described with alarm their 'predominance and ascendancy' (cited in Topik, 1987, 32).

Elections, though decided via informal elite competition, did offer a mechanism through which incumbents could be held accountable

---

[5] Jacobin newspapers blamed inflation on the Portuguese who controlled the retail trade in urban centres, accusing them of 'speculating in food' and monopolizing commerce at the expense of Brazilians (Cable, 1976, 93).

[6] Author calculations using data from Bueno de Mesquita et al. (n.d., 2003).

by a limited number of individuals. Incumbency survival was not guaranteed; rather, it had to be carefully negotiated with state elites. Even then, as discussed below, the incumbent party could not guarantee a majority in all states. In the federal capital, where Jacobinist sympathies ran high and literacy rates reached nearly two-thirds of population, the incumbent party often relied on extensive political repression to limit support for the opposition.[7] As a result, public opinion was often expressed outside the electoral process via occasional outbreaks of demonstrations and violence. Such expressions were not without influence on policy.

11.3   The *Encilhamento* and its Aftermath

The interim government that came to power in 1889 needed to curry political favour with agrarian interests. These interests wanted a return to multiple sources of note issuance and continued easy credit, a policy that had been initiated in the final years of the monarchy as a way of appeasing planters following the abolition of slavery without compensation in 1888 (Ridings, 1994, 150).[8] In the final year of the Empire, the prime minister and minister of finance, the Viscount of Ouro Preto, had signed agreements with leading banks, including the Banco do Brasil (BB), the country's largest institution, to provide long-term low-interest loans to planters, with half of the money coming from the sale of government bonds and the rest from the banks. The banks duly lent out the government's money, provided to them interest-free, but failed to provide any of their own. Ouro Preto then signed similar contracts with seventeen other banks, which also lent out the funds allocated to them but reneged on committing their own.

Departing from a twenty-four-year campaign to regain a monopoly of note issue for the Treasury, Ouro Preto also permitted some banks to print their own banknotes. Banks were not required to redeem their notes for currency; instead notes were redeemable 20 per cent in currency and 80 per cent in Treasury bonds that the banks had been

---

[7] In 1900, whereas the literacy rate in the Federal District reached 63 per cent, the national average was 35 per cent (Cable, 1976, 34).

[8] Abolition had deprived planters of their traditional security for loans at precisely the time when economic expansion and salaries for newly freed slaves and European immigrants heightened the demand for currency.

required to purchase to back their note issues. The government did not accept the banknotes as payment for import tariffs, its biggest source of revenue. Not surprisingly, the prospect of interest-free government loans induced the formation of new banks, while existing banks increased their capital to qualify for even greater sums of public money. The measures created a boom for bank shares on the stock market, with some of the interest-free public money probably diverted from planters to individuals who used it to purchase bank shares (Schulz, 2008, 74–7). Between May 1888 and the Empire's fall in November 1889, the stock market capitalization of banks more than doubled. But the credit and asset boom did not ensure the monarchy's survival.

In addition to courting agrarian interests, the new interim government needed the support of the still-influential monarchists, who comprised the country's leading financial interests and would become involved in banking and stock market speculation. Moreover, since Brazil's 1891 federal constitution gave states rather than the central government the authority to collect export tax revenue, the government needed to tap into a new source of income. The interim and republican government's first finance minister, Rui Barbosa, continued Ouro Preto's expansionary programme, arranging a loan for his government from the banks and authorizing a massive expansion of credit. The result was the *Encilhamento*.

In January 1890, Barbosa implemented banking reforms that made it easier to establish a commercial bank, encouraged the formation of universal banks, and authorized three of these universal banks to issue up to 450,000 contos[9] in notes backed by government bonds. The controversial measure, drafted with the assistance of leading financier Francisco de Paula Mayrink, a monarchist and owner or leading shareholder of many of the note-issuing banks, signified Brazil's abandonment of the gold standard.[10] The three banks, the Banco dos Estados Unidos do Brasil (BEUB), the Banco Nacional and BB, all concentrated in Rio and dominated by monarchists, controlled, through their privileges and the banks they owned, 95 per cent of the notes issued

---

[9] A conto is a thousand milreis. Using the exchange rate prevailing at the time, this amounted to roughly £20 million added to circulation.

[10] The controversial measure had been issued without consultation with other ministers, who later expressed their opposition. Deodoro then threatened to resign unless debate on the subject was ended. This seems to have worked, with opponents agreeing to accept the measure with revisions reducing total note issuance to 250,000 (Bello, 1966, 70).

(Topik, 1987, 31). Close connections existed among these financial interests, with family ties present among the overlapping directors of these banks.

Barbosa in effect traded a loan to the government in exchange for the right to print notes that could be lent at interest. Under the terms of the agreement the government bonds carried a below-market rate of interest that reduced to zero after two years, while the banks extracted additional concessions that included free land, preferential consideration for contracts for public works and mining projects, the right to expropriate land to carry out these projects, and tax exemptions from import tariffs on inputs needed to carry out the projects. By permitting the creation of universal banks with the right of note issuance, Barbosa gave licence to banks to print money that could be lent to their own firms, collateralized by stock in those same firms. The three banks used their privileges to make significant investments in the stock market (Topik, 1987, 31). As Calomiris and Haber (2014, 421) suggest, 'In short, he [Barbosa] traded a loan to the government for the right to build a house of cards.'

On the same day this package was agreed, Barbosa reformed the general incorporation law, weakening the requirements for reserve liability and thereby reducing the amount of paid-up capital necessary to trade shares. Until 1890, all corporations in Brazil had a form of reserve liability similar to that present in Britain,[11] which made a shareholder who had not yet paid in the full value of his shares liable for their full face value for a period of five years, even if the partially paid-in shares had been sold. According to supporters of Barbosa's reforms, this had reduced incentives for investors to purchase shares and inhibited industrial development. The reforms reduced the period of reserve liability from five years to when the annual shareholders' meeting approved the company accounts. Whereas in Britain reserve liability provided a form of private sector insurance for depositors, in Brazil the system had offered weaker protection, with many shareholders often refusing to pay in their shares when called and instead *roeram a corda* (literally 'chewing off the leash'), walking away from their subscriptions with impunity.

---

[11] In Britain, reserve liability remained a common practice for banks until 1878, when the City of Glasgow bank was suspended and its shareholders, many of whom had paid in only a fifth of their subscribed capital, had to pay in the remainder.

As suggested, the aim of these reforms was to hasten Brazil's transition from an agrarian economy based on slave labour to a modern industrial and commercial economy. In fact, together with expansionary monetary policy, they did significantly boost the rate at which new firms were created and they contributed to the development of Brazil's equity and long-term corporate debt markets (Haber, 1997). But the reforms also created an incentive for corporate fraud and for firms with little underlying value and good banking connections to sell their shares at inflated prices to uninformed investors on the exchange.

Banks that initially had not been granted note issuance rights soon pressured the government for similar privileges. In March 1890, Barbosa granted two additional banks the right to issue notes equal to twice their capital, up to 50,000 contos each. The issues were to be 'gold-backed' but not convertible into gold – essentially unbacked non-convertible notes. It was later discovered that another Mayrink-owned bank, which had earlier been authorized to issue notes against government bonds, had in fact simply printed money without any backing (Schulz, 2008, 81). Barbosa then extended the right to issue interest-bearing non-convertible gold-backed notes to five additional banks. Mayrink, who had significant financial interests in many of the note-issuing banks, benefited greatly from these arrangements, as did Barbosa himself, who was awarded a luxurious mansion from Mayrink while still finance minister. Later, after departing as finance minister in January 1891, Barbosa held directorships in several of Mayrink's companies.

By December 1890, two of the largest note-issuing banks – the BEUB, controlled by Mayrink, and the Banco Nacional – had large portfolios of unrealizable loans to fraudulent or incompetent firms. Their owners proposed a merger to create a single, almost monopolistic, bank of issue, to which Barbosa readily agreed. Barbosa recognized the merger of the two banks to form the Banco da República dos Estados Unidos do Brasil (BREUB), conferring on the new institution the privileges of the predecessor institutions as well as the issue rights of the BB, which had sold this facility to Mayrink and his associates. The new BREUB, led by Mayrink, was authorized to issue 50,000 contos against bonds that the old BEUB had already put in circulation. In addition, the new megabank was permitted to issue notes up to three times the value of its capital. The notes were convertible into gold, but only if the value of the milreis exceeded 27 British pence for an entire year – an extremely unlikely occurrence given that the rapid increase in the money supply had pushed the milreis down to 20 pence at the time of the merger. Within a year, the currency stood at 12 pence.

A spectacular bubble continued as Henrique Pererira de Lucena, Barbosa's successor as finance minister, continued his predecessor's policies. Brazil's money supply, which had grown at roughly 1 per cent since the 1870s, experienced a fourfold increase in the twelve months between December 1889 and December 1890 (Haber, 1997, 152). The deflation of most of the preceding decade gave way to annual inflation of above 20 per cent between 1890 and 1893 (Calomiris and Haber, 2014, 391). Much of the monetary growth was channelled into loans to fictitious or quasi-fictitious corporate entities, including many founded by Mayrink and his associates. Banks also used the note issuance to purchase shares of corporations owned by their directors, and the run-up in stock prices led to hundreds of IPOs for new companies, with their shares fully subscribed in days, if not hours. The number of firms traded on the Rio de Janeiro Stock Exchange jumped from four to eight per million people in 1890 alone, and the number of firms registered reached record levels of more than 100 per year between 1890 and 1891 (Musacchio, 2009, 43). By December 1891, the stock market capitalization of the firms listed on the Rio de Janeiro and São Paulo exchanges had experienced a fourfold increase in a span of three years, with market capitalization rising from 15 per cent of GDP in the late 1880s to 40 per cent at the height of the boom in 1891 (Musacchio, 2009, 43). The banking system also experienced similarly spectacular growth, with the number of banks rising from 27 in 1888 to 133 in 1891 (see Figure 11.3). During this period, their market capitalization grew to more than four times their 1888 level.

Inevitably, this bubble eventually burst. At the end of 1891, as the currency declined, many banks suffered losses on foreign exchange trading and their large portfolios of Treasury *apólices* (federal and state domestic debt), which were linked to the value of the milreis (Triner, 2000, 70). To avert failure, some banks successfully called in partially paid capital, enabling depositors to redeem their claims; others were less successful. Many banks failed and depositors incurred losses as investors walked away from their subscriptions due to concerns about the viability of the banks (Triner, 2000, 71). In some cases, stronger rivals acquired failing institutions.

From this time, stock prices fell rapidly, with market capitalization falling to 20 per cent of GDP. Many uninformed investors in fraudulent firms lost their money as bankruptcies multiplied (Musacchio, 2009, 43). The number of banks fell steadily from a peak of 133 in 1891 to 110 in 1894 (see Figure 11.3). The total real stock market capitalization of banks (in 1900 milreis) returned to its pre-boom level over the course of the year.

In addition to the many loans to incompetent or fraudulent firms, laws governing property rights in Brazil contributed to the build-up of unrecoverable assets in the agricultural mortgage portfolios of the universal banks. These laws prohibited the break-up of estates for the settlement of debts, preventing banks from seizing any part of an estate to settle a delinquent debt if doing so diminished its productive capacity. Banks that did accept rural properties as collateral did so at deeply discounted values. Even then, problems arose, such as in the case of the largest mortgage lender in the state of São Paulo, which collapsed in 1905 due to extensive holdings of uncollectable mortgage loans.

11.3.1   Policy Responses

Deodoro formally became the first president of the Republic after contentious elections in February 1891 (see below). He faced growing hostility in Congress from an alliance of radical and moderate republicans led by the Republican Party of São Paulo (PRP). Despite the rapid increase in prices that had followed from the collapse of the milreis and the programme of monetary expansion, the Deodoro government did not attempt to rein in inflation. It sought instead to sustain the boom by issuing yet more banknotes. It asked Congress to authorize BREUB, which had already increased the circulating medium by nearly 50 per cent since the start of the year, to issue up to 600,000 additional contos in unbacked notes. Some in the opposition viewed the proposal as a scheme to protect the monarchist financial and commercial interests connected to the finance minister (Topik, 1987, 31). Angered by this prospect as well as by the depreciation of the milreis, fraudulent schemes on the stock market, and Deodoro's increasing use of arbitrary decrees, the PRP-led opposition in Congress refused to offer its support (Schulz, 2008, 93). On 3 November, Deodoro executed the so-called 'stock market coup,' dissolving Congress and declaring a state of emergency. Deodoro's explanation to the nation listed congressional opposition to unbacked note issuance as one of the principal reasons for the move (Bello, 1966, 86).

The coup lasted just twenty days. As discussed below, Deodoro never enjoyed widespread popular support. A combined civilian–military revolt removed him from office, installing Vice President Marshal Floriano Peixoto in his place. The PRP pressed Floriano to respect the Constitution, which required new elections if the president did not complete half of his term. Yet Floriano insisted on serving until November 1894, retaining the title of vice president and claiming that the constitutional provision applied only to future presidents elected by direct popular vote (Bello, 1966, 68). The PRP acquiesced in return for control of the state of São Paulo and the appointment of one of its party members, Francisco de Paula Rodrigues Alves, as finance minister. Rodrigues Alves represented the interests of his state's coffee planters, who, due to high international coffee prices and a weak milreis, supported the implementation of orthodox monetary and financial policies (Topik, 1987, 33; Triner, 2000, 36).

Floriano's regime was based principally on support from junior military officers and the urban middle and working classes, particularly from Rio de Janeiro, the latter group forming the heart of the Jacobinist movement. The junior military officers were committed to the development of Brazil through activist state-led industrialization. This group backed Colonel Serzedelo Correia, Floriano's second finance minister, when he lamented that while Brazil was politically independent, 'in terms of economic interest [it was still] a colony' (as cited in Topik, 1987, 32). The large import component of inputs for Brazilian industry during the period also led industrial interests to support measures to strengthen the milreis (Topik, 1987, 33, 134). The urban middle and working classes, while offering important support for Floriano's regime, were also a potential source of social unrest, which made the regime highly sensitive to their concerns about inflation. Indeed, Floriano's minister of justice advised that the cost of living, which had doubled during the *Encilhamento*, would create enemies of the regime if left unaddressed (Topik, 1987, 33).

Although their rationale differed, the various interests represented in Floriano's regime thus shared a similar preference for returning to orthodox policies. Foreign bankers had not made any new loans to Brazil since the proclamation of the Republic. Subsidized government loans and excessive banknote issues had increased corruption, fostered currency depreciation, inflation and budgetary deficits, and led to a decline in foreign investment. These developments, which had helped to generate growing public disillusionment with the Republic, led all three finance ministers who served under Floriano to break sharply with the policies of the previous government, seeking to restore fiscal discipline, restrict monetary growth and return to the gold standard. In his manifesto explaining to the country his reasons for taking office, Floriano indicated, 'The administration of fiscal affairs will be one of my major concerns.' Later, he would describe his concern more directly, claiming he was the 'sentinel of the Treasury' (as cited in Bello, 1966, 94–5).

Yet Floriano was soon forced to discard this pledge. Fiscal and monetary discipline proved difficult due to the ongoing costs of responding to armed uprisings in many states, including civil war in the country's South and a naval revolt in Rio de Janeiro. Since the majority of state governors had accepted Deodoro's coup in November 1891 (Bello, 1966, 86), Floriano sought to remove them from office. Without any legal mechanism to do so, he supported rival state factions that rose up and removed them from power. These ousted state officials and their supporters joined the ranks of the opposition to Floriano, including *adesistas*, who had a strong base in the South, and higher officers of the navy. The costs of fighting these battles from July 1893 until the end of Floriano's term in office meant that while real federal spending and monetary growth declined, the government was unable to reduce the money supply.

The government also faced the problem of what to do about the many unbacked banknotes issued during the *Encilhamento*. Rodrigues Alves recognized that restoring monetary stability and returning to a monopoly on note issuance meant the government would need to assume control over these notes, which had become the national currency. As a first step, he sought to secure the passage of legislation that would have prohibited BREUB and others from further note issuance. The measure passed the Chamber of Deputies, but it stalled in the Senate, where financial interests allied with Mayrink still wielded considerable influence (Schulz, 2008, 101). Thus, the BREUB retained its note issuance privilege, though it apparently refrained, at least temporarily, from exercising this power. However, other bankers, who resolved not to surrender control over note issuance, reacted to the potential loss of their note issuance privileges by financing a conspiracy to overthrow Floriano. This uprising was put down and its leaders were exiled to remote unhealthy villages in the Amazon, thus clearing the way for financial reform (Schulz, 2008, 102).

Under the monarchy, an 1885 law allowed the Treasury to serve as a lender of last resort and had institutionalized the practice of lending public money directly to banks in times of crisis in return for good collateral. The Treasury could lend up to 25,000 contos (£2.5 million) on the security of government bonds, guaranteeing that no public funds would be lost in the process. Invoking the 1885 law, Rodrigues Alves provided emergency credit of 25,000 contos each to BB and BREUB. According to Schulz (2008, 101), despite some uncertainty as to the latter's solvency, Rodrigues Alves 'administered this rediscount honestly, insisting that the borrowing banks deliver government bonds as security'. In line with Bagehot's rule, whereas both banks could furnish these bonds and thus received assistance, many smaller institutions could not and were refused credit.

The collapse of the *Encilhamento* had also left many commercial and industrial firms unable to obtain additional capital from banks or the stock market. Banks had called in debts and restricted the amount of credit, being reluctant to lend against bonds of industrial and commercial firms issued on the security of mill property, construction and/ or equipment (Stein, 1957, 90–1). The fall in the milreis meant that factories that had ordered foreign inputs during the height of the stock market boom now found themselves facing higher import costs. Commercial and industrial interests thus began an 'aid for industry' campaign for collateralized loans from the government. In approaching the government for assistance, the industrialists, the *Jornal do Commércio* claimed approvingly, were repeating the example of Rio's 'worthy' bankers who had recently requested and received similar loans from the Treasury (as cited in Stein, 1957, 90).

Floriano had appointed Rodrigues Alves to the post of finance minister because he needed the support of the PRP while he consolidated power, which he had more or less accomplished by this time. Thus, when the aid to industry campaign emerged, Floriano – who like many other military officers believed in the need to industrialize the country – expressed his desire to 'improve the situation of those industries that merit aid through measures that protect the interest of the Treasury' (as cited in Topik, 1987, 135). Although Rodrigues Alves stood 'in principle against the intervention of the government in industrial matters', Floriano appointed a committee to study the issue, which included among its members the presidents of BREUB and BB.

The committee proposed that the federal government float a 100,000 conto bond issue for collateralized loans to industry (Stein, 1957, 92–3). Legislation was soon submitted to Congress for approval. Shortly thereafter, Rodrigues Alves resigned. The opposition in Congress claimed the bond issue would ignite inflation and produce further currency depreciation. The Rothschilds, who in June had helped Brazil to re-enter international debt markets for the first time since the establishment of the Republic, agreed. Other foes of aid to industry argued that subsidies and privileges were in and of themselves unfair, inefficient and corrupting. Critics claimed the measure would not help needy industries, but rather fraudulent ones and the bankers who had already profited mightily during the *Encilhamento* (Stein, 1957, 93; Topik, 1987, 136).

The bill's advocates countered that only genuine and worthy firms would receive assistance, claiming that without this 'the majority of factories will have to close down and more than twelve thousand workers will be fired and sent into the streets' (as cited in Topik, 1987, 137). Moreover, they claimed, by reducing Brazil's dependence on foreign markets and producers, the aid would strengthen the economy and the currency (Stein, 1957, 93–5). The reported interference of British bankers and foreign merchants heightened patriotic sentiment in favour of aiding industry.

A simultaneous debate developed over government responsibility for banknote issues. A consensus had developed within Congress in favour of the unification of banknote issues under government control, but strong disagreement emerged over how to do so. A three-cornered fight emerged between the financial and commercial interests responsible for the *Encilhamento*, Floriano, and the PRP. Financial and commercial interests advocated aid to industry and sought to maintain control over their banks and to gain compensation for any lost issue rights. Floriano and his supporters wanted aid to industry and government control, if not outright ownership, of the banks of issue. The PRP, dominated by financial conservatives, wanted the government to assume responsibility for the banknotes and opposed both aid to industry and compensation for bank shareholders.

Congressional deadlock meant that no measures were passed. The Chamber of Deputies passed Floriano's preferred measures, but the

Senate rejected them. When Congress adjourned, Floriano instituted them by decree in December 1892. The decree merged BREUB and BB to create the Banco da República do Brasil (BRB), to which he gave a monopoly over all new note issues. The government appointed three of the nine directors of the BRB, including its president and vice president. It became the official government agent in paying international debt, receiving Treasury surpluses on deposit and extending advances to the Treasury on the basis of future revenues.

Unlike the previous merger under Deodoro, the new merger did not further concentrate control of the banking system in the hands of interests associated with BREUB, with Mayrink himself ousted from the bank and forced into internal exile (Topik, 1987, 34).[12] BRB assumed responsibility for the banknotes of its predecessor banks, but what, if any, responsibility the government would take was left unresolved. The BRB became a semi-public institution and the merger itself would prove to be a compromise: the *Encilhamento* bankers kept their shares in the newly merged bank that the government appeared committed to support, but they lost control over the institution and received no compensation for their loss of note issuance. The measure constituted a government-supported merger without taxpayer expense or government guarantee of liabilities at this point, though the BRB's semi-public status suggested an ongoing implicit government commitment. The creation of the BRB furthered the move toward the creation of a central banking system that had started with the formation of BREUB in 1890. In the coming years, the BRB would provide liquidation assistance to other failed banks and often acquire assets of failing smaller organizations as part of restructurings. In the years that followed the merger, failing banks would liquidate their investments to the extent possible, use capital to redeem deposits, and sell any remaining assets to the BRB (Triner, 2000, 46, 71).

As part of the merger decree, the government also granted BRB the authority to issue 100,000 contos of bonds guaranteed by the government and acceptable as legal tender for payment of taxes. The bank could lend these bonds on the security of collateral to 'national industries in healthy conditions', which in turn could use these

---

[12] Another leading financier of the time, the Conde de Leopoldina, was also sent into exile. The government initiated bankruptcy proceedings against him and caused him to lose most of his fortune.

instruments to pay off their creditors, including the BRB and other banks (as cited in Topik, 1987, 137). As they had done before the decree, financial conservatives in Congress condemned this measure, claiming that the BRB would lend only to firms concentrated in Rio de Janeiro in which it owned stock or for which it was a creditor. Floriano compromised by mandating loans for other states.

The government did not administer the collateralized loans, but it did exert control over them via its appointment of the BRB's president. Industry received most of the loans, with about a quarter flowing to agriculture and other non-industrial sectors receiving a lesser share. The loans provided assistance to industries largely via the provision of working capital, though there is some evidence that the bank lent some of these instruments to firms in which it had an interest (Schulz, 2008, 107, 119; Topik, 1987, 137). The government used an industry-wide approach that, according to Stein (1957, 96), meant that the 'blessings of the treasury fell upon the needy and the prosperous alike'. Yet, importantly, the key element requiring the loans to be collateralized appears to have been maintained. Thus, the aid-to-industry loans parallel the collateralized assistance that the Bank of England provided to non-banks prior to the late nineteenth century (see Chapter 7).

These policy measures had some success in stabilizing the economy and in allowing Brazil to return to international capital markets, with the Rothschilds undertaking the issuance. But revolts and civil war in the South undermined monetary discipline. The milreis, which had stabilized, resumed its downward trajectory. Violence and unrest increased in the capital as living standards declined.

In July 1893, the Paulistas organized an inclusive loose confederation of state republican parties, the Federal Republican Party (PRF), to prepare for presidential elections. In March 1894, in the first presidential election to be decided by direct vote, Brazil elected Prudente de Morais, the former governor of São Paulo and leading member of the PRP, as it first civilian president (see below). The era of Paulista hegemony had begun. Under Deodoro and Floriano, the military-led governments had exhibited a preference for industrialization, which drew support from the urban middle and working classes. Prudente's election marked the coming to power of the Paulista coffee oligarchy whose ambitions contravened those favouring industrial expansion. However, the new government also faced serious challenges to its rule, including continual military revolts, a winding-down civil war in the south, conflict with religious fanatics in Canudos, and urban uprisings often led by the Jacobins.

Amidst this continuing unrest, the economy experienced a significant downturn during the worldwide depression in 1893, which reduced foreign investment and demand for exports. The price of coffee fell by nearly two-thirds between 1891 and 1898. In addition, by 1898, the milreis had fallen to what was then an all-time low of 7.2 pence (Triner, 2000, 214). The depreciation had a significantly adverse effect on Brazil's large stock of external debt, which was denominated in gold and sterling. As Conant (1915, 503) observes, 'the difficulties of the government grew constantly worse'. The country's debt-servicing capacity increasingly became a cause for concern, as did the cost of living, which rose 60 per cent between 1895 and 1898 (Topik, 1987, 36). By 1898, servicing the foreign and domestic public debt consumed more than half of the federal budget and fostered unprecedented deficits.

Despite these mounting economic problems, the era of Paulista hegemony did not bring any major changes in financial policy. Prudente had recalled Rodrigues Alves to the finance ministry. Together they continued with deflationary policies to combat the hangover from the *Encilhamento*, which included continuing bank failures throughout the 1890s (Figure 11.3). Even so, the government remained opposed to rescuing insolvent institutions (Triner, 2000, 71). Prudente also refused requests from his own constituents, Paulista coffee planters, for government loans (Schulz, 2008, 113).

Prudente and Rodrigues Alves had as their objective the government's assumption of the BRB's banknotes. Yet the BRB and Prudente's opponents still wielded considerable influence in Congress, which refused to pass the necessary legislation. These congressional opponents comprised defenders of the radical Republican line, which included the representatives of state governors in Congress who owed their appointment to Floriano.[13] The 'politics of the governors' arrangement described earlier was not institutionalized until 1900, and thus conflict between Prudente and his opponents eventually led to the disintegration of the PRF in 1897. Outside the Congress, Prudente's opponents included military officers and Jacobins in urban centres.

---

[13] With the exception of Rio Grande do Sol, these governments from seven smaller states were not doctrinaire or even historic republicans but they feared that a reversal of Floriano's policies would jeopardize their hold on power.

When Prudente fell ill in November 1896, his vice president Manuel Vitorino Pereira assumed office and appointed his own cabinet. Vitorino, who had the support of the Jacobins, decreed that the government would assume responsibility for the BRB's banknotes, which now became paper money. In reassuming monopoly of currency emissions and regaining control of the money supply, the government refused to compensate the BRB for its loss of note issuance privileges because it was heavily indebted to the Treasury. In addition, the BRB, as part of this fairly tough settlement, transferred most of its assets to the Treasury to cover part of the value of its notes (Topik, 1987, 36).

Prudente returned to office in March 1897. The pro-government party, which chose to call itself the Republican Party (PR), saw its candidate, Manuel Ferraz de Campos Sales, the governor of São Paulo, win the presidential election the following year (see below). Under Campos Sales, Brazil would regain the financial stability it had lost during and after the *Encilhamento*, but not before experiencing additional bank failures. Campos Sales successfully continued the orthodox policies pursued by his predecessors and is often regarded as 'the savior of Brazilian finances' (Topik, 1987, 37). He achieved balanced budgets in two of his four terms, reduced the money supply, and raised the value of the milreis.

In June 1898, a few months before Campos Sales came into office, but with his full endorsement, a £10 million funding loan was arranged with the Rothschilds that enabled Brazil to avoid default.[14] Under the terms of the arrangement, the loan consolidated Brazil's foreign debt and provided a three-year interest payment moratorium and a thirteen-year grace period of payments of principal. In return, Campos Sales committed to reduce the money supply, to refrain from issuing any additional paper money or contracting additional foreign loans, and pledged Rio customs house revenues against the loan. Foreign banks oversaw compliance.

Critics complained that the government had ceded control and national sovereignty to foreign bankers (Schulz, 2008, 118; Topik, 1987, 37). Campos Sales is reported to have said in 1899 that 'my government is better [received] abroad than here' (as cited in Topik, 1987, 38). Yet he drew support from merchants, some in the urban

---

[14] As president-elect, Campos Sales had helped negotiate the loan with the Rothschilds in London.

middle and working classes, as well as from foreign investors. In addition to retiring paper money from circulation, the government cut back sharply on spending. The result was a 13 per cent drop in the money supply, a sixfold increase in the trade surplus, and a doubling of the value of the milreis (Topik, 1987, 37). Brazil also benefited from stronger foreign demand and investment following the end of the world depression in 1897.

Yet the deflationary policies and the appreciation of the milreis set off a two-year recession. The government was attacked in the press, by commerce, by agricultural interests, and even by the PRP. To balance the budget the government reduced military spending, cut back on public sector employment and limited the granting of public pensions. Following Prudente's precedent, despite repeated requests, the government also refused to grant loans to agricultural interests, even though this decision caused losses for both Campos Sales and his finance minister, both of whom had considerable wealth linked to agricultural estates (Topik, 1987, 38; Triner, 2000, 258n37).

The result of these deflationary policies, according to Topik (1987, 38), was one of the 'worst banking crises the country had known'. The crisis started with the collapse of the BRB in September 1900, which triggered a run on several other banks that either failed or were forced to temporarily suspend payments. The number of banks in Brazil dropped precipitously in the period that followed (see Figure 11.3).

The portfolio of the BRB, like that of other institutions, had steadily deteriorated under the weight of loans granted by its predecessor institutions during the *Encilhamento* and those it had acquired in helping to liquidate failed banks. This portfolio constituted roughly one-third of all banking system assets, of which more than 70 per cent was distressed (Triner, 2000, 257n30). The market value of these assets had declined significantly since the *Encilhamento*, but current accounting practice forced the bank to report all assets at their original (par) value. At the time of its closure, the market value of the BRB's assets was only slightly more than half their stated value, and thus could not be liquidated to meet the bank's liabilities (Triner, 2000, 73).

This casts doubt on whether BRB was in fact solvent. Triner (2000, 47; see also 72, 257n26) suggests that the BRB ultimately failed because the 'Treasury refused to support it through a liquidity crisis', a view supported by Calomiris and Haber (2014, 427), who suggest a definitive state of insolvency had not been reached at the time of the withdrawal of support. Schulz (2008, 121) is more sceptical, claiming the bank had 'negative worth'. Yet some observers at the time, such as Serzedello Correria, who had been responsible for the creation of the BRB and was then a leading member of the finance committee of the Chamber of Deputies, attested to the bank's solvency (Schulz, 2008, 121). As we note throughout this book, measuring bank solvency in a crisis requires judgement and is often contested.

Irrespective of the bank's solvency, its liquidity problems had been recurrent. Under the terms of the 1885 banking law discussed earlier, the Treasury issued paper money to provide collateralized lending on multiple occasions (Neuhaus, 1974, 8). However, this support mechanism was no longer available after the passage of a July 1899 law that repealed the right of the Treasury to create paper money.

The next shock for the BRB occurred in February 1900 when an accord was reached to settle 186,000 contos of the bank's debt with the Treasury. Much of the bank's large portfolio of distressed assets had been funded by government money, with 80,000 contos arising from the aid-to-industry bonds, another 40,000 representing Ouru Preto's agricultural loans to the bank's predecessor institutions, and the remaining 66,000 arising from Treasury advances to provide the bank with liquidity (Schulz, 2008, 119–20). Recognizing the large stockpile of distressed assets on the bank's balance sheet, the government agreed to accept 50,000 contos in payment for the bank's total debt, a write-down of nearly 75 per cent. While Topik (1987, 38) describes this as 'an incredible windfall' for the bank, the write-down meant that government (and ultimately taxpayers) had suffered considerable losses. As part of its effort to strengthen the BRB as a private enterprise, the government relinquished its right to name the bank's president, a power it had held since Floriano's decree in 1892.

Rather than poor management, supporters of the bank argued that responsibility for the write-down lay with past government policies, which had used the bank and its predecessors to advance political interests. Moreover, the BRB, as the Treasury's agent, had purchased large volumes of government debt, which at the time of its failure traded at less than two-thirds of their par value, leaving it with an inflated balance sheet that had served the Treasury's financing needs rather than its own interest (Triner, 2000, 72, 258n31).

By the end of 1899 the total currency circulation in Brazil was only 734,000 contos. Thus, the BRB's repayment to the government

430 / Banking Crises, Policy and Politics in the UK, US and Brazil

represented a severe drain on its scarce reserves. To relieve the shock, the government provided liquidity support by depositing 10,000 contos of Treasury funds in the BRB and ordered the balances of tax-collecting agencies of all states to be transferred to the bank (Neuhaus, 1974, 9). A run on the bank, which had been under private management since March, occurred in July. The BRB turned to the government for additional liquidity support of £400,000 in government loans, equivalent at the time to 12,000 contos. Since the Rothschild loan prohibited the issue of paper money, the government extended a second sterling-denominated loan to BRB of £600,000 in August, equivalent to 18,000 contos. In September, after having incurred a heavy loss from speculative positions in the foreign exchange market, the BRB's directors called for the Treasury to issue paper money to provide it with liquidity, but the government remained firmly opposed.

Sustained liquidity support could have continued to delay closure of the BRB. But with Brazil under much greater fiscal constraint than Britain in the same decade (Fritsch, 1988, 9), the Treasury withdrew support, prompting the BRB to suspend payments. A number of other banks, which failed to receive any ongoing Treasury support during this time, suspended payments on the same and following days. The effect of the BRB's suspension quickly spread throughout the financial system.

Reflecting the prevailing orthodox ideas of the time, Joaquim Murtinho, the finance minister, and strong proponent of what Mettenheim (2015, 67) calls 'financial Darwinism', was not inclined to help banks survive pressure during the crisis (Bello, 1966, 164–7; Topik, 1987, 38; Triner, 2000, 72). As a result, Brazil experienced widespread bank failures and suspensions, with the number of operating banks falling by roughly 20 per cent over the course of Campos Sales's term in office (see Figure 11.3). Even Murtinho's own bank, the Banco Rio e Matto Grasso, founded during the *Encilhamento*, suffered under the weight of unrealizable loans and was liquidated in 1900 (Schulz, 2008, 168n28). At one point in September 1900, all domestic banks suspended payments, leaving the economy virtually without liquidity. The shock proved worse than previous ones because, unlike previous episodes, the government refused to issue paper money for fear of undermining its stabilization programme (Schulz, 2008, 121).

While it permitted other banks to fail, the Treasury proposed to take administrative control of the BRB and close its commercial operations. Murtinho labelled this restructuring proposal a 'liquidation plan', though it had elements of both the Bagehot and bailout policy models. As the funding loan prohibited the issuance of paper money, the government proposed to lend the bank 100,000 contos via five-year bonds paying 3 per cent interest per annum plus an additional 25,000 contos of paper money at 2 per cent per annum that it had previously retired. As collateral for these credits, the government proposed to take all of the stock of the BRB and resume the right to name its executive officers, which would have amounted to full nationalization (Schulz, 2008, 122).

Under the restructuring proposal, the government would supervise the settlement of the BRB's other liabilities, while new operations would be carried out under a separate, sound portfolio. Shareholders would be wiped out and the BRB would use the bonds as payment for depositors. Since both instruments were extended at well below the market rate (nearly 7 per cent at the time), depositors suffered a loss in accepting the bond payments while the BRB received a subsidy from the loan based on collateral of uncertain value. Within a period of only two weeks, the BRB's shareholders and depositors accepted the government's plan. After the arrangement, numerous weaker banks collapsed while more prudent banks survived, though often with depositors suffering losses in a similar manner to those who had savings at the BRB.

The liquidation plan of the BRB terminated in 1905, though the bank had continued to function during this period. At this point, the BRB was restructured and renamed the Banco do Brasil (BB). The liabilities to the government were transferred to share capital, with the government now holding nearly a third of the shares (the largest block) in the newly recapitalized entity. Former shareholders of the bank received the same amount and the remainder was sold to new shareholders. The capital of the new bank was 30 per cent lower than that of the BRB, which meant that former shareholders suffered both a loss of control and 'paper' capital. Initially, the government had proposed that the recapitalization be accomplished by private capital alone. The minister of finance later agreed to turn the BRB's liabilities to the government into share capital at the request of the bank's shareholders, who sought continued government involvement (Topik, 1987, 39).[15]

---

[15] Shareholders would find the restructuring to be rewarding, with the BB's stock quotation rising from 49 milreis in 1905 to 250 milreis in 1908 (Topik, 1987, 39).

The new BB was a public–private institution with the government still in the dominant position as its largest shareholder and main client, with the power to appoint its president and director of the foreign exchange department and the ability to grant special privileges, such as exclusive national banking rights among domestic banks. The Treasury deposited its funds with the BB and the BB would make loans to the Treasury. The bank was also made the Treasury's sole agent in foreign currency transactions, thus helping to stabilize the value of the milreis under the new currency board that would be put in place, ending the domination of the foreign banks despite their protests (Triner, 2000, 77). In addition to these roles, the BB also retained a commercial function but it could not act as a universal bank or extend loans with a maturity longer than six months. These commercial functions would remain subordinate to the bank's public responsibilities.[16]

The BB was designed to develop gradually some central banking functions (Neuhaus, 1974, 16). It was expected to maintain a high level of liquidity to allow it to finance the Treasury and to make countercyclical loans during times of instability. Some of Rio's largest banks had been major private shareholders of the BRB and these banks embraced the restructuring because, as the *Jornal do Commercio* observed, the new bank would 'be able to exercise the functions of a central bank, having abundant capital to rediscount the paper of other banks, make advances to other banks, and finally aid them in moments of crisis' (as cited in Topik, 1987, 40). But the BB was not a fully fledged central bank and its role as a lender of last resort remained informal at this time.

Ultimately, the government response to the crisis involved liquidity support (which was eventually withdrawn), the closure and restructuring of insolvent banks, the imposition of losses on shareholders and creditors, and nationalization. The BRB did receive a subsidized loan as part of the liquidation plan but the government seized all of its stock as collateral, wiping out private shareholders (who, as already indicated, included other banks). Public funds were converted into share capital for the new BB, but only at the request of the bank's shareholders and with substantial private sector participation. The response thus

---

[16] Put differently, as Calomiris and Haber (2014, 428) observe, the BB 'was set up as a commercial bank that, because of its ownership structure, would be inclined to invest in treasury notes and bills'.

departed from the market pole of non-intervention, for which, as discussed below, the government received some criticism.

Contemporaries considered the aftermath of the 1900 crisis to be the final resolution of the 1890 crisis (Schulz, 2008, 122). Murtinho is often remembered in Brazil as the 'financial strongman'. His refusal to print money during the crisis certainly contrasts with that of previous finance ministers during times of financial instability. Elite opinion at the time largely supported the contraction of the money supply that had occurred since Prudente's time in office (Schulz, 2008, 123; Triner, 2000, 73). Yet, as its handling of the BRB reveals, the government was not fully committed to the market pole of doctrinaire non-interventionism. Indeed, its contemporaries in Britain opined that Murtinho was a bit too permissive compared to their own financial authorities. In Brazil, some praised the government for its willingness to resist resolving the crisis via printing money, but chastised it for not allowing failed banks to collapse without any government involvement (Schulz, 2008, 123). Yet, at the same time, others berated Murtinho for doing too little to assist the banks' shareholders and creditors (Schulz, 2008, 126).

In this environment, Murtinho felt compelled to defend his actions against those who thought the government should not have intervened at all in the crisis:

> But, Mr. President, if we refused to follow the policies assumed until then regarding this credit institution, we did not have the right to abandon its [BRB's] creditors and shareholders.
>
> Two motives, one moral, the other social, obliged us to intervene.
>
> From the moral point of view, we could not forget that the government was mostly to blame for the madness at the stock exchange and for all the economic and financial confusion accompanying devaluation of our currency.
>
> It was the government that authorized the issue of bank notes which generated these acts of insanity whose colossal losses became concentrated in the portfolio of the Banco da República. (as cited in Schulz, 2008, 126)

Murtinho's public justification of the intervention invokes the failures of the expansionary policies of past administrations. Indeed, some scholars suggest that the government's steadfast refusal to print money to resolve the crisis was due both to its intellectual attachment to monetary orthodoxy and its commitment, highly constrained after the funding loan, to maintaining Brazil's credibility with foreign investors (Schulz, 2008, 121; Triner, 2000, 47, 72–3). As Neuhaus (1974, 11) observes, the widespread failure of numerous banks 'was regarded as the price to be paid for restoring order in monetary and financial affairs'. Remarkably, Campos Sales and Murtinho pursued this policy even though they and their fellow agricultural interests also paid the price. It is thus difficult to sustain the claim that the intervention was due to rent-seeking or a desire for personal gain.

Others suggest that although the public justification was to atone for the errors of previous administrations, the BRB, as the Treasury's agent and the largest bank by total assets, also had become too important, perhaps too big, to fail (Calomiris and Haber, 2014, 427; Topik, 1987, 38). Topik (1987, 38) points out, 'As the largest native bank and the most active in the exchange market, it was simply too important to sacrifice to Murtinho's cherished law of survival of the economically fittest.' Of course, possible concerns about systemic risk did not prevent the government from standing by during the liquidity shock and widespread bank failures that followed closure of the BRB. As such, some suggest the government intervened in the BRB mainly to ensure that the bank repaid the £1 million it was owed (Schulz, 2008, 121; Topik, 1987, 38).

Murtinho's intervention may have been driven as much by these concerns as by the desire to strengthen the BRB against competition from foreign banks (Schulz, 2008, 125–6; Topik, 1987, 39). In 1893, after currency mismatches had created severe problems for many banks during the *Encilhamento*, the government had prohibited all foreign exchange trading by domestic banks that did not support underlying business transactions, exempting the BRB. This had left the BRB competing against foreign banks for exchange business. Indicative of his desire to strengthen the position of the BRB, Murtinho at the height of the crisis had proposed prohibiting all banks, including foreign ones, that dealt with exchange from taking deposits, once again exempting the BRB. Had the proposal been implemented, foreign banks, which held nearly half of all deposits (Triner, 2000, 210), would have lost one of their principal sources of profit in the exchange business.

The five-year period of government control of the BRB led to growing support for the idea that it was desirable to have some official control over the exchange rate. This would enable the government to smooth the seasonal pressures on the exchange rate arising from fluctuations in the trade balance. Moreover, as Fritsch (1988, 9) observes, after a decade of currency instability, 'government officials and public opinion in general were very critical of the alleged destabilising influence that speculation by the larger foreign banks could have on the market', and recognized that BRB, as a private concern, would have no obligation to countervail those influences; in fact, it had previously contributed to them. The government had attached such great importance to breaking the oligopoly of foreign banks in the exchange market that its responsibility for exchange market stability dominated the 1905 debate on the creation of the BB (Neuhaus, 1974, 16fn4). In this way, a desire to avoid external dependence, expressed initially as part of the radical republican and Jacobin movement aligned with Floriano, may have favoured state intervention in the financial system.

Yet the government did not opt for full-blown economic nationalism and remained largely committed to liberal economic orthodoxy. Although the nationalization of the BRB had been undertaken in part to combat the dominant position of foreign banks in the exchange market, the finance minister had initially sought foreign investors to provide as much as one-third of the bank's capital. The government is said to have changed its mind only when foreign investors became 'very demanding' about the terms (Topik, 1987, 39). The nationalization would also serve to further a key liberal reform: the return to gold convertibility, which was achieved in 1906 with the creation of a new currency board (the Caixa de Conversão). The creation of the BB called for state profits to be invested in a fund that had been established to start amortizing the 1898 Funding Loan when payments became due in 1911. The BB would work with the Caixa to stabilize the exchange rate, which, according to the finance minister, was 'essential to guarantee the efficiency of the redemption policy [of paper money] into gold' (as cited in Topik, 1987, 42).

The Paulistas' commitment to orthodox policies protected the extensive bond holdings (both domestic and foreign) of agrarian and commercial elites from inflation and later from default. Although bank failures and inflation threatened the wealth stored in deposits, these savings comprised a small share in the portfolios of elites. In effect, these elites limited their exposure to domestic bank failures by holding their wealth outside of this system and by maintaining large holdings with foreign banks, which held nearly half of total deposits in the banking system. Agrarian elites were thus much less at risk than financial and commercial interests connected to domestic banks. This helps to explain the ease with which the governing and opposition parties blamed speculators for financial instability (see Table 4.1), as well as the strong adherence of the Paulistas to monetary orthodoxy.[17]

The middle classes were more at risk. Outside property assets, stocks and bonds then formed the largest component of the portfolios of middle-class wealth-holders in Rio de Janeiro, followed by bank deposits and a considerably smaller sum held in cash (Frank, 2005, 95, and Chapter 3). Given the likely importance of deposit wealth for the middle class in general, it seems reasonable to presume that many also sought the comparative safety of foreign banks to minimize their vulnerability to domestic bank failures. Accordingly, the principal threat to this group, and the largely unbanked working and peasant classes, was inflation, which threatened to erode the real value of wages and savings. This policy preference was therefore broadly shared across different social classes.

Thus, among the narrow group of voting elites and probably among significant elements of the middle class, the bailout constituency was of limited size and influence. The strength of the coalition favouring orthodoxy was such that it would be maintained throughout the period of Paulista hegemony despite three successive systemic crises. This meant that, as in Britain following its 1825 crisis, even among distressed financial and commercial interests there was a low expectation that government would intervene beyond limited collateralized lending. One reason the aid to industry campaign proved so controversial was because it broke with the principle of laissez-faire by offering state support for private enterprise in periods of crisis (Stein, 1957, chap. 7). The Paulistas strongly opposed the measures and, once in office, refused to offer similar support even when their own interests and those of their constituents were threatened.

As in Britain, low expectations for intervention at this time in Brazil likely also rested on the absence of any prior government commitment to prevent crises via financial regulation. Although required to

---

[17] Importantly, as we discuss in the next chapter, this low expectation of support for private sector banks reinforced the position of BB and other state-owned banks, which came to be perceived as enjoying an implicit guarantee.

publish monthly balance sheets in the local financial press and audited semi-annual reports to their shareholders, banks were not subject to minimum capital or reserve requirements (Triner, 2000, 145). Bank shareholders were subject to reserve liability for losses, which provided an additional signal that government protection would not be forthcoming, particularly after Barbosa's reforms and in an environment where investors often walked away from their subscriptions with impunity. 'In essence,' as Triner (2000, 146) observes, 'private-sector banks were left to determine, establish, and maintain their own credibility ... Risk protection was an area in which the State did not involve itself in private-sector concerns.' This is striking in an era in which wealthy and comparatively financialized elites dominated politics.

Overall, the government's response to the 1900 crisis entailed greater intervention than in previous crises but it was still limited. With the exception of the BRB, the government permitted widespread bank failures and refrained from offering liquidity support. Since Brazil at this time fell short of the democratic thresholds in the Boix and Polity databases, the crises examined here do not appear in our analysis in Chapter 5. Nonetheless, the data we collected indicates that our assessment of its policy response is consistent with the index score for the 1900 crisis, which shows that the government leaned strongly towards the market-conformist pole of the policy spectrum, even if its intervention in the BRB made it less so than the responses to earlier crises (see Figure 11.4). Interestingly, in crises that followed in the 1920s, the government returned to its previous stronger adherence to market-conforming policies. This relatively market-conforming policy stance continued until the early 1990s, with the crisis that followed in 1994 involving a much more interventionist response (discussed in the following chapter).

11.3.2 Political Effects

In considering the political effects of the crises of this period, Deodoro's measures to delay the collapse of the *Encilhamento* appear to have been the final straw for his opponents. Even before the bubble began to deflate, the legitimacy of the Deodoro-led interim military government had been called into question with repeated accusations of corruption and authoritarianism. Republicans were particularly critical of Barbosa, the banking measures, and the close links that

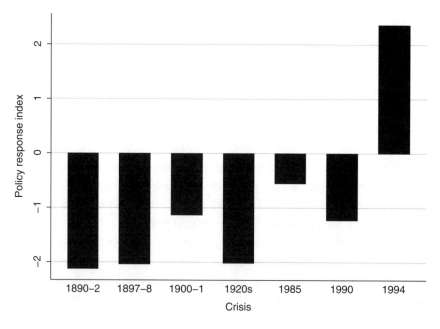

Figure 11.4: Policy responses to banking crises in Brazil, 1890–1994.
Note: With the exception of 1985, crisis dating is taken from those crises designated as systemic by Laeven and Valencia since 1970 and by Reinhart and Rogoff before 1945 (Laeven and Valencia, 2013; Reinhart, 2010).

monarchist financiers had to the regime. Afonso Pena, a leading Republican who would later become governor of Minas Gerais and the sixth president of Brazil, observed, 'The center of all fraud is the Banco da República, which wants to impose itself ... as the incarnation of the new regime, making the stability of the latter depend on the success of the former' (cited in Topik, 1987, 31).

In September 1890, after a period of delay, Deodoro permitted elections for a Constituent Assembly that he regulated to ensure that military officers comprised roughly one-fourth of the Assembly and that all of the ministers of the interim government, except one, were elected (Hahner, 1969, 40). Yet in an indication of the considerable degree of political competition that existed, historic republicans managed to command a majority in the Assembly, a position they would increasingly use to undermine Deodoro's authority. The historic republicans understood that they had little power regarding military matters, but that the Assembly was to indirectly elect the first constitutional president of Brazil to replace the interim government. Importantly, they had sufficient seats in the Assembly to prevent Deodoro from securing this new office, a cause that would be led by the radicals.

Momentum was added to these efforts when, in January 1891, following the resignation of the entire first cabinet in protest at Deodoro's attempt to award a public works concession to one of his supporters, a new cabinet was appointed consisting of many prominent monarchists. Whereas initially Deodoro had obtained overwhelming support for his policies in the Assembly, by the end of January 1891, the radical republicans obtained the support of almost half of the representatives in their motions of censure against the provisional president (Cable, 1976, 60).

Competition for office among elites intensified when historic republicans united in endorsing the candidacy of Prudente for president and threw their support behind Floriano for vice president. The Republican Party of São Paulo (PRP) constituted the most powerful group in the Assembly and had managed to elect Prudente as its president. Floriano had been serving as interim vice president, but was not Deodoro's preferred choice.

In the face of such hostile opposition, Deodoro was forced to rely on the threat of military force to secure victory in the indirect election (Cable, 1976, 66–7; Hahner, 1969, 45). Despite this, many republicans and dissident military officers still cast their vote for Prudente, who secured over 40 per cent of the votes. The Assembly underscored its opposition to Deodoro by electing Floriano as vice president by a much larger margin.

After the presidential election the Constituent Assembly became an ordinary legislature, consisting of a separate Senate and Chamber of Deputies. The radicals continued to offer their opposition in alliance with the moderate Paulistas, but it was the PRP that led the coalition against Deodoro. The exchange rate had declined steadily due to Barbosa's inflationary bank reform in December, the threat of military force during the election in February, and the Barings crisis taking place in neighbouring Argentina. The citizens of Rio, who spent a large proportion of their budgets on imported items, found their cost of living had doubled while their salaries had barely increased. Violence in the streets of the capital also became much more common than it had been under the monarchy, much of it directed at Portuguese merchants whom the populace blamed for the inflation (Schulz, 2008, 90–2, 110).

The expansionary measures of Deodoro's finance ministers were aimed at winning the support of agrarian interests, merchants and financiers. But as the costs of inflation and currency depreciation accumulated and evidence of corruption and corporate fraud mounted, Deodoro lost the support of most elites except for the narrow group of financial and commercial interests who continued to receive concessions owing to their close ties to the government.[18]

At the time Deodoro still enjoyed considerable support among the state governors and elements of the military. Thus, the decision to risk civil war to depose Brazil's first president suggests that most agricultural and commercial elites experienced negative fallout from the *Encilhamento*. As detailed in Chapter 3, agricultural and commercial elites at the time stored a great deal of their wealth in government bonds and increasingly in private securities traded on the stock exchanges and bank deposits. These elites would have lost significant wealth due to inflation and the stock market collapse, not to mention the purchases of the stocks of fraudulent firms.[19] Thus, rather than accommodate Deodoro's attempt to continue monetary expansion in an effort to delay the stock market correction and restructuring of the increasingly insolvent banking system, these elites instead insisted upon a return to orthodox monetary and financial policies. Indeed, in this era of low expectations Deodoro's opponents removed him from office precisely because he sought to break even further, in an unconstitutional manner, with market-conforming policy responses.

To be sure, these policies would bring widespread bank failures and a shortage of credit that inflicted additional harm on these elites. In fact, the aid-to-industry campaign followed on the implementation of these policies. But this additional harm was, in all likelihood, viewed as smaller than that which would have resulted from continued inflationary note issuance, which had served as a tax on their deposit and securities holdings, weakened the exchange rate and deterred foreign investment.

The agrarian Paulista oligarchy maintained largely unchallenged hegemony after the first direct presidential election in 1894. This

[18] The British ambassador described the head of the new ministry formed in January 1891 as a 'plunderer' (as cited in Schulz, 2008, 91). Schulz (2008, 91) details some of the concessions granted to closely connected financial and commercial interests during the period before the coup.

[19] Recall from Chapter 3 that the wealth share of the top 1 per cent of wealth-holders in Rio de Janeiro fell considerably during the period of financial instability in the 1890s and 1900s.

was despite the continued application of largely market-conforming policies, the costs of which were at times severe, particularly, as we saw in Chapter 3, for wealthy elites in Rio de Janeiro (and likely elsewhere). The platform of the PRF, which had been formed to contest the 1894 election, reflected Paulista interests, which, with the coffee economy dependent on stability to attract European immigrant labour and foreign investment and loans, supported fiscal and monetary orthodoxy to restore confidence (Cable, 1976, 81). The programme also opposed any government intervention in the economy, as had been favoured by supporters of industrialization, and instead pledged to advance private enterprise and by implication agricultural exporting interests. In the end, the election was uneventful, as no alternative candidate stood in opposition to Prudente.

As the 1898 election approached, the radicals organized themselves under a new party, the Partido Concentração (PC) or 'Majority Party', suggesting they represented the majority of republicans. The PC comprised a coalition of the ruling state parties – including Rio Grande do Sul and five minor states – that had opposed Prudente, as well as dissident factions from other states.

The manifestos of the competing PR and PC differed little on the banking crisis and its aftermath. Anti-speculation rhetoric drove the electoral campaigns of both parties (Mettenheim, 2015, 67). Both also reiterated the programme that had been outlined by the PRF in 1894, including, despite the steady stream of bank failures since the previous election, a commitment to fiscal and monetary orthodoxy (Bello, 1966, 164; Cable, 1976, 107). The main difference between the two parties was that the PC manifesto accused the PR of being controlled by the 'conservative elements of the Empire which had systematically opposed all liberal reform' (as cited in Cable, 1976, 107). Arguments raged not over economic policy, but over responsibility for continued conflict between the radical republicans and *adesistas* since 1894.

It soon became clear that the PR would poll the most votes at the election. The PR had the support of the majority of state governments, and the vote for the opposition would be reduced through government control of the electoral machinery. Yet certification of the winner would depend on control of the Congress, where allegiances were evenly split between the PR and PC (Cable, 1976, 108). What appears to have tipped the balance in favour of the PR was a failed assassination attempt against Prudente in November 1897 but which resulted in the death of the minister of war. The vice president and leaders of the opposition were implicated in the plot. Anti-monarchist demonstrations were replaced with violent anti-Jacobin ones.

From this point, Prudente consolidated his power relative to the PC opposition as well as the military. A PR majority in the Congress and the ballot box was assured, though continued apprehension about support for the opposition in the capital led the government to extend a state of emergency that had been imposed after the assassination attempt. The majority of election booths in the capital were closed, and the government resorted to extensive fraud in states where support for the opposition was expected to continue (Cable, 1976, 112). In the end, Campos Sales, the PR candidate, captured over 90 per cent of the votes.

By the time of the 1902 election, Campos Sales had institutionalized the politics of the governors. He was able to secure widespread support from this group for his chosen successor, the former finance minister Rodrigues Alves, who offered a platform that undertook primarily to continue the financial programme of Campos Sales and to leave in place those in power in the states. The crisis itself and the BRB intervention featured little in the internal PR discussions undertaken to nominate Campos Sales's successor. Rodrigues Alves was above all noted for his financial expertise and his commitment to orthodoxy (Cable, 1976, 125–30).

To the extent that debate arose, it focused on the fact that Campos Sales would be the third Paulista nominated since 1894, that he had been selected by the president, and that as an *adesista*, he would be the first candidate from the PR not to have been a 'historic' republican. However, Campos Sales was able to rely on his support among the state governors to overcome these objections. Of importance was his willingness to accept that the vice presidency should go to a candidate from Minas Gerais.

Rival factions did emerge to contest the election, but their opposition focused not on the crisis and its aftermath but rather on the gradual concentration of power in the hands of the president at the expense of the Congress, the consolidation of oligarchic rule and the exclusion of minority views (Cable, 1976, 130). But the politics of the governors ensured an almost total suppression of opposition votes in most states.

Only in Rio did the PRP fail to crush the opposition. Here the costs of the deflationary programme had been most severe, producing a high number of unemployed in a city where the cost of living remained high. The government permitted only half of the voting sections in the capital to open; only 31 per cent of registered voters ultimately cast their vote. Those that did opted overwhelmingly in favour of the candidate of the local ruling party rather than the opposition. Yet the outcome of the election was never in doubt. The Paulistas triumphed for a third consecutive election, once again capturing over 90 per cent of the vote. Interstate rivalry and concerns about Paulista hegemony led the PRP to acquiesce in the uncontested victory of the Mineiro Republican Party in the following election in 1906.

Thus, the ruling Paulistas maintained political power despite continued distress in the banking system that was at times exceptionally severe, and, in part, amplified by their policy choices. To be sure, the constrained nature of Brazil's democracy meant that informal intra-elite competition heavily influenced the vote shares in each election. In the federal capital, where the deflationary policies were often felt in the large number of unemployed and where civil unrest was sometimes extensive, the ruling party sometimes relied on voter exclusion tactics.

Sometimes this urban unrest was driven by nationalist and anti-monarchist sentiment, at other times by declining living standards. It is relevant that popular unrest during this period focused largely on inflation rather than on bank failures. If anything, the Jacobin press depicted any effort to support financial and commercial interests as a monarchist plot and stressed the harmful effects of inflation. They also expressed support for policies such as compulsory primary education and pensions for all state workers, aimed at improving the living conditions of the growing urban working class (Cable, 1976, 75–6, 92–3, 102, 109; Schulz, 2008, 114–15) As a result, though their rationale differed, these groups joined Paulista coffee interests and other elites in supporting a return to policy orthodoxy, though as the effects of deflation accumulated it did stir increasing resentment.

Yet, outside the federal capital, in the three direct presidential elections examined in this chapter, the opposition party managed to secure the support of only two minor state governments in just one election.[20]

---

[20] Rio Grande do Norde and Paraná in the 1898 election (Cable, 1976, 86–7, 113–15, 134–5). In some cases, state governments abstained from voting, permitting only the pro-government minority factions to vote. Opposition parties also captured significant minority factions in some states across the three elections.

As with Britain in the 1826 election (see Chapter 7), the presence of state government support for the opposition party may have been endogenous to voter sentiment. The widespread absence of support for opposition parties across all three elections likely reflects the limited impact that banking system distress had on the Paulistas' prospects for defeat. Even when elites formed opposition parties to contest the elections, they did so without departing from the governing party's monetary and financial policies. In fact, the 1902 election marked the end of remaining ideological divisions that had dominated the Old Republic (Cable, 1976, 100–3). From then onward, all state parties would be part of a unified Republican Party.

11.4   Conclusion

The first decade of the Old Republic was a period of recurrent systemic crises that began with the *Encilhamento*. At this time financialization was limited, wealth was concentrated in the hands of agrarian oligarchs, and the government refrained from any formal commitment to prevent financial instability. The wealth holdings of the elite largely comprised land and public securities, and the opportunity to store deposits in foreign banks minimized vulnerability to domestic bank failures. Inflation and currency instability emerged as the principal threat to this group's interests, and to those of the urban middle and working classes dependent on wage income. The prospect of default only served to reinforce these preferences, particularly among the wealthier elite.

Banking crises, on the other hand, posed a far smaller risk to these groups than to the financial and commercial interests that were threatened with losses. The dominance of agrarian over commercial interests during this period meant that the size and influence of the Bagehot constituency was substantial. Crisis resolution policies were thus largely market-conforming. Collateralized lending was offered to distressed financial and commercial interests, but in many cases these firms were permitted to fail and depositors and shareholders suffered losses.

The political fallout from these responses, as our theory expects, was limited. The Paulistas enjoyed a period of extended hegemony that stretched across much of this period of instability. These governments made few efforts to limit the closure of insolvent banks, despite the costs to the economy and, at times, their direct personal interests and those of their party's main constituents. It is worth reiterating that Deodoro was removed from office in large part because his government sought to pursue the opposite course of action.

In the next chapter we show that Brazil's experience with systemic crises a century later was quite different. Brazil remained a highly unequal society and inflation continued to pose severe challenges, but financialization had boosted the wealth of the recently enfranchised middle class and exposed them to much greater risk from banking crises. By this time the prevalence of state-owned banks and the presence of an explicit regulatory framework also provided voters with a clear signal of the government's greater commitment to financial stability. The emergence of great expectations among Brazilian voters fostered dramatically different policy and political consequences than those examined in this chapter, particularly when the government made an initial attempt to reprise Bagehot policies.

12 BANKING CRISES IN BRAZIL IN AN ERA OF RISING EXPECTATIONS

In this chapter we explore the political and policy aftermaths of a series of extended crises in Brazil in the 1990s. These occurred after the end of military rule in the mid-1980s in a new era of rapid democratization, declining economic inequality and rising financialization, including for the country's rising middle class. The combination of the last two factors distinguishes the Brazilian case from the British and American cases discussed in Chapters 8 and 10, where rising financialization accompanied rising inequality.

Indeed, in important respects, Brazil in the 1990s is a less likely case for our argument than these more advanced countries. As a relatively recent democratizer with lower levels of middle-class wealth, we might expect the development and strength of the bailout constituency in Brazil to be comparatively weaker. Brazil also has a long experience, stretching back at least to the early twentieth century, of close connections between political, business and financial elites. Since the 1930s and especially under the military dictatorship (1964–85), banks were used by governments at the federal and state levels to finance chronic fiscal deficits.[1] Banks were in turn provided with easy access to central bank credit and periodic government bailouts.

This system, which generated high and rising inflation and was beset with moral hazard, did not disappear with the emergence of the new democracy. Government and banking sector reliance on the

---

[1] A similar arrangement operated during the Empire and Old Republic (Calomiris and Haber, 2014, chap. 12; Topik, 1987, chap. 2).

inflation tax actually grew after 1985. Politically empowered and increasingly influential state governors also used locally controlled banks to direct credit towards favoured projects and groups to garner votes. This eventually prompted more bank bailouts, in part because national leaders could not afford to punish states important to their own political survival. Thus, one might expect many voters to have supported a less interventionist state that hewed more closely to market principles and engaged in fewer cronyistic bank bailouts. In this way, Brazil's transition from military dictatorship to vibrant democracy should be an ideal test of Rosas's argument about the constraining effects of democracy (Rosas, 2009).

Our argument suggests this narrative is at best incomplete. There has not been an end to bailouts in democratic Brazil, in part because there are new sources of demand for bailouts in a nation of rising middle-class wealth and exposure to the financial system. Major banks have remained under state control and are still important tools of policy intervention and political survival for elected governments. Although a majority of Brazilian voters do seem to have accepted in the mid-1990s that radical reform was necessary and that many banks should be closed, the evidence suggests that this acceptance was conditional on the protection of their own wealth. In this emerging democracy, then, great expectations among a rising middle class were sufficiently substantial by the 1990s that the Cardoso government took considerable pains to protect citizens' wealth much more assiduously than had its predecessors. To achieve this, Cardoso undertook the most extensive bailout response in Brazil's history (see Figure 11.4).

The rest of this chapter proceeds as follows. The first section describes the changing political-institutional context of banking in Brazil under authoritarianism and during the era of democratization from the mid-1980s. The second briefly describes the origins and nature of the extended period of banking crises from 1990. The third compares the policy responses of the Collor and Cardoso governments to the crises beginning in 1990 and 1994 respectively.[2] The fourth considers the political aftermaths of these crises, and a final section concludes by discussing the relationship between democratization and financial stability in contemporary Brazil.

---

[2] See Chapter 11 for the rationale for considering these crises.

12.1 The Evolving Political and Institutional Context of Banking in Brazil

Despite recurring financial instability, the government did not take explicit responsibility for financial stability until the 1930s. Before this, a basic form of banking regulation operated through public incorporation laws dating from 1891 that required all companies to publish their balance sheets monthly in the financial press and to provide audited semi-annual financial reports to shareholders. In 1918, banks were required to report their financial data to the Treasury, but this decree was not implemented until 1922, when a national banking inspectorate was established.

However, this inspectorate did not represent a new, explicit commitment to financial stability as it did not request data in excess of existing 1918 standards, strictly enforce the regulation or verify the reported data (Triner, 2000, 146). Nor did it specify minimum standards of bank safety, such as reserve and capital requirements. The government's principal motivation for creating the inspectorate appears to have been to enhance the Treasury's capacity to monitor the foreign exchange operations of foreign banks (Topik, 1987, 47; Triner, 2000, 146). Thus, the creation of the banking inspectorate gave the public little reason to expect that the government would henceforth protect their deposits and investments from private banking failures. The same could not be said for the Banco do Brasil (BB) and the growing network of state-owned banks, which increasingly benefited from an implicit government guarantee (Triner, 2000, 146).

Differential public expectations regarding the safety of private and state-owned banks were reinforced by widespread private banking failures during the 1920s. These undermined confidence in private domestic banks, which saw their share of deposits fall from more than 50 per cent to less than 30 per cent. Meanwhile, the deposit share of state-owned banks rose from less than 2 per cent to nearly 25 per cent, while that of BB more than doubled from roughly 13 per cent to nearly 29 per cent (Triner, 2000, 210). As we saw in Chapter 4, the 1920s banking failures prompted newspaper opinion to call on the government to take greater responsibility for general financial stability.[3]

---

[3] *O Paiz*, Os Bancos e a Fiscalização Bancaria [The Banks and Banking Supervision], 14 May 1929; *Folha da Manha*, O banco do Brasil e a crise financeira [Banco do Brasil and the financial crises], 28 June 1926.

The government did so explicitly in the early 1930s. In 1932, it opened a Banking Mobilization Office within BB to serve as a lender of last resort for failing banks. BB continued to operate as the de facto central bank until the 1960s, when the Central Bank of Brazil (BACEN) was created. In 1933, the Treasury imposed reserve requirements for the first time on banks (Triner, 2000, 254n136). The government also introduced a range of measures that were aimed at limiting and undermining the position of foreign banks operating in Brazil, including a commitment in the 1934 Constitution (though never acted upon) to nationalize all banks. In 1945, the government created the Superintendency of Money and Credit (SUMOC) by decree to oversee monetary policy as well as banking supervision and regulation that was implemented by BB.

Brazil's increasingly state-dominated banking system was an arrangement supported by both the elite-democratic governments and the authoritarian regimes that followed them (Elliot Armijo, 1993; Martinez-Diaz, 2009, 5, 14). State dominance suited the developmentalist coalition that sought to use national finance to promote industrialization and national autonomy, as well as political executives who came to rely heavily on inflation tax revenue and employment programmes to maintain their support coalitions. Private domestic banks were accommodated within the system but lacked the political influence to capture policy, with the state and the political elites that controlled it using the banking system for their own ends. Despite successive attempts to ban them entirely, foreign banks were tolerated though discouraged.

Individual banks, however, continued to enjoy powerful and privileged positions. As discussed in Chapter 11, BB had been serially restructured in the late nineteenth and early twentieth centuries but it remained the dominant commercial bank with a special relationship with the government, which had become its majority shareholder in 1923. It was particularly close to agricultural interests and possessed the sole interstate branching licence, which allowed it to collect nationwide deposits and thereby to fund the Treasury. The BNDES, the state-owned development bank established under Getúlio Vargas's second administration in 1952, was used by successive governments to pursue import-substitution industrialization objectives and to secure political support (Ferreira and Rosa, 2017).[4] This included the military, who considered

---

[4] Until 1982, the bank was formally BNDE; the 'S' for Social was added in 1982.

national development a precondition for the achievement of great power status. Caixa Econômica Federal (CEF) provided infrastructure financing and came to dominate the provision of housing finance.[5] It enjoyed a near-monopoly in the market for savings by the relatively poor, in the provision of pawnshops (an important source of credit) and in the management of the national lottery and government savings funds (the Programa de Integração Social and the Fundo de Assistência Social). Effectively, CEF became a tool for social and financial inclusion (von Mettenheim, 2006).

Inflation and financial repression, which ensured inflation tax revenues shared between the state and the banking sector, became integral to this system (Calomiris and Haber, 2014, 415–34). However, it also produced gradual financial disintermediation and discouraged the development of the stock market as individuals held assets outside the financial system in vehicles such as land and jewellery (Elliot Armijo, 1993, 266).

The military dictatorship from 1964 initially responded by attempting to impose a more liberal economic system with lower inflation and more incentives to save and invest. It promoted policies popular with business elites and the middle class including housing finance, stocks, inflation-indexed savings instruments with guarantees from the National Housing Bank (BNH), and a central bank (BACEN) managed by a National Monetary Council (NMC).[6] To appeal to the working class, in 1966 it established a system of compulsory savings (FGTS) to provide employer-funded unemployment compensation. These funds were also used to provide federally directed bank financing for infrastructure investment, primarily through CEF (World Bank, 1995, 3). Workers and their families could use FGTS funds in specific circumstances such as dismissal without just cause and death, as well as for the purchase of their own home (Deos, Ruocco & Rosa, 2017, 72).

Ultimately, however, the generals would prove as unwilling as their democratic predecessors to raise taxes on the private sector or to cut public expenditure to close the fiscal gap. BACEN struggled to maintain its political independence under the authoritarian regime as

---

[5] The Caixas were a decentralized association of state savings institutions until 1970, when they were merged into a single bank.

[6] After the creation of BACEN, BB retained its position as the government's banker and the most important commercial bank.

it was increasingly subordinated to the government's development objectives, heavily oriented to supporting lending by development banks such as BNDES to state-owned firms in key sectors (Elliot Armijo, 1993, 268–72). Moral hazard spread through the banking system. Many private banks were strongly associated with clientilism, often closely connected to agricultural and industrial interests that had supported the military government. Like state-controlled banks, they also came to enjoy effective government protection, weakening credit discipline. Some attempts were made to inject greater market discipline but these were not sustained. For example, the technocratic finance minister Mario Enrique Simonsen announced in 1974 that weak banks should expect no state bailouts, but soon afterwards President Goulart authorized BACEN to rescue a failing bank associated with an industrial conglomerate, Banco Halles, to prevent a wider financial panic (Elliot Armijo, 1993, 276; Mezarobba, 1995).

High growth shored up the military regime's support base only temporarily. The government increasingly relied on foreign borrowing, BNDES development finance and a rising inflation tax to sustain high growth, especially after the first oil shock in the early 1970s. From the late 1970s, rising inflation and declining growth eroded the political foundations of authoritarianism. By the early 1980s the military's grip on political power was weak. Despite its efforts to cultivate the support of the poor and workers, the influence of social forces beyond its traditional support base had increased steadily, promoted by rising literacy, industrialization and urbanization. Free elections for state governors, municipal councils and mayors were held across the country in 1982 in which large losses were suffered by the military's party (Elliot Armijo, 1993, 280). In 1985, in conjunction with the transition to civilian rule at the national level, the franchise was extended to all citizens above fifteen years.

Yet many of the financial policies set in previous decades continued in the early years of democratic governance, resulting in persistent high inflation and financial disintermediation. State-controlled banks came to provide the bulk of lending. By the late 1980s, the CEF was providing nearly half of all private sector lending (Figure 12.1). Following the creation of a new housing finance system, the CEF became Brazil's main source of loans for residential construction and mortgage loans to individuals, directly benefiting the country's urban middle class (Elliot Armijo, 1993). From 1986, CEF managed the FGTS

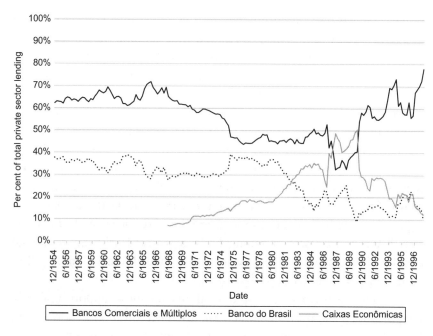

Figure 12.1: Credits to the private sector by major lenders (per cent of total private sector lending), 1954–97.

Source: Instituto Brasileiro de Geografia e Estatistica (2018).

Note: *Bancos comerciais e múltiplos* may be public or private institutions that are multi-function finance firms or universal banks engaging in commercial, investment and development lending, as well as real estate finance and leasing activities. BNDES is included in this category.

unemployment insurance fund, which enabled it to become a crucially important institution for social policy in Brazil: 'By 1993, the Caixa had unified over 130 million FGTS accounts once dispersed across 76 banks, eliminating over 72 million inactive accounts' (von Mettenheim, 2006, 50). This is likely to have reinforced societal support for the protection of CEF in particular.

As the centre's political control declined, elected state governors actively used their new authority to secure their political positions, including by using state-controlled banks to finance local development projects. The 1988 Constitution also gave states access to largely automatic federal fiscal transfers, and municipalities could in turn draw on state revenues (Fishlow, 2011, 23–4). State-controlled banks could borrow from BACEN or BB. In 1989 and 1993, the national government federalized state debts, completing the circle of moral hazard. As the autonomy of national technocrats declined further, politically connected lending by state-owned banks led to deteriorating credit standards.

Worker financial protection policies established under the military were also extended under democratic governments and contributed to financialization. Additional workers' support funds were created in the late 1980s, which became important sources of funding for BNDES (Ferreira and Rosa, 2017, 107–11). Later, in July 1996, a new law allowed workers to use up to 50 per cent of their FGTS deposits to purchase shares in Mutual Privatization Funds (FMP). This encouraged workers to undertake riskier investments in stocks rather than to retain these in the form of guaranteed deposits (which continued to be indexed to the Reference Rate (TR) plus interest of 3 per cent per year) (Banco Central do Brasil, 1997, 82). Democratization, in short, has not necessarily promoted financial stability.

It was also associated with considerable political instability, at least in its early stages. The new indirectly elected civilian administration that took office in March 1985 suffered an immediate blow when the victorious Brazilian Democratic Movement Party (PMDB) candidate, Tancredo Neves, died before his presidential inauguration. His vice president-elect and successor, José Sarney, would expend much of his political capital over the following five years in a series of vain attempts to defeat inflation. The PMDB, the sole opposition party under the military regime, won a large majority in the constituent assembly in 1986 but then split over a range of issues, including the party's stance towards Sarney. As the end of Sarney's term loomed, the political and economic elite feared that the 1989 election – the first time that Brazilians could vote directly for a president – might produce a victorious candidate from the left. The right offered no viable candidate of its own but rallied around a young opportunist, Fernando Collor de Mello, who ran on an anti-corruption programme as a political outsider leading a new political party, the Party of National Reconstruction (PRN) (Bethell and Nicolau, 2008, 246–50). After a first round of voting in the presidential election of 1989 failed to produce a clear winner, the election became a contest between Collor on the right and the remaining candidate of the left, Luiz Ignácio Lula da Silva ('Lula'), of the grassroots Workers' Party (PT). Lula's radicalism worried banks and business generally. Capital flight accelerated in the months before the election and during the ensuing run-off (Welch, 1991, 18–19). Collor won the run-off fairly easily, assisted in part by support from dominant media outlets. Whether Brazil's new and very young democratic order would have survived had Lula been elected (his platform then included nationalizing the banks and the press) remains uncertain (Bethell and Nicolau, 2008, 250).

Political instability continued during Collor's short presidency, which ended abruptly with charges of grand corruption and impeachment in September 1992. Perhaps in part because Collor was removed peaceably, the democratic political system stabilized in the following years. He was succeeded by his vice president, Itamar Franco, who served out the remaining two years of Collor's term. Franco built a more stable coalition based on the three major parties, the PMDB, the Liberal Front Party (PFL) and the Social Democratic Party of Brazil (PSDB), and maintained good relations with the military, which retained three ministries. As we discuss in the following section, his government also succeeded in reducing inflation, the key challenge that his predecessors failed to overcome.

The political system in the democratization era was characterized by high party fragmentation and low party loyalty, with continuing high rates of party defection by deputies. Smaller states are also relatively over-represented in the Congress, both in the Chamber of Deputies and in the Senate, which contains three senators from every state or federal district. Civilian presidents elected after 1985 constantly had to negotiate with other parties in Congress, as well as key individuals and state governors who also controlled congressional votes. As Bethell and Nicolau note, presidents were forced to appeal to the pragmatic centre; worse, '*Presidentialismo de coalizão* [coalition presidentialism] led inevitably to *fisiologismo* (pork-barrel politics) and corruption. Many of the medium-sized and smaller parties simply became *partidos de aluguel* (parties for rent)' (Bethell and Nicolau, 2008, 269). Democratization was thus also associated with continuing clientilism and corruption.

The 1988 Constitution, intended to prevent a return to a centralized authoritarian state, formally decentralized power. The power of Congress to draft legislation was enhanced, including in areas such as budget preparation (Câmara dos Deputados (Brazil), 2010, 53-7). Other populist provisions included referenda and citizens' right to propose laws, as well as a long list of specific guaranteed 'social rights' for particular groups (Câmara dos Deputados (Brazil), 2010, 21-3, 25). Populism was also arguably facilitated by continuing high rates of illiteracy and low levels of education; as late as 2014, 44 per cent of the population over twenty-five years had no more than primary school education.[7]

At the same time, the 1988 Constitution retained a substantial degree of executive power. The president would be directly elected but under Article 62 could avoid legislative vetoes through the use of temporary executive decrees, which have immediate effect but require approval by Congress within sixty days – a method used heavily by Collor in 1991 but restricted by Congress as power shifted back towards the legislative branch in 1992. The president was also granted discretion in particular areas. For example, foreign bank branches and subsidiaries were banned, but the president could override this (Martinez-Diaz, 2009, 80).[8] Skilled presidents could also dominate the policy agenda by exploiting the weak party system – in some cases, literally by buying votes. Another clause required a referendum after five years on whether the political system should be modified, but in April 1993 voters reaffirmed that it should remain republican and presidential. The following year, Congress passed another amendment that reduced presidential terms to four years, which had the practical effect of harmonizing the timetables for presidential and congressional elections (Bethell and Nicolau, 2008, 256). This increased the likelihood that a strong president would enjoy a workable majority in Congress.

The potential power of the presidency became apparent in the second half of the 1990s. The 1994 presidential elections were a contest between Fernando Henrique Cardoso of the PSDB, formerly the foreign and finance minister of the Franco government, and Lula of the PT. This open contest between two candidates of the centre-left and left, both with strong democratic credentials, was a promising indicator of demo-cratic consolidation. Cardoso's ability to appeal to centre-right constitu-encies and his association with the successful *Plano Real*, which was highly popular among the poor (see below), dramatically boosted his standing. He won resoundingly in the first round with 54 per cent of the vote against 27 per cent for Lula. Although Cardoso's political coalition won only 35 per cent of the seats in the Chamber and 45 per cent of seats in the Senate, the PMDB lent its support to the government and

---

[7] World Bank, World Development Indicators, accessed 2 March 2018.
[8] As discussed below, these restrictive provisions were later revoked in constitutional amendments.

assured it a working congressional majority. When in 1996 the PPB (Partido Progressista Brasileiro) also joined this coalition, the government in principle had sufficient votes in Congress to pass reforms requiring constitutional amendment. This would include an amendment to allow presidents to serve for two terms rather than only one – of immediate benefit to Cardoso himself. Nevertheless, Cardoso would also rely heavily on executive decrees to govern (Bethell and Nicolau, 2008, 259–61).

Cardoso's first term was widely seen as successful and, as we discuss below, he was re-elected in 1998. He also limited the military's political role, appointing a civilian in charge of a new defence ministry at the end of 1998 and ending the military's hitherto privileged position in the cabinet. That Cardoso's long-term rival on the centre-left, Lula, was finally elected president in 2002 despite his modest background and radical past was another indication of further democratic consolidation. Nevertheless, scepticism about democracy persisted. In a Latinobarómetro poll in 1998, 71.3 per cent of respondents said they were 'not very' or 'not at all' satisfied with the way democracy works in Brazil, an increase of 6 per cent from 1995. Almost 80 per cent over this period also professed 'little' or 'no' confidence in Brazil's political parties, and two-thirds thought elections were 'rigged'.[9] These results owed much to persisting perceptions of political corruption and the focus of governments in the 1990s on macroeconomic stabilization, which meant that there was limited progress in addressing Brazil's major structural challenges, including education, inequality and poverty (Bethell and Nicolau, 2008, 273–4).

12.2 The Banking Crises of the 1990s

The crisis of 1990–3 may be seen as the final crisis of the high inflation era. The considerably deeper banking crisis that began in 1994 and continued to at least 1998,[10] by contrast, was closely associated with the period of disinflation initiated by the *Real* Plan. As noted in Chapter 11, there is also inconsistency in the economic literature as to whether both crises were systemic. Our analysis suggests that both were

---

[9] http://www.latinobarometro.org/, accessed 2 March 2018.
[10] As we note below, the restructuring and recapitalization of federal government-owned banks continued through 2001.

very serious and, had it not been for government interventions in 1990, the earlier crisis could easily have spread in scope and intensity. Indeed, from a longer perspective, both crises are best seen as related and a consequence of a gradual build-up in financial fragility over the course of the 1970s and 1980s. The disinflation that was finally achieved from 1994 exposed longstanding weaknesses in the banking system that had been masked during the high inflation period.[11]

Severe problems emerged in Brazil's banking sector not long after the onset of the Latin American debt crisis in 1982 (Ness, 2000, 72). In February 1985, the government intervened in Banco Sul Brasileiro, then the country's thirteenth largest bank, and a related mortgage lender, Habitasul. BACEN injected liquidity into the banking system to prevent the crisis from spreading. Then, in March, the newly installed Sarney government immediately took action to close a major investment bank, Brazilinvest. The government warned Brazilinvest's owners that their personal assets would be seized to cover the bank's liabilities, which was notable because one of the bank's directors was also a cabinet minister. It was intended as an early signal to bankers that the Sarney government would not bail them out and that it intended to 'clean up the mess' left by the military government, including by adopting austerity measures demanded by the IMF (Foster and Witcher, 1985).

When the crisis worsened in November 1985, three large banks (Comind (Banco de Comércio e Indústria de São Paulo), Maisonnave and Auxiliar) were taken over and closed by the government, an indication of this tougher approach. However, the government guaranteed deposits in the failed banks. As a result, our policy response index score for the 1985 crisis suggests one that was decidedly less market-conforming than any previous crisis in Brazil's history, though it still leaned in that direction (see Figure 11.4). Although BACEN had earlier provided finance to Comind to protect Brazil's foreign debt credibility, relations with foreign bankers soured when shortly thereafter the government decided to reimburse only 25 per cent of the losses they had suffered due to the failures. Concerted pressure from foreign banks

---

[11] Notably, Brazil was only one of two countries in the R&R dataset that experienced a banking crisis (a non-systemic crisis in 1963) in the otherwise extraordinarily tranquil period in the global economy over 1940–70 (Reinhart, 2010; Reinhart and Rogoff, 2009). The other was India over 1947–8, associated with the upheaval of independence and division.

forced the government to improve this offer (Reuters, 1985; Witcher and Conroy, 1985).

The new government's efforts to clean up the banking sector legacies of the military regime also caused problems for state-connected banks, particularly the largest, BB. The National Housing Bank (BNH) was clearly bankrupt and was merged with CEF in 1986, which was forced to absorb its large and distressed real estate loan portfolio. The government ended the policy of subsidized agricultural lending, rendering a number of borrowers in this sector insolvent. This raised NPLs at BB, the major lender in this sector. The government also removed BB's privileged access to BACEN credit via its 'movement account' in early 1986, but partly compensated BB by permitting it to become a financial conglomerate. Despite this, by October 1991 BB's NPL portfolio had reached US$636 million (Elliot Armijo, 1993, 280–1). It would also prove to be too important to fail.

As we saw in Chapter 4, newspaper opinion in the mid-1980s was already pointing to the state banks as the 'Achilles heel' of the national financial system (*Jornal do Brasil*, 1986). In 1983 and 1984, the military government had given these banks favourable terms to refinance their existing debts and fines owed to BACEN. Then, in February 1987, the Sarney government adopted the Temporary Special Administration Regime (RAET), which allowed BACEN to deal with failing banks via liquidation, recapitalization, merger and acquisition, and restructuring and resale. Under RAET, BACEN takes temporary control of a bank's liabilities and administration, fully protecting depositors. It was initially used to support and stabilize state banks and to return them to state government control (Ness, 2000, 72–3).

The underlying chronic problem, as noted above, was that military and civilian governments in the 1980s and early 1990s continued to rely on the banking sector, and ultimately BACEN, to finance a continuing fiscal gap. As Fishlow notes, 'There was no real budget constraint operating; it was, at best, a very 'soft' limitation' (Fishlow, 2011, 25). State-owned banks were also used by politicians to achieve redistributionist objectives and to buy votes by boosting lending in targeted districts before elections – a practice that did not disappear after the banking crises of the 1980s and 1990s (Carvalho, 2014; Ness, 2000, 72). Bank failures would also expose depositors to losses, which, as Sarney's successor would find, was politically disastrous in an era of rising middle-class wealth and exposure to the financial system. For all

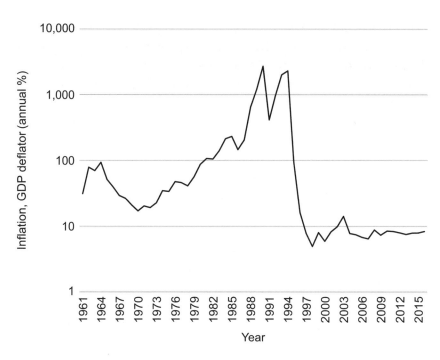

Figure 12.2: Inflation, GDP deflator, 1961–2016 (annual percentage change, log scale).
Source: World Bank, World Development Indicators.

these reasons, the state had strong political incentives to guarantee many banks' survival even when they were very weak (Beck, Crivelli & Summerhill, 2005, 2226–7).

The main thing keeping weak banks operating by the late 1980s was high inflation (Bridges, 1988). This had accelerated under democratic government, reaching about 2,700 per cent by 1990, before falling to 414 per cent in 1991 (Figure 12.2). Banks thrived under high inflation by collecting easy revenue on the 'float' between check payments and clearing, by which time the real value of their demand deposit liabilities had fallen. By the early 1990s, this 'inflation revenue' had grown to about 4 per cent of GDP and represented about 40 per cent of bank income. The number of banks also grew rapidly (Goldfajn, Hennings and Mori, 2003, 12). Thus, any attempt to control inflation entailed serious risks for the country's banking sector, as a series of mostly unsuccessful macroeconomic stabilization plans would demonstrate.

Serial attempts were made to bring inflation under control before the mid-1990s, including the Cruzado Plan (1986), the Bresser

Plan (1987) and the Summer (*Verão*) Plan (1989). None had a lasting impact because they failed to tackle the financing of public sector deficits (Fishlow, 2011, 38–9). Nevertheless, there was a growing political constituency favouring disinflation by this time. Business elites and the middle classes had become disenchanted with hyperinflation, and the poor, who had always lost most from inflation, were also newly empowered by democratization.

Immediately on taking office in March 1990, Collor sought to implement his own macroeconomic stabilization plan, *Plano Brasil Novo*, better known as Collor Plan I. It was a heterodox package of radical economic opening, privatization and stabilization measures that included elements of Lula's proposals, including a moratorium on internal public debt, the introduction of a new currency (the new cruzeiro), the freezing of demand, savings and overnight deposits, and a three-day bank holiday. We discuss the banking sector measures in the following section. The plan's main inspiration for achieving price stability, West Germany's 1948 Erhard Plan, suggested that the excess money supply first needed to be wiped out (de Paiva Abreu, 2008, 418–19). Financial institutions were also initially required to purchase shares in state privatizations with government certificates that lost 1 per cent of their value monthly until used. Collor's untested economy minister, Zélia Cardoso de Mello, promised that the budget balance would swing from an 8 per cent deficit to a 2 per cent surplus by the end of the year (Brooke, 1990).

As Collor's predecessors had found, his government lacked support in Congress and among economic elites to enact the necessary fiscal adjustment (Bresser-Pereira and Nakano 1991, 50–2). The political opposition was also bolstered by the fact that the administration's policy measures were generally very unpopular, as reflected in contemporary newspaper opinion (see Chapter 4). Inflation fell initially but the absence of real fiscal reform meant that it quickly accelerated when wage and price controls were removed (Welch, 1991, 21–2). Retail sales fell by a third (Brooke, 1991) and GDP fell by nearly 5 per cent over the year, a record (de Paiva Abreu, 2008, 420).

The Collor Plan II, announced at the end of January 1991, included additional wage and price freezes, after talks with unions and employers' organizations to end automatic wage indexation broke down (Brooke, 1991). This plan was widely flouted and predictably it also failed to reduce inflation. Four months later Collor's unpopular economy minister was forced to resign. A more orthodox plan followed led by a new economy minister, Marcilio Marques Moreira, with further tightening of monetary and fiscal policy, unfreezing of prices and a release of the remaining frozen deposits. Real interest rates rose sharply and heavily indebted states began to default (World Bank, 1995, 4). The government's credibility was in tatters, well before the corruption scandal broke that led to Collor's impeachment.

The next banking crisis also grew out of a new macroeconomic stabilization plan, this time successful. The *Real* Plan, introduced by Cardoso in 1994 after he became finance minister (in 1993) under Franco (December 1992–January 1995), was thought likely to fail by institutions such as the IMF. The plan introduced first a voluntary transitional unit of account and daily indexing mechanism, the *Unidade Real de Valor*, alongside cruzeiros. In July 1994 a new currency, the *real*, was introduced. It was underpinned by a 'triple anchor' comprising a managed exchange rate, a firm commitment to tight money and a primary fiscal surplus, which required debt renegotiations with the states, a number of which were close to default (Cardoso and Graeff, 2012, 18). In the latter respect, the administration achieved congressional agreement in early 1994 to substantial fiscal reform via the *Fundo Social de Emergência*, which suspended existing legislation on earmarked revenues for two years (de Paiva Abreu, 2008, 426). A new financial transactions tax, including on the cashing of cheques, was introduced. The administration also reached agreement with foreign banks to end the default that had lasted since 1987 and which wrote off a third of the face value of this external debt. Despite the continued deterioration of the fiscal position, tight monetary policy and rising real interest rates ensured rapid disinflation after 1994, falling from about 2,300 per cent to below 5 per cent by 1998.

To constrain state government borrowing credibly, it was essential that the Franco and then Cardoso governments wrest control of state banks from their political principals (Sola, da Cunha Bueno Garman and Marques, 2001, 54–5). Cardoso's team planned to do this by ensuring their closure or privatization. Many public banks were by this time in dire straits and most state governments were in no shape to rescue them (Bevilaqua, 2002, 21–3). Inflation float revenues became negligible by 1995, requiring banks to find new sources of revenue (Goldfajn et al., 2003, 17; Maia, 1999, 107–8). State banks lent heavily to state governments; others rapidly expanded lending to business and individuals.

Despite precautionary increases in reserve requirements by BACEN, poor credit risk assessments and continuing expectations of federal government support generated rising balance sheet risk for many banks (Baer and Nazmi, 2000, 8–9). As interest rates rose and the economy deteriorated in the aftermath of the Mexican peso crisis of 1994–5, NPLs rose to over 15 per cent of total loans (Maia, 1999, 108; Takami and Tabak, 2007, 5). Dozens of state-owned banks, including Banespa, the largest state bank based in São Paulo state, faced bankruptcy. The government's woes were compounded because major national banks, including BB and CEF, also experienced large losses in 1995 and the former at least was technically insolvent; so too were a number of private banks (Deos et al., 2017, 71; Martinez-Diaz, 2009, 90). Over the period July 1994 to December 1998, fifty-nine banks failed, representing 22 per cent of all banks (Sales and Tannuri-Pianto, 2007, 4)

It was widely believed that state governments and their captive banks would ultimately be rescued by the federal government, as they had been in the 1980s. State debts to federal banks, especially the CEF, had been transferred to the Treasury in 1993. Federal bailouts created few political incentives for voters to punish state governments for continuing to spend on local projects above and beyond local tax receipts (Rodden, 2006, 205; World Bank, 1995, 5–6). The federal government was thus faced simultaneously with both failing banks and failing states. With real interest rates rising and a new fiscal framework in place, governments such as São Paulo's had ceased servicing their debt. A federal government rescue plan in November 1995 extended another lifeline to states in the form of CEF loans with fiscal conditionality attached, but this conditionality lacked credibility and only shifted financial risk onto another public sector institution (Bevilaqua, 2002, 27). We describe below how an eventual deal between the federal and state governments was reached that restructured state debts and which provided for the privatization or closure of most state banks.

12.3   Policy Responses in the 1990s Crises

We pointed in the previous chapter to the largely market-conforming nature of the policy responses to Brazil's banking crises of the pre-1945 period. As noted above, the Sarney government also closed some failing banks in November 1985, though it protected domestic depositors. Banking crises may also have been avoided because of explicit or implicit protection of banks – as noted above, the insolvent National Housing Bank was merged with CEF in 1986 and BB, which was too big and politically important to fail, continued to operate despite growing losses. As shown in Figure 11.4, this policy tendency continued in the early 1990s but not from 1994, where there is a clear shift from a relatively market-conforming policy response to a bailout response. As we describe in more detail, the crisis policies in the early 1990s were unusual for modern governments in that they imposed substantial costs on depositors. The responses of the Cardoso government to the crisis of the mid-1990s were more consistent with the trend towards bailout responses we identify in this book, though this government was tougher than its predecessors in closing or privatizing some failing banks.

As noted above, a deposit freeze was a central component of the Collor Plan I and based on the post-war West German approach of confiscating a large proportion of the existing money supply. The political context of the German plan was, however, fundamentally different: the massive confiscation of old Reichmarks in 1948 occurred under allied military occupation and at the primary insistence of the American government, predating the formation of the Federal Republic of Germany (Tribe, 2001). Stolper and Roskamp note that it 'was perhaps fortunate for the future political stability of the Federal Republic that the currency reform was designed and executed by the Allies' (Stolper and Roskamp, 1979, 384). Collor seems not to have understood that Brazilians might react badly to an attempt by their own government to confiscate wealth in a newly democratizing free country, even if most accepted that hyperinflation had to be stopped (see Chapter 4).

The freeze was applied to all but the smallest accounts and amounted to about 30 per cent of GDP and 80 per cent of financial system liabilities. Individuals could withdraw and convert into cruzeiros a maximum of about US$1,000 from deposit and savings accounts, and the higher of 25,000 cruzados and 20 per cent from 'overnight' accounts that paid daily interest on short-term government bills.[12] For the following eighteen months all remaining deposits were to be frozen

[12] The latter had become very popular because they paid high interest and could be less risky than holding US dollars, due to exchange rate volatility. These bills had also become an important source of government finance – an indication of the government's declining creditworthiness – but had contributed to escalating interest costs on public debt (Bresser-Pereira and Nakano, 1991, 43–5).

and used only to pay past debts (in cruzados), then released in annual instalments in cruzeiros from September 1991, with indexation and accumulated interest of 6 per cent per annum. However, these measures failed to protect the wealth of depositors who saw their frozen assets suffer losses due to rapidly accelerating inflation, which reached a monthly rate of nearly 8 per cent in May 1990, 13 per cent in August 1990, and 20 per cent by January 1991 (de Paiva Abreu, 2008, 419). The government also imposed sweeping new fiscal measures, including a new tax on financial operations (*Imposto sobre Operações Financeiras* – IOF) charged on the stock of financial assets, on transactions in gold and stocks, and on withdrawals from savings accounts.

Along with BACEN assistance to failing banks, the deposit freeze may have (temporarily) rescued the banking sector (Elliot Armijo, 1993, 283). However, it was deeply unpopular among businesses and depositors. As noted in Chapter 4, it was commonly referred to as a 'confiscation' of private savings by the government (Fishlow, 2011, 39; Welch, 1991, 19). Over 70,000 lawsuits were filed against the government action, many successfully (Kamm and Michaels, 1991). After loud complaints from business, companies were allowed to pay wages from blocked accounts by bidding in BACEN auctions for the right to convert their cruzado deposits into cruzeiros. This helped to feed perceptions of policy instability and corruption under Collor and was perceived as shifting the burden to ordinary Brazilians (de Paiva Abreu, 2008, 419; Gall, 1992; Long, 1990). Frequent discretionary deviations from the plan both undermined its effectiveness and increased perceptions of injustice. Due to lobbying and legal action, nearly half the frozen accounts were unblocked within months, but they had lost about 30 per cent of their real value due to inflation (Bethell and Nicolau, 2008, 251).

Collor Plan II also included new measures that hurt depositors. In its effort to 'de-index' the economy, it abolished the popular overnight accounts, forcing depositors into new funds that banks were then required to use in part to purchase government bonds. Another short bank holiday was decreed to allow banks to prepare. Creditor interests were also damaged by new proposals to lengthen effective debt maturities based on the delusional assumption that inflation would immediately fall to zero. This invited further legal challenge (de Paiva Abreu, 2008, 421).

Since hyperinflation itself was a source of wealth confiscation, especially for the poor, there was growing political support for policies that could bring inflation under control. In fact, the transition from authoritarianism initially produced a shift back towards a more market-conformist policy approach (see Figure 11.4). However, the Collor administration's confiscation of societal wealth was not tolerated in an era of rising expectations in which many voters expected government to protect it. Furthermore, its policies were implemented in ways widely perceived as unfair and, ultimately, because it failed to end the hyperinflation for which the sacrifice was said to be necessary.

It is striking that this apparently widespread intolerance for deposit confiscation occurred in circumstances in which the wealth of the middle and lower classes in Brazil was significantly less than that in the United States around the time of the 1907 banking crisis (Chapter 3). Yet the political context of 1990s Brazil was very different. The Brazilian middle class aspired to the better conditions of life that prevailed elsewhere, and had been deeply disappointed by the results of democratization. For example, Brazilians – especially those in the middle and upper-middle quintiles – enjoyed less access to public welfare services such as government-provided healthcare than their counterparts in most upper-middle- and high-income countries and paid higher average out-of-pocket expenses for medical care.[13] Lower public welfare provision, in turn, generally increases the reliance on personal savings for unexpected or emergency expenditures. Thus, even at relatively low levels of wealth, government confiscation in Brazil was likely to be badly received.

The underlying problems with the banking sector only came to a head after Collor's ignominious exit, in the final year of Franco's term. In 1994, the government liquidated seventeen small banks, intervened in three private banks, and placed eight state banks under administration. Shortly before Cardoso was inaugurated in January 1995, BACEN took over two large state banks, Banespa and Banerj, from São Paulo and Rio de Janeiro states respectively, under its RAET authority.[14] The shift towards bank bailouts accelerated after Cardoso took office.

[13] In 1996, out-of-pocket healthcare expenditures for Brazilians averaged 41 per cent of total health expenditure, compared to 14.2 per cent and 11 per cent in the United States and United Kingdom respectively. A fifty-nine-country study using data from the 1990s found that Brazil and Vietnam were the countries where households were most likely to experience 'catastrophic' healthcare expenditures beyond their capacity to pay (Barros and Bertoldi, 2008; OECD, 2014; Xu et al., 2003).

[14] Cardoso had ceased to be finance minister in March 1994 to run for the presidency.

The government recapitalized Banespa in May 1995 to improve its attractiveness to foreign buyers (Martinez-Diaz, 2009, 88). This recapitalization followed the government's attempt to prop it up by having federal banks, especially BB, purchase Banespa's bonds that private banks and other investors would no longer hold (World Bank, 1995, 7). Banespa was the main remaining source of lending to state governments and two-thirds of its loans to São Paulo state had been funded by loans it contracted with foreign banks. By providing an effective guarantee of Banespa's and Banerj's liabilities, the government allowed these politically important banks to continue operations; it also shifted the risk of São Paulo state's defaulting from the banks to the federal government (World Bank, 1995, 1, 6). These rescues were followed by others in 1995, including Credireal from Minas Gerais (Ness, 2000, 77). However, the federal government lacked the resources to bail out all of the distressed banks. As Pérsio Arrida, a key member of Cardoso's economic team, noted, 'We had to avoid a banking crisis, and we didn't have enough capital to absorb all the weak banks' (cited in Martinez-Diaz, 2009, 91). This forced them to look to foreign buyers. With insufficient time to amend the constitutional ban and due to the uncertainty regarding the outcome of any such attempt, Cardoso invoked his constitutional right to exercise discretion on foreign ownership of banks (Martinez-Diaz, 2009, 91–2).

The Cardoso government then introduced two new programmes to deal with troubled private and state-owned banks respectively. Both regimes also fully protected depositors and aimed to transfer control of the banks to new owners or to close them (Baer and Nazmi, 2000, 12–13; Maia, 1999, 107). Some argue that executive autonomy was maintained in the bank restructuring process in part due to the ability of the president to issue decrees and that the legislature played little role (Martinez-Diaz, 2009, 83, 104–5). However, this conclusion seems more applicable to the restructuring of private banks than of state-owned banks.

The first programme, the Programme of Incentives for the Restructuring and Strengthening of the National Financial System (PROER), was introduced in November 1995 in the wake of some prominent bank rescues. These included Banco Econômico in August 1995 and Banco Nacional in November 1995, then the eighth- and sixth-largest private banks respectively (Mettenheim, 2015, 121–2; Sales and Tannuri-Pianto, 2007, 8). Their depositors had moved funds to banks perceived as safer, destabilizing the interbank market and prompting the government intervention (Goldfajn et al., 2003, 16). PROER provided BACEN with new authority to restructure the private bank sector via liquidations, recapitalizations, restructuring and sales. It also allowed regulatory forbearance in the form of a temporary waiver on minimum capital requirements for intervened banks (Nakane and Weintraub, 2005, 2262). BACEN restructured six private banks, separating the largest into good and bad banks and providing credit lines from federal government banks to the banks acquiring the good assets. Managements were typically replaced in restructured banks. In the case of major banks, PROER also allowed for their mortgage portfolios to be acquired by CEF, continuing a policy precedent that would eventually prove costly for the government (Maia, 1999, 114).

In contrast to the treatment of depositors under Collor, the Cardoso government took great care to communicate to depositors that their wealth would be protected. Following the RAET interventions in Banerj and Banespa in 1994, the government committed to the protection of depositor accounts. Pedro Malan, BACEN president, affirmed that 'anyone who wants to go to the banks on Monday to take out their money will encounter plenty of cash at their disposal' (Beck et al., 2005, 2228). There was no formal deposit insurance system in Brazil before 1995, when the government introduced a Credit Guarantee Fund financed by bank levies, providing for coverage of up to R$20,000 per account (Banco Central do Brasil, 1995; Maia, 1999, 112).[15]

A decision to close Banco Econômico in 1996 was particularly controversial because it was located in Bahia, a politically crucial state, and closely connected with the right-wing Liberal Front Party (PFL), one of the parties in the government's coalition (Sola et al., 2001, 52–7). Cardoso argued that politically connected bailouts had to cease, though the decision nearly precipitated a mass resignation of directors on the NMC (Fishlow, 2011, 61). Yet this seems to have strengthened BACEN's hand to take more decisive action against some failing banks. The assets of closed banks were acquired by the largest private banks, Bradesco, Itaú and Unibanco, though from 1997 foreign banks were

---

[15] In the preceding year, the banks provided an industry-funded scheme but this seems not to have deterred anxious depositors from moving deposits from weak to protected banks. The government scheme covered all deposits as well as exchange, mortgage and real estate bills (Baer and Nazmi, 2000, 12). The insured amount was increased in 2006, 2010 and 2013 and today stands at R$250,000.

permitted to enter the market by purchasing problem banks (a restructured Banco Econômico being one of these). An important first step was taken in March 1997 when BACEN rejected a restructuring proposal by the politically influential controlling family of Bamerindus. BACEN seized the bank and encouraged HSBC to purchase it by offering the British bank a number of financial incentives.[16]

The second government programme, the Programme of Incentives to Reduce the State-Owned Banking Sector (PROES), was adopted in August 1996 and operated over 1997–9. It encouraged states to liquidate, privatize or transform[17] their problem banks, with the national government assuming all of the losses incurred during the process (it assumed only half the losses if states chose to restructure and retain control of a bank) (Beck et al., 2005, 2224). PROES also allowed the government and BACEN to provide finance to intervened banks to prepare them for privatization, to purchase their public sector loans, to provide recapitalizations, to fund employee pension plans and to install new bank management (Ness, 2000, 78–9). Like intervention under RAET, PROES made clear that depositors would be safeguarded while the state bank's final fate was decided.

This programme was the most important because of the greater size of the public bank sector and the dire need to reduce the reliance of the states on bank finance. As Martinez-Diaz notes, the federal government had been trying and failing for a decade to close major state banks (Martinez-Diaz, 2009, 87). From 1994, BACEN enforced a longstanding formal prohibition on bank lending to major shareholders, preventing state banks from extending further credits to their state governments (via loans or bonds, which were typically underwritten by state banks). Private banks were also barred from increasing credits to state governments, excepting bonds (World Bank, 1995, 11). Heavy state indebtedness to the national government, and a 1994 constitutional amendment that limited the automaticity of fiscal transfers from the federal government to states and municipalities, put the latter in a stronger position to insist on linking the reform of the state banking sector to state fiscal reform (Fishlow, 2011, 25). States that were

---

[16] HSBC received $2.5 billion from the federal deposit insurance fund, credits from the PROER fund, and Bamerindus's bad real estate loan portfolio was bought by the CEF (Martinez-Diaz, 2009, 99).

[17] States could transform their state banks into non-bank development agencies.

relatively dependent on federal fiscal transfers were more likely to give up control of their banks in return for the federal government absorbing the full costs of bank restructuring as well as their debt (Beck et al., 2005, 2234). But states' access to federal funds had not yet been entirely controlled: over 1995–6, state governors enjoyed continued access to BNDES loans using anticipated privatization proceeds as collateral (de Paiva Abreu and Werneck, 2008, 435).

Banerj and Credireal were eventually sold to private banks in 1997. Over 1997–9, twenty-seven state government banks were privatized under PROES (Mettenheim, 2015, 122). Banks were rehabilitated by swapping state debt for national government debt. State banks were generally federalized, recapitalized, restructured and privatized. Acquiring banks were often provided with state-subsidized credit lines (from BACEN, BB and CEF) and were also permitted to reduce losses via tax write-offs.

Banespa, after having been rescued by BACEN in December 1994, was a greater political challenge and a crucial test case of the willingness of states to relinquish their banks and of the *desenvolvimentista* (developmentalist) group in the Cardoso government to give way to neoliberal ministers associated with BACEN and the Ministry of Finance (de Paiva Abreu and Werneck, 2008, 435). Years of opposition from Banespa's employees and unions, and more importantly, influential veto players at the sub-national and national level – the São Paulo governor and members of Congress protecting state interests – delayed a resolution. Despite being in default, São Paulo state was in a strong position to hold out to extract a high price for ceding control of Banespa because of the size of its population, its economic importance and Banespa's own strategic importance. The federal-state negotiations that ensued extended over much of Cardoso's period as finance minister and his first presidential term.

One year after having intervened in Banespa, the federal government proposed settling half of the state government's R$15 billion debt to the bank by issuing federal bonds, which would be given to São Paulo and transferred to the bank. The state government was to raise the remaining half through asset sales. The bonds would carry 30 years' maturity and an interest rate of 6 per cent, with exchange rate indexation. But a group of senators from the North, North-east and Midwest regions blocked approval of the rescue operation, demanding similar treatment for their states, which were paying interest rates at least five times higher than the rate offered to São Paulo (Bevilaqua, 2002, 28). Other states crucial to Cardoso's coalition – including Rio de Janeiro, Minas Gerais and Rio Grande do Sul – soon followed with similar demands.

The federal government reached a deal with Minas Gerais and Rio Grande do Sul, but pressure to extend similar terms to other states, particularly poorer ones in the north-east, mounted when the leader of the PFL in Senate issued a formal statement demanding identical terms for all states (Bevilaqua, 2002, 29). Poorer states complained that renegotiation emphasizing state bonds would disproportionately favour the four richest states (São Paulo, Rio de Janeiro, Minas Gerais and Rio Grande do Sul), which were responsible for 90 per cent of the stock of state bonds. The presence of São Paulo in this group enhanced their influence, since the state was both the largest bond debtor and governed by one of the main leaders of the PSDB.

In November 1996, the São Paulo state governor agreed to surrender control of Banespa, though the bank was only sold to Santander (from Spain) in 2000 (Martinez-Diaz, 2009, 106). Finally, in September 1997, nearly three years after the initial intervention in Banespa, the federal government agreed to assume all of São Paulo's bond debt and in December 1997 its debt to Banespa and other banks – a deal that also suited Cardoso, who was then running for re-election and who needed votes in this crucial state (Bevilaqua, 2002, 39; Rodden, 2006, 188–225). This deal, which was considerably more costly than that first proposed in December 1995, was then extended to other states and municipalities, meeting their demands for equal treatment. The national government forgave part of the state debt it assumed, asked for some repayment via privatization receipts, but restructured about 80 per cent, amortized over thirty years at a subsidized interest rate and with a cap on state debt service payments (Bevilaqua, 2002, 31). This in turn bolstered the balance sheets of the state-controlled banks since their debt was now owed to the centre.

In return, the federal government succeeded in obtaining limits on future debt issuance by states. The IMF supported PROES in the conditions attached to its 1998 lending package to Brazil, but international institutions did not play a significant role in its elaboration or implementation (Martinez-Diaz, 2009, 94–5). In May 2000, in Cardoso's second term, Congress passed the Law of Fiscal Responsibility, which required greater fiscal transparency of all levels of government and in principle prevented the federal government from bailing out states and municipalities in the future.

A third banking sector programme was introduced in Cardoso's second term in June 2001, the Program to Strengthen Federal Financial Institutions (PROEF), focused on rehabilitating federal government banks. It can be seen as a delayed consequence of years of federal government interference in the national banking sector for developmental and narrower political reasons, as well as a tendency throughout the 1980s and 1990s to use these banks to resolve problems with other banks and with states and municipalities. The country's largest bank, BB, was recapitalized in 1996 with R$8 billion, financed by BACEN, sales of BB's shares in state companies and by its pension fund (Fishlow, 2011, 64). In June 2001, bad assets from the CEF, which as noted above had acquired mortgage assets from other restructured banks, were transferred to a new asset management corporation (Empresa Gestora de Ativos, EMGEA) at the Ministry of Finance. Three of the four federal banks (CEF, BNB and Basa) were also bolstered by direct capital injections at this time and by swapping other low-interest bearing assets for new Treasury bonds paying market interest rates. CEF's 2001 recapitalization cost R$9.3 billion (Mettenheim, 2015, 122; Nakane and Weintraub, 2005, 2263). Combined, the BB and CEF recapitalizations were the equivalent of about US$28 billion in 2012 values (Deos et al., 2017, 71).

In terms of fiscal consequences, the PROES programme was the largest, estimated to have cost the public budget the equivalent of 5.7 per cent of GDP; the PROEF and PROER programmes represented an estimated 2.1 per cent and 0.9 per cent of GDP respectively (Goldfajn et al., 2003, 19).[18] Of 48 problem banks dealt with between 1994 and 1998, 31 were liquidated (most of which were private banks), 10 were dealt with under bankruptcy law, 5 were placed under RAET administration, and 2 were intervened by freezing deposits (Baer and Nazmi, 2000, 12–14; Maia, 1999, 110–12).

These three programmes significantly reduced the number of banks, increased concentration and reduced employment in the banking sector. After 1997, foreign bank participation was also allowed to rise as domestic capital proved insufficient and as the government's interest

---

[18] Fishlow offers a slightly higher estimate of the total cost of PROES and PROER at 10.4 per cent of GDP (Fishlow, 2011, pp. 63–5).

in maximizing revenue from bank sales increased. As the public banking sector retreated, foreign banks were the main beneficiaries, increasing their share of total sector assets from 8.7 per cent at the end of 1993 to 30.4 per cent by June 2002 (Goldfajn et al., 2003, 8).

In 2000, the government legislated to prevent either BACEN or the finance ministry from undertaking bailouts of insolvent banks without congressional approval. This constraint seemed to work, though only in part: BACEN refused to provide short-term liquidity over 2008–9, but the deposit insurance fund instead was persuaded to extend its coverage and BACEN encouraged larger banks to lend to smaller banks (Calomiris and Haber, 2014, 443–5). BACEN then avoided rescuing one medium-sized bank in 2010 and it closed two smaller bankrupt lenders in 2012 (Pearson, 2012). Yet the government retained the option of bailing out insolvent banks via takeovers by government-owned banks – as in fact it did in BB's takeover of Banco Votorantim in 2013.[19]

Furthermore, although the Cardoso administration largely succeeded in its objective of severing the close links between politicians and banks at the state level, the federal government retained its control of three major banks: BB, BNDES and CEF. Under the more leftist presidents Lula and Rousseff, the government's commitment to using these banks to promote development via subsidized loans returned in dramatic fashion. State-subsidized lending by BNDES in particular grew dramatically after the 2008 global crisis. By 2014, outstanding Treasury credit to BNDES reached an astounding 9 per cent of GDP (though the bank returns large dividends to the government). BNDES had become a bigger lender than the World Bank amid widespread allegations that large and politically connected borrowers still obtained privileged access to its loans (Leahy, 2015). The government also encouraged the CEF to increase household credit to boost demand, rather than relying on traditional fiscal stimulus (Sobreira and Paula, 2010, 90).

Thus, the Cardoso team reduced the size of the state-owned banking sector in Brazil and achieved fundamental reforms of fiscal federalism that had eluded previous governments. This was crucial in ending the system of high inflation associated with rising inequality, financial disintermediation and which masked chronic weakness in the banking sector. At the same time, in contrast to Collor, the Cardoso

[19] Provisional Act 443 (2008) and Law 11908 (2009).

government prioritized the protection of depositors, laying the foundations for a rapid growth in the deposits and other forms of wealth of the middle class in Brazil. Consumer credit also grew rapidly; in 1994 alone, it rose by 180 per cent (Baer and Nazmi, 2000, 9–10). The democratization of credit, which, as we saw in Chapter 4, provided a basis of support in newspaper opinion for financial rescues, has continued since then, with household debt approximately doubling as a proportion of GDP in the 2000s (Figure 3.23). This increasing exposure to financial risk has arguably expanded the political constituency supporting financial stabilization.

The political costs for the Cardoso government of not providing bailouts to key parts of the financial system likely proved highly relevant for policy decisions. This can be seen in the rescue package that allowed São Paulo state to settle its debts to Banespa. As the country's third largest bank, Banespa's failure could have provoked a systemic economic and financial collapse at a critical phase in the stabilization process, as politicians on all sides well understood. This would have jeopardized recent gains in macroeconomic stability and in the stock market, posing a serious threat to the growing middle-class household wealth invested in private pensions and other market-traded assets after monetary stabilization. As early as 1988, high inflation had encouraged over seven million Brazilians, roughly 11 per cent of the adult population, to become stock market investors (Lees, Botts and Cysne, 1990, 286). Given the upward trend we observed across other measures in Chapter 3, the number of Brazilians with a stake in the stock market almost certainly increased significantly after the success of the *Real* Plan. Brazil's large and growing closed private pension funds in the mid-1990s, on average, allocated roughly 34 per cent of their portfolio to domestic equities (Reis and Paixão, 2004, 10).[20] The boom in the stock market delivered substantial gains to investors, and there is little evidence that the markets seriously expected the government to allow a failure that would put these wealth gains at risk (Figure 12.3).

Cardoso grasped the importance of responding to the rising effective demand for stabilization. He later recalled that 'in conversations with President Rafael Caldera [of Venezuela], his description of

---

[20] Private pension assets grew from 7.2 per cent of GDP in 1993 to 10.8 per cent of GDP in 1997.

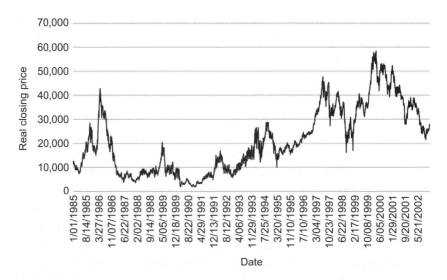

Figure 12.3: Brazil Bolsa de Valores de São Paulo (Bovespa) Index, inflation-adjusted, 1985–2002.
Source: Globalfinancialdata.com, last accessed 30 March 2018. Daily (close) data, inflation and split-adjusted.

the banking crisis experienced by that country the previous year made a big impression on me. The bankruptcy of one bank would unleash a formidable chain reaction' (as cited in Martinez-Diaz, 2009, 90). In addition to the risk of systemic collapse, not extending a bailout would also have threatened to unravel the delicate fiscal deal with the states and, with it, the achievements of the *Real* Plan. Cardoso risked being a victim of his own success: monetary stabilization came at the price of consistently high real interest rates that raised state debt burdens, typically on variable rates, to potentially explosive levels. As we observed in Chapter 4, the federal government did not escape responsibility for the crisis, yet the success of the anti-inflationary programme now depended on stabilizing the financial sector. Thus, the 1997 bailout was negotiated in two stages, both seemingly timed to gain maximum political benefit (Bevilaqua, 2002, 39). The first stage corresponded to agreement with Minas Gerais and Rio Grande do Sul, coinciding with the 1996 municipal elections and the discussion in Congress of the constitutional amendment to authorize a second term in office for the president, state governors and city mayors. The second stage aligned with the final negotiation with other states, when Cardoso and many state governors began their re-election campaigns.

12.4   Political Consequences of the 1990s Crises

It is difficult to disentangle the political impact of the banking crisis of the early 1990s and associated policy interventions from other economic and non-economic factors. It is likely that the Collor administration's policy interventions, especially the deposit freeze, played a role in reducing public support for the government, even if they were not decisive in Collor's untimely removal from office. Collor began his presidency with high public expectations and approval ratings – a reflection of the promise of a young and vigorous candidate, and a marked contrast with Sarney's low approval ratings at the end of his term. Collor was also successful in securing passage of key legislation (Saiegh, 2014), though as noted earlier he also relied heavily on executive decrees. But his economic programme proved deeply unpopular for a mix of reasons.

First, its impact on the economy was immediate and very negative: after rising strongly in the first quarter of 1990, real GDP fell by nearly a third in April – the equivalent of the economic collapse experienced by the United States over the period of the Great Depression in a single month. Economic activity remained depressed for the rest of Collor's term (Figure 12.4). Second, as noted earlier, the deposit freeze 'confiscation' was especially unpopular among the middle classes and business elites. An historian describes it as causing 'a trauma among Brazilians that was to last for years' (Fausto, 2014, 330). Its implementation was also perceived as unfair, with powerful interests seemingly able to unfreeze their deposits more easily than most (de Paiva Abreu, 2008, 419). Third, the government, especially its controversial first economy minister Zélia Cardoso de Mello, quickly obtained a reputation both for obstinacy and policy instability. Fourth, and crucially, the administration's policies failed in their stated objective of defeating inflation, which remained a highly regressive tax on wealth.

The political impact of these problems was considerable. As Figure 12.5 indicates, Collor's approval ratings fell sharply in his first few months of office, which followed on the implementation of the deposit freeze. Later that year, in November 1990, elections were held for the Chamber of Deputies, a third of Senate seats, state legislatures and governors. Collor's own party, the PRN, took part in congressional elections for the first time, but won only 40 (8 per cent) of the seats, well below what he had hoped for only months earlier. Together with the three other parties supporting his government, the PRN, PFL and PDS,

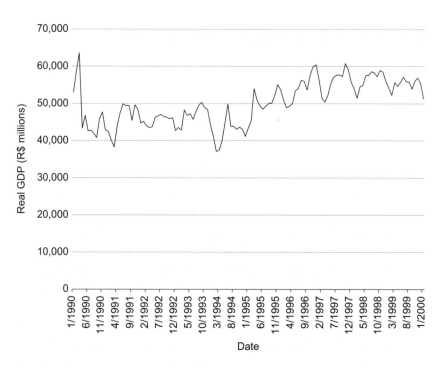

Figure 12.4: Real GDP, monthly, January 1990 to December 2000 (R$ millions, August 1994=100).

Source: www.ipeadata.com. GDP data is from BACEN, *Boletim, Seção Atividade Econômica BM12_PIB12* and is deflated using the IGP-M general price index (August 1994 = 100) from Fundação Getúlio Vargas, *Conjuntura Econômica.*

they commanded only a third of parliamentary seats and a quarter of the Senate's. The opposition also controlled most of the major states, with only four allies loyal to Collor among the governors (Bethell and Nicolau, 2008, 252). Thus, the government constantly had to negotiate with other parties hostile to its agenda. It is notable that the steepest rise in disapproval of Collor's performance occurred in his first two months in office following implementation of the deposit freeze. As his keynote policy of inflation reduction failed and the economy shrank, Collor's approval ratings continued to fall. By the beginning of 1991, poll respondents who evaluated his performance as poor outnumbered those who approved or strongly approved. By September 1991 a plurality thought Collor was performing poorly; within a few months this would become the majority view.

Collor's popularity was already very low in May 1992 when his brother dramatically accused him of corruption, leading to

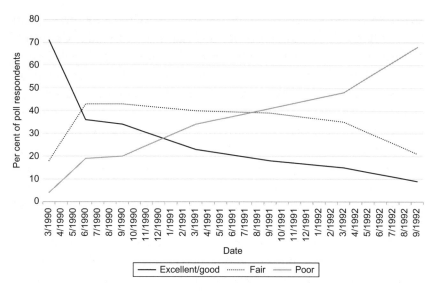

Figure 12.5: President Collor de Mello: evaluations of performance, 1990–2.
Source: Datafolha, http://datafolha.folha.uol.com.br/opiniaopublica/
avaliacaodegoverno/presidente/fhc/indice-1.shtml, last accessed 2 March 2018.
The remainder of respondents indicated 'don't know'.

congressional hearings over which he had no control (Brooke, 1992; Preston, 1992). This seems to have had a direct effect on public perception of his performance, which deteriorated further thereafter, but it is likely that the generalized disapproval of the policies of his first two years in office had already primed voters not to side with the embattled president. The great majority of Brazilians were evidently relieved when Collor resigned in September 1992, only hours before he would have been impeached by the Senate.

Polls indicated that initially voters were not greatly enamoured with his successor Itamar Franco, who had a reputation for volatility. Later in Franco's two-year term, however, the *Plano Real* transformed his presidency: his approval ratings improved sharply from mid-1994 and by its end, 89 per cent of poll respondents thought he was doing an excellent, good or fair job; only 8 per cent thought his performance poor (Datafolha, 1994). The unexpected success of the *Real* Plan also placed Cardoso, the minister primarily associated with it, in a commanding position in the 1994 elections. In contrast to Collor's populist, personality-centred campaign, Cardoso's was very policy-oriented, which set the tone of future presidential election campaigns (Boas,

2016, 89). Voters generally approved of this technocratic orientation after Collor's disastrous presidency and many were to judge Cardoso's performance in office based on the perceived success of his policies.

Although the popular *Real* Plan continued to bear down on inflation over the next few years, as discussed earlier it was instrumental in precipitating a deeper banking crisis. But Cardoso's government appears not to have been punished for this crisis or the extensive policy interventions associated with it. Why, in this case, were voters seemingly so forgiving? Ongoing banking sector problems over the preceding decade, the perception that banks and wealthier households had profited at the expense of the middle class from high inflation, and extensive related media discussion had led most Brazilians to perceive that the ultimate cause of the weak banking sector had little to do with Cardoso or his government. Middle-class voters also likely attached greater importance to the achievements of the *Real* Plan, which alongside Cardoso's consistent reassurance to depositors, formed a crucial part of the government's wealth protection strategy that voters would perceive as being reasonably fair, at least when compared to the previous government.

Cardoso's approval ratings declined somewhat in the first half of 1996, when the banking crisis was intense in the private and state-owned banking sectors, but it recovered thereafter. There is also some evidence to suggest that the banking crisis was itself not the primary cause of this temporary decline in approval. In 1996, at the peak of the banking crisis, most poll respondents (17 per cent) listed health as the most important challenge facing the nation, with 14 per cent each naming low salaries, education and unemployment as most important, and 13 per cent naming corruption. Although we cannot conclude that this shows that relatively few were dissatisfied with Cardoso's interventions, since no policy challenge directly relevant to financial stability was presented to respondents, there was an 'other' category available that was chosen by only 1 per cent of respondents.[21]

Throughout the banking crisis and for the remainder of his first term, polls indicated that no less than 70 per cent of voters thought Cardoso's performance was fair, good or excellent (Figure 12.6). In view of the general results we reviewed in Chapter 5 and in recent crises in the United States and United Kingdom reviewed in Chapters 8 and

---

[21] www.latinobarometro.org/latOnline.jsp, accessed 2 March 2018.

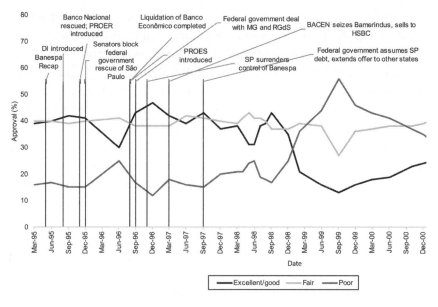

Figure 12.6: President Cardoso: evaluations of performance, 1995–2002.
Source: Datafolha, http://datafolha.folha.uol.com.br/opiniaopublica/
avaliacaodegoverno/presidente/fhc/indice-1.shtml, last accessed 2 March 2018.
The remainder of respondents indicated 'don't know'.

10, this performance might be seen as remarkable. Could this be because the relatively low levels of wealth among Brazil's middle class meant that low mass expectations prevailed at this time regarding the protection of wealth compared to these much wealthier countries? This is possible but it seems unlikely, given the intensity with which Brazilians reacted to the Collor administration's confiscation of wealth and the newspaper evidence we reviewed in Chapter 4. Rather, as newspaper opinion at the time suggested, many Brazilians appeared to understand that tackling the deep problems in the banking sector and the associated link with chronic fiscal incontinence was well overdue.

It was almost certainly also crucial that Cardoso's government was careful to build a sustainable political constituency for reform. First, much more consistently than its predecessor, the administration protected citizens' savings in the process of liquidating and restructuring many banks. Cardoso's economic policy team knew that this was politically essential and pursued stabilization reforms that were transparent to voters and used ideas of voluntary participation to build trust in key constituencies, including the middle class (Alston, Melo, Mueller and Pereira, 2016, 98–100). Second, ending high inflation also contributed substantially to the administration's wealth protection strategy aimed at voters, as wage indexation and interest on deposits had never been fully sufficient to compensate for inflation, which had shifted wealth to banks, the government and the rich. Third, falling income and wealth inequality in Brazil from this time also likely contributed to a general perception that Cardoso's policies were reasonably fair, particularly when compared to interventions taken under Collor.[22] The government's policy of replacing the management of intervened banks may also have helped in this regard. Downsizing state-owned banks was not unpopular, perhaps in part because public sector and financial sector wages were generally higher than in other industries.[23] Opinion polls late in Cardoso's first term also reveal that a majority of respondents supported privatization of state-owned companies, which would include banks (Latinobarómetro, n.d., 1998).

However, as in Britain and the United States, voters in Brazil appear to have responded negatively to policy delays associated with veto players. It is noteworthy that the percentage of respondents rating Cardoso's performance as excellent/good (poor) falls (rises) to its lowest (highest) point in his first term in the period following the group of senators' rejection of the December 1995 proposal to rescue São Paulo. His approval rating then rebounded sharply in September and November 1996 after a debt settlement was reached with Minas Gerais and Rio Grande do Sul, and São Paulo agreed to surrender control of Banespa. Voters appear to have responded favourably to these developments, the former, as mentioned earlier, timed days before the municipal elections in which Cardoso's coalition won seventeen of the contested twenty-six mayoralties (Political Database of the Americas, 1999). Cardoso received another bounce in opinion polls when the debt settlement was extended to all states.

---

[22] Evidence from Latinobarometer surveys taken at different points (1997, 2001 and 2002) in Cardoso's first and second terms in office is revealing in this regard. Over this period, the percentage of respondents who perceived the income distribution in Brazil to be 'very fair' or 'fair' increased from 7 per cent to 14 per cent, while the proportion of respondents who answered 'unfair' or 'very unfair' fell from 91 per cent to 83 per cent. Throughout, Brazilians remained very concerned about poverty and distribution.

[23] In 2000, average financial sector wages were nearly three times higher than in manufacturing (International Labor Organization, n.d.). Public sector wages, including at local levels, continue to be significantly higher than average private sector wages (*The Economist*, 2012).

Despite these policy delays, Cardoso's generally effective management of the policy process likely contributed to his relatively strong and consistent approval rating during this very difficult period for the Brazilian financial system and economy. Although his government enjoyed a modest working majority in Congress, low party loyalty and high fragmentation meant that Cardoso's negotiation skills were an essential component of his policy success. This helped to reduce the importance of resistance from state governors as well as from the PT in Congress and that part of the labour movement associated with the public sector and state-owned enterprises (Cardoso and Graeff, 2012, 35). Cardoso's continued use of executive orders might be seen as suggesting that he resorted to these to avoid legislative gridlock, but this interpretation would undervalue his ability to build legislative coalitions. As Saiegh concludes from a comparative analysis of chief executive performance, Cardoso was on average unusually successful in this regard given his coalition size and country characteristics: 'Fernando Henrique Cardoso was the most accomplished president of the 1985–2006 era in terms of legislative success, while José Sarney was the least effective one' (Saiegh, 2014). Saiegh also shows that such legislative success was generally rewarded by voters (Saiegh, 2011, 2014).

This interpretation is also supported by the obvious fact that Cardoso was rewarded with another overwhelming victory in the 1998 elections. Lula, running for the third time, mounted a stronger challenge than in 1994 by building a broad centre-left political coalition, but Cardoso gained 53.1 per cent of the votes to Lula's 37.1 per cent, once again winning easily in the first round. He was the first Brazilian president ever to be re-elected to office. The elections also confirmed the government's working majority in the Chamber and Senate, albeit in the context of continuing high party fragmentation. Cardoso's own Social Democrats increased their seats in the Chamber from 62 to 99, or from 12.3 to 19.3 per cent of the total seat share (Bethell and Nicolau, 2008, 238). Although the PT party improved its electoral performance at both national and local levels, in 1998 Lula was unable to appeal to the large bloc of voters who wanted more stability and the protection of their incomes and wealth. As Bethell and Nicolau summarize:

> the PT also contributed to its own defeat: it remained rooted in the socialist Left; it was internally divided; many of its economic policies in particular were unconvincing; its social base in the

industrial working class was too narrow; it could never decide whether to bid for the support of the very poor and underprivileged or to look for alliances in the centre ground beyond the small parties of the Left. (Bethell and Nicolau, 2008, 264)

Cardoso's second term was less successful and his approval ratings declined sharply after his re-election (Figure 12.6). It is possible that this was in part a delayed effect of the 1994–8 banking crisis, including the costly rescues of federally owned banks in 2001. More likely, it was shaped by other factors. The sharp deterioration in Cardoso's approval ratings occurred at the beginning of his second term, bottoming out in the second half of 1999 and recovering gradually thereafter. The primary driver appears to be the emergence of turmoil in global financial markets following the Asian financial crises of 1997–8. These were followed by a Russian crisis that affected many emerging countries, Brazil included. The real came under serious pressure in late 1998 and the government was forced in December to accept a $43 billion IMF-led rescue package, with politically unpopular conditionality including substantial fiscal tightening. Brazil's international position was also worsened by the decision of Minas Gerais state (governed by former president Itamar Franco, whose personal relations with Cardoso had worsened before the election) in early 1999 to default on its federal debt (de Paiva Abreu and Werneck, 2008, 438). In mid-January, the government abandoned the crawling peg regime – belatedly in the opinion of many critics.

These events indicated Brazil's continuing vulnerability to external financial shocks and took a toll on its economy, which was already suffering from low growth. The government had successfully reassured voters that their wealth was safe, but other concerns now loomed larger. By 1998, unemployment was consistently cited by poll respondents as the major problem facing the country; this persisted throughout Cardoso's second term.[24] There are some indications that Brazilian voters may also have perceived more distributional unfairness in the Cardoso government's second term policies. In 2002, respondents to one poll listed politicians (33 per cent) and banks (29 per cent) as the major beneficiaries of Cardoso's policies. Only 7 per cent of respondents saw

[24] Datafolha (2002); Latinobarómetro (n.d., secs 1998–2002). See also Ferreira and Sakurai (2013).

industry and agriculture as major beneficiaries and only 5 per cent thought workers were (Datafolha, 2002). It is likely that the latter result was due to continuing high rates of unemployment and underemployment. The majority of respondents to another poll identified the government's economic policy as responsible for Brazil's economic problems (53 per cent), with banks attracting a considerable amount of blame as well (11 per cent). The same poll revealed that support for privatization – a key element of Cardoso's bank restructuring plan – had fallen from 51 per cent at the time of his re-election in 1998 to 38 per cent when his party's successor faced defeat four years later (Latinobarómetro, n.d., 2002). Nevertheless, it is arguably more remarkable that voters demonstrated considerable tolerance for low growth during Cardoso's presidency for as long as they did.

As noted earlier, Lula's eventual victory in the 2002 presidential elections reflected these growing concerns among voters about unemployment and low growth. Although he did not win an outright victory in the first round of voting (winning 46.4 per cent of the vote), he easily beat his rival José Serra, an uncharismatic candidate closely associated with Cardoso's government, in the second round. Cardoso's PSDB also lost 28 of its 99 seats in the Chamber. In government, Lula's policies were more orthodox than many expected and mainly continued those adopted by Cardoso (de Paiva Abreu and Werneck, 2008, 431). Notably, Lula abandoned his earlier positions favouring the nationalization of banks and industry, and his government accommodated itself to the financial and economic reforms set in train by its predecessors in the 1990s. Notably for this study, centre-left governments throughout the 2000s continued to promote financial inclusion and access to credit for poorer Brazilians and did not revert to wealth confiscation of the middle class. The promotion of financial inclusion may have linked the welfare of ever-larger proportions of the Brazilian population to financial markets (Lavinas de Morais, 2017).

Lula's government – and that of his less successful appointed successor, Dilma Rousseff – also continued to use the large federally owned banks to pursue developmental and narrower political objectives. One recent study, for example, finds that federal government banks lent countercyclically after the collapse of Lehman Brothers in September 2008 and that increased lending was targeted towards localities aligned with the incumbent Workers' Party (Coleman and Feler, 2015). These authors also note that about a third of bank branches in

Brazil still belong to federal government banks, with BB and CEF the most important. But this too was a legacy of Cardoso's government: as of the early 2000s, government-owned banks still accounted for nearly half of total sector assets, despite the closure or privatization of banks owned by the states. Despite the substantial restructuring of the financial sector during this period, state control of finance remains considerable amidst an acceleration of financialization among the general population.

12.5 Conclusion

As we noted at the beginning of this chapter, one might have expected Brazilian governments facing financial instability to have moved from extensive and cronyistic bailouts under authoritarianism before 1985 towards great market conformity under democracy in the 1990s. There were early indications of such a shift when the new Sarney government announced in 1985 that it would end the clientilistic protection of the financial sector. However, this policy tendency was not sustained. The Collor government favoured banks over depositors, but this policy was so unpopular with voters that it was soon abandoned. By the mid-1990s, the Cardoso government dealt with a deep banking crisis by closing a number of mostly private sector banks and restructuring, recapitalizing and privatizing much of the state-owned banking sector. Depositors were protected and wealth-holders generally, especially those outside of the richest households, benefited from the end of hyperinflation. By preventing systemic collapse, government interventions also protected households increasingly connected to the financial system as investors and borrowers. Major federal government-owned banks, by contrast, were kept in state ownership and were used throughout the period to manage the process of bank restructuring; where necessary, they were also recapitalized by the government.

Voters in this new era of democracy broadly approved of the Cardoso government's policies, electing Cardoso to an unprecedented second term. The president's skill in managing a highly fragmented policy process with large numbers of potential veto players was an essential component of crisis management, although there were important cases where opponents were able to delay reform (the Banespa case being a prominent example). The government's policy of favouring depositors and preventing systemic collapse, as well as the general decline in inequality from the mid-1990s, likely also served to underpin voter support for its crisis management strategy. Critically, the government's response to the crisis also protected what Martinez-Diaz calls the 'administration's most important political asset, the success of the inflation control program' (Martinez-Diaz, 2009, 91). The banking system was stabilized, the achievements of the *Real* Plan sustained, and, in contrast to the experience under Collor, middle-class wealth was protected in ways broadly perceived as fair – or at least sufficiently so. This outcome was far from inevitable. After all, it eluded political incumbents in the United Kingdom and the United States, among many others, in the following decade. On the basis of these accomplishments, Cardoso secured re-election and the foundation for deepening financialization – and possibly future financial fragility – was laid.

13 CONCLUSION

A long historical perspective generates significant analytical pay-offs, enabling scholars to uncover trends and forces that might otherwise be overlooked but which have fundamentally altered the conditions shaping policy choices and political outcomes. This is the case, we have shown, regarding evolving societal expectations of government responsibility for financial stabilization over the past century and more.

In the environment of comparatively low expectations of government that prevailed in the aftermath of major banking crises from (at least) the early nineteenth century to the period before the Second World War most elected governments implemented policy responses that by recent standards were relatively market-conforming but posed little threat to their hold on political office. By contrast, the emergence of great expectations among much of what became the middle class in many countries during the course of the twentieth century made it increasingly untenable for elected governments to pursue the Bagehot ideal during systemic crises.

The wealth effect has had powerful consequences. Increasingly, governments and associated policy agencies that attempted to adhere to relatively market-conforming policies became subject to overwhelming political pressure to depart from them during crises. We saw this, for example, in the increasingly extensive departures from market conformity in Britain and America as the crisis that began in mid-2007 deepened over the following year. By October 2008, the rhetorically pro-market governments of New Labour in Britain and the Bush administration in the United States had opted for a wholesale bailout of the financial system unprecedented in its scope and depth. As we showed in Chapter 5, this outcome was largely replicated across virtually all other crisis-hit democracies, irrespective of the partisan colour of government or other institutional characteristics.

Despite this, in the British and American cases incumbent political parties, with their reputations for economic competence eroded, soon lost office due to the considerable delays that hampered the response of governments to the deepening crisis and to perceptions that the bailouts unfairly distributed costs and benefits among different economic and social groups. These cases were two prominent examples of our more general finding in Chapter 5 that the rise of great expectations altered the political significance of institutional constraints on policy interventions. This point is underplayed in literature that emphasizes continuity rather than change in the way that institutions shape political outcomes over time, including some in the historical institutionalist tradition (Calomiris and Haber, 2014; Capoccia, 2016; Lieberman, 2003).

As the long-run shift from relatively market-conforming policy interventions in systemic crises towards extensive financial sector bailouts over the course of the twentieth century became increasingly ubiquitous, such institutional constraints made it difficult for political incumbents to reap political benefits. As we saw in Chapter 12, the Cardoso government in Brazil after 1994 was one of the few to do so – partly because of Cardoso's political skills and partly because, unlike his predecessor, Cardoso's response, which sustained the achievements of the *Real* Plan and protected depositor wealth, was perceived as reasonably fair in its distributional consequences. More often, incumbent governments lost office even after providing costly financial sector bailouts because it often proved impossible for them to prevent large absolute and relative wealth losses for a significant proportion of voters and – equally importantly – for government leaders and policymakers to convey effectively the message that such losses would have been far greater had they chosen a narrower, market-conforming policy response. These findings lead us to be sceptical about the possibility that setting actual outcomes in a counterfactual context for individual voters will allow policymakers to avoid blame.[1]

---

[1] For a more optimistic argument of this kind, see Haldane (2018).

The higher political costs of not providing bailouts under circumstances of high financialization and the great expectations of voters also suggest why incumbents ultimately choose bailouts even if they anticipate they will not be rewarded for them. The dissenting report by three Republican members of the US Financial Crisis Inquiry Commission in 2011 illustrates this dilemma for policymakers:

> For a policymaker, the calculus is simple: if you bail out AIG and you're wrong, you will have wasted taxpayer money and provoked public outrage. If you don't bail out AIG and you're wrong, the global financial system collapses. It should be easy to see why policymakers favored action – there was a chance of being wrong either way, and the costs of being wrong without action were far greater than the costs of being wrong with action. (Financial Crisis Inquiry Commission, 2011, 433)

If, then, the rise of great expectations was transformative for both policy responses and political survival after major banking crises, what accounts for their emergence in the first place? We have emphasized the importance of the evolving material stake of most voters in financial stability. This is not because we think ideas are unimportant in shaping the identities, interests and policy preferences of actors. Indeed, like others, we see financialization as often associated with the acquisition of new social identities, notably among households in the middle and upper parts of the wealth distribution (Fligstein and Goldstein, 2015; Langley, 2009). Leaving aside the bust phase of the cycle, these authors instead focus on the credit boom phase when some individuals in the middle class became 'investor subjects', embracing financial risk-taking. Our research follows on from this work showing that during crises, when asset prices were falling, many of these individuals apparently shifted towards more protective orientations towards the preservation of the value of their assets, suggesting that these new identities may not be fixed.

Alongside these identity shifts, we see the primary drivers of the emergence of great expectations among the rising middle class as the new material wealth of this group and its increasing exposure to financial instability. As we argued in Chapter 3, political parties and elected governments reinforced these new expectations regarding wealth protection by making increasingly explicit policy commitments to financial regulation and stabilization. These commitments were of course connected to the economic policy revolution of the mid-twentieth century, so Keynesian and social democratic ideas, as well as nationalist goals of industrial development and nation-building in the developing world, are accordingly likely to have played an indirect role in fostering great expectations. This at-risk wealth provided middle-class households with strong incentives to align with a pre-existing but hitherto much narrower bailout constituency who offered other justifications for government efforts to protect wealth during crises.

The second-order consequences of the rise of great expectations have also been extensive. It has given large financial institutions more leverage in crises because they can point to the electoral costs for governments of any failure to provide bailouts – essentially, a political form of structural power. The sharp increase in the probability of financial sector bailouts also gave the large and complex financial institutions that received a form of public insurance powerful incentives to take on more risk. They did so in large part by increasing their leverage, enhancing their return on shareholder equity by purchasing risky assets through the issuance of debt. Businesses and, especially, households also responded by taking on more debt to purchase housing assets, which generated high returns during credit booms but which thereby placed even more wealth at risk during busts. We saw this operate in our three country cases since the 1970s, but rising leverage, wealth and financial fragility can be observed in most democracies since this time (Jordà, Schularick and Taylor, 2014, 2015). Thus, the rise of great expectations and increased risk to accumulated wealth have become mutually self-reinforcing. Put differently, a rising effective demand for financial stabilization has undermined the effectiveness of the growing state commitment to financial stability.

In our view, this suggests a political interpretation of the 'Minskian' cycle of credit boom and bust that gained renewed attention after 2007 (Minsky, 1992), and one that suggests that its origins lie partly with the very households often most threatened by it. The middle class is thus not the progressive force for financial stability some have claimed (Hoffman et al., 2009). By implication, our argument also casts doubt on the claim that democratic institutions provide a credible commitment to public debt repayment (North and Weingast, 1989; Schultz and Weingast, 2003). If democracy increasingly favours extensive bailouts, this is likely gradually to erode rather than sustain creditworthiness.

13.1   More Market Discipline?

Can this dangerous feedback loop be avoided or mitigated by new policy regimes that commit governments to avoid bailouts? We have seen that attempts in highly financialized democracies such as Britain and the United States to set lower societal expectations concerning the likelihood of government support during crises have largely proven futile. The Reagan and Thatcher 'revolutions' were in part built on the idea that governments should adopt market-conforming policies, even when it was politically painful to do so, on the grounds that such tough love would reduce reliance on government and enhance productivity and resilience. Consistent with this, central banks and financial regulators in recent decades also articulated 'non-zero failure' policy regimes on the principle that enforcing market discipline required that no entity should be too large or important to fail.

The main achievement of these new policy ideas was to increase the level of 'revealed hypocrisy', or the size of the gap between the new market-oriented policy rhetoric and policy practice during banking crises. After having been lectured over the previous decade by advanced countries on the need to restore confidence by implementing Bagehot policies following a crisis, emerging market officials, historically constrained by their more limited fiscal capacity, exploited this gap and their accumulation of unprecedented levels of foreign reserve stockpiles to enlarge their policy space after the 2007–9 crises (Chwieroth, 2015). The growing ideological strain created by this gap may be particularly acute in liberal market economies. Esping-Andersen famously argued that the welfare state was most politically fragile in liberal systems because it was focused on residual safety nets that stigmatized redistribution (Esping-Andersen, 1990). Our argument suggests another point of fundamental vulnerability for these political economies: in fostering financial liberalization and the financialization of middle-class wealth they have made it increasingly difficult for political incumbents to live up to their pro-market rhetoric. Many voters reject the Thatcherite narrative of personal financial responsibility in crises, in part because relatively few perceive the processes of financialization as an outcome of inclusive democratic deliberation. In some contexts, however, neoliberal ideas can help: Cardoso's team in Brazil deployed them to support their argument for the reform and transformation of state-owned banks.

Nevertheless, despite the achievements of the *Real* Plan, ideological strain also developed in Brazil as neoliberalism failed to address the country's major structural challenges, including education, inequality and poverty, culminating in Lula's election in 2002. Moreover, as we saw in Chapters 8 and 10, neoliberal ideology in the UK and US contributed to the polarization that was a source of delay in adopting the extensive interventions that ultimately resulted, by motivating pro-market actors to use institutional veto points to oppose bailouts. In the United States, a radical anti-big-government movement fought within the Republican Party and with the Bush and Obama administrations to oppose bailouts of Wall Street and even of other distressed households. This was also apparent even in comparatively politically centralized Britain, where the central bank initially sought to enforce a policy of market discipline through bank exit, and where the leadership of the New Labour government feared that policy interventions indicating a reversion to the ways of 'old' Labour would undermine their electoral appeal. In this way, the revival of pro-market ideas interacted with domestic institutions to produce blockages and delays that resulted in large, unevenly distributed wealth losses. Ultimately, however, these governments reluctantly agreed to extensive bailouts anyway because risking wholesale financial collapse was even less tolerable than setting aside ideological neoliberalism. The overall effect was that neither those societal groups demanding stricter adherence to market principles nor those demanding bailouts were satisfied with the results, producing rising dissatisfaction with government across the political spectrum. That this effect was particularly pronounced in the two countries most associated with the neoliberal policy trend since the 1970s was not foreseen by its most ardent proponents.

Yet despite the growing credibility problem attached to market-conforming policy principles in the era of great expectations, new proposals in this vein have become popular since 2008. For example, these have sought to 'bail-in' creditors of distressed or failing financial institutions so as to eliminate the need for taxpayer support in future crises.[2] In addition, new 'resolution' regimes are aimed at ensuring that large and complex financial institutions produce *ex ante* plans ('living

---

[2] The main elements of these reforms include new capital instruments that increase banks' loss-absorbency. At the global level, the Basel Committee recommended increases in required equity and later a 'TLAC' standard specifying additional minimum loss-absorbing capacity for G-SIBs from 2019. At the European level, the 'MREL' standards impose similar requirements on European banks (Deutsche Bundesbank, 2016; Restoy, 2018).

wills') for winding up their business in the event of bankruptcy (Financial Stability Board, 2017). Do these reforms offer an escape from the implications of great expectations?

We remain sceptical. In post-2007 crises, creditor bail-in was relatively rare and even then, according to a recent World Bank study, 'the decision to bail-in [was] taken only after repeated bail-outs and at a point when there had been substantial erosion of the "bail-inable" base' (World Bank, FinSAC, 2017, 2). It is also notable that these reform proposals have generally not sought to reduce the protection afforded to depositors and households. In the United States, for example, the intra-crisis increase in deposit insurance to $250,000 per account was made permanent by the Dodd–Frank Act, which also increased the protection afforded to individuals by establishing the controversial Consumer Financial Protection Board. Indeed, in no crisis-hit country in which deposit insurance was raised after 2007 have these limits subsequently been reduced to their pre-crisis level. This suggests that the ratchet effect to which we pointed in Britain since the 1857 crisis continues, whereby new crises generate higher levels of intervention and societal expectations of government protection. It also casts doubt on the political credibility of creditor bail-in reforms. To the extent that these reforms risk forcing losses onto middle-class households either directly as creditors or indirectly by increasing systemic risk, politicians will be incentivized to set them aside when crises strike.

A recent illustration can be found in Italy, where by 2016 the incumbent Democratic Party government faced a major crisis: due to a stagnant economy, over 100 banks had net NPLs that exceeded the value of their tangible equity (Pavesi, 2017). Italian banks then accounted for about a third of all European bank NPLs. The new European bail-in rules, in force from January 2016 with the issuance of the EU's Bank Recovery and Resolution Directive (BRRD), were intended to prevent taxpayer-funded bailouts. In the looming Italian banking crisis this regime encountered its first major test. The new rules required the bail-in of bank bondholders, including retail household investors who held about one-third of bank bonds partly due to their favourable tax treatment without fully understanding their increased riskiness (Merler, 2016).[3] Rather than enforce these new rules, the

---

[3] Italian deposit accounts are insured up to €100,000, but customers' bond holdings are not included.

centre-left government used a national interest loophole in the BRRD to undertake its largest banking bailouts since the 1930s. In June 2017, the government liquidated two Venetian banks, Veneto Banca and Banca Popolare di Vicenza, creating a bad bank and passing the remaining assets to Italy's largest retail bank, Intesa Sanpaolo. Intesa was paid €5.2 billion by the government, which also agreed to provide an additional €12 billion of guarantees (Merler, 2017). The following month, the government injected €5.4 billion into Banca Monte dei Paschi di Siena, the country's oldest bank – also based in a politically important region (Sanderson, 2017). This was the third state bailout of Monte dei Paschi since 2008. Like the interventions in the Venetian banks, it too was ultimately approved by the European Commission. Even so, in elections in 2018 the Democratic government lost badly to populist parties who decried the 'cronyism' of the bailouts while defending the interests of savers (Sanderson, 2018).

The political importance of banks across much of Europe suggests that this is unlikely to be an isolated case. Portugal's government in late 2015 also announced that they would impose losses on senior institutional bondholders of the restructured Novo Banco while protecting its retail bondholders (Wise and Arnold, 2015). In Germany, local savings banks are still subject to considerable political influence and, at the insistence of the German government, are not subject to European Central Bank supervision (Englmaier and Stowasser, 2017). If departures from market-conforming principles still occur with politically important but relatively small banks, our argument suggests that it is even less likely that systemically important financial institutions will be allowed to fail in accordance with the new resolution rules, with all the attendant economic and political consequences this would entail. It is thus not surprising to hear it reported that although the German government was among the leading voices calling for an end to bank bailouts in Europe, 'German officials acknowledge in private that they would be tempted to skirt European rules if one of the country's top banks needed a bailout' (Comfort, 2018). Politics may inevitably entail to some degree the management of hypocrisy, but we have seen that there have been substantial political costs for governments that have notionally adhered to market principles only to depart from them during major banking crises.

More generally, banks and private investors will always prefer the public socialization of losses to bail-in, and so have strong incentives to avoid committing new funds to cover potential losses in the knowledge that such avoidance increases the probability of state bailouts. Recent research suggests that bail-ins will be more credible if the size of the shock to the financial system is low and the density of the financial network is also low (Bernard, Capponi and Stiglitz, 2017). Large shocks in dense financial networks increase the likelihood that the authorities will need to intervene to prevent systemic collapse, thus reducing the credibility of creditor bail-in strategies. Financial firms also have an incentive to maximize their network interconnectedness – not only their size – in order to minimize the probability of bail-in requirements (Bernard et al., 2017). This provides a public policy interest in limiting network complexity and density, but financial firms have obvious incentives to argue that this would produce lower credit provision. As our analysis suggests, such arguments are likely to resonate powerfully with the interests of the middle class, which banks are keen to exploit to leverage political pressure from below.[4]

13.2 Tackling the Root Cause? Financialization and Democratic Politics

We have argued so far that neither communicative strategies emphasizing market discipline nor even direct legal efforts to proscribe bank bailouts are likely to be very effective in resisting the policy implications of the accumulation of at-risk middle-class wealth and the great expectations it has entailed. Might it be possible instead to address the root causes of the problem by breaking the link between financialization, democratic politics and bailouts?

Although we have argued that under circumstances of financialization, democratic politics has facilitated bailouts and rising financial instability, we would not advocate any curtailment of representative government and associated political institutions, which have inherent benefits that extend well beyond the narrow concerns of this book. We would, however, note that direct democracy has the potential to amplify the links between financialization, democratic politics, bailouts, and

---

[4] One example of this strategy has been the post-2009 campaign by major banks to argue that tighter regulation will hurt economic growth and employment and thus the interests of average households (Global Financial Markets Association, 2010; Institute for International Finance, 2011).

rising financial instability. Italy in 2016 is again a case in point. The bank bailout was arranged ahead of a constitutional referendum on which the prime minister at the time had wagered his job, but which he ultimately lost. Similarly, in Britain, the large losses inflicted on many middle-class and poorer households after the 2007–9 banking crisis were layered onto other losses suffered by particular regions over decades. The 2016 Brexit referendum gave voters 'left behind' in these deprived regions an opportunity to punish a political establishment which they saw as having abandoned them time and again.[5] With much of the outcome of Brexit still to be determined, the Bank of England has continued to warn, as it did in the lead-up to the vote, that the risks around the referendum posed the most significant, near-term threat to the country's financial stability (Bank of England Financial Policy Committee, 2018).

Authoritarian regimes are also far from immune to the pressures generated by the expectations of rising middle classes. The rising importance of housing assets as a component of middle-class wealth in China, for example, has created new dilemmas for Chinese policymakers in managing a market that is overheated in major cities and suffering from excess supply in second- and third-tier cities. Since 2013, Russia's central bank has provided stronger banks with subsidized finance to acquire hundreds of smaller failed banks, and in 2017 it nationalized three major private banks to prevent a wider financial collapse (Seddon, 2018). In both countries, state control of banking remains a dominant factor, and cronyistic ties may be at work in particular cases. But depositors have also been systematically protected, suggesting the sensitivity of these governments to middle-class interests (Rudnitsky and Baraulina, 2017; *The Economist*, 2017).

Nor do we advocate a return to market-conformist policies in crises in the context of high financialization, since the consequences of systemic financial collapse would likely be even worse than those of bailouts. Yet Bagehot's core principle of placing the burden of permanent insolvency on banks, their management and their major creditors rather than taxpayers remains as appropriate today as it did in the nineteenth century. Ideally, governments hoping to avoid the political backlash that so often accompanies modern bailouts should intervene

---

[5] On the role of longstanding regional inequalities in these populist revolts, see Essletzbichler, Disslbacher and Moser (2018); Lee, Morris and Kemeny (2018); Rodríguez-Pose (2018).

early and decisively, seeking to ensure that the costs and benefits of such bailouts are as fairly distributed as possible, with sufficient creditor bail-in to minimize moral hazard and losses to the taxpayer. This does not necessarily mean that home owners with underwater mortgages must be rescued alongside systemic banks. As we argued in the case of the United States (Chapter 10), the cost of doing so for current and future taxpayers and welfare recipients would be prohibitive and regarded by some as unfair.

Instead, policies that create incentives for greater burden-sharing between groups in advance of asset price declines would make sense. This includes government policies specifying that creditors and home owners share equity gains and losses in booms and busts, and policies promoting pension arrangements that divide risks more evenly between employers and employees and across generations (as has been tried in the Netherlands, Norway and parts of Canada). We also support post-2008 policies that aim to reduce moral hazard by imposing more automatic and transparent costs on institutions that receive bail-outs – especially shareholders, senior creditors, managements and large depositors. Sweden in the 1990s and again after 2008 provides a positive example of how this may be done. This included swift and transparent nationalization of failing banks, which governments in Britain and the United States sought desperately and ultimately unconvincingly to avoid. The relative rarity of successful examples, like Sweden, in the modern era also indicates the political difficulties involved (Ergungor and Cherny, 2009; Ingves, Lind, Shirakawa, Caruana and Ortiz Martínez, 2009; Lindvall, 2012).

Would it be possible to curtail financialization and thereby to lower the level of systemic risk that now often pertains to crucial middle-class assets such as housing and pensions? Such policies have become increasingly discussed as part of the post-2008 emphasis on 'macro-prudential' regulation (Borio, 2009). Yet these proposals allude to systemically beneficial outcomes that are difficult to translate into straightforward gains for voters. Capturing the difficulty of mobilizing voter support for such measures, Claudio Borio has remarked: 'while there is a constituency against inflation, there is hardly any against the inebriating feeling of getting richer' (Borio, 2014, 80).

On housing, it is difficult to imagine most democratic governments sustaining measures such as those undertaken in major Chinese cities to set lower maximum loan-to-value ratios aimed at limiting household and bank leverage and property price inflation.[6] The perceived right to take on debt, even at levels that would have seemed absurdly risky to previous generations, appears to have become entrenched in many contemporary societies. This is closely related to the view – encouraged by politicians of different partisan stripes going back at least as far as the Conservative Salisbury government in Britain in the 1880s – that property ownership is a necessary condition of middle-class status and an attribute of engaged citizenship. High house price inflation in many cities and other desirable locations also means that middle-class property ownership has become dependent on greater access to credit in recent decades. Thus, policymakers in many democratic countries have taken very modest steps by comparison with Chinese local authorities. For example, the Canadian central bank required minimum downpayments on properties of 5 per cent (an increase from 0 per cent) in July 2008, and increased this to 10 per cent in December 2015 (National Bank of Canada, 2018, 16). As of 2017, only a handful of emerging market democracies had implemented maximum LTVs despite ongoing concerns about credit booms in many (International Monetary Fund 2017a, 23–4).

In the Netherlands, where more than half of all mortgages require no contractual repayments during the term of the mortgage, maximum loan-to-value ratios for house purchases were reduced from 101 per cent to 100 per cent in 2018. The Dutch Financial Stability Committee has recommended since 2015 that the government agree to a gradual reduction in maximum LTVs to 90 per cent, but the new centre-right coalition government ignored this, agreeing in October 2017 that 'the maximum loan-to-value ratio will not be reduced any further in order to avoid making it more difficult for first-time buyers to access the housing market' (Government of the Netherlands, 2017, 35). Like many elected governments, it seems more convenient to postpone tough measures that would hurt large numbers of voters, even though many Dutch households are not expected to have acquired sufficient assets to repay interest-only mortgages when they expire. A substantial proportion of these loans will be due for repayment in the mid-2030s, when their mortgage interest tax relief will also expire (De Nederlandsche

---

[6] In 2016, some Tier 1 cities in China increased required downpayments on first properties to 30–5 per cent of the total value and downpayments on second properties to 50–70 per cent (Chiu, 2016).

Bank, 2017, 7, 23–30). In Norway, members of parliament even threatened to remove the regulator's power to set LTV ratios after it proposed lowering them. Meanwhile, governments in Australia, Canada and New Zealand have been more inclined to raise taxes on foreign property buyers to reduce demand pressure in their housing markets than to discourage purchases by citizens. Other policies that subsidize leverage, including mortgage interest deductions for income taxes, have also contributed to rising property prices, financial fragility and greater wealth inequality. Yet some countries have reduced or eliminated these distorting subsidies, including Britain in the early 1990s, the Netherlands for new interest-only mortgages in 2013, and more recently the United States in 2017.

It is not easy to see how a grand social bargain of the kind envisaged at the end of the Second World War could be constructed today (Polanyi, 1957). Continuing pressures on public and private pension schemes due to demographic change and lower than expected returns suggest that it is unlikely that the trend away from defined benefit to defined contribution schemes will be reversed in the near future (OECD, 2016). The decline of organized labour unions in many countries in recent decades has arguably contributed to this trend, which has shifted financial risk from employers to employees (Pierson, 1996). Globalization and technological change have accelerated the decline in employee bargaining power. Meanwhile, the size and political importance of the fund management industry has continued to rise.[7] As suggested above, however, promising new forms of risk-sharing in pensions are emerging that may achieve some easing of distributive conflict in this area.

Nevertheless, structural trends in property markets, mortgage finance, fund management and the wider political economy suggest that it is unlikely that the financialization of middle-class wealth will be reduced substantially in the near future. If anything, there are reasons to believe that it will continue to deepen, especially in emerging and developing countries that currently lag behind more advanced countries

---

[7] Although the wealth management industry that caters to the very wealthy has received recent attention (Harrington, 2016), the onshore funds management industry that manages middle-class pensions and other financial investments has become very large in many countries. As of the end of 2017, the average net asset size of the sector (excluding funds of funds) was 72 per cent of GDP for G7 countries. It was 59 per cent for Brazil and over 100 per cent for Australia, the Netherlands and the United States (Investment Company Institute, 2018).

in these areas. We noted in Chapter 12 that financialization and leverage is rising quickly in Brazil, posing policy challenges now familiar in more advanced countries. It is difficult to imagine governments embracing other policy interventions to reduce the demand for housing and other positional assets, such as more progressive wealth taxes (Atkinson, 2015, 179–204; Sandbu, 2017; Turner, 2015, 180). Such reforms may have additional merits beyond contributing to lower levels of financialization, but to the extent that they impose perceived costs on significant groups of wealthy and middle-class voters, politicians will be reluctant to take radical action along these lines. These considerations suggest that the self-reinforcing relationship between financialization, great expectations and financial instability may be set to continue. Since this is likely to produce new crises, it implies that the demand pressure from large numbers of voters that governments provide extensive financial protection is likely to remain high.

To what extent might governments resist this pressure by delegating financial stabilization policy to politically independent agencies? There have been moves in a number of countries in this direction since 2008, with independent central banks often being given greater statutory responsibility to manage and limit systemic financial stability, including via discretionary regulation. The limited appetite for such political delegation should already be clear – as for example in the Dutch case already mentioned, where the government has ignored key recommendations from the inter-agency Financial Stability Committee. Similar institutional bodies responsible for setting overall financial stability policy have been established in recent years in major countries, often with government participation and possessing limited authority to set policy without government approval.

Even so, the trend to place more responsibility for financial stability on central banks has led to fears that central bank independence will ultimately be compromised (Chwieroth and Danielsson, 2013). This is a real concern since, as we have argued, the deepening of links between the activities of systemically important financial institutions and the household sector has politicized financial regulation, especially during and after crises. It may be tempting for politicians to shift some politically difficult decisions regarding financial sector policy to formally independent agencies, but the former have strong incentives to limit such delegation or to reassert control if these agencies take decisions with significant electoral consequences. Regulators may also be biased against intervention because the costs of puncturing bubbles are greater than the rewards for preventing a crisis. If regulators do take a hard line, it may only reinforce voter perceptions that political and financial elites prefer to disempower the common people, which as we discuss below can be politically counterproductive.

Governments, including those in Britain and the United States, also delegated significant discretionary authority to financial regulators to negotiate tighter agreed regulatory standards with international counterparts after 2008, especially for systemically important financial institutions. In some countries, domestic financial regulators were also given authority to adopt more stringent national regulations than these agreed international minima where this was thought necessary to promote national financial stability. The Bank of England, the Federal Reserve Board, the Swiss National Bank and a number of other regulatory authorities have since used this authority to impose relatively high capital standards on their largest banks.

Our argument implies that this makes eminent sense from a public policy perspective. Differences in levels of financialization and financial structure suggest that individual countries may need to adopt more stringent regulatory standards than elsewhere so as to promote financial stability. If bailouts are virtually inevitable once systemic crises occur given great expectations, the obvious solution is to seek to minimize the likelihood of their occurrence. Thus, an important implication of our argument is that political parties must seek to engage voters in a constructive conversation during stable periods that more radical crisis prevention measures are necessary in circumstances of high and rising financialization, for the sake both of their wealth and of the stability of democracy. This conversation must be open and honest. It will require regulators to undertake considerable investment in the art of political communication so as to develop frames that resonate with the interests of voters. The underlying problem cannot be resolved by attempts to delegate key regulatory decisions to technical agencies and hoping that the next crisis will not happen during the term of the current government. Experience shows that this strategy has consistently failed.

Of course, there are obvious political limits to this recommendation. First, there is little agreement on the optimal level of bank equity capital, let alone the macroprudential settings that would balance the minimization of the probability of crises and the desirability of retaining the positive role of credit in supporting growth (Admati and Hellwig,

2013; Calomiris, 2013; Miles, Yang and Marcheggiano, 2013). Second, both the middle classes and the financial sector have incentives to resist very tight financial regulation, and politicians have incentives to respond by pressuring regulators not to go too far. Although we have focused on the negative political effects of banking crises on political incumbency, a number of authors have shown that incumbents, at least in recent decades, can derive political benefits from credit booms in the period before an election (Chavaz and Rose, 2016; Dinç, 2005; Englmaier and Stowasser, 2017; Illueca, Norden and Udell, 2014; Kern and Amri, 2016). Some voters might also interpret restrictive policies as an attempt by those who used leverage in the past to acquire positional assets to deny the same possibility to others. Third, regulators are also aware that unilateral increases in regulatory stringency will increase industry resistance on the grounds that they create an international competitive disadvantage (Singer, 2007). All these dynamics played out within and between a number of jurisdictions in the negotiations over Basel III standards over 2009–10 and since. These agreed standards may be seen as a welcome move in the right direction but are likely insufficient to prevent future major crises (Admati and Hellwig, 2013).

13.3 Implications for Democratic Politics

Despite these difficulties, those who believe that bolstering support for democratic political institutions is vital, as we do, should not decide that achieving greater financial stability is a lost cause. Middle-class households, as we have noted, are increasingly anxious about their wealth and may respond positively to policy proposals that link more effective crisis prevention measures with risk-sharing in housing and savings perceived as fairer than current arrangements.

We noted at the outset of this book that our analysis identifies another possible trilemma, raising serious concerns about the ability of contemporary societies simultaneously to sustain democratic politics, rising financialization and financial stability over time. If financialization, great expectations and associated financial instability are probably here to stay, the potential implications for democracy are not encouraging. This is in part because this additional trilemma is layered on top of associated long-term structural changes – notably globalization and continuing technological change – that have driven rising social polarization and anxiety. In the United States, for example, bailouts after 2007 favoured incipient populist political movements outside and within both major parties – even though governments were responding to pressure for intervention from much of the electorate. By sustaining high and rising leverage, bailouts may also contribute to rising economic volatility and slower growth, further feeding popular discontent (Jordà, Schularick and Taylor, 2015; Mian and Sufi, 2014a, 7; Reinhart and Rogoff, 2009, 145–7).

From a longer perspective, the rising propensity for bailouts and the perceived asymmetries in their effects on the distribution of wealth have occurred in the context of rising inequality, job losses and social change over a generation or more and have been concentrated in particular regions (Rodríguez-Pose, 2018). The Italian case that we discussed briefly above is in many ways an even starker illustration of these layering effects, and the demise of mainstream political parties even more pronounced. These forces have encouraged the trend towards rising dissatisfaction with mainstream politics and even with democratic institutions over the past few decades (Foa and Mounk, 2016, 2017; Inglehart and Norris, 2016). In many contemporary democracies, growing numbers of citizens appear to believe that economic and political elites have managed systematically to skew outcomes in their favour, creating opportunities for 'anti-establishment' political entrepreneurs. Costly financial sector bailouts that appear to leave middle-class and poorer households relatively worse off – even if the truth is more complex – may be seen to epitomize this broader, long-standing tendency. After 2007, many middle-class households, who in a previous long period of asset price growth felt they could just about keep up, now also saw this wealth – and perhaps what remained of their status and dignity – being taken from them.

The greater success of anti-establishment politicians in the aftermath of modern banking crises is not unique to advanced economies. Following a deep systemic crisis in Venezuela in 1994–5 that was followed by IMF intervention, Hugo Chávez gained power in a landslide election on an anti-corruption platform that condemned the two major political parties that had dominated politics since 1958 (de Krivoy, 2003). More recently, in Hungary, Viktor Orbán capitalized on the political fallout from the 2008 systemic crisis, which included a rescue package from the IMF and European Union that was followed by the then prime minister being caught on tape explaining to party officials the inadequacy of his policies and that he had lied to the public over an extended period. In 2010, Orbán secured nearly 70 per cent of the vote on a platform that claimed the near bankruptcy of the Hungarian economy had been brought about by a corrupt political system still dominated by the old communist regime (Djankov, 2015). In these and other emerging markets, as well as developing countries, where fiscal capacity is also historically more limited, the need for costly external financial interventions likely amplified citizen frustration with economic and political elites.

Financialization, crises and bailouts pose challenges to most political parties, but they may pose particularly acute challenges to mainstream centre-left political parties. These parties arguably suffer greater ideological strain than centre-right parties when they are perceived as intervening in favour of the financial sector, as in Britain over 2008–9, in the United States during the first term of the Obama administration, and in Brazil during Cardoso's second term. The growing cost of bailouts as financialization and leverage grow also means that the redistributive effects of bailouts have increased over time. More leveraged households generally suffer larger proportional wealth losses than richer households when house prices fall. This can be seen in the United States on the eve of the crisis in 2007, where the leverage ratio (debt to total assets) of the richest quintile of households was 7 per cent, while that for the poorest quintile had risen to 80 per cent. After 2006, house price declines of about 30 per cent on average wiped out the net wealth of relatively poor US households (Mian and Sufi, 2014a, 17). This led to forced asset sales and sustained losses for poorer households, amplifying pre-existing wealth inequality between richer and poorer households. To the extent that costly bailouts also increase the likelihood of fiscal austerity in the aftermath of such interventions, less affluent households and the unemployed can also suffer more through this channel. This may increase the tendency of such households to abandon centre-left parties, as was seen in Britain in the elections of 2010 and 2015, and the Brexit referendum and the US elections of 2016.[8]

---

[8] Of course, this factor is not the only reason for the decline of centre-left parties. Other factors, often associated with financialization, eroding the traditional base of centre-left parties include: the rise of middle-class wealth, including housing and pension equity; the relative growth of the financial sector and of the service sector generally; relatively high growth in manufacturing productivity; and the effects of capital account openness and associated exchange rate volatility on manufacturing-sector employment and output.

It is striking that in the two countries at the centre of the deep financial and economic crises that began in 2007, Britain and the United States, conservative political parties considerably improved their position in Parliament and Congress respectively by 2010 and eventually recaptured government. Since then, right-wing populist insurgencies have been increasingly influential within both the British Conservative Party and the US Republican Party. In both countries, which by the early 2000s were thought to have managed immigration, cultural and economic change relatively successfully compared to other advanced democracies, political polarization has risen. Government leaders in Britain and America have come to adopt policies previously seen as the preserve of radical fringe parties, have openly disdained democratic institutions and cast groups that oppose their agendas as enemies. Although it is not easy to draw a straight line from the 2007–9 banking crisis to these political outcomes, it seems likely that this crisis, which triggered each country's most extensive peacetime economic interventions, was an important contributing factor.

Great expectations thus appear destined to produce great disappointments. As Pip came to understand in Dickens's novel, that heady feeling of new-found wealth eventually jeopardized all that was important to him. These great disappointments are increasingly shaping politics and policy in hitherto stable democracies, to our common detriment. Governments must engage the general public, especially the now wealthy but anxious middle class, in a policy conversation that recognizes that the current path is unsustainable and fundamental change is needed.

BIBLIOGRAPHY

'1830 | History of Parliament Online'. n.d. Last accessed 23 January 2017. www
.historyofparliamentonline.org/volume/1820-1832/parliament/1830-0.

Aaronson, Daniel, Daniel Hartley and Bhashkar Mazumder. 2017. 'The Effects
of the 1930s HOLC "Redlining" Maps'. Working Paper, WP-2017-12.
Federal Reserve Bank of Chicago.

Abbas, S. M. Ali, Nazim Belhocine, Asmaa A. ElGanainy and Mark Horton.
2011. 'Historical Patterns and Dynamics of Public Debt – Evidence from a
New Database'. *IMF Economic Review* 59 (4): 717–42.

Abiad, Abdul, Enrica Detragiache and Thierry Tressel. 2008. 'A New Database of
Financial Reforms'. IMF Working Paper, WP/08/266. New York, NY:
International Monetary Fund.

Acemoglu, Daron, and James A. Robinson. 2006. *Economic Origins of
Dictatorship and Democracy*. New York, NY: Cambridge University Press.

Acharya, Viral V., Deniz Anginer and A. Joseph Warburton. 2016. 'The End of
Market Discipline? Investor Expectations of Implicit Government Guarantees'.
SSRN Scholarly Paper ID 1961656. Rochester, NY: Social Science Research
Network.

Acharya, Viral V., Lasse H. Pedersen, Thomas Philippon and Matthew Richardson.
2017. 'Measuring Systemic Risk'. *The Review of Financial Studies* 30 (1): 2–47.

Acharya, Viral V., and Matthew Richardson. 2009. 'Causes of the Financial
Crisis'. *Critical Review* 21 (2–3): 195–210.

Acharya, Viral V., Matthew Richardson, Stijn van Nieuwerburgh and Lawrence
J. White. 2011. *Guaranteed to Fail: Fannie Mae, Freddie Mac, and the Debacle
of Mortgage Finance*. Princeton, NJ: Princeton University Press.

Achen, Christopher H., and Larry M. Bartels. 2012. 'Blind Retrospection: Why
Shark Attacks Are Bad for Democracy'. Working Paper, Center for the Study
of Democratic Institutions, Vanderbilt University.

Admati, Anat, and Martin Hellwig. 2013. *The Bankers' New Clothes*. Princeton, NJ: Princeton University Press.

Ahlquist, John S., and Ben W. Ansell. 2017. 'Taking Credit: Redistribution and Borrowing in an Age of Economic Polarization'. *World Politics* 69 (4): 640–75.

Albanesi, Stefania, Giacomo De Giorgi and Jaromir Nosal. 2017. 'Credit Growth and the Financial Crisis: A New Narrative'. Working Paper 23740. National Bureau of Economic Research. https://doi.org/10.3386/w23740.

Alemanno, Alberto, Frank den Butter, André Nijsen and Jacopo Torriti. 2013. *Better Business Regulation in a Risk Society*. New York, NY: Springer Science & Business Media.

Alesina, Alberto, and Allan Drazen. 1991. 'Why Are Stabilizations Delayed?' *The American Economic Review* 81 (5): 1170–88.

Alesina, Alberto, Sule Özler, Nouriel Roubini and Phillip Swagel. 1996. 'Political Instability and Economic Growth'. *Journal of Economic Growth* 1 (2): 189–211.

Alesina, Alberto, and Howard Rosenthal. 1989. 'Partisan Cycles in Congressional Elections and the Macroeconomy'. *American Political Science Review* 83 (2): 373–98.

Alesina, Alberto, and Howard Rosenthal. 1995. *Partisan Politics, Divided Government, and the Economy*. Cambridge and New York, NY: Cambridge University Press.

Alessandri, Piergiorgio, and Andrew G. Haldane. 2009. 'Banking on the State'. www.bis.org/review/r091111e.pdf.

Allen, A. M., S. R. Cope, L. J. H. Dark and H. J. Witheridge. 1938. *Commercial Banking Legislation and Control*. London: Macmillan.

Alston, Lee J., Marcus André Melo, Bernardo Mueller and Carlos Pereira. 2016. *Brazil in Transition: Beliefs, Leadership, and Institutional Change*. Princeton, NJ: Princeton University Press.

Amyx, Jennifer. 2013. *Japan's Financial Crisis: Institutional Rigidity and Reluctant Change*. Princeton, NJ: Princeton University Press.

Anderson, Christopher J. 2000. 'Economic Voting and Political Context: A Comparative Perspective'. *Electoral Studies* 19 (2–3): 151–70.

Anderson, Christopher J. 2007. 'The End of Economic Voting? Contingency Dilemmas and the Limits of Democratic Accountability'. *Annual Review of Political Science* 10 (1): 271–96.

Andrews, Edmund L. 2009. 'After "Stress Tests," Banks Told to Raise Money'. *New York Times*, 7 May 2009, sec. Business Day.

Andrews, Edmund L., and Peter Baker. 2009. 'A.I.G. Planning Huge Bonuses After $170 Billion Bailout'. *New York Times*, 14 March 2009, sec. Business Day.

Andrews, Edmund L., Michael J. de la Merced and Mary Williams Walsh. 2008. 'Fed's $85 Billion Loan Rescues Insurer'. *New York Times*, 16 September 2008, sec. Business Day.

Ansell, Ben W. 2012. 'Assets in Crisis: Housing, Preferences and Policy in the Credit'. *Swiss Political Science Review* 18 (4): 531–7.

Ansell, Ben W. 2014. 'The Political Economy of Ownership: Housing Markets and the Welfare State'. *American Political Science Review* 108 (2): 383–402.

Ansell, Ben W., and David Samuels. 2010. 'Inequality and Democratization: A Contractarian Approach'. *Comparative Political Studies* 43 (12): 1543–74.

Anson, Mike, David Bholat, Miao Kang and Ryland Thomas. 2017. 'The Bank of England as Lender of Last Resort: New Historical Evidence from Daily Transactional Data'. Bank of England.

Antoniades, Alexis, and Charles W. Calomiris. 2018. 'Mortgage Market Credit Conditions and U.S. Presidential Elections'. Working Paper 24459. National Bureau of Economic Research.

Aron, Janine, John Muellbauer and Johan Prinsloo. 2008. 'Estimating the Balance Sheet of the Personal Sector in an Emerging Market Country: South Africa, 1975–2005'. In *Personal Wealth from a Global Perspective*, edited by James B. Davies, 196–223. Oxford: Oxford University Press.

Associação Brasileira das Entidades Fechadas de Previdência Complementar. n.d. 'Brazilian Pension System: Country Profile'. www.abrapp.org.br/Paginas/Brazilian-Pension-System.aspx.

Assunção, Juliano J. 2008. 'Rural Organization and Land Reform in Brazil: The Role of Nonagricultural Benefits of Landholding'. *Economic Development and Cultural Change* 56 (4): 851–70.

Atkinson, Anthony B. 2015. *Inequality: What Can Be Done?* Cambridge, MA: Harvard University Press.

Atkinson, Anthony B., and Andrea Brandolini. 2013. 'On the Identification of the Middle Class'. In *Income Inequality: Economic Disparities and the Middle Class in Affluent Countries*, edited by Janet C. Gornick and Markus Jäntti, 77–100. Stanford, CA: Stanford University Press.

Atkinson, Anthony B., Joe Hasell, Salvatore Morelli and Max Roser. 2017. 'The Chartbook of Economic Inequality – Data on Economic Inequality over the Long-Run'. Oxford: Institute for New Economic Thinking, Oxford Martin School.

Atkinson, Anthony B., and Salvatore Morelli. 2011. 'Economic Crises and Inequality'. Human Development Research Paper 2011/06. United Nations Development Programme.

Badev, Anton, Thorsten Beck, Ligia Vado and Simon Walley. 2014. 'Housing Finance across Countries: New Data and Analysis'. World Bank Policy Research Working Papers.

Baer, Werner, and Nader Nazmi. 2000. 'Privatization and Restructuring of Banks in Brazil'. *The Quarterly Review of Economics and Finance* 40 (1): 3–24.

Bagehot, Walter. 1882. *The English Constitution*. 3rd edn. London: Kegan Paul, Trench & Co.

Bagehot, Walter. 1962 [1873]. *Lombard Street: A Description of the Money Market*. Homewood, IL: R. D. Irwin.

Bair, Sheila. 2012. *Bull by the Horns: Fighting to Save Main Street from Wall Street and Wall Street from Itself*. New York, NY: Free Press.

Banco Central do Brasil. 1995. 'PROER – Program of Incentives to the Restructuring and Strengthening of the National Financial System'. Brasilia: Banco Central do Brasil.

Banco Central do Brasil. 1997. 'Annual Report 1997'. Brasilia: Banco Central do Brasil.

Bank for International Settlements. 2017a. 'Residential Property Prices: Selected Series (Nominal and Real)'. 30 August 2017.

Bank for International Settlements. 2017b. 'Long Series on Credit to the Non-Financial Sector'. 3 December 2017.

Bank of England. 1978. 'The Secondary Banking Crisis and the Bank of England's Support Operations'. *Bank of England Quarterly Bulletin* 18 (2): 230–9.

Bank of England. 2008. 'Financial Stability Report October 2008'.

Bank of England. 2009a. 'News Release: Special Liquidity Scheme'.

Bank of England. 2009b. 'Financial Stability Report December 2009'. Bank of England.

Bank of England. 2011. 'Quarterly Bulletin 2011 Q3, Volume 51 No. 3'. Bank of England.

Bank of England. 2014. 'Inflation Report, February 2014'. Bank of England.

Bank of England. 2016. 'Financial Stability Report November 2016'. Bank of England.

Bank of England. n.d. 'Money and Lending Database'. www.bankofengland.co.uk/boeapps/iadb/index.asp?first=yes&SectionRequired=A&HideNums=-1&ExtraInfo=false&Travel=NIxSTx.

Bank of England Financial Policy Committee. 2018. 'Financial Policy Committee Statement from Its Meeting – 12 March 2018'. Bank of England.

Banking Supervision and Regulation – Economic Affairs Committee, House of Lords (UK). 2009. 'Financial Supervision in the United Kingdom'.

'BankRegData'. n.d. bankregdata.com.

Banks, James, and Sarah Tanner. 2002. 'Household Portfolios in the United Kingdom'. In *Household Portfolios*, edited by Luigi Guiso, Michael Haliassos and Tullio Jappelli, 219–50. Cambridge, MA: MIT Press.

Barker, Alex. 2008. 'Brown Says UK Leads World with Rescue'. *Financial Times*, 9 October 2008.

Barman, Roderick J. 1988. *Brazil: The Forging of a Nation, 1798–1852*. Stanford, CA: Stanford University Press.

Barnes, Lucy, and Timothy Hicks. 2012. 'Left Behind? Partisan Politics after the Financial Crisis'. SSRN Scholarly Paper ID 2105310. Rochester, NY: Social Science Research Network.

Barofsky, Neil M. 2012. *Bailout: An Inside Account of How Washington Abandoned Main Street while Rescuing Wall Street*. New York, NY: Free Press.

Barro, Robert. 1973. 'The Control of Politicians: An Economic Model'. *Public Choice* 14 (1): 19–42.

Barro, Robert J., and José F. Ursua. 2008. 'Macroeconomic Crises since 1870'. *Brookings Papers on Economic Activity* 39 (1 (Spring)): 255–350.

Barros, Aluísio J. D., and Andréa D. Bertoldi. 2008. 'Out-of-Pocket Health Expenditure in a Population Covered by the Family Health Program in Brazil'. *International Journal of Epidemiology* 37 (April): 758–65.

Bartels, Larry M. 2008. *Unequal Democracy: The Political Economy of the New Gilded Age*. New York, NY: Russell Sage Foundation; Princeton, NJ: Princeton University Press.

Bartels, Larry M. 2013. 'Political Effects of the Great Recession'. *The ANNALS of the American Academy of Political and Social Science* 650 (1): 47–76.

Bartels, Larry M. 2014. 'Ideology and Retrospection in Electoral Responses to the Great Recession'. In *Mass Politics in Tough Times: Opinions, Votes and Protest in the Great Recession*, edited by Larry M. Bartels and Nancy Bermeo, 185–224. Oxford and New York, NY: Oxford University Press.

Bartels, Larry M., and Nancy Bermeo, eds. 2014. *Mass Politics in Tough Times: Opinions, Votes and Protest in the Great Recession*. Oxford and New York: Oxford University Press.

Barth, James R., Gerard Caprio and Ross Levine. 2006. *Rethinking Bank Regulation: Till Angels Govern*. Cambridge and New York, NY: Cambridge University Press.

Basel Committee on Banking Supervision. 1988. 'International Convergence of Capital Measurement and Capital Standards'. www.bis.org/publ/bcbs04a.htm.

Basel Committee on Banking Supervision. 2015. 'Glossary'. 16 June. www.bis.org/cpmi/publ/d00b.htm?&selection=68&scope=CPMI&c=a&base=term.

BBC News. 2007. 'Brown Attacked over Northern Rock'. 17 September. www.reuters.com/article/northernrock-brown-crisis/bank-crisis-deals-blow-to-browns-reputation-idUKNOA92342420070919.

BBC Press Office. 2010. 'Global Poll: Governments Misspend More than Half Our Taxes'. 27 September. www.bbc.co.uk/pressoffice/pressreleases/stories/2010/09_september/27/poll.shtml.

BBC World Service. 2009. 'Global Poll Shows Support for Increased Government Spending and Regulation'. www.globescan.com/news_archives/bbc2009_globalPoll-04/backgrounder.html.

BBC World Service. 2010. 'Governments Misspend More Than Half of Our Taxes – Global Poll'. www.globescan.com/news_archives/bbc2010_economics/keyfindings.html.

BBC World Service. 2012. 'Economic System Seen as Unfair: Global Poll'. https://globescan.com/wp-content/uploads/2012/03/BBC12_Economics.pdf.

Beck, Thorsten, Büyükkarabacak Berrak, Felix Rioja and Neven T. Valev. 2012. 'Who Gets the Credit? And Does It Matter? Household vs. Firm Lending Across Countries'. *The B.E. Journal of Macroeconomics* 12 (1): 1–46.

Beck, Thorsten, George Clarke, Alberto Groff, Philip Keefer and Patrick Walsh. 2001. 'New Tools in Comparative Political Economy: The Database of Political Institutions'. *The World Bank Economic Review* 15 (1): 165–76.

Beck, Thorsten, Juan Miguel Crivelli and William Summerhill. 2005. 'State Bank Transformation in Brazil: Choices and Consequences'. *Journal of Banking & Finance*, 29 (8): 2223–57.

Beck, Ulrich. 1992. *Risk Society: Towards a New Modernity*. London: Sage.

Behn, Markus, Rainer Haselmann, Thomas Kick and Vikrant Vig. 2015. 'The Political Economy of Bank Bailouts'. Working Paper 86. Goethe University Frankfurt, Institute for Monetary and Financial Stability (IMFS).

Belfield, Chris, Daniel Chandler and Robert Joyce. 2015. 'Today's Young Adults Are Much Less Likely to Own a Home Than Their Parents' Generation, But Those Owning a Home Well Before the Crisis Have Gained From House Price Increases and a Sharp Fall in Housing Costs'. 19 February. www.ifs.org.uk/publications/7594.

Bello, José Maria. 1966. *A History of Modern Brazil, 1889–1964*. Stanford, CA: Stanford University Press.

Bergad, Laird W. 1999. *Slavery and the Demographic and Economic History of Minas Gerais, Brazil, 1720–1888*. Cambridge: Cambridge University Press.

Berman, Sheri. 2006. *The Primacy of Politics: Social Democracy and the Making of Europe's Twentieth Century*. New York, NY: Cambridge University Press.

Bermeo, Nancy Gina, and Jonas Pontusson. 2012. *Coping with Crisis: Government Reactions to the Great Recession*. New York, NY: Russell Sage Foundation.

Bernanke, Ben S. 1983. 'Nonmonetary Effects of the Financial Crisis in Propagation of the Great Depression'. *American Economic Review* 73 (3): 257–76.

Bernanke, Ben S. 2015. *The Courage to Act: A Memoir of a Crisis and Its Aftermath*. New York, NY: W. W. Norton.

Bernard, Benjamin, Agostino Capponi and Joseph E. Stiglitz. 2017. 'Bail-Ins and Bail-Outs: Incentives, Connectivity, and Systemic Stability'. Working Paper 23747. National Bureau of Economic Research.

Bértola, Luis, and José Antonio Ocampo. 2012. *The Economic Development of Latin America since Independence*. Oxford: Oxford University Press.

Bethell, Leslie, and Jairo Nicolau. 2008. 'Politics in Brazil, 1985–2002'. In *The Cambridge History of Latin America. Volume 9: Brazil since 1930*, edited by Leslie Bethell: 231–80. Cambridge: Cambridge University Press.

Bevilaqua, Afonso S. 2002. 'State Government Bailouts in Brazil'. IDB Working Paper No. 153. Rochester, NY: Social Science Research Network.

Bhutta, Neil, and Daniel Ringo. 2015. 'Assessing the Community Reinvestment Act's Role in the Financial Crisis, FEDS Notes'. 26 May.

Bignon, Vincent, Marc Flandreau and Stefano Ugolini. 2012. 'Bagehot for Beginners: The Making of Lender-of-Last-Resort Operations in the Mid-Nineteenth Century'. *Economic History Review* 65 (2): 580–608.

Binder, Sarah. 2003. *Stalemate: Causes and Consequences of Legislative Gridlock*. Washington DC: Brookings Institution Press.

Binder, Sarah. 2015. 'The Dysfunctional Congress'. *Annual Review of Political Science* 18 (1): 85–101.

Blick, Andrew, and George Jones. 2010. *Premiership: The Development, Nature and Power of the Office of the British Prime Minister*. Exeter: Imprint Academic.

Blinder, Alan S. 2012. 'Central Bank Independence and Credibility during and after a Crisis'. Working Paper 1401. Princeton University, Department of Economics, Center for Economic Policy Studies.

Blinder, Alan S., and Mark Zandi. 2010. 'How the Great Recession Was Brought to an End'. Princeton University and Moody's Analytics. www.economy.com/mark-zandi/documents/End-of-Great-Recession.pdf.

Blinder, Alan S., and Mark Zandi. 2015. 'The Financial Crisis: Lessons for the Next One'. Center on Budget and Policy Priorities. www.cbpp.org/research/economy/the-financial-crisis-lessons-for-the-next-one.

Blyth, Mark. 2002. *Great Transformations: The Rise and Decline of Embedded Liberalism*. New York, NY: Cambridge University Press.

Blyth, Mark, and Matthias Matthijs. 2017. 'Black Swans, Lame Ducks, and the Mystery of IPE's Missing Macroeconomy'. *Review of International Political Economy* 24 (2): 203–31.

Board of Governors of the Federal Reserve System. 2014. 'Report on the Economic Well-Being of U.S. Households in 2013'. www.federalreserve.gov/econresdata/2014-economic-well-being-of-us-households-in-2013-retirement.htm.

Board of Governors of the Federal Reserve System. 2015. 'Federal Reserve Board Approves Final Rule Specifying Its Procedures for Emergency Lending under Section 13(3) of the Federal Reserve Act'. Board of Governors of the Federal Reserve System. 30 November. www.federalreserve.gov/newsevents/pressreleases/bcreg20151130a.htm.

Board of Governors of the Federal Reserve System. 2017a. 'Report on the Economic Well-Being of U.S. Households in 2016'. Federal Reserve Board.

Board of Governors of the Federal Reserve System. 2017b. 'The Fed – Recent Balance Sheet Trends'. Board of Governors of the Federal Reserve System. 29 December. www.federalreserve.gov/monetarypolicy/bst_recenttrends.htm.

Board of Governors of the Federal Reserve System, and Federal Deposit Insurance Corporation. 2017. 'Agencies Announce Joint Determinations for Living Wills'. Board of Governors of the Federal Reserve System. 19 December. www.federalreserve.gov/newsevents/pressreleases/bcreg20171219a.htm.

Boas, Taylor C. 2016. *Presidential Campaigns in Latin America: Electoral Strategies and Success Contagion*. New York, NY: Cambridge University Press.

Boin, Arjen, Paul t'Hart and Allan McConnell. 2009. 'Crisis Exploitation: Political and Policy Impacts of Framing Contests'. *Journal of European Public Policy* 16 (1): 81–106.

Boix, Carles, Michael Miller and Sebastian Rosato. 2013. 'A Complete Data Set of Political Regimes, 1800–2007'. *Comparative Political Studies* 46 (12): 1523–54.

Boix, Carles, Michael Miller and Sebastian Rosato. 2014. 'Boix–Miller–Rosato Dichotomous Coding of Democracy, 1800–2010'. Harvard Dataverse. https://doi.org/10.7910/DVN/28468.

Boothroyd, David. n.d. 'General Election Results 1885–1979'. www.election .demon.co.uk/geresults.html.

Bordo, Michael D., and Barry J. Eichengreen. 1999. 'Is Our Current International Economic Environment Unusually Crisis Prone?' In *Capital Flows and the International Financial System*, edited by David Gruen and Luke Gower, 18–74. Sydney: Reserve Bank of Australia.

Bordo, Michael D., Barry Eichengreen, Daniela Klingebiel and Maria Soledad Martinez-Peria. 2001. 'Is the Crisis Problem Growing More Severe?' *Economic Policy* 16 (32): 52–82.

Bordo, Michael D., and Christopher M. Meissner. 2006. 'The Role of Foreign Currency Debt in Financial Crises: 1880–1913 versus 1972–1997'. *Journal of Banking & Finance* 30 (12): 3299–329.

Borio, Claudio. 2009. 'Implementing the Macroprudential Approach to Financial Regulation and Supervision'. *Banque de France Financial Stability Review*, 13: 31–41.

Borio, Claudio. 2014. 'Macroprudential Policy and the Financial Cycle: Some Stylized Facts and Policy Suggestions'. In *What Have We Learned? Macroeconomic Policy after the Crisis*, edited by George A. Akerlof, Olivier Blanchard, David Romer and Joseph E. Stiglitz, 71–86. Cambridge, MA: MIT Press.

Bourguignon, François, and Christian Morrisson. 2002. 'Inequality among World Citizens: 1820–1992'. *American Economic Review* 92 (4): 727–44.

Bovens, Mark, and Paul t'Hart. 1996. *Understanding Policy Fiascoes*. New Brunswick, NJ: Transaction Publishers.

Box-Steffensmeier, Janet M., and Bradford S. Jones. 2004. *Event History Modeling: A Guide for Social Scientists*. New York, NY: Cambridge University Press.

Brambor, Thomas, William Roberts Clark and Matt Golder. 2006. 'Understanding Interaction Models: Improving Empirical Analyses'. *Political Analysis* 14 (1): 63–82.

Brambor, Thomas, and Johannes Lindvall. 2017. 'The Ideology of Heads of Government, 1870–2012'. *European Political Science*.

Branham, J. Alexander, Stuart N. Soroka and Christopher Wlezien. 2017. 'When Do the Rich Win?' *Political Science Quarterly* 132 (1): 43–62.

Bresser-Pereira, Luiz Carlos and Yoshiaki Nakano. 1991. 'Hyperinflation and Stabilization in Brazil: The First Collor Plan'. In *Economic Problems of the 1990s*, edited by Paul Davidson and Jan Kregel, 41–68. London: Edward Elgar.

Bricker, Jesse, Lisa J. Dettling, Alice Henriques, Joanne W. Hsu, Lindsay Jacobs, Kevin B. Moore, Sarah Pack, John Sabelhaus, Jeffrey Thompson and Richard A. Windle. 2017. 'Changes in US Family Finances from 2013 to 2016: Evidence from the Survey of Consumer Finances'. *Federal Reserve Bulletin* 103 (3): 1–42.

Bridges, Tyler. 1988. 'Brazil's Banks, Hooked on Inflation, Yearn for Stability: The Americas'. *Wall Street Journal*, 1 April.

Briggs, Asa. 1961. 'The Welfare State in Historical Perspective'. *European Journal of Sociology / Archives Européennes de Sociologie* 2 (2): 221–58.

British Electoral Study. 2010. 'Continuous Monitoring Survey'. http://bes2009–10.org./.

British Social Attitudes. n.d. 'Key Findings'. www.bsa.natcen.ac.uk/latest-report/british-social-attitudes-30/key-findings/trust-politics-and-institutions.aspx.

Brock, W. R. 1967. *Lord Liverpool and Liberal Toryism 1820 to 1827*. 3rd edn. London: Cass & Co.

Brooke, James. 1990. 'Brazil's New Chief Gives Radical Plan to Halt Inflation'. *New York Times*, 17 March.

Brooke, James. 1991. 'Brazil Freezes All Wages and Prices'. *New York Times*, 1 February.

Brooke, James. 1992. 'Corruption Charge Taints Brazil Leader'. *New York Times*, 25 May.

Brooker, Nathan. 2018. 'How the Financial Crash Made Our Cities Unaffordable'. *Financial Times*, 15 March.

Brooks, Sarah M. 2005. 'Interdependent and Domestic Foundations of Policy Change: The Diffusion of Pension Privatization Around the World'. *International Studies Quarterly* 49 (2): 273–94.

Brooks, Sarah M. 2007. 'When Does Diffusion Matter? Explaining the Spread of Structural Pension Reforms Across Nations'. *Journal of Politics* 69 (3): 701–15.

Brown, Gordon. 2010. *Beyond the Crash: Overcoming the First Crisis of Globalisation*. London: Simon & Schuster.

Browne, James, and David Phillips. 2010. 'Tax and Benefit Reforms under Labour'. Briefing Note No. 88. Institute for Fiscal Studies.

Broz, J. Lawrence, and Richard S. Grossman. 2004. 'Paying for Privilege: The Political Economy of Bank of England Charters, 1694–1844'. *Explorations in Economic History* 41 (1): 48–72.

Bruner, Robert F., and Sean D. Carr. 2007. *The Panic of 1907: Lessons Learned from the Market's Perfect Storm*. Hoboken, NJ: John Wiley & Sons.

Brunnermeier, Markus K., Harold James and Jean-Pierre Landau. 2016. *The Euro and the Battle of Ideas*. Princeton, NJ: Princeton University Press.

Brunnermeier, Markus K., and Christian Julliard. 2008. 'Money Illusion and Housing Frenzies'. *The Review of Financial Studies* 21 (1): 135–80.

Brunnermeier, Markus K., and Isabel Schnabel. 2015. 'Bubbles and Central Banks: Historical Perspectives'. SSRN Scholarly Paper ID 2592370. Rochester, NY: Social Science Research Network.

Bueno de Mesquita, Bruce, Alastair Smith, Randolph M. Siverson and James D. Morrow. n.d. 'The Logic of Political Survival Data Source'. www.nyu.edu/gsas/dept/politics/data/bdm2s2/Logic.htm.

Bueno de Mesquita, Bruce, Alastair Smith, Randolph M. Siverson and James D. Morrow. 2003. *The Logic of Political Survival*. Cambridge, MA: MIT Press.

Burn-Murdoch, John. 2017. 'Youth Turnout at General Election Highest in 25 Years, Data Show'. *Financial Times*, 20 June.

Burns, Helen M. 1974. *The American Banking Community and New Deal Banking Reforms, 1933–1935*. Westport, CT: Greenwood Press.

Busch, Andreas. 2009. *Banking Regulation and Globalization*. New York, NY: Oxford University Press.

Bush, George W. 2011. *Decision Points*. Reprint edition. New York, NY: Broadway Books.

Butkiewicz, James L. 1995. 'The Impact of a Lender of Last Resort during the Great Depression: The Case of the Reconstruction Finance Corporation'. *Explorations in Economic History* 32 (2): 197–216.

Cable, Olympia. 1976. 'Brazilian Presidential Elections of the First Republic, 1889–1930'. PhD dissertation, University of Glasgow.

Cain, P. J., and A. G. Hopkins. 2016. *British Imperialism: 1688–2015*. London: Routledge.

Cairncross, Alec K., and Barry J. Eichengreen. 1983. *Sterling in Decline: The Devaluations of 1931, 1949, and 1967*. Oxford: Basil Blackwell.

Calmes, Jackie. 2008. 'Fed Official Is Said to Be Choice for Treasury'. *New York Times*, 21 November, sec. Politics.

Calomiris, Charles W. 2013. 'Is a 25% Bank Equity Requirement Really a No-Brainer?' *VoxEU.Org* (blog). 28 November. https://voxeu.org/article/25-bank-equity-requirement.

Calomiris, Charles W., and Gary Gorton. 1991. 'The Origins of Banking Panics: Models, Facts, and Bank Regulation'. In *Financial Markets and Financial Crises*, edited by Robert Hubbard, 109–74. National Bureau of Economic Research, Inc.

Calomiris, Charles W., and Stephen H. Haber. 2014. *Fragile by Design: The Political Origins of Banking Crises and Scarce Credit*. Princeton, NJ: Princeton University Press.

Calomiris, Charles W., and Eugene N. White. 1994. 'The Origins of Federal Deposit Insurance'. In *The Regulated Economy: A Historic Approach to Political Economy*, edited by Claudia Goldin and Gary D. Libecap, 145–88. Chicago, IL: University of Chicago Press.

Câmara dos Deputados (Brazil). 2010. *Constitution of the Federative Republic of Brazil*. 3rd edn. Brasilia: Biblioteca Digital da Câmara dos Deputados.

Cameron, Rondo E. 1967. *Banking in the Early Stages of Industrialization: A Study in Comparative Economic History*. New York, NY: Oxford University Press.

Cannon, James Graham. 1910. 'National Monetary Commission: Clearing Houses'. Senate Document No. 491, 61st Congress, 2nd Session. Washington DC: Government Printing Office.

Capie, Forrest. 2014. 'British Financial Crises in the Nineteenth and Twentieth Centuries'. In *British Financial Crises since 1825*, edited Nicholas Dimsdale and Anthony Hotson, 9–23. Oxford: Oxford University Press.

Capoccia, Giovanni. 2016. 'When Do Institutions "Bite"? Historical Institutionalism and the Politics of Institutional Change'. *Comparative Political Studies* 49 (8): 1095–1127.

Caprio, Gerard, and Daniela Klingebiel. 2003. 'Episodes of Systemic and Borderline Financial Crises: World Bank Research Dataset'. New York: World Bank.

Carcasson, Martin. 1998. 'Herbert Hoover and the Presidential Campaign of 1932: The Failure of Apologia'. *Presidential Studies Quarterly* 28 (2): 349–65.

Cardoso, Fernando Henrique, and Eduardo Graeff. 2012. 'Political Leadership and Economic Reform: The Brazilian Experience in the Context of Latin America'. In *The Oxford Handbook of Latin American Political Economy*, edited by Javier Santiso and Jeff Dayton-Johnson, 13–42. Oxford and New York, NY: Oxford University Press.

Carr, Jack, Frank Mathewson and Neil Quigley. 1995. 'Stability in the Absence of Deposit Insurance: The Canadian Banking System, 1890–1966'. *Journal of Money, Credit and Banking* 27 (4): 1137–58.

Carroll, Royce, Jeff Lewis, James Lo, Nolan McCarty, Keith Poole and Howard Rosenthal. 2015. "Common Space" DW-NOMINATE Scores With Bootstrapped Standard Errors'. 2 September. https://legacy.voteview.com/dwnomin_joint_house_and_senate.htm.

Carruthers, Bruce G. 2015. 'Financialization and the Institutional Foundations of the New Capitalism'. *Socio-Economic Review* 13 (2): 379–98.

Carvalho, Daniel. 2014. 'The Real Effects of Government-Owned Banks: Evidence from an Emerging Market'. *The Journal of Finance* 69 (2): 577–609.

Cassidy, John. 2008. 'Anatomy of a Meltdown'. *The New Yorker*, 24 November.

Cassis, Youssef. 2010. *Capitals of Capital: The Rise and Fall of International Financial Centres, 1780–2009*. New York, NY: Cambridge University Press.

Cassis, Youssef. 2013. *Crises and Opportunities: The Shaping of Modern Finance*. Oxford: Oxford University Press.

Catellani, Patrizia, Patrizia Milesi and Augusta Isabella Alberici. 2014. 'Counterfactuals, the National Economy, and Voting Choice'. *Current Psychology* 33 (1): 47–63.

Cawood, Ian. 2010. 'The 1892 General Election and the Eclipse of the Liberal Unionists'. *Parliamentary History* 29 (3): 331–57.

CBOE. 2018. 'SPX Historical Data'. www.cboe.com/products/stock-index-options-spx-rut-msci-ftse/s-p-500-index-options/s-p-500-index/spx-historical-data.

CBS News. 2008. 'CBS Poll: Presidential Race Tightens'. 6 October. www.cbsnews.com/news/cbs-poll-presidential-race-tightens/.

CBS News. 2009. '$90B of AIG's Federal Rescue Went to Banks'. 16 March. www.cbsnews.com/news/90b-of-aigs-federal-rescue-went-to-banks/.

Cerutti, Eugenio M., Jihad Dagher and Giovanni Dell'Ariccia. 2015. 'Housing Finance and Real-Estate Booms: A Cross-Country Perspective'. IMF Staff Discussion Notes No. 15/12. New York: International Monetary Fund.

Chan, Sewell. 2010. 'Senate, Weakly, Backs New Term for Bernanke,' 28 January.

Chandler, Lester V. 1971. *American Monetary Policy, 1928–1941*. New York, NY: Harper & Row.

Chavaz, Matthieu, and Andrew K. Rose. 2016. 'Political Borders and Bank Lending in Post-Crisis America'. Working Paper 22806. National Bureau of Economic Research.

Chetty, Raj, Nathaniel Hendren, Patrick Kline and Emmanuel Saez. 2014a. 'Where Is the Land of Opportunity? The Geography of Intergenerational Mobility in the United States'. *The Quarterly Journal of Economics* 129 (4): 1553–1623.

Chetty, Raj, Nathaniel Hendren, Patrick Kline, Emmanuel Saez and Nicholas Turner. 2014b. 'Is the United States Still a Land of Opportunity? Recent Trends in Intergenerational Mobility'. *American Economic Review* 104 (5): 141–7.

Chiu, Dominic. 2016. 'Housing Bubble, Politics and Trouble: Problems and Policies for China's Real Estate Market'. *China Business Review* (blog). 4 November. www.chinabusinessreview.com/housing-bubble-politics-and-trouble-problems-and-policies-for-chinas-real-estate-market/.

Christie, I. R. 1982. *Wars and Revolutions: Britain 1760–1815*. London: Edward Arnold.

Chwieroth, Jeffrey M. 2015. 'Managing and Transforming Policy Stigmas in International Finance: Emerging Markets and Controlling Capital Inflows after the Crisis'. *Review of International Political Economy* 22 (1): 44–76.

Chwieroth, Jeffrey M., and Jon Danielsson. 2013. 'Political Challenges of the Macroprudential Agenda'. *VoxEU.Org* (blog). 6 September. https://voxeu .org/article/political-challenges-macroprudential-agenda.

Chwieroth, Jeffrey M., and Andrew Walter. 2017. 'Banking Crises and Politics: A Long-Run Perspective'. *International Affairs* 93 (5): 1107–29.

Clark, William R., Sona N. Golder and Paul Poast. 2013. 'Monetary Institutions and the Political Survival of Democratic Leaders'. *International Studies Quarterly* 57 (3): 556–67.

Coates, David. 2009. 'Chickens Coming Home to Roost? New Labour at the Eleventh Hour'. *British Politics* 4 (4): 421–33.

Coleman, Nicholas, and Leo Feler. 2015. 'Bank Ownership, Lending, and Local Economic Performance during the 2008–2009 Financial Crisis'. *Journal of Monetary Economics* 71 (2): 50–66.

Collins, Michael. 1988. *Money and Banking in the UK: A History*. London and New York, NY: Croom Helm.

Colvin, Christopher L. 2014. 'Interlocking Directorates and Conflicts of Interest: The Rotterdamsche Bankvereeniging, Müller & Co. and the Dutch Financial Crisis of the 1920s'. *Business History* 56 (2): 314–34.

Comfort, Nicholas. 2018. 'ECB's Record as a Bank Supervisor? Barely a Pass, Experts Say'. Bloomberg.com. 12 February. www.bloomberg.com/news/articles/ 2018-02-12/ecb-told-it-must-do-better-as-soured-loans-crisis-rumbles-on.

Comptroller of the Currency (US). 1909. 'Annual Report of the Comptroller of the Currency to the Second Session of the Sixty-First Congress of the United States'. US Treasury.

Conant, Charles A. 1902. *A History of Modern Banks of Issue*. Accessed from http://nla.gov.au/nla.cat-vn738934. New York, NY: G. D. Putnam's Sons.

Conant, Charles A. 1915. *A History of Modern Banks of Issue*. New York, NY: G. D. Putnam's Sons.

Conservative Party (UK). 2010. 'Invitation to Join the Government of Britain: The Conservative Manifesto 2010'. The Conservative Party.

Cook, Chris, and John Stevenson. 2014. *A History of British Elections since 1689*. Oxford: Taylor & Francis Group.

Corlett, Adam, and Lindsay Judge. 2017. 'Home Affront: Housing across the Generations'. Intergenerational Commission Report. Wealth Series. London: Resolution Foundation.

Craig, Fred W. S. 1976. *British Electoral Facts 1885–1975*. London: Macmillan.

Cramer, Katherine J. 2014. 'Political Understanding of Economic Crises: The Shape of Resentment toward Public Employees'. In *Mass Politics in Tough Times: Opinions, Votes and Protest in the Great Recession*, edited by Larry M. Bartels and Nancy Bermeo, 72–104. Oxford and New York, NY: Oxford University Press.

Crawford, Rowena, David Innes and Cormac O'Dea. 2015. *The Evolution of Wealth in Great Britain: 2006–08 to 2010–12*. London: Institute for Fiscal Studies.

Crawford, Rowena, David Innes and Cormac O'Dea. 2016. 'Household Wealth in Great Britain: Distribution, Composition and Changes 2006–12'. *Fiscal Studies* 37 (1): 35–54.

Credit Suisse Research Institute. 2012. *Global Wealth Databook 2012*. Zurich: Credit Suisse.

Credit Suisse Research Institute. 2014. *Global Wealth Databook 2014*. Zurich: Credit Suisse.

Credit Suisse Research Institute. 2015. *Global Wealth Databook 2015*. Zurich: Credit Suisse.

Credit Suisse Research Institute. 2016. *Global Wealth Databook 2016*. Zurich: Credit Suisse.

Credit Suisse Research Institute. 2017a. *Global Wealth Databook 2017*. Zurich: Credit Suisse.

Credit Suisse Research Institute. 2017b. *Global Wealth Report 2017*. Zurich: Credit Suisse.

Crespo-Tenorio, Adriana, Nathan M. Jensen and Guillermo Rosas. 2014. 'Political Liabilities: Surviving Banking Crises'. *Comparative Political Studies* 47 (7): 1047–74.

Cribb, Jonathan, Andrew Hood and Robert Joyce. 2016. 'The Economic Circumstances of Different Generations: The Latest Picture'. Briefing Note 187. London: Institute for Fiscal Studies.

Cribb, Jonathan, Andrew Hood, Robert Joyce and Agnes Norris Keiller. 2017. 'Living Standards, Poverty and Inequality in the UK: 2017'. Report 129. London: Institute for Fiscal Studies.

Croft, Adam. 2007. 'Bank Crisis Deals Blow to Brown's Reputation'. 19 September. Reuters.com. www.reuters.com/article/northernrock-brown-crisis/bank-crisis-deals-blow-to-browns-reputation-idUKNOA92342420070919.

Crouch, Colin. 2009. 'Privatised Keynesianism: An Unacknowledged Policy Regime'. *The British Journal of Politics & International Relations* 11 (3): 382–99.

Cruz, Cesi, Philip Keefer and Carlos Scartascini. 2016. 'The Database of Political Institutions 2015 (DPI2015)'. January. www.iadb.org/en/research-and-data/publication-details,3169.html?pub_id=IDB-DB-121.

Culpepper, Pepper D. 2010. *Quiet Politics and Business Power: Corporate Control in Europe and Japan*. Cambridge: Cambridge University Press.

Culpepper, Pepper D., and Raphael Reinke. 2014. 'Structural Power and Bank Bailouts in the United Kingdom and the United States'. *Politics & Society* 42 (4): 427–54.

Darling, Alistair. 2011. *Back from the Brink*. London: Atlantic Books.

Dash, Eric, and Andrew Ross Sorkin. 2008. 'Government Seizes WaMu and Sells Some Assets'. *New York Times*, 25 September, sec. Business Day.

Datafolha. 1994. 'Evaluation of the Government of Itamar Franco'. 12 January. http://datafolha.folha.uol.com.br/opiniaopublica/1994/12/1222332-avaliacao-do-governo-itamar-franco.shtml.

Datafolha. 2002. 'FHC Closes Mandate with Greater Disapproval than Approval'. 15 December. http://datafolha.folha.uol.com.br/opiniaopublica/2002/12/12223 26-fhc-encerra-mandato-com-reprovacao-maior-do-que-aprovacao.shtml.

Davidson, Adam, and Liane Hansen. 2008. 'Federal Mortgage Takeover Plan Prompts Questions'. NPR.Org. 7 September. www.npr.org/templates/story/story.php?storyId=94367320.

Davies, Howard, and David Green. 2010. *Banking on the Future*. Princeton, NJ: Princeton University Press.

Davies, James B., ed. 2008. *Personal Wealth from a Global Perspective*. Oxford: Oxford University Press.

Davies, James B., Susanna Sandström, Anthony Shorrocks and Edward N. Wolff. 2008. 'The World Distribution of Household Wealth'. In *Personal Wealth from a Global Perspective*, 395–418. Oxford: Oxford University Press.

Dayen, David. 2015. 'Obama Program That Hurt Homeowners and Helped Big Banks Is Ending'. *The Intercept* (blog). 28 December. https://theintercept.com/2015/12/28/obama-program-hurt-homeowners-and-helped-big-banks-now-its-dead/.

De Ferranti, David, Guillermo E. Perry, Francisco H. E. Ferreira and Michael Walton. 2004. *Inequality in Latin America: Breaking with History?* Washington DC: World Bank.

De Ferranti, David, Guillermo E. Perry, Francisco H. G. Ferreira, Michael Walton, David Coady, Wendy Cunningham, Leonardo Gasparini *et al.* 2003. *Inequality in Latin America and the Caribbean: Breaking with History?* Advance Conference Edition. World Bank.

De Haan, Jakob de, and Sylvester Eijffinger. 2016. 'The Politics of Central Bank Independence'. DNB Working Paper. Amsterdam: Netherlands Central Bank, Research Department.

de Krivoy, Ruth. 2003. 'The Venezuelan Banking Crisis – Epilogue'. Toronto International Leadership Centre for Financial Sector Supervision. http://sitere sources.worldbank.org/EXTFINANCIALSECTOR/Resources/282884-12398

31335682/6028531-1239831365859/K2_Toronto_Center_Venezuela_Bkg_
Epil.pdf.

De Nederlandsche Bank. 2017. 'Financial Stability Report, Autumn 2017'.
Amsterdam: De Nederlandsche Bank.

de Paiva Abreu, Marcelo. 2008. 'The Brazilian Economy, 1980–1994'. In *The
Cambridge History of Latin America. Volume 9: Brazil since 1930*, edited by
Leslie Bethell: 395–430. Cambridge: Cambridge University Press.

DeLong, J. Bradford. 2012. 'This Time, It Is Not Different: The Persistent
Concerns of Financial Macroeconomics'. Equitable Growth. http://equitable
growth.org/equitablog/j-bradford-delong-2012-this-time-it-is-not-different-the-
persistent-concerns-of-financial-macroeconomics/.

Demirgüç-Kunt, Asli, and Leora Klapper. 2012. 'Measuring Financial Inclusion:
The Global Findex Database'. Working Paper. Policy Series. The World
Bank.

Demirgüç-Kunt, Asli, and Ross Levine. 2001. *Financial Structure and Economic
Growth: A Cross-Country Comparison of Banks, Markets, and Development*.
Cambridge, MA: MIT Press.

Democratic Party, United States. 1912. 'Democratic Party Platforms:
1912 Democratic Party Platform'. 25 June. www.presidency.ucsb.edu/ws/
index.php?pid=29590.

Dennis, Brady, and David Cho. 2009. 'Rage at AIG Swells As Bonuses Go Out',
17 March. www.washingtonpost.com/wp-dyn/content/article/2009/03/16/AR
2009031602961.html.

Deos, Simone, Camilla Ruocco and Everton Sotto Tibiriçá Rosa. 2017.
'Federal Public Banks in Brazil: Historical Overview and Role in the Recent
Crisis'. In *Public Banks in the Age of Financialization: A Comparative
Perspective*, edited by Christoph Scherrer, 67–82. Cheltenham: Edward
Elgar Publishing.

Deutsche Bundesbank. 2016. 'Bank Recovery and Resolution – The New TLAC
and MREL Minimum Requirements'. Deutsche Bundesbank Monthly Report.
Frankfurt: Deutsche Bundesbank.

Diamond, Larry, Marc F. Plattner and Christopher Walker. 2016.
Authoritarianism Goes Global: The Challenge to Democracy. Baltimore, MD:
Johns Hopkins University Press.

Dimsdale, N. H., and A. Hotson. 2014. 'Financial Crises and Economic Activity
in the UK since 1825'. In *British Financial Crises since 1825*, 24–57. Oxford:
Oxford University Press.

Dimson, Elroy, Paul Marsh and Mike Staunton. 2016. *Credit Suisse Global
Investment Returns Yearbook 2016*. Zurich: Credit Suisse.

Dinç, I. Serdar. 2005. 'Politicians and Banks: Political Influences on Government-
Owned Banks in Emerging Markets'. *Journal of Financial Economics* 77 (2):
453–79.

Djankov, Simeon. 2015. 'Hungary under Orbán: Can Central Planning Revive Its Economy?' PB15-11. Peterson Institute Policy Briefs. Washington DC: Peterson Institute for International Economics.

Douglas, Paul Howard, and Aaron Director. 1931. *The Problem of Unemployment*. New York, NY: Macmillan.

Drake, Bruce. 2013. 'Public Has Mixed Views about Government Regulation of Banks'. *Pew Research Center* (blog). 20 November. www.pewresearch.org/fact-tank/2013/11/20/public-has-mixed-views-about-government-regulation-of-banks/.

Drezner, Daniel W. 2014. *The System Worked: How the World Stopped Another Great Depression*. Oxford: Oxford University Press.

Duch, Raymond M., and Randolph T. Stevenson. 2008. *The Economic Vote: How Political and Economic Institutions Condition Election Results*. New York, NY: Cambridge University Press.

Dungan, Adrian. 2014. 'Individual Income Tax Shares, 2014. Statistics of Income Bulletin, SOI Tax Stats'. US Internal Revenue Service. www.irs.gov/pub/irs-soi/soi-a-ints-id1704.pdf.

Dunkley, Emma. 2017a. 'Philip Hammond Warns State-Owned RBS Stake Could Be Sold at a Loss'. *Financial Times*, 18 April.

Dunkley, Emma. 2017b. 'UK Government Sells Remaining Stake in Lloyds'. *Financial Times*, 16 May.

Eaglesham, Jean, Peter Thal Larson, Chris Giles and Lina Saigol. 2007. 'UK to Guarantee Northern Rock Deposits'. *Financial Times*, 18 September.

Easterly, William, and Stanley Fischer. 2001. 'Inflation and the Poor'. *Journal of Money, Credit and Banking* 33 (2): 160–78.

The Economist. 2012. 'Shaming the Unshameable'. *The Economist*, 16 June.

The Economist. 2017. 'A Purge of Russia's Banks Is Not Finished Yet'. *The Economist*, 23 November.

Edwards, Sebastian, and Guido Tabellini. 1991. 'Explaining Fiscal Policies and Inflation in Developing Countries'. *Journal of International Money and Finance* 10 (Supplement 1): S16–48.

Eichengreen, Barry J. 1992. *Golden Fetters: The Gold Standard and the Great Depression, 1919–1939*. New York, NY: Oxford University Press.

El-Erian, Mohamed A. 2016. *The Only Game in Town: Central Banks, Instability, and Avoiding the Next Collapse*. Reprint edition. New York, NY: Random House Trade Paperbacks.

Elliot, A. R. D. 1911. *The Life of George Joachim Goschen, First Viscount Goschen (1831–1907). Volume 2*. London: Longmans, Green, and Co.

Elliot Armijo, Leslie. 1993. 'Brazilian Politics and Patterns of Financial Regulation, 1945–1991'. In *The Politics of Finance in Developing Countries*, edited by Stephan Haggard, Chung H. Lee and Sylvia Maxfield., 259–92. Ithaca, NY: Cornell University Press.

Employee Benefit Research Institute. 1998. 'History of Pension Plans'. March. www.ebri.org/publications/facts/index.cfm?fa=0398afact.

Enderle-Burcel, Gertude. 1994. 'The Failure of Crisis Management: Banking Laws in Interwar Austria'. In *Universal Banking in the Twentieth Century: Finance, Industry and State in North and Central Europe*, edited by T. R. Gourvish, Ágnes Pogány and Alice Teichova, 116–30. Aldershot: Edward Elgar.

Englmaier, Florian, and Till Stowasser. 2017. 'Electoral Cycles in Savings Bank Lending'. *Journal of the European Economic Association* 15 (2): 296–354.

Enns, Peter K. 2015. 'Relative Policy Support and Coincidental Representation'. *Perspectives on Politics* 13 (4): 1053–64.

Epstein, Gerald A. 2005. 'Introduction: Financialization and the World Economy'. In *Financialization and the World Economy*, edited by Gerald A. Epstein, 3–16. Cheltenham: Edward Elgar.

Epstein, Lee, and Jeffrey A. Segal. 2000. 'Measuring Issue Salience'. *American Journal of Political Science* 44 (1): 66–83.

Ergungor, Emre, and Kent Cherny. 2009. 'Sweden as a Useful Model of Successful Financial Crisis Resolution'. *VoxEU.Org* (blog). 19 March. https://voxeu .org/article/resolving-banking-crisis-should-we-follow-sweden-s-example.

Erturk, Ismail, Julie Froud, Sukhdev Johal, Adam Leaver and Karel Williams. 2007. 'The Democratization of Finance? Promises, Outcomes and Conditions'. *Review of International Political Economy* 14 (4): 553–75.

Esping-Andersen, Gøsta. 1990. *The Three Worlds of Welfare Capitalism*. Princeton, NJ: Princeton University Press.

Essletzbichler, Jürgen, Franziska Disslbacher and Mathias Moser. 2018. 'The Victims of Neoliberal Globalisation and the Rise of the Populist Vote: A Comparative Analysis of Three Recent Electoral Decisions'. *Cambridge Journal of Regions, Economy and Society* 11 (1): 73–94.

European Central Bank. 2013. 'The Eurosystem Household Finance and Consumption Survey – Results from the First Wave'. Statistics Paper Series No. 2. Frankfurt: ECB.

European Central Bank. 2016. 'The Household Finance and Consumption Survey: Results from the Second Wave'. Statistics Paper Series No. 18. Frankfurt: ECB.

Eurostat. 2017. 'Housing Statistics – Statistics Explained'. February. http://ec .europa.eu/eurostat/statistics-explained/index.php/Housing_statistics#Type_of_ dwelling.

Evans, Eric J. 2011. *The Shaping of Modern Britain: Identity, Industry and Empire, 1780–1914*. Abingdon and New York, NY: Routledge.

Eymann, Angelika, and Axel Börsch-Supan. 2002. 'Household Portfolios in Germany'. In *Household Portfolios*, edited by Luigi Guiso, Michael Haliassos and Tullio Jappelli, 291–340. Cambridge, MA: MIT Press.

Farrell, Diana, Kanav Bhagat, Peter Ganang and Pascal Noel. 2017. 'Mortgage Modifications after the Great Recession'. New York: JP Morgan Chase Institute.

Fausto, Boris. 1989. 'Society and Politics'. In *Brazil: Empire and Republic, 1822–1930*, edited by Leslie Bethell, 257–308. Cambridge: Cambridge University Press.

Fausto, Boris. 2014. *A Concise History of Brazil*. Cambridge: Cambridge University Press.

Fay, Marianne, and Anna Wellenstein. 2005. 'Keeping a Roof over One's Head: Improving Access to Safe and Decent Shelter'. In *The Urban Poor in Latin America*, edited by Marianne Fay, 91–124. Washington DC: World Bank.

Federal Deposit Insurance Corporation (US). 1997. *History of the Eighties – Lessons for the Future. Volume I: An Examination of the Banking Crises of the 1980s and Early 1990s*. Washington DC: FDIC.

Federal Deposit Insurance Corporation (US). 1998. 'A Brief History of Deposit Insurance in the United States'. Prepared for the International Conference on Deposit Insurance, Washington DC. Washington DC: FDIC.

Federal Deposit Insurance Corporation (US). 2007. 'Failed Bank Capital Ratios'. www.fdic.gov/about/learn/board/hoenig/failed-bank-capital-ratios.pdf.

Federal Deposit Insurance Corporation (US). 2014. 'Resolutions Handbook'. Washington DC: FDIC.

Federal Housing Finance Agency. 2011. 'A Brief History of the Housing Government-Sponsored Enterprises'. FHFA, Office of the Inspector General.

Federal Reserve Bank of New York. 2017. 'Quarterly Report on Household Debt and Credit 2017 Q3'. www.newyorkfed.org/medialibrary/interactives/house holdcredit/data/pdf/HHDC_2017Q3.pdf.

Federal Reserve Board (US). 2017a. 'Financial Accounts Guide – All Tables'. www.federalreserve.gov/apps/fof/FOFTables.aspx.

Federal Reserve Board (US). 2017b. 'The Fed – Section 13. Powers of Federal Reserve Banks'. Board of Governors of the Federal Reserve System. 13 February. www.federalreserve.gov/aboutthefed/section13.htm.

Feenstra, Robert C., Robert Inklaar and Marcel P. Timmer. 2015. 'The Next Generation of the Penn World Table'. *American Economic Review* 105 (10): 3150–82.

Ferejohn, John. 1986. 'Incumbent Performance and Electoral Control'. *Public Choice* 50 (1/3): 5–25.

Ferns, H. S. 1992. 'The Baring Crisis Revisited'. *Journal of Latin American Studies*. May.

Ferreira, Adriana Nunes, and Everton Sotto Tibiriçá Rosa. 2017. 'The Role of the Brazilian Development Bank (BNDES) in Brazilian Development Policy'. In *Public Banks in the Age of Financialization: A Comparative Perspective*, edited by Christoph Scherrer, 101–15. Cheltenham: Edward Elgar.

Ferreira, Alex Luiz, and Sérgio Naruhiko Sakurai. 2013. 'Personal Charisma or the Economy? Macroeconomic Indicators of Presidential Approval Ratings in Brazil'. *Economia* 14 (3): 214–32.

Ferreira, Francisco, Phillippe Leite and Julie Litchfield. 2008. 'The Rise and Fall of Brazilian Inequality: 1981–2004'. *Macroeconomic Dynamics* 12 (S2): 199–230.

Ferreira, Francisco H. G., Julian Messina, Jamele Rigolini, Luis-Felipe López-Calva, Maria Ana Lugo and Renos Vakis. 2013. 'Economic Mobility and the Rise of the Latin American Middle Class'. *Latin America and Caribbean Studies*. Washington DC: The World Bank.

Fetter, Frank W. 1965. *Development of British Monetary Orthodoxy, 1797–1875.* Cambridge, MA: Harvard University Press.

Fettig, David. 2002. 'Lender of More Than Last Resort. Federal Reserve Bank of Minneapolis Note'. 1 December. www.minneapolisfed.org/publications/the-region/lender-of-more-than-last-resort.

Financial Crisis Inquiry Commission. 2011. 'The Financial Crisis Inquiry Report. Final Report of the National Commission on the Causes of the Financial and Economic Crisis in the United States'. US Government Printing Office.

Financial Services Authority Board. 2011. 'The Failure of the Royal Bank of Scotland'. Financial Services Authority.

Financial Services Authority (UK). 2008. 'Compensation Scheme to Cover Savers' Claims Up to £50,000'. FSA/PN/114/2008. FSA.

Financial Services Authority (UK). 2012. 'Consumer Awareness of the FSA and Financial Regulation, Fieldwork Conducted by TNS Research International'. Financial Services Authority.

Financial Stability Board. 2017. 'Ten Years On: Taking Stock of Post-Crisis Resolution Reforms'. Sixth Report on the Implementation of Resolution Reforms. Basel: Financial Stability Board.

Finlayson, Alan. 2009. 'Financialisation, Financial Literacy and Asset-Based Welfare'. *The British Journal of Politics & International Relations* 11 (3): 400–21.

Fishback, Price V. 2017. 'How Successful Was the New Deal? The Microeconomic Impact of New Deal Spending and Lending Policies in the 1930s'. *Journal of Economic Literature* 55 (4): 1435–85.

Fishback, Price V., Jonathan Rose and Kenneth A. Snowden. 2013. 'An HOLC Primer'. In *Well Worth Saving: How the New Deal Safeguarded Home Ownership*, edited by Price V. Fishback, Jonathan Rose and Kenneth A. Snowden, 54–69. Chicago, IL: National Bureau of Economic Research (NBER) & University of Chicago Press.

Fisher, D. R. 2009. *The History of Parliament: The House of Commons 1820–1832. Volume I: Introductory Survey, Appendices.* Cambridge: Cambridge University Press.

Fishlow, Albert. 2011. *Starting Over: Brazil since 1985*. Washington DC: Brookings Institution Press.

Flandreau, Mark, and Stefano Ugolini. 2014. 'The Crisis of 1866'. In *British Financial Crises since 1825*, edited by Nicholas Dimsdale and Anthony Hotson, 76–93. Oxford: Oxford University Press.

Flandreau, Marc, and Frédéric Zumer. 2004. *The Making of Global Finance, 1880–1913*. Paris: OECD Development Studies Centre.

Fletcher, W. Miles. 1991. 'Japanese Banks and Economic Policy'. In *The Role of Banks in the Interwar Economy*, edited by Harold James, Håkan Lindgren and Alice Teichova, 251–71. Cambridge: Cambridge University Press.

Fligstein, Neil, and Adam Goldstein. 2015. 'The Emergence of a Finance Culture in American Households, 1989–2007'. *Socio-Economic Review* 13 (3): 575–601.

Foa, Roberto Stefan, and Yascha Mounk. 2016. 'The Democratic Disconnect'. *Journal of Democracy* 27 (3): 5–17.

Foa, Roberto Stefan, and Yascha Mounk. 2017. 'The Signs of Deconsolidation'. *Journal of Democracy* 28 (1): 5–15.

Foley, Michael. 2009. 'Gordon Brown and the Role of Compounded Crisis in the Pathology of Leadership Decline'. *British Politics* 4 (4): 498–513.

Fong, Christina M., Samuel Bowles and Herbert Gintis. 2006. 'Strong Reciprocity and the Welfare State'. In *Handbook of the Economics of Giving, Altruism and Reciprocity*, edited by S. Kolm and Jean Mercier Ythier, 1: 1439–64. Amsterdam and New York, NY: Elsevier.

Foote, Christopher L., Kristopher S. Gilardi and Paul S. Willen. 2012. 'Why Did So Many People Make So Many Ex Post Bad Decisions? The Causes of the Foreclosure Crisis'. Public Policy Discussion Papers 12-2. Federal Reserve Bank of Boston.

Forsyth, Douglas J. 1991. 'The Rise and Fall of Mixed Banking in Italy'. In *The Role of Banks in the Interwar Economy*, edited by Harold James, Håkan Lindgren and Alice Teichova, 179–205. Cambridge: Cambridge University Press.

Foster, Richard W., and S. Karene Witcher. 1985. 'New Leadership of Brazil Closes Troubled Bank'. *Wall Street Journal*, 20 March.

Fox News. 2009. 'Watchdog: Financial Bailout Support Could Reach $23.7 Trillion'. Fox News.com. 20 July. www.foxnews.com/politics/2009/07/20/watchdog-financial-bailout-support-reach-trillion.html.

Frame, W. Scott, Andreas Fuster, Joseph Tracy and James Vickery. 2015. 'The Rescue of Fannie Mae and Freddie Mac'. *Journal of Economic Perspectives* 29 (2): 25–52.

Frank, Robert H. 2013. *Falling Behind: How Rising Inequality Harms the Middle Class*. The Aaron Wildavsky Forum for Public Policy: 4. Berkeley, CA: University of California Press.

Frank, Zephyr L. 2004. *Dutra's World: Wealth and Family in Nineteenth-Century Rio de Janeiro*. Albuquerque, NM: University of New Mexico Press.

Frank, Zephyr L. 2005. 'Wealth Holding in Southeastern Brazil, 1815–1860'. *Hispanic American Historical Review* 85 (2): 223–57.

Franko, William W., Nathan J. Kelly and Christopher Witko. 2016. 'Class Bias in Voter Turnout, Representation, and Income Inequality'. *Perspectives on Politics* 14 (2): 351–68.

FRED Database. 2016a. '3-Month Treasury Bill: Secondary Market Rate'. Federal Reserve Bank of St Louis. 2016. https://fred.stlouisfed.org/series/DTB3.

FRED Database. 2016b. 'Overnight London Interbank Offered Rate (LIBOR), Based on British Pound'. Federal Reserve Bank of St Louis. https://fred.stlouisfed.org/series/GBPONTD156N.

FRED Database. 2017a. 'Federal Funds Target Range – Upper Limit (DFEDTARU)'. Federal Reserve Bank of St Louis. https://fred.stlouisfed.org/series/DFEDTARU.

FRED Database. 2017b. 'Federal Funds Target Rate (DISCONTINUED) [DFEDTAR]'. Federal Reserve Bank of St Louis. https://fred.stlouisfed.org/series/DFEDTAR.

FRED Database. 2017c. 'S&P/Case-Shiller U.S. National Home Price Index (CSUSHPINSA)'. Federal Reserve Bank of St Louis. https://fred.stlouisfed.org/series/CSUSHPINSA.

Frieden, Jeffry A. 2006. *Global Capitalism: Its Fall and Rise in the Twentieth Century*. New York, NY: W. W. Norton.

Friedman, Milton, and Anna Jacobson Schwartz. 1963. *A Monetary History of the United States, 1867–1960*. Princeton, NJ: Princeton University Press.

Fritsch, Winston. 1988. *External Constraints on Economic Policy in Brazil: 1889–1930*. Pittsburgh, PA: University of Pittsburgh Press.

Funke, Manuel, Moritz Schularick and Christoph Trebesch. 2016. 'Going to Extremes: Politics after Financial Crises, 1870–2014'. *European Economic Review* 88 (C): 227–60.

Gai, Prasanna, Andrew Haldane and Sujit Kapadia. 2011. 'Complexity, Concentration and Contagion'. *Journal of Monetary Economics*, Carnegie-Rochester Conference on Public Policy: Normalizing Central Bank Practice in Light of the Credit Turmoil, 12–13 November 2010, 58 (5): 453–70.

Galbraith, John Kenneth. 1955. *The Great Crash, 1929*. Boston, MA: Houghton Mifflin.

Gall, Norman. 1992. 'After the Impeachment in Brazil, the Abyss Still Looms'. *Wall Street Journal*, 2 October.

Gallup. n.d. 'Presidential Approval Ratings – Barack Obama'. Gallup.Com. http://news.gallup.com/poll/116479/barack-obama-presidential-job-approval.aspx.

Gallup. n.d. 'Presidential Approval Ratings – George W. Bush'. Gallup.Com. http://news.gallup.com/poll/116500/Presidential-Approval-Ratings-George-Bush.aspx.

Gallup. 2009. 'Views on Government Aid Depend on the Program'. Gallup. Com. 24 February. www.gallup.com/poll/116083/Views-Government-Aid-Depend-Program.aspx.

Galston, William A. 2010. 'President Barack Obama's First Two Years: Policy Accomplishments, Political Difficulties'. Governance Studies, Brookings Institution, Washington DC.

Gamble, Andrew. 2009. 'British Politics and the Financial Crisis'. *British Politics* 4 (4): 450–62.

Gandrud, Christopher. 2013. 'The Diffusion of Financial Supervisory Governance Ideas'. *Review of International Political Economy* 20 (4): 881–916.

Gandrud, Christopher. 2015. 'Corrections and Refinements to the Database of Political Institutions' Yrcurnt Election Timing Variable'. *The Political Methodologist* (blog). 3 March. https://thepoliticalmethodologist.com/2015/03/03/corrections-and-refinements-to-the-database-of-political-institutions-yrcurnt-election-timing-variable/.

Gandrud, Christopher, and Mark Hallerberg. 2013. 'Bad Banks as a Response to Crises: When Do Governments Use Them, and Why Does Their Governance Differ?' SSRN Scholarly Paper ID 2241290. Rochester, NY: Social Science Research Network.

Gandrud, Christopher, and Mark Hallerberg. 2015a. 'When All Is Said and Done: Updating "Elections, Special Interests, and Financial Crisis"'. *Research & Politics* 2 (3): 1–9.

Gandrud, Christopher, and Mark Hallerberg. 2015b. 'What Is a Financial Crisis? Efficiently Measuring Real-Time Perceptions of Financial Market Stress with an Application to Financial Crisis Budget Cycles'. SSRN Scholarly Paper ID 2706508. Rochester, NY: Social Science Research Network.

Garvy, George. 1977. *Money, Financial Flows, and Credit in the Soviet Union.* New York, NY: National Bureau of Economic Research.

Gayer, Arthur D., W. W. Rostow and Anna Jacobson Schwartz. 1975. *The Growth and Fluctuation of the British Economy, 1790–1850: An Historical, Statistical, and Theoretical Study of Britain's Economic Development. Volume 1.* Hassocks: Harvester Press.

Geithner, Timothy F. 2015. *Stress Test: Reflections on Financial Crises.* New York, NY: Crown.

Gentzkow, Matthew, and Jesse M. Shapiro. 2010. 'What Drives Media Slant? Evidence from U.S. Daily Newspapers'. *Econometrica* 78 (1): 35–71.

Gerdrup, Karsten. 2003. 'Three Episodes of Financial Fragility in Norway since the 1890s'. BIS Working Paper 142. Basel: Bank for International Settlements.

Gerschenkron, Alexander. 1962. *Economic Backwardness in Historical Perspective: A Book of Essays.* Cambridge, MA: Belknap Press of Harvard University Press.

Gilens, Martin. 2012. *Affluence and Influence: Economic Inequality and Political Power in America.* Princeton, NJ, and Oxford: Princeton University Press.

Glassman, Ronald M. 1995. *The Middle Class and Democracy in Socio-Historical Perspective.* Leiden: E. J. Brill.

Global Financial Data. n.d. www.globalfinancialdata.com/.

Global Financial Markets Association. 2010. 'Rushing Basel Could Stifle Future Economic Growth, Say Financial Services Firms'. 20 April. www.gfma.org/initiatives/basel-iii/rushing-basel-could-stifle-future-economic-growth,-say-financial-services-firms/.

Glover, Julian. 2008. 'Labour Fails to Win Poll Boost from Banking Crisis'. *The Guardian*, 20 October, sec. Politics.

Glover, Julian. 2009. 'Divided, Out of Touch, Heading For Defeat: How Public Sees Labour in ICM Poll'. *The Guardian*, 15 June, sec. Politics.

Goldfajn, Ilan, Katherine Hennings and Hélio Mori. 2003. 'Brazil's Financial System: Resilience to Shocks, No Currency Substitution, but Struggling to Promote Growth'. Working Papers Series 75. Central Bank of Brazil, Research Department.

Goldman, David. 2008. 'Americans Want Bailout, But Cost a Concern'. *CNN Money*, 3 April.

Goldsmith, R. W. 1986. *Desenvolvimento Financerio soh um Seculo de Inflação.* São Paulo: Banco Bamerindus do Brasil, S.A. and Editora Harper & Row do Brasil Ltda.

Goldthorpe, John H. 2010. 'Analysing Social Inequality: A Critique of Two Recent Contributions from Economics and Epidemiology'. *European Sociological Review* 26 (6): 731–44.

Goodhart, Charles A. E. 1999. 'Myths about the Lender of Last Resort'. FMG Special Paper. Financial Markets Group, London School of Economics.

Goodhart, Charles A. E. 2000. 'The Organisational Structure of Banking Supervision'. FSI Occasional Papers 1. Financial Stability Institute, Bank for International Settlements, Basel.

Goodhart, Charles A. E. 2014. 'Competition and Credit Control'. FMG Special Paper sp229. Financial Markets Group, London School of Economics.

Goodhart, Charles A. E., and Philipp Erfurth. 2014. 'Monetary Policy and Long-Term Trends'. *VoxEU.Org* (blog). 3 November 2014.

Goolsbee, Austan D., and Alan B. Krueger. 2015. 'A Retrospective Look at Rescuing and Restructuring General Motors and Chrysler'. *Journal of Economic Perspectives* 29 (2): 3–24.

Gorton, Gary. 1984. 'Private Clearinghouses and the Origins of Central Banking'. *Federal Reserve Bank of Philadelphia Business Review*, February.

Gorton, Gary. 1988. 'Banking Panics and Business Cycles'. *Oxford Economic Papers* 40 (4): 751–81.

Gourevitch, Peter A., and James Shinn. 2006. *Political Power and Corporate Control.* Princeton, NJ: Princeton University Press.

Government of the Netherlands. 2017. 'Confidence in the Future: 2017–2021 Coalition Agreement, People's Party for Freedom and Democracy (VVD), Christian Democratic Alliance (CDA), Democrats '66 (D66) and Christian Union (CU)'. Government of the Netherlands.

Green, E. H. H. 1995. *The Crisis of Conservatism: The Politics, Economics, and Ideology of the British Conservative Party, 1880–1914*. London and New York, NY: Routledge.

Green, Matthew, and Kristen Hudak. 2009. 'Congress and the Bailout: Explaining the Bailout Votes and Their Electoral Effect'. *Legislative Studies Section Newsletter* 32 (1).

Greene, Stephen. 2013. 'Emergency Banking Act of 1933'. Federal Reserve History. 22 November. www.federalreservehistory.org/essays/emergency_banking_act_of_1933.

Grice, Andrew. 2009. '£850bn: Official Cost of the Bank Bailout'. *The Independent*, 4 December.

Griffiths, Katherine. 2007. 'Call to Nationalise Northern Rock'. *The Telegraph*, 6 December, sec. Finance.

Grossman, Emiliano, and Cornelia Woll. 2014. 'Saving the Banks: The Political Economy of Bailouts'. *Comparative Political Studies* 47 (4): 574–600.

Grossman, Richard S. 2001. 'Double Liability and Bank Risk Taking'. *Journal of Money, Credit and Banking* 33 (2): 143–59.

Grossman, Richard S. 2007. 'Fear and Greed: The Evolution of Double Liability in American Banking, 1865–1930'. *Explorations in Economic History* 44 (1): 59–80.

Grossman, Richard S. 2010. *Unsettled Account: The Evolution of Banking in the Industrialized World since 1800*. Princeton, NJ: Princeton University Press.

Guha, Krishna, James Politi and Michael Mackenzie. 2008. 'US Injection Lifts Confidence'. *Financial Times*, 14 October 2008.

Guiso, Luigi, Michael Haliassos and Tullio Jappelli, eds. 2002. *Household Portfolios*. Cambridge, MA: MIT Press.

Guiso, Luigi, Michael Haliassos, Tullio Jappelli and Stijn Claessens. 2003. 'Household Stockholding in Europe: Where Do We Stand and Where Do We Go?' *Economic Policy* 18 (36): 125–70.

Guiso, Luigi, and Tullio Jappelli. 2002. 'Household Porfolios in Italy'. In *Household Portfolios*, edited by Luigi Guiso, Michael Haliassos and Tullio Jappelli, 251–90. Cambridge, MA: MIT Press.

Guriev, Sergei, and Andrei Rachinsky. 2008. 'Evolution of Personal Wealth in the Former Soviet Union and Central and Eastern Europe'. In *Personal Wealth from a Global Perspective*, edited by James B. Davies, 134–49. Oxford: Oxford University Press.

Haber, Stephen H. 1997. 'Financial Markets and Industrial Development: A Comparative Study of Government Regulation, Financial Innovation, and Industrial Structure in Brazil and Mexico, 1840–1930'. In *How Latin America Fell behind: Essays on the Economic Histories of Brazil and Mexico, 1800–1914*, edited by Stephen H. Haber, 146–78. Stanford, CA: Stanford University Press.

Hacker, Jacob S., and Paul Pierson. 2010. *Winner-Take-All Politics: How Washington Made the Rich Richer, and Turned Its Back on the Middle Class*. New York, NY: Simon & Schuster.

Hackley, Howard H. 1973. *Lending Functions of the Federal Reserve Banks: A History*. Washington DC: Board of Governors of the Federal Reserve.

Haggard, Stephan. 2000. *The Political Economy of the Asian Financial Crisis*. Washington DC: Institute for International Economics.

Haggard, Stephan, and Robert R. Kaufman. 1995. *The Political Economy of Democratic Transitions*. Princeton, NJ: Princeton University Press.

Hahner, June Edith. 1969. *Civilian–Military Relations in Brazil, 1889–1898*. Columbia, SC: University of South Carolina Press.

Haldane, Andrew G. 2011. 'Control Rights (and Wrongs)'. Wincott Memorial Lecture. London: Bank of England.

Haldane, Andrew G. 2013. 'Rethinking the Financial Network'. In *Fragile Stabilität – stabile Fragilität*, edited by Stephan A. Jansen, Eckhard Schröter and Nico Stehr, 243–78. Wiesbaden: Springer Fachmedien Wiesbaden.

Haldane, Andrew G. 2016. 'Whose Recovery?' Speech given by Andrew G. Haldane, Chief Economist, Bank of England. Bank of England.

Haldane, Andrew G. 2018. 'How Monetary Policy Affects Your GDP'. 2018 Finch Lecture, University of Melbourne. Bank of England

Haldane, Andrew G., David Aikman, Sujit Kapadia and Marc Hinterschweiger. 2017. 'Rethinking Financial Stability'. Speech given by Andrew G Haldane, Chief Economist, Bank of England, at the 'Rethinking Macroeconomic Policy IV' Conference.

Haldane, Andrew G., and Robert M. May. 2011. 'Systemic Risk in Banking Ecosystems'. *Nature* 469 (7330): 351–5.

Hall, Maximilian. 1993. *Banking Regulation and Supervision: A Comparative Study of the UK, USA and Japan*. Aldershot: Edward Elgar.

Hall, P. A., and D. Soskice. 2001. *Varieties of Capitalism: The Institutional Foundations of Comparative Advantage*. Oxford: Oxford University Press.

Hammond, Bray. 1933. 'The Banks, the States and the Federal Government'. *The American Economic Review* 23 (4): 622–36.

Hanley, Anne G. 2005. *Native Capital: Financial Institutions and Economic Development in São Paulo, Brazil, 1850–1920*. Stanford, CA: Stanford University Press.

Hansen, Per H. 1994. 'Production versus Currency: The Danish Central Bank in the 1920s'. In *Universal Banking in the Twentieth Century: Finance, Industry and State in North and Central Europe*, edited by T. R. Gourvish, Ágnes Pogány and Alice Teichova, 59–78. Aldershot: Elgar.

Hardie, Iain, David Howarth, Sylvia Maxfield and Amy Verdun. 2013. 'Banks and the False Dichotomy in the Comparative Political Economy of Finance'. *World Politics* 65 (4): 691–728.

Harrington, Brooke. 2016. *Capital without Borders: Wealth Managers and the One Percent*. Cambridge, MA: Harvard University Press.

Healy, Andrew, and Neil Malhotra. 2013. 'Retrospective Voting Reconsidered'. *Annual Review of Political Science* 16 (1): 285–306.

Heimlich, Russell. 2010. 'Was TARP Passed under Bush or Obama?' *Pew Research Center* (blog). 10 August 2010. www.pewresearch.org/fact-tank/2010/08/10/was-tarp-passed-under-bush-or-obama/.

Helleiner, Eric. 1994. *States and the Reemergence of Global Finance: From Bretton Woods to the 1990s*. Ithaca, NY: Cornell University Press.

Helleiner, Eric. 2003. 'The Southern Side of Embedded Liberalism: The Politics of Postwar Monetary Policy in the Third World'. In *Monetary Orders: Ambiguous Economics, Ubiquitous Politics*, edited by Jonathan Kirshner, 55–77. Ithaca, NY: Cornell University Press.

Hellwig, Timothy. 2008. 'Globalization, Policy Constraints, and Vote Choice'. *The Journal of Politics* 70 (4): 1128–41.

Hellwig, Timothy, and Eva Coffey. 2011. 'Public Opinion, Party Messages, and Responsibility for the Financial Crisis in Britain'. *Electoral Studies, Special Symposium on the Politics of Economic Crisis*, 30 (3): 417–26.

Hellwig, Timothy, and David Samuels. 2007. 'Voting in Open Economies: The Electoral Consequences of Globalization'. *Comparative Political Studies* 40 (3): 283–306.

Henisz, Witold J. 2002. 'The Institutional Environment for Infrastructure Investment'. *Industrial and Corporate Change* 11 (2): 355–89.

Henisz, Witold J. 2017. 'POLCON Database'. Management Department. 2017. http://mgmt.wharton.upenn.edu/profile/henisz/.

Herszenhorn, David M. 2008. 'Bailout Plan Wins Approval; Democrats Vow Tighter Rules'. *New York Times*, 3 October 2008, sec. Economy.

Herszenhorn, David M., and Carl Hulse. 2009. 'Deal Reached in Congress on $787Billion Stimulus Plan'. *New York Times*, 11 February 2009.

Herszenhorn, David M., and Edward Wyatt. 2010. 'Financial Reform Bill Heads to Senate Floor'. *New York Times*, 28 April, sec. Business Day.

Hetherington, Marc J., and Thomas J. Rudolph. 2015. *Why Washington Won't Work: Polarization, Political Trust, and the Governing Crisis*. Chicago Studies in American Politics. Chicago, IL: The University of Chicago Press.

Hill, Seth J., Michael C. Herron and Jeffrey B. Lewis. 2010. 'Economic Crisis, Iraq, and Race: A Study of the 2008 Presidential Election'. *Election Law Journal: Rules, Politics, and Policy* 9 (1): 41–62.

Hoenig, Thomas M. 2013. 'Basel III Capital: A Well-Intended Illusion. Remarks by FDIC Vice Chairman Thomas M. Hoenig to the International Association of Deposit Insurers 2013 Research Conference'. Basel: Federal Deposit Insurance Corporation.

Hoffman, Philip T., Gilles Postel-Vinay and Jean-Laurent Rosenthal. 2009. *Surviving Large Losses: Financial Crises, the Middle Class, and the Development of Capital Markets.* Cambridge, MA: Harvard University Press.

Holmes, Richard. 2002. *Wellington: The Iron Duke.* London: HarperCollins.

Honohan, Patrick. 2008. 'Household Financial Assets in the Process of Development'. In *Personal Wealth from a Global Perspective*, edited by James B. Davies, 271–93. Oxford: Oxford University Press.

Honohan, Patrick, and Daniela Klingebiel. 2000. 'Controlling the Fiscal Costs of Banking Crises'. Policy Research Working Paper Series 2441. The World Bank.

Honohan, Patrick, and Daniela Klingebiel. 2003. 'The Fiscal Cost Implications of an Accommodating Approach to Banking Crises'. *Journal of Banking & Finance* 27 (8): 1539–60.

Hoover, Herbert. 1930. 'Herbert Hoover: Annual Message to the Congress on the State of the Union'. 2 December 1930. www.presidency.ucsb.edu/ws/index.php?pid=22458.

Hopkin, Jonathan, and Martina Viarengo. 2012. 'Inequality, Poverty and the 2010 Election'. In *Coalition Britain: The UK Election of 2010*, edited by Gianfranco Baldini and Jonathan Hopkin, 111–30. Manchester: Manchester University Press.

'House of Commons Debate 14 January 2009'. n.d. www.publications.parliament.uk/pa/cm200809/cmhansrd/cm090114/debtext/90114-0004.htm.

'House of Commons Debate 19 January 2009'. n.d. www.publications.parliament.uk/pa/cm200809/cmhansrd/cm090119/debtext/90119-0004.htm.

House of Commons Library, United Kingdom. 2013. 'The History of the Parliamentary Franchise'. Research Paper 13/14.

House of Commons Public Accounts Committee. 2009. 'The Nationalisation of Northern Rock. Thirty-First Report of Session 2008–09. HC 394'. London: The Stationery Office.

House of Commons Treasury Committee. 2012. 'The FSA's Report into the Failure of RBS'. Fifth Report of Session 2012–13. HC 640, Incorporating HC 1780, Session 2010–12. London: The Stationery Office Limited.

House of Commons Treasury Committee, United Kingdom. 2008. 'The Run on The Rock: HC 56-I'. Fifth Report of Session 2007–8 – Volume I: Report, Together with Formal Minutes. The Stationery Office.

Housing Finance Information Network. 2018. 'Research Centre'. 2018. www
.hofinet.org/documents/index.aspx.

Housing Finance Policy Center, Urban Institute. 2017a. 'Housing Credit
Availability Index'. Urban Institute. www.urban.org/policy-centers/housing-
finance-policy-center/projects/housing-credit-availability-index.

Housing Finance Policy Center, Urban Institute. 2017b. 'Housing Finance at a
Glance: A Monthly Chartbook, November 2017'. Urban Institute.

Huang, Huaxiang, and Ryland Thomas. 2016a. 'The Weekly Balance Sheet of the
Bank of England 1844–2006'. Bank of England.

Huang, Huaxiang, and Ryland Thomas. 2016b. 'The Ghost of Crises Past, Present
and Future: The Bank Charter Act Goes on Trial in 1847'. *Bank Underground*
(blog). 19 December. https://bankunderground.co.uk/2016/12/19/the-ghost-of-
crises-past-present-and-future-the-bank-charter-act-goes-on-trial-in-1847/.

Hulse, Carl, and David M. Herszenhorn. 2008. 'Defiant House Rejects Huge
Bailout; Next Step is Uncertain'. *New York Times*, 29 September 2008, sec.
Business Day.

ICM Research. n.d. 'State of the Parties'. All Guardian/ICM Poll Results. n.d.
https://docs.google.com/spreadsheets/d/10HcxlAbkTJmqfOxYQM22cvjjjRf5
pETIF30x7L-qybc/edit?usp=embed_facebook.

Ikenberry, G. John. 1992. 'A World Economy Restored: Expert Consensus and
the Anglo-American Postwar Settlement'. *International Organization* 46 (1):
289–321.

Illueca, Manuel, Lars Norden and Gregory F. Udell. 2014. 'Liberalization and
Risk-Taking: Evidence from Government-Controlled Banks'. *Review of
Finance* 18 (4): 1217–57.

Ilzetzki, Ethan, Carmen M. Reinhart and Kenneth S. Rogoff. 2017. 'Exchange
Arrangements Entering the 21st Century: Which Anchor Will Hold?' Working
Paper 23134. National Bureau of Economic Research.

Inglehart, Ronald, and Pippa Norris. 2016. 'Trump, Brexit, and the Rise of
Populism: Economic Have-Nots and Cultural Backlash'. SSRN Scholarly
Paper ID 2818659. Rochester, NY: Social Science Research Network.

Ingves, Stefan, Göran Lind, Masaaki Shirakawa, Jaime Caruana and Guillermo
Ortiz Martínez. 2009. *Lessons Learned from Previous Banking Crises:
Sweden, Japan, Spain, and Mexico*. Group of Thirty Occasional Paper 79.
Washington DC: Group of Thirty.

Institute for International Finance. 2011. 'The Cumulative Impact on the Global
Economy of Changes in the Financial Regulatory Framework'. Institute for
International Finance. www.iif.com/system/files/ncseptember2011.pdf.

Instituto Brasileiro de Geografia e Estatística. 2018. '20th Century Statistics:
Economic Statistics, Currency and Credit'. https://seculoxx.ibge.gov.br/
economicas/moeda-e-credito.

International Labor Organization. n.d. 'Brazil'. www.ilo.org/wcmsp5/groups/
   public/—ed_dialogue/—sector/documents/publication/wcms_161276.pdf.
International Monetary Fund. 2009. 'IMF Global Financial Stability Report:
   Responding to the Financial Crisis and Measuring Systemic Risks'. April. IMF.
International Monetary Fund. 2013. 'Brazil: Technical Note on Consumer Credit
   Growth and Household Financial Stress'. IMF Country Report 13/149.
   Washington DC: IMF.
International Monetary Fund. 2014. 'From Banking to Sovereign Stress –
   Implications For Public Debt'. Policy Papers. IMF.
International Monetary Fund. 2017a. 'Kingdom of the Netherlands – Netherlands:
   Financial Sector Assessment Program'. Technical Note – Macroprudential
   Policy Framework. IMF.
International Monetary Fund. 2017b. 'Global Financial Stability Report, October
   2017: Getting the Policy Mix Right'. IMF.
International Monetary Fund. 2017c. 'Global Financial Stability Report, October
   2017: Is Growth at Risk?' IMF.
International Monetary Fund, Basel Committee on Banking Supervision, and
   Financial Stability Board. 2009. 'Guidance to Assess the Systemic Importance
   of Financial Institutions, Markets and Instruments: Initial Considerations'.
   7 November.
International Organisation of Pension Supervisors. 2017. 'Member Country
   Profiles'. www.iopsweb.org/researchbycountry/.
International Social Security Association. 2017. 'Social Security Country Profiles –
   ISSA.' www.issa.int/en_GB/country-profiles. Last accessed 4 December 2017.
Investment Company Institute. 2018. 'Worldwide Regulated Open-End Fund
   Assets and Flows, Fourth Quarter 2017'. 27 March. www.ici.org/research/
   stats/worldwide/ww_q4_17.
Jabłecki, Juliusz, and Mateusz Machaj. 2009. 'The Regulated Meltdown of
   2008'. *Critical Review* 21 (2–3): 301–28.
Jackson, Kenneth T. 1980. 'Race, Ethnicity, and Real Estate Appraisal: The
   Home Owners Loan Corporation and the Federal Housing Administration'.
   Journal of Urban History 6 (4): 419–52.
Jacobe, Dennis. 2008. 'Six in 10 Oppose Wall Street Bailouts'. Gallup.Com. 3 April.
   http://news.gallup.com/poll/106114/Six-Oppose-Wall-Street-Bailouts.aspx.
Jacobs, Alan M. 2010. 'Policymaking as Political Constraint: Institutional
   Development in the U.S. Social Security Program'. In *Explaining Institutional
   Change: Ambiguity, Agency, and Power*, edited by James Mahoney and
   Kathleen Ann Thelen, 94–131. Cambridge and New York, NY: Cambridge
   University Press.
Jacobson, Gary C. 2010. 'George W. Bush, the Iraq War, and the Election of
   Barack Obama'. *Presidential Studies Quarterly* 40 (2): 207–24.

Jacobson, Gary C. 2011. 'The Republican Resurgence in 2010'. *Political Science Quarterly* 126 (1): 27–52.

Jaevicius, Arvydas, Simon Huston and Andrew Baum. 2015. 'Two Centuries of Farmland Prices in England'. Oxford Saïd Research Paper. 5 August.

Jahn, Detlef. 2011. 'The Veto Player Approach in Macro-Comparative Politics: Concepts and Measurement'. In *Reform Processes and Policy Change*, 43–68. New York, NY: Springer.

Jalil, Andrew J. 2014. 'Monetary Intervention Really Did Mitigate Banking Panics during the Great Depression: Evidence along the Atlanta Federal Reserve District Border'. *The Journal of Economic History* 74 (1): 259–73.

James, Estelle, and Sarah Brooks. 2001. 'The Political Economy of Structural Pension Reform'. In *New Ideas about Old Age Security*, edited by Robert Holzmann and Joseph Stiglitz, 133–70. Washington DC: World Bank.

James, Harold. 1991. 'Introduction'. In *The Role of Banks in the Interwar Economy*, edited by Harold James, Håkan Lindgren and Alice Teichova, 1–12. Cambridge: Cambridge University Press.

James, Harold. 2009. *The Creation and Destruction of Value: The Globalization Cycle*. Cambridge, MA: Harvard University Press.

Jaremski, Matthew, and Peter L. Rousseau. 2018. 'The Dawn of an "Age of Deposits" in the United States'. *Journal of Banking & Finance* 87 (Supplement C): 264–81.

Johnson, Louis, and Samuel H. Williamson. 2017. '"What Was the U.S. GDP Then?" Measuring Worth'. https://measuringworth.com/usgdp12/.

Johnson, Simon, and James Kwak. 2010. *13 Bankers: The Wall Street Takeover and the Next Financial Meltdown*. New York, NY: Pantheon Books.

Jones, Bryan D. 2005. *The Politics of Attention: How Government Prioritizes Problems*. Chicago, IL, and London: University of Chicago Press.

Jones, Bryan D., and Frank R. Baumgartner. 2012. 'From There to Here: Punctuated Equilibrium to the General Punctuation Thesis to a Theory of Government Information Processing'. *Policy Studies Journal*, 40(1): 1–20. doi:10.1111/j.1541-0072.2011.00431.x.

Jordà, Òscar, Björn Richter, Moritz Schularick and Alan M. Taylor. 2017. 'Bank Capital Redux: Solvency, Liquidity, and Crisis'. Working Paper 23287. National Bureau of Economic Research.

Jordà, Òscar, Moritz Schularick and Alan M. Taylor. 2013. 'When Credit Bites Back'. *Journal of Money, Credit and Banking* 45 (s2): 3–28.

Jordà, Òscar, Moritz Schularick and Alan M. Taylor. 2014. 'The Great Mortgaging: Housing Finance, Crises, and Business Cycles'. w20501. Cambridge, MA: National Bureau of Economic Research.

Jordà, Òscar, Moritz Schularick and Alan M. Taylor. 2015. 'Leveraged Bubbles'. *Journal of Monetary Economics*, Supplement Issue: 7–8 November 2014

Research Conference on 'Asset Price Fluctuations and Economic Policy', 76, Supplement (December): S1–20.

Jordà, Òscar, Moritz Schularick and Alan M. Taylor. 2016. 'The Great Mortgaging: Housing Finance, Crises and Business Cycles'. *Economic Policy*, 85 (January): 107–40.

Jordà, Òscar, Moritz Schularick and Alan M. Taylor. 2017. 'Macrofinancial History and the New Business Cycle Facts'. In *NBER Macroeconomics Annual 2016*, edited by Martin Eichenbaum and Jonathan A. Parker. Volume 31. Chicago, IL: University of Chicago Press.

Jordà, Òscar, Alan Taylor and Moritz Schularick. 2014. 'The Great Mortgaging'. *VoxEU.Org* (blog). 12 October 2014. http://voxeu.org/article/great-mortgaging.

Jordan, William. 2015. 'Americans No Longer Want "More" Financial Regulation'. YouGov: What the World Thinks (blog). 23 January 2015. //today.yougov.com/news/2015/01/23/americans-no-longer-want-more-financial-regulation/.

Jordana, Jacint, David Levi-Faur and Xavier Fernández-i-Marín. 2011. 'The Global Diffusion of Regulatory Agencies: Channels of Transfer and Stages of Diffusion'. *Comparative Political Studies* 44 (10): 1343–69.

Jornal do Brasil. 1986. 'O Absurdo Problema dos Bancos Estaduais'. *Jornal do Brasil*, 13 October.

Kahler, Miles, and David A. Lake, eds. 2013. *Politics in the New Hard Times: The Great Recession in Comparative Perspective*. Ithaca, NY: Cornell University Press.

Kahneman, Daniel, and Amos Tversky. 1984. 'Choices, Values, and Frames'. *American Psychologist* 39 (4): 341–50.

Kalleberg, Arne L. 2009. 'Precarious Work, Insecure Workers: Employment Relations in Transition'. *American Sociological Review* 74 (1): 1–22.

Kamm, Thomas, and Julia Michaels. 1991. 'Brazil Picks a New Economics Minister Who Is Likely to Back Orthodox Policies'. *Wall Street Journal*, 10 May.

Kapstein, Ethan B. 1996. *Governing the Global Economy*. Cambridge, MA: Harvard University Press.

Katznelson, Ira. 2006. *When Affirmative Action Was White: An Untold History of Racial Inequality in Twentieth-Century America*. Reprint edition. New York, NY: W. W. Norton.

Kavanagh, Dennis, and Philip Cowley. 2010. *The British General Election of 2010*. Basingstoke and New York, NY: Palgrave Macmillan.

Kay, John A. 2015. *Other People's Money: Masters of the Universe or Servants of the People?* London: Profile Books.

Kayser, Mark Andreas, and Michael Peress. 2012. 'Benchmarking across Borders: Electoral Accountability and the Necessity of Comparison'. *American Political Science Review* 106 (3): 661–84.

Keefer, Philip. 2007. 'Elections, Special Interests, and Financial Crisis'. *International Organization* 61 (3): 607–41.

Keeler, John T. S. 1993. 'Opening the Window for Reform: Mandates, Crises, and Extraordinary Policy-Making'. *Comparative Political Studies* 25 (4): 433–86.

Kennedy, Susan Estabrook. 1973. *The Banking Crisis of 1933*. Lexington, KY: University Press of Kentucky.

Kern, Andreas, and Puspa Delima Amri. 2016. 'Political Credit Cycles – Myth or Reality?' SSRN Scholarly Paper ID 2865817. Rochester, NY: Social Science Research Network.

Kessler-Harris, Alice. 2003. *In Pursuit of Equity: Women, Men, and the Quest for Economic Citizenship in 20th-Century America*. Oxford and New York, NY: Oxford University Press.

Kiel, Paul. 2013. 'Bank of America Lied to Homeowners and Rewarded Foreclosures'. ProPublica. 14 June. www.propublica.org/article/bank-of-america-lied-to-homeowners-and-rewarded-foreclosures.

Kimber, Richard. 2017. 'United Kingdom Politics Resources'. Richard Kimber's Political Science Resources. www.politicsresources.net/area/uk/man.htm.

Kindleberger, Charles Poor, and Robert Z. Aliber. 2011. *Manias, Panics and Crashes: A History of Financial Crises*. Basingstoke and New York, NY: Palgrave Macmillan.

King, Mervyn A. 2016. *The End of Alchemy: Money, Banking and the Future of the Global Economy*. New York, NY: W. W. Norton.

Klott, Gary. 1988. 'Interest Deductions Limited by Maze of New Regulations'. *New York Times*, 12 February.

Knoll, Katharina, Moritz Schularick and Thomas Steger. 2017. 'No Price Like Home: Global House Prices, 1870–2012'. *American Economic Review* 107 (2): 331–53.

Knutsen, Sverre. 1994. 'Norwegian Banks and the Legacy of the Interwar Years'. In *Universal Banking in the Twentieth Century: Finance, Industry and State in North and Central Europe*, edited by T. R. Gourvish, Ágnes Pogány and Alice Teichova, 77–95. Aldershot: Edward Elgar.

Krippner, Greta R. 2005. 'The Financialization of the American Economy'. *Socio-Economic Review* 3 (2): 173–208.

Kroszner, Randall S. 1998. 'Is It Better to Forgive than to Receive? Repudiation of the Gold Indexation Clause in Long-Term Debt during the Great Depression'. CRSP Working Paper. Center for Research in Security Prices, Graduate School of Business, University of Chicago.

Kuhn, Moritz, Moritz Schularick and Ulrike Steins. 2017. 'Income and Wealth Inequality in America, 1949–2013'. CEPR Discussion Paper 20547-1502139867. London: Centre for Economic Policy Research.

La Porta, Rafael, Florencio Lopez-De-Silanes and Andrei Shleifer. 2002. 'Government Ownership of Banks'. *The Journal of Finance* 57 (1): 265–301.

Laeven, Luc, and Fabián Valencia. 2008. 'Systemic Banking Crises: A New Database'. SSRN Scholarly Paper ID 1278435. Rochester, NY: Social Science Research Network.

Laeven, Luc, and Fabián Valencia. 2013. 'Systemic Banking Crises Database'. *IMF Economic Review* 61 (2): 225–70.

Landler, Mark. 2008. 'U.S. Investing $250 Billion in Banks'. *New York Times*, 13 October, sec. Economy.

Langley, Paul. 2009. *The Everyday Life of Global Finance: Saving and Borrowing in Anglo-America.* Oxford and New York, NY: Oxford University Press.

Larsson, Mats. 1991. 'State, Banks and Industry in Sweden, with Some Reference to the Scandinavian Countries'. In *The Role of Banks in the Interwar Economy*, edited by Harold James, Håkan Lindgren and Alice Teichova, 80–103. Cambridge: Cambridge University Press.

Latinobarómetro. n.d. 'Latinobarómetro Database'. www.latinobarometro.org/latOnline.jsp.

Lavinas de Morais, Lena. 2017. *The Takeover of Social Policy by Financialization: The Brazilian Paradox.* New York, NY: Palgrave Macmillan.

Leahy, Joe. 2015. 'BNDES: Lender of First Resort for Brazil's Tycoons'. *Financial Times*, 11 January.

Lee, Neil, Katy Morris and Thomas Kemeny. 2018. 'Immobility and the Brexit Vote'. *Cambridge Journal of Regions, Economy and Society* 11 (1): 143–63.

Lees, Francis A., James M. Botts and Rubens Penha Cysne. 1990. *Banking and Financial Deepening in Brazil.* London: Palgrave Macmillan.

Léon, Florian. 2017a. 'Credit Structure Database'. https://sites.google.com/site/florianleon/research/data.

Léon, Florian. 2017b. 'Convergence of Credit Structure around the World'. *Economic Modelling*, August.

Leuchtenburg, William E. 2009. *Herbert Hoover: The American Presidents Series: The 31st President, 1929–1933.* New York, NY: Henry Holt and Company.

Lewis, W. Arthur. 1950. *The Principles of Economic Planning: A Study Prepared for the Fabian Society.* London: Allen and Unwin.

Lieberman, Evan S., ed. 2003. 'The Rise of the Modern Tax State in Brazil and South Africa'. In *Race and Regionalism in the Politics of Taxation in Brazil and South Africa*, 106–72. Cambridge Studies in Comparative Politics. Cambridge: Cambridge University Press.

Lindert, Peter H. 1986. 'Unequal English Wealth since 1670'. *Journal of Political Economy* 94 (6): 1127–62.

Lindert, Peter H. 2017. 'The Rise and Future of Progressive Redistribution'. Working Paper 73. Commitment to Equity (CEQ) Institute, Tulane University.

Lindgren, Carl J. 2005. 'Pitfalls in Managing Closures of Financial Institutions'. In *Systemic Financial Crises: Containment and Resolution*, edited by Patrick Honohan and Luc Laeven, 76–108. Cambridge: Cambridge University Press.

Lindvall, Johannes. 2012. 'Politics and Policies in Two Economic Crises: The Nordic Countries'. In *Coping with Crisis: Government Reactions to the Great Recession*, edited by Nancy Gina Bermeo and Jonas Pontusson, 233–60. New York, NY: Russell Sage Foundation.

Littrell, Jill, Fred Brooks, Jan Ivery and Mary Ohmer. 2010. 'Why You Should Care about the Threatened Middle Class'. *The Journal of Sociology & Social Welfare* 37 (2): 85–112.

Lodge, Martin, and Kai Wegrich. 2011. 'Arguing about Financial Regulation: Comparing National Discourses on the Global Financial Crisis'. *PS: Political Science & Politics* 44 (4): 726–30.

Long, William R. 1990. 'Brazilians Stay Wary of Collor's Inflation Cure: Economy: President's Plan Put an Immediate Halt to Soaring Prices. Now Consumers, Merchants and Laborers Await the Long-Term Consequences'. *Los Angeles Times*, 17 June.

Love, Joseph L. 1970. 'Political Participation in Brazil, 1881–1969'. *Luso-Brazilian Review* 7 (2): 3–24.

Lucas, Deborah. 2017. 'Valuing the GSEs' Government Support'. Shadow Open Market Committee and E21 Manhattan Institute memo. http://shadowfed.org/wp-content/uploads/2017/05/LucasSOMC-May2017.pdf.

Lupia, Arthur. 1998. *The Democratic Dilemma: Can Citizens Learn What They Need to Know?* Cambridge: Cambridge University Press.

Macey, Jonathan R., and Geoffrey P. Miller. 1992. 'Double Liability of Bank Shareholders: History and Implications'. *Wake Forest Law Review* 31.

MacIntyre, Andrew J. 2003. *The Power of Institutions: Political Architecture and Governance*. Ithaca, NY: Cornell University Press.

Maddison Project. 2013. 'New Maddison Project Database, 2013 Version'. The Maddison-Project. www.ggdc.net/maddison/maddison-project/data.htm.

Mahler, Vincent. 2008. 'Electoral Turnout and Income Redistribution by the State: A Cross-National Analysis of the Developed Democracies'. *European Journal of Political Research* 47 (2): 161–83.

Mahler, Vincent, David Jesuit and Piotr R. Paradowski. 2014. 'Electoral Turnout and State Redistribution: A Cross-National Study of Fourteen Developed Countries'. *Political Research Quarterly* 67 (June): 361–73.

Maia, Geraldo. 1999. 'Restructuring the Banking System – the Case of Brazil'. BIS Policy Papers 6. Bank of International Settlements.

Malik, Sheheryar, and TengTeng Xu. 2017. 'Interconnectedness of Global Systemically-Important Banks and Insurers'. International Monetary Fund.

Mann, Thomas E. 2010. 'American Politics on the Eve of the Mid-Term Elections: Fall from Grace'. *The World Today* 66 (11): 20–2.

Mansfield, Edward D., and Helen V. Milner. 2012. *Votes, Vetoes, and the Political Economy of International Trade Agreements.* Princeton, NJ: Princeton University Press.

Marshall, Monty G., Ted Robert Gurr and Keith Jaggers. 2017. 'POLITY IV Project: Political Regime Characteristics and Transitions, 1800–2016'. Vienna: Center for Systemic Peace.

Martin, Randy. 2002. *Financialization of Daily Life.* Philadelphia, PA: Temple University Press.

Martinez-Diaz, Leonardo. 2009. *Globalizing in Hard Times: The Politics of Banking-Sector Opening in the Emerging World.* Ithaca, NY: Cornell University Press.

Maues, Julia. 2013. 'Banking Act of 1933 (Glass-Steagall)'. Federal Reserve History. 22 November. www.federalreservehistory.org/essays/glass_steagall_act.

Mauro, Paolo, Rafael Romeu, Ariel J. Binder and Asad Zaman. 2013. 'A Modern History of Fiscal Prudence and Profligacy'. Working Paper 13/5. International Monetary Fund.

Maxfield, Sylvia. 1997. *Gatekeepers of Growth: The International Political Economy of Central Banking in Developing Countries.* Princeton, NJ: Princeton University Press.

Mayhew, David. 2005. *Divided We Govern.* New Haven, CT: Yale University Press.

Mazur, Christopher, and Ellen Wilson. 2011. 'Housing Characteristics: 2010, 2010 Census Briefs C2010BR-07'. US Department of Commerce, Economics and Statistics Administration, US Census Bureau.

McCain, John, and Sarah Palin. 2008. 'We'll Protect Taxpayers from More Bailouts'. *Wall Street Journal*, 9 September.

McCarty, Nolan, Keith T. Poole and Howard Rosenthal. 2013. *Political Bubbles: Financial Crises and the Failure of American Democracy.* Princeton, NJ: Princeton University Press.

McCarty, Nolan, Keith T. Poole and Howard Rosenthal. 2015. *Polarized America: The Dance of Ideology and Unequal Riches.* 2nd edn. Cambridge, MA: MIT Press.

McCloud, Laura, and Rachel E. Dwyer. 2011. 'The Fragile American: Hardship and Financial Troubles in the 21st Century'. *Sociological Quarterly* 52 (1): 13–35.

McCulley, Richard T. 1992. *Banks and Politics during the Progressive Era: The Origins of the Federal Reserve System, 1897–1913.* New York, NY, and London: Garland.

McGhee, Eric. 2010. 'Which Roll Call Votes Hurt the Democrats?' *The Monkey Cage* (blog). 9 November. http://themonkeycage.org/2010/11/which_roll_call_votes_hurt_the/.

Meltzer, Allan H. 2010. *A History of the Federal Reserve. Volume 1: 1913–1951*. Chicago: The University of Chicago Press.

Merler, Silvia. 2016. 'Italy's Bail-in Headache'. *Bruegel Blog Post* (blog). 19 July. http://bruegel.org/2016/07/italys-bail-in-headache/.

Merler, Silvia. 2017. 'A Tangled Tale of Bank Liquidation in Venice'. *Bruegel Blog Post* (blog). 26 June. http://bruegel.org/2017/06/a-tangled-tale-of-bank-liquidation-in-venice/.

Mettenheim, Kurt von. 2006. 'Still the Century of Government Savings Banks? The Caixa Econômica Federal'. *Brazilian Journal of Political Economy* 26 (1): 39–57.

Mettenheim, Kurt von. 2015. *Monetary Statecraft in Brazil: 1808–2014*. London: Routledge.

Mezarobba, Glenda. 1995. 'Expropriations Reach More Banks'. *Folha de São Paulo*, 16 August.

Mian, Atif, and Amir Sufi. 2014a. *House of Debt: How They (and You) Caused the Great Recession, and How We Can Prevent It from Happening Again*. Chicago, IL: University of Chicago Press.

Mian, Atif, and Amir Sufi. 2014b. 'Why Tim Geithner Is Wrong on Homeowner Debt Relief'. *Washington Post*, 14 May, sec. Wonkblog. www.washingtonpost.com/news/wonk/wp/2014/05/14/why-tim-geithner-is-wrong-on-homeowner-debt-relief/.

Mian, Atif, Amir Sufi and Francesco Trebbi. 2013. 'The Political Economy of the Subprime Mortgage Credit Expansion'. *Quarterly Journal of Political Science* 8 (4): 373–408.

Mian, Atif, Amir Sufi and Francesco Trebbi. 2014. 'Resolving Debt Overhang: Political Constraints in the Aftermath of Financial Crises'. *American Economic Journal: Macroeconomics* 6 (2): 1–28.

Miles, David, Jing Yang and Gilberto Marcheggiano. 2013. 'Optimal Bank Capital'. *The Economic Journal* 123 (567): 1–37.

Minsky, Hyman P. 1992. 'The Financial Instability Hypothesis'. Economics Working Paper Archive 74. Annandale, NY: Levy Economics Institute.

Mishkin, Frederic S., and Stanley Eakins. 2014. *Financial Markets and Institutions*. 8th edn. Boston, IL, Columbus, OH, and Indianapolis, IN: Pearson.

Mishkin, Frederic S., and Eugene N. White. 2016. 'Unprecedented Actions: The Federal Reserve's Response to the Global Financial Crisis in Historical Perspective'. In *The Federal Reserve's Role in the Global Economy: A Historical Perspective*, edited by Michael D. Bordo and Mark A. Wynne, 220–58. New York, NY: Cambridge University Press.

Mitch, David. 2004. 'Education and Skill of the British Labour Force'. In *The Cambridge Economic History of Modern Britain. Volume 1: Industrialisation, 1700–1860*, edited by Roderick Floud and Paul Johnson, 332–56. Cambridge: Cambridge University Press.

Mitchener, Kris James, and Gary Richardson. 2013. 'Does "Skin in the Game" Reduce Risk Taking? Leverage, Liability and the Long-Run Consequences of New Deal Banking Reforms'. *Explorations in Economic History* 50 (4): 508–25.

Moen, Jon, and Ellis W. Tallman. 1992. 'The Bank Panic of 1907: The Role of Trust Companies'. *The Journal of Economic History* 52 (3): 611–30.

Moley, Raymond. 1966. *The First New Deal*. New York, NY: Harcourt, Brace & World.

Moody's Investor Services. 2016. 'Rating Methodology: Banks'. Moody's.

Moore, Barrington, Jr. 1966. *Social Origins of Dictatorship and Democracy: Lord and Peasant in the Making of the Modern World*. Boston, MA: Beacon Press.

Moore, John L. 1985. *Congressional Quarterly's Guide to U.S. Elections*. 2nd edn. Washington DC: Congressional Quarterly, Inc.

Morales, Lymari. 2008. 'Initial Bailout Falling Out of Favor With Americans'. Gallup.Com. 9 December. http://news.gallup.com/poll/113047/Americans-Falling-Favor-Initial-Bailout.aspx.

Morin, Rich, and Paul Taylor. 2009. 'Different Age Groups, Different Recessions'. *Pew Research Center's Social & Demographic Trends Project* (blog). 14 May.

Mounk, Yascha. 2018. *The People vs. Democracy: Why Our Freedom Is in Danger and How to Save It*. Cambridge, MA: Harvard University Press.

Muellbauer, John. 2008. 'Housing and Personal Wealth in a Global Context'. In *Personal Wealth from a Global Perspective*, edited by James B. Davies, 293–311. Oxford: Oxford University Press.

Musacchio, Aldo. 2009. *Experiments in Financial Democracy: Corporate Governance and Financial Development in Brazil, 1882–1950*. New York, NY, and Cambridge: Cambridge University Press.

Myrdal, Gunnar. 1968. *Asian Drama: An Inquiry into the Poverty of Nations*. New York, NY: Pantheon.

Nakane, Marcio, and Daniela B. Weintraub. 2005. 'Bank Privatization and Productivity: Evidence for Brazil'. *Journal of Banking & Finance* 29 (8–9): 2259–89.

National Audit Office (UK). 2009a. 'HM Treasury: The Nationalisation of Northern Rock'. National Audit Office. www.nao.org.uk/report/hm-treasury-the-nationalisation-of-northern-rock/.

National Audit Office (UK). 2009b. 'Maintaining Financial Stability across the United Kingdom's Banking System'. Report by the Comptroller and Auditor General HC 91. National Audit Office.

National Audit Office (UK). 2010. 'HM Treasury: Maintaining the Financial Stability of UK Banks: Update on the Support Schemes'. Report by the Comptroller and Auditor General HC 676 Session 2010–2011. London: The Stationery Office.

National Bank of Canada. 2018. 'Special Report: Is Canada's Household Leverage Too High – or on the Low Side?' National Bank of Canada.

National Bureau of Economic Research. n.d. 'Unemployment Rate for United States'. FRED, Federal Reserve Bank of St Louis. https://fred.stlouisfed.org/series/M0892AUSM156SNBR.

National Bureau of Economic Research. n.d. 'NBER Macrohistory: X. Savings and Investment'. n.d. www.nber.org/databases/macrohistory/contents/chapter10.html.

Neri, Marcelo C. 1995. 'Sobre a Mensuração dos Salários Reais em Alta Inflação'. *Pesquisa e Planejamento Econômico* 25 (3): 497–525.

Ness, Walter L., Jr. 2000. 'Reducing Government Bank Presence in the Brazilian Financial System: Why and How'. *The Quarterly Review of Economics and Finance* 40 (1): 71–84.

Nesvetailova, Anastasia, and Ronen Palan. 2013. 'Minsky in the Shadows: Securitization, Ponzi Finance, and the Crisis of Northern Rock'. *Review of Radical Political Economics* 45 (3): 349–68.

Neuhaus, Paulo. 1974. 'A Monetary History of Brazil, 1900–1945'. PhD dissertation, University of Chicago.

New York Times. 1907. 'Latest Thing in Paternalism'. *New York Times*, 23 November.

New York Times. 2007. 'BNP Paribas Freezes Funds over Subprime Plunge'. *New York Times*, 9 August, sec. International Business.

New York Times. 2008. 'President Bush's Speech to the Nation on the Economic Crisis'. *New York Times*, 24 September, sec. Economy.

New York Times. 2010. 'Polling the Tea Party'. *New York Times*, 14 April.

North, Douglass C., and Robert Paul Thomas. 1973. *The Rise of the Western World: A New Economic History*. Cambridge: Cambridge University Press.

North, Douglass C., and Barry R. Weingast. 1989. 'Constitutions and Commitment: The Evolution of Institutions Governing Public Choice in Seventeenth-Century England'. *The Journal of Economic History* 49 (4): 803–32.

Oatley, Thomas. 2004. 'Why Is Stabilization Sometimes Delayed? Reevaluating the Regime-Type Hypothesis'. *Comparative Political Studies* 37 (3): 286–312.

OECD. 2009. *OECD Private Pensions Outlook 2008*. Paris: OECD.

OECD. 2014. 'OECD Health Statistics 2014: How Does Brazil Compare?' OECD Health Systems Briefing Note. Paris: OECD.

OECD. 2015a. 'Pensions at a Glance 2015 – OECD and G20 Indicators'. www.oecd.org/publications/oecd-pensions-at-a-glance-19991363.htm.

OECD. 2015b. *In It Together: Why Less Inequality Benefits All*. Paris: OECD.

OECD. 2016. *OECD Pensions Outlook 2016*. Paris: OECD.

OECD. 2017. 'General Government Deficit (Indicator)'. https://data.oecd.org/gga/general-government-deficit.htm.

OECD. 2018. 'Household Financial Assets (Indicator)'. https://data.oecd.org/hha/household-financial-assets.htm#indicator-chart.

Offer, Avner. 1991. 'Farm Tenure and Land Values in England, c. 1750–1950'. *Economic History Review* 44 (1): 1–20.

Offer, Avner. 2014. 'Narrow Banking, Real Estate, and Financial Stability in the UK, c. 1870–2010'. In *British Financial Crises since 1825*, edited by Nicholas Dimsdale and Anthony Hotson, 158–73. Oxford: Oxford University Press.

Office for National Statistics. 2013. 'A Century of Home Ownership and Renting in England and Wales'. UK Government Web Archive – The National Archives. 19 April.

Office for National Statistics. 2014. 'Pension Trends: Compendium'. ONS. www.ons.gov.uk/economy/investmentspensionsandtrusts/compendium/pensiontrends/2014-11-28.

Office for National Statistics. 2016a. 'Balance Sheet Estimates (Economic Trends, 1980 and 1981)'. 12 January. www.ons.gov.uk/economy/nationalaccounts/uksectoraccounts/datasets/balancesheetestimateseconomictrends1980and1981.

Office for National Statistics. 2016b. 'Charts and Figures for Historical Estimates of Financial Accounts and Balance Sheets Article'. 12 January. www.ons.gov.uk/economy/nationalaccounts/uksectoraccounts/datasets/chartsandfiguresforhistoricalestimatesoffinancialaccountsandbalancesheetsarticle.

Office for National Statistics. 2016c. 'Pre-ESA95 Financial Accounts and Balance Sheets'. 12 January. www.ons.gov.uk/economy/nationalaccounts/uksectoraccounts/datasets/preesa95financialaccountsandbalancesheets.

Office for National Statistics. 2016d. 'Occupational Pension Schemes Survey, UK: 2015'. 22 September. www.ons.gov.uk/peoplepopulationandcommunity/personalandhouseholdfinances/pensionssavingsandinvestments/bulletins/occupationalpensionschemessurvey/2015.

Office for National Statistics. 2017a. 'Time Series: PS: Net Debt (Excluding Public Sector Banks) as a % of GDP: NSA'. www.ons.gov.uk/economy/governmentpublicsectorandtaxes/publicsectorfinance/timeseries/hf6x/pusf.

Office for National Statistics. 2017b. 'Household Disposable Income and Inequality in the UK'. ONS. www.ons.gov.uk/peoplepopulationandcommunity/personalandhouseholdfinances/incomeandwealth/bulletins/householddisposableincomeandinequality/financialyearending2016.

Office for National Statistics. n.d., a. 'Employment and Labour Market'. www.ons.gov.uk/employmentandlabourmarket.

Office for National Statistics. n.d., b. 'Time Series: Gross Domestic Product: Quarter on Quarter Growth: CVM SA %'. Last accessed 1 August 2017. www.ons.gov.uk/economy/grossdomesticproductgdp/timeseries/ihyq.

Office of the Special Inspector General for the Troubled Asset Relief Program. 2009. 'Sigtarp: Quarterly Report to Congress, July 21 2009'. Office of the Special Inspector General for the Troubled Asset Relief Program.

O'Gorman, Frank. 1997. *The Long Eighteenth Century: British Political and Social History, 1688–1832*. New York, NY: Arnold.

Ohlsson, Henry, Jesper Roine and Daniel Waldenström. 2008. 'Long-Run Changes in the Concentration of Wealth: An Overview of Recent Findings'. In *Personal Wealth from a Global Perspective*, edited by James B. Davies, 112–33. Oxford: Oxford University Press.

Olson, James S. 1972. 'The End of Voluntarism: Herbert Hoover and the National Credit Corporation'. *The Annals of Iowa* 41 (6): 1104–13.

Olson, James S. 1988. *Saving Capitalism: The Reconstruction Finance Corporation and the New Deal, 1933–1940*. Princeton, NJ: Princeton University Press.

Olsson, Ulf. 1991. 'Comparing the Interwar Banking History of Five Small Countries in North-West Europe'. In *The Role of Banks in the Interwar Economy*, edited by Harold James, Håkan Lindgren and Alice Teichova, 26–34. Cambridge: Cambridge University Press.

Orbell, John, and Alison Turton. 2001. *British Banking: A Guide to Historical Records*. Aldershot: Ashgate.

Organisation for Economic Cooperation and Development, International Social Security Association, and International Organisation of Pension Supervisors. 2008. *Complementary and Private Pensions throughout the World 2008*. Paris: Organisation for Economic Cooperation and Development. www.oecd-ilibrary.org/content/book/9789264048829-en.

Page, Benjamin I., and Robert Y. Shapiro. 1983. 'Effects of Public Opinion on Policy'. *American Political Science Review* 77 (1): 175–90.

Paiva Abreu, Marcelo de, and Rogério Werneck. 2008. 'The Brazilian Economy, 1994–2004: An Interim Assessment'. In *The Cambridge History of Latin America. Volume 9: Brazil since 1930*, edited by Leslie Bethell: 431–54. Cambridge: Cambridge University Press.

Pallares-Miralles, Montserrat, Edward Whitehouse and Carolina Romero. 2012. 'International Patterns of Pension Provision II: A Worldwide Overview of Facts and Figures'. 70319. The World Bank. http://documents.worldbank .org/curated/en/143611468168560687/International-patterns-of-pension-provision-II-a-worldwide-overview-of-facts-and-figures.

Parker, George, and Jim Pickard. 2009. 'Myners Rejects Bank Nationalisation'. *Financial Times*. 21 January.

Patch, B. W. 1935. 'The R.F.C. under Hoover and Roosevelt. Editorial Research Reports 1935, Vol. II'. Washington DC: CQ Press.

Pattie, Charles, Daniel Dorling and Ron Johnston. 1995. 'A Debt-Owing Democracy: The Political Impact of Housing Market Recession at the British General Election of 1992'. *Urban Studies* 32 (8): 1293–1315.

Paul, Ellen F. 1980. 'Laissez Faire in Nineteenth-Century Britain: A Bibliographical Essay'. Washington DC: Cato Institute.

Paulson, Henry M. 2010. *On the Brink: Inside the Race to Stop the Collapse of the Global Financial System*. New York, NY: Business Plus.

Pavesi, Fabio. 2017. 'Ecco le 114 Banche Italiane a Rischio per le Sofferenze'. *Il Sole 24 ORE*, 25 March.

Pearce, Malcolm, and Geoffrey Stewart. 2002. *British Political History, 1867–2001: Democracy and Decline*. New York: Routledge.

Pearson, Samantha. 2012. 'Brazil Liquidates Two Banks amid Slowdown'. *Financial Times*, 14 September.

Pelosi, Nancy. 2008. *Housing and Economic Recovery Act of 2008*. www.congress.gov/bill/110th-congress/house-bill/3221/all-actions.

Pepinsky, Thomas B. 2012. 'The Global Economic Crisis and the Politics of Non-Transitions'. *Government and Opposition* 47 (2): 135–61.

Pew Research Center. 2008. 'Obama Seen as Better Able to Address Crisis; 57% of Public Favors Wall Street Bailout'. Washington DC. http://assets.pewresearch.org/wp-content/uploads/sites/5/legacy-pdf/452.pdf.

Pew Research Center. 2013. 'Economies of Emerging Markets Better Rated during Difficult Times'. www.pewglobal.org/2013/05/23/chapter-3-inequality-and-economic-mobility/.

Philippon, Thomas, and Ariell Reshef. 2012. 'Wages and Human Capital in the U.S. Finance Industry: 1909–2006'. *The Quarterly Journal of Economics* 127 (4): 1551–1609.

Pierson, Paul. 1996. 'The New Politics of the Welfare State'. *World Politics* 48 (2): 143–79.

Piketty, Thomas, and Emmanuel Saez. 2014. 'Inequality in the Long Run'. *Science* 344 (6186): 838–43.

Piketty, Thomas, and Gabriel Zucman. 2014. 'Capital Is Back: Wealth-Income Ratios in Rich Countries 1700–2010'. *The Quarterly Journal of Economics* 129 (3): 1255–310.

Piketty, Thomas, and Gabriel Zucman. 2015. 'Wealth and Inheritance in the Long Run'. In *Handbook of Income Distribution*, edited by Anthony B. Atkinson and François Bourguignon, 1303–68. Amsterdam: Elsevier.

Pirrong, Craig. 2009. 'AIG Bailout: A Goldman Rescue in Drag?' Seeking Alpha. 22 November. https://seekingalpha.com/article/174686-aig-bailout-a-goldman-rescue-in-drag.

PM Special Podcast on the Financial Stability Programme. n.d. www.youtube.com/watch?v=7KQXwwbCSLo. Last accessed 17 July 2017.

Polanyi, Karl. 1957. *The Great Transformation*. Boston, MA: Beacon Press.

Political Database of the Americas. 1999. 'Brazil: Municipal Elections of 1996 – State Capitals'. http://pdba.georgetown.edu/Elecdata/Brazil/96first.html.

Popkin, Samuel L. 1994. *The Reasoning Voter: Communication and Persuasion in Presidential Campaigns*. Chicago, IL: Chicago University Press.

Powdthavee, Nattavudh, and Andrew Oswald. 2016. 'Does Money Make People Right-Wing and Inegalitarian? A Longitudinal Study of Lottery Winners'. PIER Discussion Paper 16. Bangkok: Puey Ungphakorn Institute for Economic Research.

Powell, G. Bingham, and Guy D. Whitten. 1993. 'A Cross-National Analysis of Economic Voting: Taking Account of the Political Context'. *American Journal of Political Science* 37 (2): 391–414.

Pressnell, L. S. 1956. *Country Banking in the Industrial Revolution*. Oxford: Clarendon Press.

Pressnell, L. S. 1968. 'Gold Reserves, Banking Reserves, and the Baring Crisis of 1890'. In *Essays in Money and Banking: Essays in Honour of R. S. Sayers*, edited by C. R. Whittlesey and J. S. G. Wilson, 167–228. Oxford: Clarendon Press.

Preston, Howard H. 1933. 'The Banking Act of 1933'. *The American Economic Review* 23 (4): 585–607.

Preston, Julia. 1992. 'Brazil's Press Presses'. *Washington Post*, 6 July.

Pruzan, Jeff. 2008. 'Timeline: Bear Stearns' Year of Turmoil'. *Financial Times*, 14 March.

Przeworski, Adam. 2009. 'Conquered or Granted? A History of Suffrage Extensions'. *British Journal of Political Science* 39 (2): 291–321.

Pugh, Colin. 2009. 'Brazil – Regulation and Supervision of Closed Pension Funds'. Presented to the IOPS/OECD Global Forum, October, Rio de Janeiro.

Pugh, Colin, and Ricardo Pena Pinheiro. 2009. 'Brazilian System of Pension Funds in the Context of the International Environment'. Presented to the Global Forum of IOPS, October, Rio de Janeiro.

Quaglia, Lucia. 2009. 'The "British Plan" as a Pace-Setter: The Europeanization of Banking Rescue Plans in the EU?' *Journal of Common Market Studies* 47 (5): 1063–83.

Quennouëlle-Corre, Laure. 2016. 'State and Finance'. In *The Oxford Handbook of Banking and Financial History*, edited by Youssef Cassis, Richard S. Grossman and Catherine R. Schenk, 420–36. Oxford: Oxford University Press.

Rajan, Raghuram. 2010. *Fault Lines: How Hidden Fractures Still Threaten the World Economy*. Princeton, NJ: Princeton University Press.

Rawnsley, Andrew. 2010. 'The Weekend Gordon Brown Saved the Banks from the Abyss'. *The Observer*, 21 February, sec. Politics.

RealClearPolitics. n.d. 'General Election 2008 – McCain vs. Obama'. /epolls/2008/president/us/general_election_mccain_vs_obama-225.html.

Reinhart, Carmen M. 2010. 'This Time Is Different Chartbook: Country Histories on Debt, Default, and Financial Crises'. Working Paper 15815. National Bureau of Economic Research.

Reinhart, Carmen M., and Kenneth S. Rogoff. 2009. *This Time Is Different: Eight Centuries of Financial Folly*. Princeton, NJ: Princeton University Press.

Reinhart, Carmen M., Kenneth Rogoff and Miguel A. Savastano. 2003. 'Debt Intolerance'. NBER Working Paper 9908. National Bureau of Economic Research, Inc.

Reis, Adacir, and Leonardo André Paixão. 2004. 'Private Pensions in Brazil'. Paris: OECD.

Restoy, Fernando. 2018. 'Bail-In in The New Bank Resolution Framework: Is There an Issue With the Middle Class?' Basel: Bank for International Settlements.

Reuters. 1985. 'Brazil Raises Bank Failure Payment'. *New York Times*, 23 December.

Revell, Jack, John J. Moyle and Graham C. Hockley. 1967. *The Wealth of the Nation: The National Balance Sheet of the United Kingdom, 1957–1961*. Cambridge: Cambridge University Press.

Richardson, Gary. 2013. 'Banking Panics of 1930–31'. Federal Reserve History. 22 November. www.federalreservehistory.org/essays/banking_panics_1930_31.

Richardson, Gary, and William Troost. 2009. 'Monetary Intervention Mitigated Banking Panics during the Great Depression: Quasi-Experimental Evidence from a Federal Reserve District Border, 1929–1933'. *Journal of Political Economy* 117 (6): 1031–73.

Ridings, Eugene. 1994. *Business Interest Groups in Nineteenth-Century Brazil*. Cambridge: Cambridge University Press.

Robb, Victoria. 1997. 'The Genesis of Regulation'. *Bank of England Financial Stability Review* 3: 29–41.

Roberts, Richard. 2013a. *Saving the City: The Great Financial Crisis of 1914*. Oxford: Oxford University Press.

Roberts, Richard. 2013b. 'The Impact of Crises on Savings Banks Institutions in the United Kingdom'. ESBG Perspectives No. 66. European Savings and Retail Banking Group.

Rodden, Jonathan A. 2006. *Hamilton's Paradox: The Promise and Peril of Fiscal Federalism*. New York, NY: Cambridge University Press.

Rodems, Richard, and H. Luke Shaefer. 2016. 'Left Out: Policy Diffusion and the Exclusion of Black Workers from Unemployment Insurance'. *Social Science History* 40 (3): 385–404.

Rodríguez-Pose, Andrés. 2018. 'The Revenge of the Places That Don't Matter (And What to Do about It)'. *Cambridge Journal of Regions, Economy and Society* 11 (1): 189–209.

Rodrik, Dani. 2012. *The Globalization Paradox: Why Global Markets, States, and Democracy Can't Coexist*. New York, NY: Oxford University Press.

Roe, A. 1971. *The Financial Interdependence of the Economy*. London: Chapman and Hall.

Romer, Christina, and David Romer. 1999. 'Monetary Policy and the Well-Being of the Poor'. Federal Reserve Bank of Kansas City.

Roosevelt, Franklin Delano. 1932. 'Acceptance Speech at the Democratic Convention, Chicago, July 2, 1932'. http://www.presidency.ucsb.edu.ws/?pid=75174.

Rosas, Guillermo. 2006. 'Bagehot or Bailout? An Analysis of Government Responses to Banking Crises'. *American Journal of Political Science* 50 (1): 175–91.

Rosas, Guillermo. 2009. *Curbing Bailouts: Bank Crises and Democratic Accountability in Comparative Perspective*. Ann Arbor, MI: University of Michigan Press.

Ross, Duncan. 2013. 'Savings Bank Depositors in a Crisis: Glasgow 1847 and 1857'. *Financial History Review* 20 (2): 183–208.

Roth, Kenneth. 2017. 'The Dangerous Rise of Populism: Global Attacks on Human Rights Values'. In *Human Rights Watch World Report 2017*, 1–17. New York, NY: Human Rights Watch.

Rudnitsky, Jake, and Anna Baraulina. 2017. 'The Russian Banking Analyst Who Predicted Deluge of Bailouts'. *Bloomberg.Com*, 21 September. www.bloomberg.com/news/articles/2017-09-21/the-russian-banking-analyst-who-predicted-a-deluge-of-bailouts.

Ruggie, John Gerard. 1982. 'International Regimes, Transactions, and Change: Embedded Liberalism in the Postwar Economic Order'. *International Organization* 36 (2): 379–415.

Saad, Lydia. 2010. 'Among Recent Bills, Financial Reform a Lone Plus for Congress'. Gallup.Com. September 13, 2010. http://news.gallup.com/poll/142967/Among-Recent-Bills-Financial-Reform-Lone-Plus-Congress.aspx.

Saad, Lydia, Jeffrey M. Jones and Frank Newport. 2008. 'Obama's Road to the White House: A Gallup Review'. Gallup.Com. 5 November. http://news.gallup.com/poll/111742/Obamas-Road-White-House-Gallup-Review.aspx.

Saiegh, Sebastian M. 2011. *Ruling by Statute: How Uncertainty and Vote Buying Shape Lawmaking*. Reprint edition. Cambridge: Cambridge University Press.

Saiegh, Sebastian M. 2014. 'Brazil's Presidents Are More Maradona Than Pelé'. *FiveThirtyEight* (blog). 18 June. https://fivethirtyeight.com/features/brazils-presidents-are-more-maradona-than-pele/.

Sales, Adriana Soares, and Maria Eduarda Tannuri-Pianto. 2007. 'Explaining Bank Failures in Brazil: Micro, Macro and Contagion Effects (1994–1998)'. 147. Working Papers Series. Central Bank of Brazil, Research Department.

Samuels, David, and Timothy Hellwig. 2010. 'Elections and Accountability for the Economy: A Conceptual and Empirical Reassessment'. *Journal of Elections, Public Opinion and Parties* 20 (4): 393–419.

Sandbu, Martin. 2017. 'Inequality Does Not Merit Fatalism'. *Financial Times*, 19 December.

Sanders, David, and Sean Carey. 2002. 'Temporal Variations in Economic Voting: A Comparative Crossnational Analysis'. In *Economic Voting*, edited by Han Dorussen and Michael Taylor, 200–32. London: Routledge.

Sanderson, Rachel. 2017. 'EU Approval of Monte Paschi Restructure Paves Way for State Control'. *Financial Times*, 5 July.

Sanderson, Rachel. 2018. 'Padoan Defends Vision for Italy in Tuscany's Vineyards'. *Financial Times*, 21 February.

Satyanath, Shanker. 2006. *Globalization, Politics, and Financial Turmoil: Asia's Banking Crisis*. New York, NY: Cambridge University Press.

Sayers, R. S. 1936. *Bank of England Operations, 1890–1914*. London: P. S. King & Son Ltd.

Scatigna, Michela, Robert Szemere and Kostas Tsatsaronis. 2014. 'Residential Property Price Statistics across the Globe'. SSRN Scholarly Paper ID 2498635. Rochester, NY: Social Science Research Network.

Scheidel, Walter. 2017. *The Great Leveler: Violence and the History of Inequality from the Stone Age to the Twenty-First Century*. Princeton, NJ: Princeton University Press.

Schenk, Catherine R. 2005. 'Crisis and Opportunity: The Policy Environment of International Banking in the City of London, 1958–1980'. In *London and Paris as International Financial Centres in the Twentieth Century*, edited by Y. Cassis and E. Bussière, 207–29. Oxford: Oxford University Press.

Schenk, Catherine R. 2016. 'Bank Regulation and Supervision'. In *The Oxford Handbook of Banking and Financial History*, edited by Youssef Cassis, Richard S. Grossman and Catherine R. Schenk, 394–419. Oxford: Oxford University Press.

Scheve, Kenneth, and David Stasavage. 2016. *Taxing the Rich: A History of Fiscal Fairness in the United States and Europe*. Princeton, NJ, and Oxford: Oxford University Press.

Schneider, Ben Ross. 2013. *Hierarchical Capitalism in Latin America: Business, Labor, and the Challenges of Equitable Development*. Cambridge: Cambridge University Press.

Schneider, Ben Ross, and David Soskice. 2009. 'Inequality in Developed Countries and Latin America: Coordinated, Liberal and Hierarchical Systems'. *Economy and Society* 38 (1): 17–52.

Schoenmaker, Dirk. 2013. *Governance of International Banking: The Financial Trilemma*. New York, NY: Oxford University Press.

Schultz, Kenneth A., and Barry R. Weingast. 2003. 'The Democratic Advantage: Institutional Foundations of Financial Power in International Competition'. *International Organization* 57 (1): 3–42.

Schulz, John. 2008. *The Financial Crisis of Abolition*. New Haven, CT, and London: Yale University Press.

Schwartz, Herman M., and Leonard Seabrooke. 2009. *The Politics of Housing Booms and Busts*. Basingstoke: Palgrave Macmillan.

Seabrooke, Leonard. 2007. 'The Everyday Social Sources of Economic Crises: From "Great Frustrations" to "Great Revelations" in Interwar Britain'. *International Studies Quarterly* 51 (4): 795–810.

Seddon, Max. 2018. 'Russia Plans "Bad Bank" for $19bn in Toxic Assets'. *Financial Times*, 3 April.

Shafir, Eldar, Peter Diamond and Amos Tversky. 1997. 'Money Illusion'. *The Quarterly Journal of Economics* 112 (2): 341–74.

Shannon, Richard. 1996. *The Age of Salisbury, 1881–1902; Unionism and Empire*. London and New York, NY: Longman.

Sharkey, Patrick. 2013. *Stuck in Place*. Chicago, IL: Chicago University Press.

Shaw, Leslie M. 1905. 'Address by Hon. Leslie M. Shaw, Secretary of the Treasury to the American Bankers Association'.

Shiller, Robert J. n.d. 'Online Data – Robert Shiller'. www.econ.yale.edu/~shiller/data.htm.

Shiller, Robert J. 2005. *Irrational Exuberance*. Princeton, NJ, and Oxford: Princeton University Press.

Shiller, Robert J. 2015. *Irrational Exuberance*. 3rd edn. Princeton, NJ: Princeton University Press.

Short, Joanna. 2002. 'Economic History of Retirement in the United States'. 30 September. https://eh.net/encyclopedia/economic-history-of-retirement-in-the-united-states/.

Sidel, Robin, David Enrich and Dan Fitzpatrick. 2008. 'WaMu Is Seized, Sold Off to J.P. Morgan, in Largest Failure in U.S. Banking History'. *Wall Street Journal*, 26 September.

SIFMA. 2016. 'Statistics'. June. www.sifma.org/research/statistics.aspx.

Silber, William L. 2009. 'Why Did FDR's Bank Holiday Succeed?' *FRBNY Economic Policy Review* 15 (1): 19–30.

Silveira, Ricardo Antonio Rocha. 1985. 'The Distribution of Wealth in Brazil – The Case of Rio de Janeiro: 1870s to 1980s'. PhD, University of California, Berkeley.

Silver, Nate. 2010. 'Health Care and Bailout Votes May Have Hurt Democrats'. 16 November. https://fivethirtyeight.com/features/health-care-and-bailout-votes-may-have-hurt-democrats/.

Simensen, Ivar. 2007. 'Subprime Woes Take Their Toll in Germany'. *Financial Times*, 30 July.

Singer, David Andrew. 2007. *Regulating Capital: Setting Standards for the International Financial System*. Ithaca, NY: Cornell University Press.

Skocpol, Theda, and Vanessa Williamson. 2016. *The Tea Party and the Remaking of Republican Conservatism*. Updated edition. New York, NY: Oxford University Press.

Smith, Henry Stooks. 1844. *The Parliaments of England, from 1st George I., to the Present Time. Volume 1*. London: Simpkin, Marshall & Co.

Smith, Mark A. 2000. *American Business and Political Power: Public Opinion, Elections, and Democracy*. Chicago, IL, and London: University of Chicago Press.

Smith, Martin J. 2010. 'From Big Government to Big Society: Changing the State–Society Balance'. In *Britain Votes 2010*, edited by Andrew Geddes and Jonathan Tonge, 233–48. Oxford: Oxford University Press.

Snowden, Kenneth A. 2010. 'The Anatomy of a Residential Mortgage Crisis: A Look Back to the 1930s'. Working Paper 16244. National Bureau of Economic Research.

Sobreira, Rogério, and Luiz Fernando de Paula. 2010. 'The 2008 Financial Crisis and Banking Behavior in Brazil: The Role of the Prudential Regulation, Abstract'. *Journal of Innovation Economics & Management*, 6 (November): 77–93.

Sola, Lourdes, Christopher da Cunha Bueno Garman and Moisés S. Marques. 2001. 'Central Banking Reform and Overcoming the Moral Hazard Problem: The Case of Brazil'. *Brazilian Journal of Political Economy* 21 (3): 40–64.

Solomou, Solomos, and Martin Weale. 1997. 'Personal Sector Wealth in the United Kingdom, 1920–56'. *Review of Income and Wealth* 43 (3): 297–318.

Solt, Frederick. 2008. 'Economic Inequality and Democratic Political Engagement'. *American Journal of Political Science* 52 (1): 48–60.

Solt, Frederick. 2016. 'The Standardized World Income Inequality Database'. *Social Science Quarterly* 97 (5): 1267–81.

Sommer, Joseph H. 2014. 'Why Bail-In? And How!' *FRBNY Economic Policy Review* December: 207–28.

Soto, Hernando de. 2000. *The Mystery of Capital: Why Capitalism Triumphs in the West and Fails Everywhere Else*. New York, NY: Basic Books.

Sparrow, Andrew. 2009. 'Labour's Bank Rescue Plan Has Failed, Opposition Tells Darling'. *The Guardian*, 20 January, sec. Politics.

Stasavage, David. 2003. *Public Debt and the Birth of the Democratic State: France and Great Britain, 1688–1789*. Cambridge and New York, NY: Cambridge University Press.

Stasavage, David. ed. 2011. *States of Credit: Size, Power, and the Development of European Polities*. Princeton, NJ: Princeton University Press.

Stein, Stanley J. 1957. *The Brazilian Cotton Manufacture: Textile Enterprise in an Underdeveloped Area, 1850–1950*. Cambridge, MA: Harvard University Press.

Stern, Gary H., and Ron J. Feldman. 2004. *Too Big to Fail: The Hazards of Bank Bailouts*. Washington DC: Brookings Institution Press.

Stiglitz, Joseph E. 2009. 'The Anatomy of a Murder: Who Killed America's Economy?' *Critical Review* 21 (2–3): 329–39.

Stolper, Wolfgang F., and Karl W. Roskamp. 1979. 'Planning a Free Economy: Germany 1945–1960'. *Zeitschrift für die Gesamte Staatswissenschaft / Journal of Institutional and Theoretical Economics* 135 (3): 374–404.

Subramanian, S., and D. Jayaraj. 2008. 'The Distribution of Household Wealth in India'. In *Personal Wealth from a Global Perspective*, edited by James B. Davies, 112–33. Oxford: Oxford University Press.

Summers, Deborah. 2008. 'Gordon Brown: We Are Taking Decisive Action on Financial Crisis'. *The Guardian*, 30 September, sec. Politics.

Svirydzenka, Katsiaryna. 2016. 'Introducing a New Broad-Based Index of Financial Development'. IMF Working Paper WP/16/5. International Monetary Fund.

Swagel, Phillip. 2015. 'Legal, Political, and Institutional Constraints on the Financial Crisis Policy Response'. *Journal of Economic Perspectives* 29 (2): 107–22.

Swaine, Jon. 2008. 'Bank Bailout: Alistair Darling Unveils £500 Billion Rescue Package', 8 October, *The Telegraph*, sec. Finance.

Sylla, Richard, Robert E. Wright and David J. Cowen. 2009. 'Alexander Hamilton, Central Banker: Crisis Management during the U.S. Financial Panic of 1792'. *Business History Review* 83 (1): 61–86.

Takami, Marcelo Y., and Benjamin M. Tabak. 2007. 'Evaluation of Default Risk for the Brazilian Banking Sector'. Working Papers Series No. 135. Central Bank of Brazil, Research Department.

Taus, Esther Rogoff. 1943. *Central Banking Functions of the United States Treasury, 1789–1941*. New York, NY: Columbia University Press.

Taylor, John B. 2009. 'Economic Policy and the Financial Crisis: An Empirical Analysis of What Went Wrong'. *Critical Review* 21 (2–3): 341–64.

Thaler, Richard H. 2015. *Misbehaving: The Making of Behavioral Economics*. New York, NY: W. W. Norton.

Thomas, Ryland, and N. H. Dimsdale. 2017. 'A Millennium of UK Data: Bank of England OBRA Dataset'. Bank of England.

Thomas, S. Evelyn. 1934. *The Rise and Growth of Joint Stock Banking. Volume 1*. London: Pitman.

Thornton, Henry. 1802. *An Enquiry into the Nature and Effects of the Paper Credit of Great Britain*. London: G. Allen & Unwin.

Timberlake, Richard H. 1978. *The Origins of Central Banking in the United States*. Cambridge, MA: Harvard University Press.

Topik, Steven. 1987. *The Political Economy of the Brazilian State, 1889–1930*. Austin, TX: University of Texas Press.

Torche, Florencia, and Seymour Spilerman. 2008. 'Household Wealth in Latin America'. In *Personal Wealth from a Global Perspective*, edited by James B. Davies, 150–77. Oxford: Oxford University Press.

Tribe, Keith. 2001. 'The 1948 Currency Reform: Structure and Purpose'. In *50 Years of the German Mark: Essays in Honour of Stephen F. Frowen*, edited by Jens Hölscher, 15–55. London: Palgrave Macmillan.

Triner, Gail D. 2000. *Banking and Economic Development: Brazil, 1889–1930*. New York, NY, and Basingstoke: Palgrave.

Tsebelis, George. 2002. *Veto Players: How Political Institutions Work*. Princeton, NJ: Princeton University Press.

Turner, Adair. 2015. *Between Debt and the Devil: Money, Credit, and Fixing Global Finance*. Princeton, NJ: Princeton University Press.

Turner, John D. 2014. *Banking in Crisis: The Rise and Fall of British Banking Stability, 1800 to the Present*. Cambridge: Cambridge University Press.

UK Financial Investments Limited. 2015. 'Annual Report and Accounts 2014/ 15'. Cm 9086. Her Majesty's Stationery Office.

UK Parliament. 2018. 'Hansard 1803–2005'. https://api.parliament.uk/historic-hansard/index.html.

United Nations Educational, Scientific and Cultural Organization. 2005. 'EFA Global Monitoring Report 2006: Literacy for Life'. UNESCO.

United Nations Human Settlements Program. 2006. 'United Nations Human Settlements Programme 2005 Annual Report'. Text. ReliefWeb. 1 June. http:// reliefweb.int/report/world/united-nations-human-settlements-programme-2005-annual-report.

United States Congress, House Committee on Banking and Currency. 1912. 'Money Trust Investigation: Investigation of Financial and Monetary Conditions in the United States Under House Resolutions Nos. 429 and 504 Before a Subcommittee of the Committee on Banking and Currency, House of Representatives'. https://fraser.stlouisfed.org/title/80.

US Bureau of the Census. 1975a. *Historical Statistics of the United States: Colonial Times to 1970. Volume 1*. Bureau of the Census, US Department of Commerce.

US Bureau of the Census. 1975b. *Historical Statistics of the United States: Colonial Times to 1970. Volume 2*. Bureau of the Census, US Department of Commerce.

US Bureau of the Census. 2017. 'Homeownership Rate for the United States'. FRED, Federal Reserve Bank of St Louis. 14 September.

US Department of Commerce and Labor. 1910. 'Statistical Abstract of the United States: 1909'. Washington DC: Government Printing Office.

US Department of the Treasury. 1959. *Final Report on the Reconstruction Finance Corporation: Pursuant to Section 6 (C), Reorganization Plan No. 1 of*

1957. https://fraser.stlouisfed.org/scribd/?title_id=134&filepath=/files/docs/
publications/rcf/rfc_19590506_finalreport.pdf.

US Department of the Treasury. 2009a. 'President Obama, Treasury Secretary Tim
Geithner, and Housing and Urban Development Secretary Shaun Donovan
Unveil The Homeowner Affordability and Stability Plan'. 18 February 2009.
www.treasury.gov/press-center/press-releases/Pages/2009218954476942
.aspx.

US Department of the Treasury. 2009b. 'Financial Regulatory Reform: A New
Foundation'. US Treasury. www.treasury.gov/press-center/press-releases/
Pages/20096171052487309.aspx.

US Department of the Treasury. 2017. 'Monthly Report to Congress, November
2017, Troubled Asset Relief Program'. US Treasury.

US Federal Reserve. 1937. 'Bank Suspensions, 1921–1936'. *Federal Reserve
Bulletin* September: 866–910.

US Government Accountability Office. 2010. 'Financial Markets Regulation:
Financial Crisis Highlights Need to Improve Oversight of Leverage at
Financial Institutions and across System'. GAO-10-555T. Washington DC:
US GAO.

US Office of Financial Research. 2016. '2016 Financial Stability Report'. Office of
Financial Research.

Van de Walle, Nicholas. 2001. *African Economies and the Politics of Permanent
Crisis, 1979–1999*. Cambridge: Cambridge University Press.

Van der Cruijsen, Carin, Jakob de Haan, David-Jan Jansen and Robert Mosch.
2013. 'Knowledge and Opinions about Banking Supervision: Evidence from a
Survey of Dutch Households'. *Journal of Financial Stability* 9 (2): 219–29.

Van der Zwan, Natascha. 2014. 'Making Sense of Financialization'. *Socio-
Economic Review* 12 (1): 99–129.

Vanguard Group, Inc. 2017. 'Global Bond Index Factsheet'. Vanguard. www
.trustnetoffshore.com/Tools/PDFViewer.aspx?url=%2FFactsheets%
2FFundFactsheetPDF.aspx%3FfundCode%3DD2FH5%26univ%3DDC.

Vanthemsche, Guy. 1991. 'States, Banks, and Industry in Belgium and the
Netherlands, 1919–1939'. In *The Role of Banks in the Interwar Economy*,
edited by Harold James, Håkan Lindgren and Alice Teichova, 104–21.
Cambridge: Cambridge University Press.

Verdier, Daniel. 2000. 'The Rise and Fall of State Banking in OECD Countries'.
Comparative Political Studies 33 (3): 283–318.

Wachman, Richard. 2007. 'Call to "Nationalise" Northern Rock'. *The Observer*,
18 November, sec. Business.

Wall Street Journal. n.d. 'Fannie Mae Timeline'. Last accessed 2 May 2018.

Wallison, Peter J. 2009. 'Cause and Effect: Government Policies and the Financial
Crisis'. *Critical Review* 21 (2–3): 365–76.

Walter, Andrew. 2008. *Governing Finance: East Asia's Adoption of International Financial Standards*. Ithaca, NY: Cornell University Press.

Warnock, Veronica Cacdac, and Francis E. Warnock. 2008. 'Markets and Housing Finance'. *Journal of Housing Economics* 17 (3): 239–51.

Washington Post. 1907. 'Two Democrats and Finance'. *Washington Post*, 29 October.

Washington Post. 2008. 'The Lehman Lesson', *Washington Post*, 16 September.

Watson, Matthew. 2007. *The Political Economy of International Capital Mobility*. Basingstoke: Palgrave Macmillan.

Weber, B., and S. W. Schmitz. 2011. 'Varieties of Helping Capitalism: Politico-Economic Determinants of Bank Rescue Packages in the EU during the Recent Crisis'. *Socio-Economic Review* 9 (4): 639–69.

Weber, Fritz. 1991. 'Universal Banking in Interwar Central Europe'. In *The Role of Banks in the Interwar Economy*, edited by Harold James, Håkan Lindgren and Alice Teichova, 19–25. Cambridge: Cambridge University Press.

Weir, Margaret. 1998. *The Social Divide: Political Parties and the Future of Activist Government*. Washington DC: Brookings Institution Press.

Welch, John H. 1991. 'Hyperinflation, and Internal Debt Repudiation in Argentina and Brazil: From Expectations Management to the "Bonex" and "Collor" Plans'. Federal Reserve Bank of Dallas Research Papers 9107.

Wessel, David. 2009. *In FED We Trust: Ben Bernanke's War on the Great Panic*. Reprint edition. New York, NY: Crown Business.

Western, Bruce, Deirdre Bloome, Benjamin Sosnaud and Laura Tach. 2012. 'Economic Insecurity and Social Stratification'. *Annual Review of Sociology* 38 (1): 341–59.

Wheelock, David C. 2008. 'The Federal Response to Home Mortgage Distress: Lessons from the Great Depression'. *Federal Reserve Bank of St. Louis Review* 90 (3): 133–48.

White, Eugene N. 1983. *The Regulation and Reform of the American Banking System, 1900–1929*. Princeton, NJ: Princeton University Press.

White, Eugene N. 2016a. 'How to Prevent a Banking Panic: The Barings Crisis of 1890'. Paper delivered to the Economic History Association conference, 16–18 September.

White, Eugene N. 2016b. 'Rescuing a SIFI, Halting a Panic: The Barings Crisis of 1890'. *Bank Underground* (blog). 10 February. https://bankunderground.co.uk/2016/02/10/rescuing-a-sifi-halting-a-panic-the-barings-crisis-of-1890/.

Wilson, Woodrow. 1913. 'Message Regarding Banking System, Speech to Congress'. Miller Center. 23 June.

Wise, Peter, and Martin Arnold. 2015. 'Novo Banco Investors Threaten Legal Action over €2bn Losses'. *Financial Times*, 30 December.

Witcher, S. Karene, and Kim Conroy. 1985. 'Brazil Won't Meet All Debts Owed By Failed Banks'. *Wall Street Journal*, 21 November.

Wolff, Edward N. 2014. 'Household Wealth Trends in the United States, 1962–2013: What Happened over the Great Recession?' Working Paper 20733. National Bureau of Economic Research.

Wolff, Edward N. 2016. 'Deconstructing Household Wealth Trends in the United States, 1983–2013'. Working Paper 22704. National Bureau of Economic Research. https://doi.org/10.3386/w22704.

Wolff, Edward N. 2017a. *A Century of Wealth in America*. Cambridge, MA: Belknap Press of Harvard University Press.

Wolff, Edward N. 2017b. 'Household Wealth Trends in the United States, 1962 to 2016: Has Middle Class Wealth Recovered?' Working Paper 24085. National Bureau of Economic Research.

Woll, Cornelia. 2014. *The Power of Inaction: Bank Bailouts in Comparison*. Ithaca, NY: Cornell University Press.

Wood, John H. 2014. *Central Banking in a Democracy: The Federal Reserve and Its Alternatives*. London: Routledge.

Woods, Ngaire. 2006. *The Globalizers: The IMF, the World Bank, and the Borrowers*. Ithaca, NY: Cornell University Press.

World Bank. 1995. 'Brazil State Debt: Crisis and Reform'. Report No. 14842-BR. Public Sector Management and Private Sector Development Division. Washington DC: The World Bank.

World Bank. 2002. 'Brazil – Progressive Low-Income Housing: Alternatives for the Poor'. The World Bank.

World Bank. 2014. 'Global Financial Development Report 2014: Financial Inclusion'. World Bank.

World Bank. 2015. 'Global Financial Development Report 2015/16: Long-Term Finance'. World Bank.

World Bank. 2016. 'Size of the Public Sector: Government Wage Bill and Employment'. World Bank. 17 February.

World Bank. 2017. 'Global Financial Development Database (GFDD)'. World Bank.

World Bank, FinSAC. 2017. *Bank Resolution and 'Bail-In' in the EU: Selected Case Studies Pre and Post BRRD*. World Bank.

World Values Survey. 2017. 'WVS Database'. www.worldvaluessurvey .org/wvs.jsp.

World Wealth & Income Database. 2017. 'WID – World Wealth & Income Database'. http://wid.world/.

Xu, Ke, David B. Evans, Kei Kawabata, Riadh Zeramdini, Jan Klavus and Christopher J. L. Murray. 2003. 'Household Catastrophic Health Expenditure: A Multicountry Analysis'. *The Lancet* 362 (9378): 111–17.

Ynesta, Isabelle. 2008. 'Household's Wealth Composition across OECD Countries and Financial Risks Borne by Households'. *Financial Market Trends* 95 (2).

Zingales, Luigi. 2015. 'Presidential Address: Does Finance Benefit Society?' *The Journal of Finance* 70 (4): 1327–63.

Zucman, Gabriel. 2015. *The Hidden Wealth of Nations*. Chicago: University of Chicago Press.

Zysman, John. 1983. *Governments, Markets, and Growth: Financial Systems and the Politics of Industrial Change*. Ithaca, NY: Cornell University Press.

INDEX